THE NORTHERN IRELAND CONFLICT

The Northern Ireland Conflict

Consociational Engagements

JOHN McGARRY
AND
BRENDAN O'LEARY

OXFORD

UNIVERSITY PRESS

OXFORD
UNIVERSITY PRESS

Great Clarendon Street, Oxford OX2 6DP

Oxford University Press is a department of the University of Oxford.
It furthers the University's objective of excellence in research, scholarship,
and education by publishing worldwide in

Oxford New York

Auckland Bangkok Buenos Aires Cape Town Chennai
Dar es Salaam Delhi Hong Kong Istanbul Karachi Kolkata
Kuala Lumpur Madrid Melbourne Mexico City Mumbai Nairobi
São Paulo Shanghai Taipei Tokyo Toronto

Oxford is a registered trade mark of Oxford University Press
in the UK and in certain other countries

Published in the United States
by Oxford University Press Inc., New York

© John McGarry and Brendan O'Leary 2004

The moral rights of the authors have been asserted
Database right Oxford University Press (maker)

First published 2004

British Library Cataloguing in Publication Data
Data available

Library of Congress Cataloging in Publication Data
Data available

ISBN 0-19-926657-3

1 3 5 7 9 10 8 6 4 2

Typeset by Newgen Imaging Systems (P) Ltd., Chennai, India
Printed in Great Britain
on acid-free paper by
Biddles Ltd., King's Lynn, Norfolk

To our daughters:
Ciara Rose McGarry
and
Anna Aisling O'Leary

Acknowledgements

Brendan O'Leary, 'The Anglo-Irish Agreement: Statecraft or Folly?' is reprinted from *West European Politics*, 10 (1): 5–32 by kind permission of Frank Cass Publishers.

Brendan O'Leary, 'The Limits to Coercive Consociationalism in Northern Ireland' is reprinted from *Political Studies*, 37 (4), 1989: 452–68 by kind permission of Blackwell Publishing.

John McGarry, 'Comparing Northern Ireland' is a revised and updated version of John McGarry, 'The Comparable Northern Ireland'. In John McGarry (ed.), *Northern Ireland and the Divided World: Post-Agreement Northern Ireland in Comparative Perspective*. Oxford: Oxford University Press, 2001: 1–33.

John McGarry and Brendan O'Leary, 'Five Fallacies: Northern Ireland and the Liabilities of Liberalism' is reprinted from *Ethnic and Racial Studies*, 18 (4), 1995: 837–61 by kind permission of the Taylor and Francis Group. The website of *Ethnic and Racial Studies* can be found at *http:// www.tandf.co.uk*.

Brendan O'Leary, 'The Labour Government and Northern Ireland, 1974–1979' will be published as 'Northern Ireland' in Kevin Hickson and Anthony Seldon (eds.), *Governing Before New Labour: Blair and the Wilson-Callaghan Government 1974–79*. Routledge. Copyright Brendan O'Leary.

Brendan O'Leary, 'The Conservative Stewardship of Northern Ireland 1979–97: Sound-Bottomed Contradictions or Slow Learning?' is reprinted from *Political Studies*, 45 (4), 1997: 663–76 by kind permission of Blackwell Publishing.

John McGarry, 'Political Settlements in Northern Ireland and South Africa' is reprinted from *Political Studies*, 46 (5), 1998: 853–70 by kind permission of Blackwell Publishing.

Brendan O'Leary, 'The Nature of the Agreement' first appeared in the *Fordham Journal of International Law* 22 (4), 1999: 1628–67.

John McGarry, 'Globalization, European Integration and the Northern Ireland Conflict' first appeared in Michael Keating and John McGarry (eds.), *Minority Nationalism and the Changing International Order*. Oxford: Oxford University Press, 2001: 295–324.

John McGarry, ' "Democracy" In Northern Ireland: experiments in Self-rule from the Protestant Ascendancy to the Good Friday Agreement' first appeared in *Nations and Nationalism*, 8 (4), 2002: 451–74.

Brendan O'Leary, 'The Protection of Human Rights under the Belfast Agreement' first appeared in *Political Quarterly*, 72 (3 (July–Sept. 2001)): 353–65.

Contents

Abbreviations

AIA	Anglo-Irish Agreement
ANC	African National Congress
AOH	Ancient Order of Hibernians
APNI	Alliance Party of Northern Ireland
ASEAN	Association of the South-East Asian Nations
AV	Alternative Vote
BIC	British-Irish Council
B-IGC	British-Irish intergovernmental conference
CIRA	Continuity IRA
DFM	Deputy First Minister
DL	Democratic Left
DPPB	District Policing Partnership Boards
DUP	Democratic Unionist Party
EEC	European Economic Community
EOC	Equal Opportunities Commission
EPA	Emergency Provisions Act
EPS	Executive power-sharing
EU	European Union
FEA	Fair Employment Agency
FEC	Fair Employment Commission
FET	Fair Employment Tribunal
FF	Fianna Fáil
FG	Fine Gael
FM	First Minister
GAA	Gaelic Athletic Association
HCNM	High Commissioner on National Minorities
IGC	Intergovernmental Conference (of the Anglo-Irish Agreement)
IIP	Irish Independence Party
ILP	Irish Labour Party
INLA	Irish National Liberation Army
IRA	Irish Republican Army
KKK	Ku Klux Klan
LVF	Loyalist Volunteer Force
MLA	Member of the Legislative Assembly
NATO	North Atlantic Treaty Organization

NICRA	Northern Ireland Civil Rights Association
NIHRC	Northern Ireland Human Rights Commission
NILP	Northern Ireland Labour Party
NIO	Northern Ireland Office (ministry of the UK government)
NSMC	North-South Ministerial Council
NUPRG	New Ulster Political Research Group
OIRA	Official IRA
OSCE	Organization for Security and Cooperation in Europe
OUP	Official Ulster Unionist Party
PACE	Protestant and Catholic Encounter
PANI	Police Authority for Northern Ireland
PCB	Police Complaints Board
PD	Progressive Democrats
PIRA	Provisional IRA
PLO	Palestine Liberation Organization
PR	Proportional Representation
PSF	Provisional Sinn Féin
PSNI	Police Service of Northern Ireland
PTA	Prevention of Terrorism Act
PUP	Progressive Unionist Party
RHC	Red Hand Commandos
RIR	Royal Irish Regiment (created from the merger of the UDR and the Royal Irish Rangers)
RIRA	Real IRA
RSF	Republican Sinn Féin
RUC	Royal Ulster Constabulary
SACHR	Standing Advisory Commission on Human Rights
SDLP	Social Democratic and Labour Party of Northern Ireland
SF	Sinn Féin
STV	Single Transferable Vote
UDA	Ulster Defence Association
UDI	Unilateral Declaration of Independence
UDP	Ulster Democratic Party
UDR	Ulster Defence Regiment
UFF	Ulster Freedom Fighters (pseudonym for the UDA)
UKUP	United Kingdom Unionist Party
UPNI	Unionist Party of Northern Ireland
UUC	Ulster Unionist Council
UULCC	United Ulster Loyalist Central Coordinating Committee
UUP	Ulster Unionist Party

UUUC	United Ulster Unionist Council
UVF	Ulster Volunteer Force
UWC	Ulster Workers' Council
WC	(Northern Ireland) Women's Coalition
WP	Workers' Party

1

Introduction: Consociational Theory and Northern Ireland

John McGarry and Brendan O'Leary

I did not draw my principles from my prejudices, but from the nature of things.

(Montesquieu 1748/1989: xliii)

'What a wonderful place the world would be', cry the devotees of each way of life, 'if only everyone were like us'. We can now see the fallacy in this frequently expressed lament: it is only the presence in the world of people who are different from them that enables adherents of each way of life to be the way they are.

(Thompson, Ellis, and Wildavsky 1990: 96)

Consociational theory, developed by Arend Lijphart and other scholars, is one of the most influential theories in comparative political science. Its key contention is that divided territories, be they regions or states, with historically antagonistic ethnically, religiously, or linguistically divided peoples, are effectively, prudently, and sometimes optimally governed according to consociational principles. Consociations can be both democratic and authoritarian (O'Leary, in progress), but complete consociational democracies respect four organizational principles.[1]

1. *Executive power-sharing* (EPS).   Each of the main communities share in executive power, in an executive chosen in accordance with the principles of representative government.

---

[1] Refinements in the definition of consociation are treated at length by one of us in a forthcoming work (O'Leary, in progress).

2. *Autonomy or Self-government.* Each enjoys some distinct measure of autonomy, particularly self-government in matters of cultural concern.
3. *Proportionality.* Each is represented proportionately in key public institutions and is a proportional beneficiary of public resources and expenditures.
4. *Veto-rights.* Each is able to prevent changes that adversely affect their vital interests.

Consociational theory has been a central part of Northern Ireland's 'meta-conflict', that is, the intellectual conflict about the nature of the conflict and the appropriate prescriptions to tackle it (McGarry and O'Leary 1995*a*: 320–6, 338–44). It was first applied to Northern Ireland by Lijphart in the *British Journal of Political Science* (Lijphart 1975). But, as he has often observed, practice does not require theory. Consociational principles had already been evident in the ill-fated Sunningdale Agreement of 1973–4, widely known locally and accurately as a power-sharing experiment. Lijphart argued that consociational democracy was the most appropriate form of government for the region, but was then pessimistic about its prospects (Lijphart 1975, 1990).[2] Consociational theory has also helped craft our joint and individual writings.[3] We have consistently shared Lijphart's normative endorsements of consociation, and often his pessimism about its prospects in the region where we grew up. We admire his works, and the man, not least because of his grace under fire from friends and foes, but regard ourselves as critical supporters rather than slavish disciples. Lijphart makes no important distinction between polities that are linguistically, ethno-nationally, or religiously divided, whereas we have argued that Northern Ireland has primarily experienced a self-determination dispute spanning two states, and that this diagnosis is crucial, both for accurate explanation and compelling prescription, consociational or not (McGarry and O'Leary 1995*a*, *b*: *passim*). We have disagreed with Lijphart, especially about the obstacles to a durable political settlement in Northern Ireland, and have insisted that such a settlement requires more than just consociational institutions. Minimally, these would include all-island and all-Ireland cross-border

---

[2] Lijphart later became more optimistic about the prospects for a consociational settlement in Northern Ireland. (Lijphart 1995, 1996).

[3] See the Bibliography which lists our writings on Irish politics, especially our earlier writings (O'Leary 1985: 39–40; O'Leary *et al.* 1993: *passim*; McGarry 1988, 1990; O'Leary 1987: 11–12, 28–9; O'Leary 1989: 562 ff; McGarry and O'Leary 1995*a*: 311–53; 1990*a*: *passim*; 1990*b*: 268–303; O'Leary and McGarry 1993: 220–326).

institutions, and institutions linking the two sovereign governments of the United Kingdom and Ireland. We have also differed from Lijphart over conceptual and explanatory matters in general consociational theory—partly because of our engagements with Northern Ireland. But we are obviously revisionist consociationalists, not anti-consociationalists. We have no desire to bury Lijphart's theses and contributions, even though there has been (and will be) consociational theory generated independently of his publications. Lastly, we have been robust, some would say controversial, consociationalists. We believe that it is vital to champion consociation normatively, but to do so carefully, respecting the canons and protocols of scrupulous political science. That is because we think it is premature, indeed false, to claim that consociational theory is a 'degenerating research programme', as our friend Ian Lustick has maintained (Lustick 1997). To the contrary, consociational theory is a 'progressive research programme', one that certainly requires revision, extension, and refinement, and which must remain amenable to empirical falsification. Being political scientists does not, however, require us to have no politics, or to be unduly polite about bad arguments. Consociationalists can and must engage in adversarial debate—if only to rebut our critics. What unites the consociational breed is scepticism about the universal merits of adversarial majoritarian and integrationist institutions.

Anti-consociationalism, implicit or overt, has formed a staple political diet for many in Northern Ireland, a diet we believe to be as bad for local public health as the 'Ulster fry'. Consociation has been condemned, sometimes in the most vehement terms, by Irish republicans, by Unionists, and by the political parties that represent what they insist is the 'middle ground' between the two ethnonational blocs, for example, members of the Alliance, Democratic Left, and the Women's Coalition. It has been opposed by a significant number of academics, as well as by 'think-tanks'. Critics accuse consociationalists of an 'uncritical acceptance of the primacy and permanency of ethnicity' (Taylor 1994: 163) and of conveying a 'rather bleak view of humanity' (Wilford 1992: 31). They maintain that consociation, far from resolving conflict, 'institutionalises' divisions, casting them in 'marble' (Rooney 1998: 21; Wilford 1992: 31). Consociation is said to be incompatible with democratic stability: a consociational democracy is, apparently, 'impermanent', 'dysfunctional', 'unworkable'; it is declared a 'macabre' parody of 'real democracy' by a man who some think excels in parody (McCartney 2000). The hostility to consociationalists has sometimes been feverish, sometimes risible, and sometimes just outrageous, for example, one of our critics has suggested that we are segregationists and that the segregationist perspective could be seen as 'condoning...."ethnic cleansing"' (Dixon 1996: 139; for our rebuttal, see McGarry and O'Leary 1996).

But despite local past and present hostility towards consociational principles, the fact is that since 10 April 1998, a very Good Friday, Northern Ireland has had an Agreement based on consociational architecture. We shall refer to this agreement as the Agreement. How secure it is, and can be, and whether it needs further institutional support, are matters we shall address. No one can be certain of its eventual triumph. In this introduction to a selection of our work written in the years 1987–2003 we use the background to the Agreement, its details, and its aftermath to reflect on two important academic and political questions:

1. What lessons does Northern Ireland have for consociational theory?
2. What lessons does Northern Ireland have for critics of consociational theory?

WHAT CONSOCIATIONALISTS CAN LEARN FROM NORTHERN IRELAND

Consociationalists may feel at least partially vindicated by the fact that eight Northern Irish political parties were able, largely voluntarily, to agree on a settlement with important consociational components, and to win endorsement for that agreement in simultaneous referendums in both parts of Ireland. The simple achievement of the Agreement confronts one important criticism of consociationalism: that it is unachievable in deeply divided societies, and has relevance only for societies with moderate divisions (Horowitz 1985: 572–3).[4] But the Northern Irish experience also highlights six important weaknesses in traditional consociational theory.

The neglected role of external actors in the promotion and operation of consociational settlements

Conventional consociational theory is overly 'endogenous' or 'internalist'; it has tended to treat states and regions as if they are sealed entities,

---

[4] Horowitz suggests that 'European conflicts are less ascriptive in character, less severe in intensity, less exclusive in their command of the loyalty of participants, and less preemptive of other forms of conflict' by comparison with African and Asian conflicts (1985: 572). He must *either* regard Northern Ireland as typical of moderately divided European societies to save his hypothesis that consociation does not work in deeply divided societies, *or* accept that his thesis is refuted.

relatively immune from exogenous forces. This has produced two related problems. First, there has been a tendency to downplay the importance of outside factors both when explaining how consociational settlements emerge, and when seeking to engineer their creation. Of the much debated nine factors initially listed by Lijphart as conducive to a consociational settlement, eight are endogenous (Lijphart 1977: 53–103).[5] According to Lijphart, if a state's warring factions perceive a common threat from an external source, this will increase the prospects of internal solidarity, an overarching loyalty. The focus on this particular exogenous factor stemmed from Lijphart's examination of a number of small European democracies (Belgium, the Netherlands, Switzerland, and Austria) all of which have been threatened by larger neighbours and have had at least partially consociational agreements during their recent histories. However, nowhere did he consider that outside forces can *facilitate* consociation by benign rather than malign intervention, for example, by mediation, or by using pressures and incentives to induce or encourage warring or potentially warring parties to reach agreement. Such benign external interventions helped produce a settlement in Northern Ireland (Doyle 1999).

The impasse that existed there until 1998 partly resulted from internal intransigence on the part of both republicans and Unionists. Exogenous changes played an important, and constructive, role in ending this impasse.[6] The most important exogenous influence, outside the region if not the state, was the UK government. After a brief fling with the option of integrating Northern Ireland with Great Britain in the late 1970s, London moved away from this option, though not consistently (see Chapter 7). Unionists had always considered direct rule—not radically different from their goal of an integrated United Kingdom—as preferable to the risks of a power-sharing settlement with nationalists. But in December 1985, the UK government abandoned unalloyed direct

---

[5] The formal headings of these eight factors on their first elaboration were: (i) no majority segment; (ii) multiparty systems; (iii) small population size; (iv) appropriately structured cleavages; (v) overarching loyalties; (vi) representative party systems; (vii) geographical concentration of segments; and (viii) traditions of elite accommodation.

[6] Endogenous factors were also important, particularly demographic change. The Protestant and Unionist share of Northern Ireland's population is in decline, and sits currently around 55 per cent. There is a possibility, and an even stronger perception, that there will be a Catholic and nationalist majority at some point in the foreseeable future (O'Leary 1990*a*: 342–57, 1990*b*: no. 281: 12–15; no. 282: 16–17, 1995*b*: 709–12, 1997*b*). This has undercut Unionists' enthusiasm for majoritarian democracy and increased their support for power-sharing. For a more extensive treatment of the exogenous and endogenous factors behind the Agreement see Chapter 9, and of exogenous and endogenous explanations in general see McGarry and O'Leary (1995*a*: *passim*).

rule from Westminster. In the Anglo-Irish Agreement the Republic of Ireland was given a limited role in policy-making in Northern Ireland and comprehensive consultative rights—with the promise that the new intergovernmental conference would decline in salience if an agreement on a devolved government could be reached between nationalists and unionists (a strategy of 'coercive consociationalism'—see Chapters 2 and 3). The UK's default policy had now shifted towards London–Dublin cooperation in and over the region. Unionists feared this shift would be irreversible and deepened in the absence of agreement between Northern Irish parties. Margaret Thatcher had several reasons for signing the Anglo-Irish Agreement, but pressure from the United States was important. From the early 1980s, leading US politicians, prompted by the Irish government and Irish Americans, encouraged Great Britain to cooperate more closely with Ireland, and President Ronald Reagan, whom Thatcher respected, put his personal clout behind this message. So American pressure prepared the groundwork for 1998 even before President Clinton was elected in 1992. There was, of course, no immediate generation of consociation through the coercive inducements of the Anglo-Irish Agreement. At first, unionists thought they could destroy that Agreement by protest, but it proved durable. They hoped it could be resisted or incrementally reversed while the Conservatives were in power in London, especially during the 1992–7 parliament when the Major government depended on Unionist support in the House of Commons.[7] The Ulster Unionist Party (UUP) began to negotiate seriously with nationalists only after Labour's landslide victory in May 1997 and the new Prime Minister Tony Blair's signal that he was committed to achieving a settlement within his first year of office (O'Leary 2001*a*).

The United States and Irish America played a constructive role in the promotion of the Anglo-Irish Agreement and would play an even more significant role in the making of the 1998 Agreement (Arthur 1991; Cox 1997; Guelke 1996; Evans 1998; Dempsey 1999). Influenced by significant Irish-American lobbies and by the end of the cold war, which freed US presidents from traditional constraints about interfering in the United Kingdom's internal affairs, the United States gave unprecedented attention to Northern Ireland in the 1990s, especially when President Clinton took office in 1992 (O'Clery 1996/1997). He approved an indirect collective envoy, the 'Morrison delegation', which visited Ireland and met all parties during the early stages of the peace process. He put

---

[7] Indeed, the option of integration, which had been abandoned since 1979, was reconsidered during the Major years (see Chapter 7).

several of his senior advisers to work on the subject, including the National Security Adviser, Anthony Lake. He ended up visiting the region three times in five years, the first US president to go there. Northern Ireland's political leaders had open access to the White House, and made frequent use of it. Clinton persuaded former Senate majority leader George Mitchell first to chair an economic initiative, then a crucial commission to arbitrate disputes between the UK and Irish governments over the decommissioning of paramilitary weapons and the timing of negotiations, and then to preside over the final negotiations that led to the Agreement (Mitchell, G. C., de Chastelain, and Holkeri 1996: Report; Mitchell, G. C. 2000). The president is known to have intervened personally and productively in the political negotiations on several occasions (MacGinty 1997b; Cox 1999).

An important consequence of American diplomatic involvement was an increase in the confidence of Irish republicans about the merits of negotiations. A 1994 document on the peace strategy, TUAS (reputedly an acronym for either Totally Unarmed Strategy or Tactical Use of Armed Struggle, although its exact meaning was never spelled out), was explicit about the importance of the American role, noting that 'there is potentially a very powerful Irish-American lobby not in hock to any particular party in Britain or Ireland' and that 'Clinton is perhaps the first US president in decades to be influenced by such a lobby' (MacGinty 1997a: 34). Washington also shored up the position of the Irish government in its negotiations with Great Britain, and of constitutional nationalists led by John Hume of the SDLP. Clinton's decision in early 1994 to issue a visa to Sinn Féin leader Gerry Adams is credited with carrying hard-line republicans behind his peace strategy.[8] Adams himself claimed that it brought forward by one year the IRA ceasefire, which occurred in August 1994. The ceasefire was a prerequisite for the possibility of comprehensive and inclusive negotiations. While the Clinton administration's role in coaxing republicans into negotiating has been acknowledged, it is less often noted that it managed this task without alienating unionists. Like constitutional nationalists, unionists were given unprecedented access to the White House and the administration was careful to appear impartial throughout. One of us personally witnessed a loyalist paramilitary leader convicted of murders and

---

[8] The complaints of the State Department were spearheaded by the US ambassador to the UK Raymond Seitz who complained bitterly at the overturning of his counsel at the time, and in his memoirs (Seitz 1998) reviewed in O'Leary (1998a). More extensive analyses of the exogenous factors that led to the Good Friday Agreement are available (McGarry 2001c; Guelke 2001; McGarry and O'Leary 1995a: ch. 10; O'Leary 2002).

republicans convicted of bombing offences happily enjoying the White House's environs in May 1995 and March 1998. The UUP leader David Trimble acknowledged that reassurances from Clinton helped convince him to sign the Agreement.[9]

Benign, or eventually benign, exogenous action has facilitated power-sharing settlements elsewhere, not just in Northern Ireland. The United States, the United Nations, NATO, and the European Union, using their good offices, sanctions, incentives, and military powers, have played pivotal roles in promoting (or establishing) power-sharing institutions in Bosnia-Hercegovina, Macedonia, and Afghanistan. Indeed, it is difficult to imagine such settlements in any of these countries without outside intervention. Traditional consociational theory neglected a benign or at least activist role for outsiders in the promotion of power-sharing, perhaps because it was initially developed during the cold war when such interventions were rare.[10] However, we now live in an era where interventions, orchestrated especially by the United States or the European Union, are more prevalent—and there is a need to think more about the effectiveness of such efforts on the viability of consociational arrangements.[11]

While outsiders can play positive roles and tip the balance in favour of negotiated or induced agreements, settlements reached primarily under exogenous pressure may have shallow endogenous foundations. This was a fatal flaw in the Cyprus power-sharing settlement of 1960–3, and may yet prove damaging to the externally-imposed Dayton Accords in Bosnia-Hercegovina. One difficulty with the Agreement is that it is not clear that it would have been signed, at least in its extant form, particularly by unionists, without outside pressures. A large number of Unionists, led by the Democratic Unionist Party (DUP), rejected the

---

[9] Personal communication from Professor Andrew Wilson, who interviewed Trimble on this matter. One of us attended two Saint Patrick's Day celebrations held at the White House (in 1994 and 1998) and the White House May 1995 investment for peace conference, and can testify to the care taken to ensure balanced invitations of unionists, nationalists, republicans, loyalists, and others.

[10] The exceptions to this rule were analyses of the Lebanon—whose arrangements were known to be crucially affected by local geopolitics. The destabilization of Lebanon's consociation in the 1970s powerfully shows the possible impact of malign external interventions (Hanf 1993).

[11] We do not think that exogenous forces can promote stable consociational settlements when endogenous forces are strongly unfavourable, but we do not subscribe to the view that outsiders can make no appreciable difference. For an interesting essay on how external governments can use food aid to promote power-sharing, see Ed Luttwak, 'Aid is a Weapon. Let's Use it', *Globe and Mail*, 22 November 2001, A25.

Agreement, as did significant numbers of unionist voters, and this remains its chief political weakness.

A related lacuna in traditional consociational theory is that it neglected the possibilities of positive roles for outsiders both in the *implementation* and in the active *operation* of power-sharing settlements. The Agreement has numerous outsiders significantly at the heart of its implementation. An international commission, headed by the Canadian general John de Chastelain, oversees the decommissioning of paramilitary weapons and disarmament. Witnesses to IRA acts of decommissioning included the former Finnish president Marti Ahtisaari and Cyril Ramaphosa of the African National Congress. Proposing the details of police reform was handed to an independent commission, with representation from the United States and Canada, as well as Great Britain and Ireland. Overseeing the implementation of the eventual police reforms was given to an American, Tom Constantine, who reports to the two sovereign governments. Amidst continuing difficulties in achieving full implementation of the Agreement in a 'Joint Declaration', released on 1 May 2003, the same two governments proposed international representation on an 'Independent Monitoring Body'. It is tasked with putting paramilitary activity under surveillance and formulating sanctions against political parties associated with offending organizations. The four-person body is to comprise two members nominated by the UK government (one from Northern Ireland); a member nominated by the Irish government; and a fourth nominated by the American administration. The European Court of Human Rights performs a role in the protection of human rights in Northern Ireland. The office of the OSCE's High Commissioner on National Minorities has advised on deliberations over the design of a local Bill of Rights.

This extensive external involvement, which could be further elaborated, mirrors developments in power-sharing agreements elsewhere. There is external representation in several of the institutions established in Bosnia-Hercegovina and Kosovo, including Bosnia's Supreme Court and Central Bank; both arrangements are presided over by external High Representatives, and have included external agents in providing security. The recent UN plan for Cyprus envisages a central tie-breaking role for outsiders in that island's Supreme Court. These developments suggest that the implementation and the operation of consociational settlements should no longer be considered the internal preserve of sovereign independent states. One can see a repertoire of international interventionist techniques and norms emerging of which Northern Ireland is perhaps the key exemplar.

Consociationalism and trans-state self-determination disputes

Traditional consociational theory developed from a concern with religious and class divisions in a number of European countries—the Netherlands, Belgium, Austria, and Switzerland (Lijphart 1977). It neglected the particularity of self-determination disputes, that is, those that involve ethno-national communities focused on contested homelands. One consequence is that the emphasis in traditional consociational theory was on *who* should exercise power at the level of the central government. But self-determination disputes are often about *how much* power should be exercised by the central government—and about whether there should be one or more central governments. Although autonomy is an important value in consociational arrangements, the emphasis is often on non-territorial, or corporate, autonomy, rather than the territorial autonomy insisted on as a minimum desideratum by most self-determination movements. Given their 'internalist' focus, addressed above, consociationalists have been historically ill equipped to address self-determination disputes that affect more than one state.

These problems were clear in Lijphart's otherwise masterly dissection of the Northern Ireland conflict in 1975. He was pessimistic about the immediate prospects for consociation—as were we (Lijphart 1975: 105; O'Leary 1987; McGarry 1988, 1990; McGarry and O'Leary 1990*a*, *b*; and see Chapter 3). However, we differed in our diagnoses. In his view, the key difficulty was the absence of support for power-sharing among Protestants because they were capable of exercising hegemonic power alone, and because they were disposed to Westminster majoritarian practices rather than continental power-sharing norms (Lijphart 1975: 100). This analysis was accurate, but limited. It overlooked the fact that nationalists were also opposed to internalist power-sharing within the United Kingdom. Irish republicans wanted Irish national self-determination and a complete withdrawal of the British state from Ireland, whereas moderate nationalists wanted any consociation to be internationalized, that is, to have a linkage to Ireland, and a role for the Irish government. This nationalist insistence on links with Ireland reinforced the resolve of many Unionists to avoid power-sharing—and, as we have seen, they had no incentive to share power since the default option was direct rule from Great Britain, their preferred nation-state.

Any feasible agreement in Northern Ireland had to deal squarely with the disputes that had flowed from the inequitable legacies of the partition of Ireland in 1920 without any formal respect for Irish self-determination. At least three parts of the Agreement reached in 1998 are relevant here, and all depart from traditional consociational accords:

1. *The NSMC and the B-IGC.* Had the Agreement included only traditional consociational institutions, not even moderate nationalists would have signed it. The Social Democratic and Labour Party (the SDLP) signed only because the Agreement provided for a number of political institutions that joined both parts of Ireland, and maintained an oversight role for the Republic's government. The most important all-island institution was a North–South Ministerial Council (NSMC), a body nominated by the Irish Republic's government and the new Northern Ireland premiers. It was agreed that it should meet in plenary twice a year, and in smaller groups to discuss specific sectors (say, agriculture or education) on a 'regular and frequent basis'. In addition, the Agreement provided for a number of cross-border or all-island 'implementation' bodies. These eventually turned out to be six in number, and they were given the task of cooperating over inland waterways, food safety, trade and business development, special EU programmes, the Irish language and Ulster Scots dialect, and aquaculture and marine matters. The Agreement committed both parts of Ireland to a further six functional areas of cooperation—including some aspects of transport, agriculture, education, health, the environment, and tourism. It also established the British–Irish intergovernmental conference (B-IGC), the successor to the Intergovernmental Conference established under Anglo-Irish Agreement. This guarantees Ireland's government access to policy formulation on all matters not—or not yet—devolved to the Northern Ireland Assembly or the NSMC. In the event of the collapse of the Agreement, this institution will resume the all-encompassing role it had under the Anglo-Irish Agreement. It also promotes bilateral cooperation between the Irish and British governments on all matters of mutual interest within their respective jurisdictions.

2. *Recognition of Irish self-determination.* Republicans would not have approved the Agreement had the UK government not recognized, in a treaty, the right of the people of Ireland, meaning the whole island, to exercise their right to self-determination, albeit conjointly and severally as 'North' and 'South', to bring about a united Ireland if that was their wish. The referendums and the British–Irish Agreement (the treaty incorporating the Agreement) endeavoured to make the partition of Ireland—and its continuation—and the Agreement and its institutions dependent upon the expressed will of the people of Ireland.

3. *Recognition of the principle of consent and the BIC.* Unionists, who were ambivalent about the Agreement, were persuaded to ratify it because it entrenched the principle of consent. That is, Northern Ireland cannot become part of Ireland unless a majority in Northern Ireland agree. Ireland's constitution was changed, after a referendum in both jurisdictions, to reflect this principle. Unionists also secured new east–west institutions to reflect their link with Great Britain. The British–Irish Council (BIC) comprises the two governments of the United Kingdom and Ireland, along with all the devolved governments of the United Kingdom and its neighbouring insular dependent territories (Scotland, Wales, the Isle of Man, Jersey, and Guernsey). (More details of the Agreement's cross-border institutions, and the federalizing and confederalizing processes that may flow from them, are contained in Chapter 9.)

Key provisions in the Agreement mark it out as a settlement between national communities rather than ethnic or religious communities. Ministers take a 'Pledge of Office', not an 'Oath of Allegiance' (see Chapter 9). This cements the bi-nationalism at the heart of the Agreement: nationalist ministers do not have to swear an Oath of Allegiance to the Crown or the Union. The Patten Report on policing, mandated by the Agreement, recommended that the name of the police be nationally impartial, and that the display of the Union flag and the portrait of the Queen in police stations should go. Policing symbols were to be 'free from association with the British or Irish states' (see Chapter 13). Mutual recognition of national claims lay at the core of the Agreement. Ireland has recognized the British political identity of unionists. The United Kingdom recognized Irish northern nationalists as a national minority, not simply as a cultural or religious minority, and as part of a possible future Irish national majority. Unionists who made the Agreement recognized nationalists as nationalists, not simply as Catholics. Nationalists recognized Unionists as Unionists, and not just as Protestants.

Self-determination disputes are central to a range of conflicts including those in Bosnia-Hercegovina, Kosovo, the Basque country, Sri Lanka, Cyprus, Kashmir, Kurdistan, Trans-Dniestria, and Nagorno-Karabakh. In these cases, the issues at stake are not simply about sharing power, or even primarily about sharing power. Questions of autonomy, sovereignty, irredentism, symbols, explicit recognition as national communities, and institutional links across state frontiers are also crucial. To increase its relevance in a range of conflict zones, consociational theory and practice have to address these aspects of self-determination disputes.

The complexity of internal consociational settlements

The first and second omissions in consociational theory arguably stem from the same cause: a now outdated tendency to treat the state as a sovereign, independent, and insulated entity. The third is different. Even within the internal state-centric approach favoured in traditional consociational accounts, there has been an overly narrow focus on the design of, and need for agreement on, political (legislative and executive) institutions. But the achievement of enduring settlements normally requires agreement on (sometimes numerous) issues that go beyond such institutions, such as the design of the police, demilitarization, the return of exiles to their homes, the management of prisoners, education reform, economic policy, and the promotion of language and other group rights.

Failure to establish agreement on any such issue can prevent, destabilize, or undermine entire settlements, even if there is broad consensus on institutions. Thus, in Northern Ireland, an agreement required a number of issues to be addressed beyond the narrow question of executive and legislature design. One such issue, which we address in Chapter 13, was police reform. While the parties failed to reach consensus on this in the Good Friday negotiations, they agreed to mandate an independent commission, and on its terms of reference. Subsequently, the failure to manage police reform satisfactorily helped to destabilize the political institutions, as it helped to delay substantive decommissioning by the IRA, which in turn made it difficult for Unionists to participate in the executive. Another aspect of internal complexity, addressed in Chapter 12, is on the design of a Bill of Rights, including the questions of whether such bills should be limited to conventional liberal (individual) rights or should also entrench group rights, including the political rights included in the Agreement. Other power-sharing agreements, whether in Bosnia-Hercegovina, Kosovo, Macedonia, or Afghanistan, are also more internally complex than is normally discussed in consociational accounts. Any theory that seeks to explain the likelihood or durability of consociational settlements, or that seeks to facilitate them, needs to confront this complexity.

The merits of PR-STV versus PR-party list electoral systems

Elections to the new 108-member Northern Ireland Assembly (first elected in 1998) are conducted under a proportional representation (PR) system, the single transferable vote (STV), in six member constituencies. This system is not what Lijphart recommends for consociational agreements. He is an advocate of party-list PR systems, principally because they are said to help make party leaders more powerful within their parties and better able to sustain inter-ethnic consociational deals. Those who would like to see David Trimble in better control of the UUP might hanker after Lijphart's preferred form of PR. The evidence from pre- and post-Agreement Northern Ireland suggests, however, that a modification of the consociational prescriptive canon is in order.

Had a region-wide list system been in operation for the elections to the Northern Ireland Assembly in June 1998, the UUP would have ended up with fewer seats, and with fewer seats than the SDLP (Mitchell, P. 1999; O'Leary 1999e: 74–5; Mitchell, P. 2001). In consequence, the implementation of the Agreement would have been even more problematic than it has been. There is a less contingent argument against party-list systems in consociations, especially important where the relevant ethnic communities are internally democratic rather than sociologically and politically monolithic. A region-wide party list election system gives incentives for the formation of a wide variety of micro-parties. It would have fragmented and shredded the votes of the major parties that made the Agreement. Hardliners under party-list systems have every reason to form fresh parties knowing that their disloyalty will penalize more moderate parties but without necessarily reducing the total vote and seat share of the relevant ethno-national bloc. This objection to Lijphart's favoured prescription is not merely speculative. The 1996 elections to the Northern Ireland Peace Forum used a mixture of a party-list system and 'reserved seats'. Party proliferation and the erosion of the UUP first-preference vote were among the more obvious consequences (Evans and O'Leary 1997a, b).[12] STV, of course, does not guarantee party discipline, as multiple candidates for the same party in a given constituency may present, tacitly or otherwise, slightly different emphases on party commitments, as indeed happened in Northern Ireland in 1998. However, STV, with higher effective thresholds than exist under most forms of party-list PR, makes it more likely that parties will remain formally unified, and therefore able to make and maintain consociational deals. At the very least, the prescriptive superiority of the party-list system for these purposes is unproven, and Lijphart's consistent counsel in this respect should be modified.

[12] The nature of executive formation in the Agreement should act as one possible check on the possibilities of fragmentation under party-list PR, because only large parties are likely to win ministries under the d'Hondt allocation process (see Chapter 9), but that is true of any electoral system combined with this executive.

Conceptual refinements

Consociational theory has been dogged by controversy over key terms. Northern Ireland practice helps refine these conceptual issues and resolve them (O'Leary, in progress). Though Lijphart has traditionally defined a consociation as requiring a grand coalition, it is evident that though this is an empirical possibility what makes consociations feasible and work is joint consent across the significant communities, with the emphasis on jointness. We may usefully distinguish unanimous consociations (grand coalitions), concurrent consociations (in which the executive has majority support in each significant segment), and weak consociations (where the executive may have only a plurality level of support amongst one or more segments). Consociations become undemocratic when elites govern with factional or lower levels of support within their segments. Northern Ireland between 1998 and 2001 operated intermittently as a concurrent consociation and sometimes looked like a weak consociation—because of a lack of majority support amongst unionists, though it had plurality support amongst Protestants for much of the time. A range of other refinements to consociational concepts, inspired by the Northern Irish experience, may also be made which we shall not elaborate on here.

Allocating ministerial portfolios through sequential proportionality rules

It is worth highlighting a final weakness of conventional consociational thinking. It was tacitly committed to power-sharing as a by-product of interparty negotiations over government formation. This, of course, was a major political problem: such coalitions might be difficult to achieve, and even more difficult to maintain. It was a key difficulty in 'incentives'; it appeared to be premised upon overcoming trust and voluntary statesmanship. Northern Ireland has not, of course, solved this key issue of political trust but it has put it in a new light. Northern Ireland's Agreement, especially if it stabilizes, promises to publicize a technique that is not widely known, and that usefully resolves the disputes that may arise between polarized parties when they must share out ministerial portfolios (O'Leary, Grofman, and Elklit 2001).[13] It is a technique for

---

[13] Elklit shows that the system has been in use in Danish local government, so Northern Ireland is not the pioneer except in using this technique to achieve power-sharing among ethno-nationally opposed parties (O'Leary, Grofman, and Elklit, at 'revise and resubmit' stage with the *American Journal of Political Science*).

speeding government formation after elections, one that conforms to the proportionality principles of consociational thinking, facilitates power sharing, and meets many tests of fairness. The d'Hondt allocation process (see Chapter 9), using divisors of 1, 2, 3, . . . , n, takes advantage of the fact that divisor rules for achieving fair proportions can also be used to determine the sequence in which parties should be entitled to nominate ministers. This system, and any system of achieving proportionality through divisors, has the decided advantage of halting protracted negotiations over ministerial portfolio allocations; and, had it been allowed to operate without interference, would have provided strong incentives for parties to stay within an executive even if they had disagreements—because if they did not, their entitlements would go to other parties, including parties from different national or ethnic blocs. We advocated such a system before the Agreement was made (McGarry and O'Leary 1995a: 373–5), though we make no claims to being the authors of the technique,[14] which seems to have emerged out of inter-party bargaining, and we would have preferred to have had another device adopted, the Sainte-Laguë method (which uses divisors of 1, 3, 5, . . . , n, and helps smaller parties). Technically, the d'Hondt process has worked well in Northern Ireland—though, of course, it has had its critics amongst smaller parties, and amongst anti-consociationalists.

WHAT CRITICS OF CONSOCIATION CAN LEARN FROM NORTHERN IRELAND

Some local critics of consociationalism are supporters of exclusionary forms of majority rule—be they unionists who see Northern Ireland as the appropriate unit of self-determination, or nationalists who see Ireland as the appropriate unit. This amounts to saying that some groups are simply entitled to govern others by virtue of their majority status in a given territory. This, we admit, is the bias of many, if not all, nation-states. That does not mean, however, that that bias should be accepted. International law and civic values emphasize individual rights and equal citizenship—and therefore unabashed ethnic majoritarianism is of questionable moral import. And most current critics of consociationalism operate from integrationist perspectives which, at least on their face, claim to transcend ethnic partisanship (see Chapters 4 and 5). Integrationists normally present themselves as exponents of civic patriotism,

---

[14] We did help in the dissemination of such ideas (McGarry and Graham 1990: 168–9; O'Leary 1995a: 864–7; O'Leary et al. 1993: 139–44).

civic nationalism, civic republicanism, or cosmopolitanism. They accuse consociationalists of exaggerating the depth and resilience of social divisions, and of downplaying the human capacity to develop new, common, or cross-cutting identities. They believe that consociational institutions may be perverse because they allegedly exacerbate conflicts through strengthening the divisions between communities. The positions of partisan ethnic elites, whom they hold responsible for division in the first place, are thereby cemented. Their claim is that consociational institutions entrench and deepen division. Therefore, they are seen not simply as undesirable, but as perverse, unstable, and unworkable.

Northern Ireland has several different varieties of integrationist. We distinguish four:

1. *Civic republicans.* Irish republicans who reject the Agreement argue that unionism is a superficial identity, maintained by the presence of the British state in Ireland (exponents and critics can be found in Porter 1998). The way forward is said to lie, not in support for institutions which reinforce intra-Irish divisions, but in the withdrawal of the British state and the incorporation of all of Northern Ireland's citizens into a thirty-two county Irish Republic (Rooney 1998).

2. *Civic Unionists.* Some of the unionists who reject the Agreement maintain that most Catholics would be happy to be citizens of the United Kingdom, provided their individual rights and culture were protected. Rather than establish institutions that encourage Catholics to look to Dublin, and that threaten the British civil liberties of all citizens, Northern Ireland, it is argued, should be integrated with Great Britain. Strong unionist integrationists reject substantive devolution of any sort, power-sharing or not. In their view, any self-government should be minimalist in scope, like that in Wales. There are also unionists who later embraced the Agreement who have espoused civic integrationism (Porter 1996, 2003).[15]

3. *Post-national transformers.* A third perspective, popular with the intellectual left, but also represented in small parties from outside the ethno-national blocs, including the Alliance, Democratic Left, the Labour party, and the Northern Ireland Women's Coalition, emphasizes the need for Northern Ireland's society to be transformed from the bottom up. 'Transformers' typically blame

---

[15] The latter was subjected to an exasperated review by the leader of the UUP (Trimble 2003).

regional divisions on social segregation, economic inequality, and ethnocentric appeals by elites in both communities. They call for policies to promote social integration, increased public spending to tackle the 'material basis' of sectarian identities,[16] and demand that sectarian elites on both sides be challenged by civil society: particularly trade unions, civic associations, and political parties outside the two main blocs, and peace and conflict resolution groups that 'cross-cut social divisions and challenge and erode the clash of opposing ethnonationalisms' (Taylor 2001: 47; Bew and Patterson 1985: *passim*; Bew and Patterson 1990: 217). Within the camp of the transformers we include the exponents of emancipation: emancipation from existing conflictual identities (Ruane and Todd 1996: ch. 11). Transformation is seen as a prerequisite for a lasting political settlement. To try the latter without the former is seen as counterproductive. Social transformers are optimistic about the prospects for transformation, with one arguing recently that there is evidence of increasing integration in housing and schools and that a significant number of voluntary associations had succeeded in producing an 'erosion of ethno-nationalism on both sides, a fading of Orange and Green, in favour of a commonality around the need for genuine structures of democracy and justice' (see Taylor 2001: 43; Douglas 1998: 220, 222).

4. *Electoral integrationists.* This perspective, especially sympathetically received by the third and second approaches, emphasizes the engineering of *political* institutions to promote integrated identities. It is associated with our friend the distinguished American political scientist, Donald Horowitz, and his supporters in Northern Ireland, Rick Wilford and Robin Wilson (Horowitz 2001; Wilson, R. and Wilford 2003; Wilson, R. 2003). Horowitz and his local endorsers argue that political institutions should be designed to encourage politicians to reach out across ethnic boundaries. They criticize the new consociational 'grand coalition' because it guarantees seats to all major parties on the executive: it provides, allegedly, for little opposition, and little incentive for its members to cooperate. It includes the rival extremists, which makes it unlikely to reach agreement; it would be better, according to this perspective, to have a 'voluntary' coalition of moderates. Parties seeking to join such a

---

[16] Taylor approvingly cited Henry Patterson for the claim that the accommodation of the minority's national identity in the Anglo-Irish Agreement was a poor substitute for dealing with the 'material basis of Catholic grievance' (Taylor 1994: 171, n. 13).

coalition would have an incentive to tone down their ethnocentric rhetoric during election campaigns, and they would be more likely to cooperate in office. Horowitz and his supporters dislike the party-list form of PR and the PR-STV system. Both are said to damage the prospects for inter-ethnic cooperation because the relatively low quota required to win seats makes it too easy for hardline parties and their candidates to be successful (Horowitz 2001). Their preferred electoral system is the Alternative Vote (AV), which involves preferential voting like STV but requires each winning candidate to win majority support in single member districts. It is said to encourage politicians to 'vote-pool' among different ethnic groups to build such a majority (for similar arguments from the experience of Papua and New Guinea, see Reilly 1997, 2001).

Having outlined the thinking of various integrationists as fairly as we can, we shall try to provide readers with food for reflection on what we regard as both utopian and mistaken analyses. Our effort at persuasion insists on recognizing realities which we like no more than integrationists: we believe the charge of wishful thinking is more accurately directed at integrationists.

Complex consociation as responsible realism

The key problem with the integrationist perspectives of republicans and unionists who reject the Agreement is rather fundamental: neither of their projects has the remotest prospect of winning cross-community support, let alone of delivering justice and stability. For over a century historic Ulster, and then the Northern Ireland that was carved from it, has been divided electorally into two rival ethno-national blocs. The divisions have become particularly intense during the past thirty years. While nationalist and unionist parties won an average of 82 per cent of the vote during the five region-wide elections held between 1973 and 1975, they received an average of 91 per cent in the five campaigns held between 1996 and 1999. Within the nationalist bloc, moreover, the republican share of the vote has been increasing. In its first five election campaigns (1982–7) Sinn Féin won an average of 37.3 per cent of the nationalist vote. In the five campaigns between 1996 and 1999 its average increased to 41 per cent. And then, more dramatically, in the Westminster 2001 and local government elections it became the majority party in votes within the nationalist bloc for the first time (Mitchell, P., O'Leary, and Evans 2001, 2002).[17] Patterns within the unionist bloc are more complex, because both major unionist parties have been equally intransigent for most of the period between 1971 and 1998. There is some evidence, however, that the UUP's increased moderation in recent years has cost it electoral support to the advantage of the DUP (Mitchell, P., O'Leary, and Evans 2001, 2002). But there has been no swing voting between the two ethno-national blocs over the last three decades, and any change in their respective shares of the poll has been caused by different birth, death, emigration, and electoral participation rates. The rising nationalist share of the vote, from 24.1 per cent in the 1973 election to the Northern Ireland Assembly, to an average of 32.5 per cent in seven region-wide elections between 1982 and 1989, and 39.8 per cent in five elections between 1996 and 1999, had nothing to do with the conversion of Unionists. It is the result of Sinn Féin's participation in electoral politics since 1982, a higher electoral participation rate by Catholics, and an increase in the Catholic share of the population (O'Leary 1990b; O'Leary and McGarry 1993: 192; O'Leary and Evans 1997; Mitchell, P. 1995, 1999, 2001). Parties formed outside the two ethno-national blocs have shown no sign of making a political breakthrough. Indeed the self-styled 'middle ground' has been squeezed in recent decades. The largest of the middle-ground parties, the Alliance Party, averaged 8.4 per cent of the vote in its first five region-wide election campaigns (1973–5), but only 6 per cent in the five election campaigns between 1996 and 1999. During the two regional elections in 1996 and 1998, the vote-share of parties outside the ethno-national blocs amounted to just 8.4 per cent on both occasions. These data are a powerful evidence of strong polarization and deeply held identifications, realities that will not be easily transformed by any electoral system changes.

The two major communities have distinct national identities, not merely ethnic heritages. Neither unionists nor nationalists want to be subsumed within the other's nation-state, even if they are guaranteed equal citizenship. Even moderate nationalists insist on, at a bare minimum, internal power-sharing and external institutional links between Northern Ireland and Ireland. Even moderate unionists, prepared to tolerate cross-border institutions to accommodate nationalists, insist on retaining strong political links with Great Britain, now and in the future. In this respect both communities are like national communities elsewhere, in Canada (Quebec), Great Britain (Scotland), or Spain (Basques

---

[17] Interested readers will find that figure 2 in Mitchell, O'Leary, and Evans (2002: 33) has a printer's error that transposes the DUP and Alliance party vote-shares.

and Catalans), all of which insist on institutional accommodation of their own identity and reject attempts by their respective majorities to treat everyone as undifferentiated citizens. But whereas the latter cases show significant evidence of people being willing to be integrated in autonomy arrangements with dual identities (Scots and British; Catalan and Spanish; and Quebeckers and Canadians), Northern Ireland's identity matrices are different. To the extent that there are significant numbers with dual identities (Northern Irish and Irish, and Ulster Scots and British) they are opposed rather than compatible, or insufficiently strong (Northern Irish) to weaken the other polarized identities (Irish or British).

While partisan nationalist and unionist versions of integrationism are unfair and unrealistic, social transformationists and emancipationists are merely unrealistic over any feasible medium-term future. It is difficult to criticize social transformation or emancipation as a long-term objective, but there is no significant evidence that it can be achieved soon, especially outside of the context of a mutually acceptable political settlement. Transformers' optimism about the feasibility of their project stems from the belief that electoral data reflect elite machinations, manipulations, and perverse incentives, and are not representative of a considerable consensus that allegedly exists outside conventional politics. But, if so, they are obliged to explain why, in free and open elections, only nationalists and unionist elites win significant numbers of votes, while elites that stress cross-cutting issues, such as class or civic values, receive small levels of support. The fact is that turnout in Northern Ireland elections is both higher than in the United Kingdom as a whole, and higher than anywhere else in Great Britain. It is also a fact that the position of the main political parties on constitutional issues broadly reflect the public preferences reported in survey data.[18]

It is not even true that the political preferences of Northern Ireland's 'civil society', that is, its large numbers of civic associations, differ from those of its political parties. The most popular civil society organizations in Northern Ireland, the Orange Order and Gaelic Athletic Association, are solidly unionist and nationalist, respectively.[19] True, several smaller

---

[18] For data on the turnout rate in Northern Ireland, see n. 46–8 in Chapter 10. Survey data ranging from the 1960s to 1980s (Moxon-Browne 1991) and the 1990s (Trew 1996), and analyses (Duffy and Evans 1997; Evans and Duffy 1997), are consistent in showing ethnic polarization—though they used to under-report extremist preferences at the ballot box. There are social bases to party competition within blocs, but they do not explain party support across blocs.

[19] Shane O'Neill has observed that 'even politically active feminists in Northern Ireland seek to be recognized as one of the national communities by women from the other

peace and conflict resolution organizations reach across the national divide and seek to promote a transcendent identity, but just as many if not more, according to the academic who has most closely studied them, are nationalist or unionist groups that want an honourable bi-national compromise (Cochrane 2001: 153). Finally, contrary to the position of a leading social transformationist, there is no unambiguous indication that the two communities desire to mix socially. It may be true, as Taylor says, that 'the extent of integrated education has widened' (2001: 43) but it has widened to only 3–4 per cent of the school-age population. Taylor cites a survey reported by Tom Hadden that indicates 'most people in Northern Ireland want to live together rather than apart', but Hadden has argued that the 'major trend' in housing since 1971 has been for both communities to 'congregate in areas where they feel safer and less exposed' (Boyle and Hadden 1994: 33). People express tolerant preferences but practice suspicion: a common feature of ethnically divided societies. Taylor also cites an article from John Whyte in support of his claim that 'there are now a number of cross-community housing projects', but in this article Whyte actually claimed that 'residential segregation is increasing' (Whyte 1993: 115). Even if there was evidence of a clear wish to mix socially and residentially, it is not clear that this would obviate the need for, or be incompatible with, a political settlement that accommodated both groups.

These realities explain why the British and Irish governments eventually converged on accepting versions of proposals first articulated by the SDLP: accommodating the two ethno-national blocs in power-sharing institutions with trans-state dimensions.[20] Such a settlement was not possible for much of the past thirty years. It became so only when republican and unionist political agents stepped away, however haltingly, from their respective integrationist absolutes. This political movement was matched in the academic community, where two leading unionist professors switched their position subtly from the integrationist position that any accommodation of nationalists was a boon to Protestant sectarianism to the view that a (minimalist) accommodation of Irish

traditions...most feminists freely acknowledge the political primacy of the national struggle...The same point might be made about activists in the gay and lesbian communities' (O'Neill 1999).

[20] Analysts differ over whether consociation has been a consistent goal of UK governments. It is a nice irony that some anti-consociationalists think it has been. Wilford refers to it as an 'ideé fixe' of British policy since 1972 (Wilford 2001: 4; another anti-consociationalist sees a continuing emphasis on power-sharing in British policy; Dixon 2001: *passim*). By contrast, pro-consociationalists believe UK policy commitments in this respect were intermittent and inconsistent (see our chapters here, especially Chapters 2, 3, 7, and 8).

nationalism was necessary for peace and the erosion of extremism (Bew, Patterson, and Teague 1997: 214; Bew and Patterson 1990).[21]

The making of the Agreement, unarguably consociational in its pre-figuration and in its content, and with all of its attendant difficulties, has been associated with a highly significant reduction in political violence. Since January of the year of composition of this chapter (2003) there has been no political death from the conflict. In the seven years up to and including 1994, the year of the first IRA and loyalists cease fires, the total loss of life because of the conflict was 622 persons. In the seven sub-sequent years to 2001 the total loss of life because of the conflict was 140 persons. That is a fall in the death toll of nearly four-fifths, despite a major break down in the IRA ceasefire in 1996–7, and despite inter-mittent breakdowns in the loyalists' ceasefires (calculated from McKittrick *et al.* 2001: 1496; for a tribute to this work see O'Leary 2000*a*). This is palpable evidence of a meaningful peace process.

Consider first the republican truce. Since the Agreement has been made, despite difficulties in its implementation, and despite potentially damaging episodes and incidents (e.g. gun-running, material aid to the FARC of Columbia, a republican spy-ring at Stormont castle), the IRA ceasefire has held. Republican breakaways from the IRA, 'dissidents', have been minimal, and, aside from the horrific Omagh bomb, have not posed major security hazards. The IRA has opened its arms dumps to weapons-inspectors, and begun a process of decommissioning. The IRA has been the major quantitative protagonist in the conflict, responsible for 49 per cent of all deaths between 1966 and 2001 (calculated from McKittrick *et al.* 2001: table 2). The Real and the Continuity IRAs pose, to date, no comparable threat. So, in any long-run assessment, the IRA ceasefires and the making of the Agreement have to be regarded as a major step towards stability. No proposed unionist, or emancipationist, integrationist solution with which we are familiar would have been likely to produce these results.

Consider now the loyalist truce. The major loyalist paramilitary organizations, the Ulster Volunteer Force (UVF) and the Ulster Defence Association (UDA), have been on formal ceasefire since 1994. They have been subject to greater fragmentation, especially since the formation of the Loyalist Volunteer Force. They have displayed greater evidence of

---

[21] Paul Bew and Henry Patterson, along with Paul Teague, called for the establishment of cross-border institutions as a 'symbolic fig leaf' for nationalists; Patterson refers to the Framework Documents of 1995 which first sketched these proposals as 'green-garlanded' (Patterson 2001: 166).

indisciplined organization than the IRA (Bruce 2001). Between them they were responsible for fourteen deaths in 2000: six UDA/UFF, six UVF/ RHC, and two LVF killings (McKittrick *et al.* 2001: table 2). Loyalists were responsible for over 29 per cent of killings between 1966 and 2001 (calculated from McKittrick *et al.*: table 3), so their formal ceasefires, conditional upon the maintenance of the IRA's ceasefires, importantly consolidated the peace process. Had their parties not been included in the negotiations it would have been far more difficult for the UUP to have made a bargain with the SDLP and other Irish nationalists. And had not proportional representation in the Peace Forum and the first Assembly elections given them reasonable opportunities for electoral gains, it is not clear what other beneficial institutional incentives would have operated on their conduct.

The release of paramilitaries, extremists par excellence, from jail, as part of the Agreement, has infused the local population with veterans of conflict who have generally been a force for calm, and who have argued for change through peaceful political means in the future. Demilitarization by the British Army and the construction of a new police service are also evident—despite difficulties. As we write, 'acts of completion' (in the case of the IRA) and a start to 'decommissioning' by the major loyalist paramilitaries remain outstanding questions. They are, however, on the agenda. No one considers either possibility 'unthinkable' any longer. These issues have been, and will be, subjected to further bouts of intensive negotiation. In different language such acts have always been *demanded* by the two governments, but now eventual compliance is *expected*. We submit that all these considerations in aggregate constitute hard evidence that the peace process has brought greater security and stability because it was attached to an inclusive consociational settlement. The key counterfactual question is whether integrationist policies and settlements would have produced a better outcome. We think not. It is true, of course, that Northern Ireland's power-sharing institutions did not have to be literally and wholly 'consociational', or 'off-the-peg', or just consociational.[22] Horowitz and his supporters suggest that a voluntary power-sharing coalition of moderates, and an electoral system based on the alternative vote rather than on PR-STV, would have been as or more successful in making and stabilizing a peace process. We shall consider these claims in sequence.

---

[22] It is wrong to claim that consociationalism is 'a kind of off-the peg model' of governance for divided societies (Wilford 2001: 4). Consociationalism has consistent principles, like good tailoring, but it has its 'bespoke' as well as its 'off-the-peg' variants.

The virtues of inclusive coalitions over minimum-winning coalitions

Critics of 'grand coalition' describe it as 'compulsory' (Horowitz 2001: 94) and their preferred option of a minimum-winning coalition as 'voluntary'. Patrick Roche describes the executive as an 'involuntary coalition brought together on the basis of a mechanical principle (outside the control of the Assembly)' (Roche 2000). Dennis Kennedy insists that it is a 'nonvoluntary coalition' (Kennedy 2000). Such language is loaded, and incorrect. Participation in Northern Ireland's executive is voluntary. Any party with entitlements to nominate ministers may choose not to take its seats. No party is required to enter government. What Horowitz, Roche, and Kennedy may mean by a 'voluntary' coalition is one in which some parties to the coalition should be free to exclude others (e.g. the DUP and Sinn Féin). We think it is at least as fair to describe the Northern Ireland executive as inclusionary (rather than compulsory), and a minimum-winning coalition as exclusionary instead of voluntary. Having cleared this rhetorical thicket we can now address substance. Horowitz's first objection to a consociational package—that a grand coalition is less stable than a minimum-winning coalition of moderates—appears intuitively plausible. But Northern Ireland's experience also suggests that such reasoning is faulty. Excluded radicals can destabilize power-sharing institutions. They may accuse included moderates from their bloc of treachery, which may prevent the latter from making the compromises necessary for successful power-sharing. Excluded radicals may engage in violence, creating a polarized atmosphere that pressurises moderates and makes compromise difficult. This, in fact, is what happened during Northern Ireland's only previous experiment with a power-sharing coalition of moderates: the Sunningdale experiment of 1973–4 (Neuheiser and Wolff 2003: 1–24; Wolff 2001). The coalition was attacked by radicals on both sides. It found it difficult to reach substantive internal agreement, amidst mounting violence, and collapsed after less than five months in office.

Inclusion in power-sharing coalitions, we submit, can make radicals less extreme, because it provides them with opportunities to have their concerns addressed constitutionally, and gives them a stake in the system. Inclusion can strengthen the position of moderates within radical factions, a possibility Horowitz and others appear to discount. We should not be misunderstood: it does not follow that the inclusion of radicals in government is always a good idea. Had they been part of Northern Ireland's coalition in 1974, they probably would have destroyed it. This is because radicals at that time were virulently opposed to power-sharing and committed to militancy. All we are suggesting is that it makes political sense to include leaders of radical parties prepared to participate in power-sharing institutions on the basis of democratic mandates and methods, particularly when they are waging internal battles with their hawks on the merits of constitutional politics.

This situation best describes UK policies towards Sinn Féin after 1997.[23] The decision of the IRA to declare a ceasefire in 1994, and Sinn Féin's subsequent decision to participate in Northern Ireland's legislature and government, was closely related to the argument of their leaders, Gerry Adams and Martin McGuinness, that republican gains could be secured through politics. This position was strengthened, and that of hardliners weakened, by Sinn Féin's rising electoral support and the rewards that this has brought, including two ministries in Northern Ireland's executive. Anti-consociationalists tend to see Sinn Féin's vote rise after the Agreement as evidence of increasing extremism—and some link this to the 'unworkable' nature of Northern Ireland's consociational institutions (Wilford and Wilson 2001). But it makes more sense, given Sinn Féin's clear movement from endorsing physical force republicanism to constitutional politics, to explain its electoral growth as a result of its increasing moderation (Mitchell, P. *et al.* 2001, 2002). Other factors are, of course, responsible for its growth, such as the party's articulate and capable leadership, and the growing cultural Catholic share of the population combined with the tendency of young Catholics to vote Sinn Féin. We submit that Sinn Féin's moderates have been strengthened by the prospect that, as long as the party sticks to its constitutional tactics, it will supplant the SDLP as the largest nationalist party in the Northern Ireland Assembly, possibly the largest party in the Assembly, and become a significant political force in Ireland as whole. These possibilities became apparent in October 2001 when the IRA announced that it had begun decommissioning its weapons. Few now believe that the IRA will return to war. In short, Sinn Féin's recent behaviour, ironically, and contrary to Horowitz's own views on the party, is a good example of Horowitz's best known underlying thesis: parties will moderate if they have to in order to win office (Horowitz 1989).

The Agreement shows that consociational institutions can be designed to mitigate the problems associated with having rival parties in

---

[23] Patterson sees these policies as having more than a whiff of 'appeasement', though he maintains that the Blair government continued the policies of its predecessor (Patterson 2001: 181). He is, however, prepared to consider that the policy might work (ibid.: conclusion).

government: executive portfolios are allocated, as we have shown, according to the d'Hondt rule (fully explained in Chapter 9, Appendix 9A.1). Any party that wins a significant share of seats in the Assembly and is willing to abide by the new rules has a reasonable chance of access to the executive. No programme of government has to be negotiated in advance between the parties entitled to government. The design creates strong incentives for parties to take up their entitlements to ministries, because if they do not then the portfolios go either to their ethno-national rivals or to their rivals in their own bloc. The d'Hondt allocation procedure means that no vote of confidence is required by the Assembly either for individual ministers or for the Executive Committee as a whole. These incentives have produced positive results. The anti-Agreement DUP has taken its seats in the Executive, and fought the 2001 Westminster general election, not on a pledge to scrap the Agreement but to renegotiate it (Mitchell, O'Leary, and Evans 2001).[24] The d'Hondt process reduced the transaction costs of bargaining over portfolios. Distinctive coalitions can form around different issues within the executive, permitting flexibility, but inhibiting chaos—given the requirement that the budget be agreed by cross-community consent. The Executive successfully agreed a budget and a programme of government through inter-ministerial bargaining during 2000–1: the DUP ministers agreed to it, though they then supported their colleagues in voting against it in the Assembly! These creative incentives to keep parties in the executive despite strong disagreements means the Assembly differs positively from the Sunningdale power-sharing experiment of 1973–4 which sought to maintain traditional UK notions of collective cabinet responsibility.

While Northern Ireland has experienced serious crises over executive formation and maintenance, this has not resulted from the d'Hondt process. The formation crisis that lasted from June 1998 until December 1999 arose from UUP First Minister David Trimble's refusal to cooperate in the running of the d'Hondt procedure, because the IRA would not decommission its weapons. Constitutionally, he had no warrant to exercise this veto. No party was entitled to veto another party's membership of the Executive, though the Assembly as a whole, through cross-community consent, could deem a party unfit for office. Trimble was facilitated in exercising his veto by the UK and Irish governments,

---

[24] It has, however, engaged in ritualized protest, rotating its ministerial positions among its Assembly ministers. This led its critics to accuse it of accumulating and distributing pension rights among its members while depriving its constituents of effective ministers.

sympathetic to his exposed position. He was also aided by a provision in the Agreement which implied that there would be at least six other Ministers apart from the premiers, but that there could be 'up to ten', with the precise number to be decided through cross-community consent.[25] This gave Trimble the opportunity to delay executive formation for eighteen months. In future, this problem is unlikely to recur. Candidates for the first Minister (FM) and Deputy first Minister (DFM) will hardly agree to be nominated without a firm agreement on the number of executive ministers and a firm date for cabinet formation.[26]

The crises over executive maintenance have stemmed largely from machinations over the institution of the dual premiership, elected by concurrent majorities of nationalist and Unionist members of the Assembly. So far these positions have been held by three moderates: David Trimble of the UUP, and Seamus Mallon and Mark Durkan of the SDLP. Mallon, the (first) Deputy First Minister, used the threat of resignation from his post in 1999 before the executive was even formed.[27] The unilateral suspension of the Agreement's institutions by the Westminster Parliament in 2000, 2001, and 2002 arose from threatened resignations by First Minister Trimble. The United Kingdom felt politically bound to act because the posts of First and Deputy First Minister are tightly interdependent: the resignation or death of one triggers the other's formal departure from office and requires fresh elections within six weeks. The UK government has consistently calculated with each threat—or manifestation—of a resignation by Trimble that he might not be able to secure his re-election, either before or after Assembly elections.[28] This has prompted the UK government to use and abuse the Suspension Act—itself a breach of the Agreement. It is ironic that the dual premiership, elected by cross-community procedures, and thus a

---

[25] The Agreement, Government of the United Kingdom (n.d. 1998: Strand One, paras 14 (explicitly) and 3 (implicitly)).

[26] The number of portfolios is now fixed at ten in the Northern Ireland Act. In future the parties could decide, during a review of the Agreement, to require candidates for First Minister and Deputy First Minister to state the number of executive portfolios that will be available—and then require the formation of the executive to follow immediately after the election.

[27] See Statement by the Deputy First Minister (Designate), Northern Ireland Assembly (1999; 325, 15 July).

[28] This pessimism was borne out in November 2001. Trimble and Durkan fell short of election by two Unionist votes, despite securing the support of over 70 per cent of the Assembly. They were rescued only because members of the Alliance Party and Women's Coalition redesignated from 'others' to 'unionists', permitting them to win a second vote, but allowing critics of the Agreement a good laugh at the nature of the 'designation' rules (see below for further discussion).

moderating 'integrative' institution of the sort recommended by Horowitz, has been the lightning rod for deep tensions between blocs, as much as it has been a mechanism for joint coordination and creation of calm by moderate leaders.

The problems attached to the operation of the dual premiership can be dealt with if changes are made (see Appendix 1A.1). One change, which we discuss in more detail later, is for the UK government to repeal its Suspension (Northern Ireland) Act 2000, a breach of the formal treaty incorporating the Agreement. The effect of the no suspension provision would mean that a resigning First Minister or Deputy First Minister would have to face the electorate, which may cause serious reflection. Another change, that might be organized under the Agreement's provisions for review, would be to alter the method by which the FM and DFM are appointed. We commend their nomination simply by the d'Hondt procedure. Alternatively, we propose that in the event that a FM/DFM team could not be appointed by concurrent majorities, the default position should be that both are appointed by the same d'Hondt allocation process as the rest of the Executive. There would have to be a proviso that both the FM or DFM could not come from either the nationalist or unionist bloc, although there would be no need, in our view, to specify that one should be nationalist and the other unionist. The positions could also be made independent, so that the death or resignation of one did not affect the position of the other. In this scenario, the FM or DFM would be replaced by d'Hondt, with the proviso that s/he could not be from the same bloc as the sitting FM or DFM. (Our reasoning is set out at greater length in Appendix 1A.1.)

Inclusivity and the issue of opposition

Another criticism of Northern Ireland's inclusive executive design is that the new Assembly has a rather small part of its membership free to serve as an opposition for standard adversarial parliamentary debating in the classic Westminster model: 'by making the mistake common in ethnic conflicts of failing to distinguish inclusion in the "political community" from inclusion in government, the arrangements left the assembly bereft of any effective opposition to challenge executive dominance' (Wilson and Wilford 2003: 8).

This is a standard complaint of critics of consociation. In the Northern Ireland case, the charge must be tempered by the fact that that the backbenchers from other parties in government are likely to hold the relevant minister of a different party to account in the Assembly.

Ironically, those critics who charge that Northern Ireland's consociation has no opposition lament the high level of adversarial debate in the Assembly between the members of the governing parties! Mechanisms for rigorous accountability exist because ministers face an Assembly Committee in their jurisdiction headed by a representative of another party.[29] This inhibits full-scale party fiefdoms in any functional sector— which cannot be said for the Westminster system. In addition, it is clear that the d'Hondt mechanism ensures that not every party is in the executive, so there are automatically some opposition backbenchers and it is up to parties to choose to be in government or in opposition (or to play both sides of the track—as the DUP has done) and be rewarded or punished by voters accordingly. Nothing about consociation, properly understood, precludes parliamentary opposition (O'Leary, in progress).

Shortcomings of the alternative vote

The Northern Ireland case suggests obvious problems with the Alternative Vote preferred by some integrationist engineers. First, the outcomes it would deliver would be majoritarian at the constituency level, and disproportional—and they would be disproportional both within blocs and across blocs. It would, additionally, have much more indirectly 'inclusive' effects than STV. In some constituencies there would be unambiguous unionist and nationalist majorities (Mitchell, O'Leary, and Evans 2001)—and thus AV would lead to the under-representation of minority voters within these constituencies. Second, while candidates would often seek support amongst voters for lower-order preferences under AV, it would not be obvious that their best strategy would be to seek lower order preferences across the ethno-national divide. That is because the imperative of staying in the count would dictate building as big an initial first and second preference vote tally as possible.[30] Third, AV would never be agreed to by hardline parties entering a constitutional settlement if they believed it would be likely to undermine their electoral support. Since the Agreement was made possible by the inclusion in negotiations of radical parties associated with paramilitary organizations,

---

[29] The Northern Ireland Act 1998 prevents the committees from being chaired or deputy-chaired by ministers or junior ministers. The committees are required, where feasible, to be organized in such a way that the Chair and Deputy Chair be from parties other than that of the relevant minister.

[30] It may be that AV's presumptively Horowitzian moderating effects materialize better in multi-ethnic political systems with no actual or potentially dominant group in given districts, but this situation does not obtain in Northern Ireland.

that is, Sinn Féin, the Ulster Democratic Party (UDP), and the Progressive Unionist Party (PUP), it would have been perverse for their leaders to agree to an electoral system that minimized their future prospects.

Single transferable votes, in fact, worked to induce moderation within Northern Ireland's political parties. To begin with, STV had already helped to moderate the policy stance of Sinn Féin. After its first phase of electoral participation in elections in Northern Ireland in the 1980s and in the Irish Republic in the latter half of the 1980s, the party discovered it was in a ghetto. Its candidates in some local government constituencies piled up large numbers of first-preference ballot papers and then sat unelected as a range of other parties' candidates passed them to achieve quotas on the basis of lower-order preferences.[31] They received very few lower-order preferences from SDLP voters. However, once the party moderated its position, promoted the IRA's ceasefire(s), and became the champion of a peace process and a negotiated settlement, it found that its first-preference vote, its transfers from SDLP voters, and the number of seats it won all increased.

The constitutional design argument that can be extracted from this story is this: once there has been party fragmentation within ethno-national blocs, then STV can assist accommodating postures and initiatives by parties and candidates, both intra-bloc and inter-bloc.[32] Our objection to Horowitz's position is that proportionality norms better match both parties' respective bargaining strengths and their conceptions of justice. Once party pluralism has emerged, some form of proportionality is more likely to be legitimate among existing parties than a shift to strongly majoritarian systems, such as AV, or to systems with ad hoc distributive requirements that will always be—correctly—represented as (negative or affirmative) gerrymanders. Horowitz's integrationist prescriptions are perhaps most pertinent at the formation of a competitive party system, but thereafter are inapplicable. Once party formation and

---

[31] STV has been used in local government elections and European parliamentary elections in Northern Ireland since 1973 and 1979, respectively. Interestingly, the hardline unionist Ian Paisley has been most successful in the three-member district used to elect Northern Ireland MEPs; in the more proportional five- or six-member local government constituencies, the DUP has not fared as well.

[32] The corollary is that STV's positive effects apply to already polarized and pluralized party systems in ethno-nationally divided societies. If there has been no prior history of ethnicized party polarization within a state, or of pluralization of parties within ethno-national blocs, the merits of its implementation may reasonably be doubted. This consideration identifies the key problem with Horowitz's electoral integrationist prescriptions: they apply best to forestalling or inhibiting ethnic conflict. They are not effective remedies for cases of developed, protracted, and intense ethnic and ethno-national conflict.

party pluralism within blocs have occurred, there will be few agents with the incentives to implement Horowitz's preferred institutions; and if a third party or outside power does so it would be a severe provocation to the less moderate parties, and would therefore likely reignite ethno-national tensions. Exclusion, after all, is a cause of conflict.[33]

Consociational democracy need not privilege particular identity groups

A frequent criticism of consociation is that it entrenches divisions rather than transcends them: 'the fundamental problem with consociationalism is that it rests on precisely the division it is supposed to solve. It assumes that identities are primordial and exclusive rather than malleable and relational' (Wilson and Wilford 2003: 6). These authors are just wrong to suggest that consociationalists are necessarily primordialists: there is a major difference between thinking that identities are durable and maintaining that they are immutably primordial. It is also wrong to suggest that consociationalists are blind to the relational character of collective identities. But the fears behind the rhetorical exaggeration exhibited by Wilson and Wilford are not groundless.

Many consociations have privileged particular identities over others: they are 'corporate' rather than 'liberal' in form (O'Leary, in progress). Some have had corporate electoral rolls: obliging citizens to vote only within their own ethnic community for their own ethnic parties. To vote for the community councils of independent Cyrus, citizens had to opt for separate Greek Cypriot or Turkish Cypriot rolls. Lebanon's electoral law has specified that successful candidates from certain constituencies must come from particular ethnic communities. And several consociations specify that particular office holders must be from one ethnic community or another. Corporate consociations create institutional obstacles to the dissolution of the protected identities, which is not to say that they would necessarily wither in the absence of such institutions.

But let us be clear about the Agreement. It does not, contrary to the assertion of a recent article in *Foreign Affairs*, 'set aside seats for Catholics and Protestants', or for Unionists and nationalists (Dawisha and Dawisha 2003: 45). Citizens vote on a common roll; vote for any candidates or parties they prefer; can vote across blocs; and can express first or

---

[33] This argument in defence of STV and against AV is qualified: STV may not be appropriate for every consociation. But we submit it can help promote accommodative moves and consolidate power-sharing deals in ways that AV in single-member districts cannot.

lower-order voting preferences outside their blocs. So the election of Assembly members (MLAs) does not privilege particular identities. Ministers become ministers by an allocation algorithm that is 'difference-blind': it operates according to strength of representation won by parties in the Assembly, not their national identity.

However, parts of the Agreement do privilege Unionism and nationalism over other forms of identity. MLAs are required to designate themselves as 'unionists', 'nationalists', or 'others'. The election of the First and Deputy First Ministers requires concurrent nationalist and unionist majorities as well as a majority of MLAs. The passage of important laws requires either such a concurrent majority, or a weighted majority—the support of 60 per cent in the Assembly, including at least 40 per cent of both registered nationalists and unionists. While Northern Ireland's voters have shown no signs of adopting new (non-unionist and non-nationalist) identities for over a century, it is therefore true that such rules arguably create disincentives for them to change their behaviour. There is an incentive for voters to choose nationalists or unionists, as members from these groups will, *ceteris paribus*, count more than 'others' or be more pivotal. The rules have the effect of predetermining, in advance of election results, that nationalists and unionists are to be better protected than 'others'. The 'others', if they were to become a majority, would be pivotal in the passage of all normal legislation, but nationalists and unionists would have more pivotality in any key decision requiring cross-community support.

Corporate mechanisms, however, are not intrinsic to consociational design. Most modern consociationalists, in fact, would eschew these devices and prefer liberal rules that equally protect whatever groups emerge in free elections. They prefer 'self-determination to pre-determination' (Lijphart 1995a). We believe that parties to consociational pacts may make entrenchment deals, that is, settlements that institutionally represent (and privilege) certain identities, and that they may do so both for self-interested reasons and because they have genuine existential anxieties about the security of the communities they represent. These reasons explain why the SDLP and the UUP converged on creating a dual premiership, and why they adopted a concurrent majority rule for electing the premiers and as one of the cross-community consent rules—both of which require the formal designation of MLAs as unionists or nationalists (see Chapter 9). These devices were inspired by the rules used in negotiations—themselves inspired by the South African negotiations (see Chapter 8)—and arguably by the institutional self-interest of the largest moderate parties in each bloc.

Since we are liberal consociationalists, we think it would be desirable to see changes in the Agreement's rules and institutions that removed as many corporate principles as possible, though we believe such changes should occur within the rules governing the Agreement. We would recommend the use of the d'Hondt formula for the nomination of the First and Deputy First Minister (see Appendix 1A.1). This would mean that that the first and second largest parties would nominate the FM and the DFM—so they could come from any party, not just a unionist or nationalist party. We would, however, commend one important qualification: we would suggest that parties rather than MLAs should designate themselves as nationalist or unionist if they so wished. The rule governing the nomination of the premiers should then be that the two premiers could not both be unionist or nationalist. We would also recommend simplifying and changing the current rules used for the passage of 'key' measures to a simple weighted majority of at least 60 per cent of MLAs. As we explain in more detail in Appendix 1A.1, this threshold would presently be sufficient for protecting both Unionists and nationalists, but without privileging their votes over those of 'others'. It would also protect the Agreement against potential wreckers. Since 40 per cent of MLAs would be necessary to mobilize a veto there would be unlikely to be enough hardline unionists or hardline republicans to veto key measures.

Having accepted the partial merits of some integrationist difficulties with the Agreement, we would, however, maintain that most of these critics fail to note that the Agreement generally is liberal rather than corporate—apart from the exceptions just considered. Its other institutional rules are *more* conducive to the emergence of new parties and identities than the majoritarian political systems typically favoured by integrationists. The Assembly uses an electoral system, the single transferable vote in multi-member constituencies, that allows parties to win seats with much smaller thresholds than is normally required under single-member plurality. Voters in Assembly elections are less likely than voters in Westminster elections to regard voting for a new party a waste of time. PR-STV provides an opportunity, though no guarantee, of both inter-communal and trans-communal transfer of lower preference votes. In this respect it is more conducive to extra-bloc voting than plurality rule. Any party, not just nationalist and unionist parties, as we have seen, is entitled to seats in the executive if it meets the quota established by the d'Hondt system. A party is entitled to membership in government with a much smaller share of seats in the legislature than is normally required in any Westminster system, so new parties have a better chance to promote their visibility, influence public policy, and demonstrate to their supporters that voting for them is a meaningful exercise.[34]

In addition, the Agreement not only stresses equality ('parity of esteem') between nationalists and Unionists, it also offers protection to individuals, including those who regard themselves as neither Unionist nor nationalist (McCrudden 1999a, b, 2001). Each minister is required under the Agreement to behave in a non-partisan way and 'to serve all the people of Northern Ireland equally, and to act in accordance with the general obligations on government to promote equality and prevent discrimination'. The Agreement looked forward to the entrenchment of the European Convention of Human Rights in Northern Ireland Law, which will make it easier for individual citizens to bring cases against authorities. It has also established a new Northern Ireland Human Rights Commission; it will lead to a Bill of Rights for Northern Ireland; and it has led to a new statutory Equality Commission. The UK government, under the Agreement and the Northern Ireland Act (1998), imposes a statutory obligation on public authorities 'to promote equality of opportunity in relation to religion and political opinion; gender; race; disability; age; marital status; dependants; and sexual orientation'. Public bodies are required to draw up statutory schemes indicating how they will implement these obligations. While education was not a negotiated part of the Agreement, Northern Ireland's current education system can also be described as liberal consociational. It allows children to attend Catholic or state (in effect, Protestant) schools without requiring them to do so, and now funds each system equally. Parents may also opt to send their children to a third, funded, integrated sector. The universities in the region are also formally liberal. Lastly, it is worth recalling that the Agreement establishes a Civic Forum alongside the elected Assembly. This institution is made up of representatives of organisations outside of conventional politics, and presents an opportunity for those who do not feel represented by conventional political parties to have their voices heard. It has no counterpart elsewhere in the United Kingdom, including in the newly devolved regimes in Scotland and Wales; and arguably it over-represents unelectable 'others'.

A last consideration must be borne in mind by integrationists of all types. In the old saw 'patience is a virtue'. Consociational democracy, be

---

[34] There are arguments for making the executive even more inclusive by extending its size. A larger executive, constituted by the d'Hondt mechanism, might give a seat to the Alliance or other small parties. Alternatively, the executive could be constituted by the Sainte-Laguë mechanism, which is more advantageous for small parties than d'Hondt (McGarry and O'Leary 1995a: 373–5).

it liberal or corporate, is based on the accommodation of rival communities. But, *ceteris paribus*, an extended period of voluntary inter-group cooperation should reduce inter-community divisions rather than maintain or deepen them. If the Agreement is consolidated, we believe that there is a greater likelihood of conventional socio-economic politics becoming more prevalent than identity politics. This appreciation explains why parties like Alliance and the Workers Party, while critical of some of the Agreement's allegedly divisive features, nonetheless strongly support it.

STABILIZING THE AGREEMENT

It is plain that we are critical admirers of the Agreement (see Chapters 8 and 9). But the same realism that drives our consociational commitments obliges us to consider how the Agreement may be best stabilized—and to consider appropriate default options if it is ineradicably ruined. The Agreement will, of course, work best if all parties and governments fulfil their obligations on its implementation.

Republican and nationalist responsibilities—and incentives

Under the Agreement Sinn Féin and the loyalist political parties are obliged to use their good offices to ensure the comprehensive decommissioning and disarmament of the paramilitary organisations respectively associated with them. As and when all major aspects of the Agreement for which it is responsible are fully implemented by the UK government (including the repeal of the Suspension Act of 2000), it would be entirely reasonable to have provisions enabling the exclusion from ministerial office of parties which maintain links with paramilitary organizations. This should occur within the provisions of the Agreement if at all possible. But what is to be done as regards Sinn Féin and the IRA? Much the best thing that could be done should be done by the two organizations themselves: the IRA should unambiguously declare its war to be over, decommission its weapons in cooperation with the international commission, and dissolve its organization; Sinn Féin should welcome all such announcements and declare current IRA membership incompatible with party membership. But what if these paths continue to be refused?

One path is a legal one: in which courts determine whether parties have associations or conduct activities in breach of the ministerial Oath of

Office, and are empowered to suspend such parties' entitlements to ministerial office until such time as their conduct is deemed fully democratic. This would probably require fresh primary legislation at Westminster, passed outside the Agreement's procedures, and would therefore be open to the valid objection that it is 'extra-Agreement' (like the 2000 Suspension Act). 'Juridification' is, moreover, a difficult road. Once judges start extensively to regulate political parties there may be undesirable repercussions. It is not evident that Spanish judges' decisions to proscribe Basque political parties are either democratic or productive. Juridification might be a less pressing an issue if judges were widely regarded as impartial in Northern Ireland, but they are not, in fact, widely representative (see Chapter 12, and below).

The second path is the internal political one. It is embedded in the Agreement. It provides for the Northern Assembly to determine whether a party entitled to ministerial nominations is in breach of its Oath of Office—which incorporates commitments to exclusively democratic means. But, complain Unionists, this provision operates under the constraint that it requires cross-community consent. And so, they correctly maintain, in the 1998–2003 Assembly Sinn Féin was protected from the possibility of suspension from the executive by the decision of the SDLP to support inclusive government (as long as the Agreement was not implemented). It may well be, however, that this is still the best way to handle republican decommissioning. If the rest of the Agreement is unambiguously implemented while the IRA remains in existence, maintains its organizational capacity, and engages in punishment beatings and self-styled policing operations then Sinn Féin will eventually pay an electoral price, North and South. There will be strong electoral incentives for Sinn Féin to repudiate the IRA or for the SDLP to consider voting for Sinn Féin's suspension from office until such time as the IRA decommissions and dissolves itself. We think, and have regularly argued, that fresh Assembly elections would create strong incentives for Sinn Féin to deliver the IRA's final dissolution or to disassociate itself from its twin (O'Leary 2001*b*, *d*, *f*). The former would be a more desirable outcome than the latter—but the latter is not without precedent in republican history. As we write the UK government is unwilling to take that risk. We believe that risk should be taken, because it is the correct path under the Agreement, and because it is good politics. If the risk is taken, and proves not to work, then other remedies should be sought for republican failures to deliver on their obligations.

The third path is intergovernmental, and has commended itself to the two governments. It is to empower an internal and international commission to determine, after due deliberation, whether a party is in breach of democratic principles. We believe that this commission has merits, though there must be some possibility that a four member commission might be stalemated 2–2 in making an appropriate and convincing determination. That said, we believe that this political mode of deciding on the merits of finding a party in breach of the Mitchell principles is better than the juridical route—though it too suffers from the fact that it has not been agreed inside the procedures for review within the Agreement. We would expect, however, that the SDLP as well as the Irish government will embrace this idea if the republican movement remains recalcitrant. We would commend one important proviso to the existing proposals: any future suspension of a party's entitlement to office triggered by the determination of the international commission should be ratified by the two governments in the British–Irish intergovernmental conference.

Unionist and loyalist responsibilities—and incentives

The loyalist parties which made the Agreement have proven electorally brittle. One has dissolved itself; the other has a tough future. Loyalists have no immediate prospects of ministerial office; in consequence the Agreement's incentives do not affect their conduct in the same way as republicans. Electoral imperatives encouraged the start of republican decommissioning; loyalists do not have such incentives with anything like the requisite intensity. Their paramilitary organizations are merely committed to decommission on receipt of confirmation of the IRA's dissolution. Loyalist—and republican—organizations which reject the Agreement must be dealt with by the new police service, fairly, impartially, and effectively. The ambiguous status of the loyalist organizations that are on formal ceasefire should be reviewed by the new police service in conjunction with the two governments. We believe that the firm and impartial handling of current crimes by loyalists will considerably strengthen the IRA's disposition to dissolve.

The unionist community was divided by the negotiation and the making of the Agreement. It remained divided in the referendum over its adoption. And public support for the Agreement has wavered significantly within this community. As we write it is low, and outnumbered by those disappointed by or hostile towards the Agreement. But sufficient support to make the Agreement work has been there when progress has been evident. Unionists, according to surveys we have conducted, are and consider themselves likely to be supportive of the

Agreement if it generates both peace and prosperity (Evans and O'Leary 2000). For reasons that we have made clear throughout this chapter, we think that it remains possible to vindicate this belief.

The unionist community's political allegiances are largely divided between two parties. One of these, the formally pro-Agreement party, the UUP, has been deeply internally divided. To manage the rejectionists within his party, its leader, at regular intervals, has breached the Agreement, both in principle and in spirit. He delayed executive formation even though it did not require prior decommissioning of weapons by the IRA. He rejected outright the recommendations of the Patten commission on policing—established under the terms of reference of the Agreement. He refused to nominate ministers to attend and carry out their functions on the North–South Ministerial Council—and was found before the courts to have acted unlawfully in doing so. He helped persuade Secretary of State Mandelson to embark on the disastrous path of diluting the Patten commission's recommendations—which, of course, made attaining republican decommissioning of their weapons less rather than more likely (see Chapter 13). He encouraged him to pass the Suspension Act of 2000, which was in breach of the United Kingdom's treaty obligations with the Irish government and with the letter and spirit of the Agreement, and which has subsequently been used both to suspend the institutions of the Agreement and legally scheduled elections—against the express wishes of the Irish government. This is a pro-Agreement leader with some difficulties in being wholeheartedly pro-Agreement.

When due allowance is made for Trimble's difficulties in managing his party, two thoughts should be uppermost in the minds of those who want to be clear-eyed about the Agreement. First: it is not sensible to provide incentives for politicians who are in difficulties with their own party to create institutional havoc. The UK government has finally promised that it will, in principle, remove the Suspension Act. Well and good. But it has also decided to postpone elections for the Assembly apparently in the belief that it must first create the best environment for returning the UUP as the majority Unionist party. This strategic choice, 'saving David', works against the UK government's other objective: ensuring that republicans deliver on their commitments. In addition, it cannot be democratic for the UK government to determine electoral processes on its judgement calls on how the Northern Irish will vote: Westminster-determination is supposed to have been superseded by self-determination under the Agreement. Second: we will only know the Agreement's institutions are secure when their offices are held and tested by those most initially opposed to or suspicious of them. It would be strange if the Agreement's stability required the permanent minority status of the DUP and Sinn Féin within their blocs. It is good that the Agreement's institutions have provided incentives to both the DUP and Sinn Féin to maximize their vote and seat shares by moderating their platforms. It is our view that the DUP and Sinn Féin must be given the chance to be the majority parties in their respective blocs—even if this generates potential difficulties. The Agreement cannot credibly endure if the Assembly is only brought out to play when Westminster thinks it will be in the hands of utterly safe unionists and nationalists. We also think there is a reasonable prospect that the leadership of the DUP would think twice about wrecking the Agreement if their party became the majority party—and if other appropriate incentives are in place to clarify their leaders' minds.

The responsibilities of the two sovereign governments

We have indicated already where the two governments might encourage the full liberalization of the consociational arrangements (as regards designation and electing the First and Deputy First Minster). The completion of policing reform, as outlined in Chapter 13, is crucial in consolidating the Agreement. Without these steps the IRA is most unlikely to fulfil its necessary acts of completion, and there will not be political stability. In the recent Joint Declaration of April 2003 the UK government provided a framework for settling policing questions. It has, in effect, repudiated Secretary of State Mandelson's disastrous handling of the Patten commission's recommendations in 2000–1. It is committed, in the context of a peaceful settlement, to a robust Policing Board; a representative police service; effective cooperation between the new PSNI and Ireland's Garda Síochána; the reform of the Special Branch; normalized and community policing; and the devolution of policing and criminal justice. The devolution of responsibility for policing will be the final proof that the settlement has taken root. It is to take place in the next Assembly provided it is 'broadly supported' by the local parties. There is no possibility of such support unless the IRA decommissions fully—it may be calculating that it would be prudent not to do so until it has a deal which trades decommissioning in return for the devolution of policing. There is also little possibility of such support if policing were to become the preserve of either nationalist or unionist ministers. We recommend therefore that policing become a joint responsibility of the two premiers, who could also take a justice portfolio, and organize their joint office to have these two jurisdictions, justice and policing, separated within their offices but reporting to both of them.[35] The April 2003 Joint Declaration, together with previous proposals on the administration of justice and developments in the pipeline on human rights, prefigure a transformation of the administration of justice along the lines we support in Chapter 12. In brief, both policing and justice reforms look primed to fulfil the promise of the Agreement. Public inquiries, present and promised, may partially redress the grievances of the relatives of the victims of unlawful state-sanctioned killings by the police and army or through collusion between public officials and paramilitaries (for a comprehensive analysis of these cases, see Ní Aoláin 2000). The merits of a Truth and Justice Commission to achieve reconciliation lies beyond our fields of research competence: We are not opposed to such a Commission, but note that it is not required by the Agreement.

Even at this late stage distrust characterizes interparty relations over the implementation of the Agreement, and things may still go badly. The governments of Ireland and the United Kingdom are the key guarantors of the Agreement. It is a legal fact that if the Assembly and the NSMC—which are mutually interdependent—cannot function, then the B-IGC reverts to the functions and capacities its predecessor enjoyed under the Anglo-Irish Agreement (see Chapter 9). It is worth publicly highlighting this fact, if only to concentrate the minds of both the DUP's and the UUP's hardliners. Destroying the local Northern Ireland dimension of the Agreement will merely restore the institutional content of the 1985 Anglo-Irish Agreement, with two important qualifications. One, the transformation of Ireland's constitution is now entrenched—though there is nothing to stop the Irish government proposing new amendments to Ireland's constitution that would reflect the demise of the Agreement. Two, the failure of the Agreement's Assembly would not preclude the UK and Irish governments from deepening their cross-border and all-island cooperation, through or outside the B-IGC. Any reasonable reading of the Downing Street Declaration (1993), the Framework Documents (1995), and the Agreement (1998) places duties on both the governments to promote and extend such cooperation. Such cooperation would be better than an immediate shift towards joint sovereignty arrangements—but in this negative scenario demands for the Irish government to purse joint sovereignty will become vigorous.

---

[35] We find this a better idea than a single Justice Department, headed by one Minister, a Justice department rotated between different parties, and separate justice and policing departments, each headed by a Minister from a different tradition.

The incentives of this default scenario are clear. The pro-devolution DUP needs to know that no working of the Agreement's institutions by the Northern Assembly means no devolution *and* the growth in the scope and influence of the B-IGC. Sinn Féin has proven, interestingly, to like devolution, albeit as a transitional arrangement. The party knows it will flourish best within the framework of a working Agreement rather than one in default. But we think these incentives are not enough. The governments must bind themselves.

The Agreement of 1998 was intended to rectify the historic denial of Irish national self-determination by the British state. It was achieved through following John Hume's proposal—of formal respect for the principle, and its expression in dual referendums, North and South. According to the Agreement, and the correct reading of Ireland's laws and constitution, the partition of Ireland now rests on a decision of the people of Ireland, North and South. The institutions of the Agreement are a product of Irish choices, North and South, and not the choices of Great Britain's parliament or people. All that separates formerly militant Irish republicans and the British state therefore are questions of trust. The British state has put almost everything that could be asked of it on the table as of May 2003—though it has wrongly unilaterally suspended the Agreement's institutions and postponed elections. The UK government has agreed that as part of the full implementation of the Agreement it is willing to repeal the Suspension Act of 2000. But it is not enough that the Suspension Act be repealed as and when the rest of the Agreement is implemented by all parties. It is not enough because the Suspension Act was proof that the United Kingdom's understanding of the Agreement did not, as promised, respect the right of the Irish people, North and South, to self-determination—as expressed in their respective endorsements of the institutions of the Agreement. In Westminster's eyes every element of the Agreement—including the portions unionists strongly like—is revisable, and alterable, according to the current will of the current UK parliament. There is nothing in the United Kingdom's constitutional arrangements to stop a future parliament behaving as Peter Mandelson proposed. It is, therefore, desirable to have the full Agreement—without the UK Suspension Act—entrenched in a treaty attached as a joint and justiciable protocol to whatever new European constitution may be proposed and agreed in the future. The European Union's new constitution has to be compatible with each member-state's constitution and this would be the best way of ensuring no clash of laws between the UK and Irish states. This proposal would constitutionalize the Agreement so that a unilateral suspension of any of the Agreement's institutions by the UK or Ireland would be regarded as a breach of the EU constitution by the appropriate court. If these ideas were followed and implemented, then as a matter of legal fact it would be true that the partition of Ireland—if it continued indefinitely—and its reunification—if that happened in the future—would both be the products of Irish national self-determination, North and South. The Agreement would be constitutionalized—and protected from the unilateral actions of either the UK or Irish parliaments. It would also, arguably, be consistent with the volitions of two types of nationalists, Irish nationalists and British Unionists.

OUTLINE OF THE BOOK

The rest of this book comprises a collection of our individual and co-authored essays on the Northern Ireland conflict, written between 1987 and 2003. Most have been published before, in journals and edited collections, but a couple have been freshly written or substantially revised for this volume. All of them touch, in various ways, on the themes outlined in this introductory chapter. They are concerned with developing consociational theory, by addressing its shortcomings and/or confronting integrationist criticisms of consociationalism.

Chapter 2, 'The Anglo-Irish Agreement: Folly or Statecraft?', analyses the significance of the Anglo-Irish Agreement of 1985, and using research and interview material critically assesses explanations as to why it was signed (O'Leary 1987). It evaluates the consequences of the Agreement (up to 12 July 1986) and considers the prospects for its survival. The article provides a normative defence of the Agreement, including its provisions for the promotion of a consociational agreement. In the light of subsequent research we modified some of its statements in a subsequent book (O'Leary and McGarry 1996: ch. 6), but we believe its general analysis withstands subsequent scrutiny. Chapter 3 reviews efforts by the UK and Irish governments to achieve a settlement in Northern Ireland during the late 1980s (O'Leary 1989). It bears the impress of its time: normatively consociational, but somewhat bleak in its assessments. Its most important error is its concluding though well-meaning afterthought: commending the threat of a new partition to concentrate minds. Since partitions of homelands have had such a disastrous record in the twentieth century (in Ireland, India, Palestine, and Cyprus), and since the threat of partition can be self-fulfilling and encourages pre-emptive ethnic expulsions, this was poor counsel. Threats are not well judged if they cannot be well used.

Chapter 4 discusses the use of the comparative method by Northern Ireland's political partisans and academics (a revised and updated version of McGarry 2001a). It shows how analogies with other conflicts have been used by partisans to further political agendas. These analogies are tied to important international norms, and their use by Northern Ireland's politicians are an attempt to influence international opinion, as well as cement group solidarity. The chapter offers more support for our long-held view that the conflict has been affected by both exogenous and endogenous influences (O'Leary 1985; McGarry and O'Leary 1995a). The latter part of the chapter summarizes how Northern Ireland has been analysed by academics employing comparative political theories, including consociationalism and integrationism. Chapter 5 criticizes five popular arguments central to the thinking of liberal integrationists (McGarry and O'Leary 1995b). These arguments have a common flaw: they each hold that the conflict can be resolved without a political settlement that meets the needs of both its (nationalist and unionist) communities.

Chapter 6 is from a recent retrospective collection on the administrative and policy performance of the UK Labour government of 1974–9. It is highly critical of the Wilson cabinet's failure to defend Northern Ireland's first consociational experiment, the Sunningdale Agreement, even though that agreement may have had an inevitable encounter with a coroner. It is paired with Chapter 7, an evaluation of the inconsistencies in the Conservatives' approach to Northern Ireland under Prime Ministers Thatcher and Major (O'Leary 1997a). It was written as part of a symposium addressing eighteen years of Conservative administration in the United Kingdom, and reflects the atmosphere of liberation felt by many in Britain and Ireland in 1997. It applauds the Tories' recognition that intergovernmental cooperation with Dublin was essential to the successful management of the conflict—even if it took some ministers nearly two decades to relearn what Ted Heath had appreciated in 1973.

Chapter 8 offers a comparative evaluation of Northern Ireland's Agreement and the one reached in South Africa, and underlines the differences between them (McGarry 1998). It argues that the analogy between Northern Ireland and South Africa should be read in different ways than it is by nationalist and Unionist integrationists, and by social transformationists. It explains that the Northern Ireland conflict has important exogenous dimensions that are missing in South Africa. This is illustrated by two central points: (i) while South Africans reached agreement largely because of endogenous factors, cooperation by the British and Irish governments was essential to the attainment of agreement in Northern Ireland; (ii) while South Africa's settlement required new political institutions internal to the country, a vital part of Northern Ireland's agreement was the construction of trans-border political institutions linking Northern Ireland with the Republic of Ireland.

Chapter 9 is the Ninth John Whyte Memorial Lecture, delivered by Brendan O'Leary in November 1998 (published for two different audiences in O'Leary 1999*d*, *e*).[36] Its ambition was to provide a comprehensive evaluation of the Agreement of April 1998. It is a pleasure to record that its reading has won the assent of left-wingers, republicans, centrists, lawyers, rightists—and generous assessments by Unionist disposed academics such as Richard English. That, at least, means it assisted in public argument, which could focus on the merits of the Agreement not what it meant. The chapter explains in detail that the Agreement was consistent with the four central pillars of consociational democracy. However, it also showed that the Agreement was more than a mere consociational document. It addressed the self-determination dispute at the heart of the Northern Ireland conflict. A number of complex federal and confederal elements address and potentially change the relationship between the north and south of Ireland, between Ireland and the United Kingdom, and between Northern Ireland and Britain. It shows how the Agreement's complexity stretched to a number of other issues not normally considered by consociational theory, including decommissioning, demilitarization, policing reform, and prisoner release. It considers the Agreement as a model of dual protection. Appendix 1 of the chapter explains the Assembly's voting rules, while Appendix 2 explains the d'Hondt formula used for executive appointment.

Chapter 10 examines the effect of a number of changes in the international order on the Northern Ireland conflict (McGarry 2001*b*). Its central argument is that while globalization and European integration have done little to transform Northern Ireland's rival identities in the way that integrationists hope or claim, the internationialization of the Northern Ireland conflict has had important and positive effects on conflict management. Chapter 11 evaluates the suitability of five ostensibly democratic models of government (herrenvolk, ethnic, liberal, multicultural, consociational) for Northern Ireland (McGarry 2002). It discusses the shortcomings of the first four, and argues for a revised version of consociational democracy.

[36] The chapter is in U.S. spelling, and is edited in accordance with the conventions of U.S. legal journals.

Chapter 12, 'The Protection of Human Rights under the Belfast Agreement', addresses another fundamental aspect of the Agreement's complexity: the need to institutionalize basic protections (O'Leary 2001e). The article emphasizes that while a Bill of Rights should uphold traditional liberal norms of freedom and individual equality, it needs to go beyond these to entrench the basic political compromise at the heart of the Agreement. It should guard the principles of inclusive power-sharing; proportionality; community self-government and the equality of groups; and community veto rights. It should also uphold the right of the current national minority and any future minority to meaningful cross-border institutional arrangements, making explicit the 'double protection model' implicit in the Agreement. We would modify its arguments in small but important respects today, especially to make it more clearly liberal, but it reflects work on legal matters within the consociational tradition where political scientists normally fear to tread.

Chapter 13, 'The Politics of Policing and Policing Reform in Northern Ireland', is new and written specifically for this volume. It builds on the arguments presented in our recent book, *Policing Northern Ireland* (McGarry and O'Leary 1999), arguments that were widely seen as influencing the findings of the Independent Commission on Policing (the Patten Commission), and which were acknowledged by the commissioners. It also reflects our involvements in public debates on these issues.[37] We would like to thank those who encouraged us to speak out, and those who shared many of our commitments. The chapter analyses the Commission's report and the controversy surrounding its implementation by Secretary of State Peter Mandelson. Policing reform is given its own chapter, because it represents a central aspect of the Agreement and because it is an institution rarely touched on by political scientists, never mind consociationalists. We discuss the relationship between the struggle over police reform and the stalemate in the political institutions, and argue that the successful completion of policing reform is essential to the Agreement's consolidation.

The Bibliography at the end of the book gathers our collected and separate publications on Irish politics, North and South, over the last eighteen years.

---

[37] Our writings and some of the debates they gave rise to are available in the following references for those interested (O'Leary 1998b, 1999a, c, 2000b, d, e, f, g; Hillyard 2000; Mageean 2000; O'Leary 2000b; Adams 2000; Attwood 2000; Cassidy 2000; Mackay 2000; Ingram 2000; Editorial 2000; Weir 2000; FitzGerald 2000; Committee on International Relations House of Representatives 1999; O'Leary 2001c; Patten 1999; McGarry 2000).

PERSONAL ODYSSEYS

We became consociational in disposition by engagements with hard realities, not by our initial political preferences. Both of us were born into Irish Catholic families—one of us was a Northerner in origin (McGarry); the other a Southerner (O'Leary). We shared the same grammar or high school experience in Garron Tower, County Antrim between 1968 and 1976. We left Northern Ireland for university education in Dublin, Ireland, and London, Canada (McGarry), and Oxford and LSE in England (O'Leary). No longer Catholics, we became leftists. We have written and rewritten together since 1989; we no longer know or care who first had an idea or argument (good or bad); we are a dual team though we have solo performances. One of us was more directly involved in political advisory work, for the British Labour party between 1988 and 1996, but O'Leary would say that any such advice that was meritorious owed as much to McGarry as to O'Leary; the mistakes were merely his own. Working for Kevin McNamara and Mo Mowlam, very different people, provided rich access to materials and evidence that contemporary analysts cannot always easily get. Since 1996 we have jointly worked on memoranda and rendered advice to numerous parties, delegations, commissions, and governments—some of which was ignored, some of which deserved to be ignored. None of it, we think, was ultimately harmful. Practice may not be guaranteed to improve theory, but it usually does it no harm.

We have both thought long and hard about political theory and comparative politics—fields that should not be separated. We have, like Rousseau in *The Social Contract*, 'sought to discover if, in the civil order, there can be any legitimate and fixed rule of administration, taking men as they are and laws as they can be' (Rousseau 1988: 85). We share Rousseau's sense of the importance of this question; but we think his answers are generally wrong. Rousseau was persuaded that a politically homogenized people sharing a general will within a unitary and centralized mode of sovereignty is the solution to the riddle of legitimate government. When that can be so it may be desirable. But Rousseau's counsel provides no guide to Northern Ireland. We are persuaded by another philosopher, Montesquieu, the father of comparative politics, that it is better to extract principles from the nature of things rather than from our prejudices. We hope we have overcome most of our prejudices in the composition of these chapters. If we have not, it was not for want of trying.

APPENDIX 1A.1 REVIEWING THE ASSEMBLY'S RULES FOR ELECTING THE FIRST MINISTER AND DEPUTY FIRST MINISTER, AND FOR PASSING KEY MEASURES[38]

Currently, the election of the First and Deputy First Ministers requires 'parallel consent', that is, concurrent majorities in the nationalist and Unionist blocs as well as a majority in the Assembly as a whole. The rule does not specify that one premier has to be Unionist and the other nationalist, but that has been its practical consequence. Critics of the rule point to the events of 2 November 2001, when David Trimble and Mark Durkan failed to be elected, even though they were supported by over 70 per cent of the Members of the Assembly (MLAs). They were two votes short of a majority among Unionists. Unionists who oppose the Agreement were able to take advantage of a rule that had been primarily designed to assure nationalists that there would be no return to the simple majority procedures of the old Stormont Parliament.

Every one should be aware that all voting rules are manipulable in some respect (there is a theorem to this effect in political science), and that there are no universally acknowledged voting procedures which meet all reasonable tests of fairness, consistency, and efficiency when there are more than three votes and three options (the Arrow theorem). Constitutional designers and rule makers should, however, be open about their preferences. We believe that a review could proceed in the spirit of the Agreement that was plainly intended to create bi-national institutions in Northern Ireland, incentives for inclusive executive power-sharing, and strong protections for minorities. In practice, that means that supporters of the Agreement should be happy with rules that make it difficult for the 'No unionists' to wreck the Agreement, but help 'Yes nationalists', 'Yes unionists', and 'Others' to govern Northern Ireland with significant consensus. Nevertheless, since the Agreement was endorsed in double referendums, and is an outcome of Irish national self-determination, it is vital that any proposed changes be minimal.

Let us consider why change is considered necessary by some. The fact that the election of a FM/DFM team needs a majority of Unionist MLAs made the Good Friday Agreement's institutions vulnerable to Unionist rejectionists, because they could muster about half of the Assembly's Unionist MLAs. This is one reason why David Trimble's threat to resign had to be taken seriously. There were doubts, that proved justified, that

---

[38] This Appendix modifies slightly a memorandum we distributed to various people in December 2001. It has, regrettably, not yet lost its relevance.

he could get re-elected. That also helps to explain, though it does not justify, why the UK government, in breach of its treaty obligations with the Irish government, unilaterally obtained the power of suspension, and why it used this power, under Secretary of State Mandelson, and later more circumspectly, under Secretary of State Reid, either to fend off a resignation threat or to prevent a resignation leading to immediate fresh elections.

The concurrent majority rule, nevertheless, has legitimacy. It is in the Agreement, and it might create an undesirable precedent if it were to be replaced entirely. It also has value, as it ensures that the FM/DFM team has substantial support amongst the two primary blocs that have had antagonistic relations within Northern Ireland. For these reasons, there is an argument that it should be kept as the rule of first resort. But, there are a number of default rules which could be used if, as on 2 November 2001, concurrent majorities cannot be achieved. It would be within the spirit of the Agreement to have such a default rule, provided that this default rule was consistent with the design of the Agreement. We also believe that the default rule we propose below is better than the existing rule.

We assume that a default of simple majority rule (50 per cent plus one) is a non-starter. This could lead to a FM/DFM team that was exclusively unionist or, in the future, exclusively nationalist. And its logic is not within the spirit of the Agreement.

We also assume that it would be unreasonable to require concurrent majorities, not just of unionists and nationalists, but also of the others. While that default rule would rectify the complaint of the 'others' that their votes are less important under parallel consent, this change would unjustifiably inflate the importance of the 'others'. It would make them the most pivotal or decisive group: in the current Assembly, five 'other' MLAs would have the same importance as twenty-two nationalist MLAs or thirty Unionist MLAs. Given that the 'others' are likely to be currently and for the foreseeable future a small group, this change would correct their current grievance, that the present rule discriminates against them, by a rule that discriminates even more heavily against nationalists and unionists.

A weighted majority (with designation)

One obvious default is a voting rule that is also in the Agreement and designed to protect minorities, but that requires a lower threshold of support. This is the Agreement's 'weighted majority' rule: 60 per cent of the MLAs voting, including 40 per cent of both nationalists and Unionists. Trimble and Durkan would have been comfortably elected by this rule on 2 November 2001. They secured over 70 per cent support in the Assembly, 100 per cent of nationalist votes, and 49 per cent of Unionist votes.

This rule has legitimacy as it is already in the Agreement for other key decisions. It does, however, require members to designate as nationalists, Unionists, or others—a requirement that Alliance thinks institutionalizes differences. Like the parallel consent rule, it discriminates against the 'others', as their votes are less pivotal.

A less obvious difficulty with this rule is that it is likely to be perceived by Sinn Féin or the DUP as a means to deprive them of one of the top two positions if (or when) they become the largest party in their bloc. One can readily conceive of the party that commands a majority of Unionists refusing to team up with Sinn Féin under the parallel consent rule, in the hope of getting a more amenable SDLP representative partner under the weighted majority default. Likewise, one can imagine nationalists refusing to team up with a DUP nominee under the parallel consent rule, in the hope of getting a more amenable UUP nominee under the weighted majority default.

Some will eagerly see these possibilities as advantages rather than as difficulties. We regard this as an outlook lacking in principle. An overriding principle of the Agreement is inclusion. If Sinn Féin and the DUP become respectively the largest parties in their blocs and the two largest parties in the Assembly then there is a sound democratic case that they should be the best placed parties to control the dual premiership. We also believe that would be prudent as well as principled. If Sinn Féin and the DUP were to win the FM or DFM positions if they become the dominant parties in their respective blocs then this would bind them further to the institutions of the Agreement—from which they have both profited. It would further consolidate republican support for constitutional politics, and it would make the DUP think twice about the advantages of destructive behaviour.

A simple weighted majority

Under this default rule the FM/DFM team would need to win the support of more than a simple majority, say two-thirds. This appears to be the favoured rule of the Alliance, which pushed for the review. It likes it because it does not require designation and it treats all MLAs as equals. It is also relatively straightforward, and echoes similar rules in other countries' constitutions. Trimble and Durkan would have been elected under this rule on 2 November 2001.

But a weighted majority of two-thirds would not ensure future stability. The number of votes required to block the election of a FM/DFM team would be a relatively low thirty six, not much higher than the thirty that rejectionists mustered on 2 November. It might also appear unreasonable, as it would mean that a FM and DFM could not be elected even if they could command as much as 66 per cent support in the Assembly.

This problem could be addressed by dropping the threshold to 60 per cent. The repercussions of lowering the threshold would be to raise the salience of the 'others', and to make it easier for the SDLP and the UUP to gang up against Sinn Féin and the DUP. For the reasons given above we believe that for the positions of FM and DFM this logic is problematic—though as we argue below there is a case for applying this rule in the Assembly for other key decisions.

d'Hondt

The d'Hondt rule is also in the Agreement, and is currently used for allocating all the other ministers in the executive. If it became the default rule for the election of the premiers, then in the absence of parallel consent the FM and DFM would go to the two largest parties in the Assembly. We believe it would be best to have this as the rule, but also consider it the best default rule.

The advantage of d'Hondt is that it is decisive. It tells us which parties get the positions in the absence of interparty agreement. No protracted bargaining or designation shifts would be required to resolve an impasse. The Assembly's current rules even cover the difficulty that might arise if the top two parties have the same number of MLAs—the First Minister position would go to the party with the highest first-preference vote share.

Using d'Hondt as the default for the election of the FM/DFM enhances the prospect of the positions being filled—rather than being used for bargaining to break the Agreement (one of the the DUP's likely preferred future tactics). If one party refused to take its position, or resigned from it, the post would go to the next largest party which did not hold the other post.

The use of d'Hondt to allocate other ministries in the Executive helps explain why the DUP has not been able to do with the cabinet what both David Trimble and Seamus Mallon have been able to do with the dual premiership. The DUP has not felt able to threaten boycotts or resignation in the hope of extracting concessions or provoking a review because the DUP knows that under the d'Hondt allocation process its ministries would simply go to other parties.

Of course, simple d'Hondt would create the possibility of a FM/DFM team that was exclusively unionist or, particularly if unionism fragments—a serious possibility—an exclusively nationalist dual premiership.

Two possible provisos might be devised to prevent this undesirable scenario. One, similar to the logic of the Agreement, would have the default rule specify that the FM and DFM must come from the largest parties in each of the nationalist and unionist blocs, with the First Minister being from the party with the largest number of MLAs. This proviso would, however, not be regarded as fair by the 'others'. A second proviso might be better. It would specify that the dual premiers cannot be from one bloc, but would come from the two largest parties allowing for this proviso. That would mean that if the 'others' grew in size then they might be able to win one of the top two positions, and that it could not be the case that the top two posts are held by one bloc.

For the foreseeable future, the effect of any version of d'Hondt as the rule or the default rule would be to entitle Sinn Féin to a position on the FM/DFM team if it becomes the largest party in the nationalist bloc. Likewise, if the DUP becomes the largest Unionist party, it would win one of the positions. But, if the DUP refused to partner Sinn Féin, then it would presumably forfeit its opportunity for one of the premierships to the UUP.

The premiers' resignation powers

Separately, but relatedly, we believe that the rule which requires that the resignation of one premier must trigger the other's loss of office might be reconsidered. This was not in the original text of the Agreement—though we concede that it is consistent with its spirit. We have all seen that this power is a most destructive bargaining chip.

We believe the review might consider a revision, namely, that the resignation of a premier leads to the immediate fresh allocation of the two posts according to the d'Hondt process, plus our favoured second proviso specified above. So, for example, if David Trimble resigned, the UUP could nominate Reg Empey to replace him, or vacate the position— in which case, on our proviso, it would go to the DUP, and if the DUP declined the offer it would go to the Alliance party, and so on. This rule would create a small incentive for executive maintenance, and weaken the incentive to behave destructively. It cannot guarantee executive maintenance, but rules can never do that.

This proposal is motivated by a simple calculation: the dual premiership has been the most vulnerable institution to date. All crises have flowed through it, and each premier has possessed a nuclear institutional weapon. They have used the weapon. We may want to disarm the premiers from having too much destructive power.

An alternative way to disarm the premiers' power to manufacture crises would be for the United Kingdom to repeal its extra-Agreement and treaty-breaking Suspension Act. If that happened then it would be clear that the resignation of a premier, and the failure to elect a new team of premiers within six weeks, would generate fresh elections. That would make any premier think very carefully before using the resignation threat.

Cross-community consent for key decisions

The election of the First Minister and the Deputy First Minister is the only activity which requires the use of the parallel consent rule—and it has no default rule for resolving a crisis. That is why we have spent such time on it. The other weighted majority rule is available for all other decisions. It presently requires 40 per cent support within each of the two major blocs (nationalist, Unionist) and 60 per cent overall.

We must reiterate that any proposal of change to make all blocs (nationalist, unionist, and other) equal, that is, that a measure would require 40 per cent support amongst each of three blocs as well as 60 per cent overall, would generate two problems. One, it would make the 'others', when they are small, much more pivotal than their numbers warrant. Two, it would retain the designation principle, which some reject.

We believe it is worth considering having a simple weighted majority, that is, 60 per cent support overall amongst MLAs for any key decision other than the election of the premiers. This change would address the designation issue. Cross-community confidence is, however, the key question, and was at the heart of the Agreement's design. We must ask several questions before considering such a change.

One, is there likely to be a majority of 60 per cent willing to consider and capable of imposing its will in an undesirable way on a minority?

Nationalists now consistently have over 40 per cent of the popular vote in recent elections—and that will show through in the next Assembly elections. So, unionists, and indeed unionists plus others, cannot in future coerce all nationalists under a simple weighted majority rule.

Nationalists, and nationalists and others, by contrast, fall short of 60 per cent, so they could not coerce all Unionists in the foreseeable future. But, under such a rule change, 'No unionists' would be unlikely to command 40 per cent support in Northern Ireland—and the Assembly—as a whole, and therefore could not block measures which enjoyed substantial support across nationalists, unionists, and others. For these reasons, amongst others, we believe this rule change might be considered.

Party interests

The decision-rules of the Assembly were designed in negotiations primarily between the UUP and the SDLP. These rules were intended to create strong incentives for power-sharing and inclusive government, and to inhibit boycotts. It will be very difficult for these parties, both for principled and party-interested reasons, to agree to any changes in the rules. That is understandable. But, we believe, it is essential that in the review the SDLP and the UUP consider the possibility—without having to assume that possibility will become reality—of what happens if Sinn Féin and the DUP become majority parties in their blocs. In that scenario the current design promises a stalemate. The DUP will hold out for the re-negotiation of the Agreement—with the UK Secretary of State obliged to hold fresh elections or trigger another (extra-Agreement) suspension. It is that possibility, as well as the concerns of the Alliance and the Women's Coalition, that should be concentrating the minds of the pro-Agreement parties and the two governments.

REFERENCES

Adams, Gerry (2000). 'British Moves on Policing Will Not Help Peace'. *Irish Times*, 9 Aug.

Arthur, Paul (1991). 'Diasporan Intervention in International Affairs: Irish America as a Case Study'. *Diaspora*, 1 (2): 143–61.

Attwood, Alex (2000). 'Essential Purpose of Patten is being Overlooked'. *Irish Times*, 3 Aug.

Bew, Paul and Henry Patterson (1985). *The British State and the Ulster Crisis*. London: Verso.

——and——(1990). 'Scenarios for Progress in Northern Ireland'. In John McGarry and Brendan O'Leary (eds.), *The Future of Northern Ireland*. Oxford: Oxford University Press, 206–18.

——, ——, and Paul Teague (1997). *Northern Ireland: Between War and Peace*. London: Lawrence and Wishart.

Boyle, K. and T. Hadden (1994). *Northern Ireland: The Choice*. Harmondsworth: Penguin.

Bruce, Steve (2001). 'Terrorists and Politics: The Case of Northern Ireland's Loyalist Paramilitaries'. *Terrorism and Political Violence*, 13 (2): 27–48.

Cassidy, Michael J. (2000). 'Letter on Patten Report and Police Bill'. *Irish Times*, 4 Aug.

Cochrane, Feargal (2001). 'Unsung Heroes? The Role of Peace and Conflict Resolution Organizations in the Northern Ireland Conflict.' In John McGarry (ed.) *Northern Ireland and the Divided World: Post-Agreement Northern Ireland in Comparative Perspective*. Oxford: Oxford University Press, 137–58.

Committee on International Relations House of Representatives (1999). The Patten Commission Report on Policing in Northern Ireland: Open Meeting before the Subcommittee on International Operations and Human Rights, 106th US Congress, Serial No. 106–103. Washington: US Government Printing Office, 126.

Cox, Michael (1997). 'Bringing in the "International": the IRA ceasefire and the end of the Cold War'. *International Affairs*, 73 (4): 671–93.

—— (1999). 'The War that Came in from the Cold: Clinton and the Irish Question'. *World Policy Journal*, 16 (1): 59–67.

Dawisha, Adeed and Karen Dawisha (2003). 'How to Build a Democratic Iraq'. *Foreign Affairs*, 82 (3): 36–50.

Dempsey, G. T. (1999). 'The American Role in the Northern Ireland Peace Process'. *Irish Political Studies*, 14: 104–17.

Dixon, Paul (1996). 'The Politics of Antagonism: Explaining McGarry and O'Leary'. *Irish Political Studies*, 11: 130–41.

Dixon, Paul (2001). *Northern Ireland: the Politics of War and Peace*. Basingstoke: Palgrave.

Douglas, Neville (1998). 'The Politics of Accommodation, social change and conflict resolution in Northern Ireland'. *Political Geography*, 17 (2): 209–29.

Doyle, John (1999). 'Governance and Citizenship in Contested States: the Northern Ireland Peace Agreement as Internationalised Governance'. *Irish Studies in International Affairs*, 10: 201–19.

Duffy, Mary and Geoffrey Evans (1997). 'Class, Community Polarisation and Politics'. In L. Dowds, P. Devine and R. Breen (eds.) *Social Attitudes in Northern Ireland*: The 6th Report, 1996–7, Belfast: Appletree Press, 102–37.

Editorial (2000). 'Clarity Needed on Policing'. *Irish Times*, 7 Aug.

Evans, Ernest (1998). 'The US Peace Initiative in Northern Ireland: A Comparative Analysis'. *European Security*, 7 (2): 63–77.

Evans, Geoffrey, and Mary Duffy (1997). 'Beyond the Sectarian Divide: The Social Bases and Political Consequences of Nationalist and Unionist Party Competition in Northern Ireland'. *British Journal of Political Science*, 27: 47–81.

——, ——, and Brendan O'Leary (1997*a*). 'Frameworked Futures: Intransigence and Flexibility in the Northern Ireland Elections of May 30 1996'. *Irish Political Studies*, 12: 23–47.

Evans, Geoffrey, and Brendan O'Leary (1997b). 'Frameworked Futures: Intransigence and Inflexibility on the Way to Two Forums: The Northern Ireland Elections of 30th May 1996 and Public Opinion'. *Representation*, 34, 208–18.

——, ——, and —— (2000). 'Northern Irish Voters and the British–Irish Agreement: Foundations of a Stable Consociational Settlement?' *Political Quarterly*, 71 (1): 78–101.

FitzGerald, Garret (2000). 'Watering Down of Patten Unnecessary'. *Irish Times*, 12 Aug.

Guelke, Adrian (2001). 'International Dimensions of the Belfast Agreement'. In Rick Wilford (ed.), *Aspects of the Belfast Agreement*. Oxford: Oxford University Press, 245–63.

Hanf, Theodor (1993). *Coexistence in Wartime Lebanon: Decline of a State and Rise of a Nation*. London: I.B. Tauris.

Hillyard, Paddy (2000). 'Police Bill is Not Faithful Reflection of Patten'. *Irish Times*, 2 Aug.

Horowitz, Donald L. (1985). *Ethnic Groups in Conflict*. Berkeley: University of California Press.

—— (1989). 'Making Moderation Pay: The Comparative Politics of Ethnic Conflict Management'. In J. P. Montville (ed.), *Conflict and Peacemaking in Multiethnic Societies*. Lexington, MA: Heath, 451–75.

—— (2001). 'The Agreement: Clear, Consociational and Risky'. In John McGarry (ed.), *Northern Ireland in a Divided World*. Oxford: Oxford University Press, 89–108.

Ingram, Adam (2000). 'NI Police Bill Critics Should Realise Radical Goals'. *Irish Times*, 5 Aug.

Kennedy, Denis (2000). 'Evidence is Growing that Agreement Did Not Work'. *Irish Times*, 16 Feb.

Lijphart, Arend (1975). 'Review Article: The Northern Ireland Problem: Cases, Theories and Solutions'. *British Journal of Political Science*, 5 (3): 83–106.

—— (1977). *Democracy in Plural Societies: A Comparative Exploration*. New Haven, London: Yale University Press.

—— (1990). 'Foreword: One Basic Problem, Many Theoretical Options—And a Practical Solution?' In John McGarry and Brendan O'Leary (eds.), *The Future of Northern Ireland*, Oxford: Clarendon Press, vi–viii.

—— (1995a). 'Self-Determination versus Pre-Determination of Ethnic Minorities in Power-Sharing Systems'. In Will Kymlicka (ed.), *The Rights of Minority Cultures*. Oxford: Oxford University Press.

—— (1995b). *Consociational Theory and the Case of Northern Ireland*. Chicago: Proceedings of the American Political Science Association.

—— (1996). 'The Framework Document on Northern Ireland and the Theory of Power-Sharing'. *Government and Opposition*. 31, 3: 267–74.

Lustick, Ian S. (1997). 'Lijphart, Lakatos and Consociationalism'. *World Politics*, 50 (1): 88–117.

MacGinty, Roger (1997*a*). 'American Influence on the Northern Ireland Peace Process'. *Journal of Conflict Studies*, (Fall): 31–50.

MacGinty, Roger (1997*b*). 'Bill Clinton and the Northern Ireland Peace Process'. *Aussenpolitik*, 48 (3): 237–44.

Mackay, Andrew (2000). 'Flawed Police Bill Could Endanger Agreement'. *Irish Times*, 4 Aug.

Mageean, Paul (2000). 'Letter on the Patten Report and Police Bill'. *Irish Times*, 8 Aug.

McCartney, Robert (2000). 'Devolution is a Sham'. *Observer*, 20 Feb. http://www.guardian.co.uk/Devolution/Story/0,2763,190960,00.html

McCrudden, Christopher (1999*a*). 'Equality and the Good Friday Agreement'. In Joseph Ruane and Jennifer Todd, *After the Good Friday Agreement: Analysing Political Change in Northern Ireland*. Dublin: University College Dublin Press, 96–121.

—— (1999*b*). 'Mainstreaming Equality in the Governance of Northern Ireland'. *Fordham International Law Journal*, 22 (April): 1696–775.

—— (2001). 'Equality'. In Colin Harvey (ed.), *Human Rights, Equality and Democratic Renewal in Northern Ireland*. Oxford: Hart.

McGarry, John (1988). 'The Anglo-Irish Agreement and Power-Sharing in Northern Ireland'. *Political Quarterly*, 59 (2): 236–50.

—— (1990). 'Northern Ireland and the Option of Consociationalism'. *Plural Societies*, XX (June): 1–20.

—— (1998). 'Political Settlements in Northern Ireland and South Africa'. *Political Studies*, 46 (5): 853–70.

—— (ed.) (2000). 'Police Reform in Northern Ireland'. *Irish Political Studies*, 15: 183–92.

—— (2001*a*). 'The Comparable Northern Ireland'. In John McGarry (ed.), *Northern Ireland and the Divided World: Post-Agreement Northern Ireland in Comparative Perspective*. Oxford: Oxford University Press: 1–33.

—— (2001*b*). 'Globalization, European Integration and the Northern Ireland Conflict'. In Michael Keating and John McGarry (eds.), *Minority Nationalism and the Changing International Order*. Oxford: Oxford University Press, 295–324.

—— (ed.) (2001*c*). *Northern Ireland and the Divided World: Post-Agreement Northern Ireland in Comparative Perspective*. Oxford: Oxford University Press.

—— (2002). '"Democracy" in Northern Ireland: experiments in Self-rule form the Protestant Ascendancy to the Good Friday Agreement'. *Nations and Nationalism*, 8 (4): 451–74.

—— and Charles Graham (1990). 'Co-determination'. In John McGarry and Brendan O'Leary (eds.) *The Future of Northern Ireland*. Oxford: Oxford University Press, 155–74.

—— and Brendan O'Leary (eds.) (1990*a*). *The Future of Northern Ireland*. Oxford: Oxford University Press.

—— and —— (1990*b*). 'Northern Ireland's Options: A Framework, Summary, and Analysis'. In Brendan O'Leary (ed.), *The Future of Northern Ireland*. Oxford: Oxford University Press, 268–303.

58 *John McGarry and Brendan O'Leary*

McGarry, John and Brendan O'Leary (1995a). *Explaining Northern Ireland: Broken Images*. Oxford and Cambridge, MA: Basil Blackwell.

—— and —— (1995b). 'Five Fallacies: Northern Ireland and the Liabilities of Liberalism'. *Ethnic and Racial Studies*, 18 (4): 837–61.

—— and —— (1996). 'Proving our points on Northern Ireland (and giving reading lessons to Dr Dixon)'. *Irish Political Studies*, 11: 142–54.

—— and —— (1998). 'RUC reform must not repeat boundary commission fiasco'. *Sunday Business Post*, April 5.

—— and —— (1999). *Policing Northern Ireland: Proposals for a New Start*. Belfast: Blackstaff.

McKittrick, David, Seamus Kelters, Brian Feeney, and Chris Thornton (2001). *Lost Lives: The Stories of the Men, Women and Children Who Died as a Result of the Northern Ireland Troubles*. Edinburgh: Mainstream.

Mitchell, George C. (2000). *Making Peace*. Berkeley: University of California Press.

——, John de Chastelain, and Harri Holkeri (1996). Report of the International Body on Arms Decommissioning (The Mitchell Report). Dublin and London.

Mitchell, Paul (1995). 'Party Competition in an Ethnic Dual Party System'. *Ethnic and Racial Studies*, 18 (4): 773–96.

—— (1999). 'The Party-System and Party Competition'. In Paul Mitchell and Rick Wilford (eds.), *Politics in Northern Ireland*. Boulder, CO: Westview, 91–116.

—— (2001). 'Transcending an Ethnic Party System? the Impact of Consociational Governance on Electoral Dynamics and the Party System'. In Rick Wilford (ed.), *Aspects of the Belfast Agreement*. Oxford: Oxford University Press, 28–48.

—— Brendan O'Leary, and Geoffrey Evans (2001). 'Northern Ireland: Flanking Extremists Bite the Moderates and Emerge in Their Clothes'. *Parliamentary Affairs*, 54, 4: 725–42.

——, ——, and —— (2002). 'The 2001 Elections in Northern Ireland: Moderating "Extremists" and the Squeezing of the Moderates', *Representation*, 39 (1): 23–36.

Montesquieu, Charles de Secondat Baron de (1748/1989). 'Preface'. In Anne M. Cohler, Basia C. Miller, and Harold S. Stone (eds.), *The Spirit of the Laws*. Cambridge: Cambridge University Press.

Moxon-Browne, Edward (1991). 'National Identity in Northern Ireland'. In Peter Stringer and Gillian Robinson (eds.), *Social Attitudes in Northern Ireland: The First Report*. Belfast: Blackstaff, 23–30.

Neuheiser, Jorg and Stefan Wolff (eds.) (2003). *Peace at Last? The Impact of the Good Friday Agreement on Northern Ireland*. Oxford: Berghahn.

Ní Aoláin, Fionnuala (2000). *The Politics of Force: Conflict Management and State Violence in Northern Ireland*. Belfast: Blackstaff.

O'Clery, Conor (1996/1997). *The Greening of the White House: The Inside Story of How America Tried to Bring Peace to Ireland*. Dublin: Gill & Macmillan.

O'Leary, Brendan (1985). 'Explaining Northern Ireland: A Brief Study Guide'. *Politics*, 5 (1): 35–41.

—— (1987). 'The Anglo-Irish Agreement: Statecraft or Folly?' *West European Politics*, 10 (1): 5–32.

O'Leary, Brendan (1989). 'The Limits to Coercive Consociationalism in Northern Ireland'. *Political Studies*, 37 (4): 452–68.

—— (1990*a*). 'Appendix 4. Party Support in Northern Ireland, 1969–89'. In John McGarry and Brendan O'Leary (eds.), *The Future of Northern Ireland*. Oxford: Oxford University Press, 342–57.

—— (1990*b*). 'More Green, Fewer Orange'. *Fortnight*: 281 and 282, 12–15 and 16–17.

—— (1995*a*). 'Afterword: What is Framed in the Framework Documents?' *Ethnic and Racial Studies*, 18 (4): 862–72.

—— (1995*b*). 'Introduction: Reflections on a Cold Peace'. *Ethnic and Racial Studies*, 18 (4): 695–714.

—— (1997*a*). 'The Conservative Stewardship of Northern Ireland 1979–97: Sound-Bottomed Contradictions or Slow Learning?' *Political Studies*, 45 (4): 663–76.

—— (1997*b*). 'Unionists Will Lose Electoral Dominance'. *Irish Times*, 2 July.

—— (1998). 'Bias in Memoirs Scores Political Own Goal'. *Scotsman*, 19 Jan.

—— (1999*a*). 'A Bright Future and Less Orange (Review of "A New Beginning" by the Independent Commission on Policing for Northern Ireland)'. *Times Higher Education Supplement*, 19 Nov.

—— (1999*b*). 'How Can the Police Survive the Peace?' *Irish News*, 23 March.

—— (1999*c*). 'The Nature of the Agreement'. *Fordham Journal of International Law*, 22 (4): 1628–67.

—— (1999*d*). 'The Nature of the British–Irish Agreement'. *New Left Review*, 233 (Jan.–Feb.): 66–96.

—— (1999*e*). 'Patten Report has Implications for All'. *Irish Independent*, 15 Oct.

—— (1999*f*). 'Remake, remodel'. *Guardian*, 18 March.

—— (2000*a*). '3,636 so far, and counting (Review of David McKittrick et al *Lost Lives: The Stories of the Men, Women and Children who Died as a Result of the Northern Ireland Troubles)'*. *Times Higher Eduction Supplement*, 3 March.

—— (2000*b*). 'Letter on Patten Report and Police Bill'. *Irish Times*, 9 Aug.

—— (2000*c*). 'The Patten, the whole Patten and nothing but the Patten'. *Irish Times*, 28 July.

—— (2000*d*). 'What a Travesty: Police Bill is Just a Parody of Patten'. *Sunday Business Post*, 30 April.

—— (2001*a*). 'The Belfast Agreement and the Labour Government: How to Handle and Mishandle History's Hand'. In Anthony Seldon (ed.), *The Blair Effect: The Blair Government 1997–2001*. London: Little, Brown: 448–88.

—— (2001*b*). 'Elections, not suspensions'. *Guardian*, 13 July.

—— (2001*c*). *The Past, Present and Future of Policing and the Belfast Agreement*. Conference: 'Whose Police Service?' organised by The Pat Finucane Centre Derry. http://www.serve.com/pfc/brendolearybs1.htm

—— (2001*d*). 'Personal View: Ignore the Prophets of Doom'. *Financial Times*, 11 June.

—— (2001*e*). 'The Protection of Human Rights under the Belfast Agreement'. *Political Quarterly*, 72 (3): 353–65.

O'Leary, Brendan (2001*f*). 'Reid Should Not Allow a New Unionist Boycott'. *Irish Times*, 4 Oct.

—— (2002). 'The Belfast Agreement and the British–Irish Agreement: Consociation, Confederal Institutions, A Federacy, and a Peace Process'. In Andrew Reynolds (ed.), *The Architecture of Democracy: Constitutional Design, Conflict Management, and Democracy*. Oxford: Oxford University Press, 293–356.

—— (in progress). *Consociation*.

—— and Geoffrey Evans (1997). 'Northern Ireland: La Fin de Siècle, The Twilight of the Second Protestant Ascendancy and Sinn Féin's Second Coming'. *Parliamentary Affairs*, 50 (4): 672–80.

——, Bernard Grofman, and Jorgen Elklit (2004). 'Divisor Methods for Sequential Portfolio Allocation in Multi-party Executive Bodies: Evidence from Northern Ireland and Denmark', *American Journal of Political Science*.

——, Tom Lyne, Jim Marshall, and Bob Rowthorn (1993). *Northern Ireland: Sharing Authority*. London: Institute of Public Policy Research.

—— and John McGarry (1993). *The Politics of Antagonism: Understanding Northern Ireland*. London and Atlantic Heights, NJ: Athlone.

O'Neill, Shane (1999). 'Mutual Recognition and the Accommodation of National Diversity: Constitutional Justice in Northern Ireland'. Unpublished manuscript.

Patten, Christopher (1999). 'A New Beginning: The Report of the Independent Commission on Policing for Northern Ireland'. Belfast: Independent Commission on Policing for Northern Ireland. Also published at www.belfast.org.uk/report.htm.

Patterson, Henry (2001). 'From Insulation to Appeasement: the Major and Blair Governments Reconsidered'. In Rick Wilford (ed.), *Aspects of the Belfast Agreement*. Oxford: Oxford University Press, 166–83.

Porter, Norman (1996). *Rethinking Unionism: An Alternative Vision for Northern Ireland*. Belfast: Blackstaff.

—— (ed.) (1998). *The Republican Ideal: Current Perspectives*. Belfast: Blackstaff.

—— (2003). *The Elusive Quest: Reconciliation in Northern Ireland*. Belfast: Blackstaff.

Reilly, Benjamin (1997). 'Preferential Voting and Political Engineering: A Comparative Study'. *Journal of Commonwealth and Comparative Politics*, 35 (1): 1–19.

—— (2001). *Democracy in Divided Societies: Electoral Enginerring for Conflict Management*. New York: Cambridge University Press.

Roche, Patrick (2000). 'A Stormont without Policy'. *Belfast Telegraph* 30 March.

Rooney, Kevin (1998). 'Institutionalising Division'. *Fortnight*, (June): 21–2.

Rousseau, Jean-Jacques (1988). *Rousseau's Political Writings: New Translations, Interpretive Notes, Backgrounds, Commentaries, edited by Alan Ritter and Julia Conaway Bondanella*. New York: W. W. Norton.

Ruane, Joseph and Jennifer Todd (1996). *The Dynamics of Conflict in Northern Ireland: Power, Conflict and Emancipation*. Cambridge: Cambridge University Press.

Seitz, Raymond (1998). *Over Here*. London: Trafalgar Square.

Taylor, Rupert (1994). 'A Consociational Path to Peace in Northern Ireland and South Africa?' In Adrian Guelke (ed.), *New Perspectives on the Northern Ireland Conflict*. Aldershot: Avebury, 161–74.

Taylor, Rupert (2001). 'Consociation or Social Transformation?' In John McGarry (ed.), *Northern Ireland and the Divided World: Post-Agreement Northern Ireland in Comparative Perspective*. Oxford: Oxford University Press, 36–52.

Thompson, Michael, Richard Ellis, and Aaron Wildavsky (1990). *Cultural Theory*. Boulder, CO: Westview.

Trew, Karen (1996). 'National Identity'. In Paula Devine, Richard Breen, and Lizanne Dowds (eds.), *Social Attitudes in Northern Ireland*. Belfast: Appletree, 140–52.

Trimble, David (2003). 'Words, Words, Words (review of Norman Porter's *The Elusive Quest)'. Times Literary Supplement*, 5220 (18 Apr.): 7–8.

Weir, Philip (2000). 'Letter on Patten Report and Police Bill'. *Irish Times*, 7 Aug.

Whyte, John (1993). 'Dynamics of Social and Political Change in Northern Ireland'. In Dermot Keogh and Michael Haltzel (eds.), *Northern Ireland and the Politics of Reconciliation*. Cambridge: Cambridge University Press, 103–16.

Wilford, Rick (1992). 'Inverting Consociationalism? Policy, Pluralism and the Post-Modern'. In Brigid Hadfield (ed.), *Northern Ireland: Politics and the Constitution*. Buckingham: Open University Press, 29–46.

—— (2001). 'Aspects of the Belfast Agreement: Introduction'. In Rick Wilford (ed.), *Aspects of the Belfast Agreement*. Oxford: Oxford University Press, 1–10.

—— and Robin Wilson (2001). 'A "Bare Knuckle Ride": Northern Ireland'. In Robert Hazell (ed.), *The State and the Nations: the First year of Devolution in the United Kingdom*. Thorverton: Imprint Academic, 79–116.

Wilson, Andrew (1997). 'From the Beltway to Belfast: The Clinton Administration, Sinn Fein, and the Northern Ireland Peace Process'. *New Hibernia Review*, 1 (3): 23–39.

—— (2000). 'The Billy boys meet Slick Willy: The Ulster Unionist Party and the American Dimension to the Northern Ireland Peace Process, 1993–1998'. *Policy Studies Journal*, 11: 121–36.

Wilson, Robin (2003). 'Belfast Agreement Power-Sharing Model Can Entrench Sectarianism'. *Irish Times*, 5 Mar.

—— and Rick Wilford (2003). 'Northern Ireland: A Route to Stability?' *Democratic Dialogue*, http://www.devolution.ac.uk/Wilson_&Wilford_Paper (accessed 13 May 2003).

Wolff, Stefan (2001). 'Context and Content: Sunningdale and Belfast Compared'. In Rick Wilford (ed.), *Aspects of the Belfast Agreement*. Oxford: Oxford University Press, 11–27.

2

The Anglo-Irish Agreement: Folly or Statecraft?

Brendan O'Leary

This article analyses the significance of the Anglo-Irish Agreement, and using research and interview material critically assesses explanations as to why it was signed. An interim evaluation of the consequences of the Agreement up to 12 July 1986 is made before considering the prospects of the Agreement's survival. A brief normative defence of the Agreement is also presented.

Rhetorical reaction to the Anglo-Irish Agreement signed by the prime ministers of the Republic of Ireland and the United Kingdom on 15 November 1985 was predictable. Irish ultra-nationalists interpreted the Anglo-Irish Agreement as an imperialist manoeuvre, targeted against the self-styled 'armalite and ballot box' school of national liberation. Gerry Adams of Sinn Féin (SF) immediately condemned the agreement for 'copper-fastening partition'.[1] Ulster Unionists, on the other hand, saw it as a victory for the Provisional IRA, the pay-off for a war of sectarian attrition, a milestone in the liquidation of their cherished union. Ian Paisley, at the Democratic Unionist Party (DUP) conference, asserted that the Anglo-Irish Agreement 'rode to victory on the back of IRA terrorism'.[2] These polarized interpretations are as incompatible as they are implausible. Understanding the significance of the Anglo-Irish Agreement requires us to bypass the brain-numbing ordinances of Green and Orange sectarianism.

Five questions provoked by the Anglo-Irish Agreement will be addressed in this article. First, what is its constitutional significance? Second, why was the Agreement signed? This account assesses the value

I should like to express my thanks to those public officials who made themselves available for non-attributable interviews, and to George Jones, Michael Hebbert, Lorelei Watson, and John Whyte for their helpful criticisms. The usual disclaimers apply.

[1] *Guardian*, 16 Nov. 1986.   [2] *Irish Times*, 21 April 1986.

of three models of explanation frequently used by analysts to illuminate major state decisions: the rational actor, the organizational process, and the political models, respectively.[3] Third, what have been the interim results of the Anglo-Irish Agreement? Fourth, will it survive? Finally, the prescriptive question will be answered: should the Anglo-Irish Agreement be supported?

MEANINGS: WHAT IS THE ANGLO-IRISH AGREEMENT?

The Anglo-Irish Agreement is best understood negatively: it is not three things which it is alleged to be. First, it is not 'joint authority', the exactly equal sharing of sovereignty of Northern Ireland by two separate states. Contrary to Unionist rhetoric, Peter Barry, the Irish Minister for Foreign Affairs, has not become joint governor of Northern Ireland.[4] The Anglo-Irish Agreement is not a complete acceptance by the British government of one of the proposals made by the New Ireland Forum which reported in May 1984.[5] The terms of the Agreement do not give London and Dublin equal responsibility for all aspects of the government of Northern Ireland. As Article 2 states: 'There is no derogation from the sovereignty of the Irish Government or the United Kingdom Government, and each retains responsibility for the decisions and administration of Government within its own jurisdiction'. The United Kingdom has not ceded sovereignty over Northern Ireland. There is no case for those who contend that the UK government's action represents a formal erosion of the Act of Union, as a judge declared when ruling against a unionist High Court action in January 1986. Second, the Anglo-Irish Agreement does not 'put the Unionists on notice that reunification of Ireland will inevitably be enacted

---

[3] The assumptions of these models are expounded by Graham Allison, *Essence of Decision*, Little, Brown and Company, 1971.

[4] Jim Allister, the DUP Chief Whip in the Northern Ireland Assembly, claims that the Accord has made Northern Ireland a 'shared colony' (*Irish Times*, 11 May 1986). Harold McCusker, Deputy Leader of the Official Unionist Party (OUP), has gone as far as to claim that the British have already conceded sovereignty over Northern Ireland to the Irish Republic (*Irish Times*, 24 Feb. 1986).

[5] New Ireland Forum, Stationery Office, Dublin, May 1984. The Forum report was agreed by the four major constitutional nationalist parties in the Irish Republic and Northern Ireland (Fianna Fáil, Fine Gael, the Irish Labour Party, and the Social Democratic and Labour Party). The Forum deliberated, received evidence, and commissioned research for a year. In conclusion it offered three possible models of a new Ireland: a unitary state, a federal/confederal state, and joint authority. FF prefered the first model. FG, the ILP, and the SDLP preferred the second, and especially the third, models. In order to obtain an agreed report FF's preference was the nominally agreed first choice.

on an as yet undetermined date', as one constitutional lawyer has asserted.[6] The first clause of the agreement simply repeats the often expressed policy of successive British governments since the abrogation of the Stormont Parliament in 1972, and enshrined in Section 1 of the Northern Ireland Constitution Act of 1973, that Irish unification will not take place without the consent of a majority of the people of Northern Ireland (Article 1a). There is nothing new about the 'notice' being given to the unionists about their constitutional status with regard to the Irish Republic, and indeed the Anglo-Irish Agreement is a formal recognition by the current Irish government of the rectitude of the British cons-titutional guarantee. If there is a 'notice' of constitutional significance embedded in the Anglo-Irish Agreement, it is that the Unionist identity, while guaranteed preservation, has been downgraded to equality with the nationalist identity in the internal affairs of Northern Ireland. Third, the Anglo-Irish Agreement does not represent the *de jure* abandonment of the Irish Republic's constitutional claim to Northern Ireland, as SF and other ultra-nationalists allege. Articles 2 and 3 of the Irish Constitution read as follows:

ARTICLE 2: The national territory consists of the whole island of Ireland, its islands and the territorial seas.
ARTICLE 3: Pending the re-integration of the national territory and without prejudice to the right of Parliament and Government established by this Constitution to exercise jurisdiction of the whole of that territory, the laws enacted by that Parliament shall have the like area and extent of application as the laws of Saorstat Éireann[7] and the like extra-territorial effect.

As the Anglo-Irish Agreement can legitimately be interpreted as an agreement over how the national territory might be 're-integrated', it is

---

[6] Claire Palley, 'When an Iron Hand Can Beckon a Federal Union', Agenda, *Guardian*, 20 Jan. 1986. Palley's article is a perfect specimen of wishful thinking: she assumes into existence what she would like to occur. She starts with the premise that in about thirty five years the Protestant and Catholic populations will be about equal, and reasons that a majority would then be forthcoming for 'reunification'. She concludes that once Protestants are aware of their demographic destiny, it will then make sense for them to negotiate their best possible position in an Irish federal union. Both her demography and psephology are dubious. Paul Compton, 'The Demographic Background', in D. Watt (ed.), *The Constitution of Northern Ireland* (1981) shows that most assumptions of an inevitable Catholic majority are ill-founded. In any case there are considerably more Catholic Unionists than Protestant Irish nationalists, so even a future hypothetical Catholic majority would be insufficient for a majority for unification—see Edward Moxon-Browne, *Nation, Class and Creed in Northern Ireland* (Aldershot: Gower, 1983). Breeding for victory, or negotiating federalism because of the other side's fertility rates, are not sound political strategies [Dr. Palley has proved a better demographer than Dr. Compton, or me, B. O'L, May 2003].
[7] Namely the twenty-six counties of the Irish Free State (1922–37).

not in violation of the letter of the Irish Constitution. Article 1c of the Anglo-Irish Agreement states that 'If in the future a majority of the people of Northern Ireland clearly wish for and formally consent to the establishment of a united Ireland', then the two governments will introduce legislation to convert that wish into reality. However, ultra-nationalists are correct to appreciate that the Anglo-Irish Agreement represents the de facto abandonment of Irish unification as a policy goal of Fine Gael (FG) and the Irish Labour Party (ILP) for the foreseeable future, which is not the same as 'in perpetuity' as Tom King, Secretary of State for Northern Ireland, bluntly suggested on 3 December 1985 when the ink on the Anglo-Irish Agreement was still fresh.[8]

If the Anglo-Irish Agreement is not a formal joint authority, neither a formal notice to unionists of eventual reunification, nor the formal abandonment of territorial irredentism by the Irish Republic, then what is its constitutional significance? First, it is the formalization of inter-state cooperation; second, a formal notice that while the unionist guarantee remains unionists have no veto on policy formulation within Northern Ireland; and, third, the formalization of a strategy which binds the Irish Republic to a constitutional mode of reunification which is known to be practically infeasible, and therefore facilitates the end of the nationalist monolith in the Republic's politics.

Let us take these points in turn. First, the Anglo-Irish Agreement is the formalization of inter-state cooperation because the Intergovernmental Conference (IGC) which it established is solely a consultative body. The IGC has no executive authority or capacity, no recognizable instruments of state [taxation and coercion], and has no formal policy implementation function. In the crudest possible terms all that the IGC represents is the institutionalization of the talks which the two governments have been having in the Anglo-Irish Intergovernmental Council established after the Thatcher–Haughey summit in 1980. (In the communiqué which accompanied the Anglo-Irish Agreement it was stated that British and Irish ministers had met on more than twenty occasions in the previous

---

[8] 'In Northern Ireland now we have signed an agreement in which the Prime Minister of Ireland, notwithstanding the fact that he faces and has to live with a Constitution which has aspirations of sovereignty over Northern Ireland, has in fact accepted that for all practical purposes and unto perpetuity, there will not be a united Ireland because he has accepted the principle of consent that the will of the majority in Northern Ireland must predominate and that Northern Ireland, which is our fervent wish, remains part of the United Kingdom' (*Irish Times*, 4 Dec. 1986). King's message was substantially accurate, but had to be 'clarified' because the gloss 'in perpetuity' is incompatible with the Irish Constitution. King's message, designed to placate Unionists, caused uproar among ultra-nationalists—the fate of all Northern Ireland Secretaries of State.

year, a clear sign of the extent of existing collaboration as much as proof of the impending agreement.) The IGC is a policy-formulation forum with which the Secretary of State for Northern Ireland can choose to concur, take into consideration, or ignore in the government of Northern Ireland. The policy-arenas open to the two governments in the IGC are spelled out in Article 2a of the Anglo-Irish Agreement: '(i) political matters; (ii) security and related matters; (iii) legal matters, including the administration of justice; (iv) the promotion of cross-border co-operation'. The possible agenda is, thus, extremely wide-ranging, as the definition of political matters is very elastic. Article 6 of the Anglo-Irish Agreement elaborates these four fields, and specifically entitles the Irish government to discuss the work of the Standing Advisory Commission on Human Rights (SACHR), the Fair Employment Agency (FEA), the Equal Opportunities Commission (EOC), the Police Authority for Northern Ireland (PANI), and the Police Complaints Board (PCB). These five agencies, the SACHR, FEA, EOC, PANI, and PCB, are the fruit of British attempts to reform Northern Ireland, and a direct input for the Irish government is clearly intended as a confidence-building measure for the nationalist population.

Second, the Anglo-Irish Agreement signifies the formal end of Unionist supremacy within Northern Ireland: unionism without an Ulster Unionist veto on the structure of the union. The unionists are denied formal access to policy formulation unless they take advantage of the possibilities for devolution which are built into the Anglo-Irish Agreement. The Assembly set up under James Prior's rolling devolution proposals in 1982 was not mentioned in the Agreement, and its subsequent demise in June 1986 in the face of continued SDLP abstention and the Unionists' abuse of its facilities for attacking the Agreement has come as no surprise.[9] Unless the Ulster Unionists accept an agreed form of devolution, the British government will speak on behalf of Unionism in the IGC. On the other hand, the Northern Ireland minority, that is, the SDLP rather than SF, can have their grievances articulated in the IGC even without substantial devolution. The fact that the Anglo-Irish Agreement gives the Irish Republic a *de jure* interest in the affairs of

---

[9] The Assembly (1982–6) was the ill-starred child of Jim Prior's rolling devolution scheme. It foundered upon a nationalist boycott by both SF and the SDLP. Since late 1985 it had become simply an agitation-forum against the Accord, prompting the moderate Unionists in the Alliance Party (APNI) to withdraw. King was forced to dissolve the Assembly as he did not want the elections due in the autumn to occur amidst the current levels of polarization.

a minority within another state border[10] is a major symbolic affirmation of the legitimacy of the minority's complaints about the government and politics of Northern Ireland, both before and after 1972. Before the signing of the Anglo-Irish Agreement the official British position blamed all the discreditable features of Northern Ireland upon the Unionist hegemony in the period of devolved government (1920–72). However the British signature affirms that direct rule (1972–85)[11] has not reformed Northern Ireland, and on its own cannot do so—a rare example of a state engaging in self-criticism? The Anglo-Irish Agreement explicitly recognizes that an Irish dimension and agreed devolution (Article 4) are necessary to complete the reform of Northern Ireland. As this strategy has been the dominant motif of the SDLP since its inception, it is plain why the Agreement symbolically establishes the constitutional equality of the Northern Ireland minority. Ian Paisley made the point graphically when he suggested that the Agreement has made John Hume the 'uncrowned king of Northern Ireland'.[12]

Third, the Anglo-Irish Agreement signifies the end of a united front among constitutional Irish nationalists. It has brought into relief divisions which have long been apparent. Fine Gael, the ILP, and the new party in the Irish Republic, the Progressive Democrats (PD), all support the Anglo-Irish Agreement, whereas Fianna Fáil (FF) opposes it. Within Northern Ireland the SDLP supports the Agreement, whereas the small Irish Independence Party (IIP) rejects it. Since the Agreement was signed FF has shown signs of wanting to support a revamped IIP against the SDLP in Northern Ireland.[13] Consequently FF and the IIP now represent the brand of constitutional nationalism which simply disagrees with the IRA and SF over means rather than ends, whereas most of the SDLP, FG, and the ILP are making the reform of Northern Ireland a higher priority than any putative unification. This fissure between constitutional

---

[10] In this respect the Accord conforms, intentionally or otherwise, with the prescriptions of the *Capotorti Report*, 1979, prepared for the United Nations Subcommission on the Prevention of Discrimination and the Protection of Minorities: 'Bilateral agreements dealing with minority rights concluded between States where minorities live and the States from which the minorities originate (especially between neighbouring countries) would be extremely useful. It must be stressed, however, that co-operation with regard to the rights of members of minority groups shall be based on mutual respect for the principles of sovereignty and territorial integrity of the States concerned and non-interference in their internal affairs', cited in Kevin Boyle and Tom Hadden, *Ireland: A Positive Proposal* (Harmondsworth: Penguin, 1985), p. 47. (However, the Northern nationalist minority did not originate in the Irish Republic so the conformity is imperfect.)

[11] Direct rule has been interrupted only by the brief power-sharing Executive in the first five months of 1974.   [12] *Irish Times*, 29 May 1986.

[13] *Irish Times*, 8 May 1986.

nationalists, if permanent, is of potentially immense significance on both sides of the border. The SDLP has its nationalist flank protected from criticism by SF and the IIP because of the Irish dimension in the Agreement, and therefore is freer to bargain for the reform of Northern Ireland, to revitalize, and ensure the implementation of, the civil rights programme of the 1960s. The consequences for the politics of the Irish Republic will also be far-reaching.

Three final points should be made about the constitutional significance of the Anglo-Irish Agreement. First, it is not permanent, and envisages renewal after three years. Second, the Agreement does not form part of the domestic law of the United Kingdom, and thus the manner in which the British government manages the IGC is not amenable to judicial regulation. Third, the Agreement is clearly a framework which permits other constitutional settlements to be built on top of it. The Anglo-Irish Agreement is compatible with substantial, albeit necessarily agreed, devolution (Article 4b and c), and it is also the basis upon which joint authority, as envisaged by the New Ireland Forum or the Kilbrandon Inquiry of November 1984,[14] might be erected. However, the Hillsborough agreement does not currently amount to joint authority.

EXPLANATIONS: WHY WAS THE AGREEMENT SIGNED?

The formal communiqué which accompanied the Anglo-Irish Agreement declared that the promotion of reconciliation was its main objective. What are we to make of this claim? Was its signing prompted by more ignoble or Machiavellian intentions? Was it, in the words of disgruntled unionists, 'a mixture of the vilest cunning on the one hand, and the most enormous stupidity on the other'?[15] There are three modes of explaining the signing of the Anglo-Irish Agreement which are worthy of serious attention.

---

[14] The Kilbrandon Committee, an unofficial all-party body established in 1984 to give a more considered response to the New Ireland Forum than Thatcher's 'Out! Out! Out!', favoured a form of joint authority which they called cooperative devolution. A five-member ministerial executive composed of one Irish Minister, one British Minister, and three Northern Ireland representatives elected by proportional representation (i.e. two Unionists and one nationalist) would make up the Government of Northern Ireland. The idea was to produce two alternating majorities (a British–Unionist majority, or an Irish–British–Northern Ireland nationalist majority) depending on the line-up of the participants.

[15] *The Equal Citizen*, No. 3, 22 Dec. 1986.

Rational actor approaches

First, the rational actor model of foreign policy analysis suggests that we should assume that the Anglo-Irish Agreement is a rational decision reached by states in pursuit of mutually acceptable goals. Indeed, we should assume that the Agreement represents the optimal strategy available to both signatories given their interests. These simple assumptions are common to different analyses of the Agreement: first, the imperialist mode of explaining Northern Ireland; second, the Machiavellian reading of the Anglo-Irish Agreement; and third, the self-presentations of the British and Irish governments.

Imperialist manoeuvres?

The Imperialist School (SF and Green Marxists) share the common assumption that the Northern Ireland conflict is caused by British imperialism and will only cease with the latter's termination.[16] According to this school the Agreement must be understood in the context of contemporary British imperialism. Fearful of what James Prior once described as the threat of an Irish Cuba off the British mainland, the Agreement represents an attempt by the British state to re-establish its hegemony in Ireland by obtaining the consent of the 'comprador' government of the twenty-six counties to the continuation of British rule in Northern Ireland, and indeed to direct British intervention in the affairs of the twenty-six counties. To these ends the Anglo-Irish Agreement was explicitly conceived to demobilize the radical nationalist movement built by SF in the wake of the hunger strikes of 1980–1, to restore the social base and credibility of the SDLP which is much less of an organizational threat to British rule, and to cement the conditions for a military and political counter-offensive against the IRA.

Promises of a symbolic gesture towards nationalist sentiment were traded by the British government in return for the Irish government's support for Britain's real objectives: a security agreement on extradition, a Europe-wide offensive against terrorists, and the Irish government's support for an assault on the American havens of support for republicans. Such an account is found in the SF press, *An Phoblacht/Republican News*, and is echoed among sections of the British ultra-left. The analysis presupposes clear and well defined objectives for the Anglo-Irish Agreement: the maintenance of British rule in Ireland, the incorporation

---

[16] See, for a good example, John Martin, 'Marxist Interpretations of Northern Ireland', *Capital and Class*, 18, 1982, and for a bad example the caucus-group journal *Labour and Ireland*.

of the Irish Republic's elites into the NATO ruling class, and the repression of SF and the IRA. The circumstantial evidence for the imperialist school includes symbolic British attempts to appease the SDLP, the Irish government's decision to join the European Convention on the Suppression of Terrorism, EEC defence arrangements which seem to violate the Republic's traditional conceptions of sovereign neutrality, and the coordinated efforts by Thatcher and Reagan to ensure that the US Senate passes an extradition treaty against the opposition of a well-organized Irish American lobby. There can be no doubt about such evidence, only about its significance.

There are fundamental problems with the analysis of the imperialist school. First, the Irish Republic is implausibly portrayed as a marionette rather than as one of the most independent of small capitalist nation-states. Second, there is no rigorous argument why the British state, let alone British capital, should be so concerned to maintain Northern Ireland as part of the United Kingdom.[17] Northern Ireland is not a good source of surplus value—which is presumbly why it is one of the few parts of the public sector which the government has not considered privatizing! It is no longer tied by aristocratic lineage networks to the dominant echelons of British society. Its Unionist political movements no longer form a key component of mainland Conservatism. Its importance as a military training ground is much disputed by army officers, and its geopolitical significance in the era of thermonuclear warfare is negligible. Indeed, Northern Ireland's principal exploitative value seems to be as a guinea pig for experiments in public and social administration. With the notable exceptions of repressive law and military policing, its use as a guinea pig is not as detrimental to the general citizenry as one might suspect.[18] Fear of an Irish Cuba exists among the more paranoid sections of the British administrative and political class, but there is little evidence that such paranoia has been paramount in British policy-making. Green Marxists and SF have a vested interest in exaggerating the mortal threat which they pose to the British state, but there is no reason why anyone

[17] See *inter alia* A. Morgan, 'Socialism in Ireland—Red, Green and Orange', in A. Morgan and B. Purdie (eds.), *Ireland: Divided Nation, Divided Class* (London: Ink Links, 1980), and P. Bew and W. Patterson, *The British State and the Ulster Crisis* (London: Verso, 1985).

[18] The scale of the British subvention for public expenditure on non-security related items, even during the high-tide of monetarism, shows that Northern Ireland has enjoyed more than the full-share of benefits of membership of the British welfare state. Fergus Pyle, 'The Price of the Union', *Irish Times*, 14–16 April 1986, cites a Coopers and Lybrand study which shows that public expenditure accounts for 75 per cent of GNP in Northern Ireland (compared with 45 per cent in the rest of the United Kingdom), and that on a per capita basis Northern Ireland citizens benefit 42 per cent more than the average Briton.

else should accept such claims. The British state exists in Northern Ireland because of past imperialism, and British policy-makers display the customary arrogance and ignorance of their imperialist precursors, but these observations should not delude us into believing that the present conflict in Northern Ireland is an artefact of current British imperialism. Successive British governments have not left Northern Ireland because they have respected the wish of the overwhelming majority of Northern Irish Protestants to remain British citizens, because the Irish Republic's governments since the 1950s have never seriously wanted the British to withdraw, and because neither state has wanted the submerged civil war to become a full-scale holocaust.

The imperialist school's rational actor explanation of the Anglo-Irish Agreement falls at the first hurdle because it has a wildly implausible notion of British objectives, based on an outmoded and falsely applied theory of imperialism. The school also lacks any well-developed account of the evolution of the Irish state. But its failings are best illustrated by its incomprehension of Ulster loyalist reaction to the Anglo-Irish Agreement. Sinn Feiners believe that the Protestant reaction to it is either wholly irrational or based upon misperceptions of perfidious Albion. Both these readings are sectarian and false. The loyalists are not stupid. The Agreement presents them with painful dilemmas, ends their supremacy within Northern Ireland, and threatens their interpretation of the Union, if not in the way that the IRA would prefer. Outside of SF supporters, the only personality to have consistently maintained an interpretation of the Anglo-Irish Agreement as an imperialist plot is Enoch Powell.[19] It is rather strange that the left takes Powell seriously only when he shares its most far-fetched conspiracy theories.

Machiavelli: From voluntary to coercive power-sharing?
The most Machiavellian interpretation of the Anglo-Irish Agreement portrays it as a rational power-game, designed to coerce the Unionists into accepting a new version of the Sunningdale agreement of 1973–4. British policy-making between 1972 and 1975 was in favour of voluntary power-sharing in a devolved regional government in Northern Ireland, and was also marked by a willingness to concede an Irish dimension in order to assuage minority grievances. The Sunningdale agreement had two features of what political scientists call the consociational model of liberal democracy which is considered appropriate for societies with

---

[19] Enoch Powell, 'Dirty Tricks That Link Dublin and Westland', Agenda, *Guardian*, 20 Jan. 1986.

deeply divisive non-class cleavages.[20] First, a power-sharing executive in which a cross-bloc majority government (Faulkner's Unionists, the SDLP, and the Alliance Party of Northern Ireland, APNI) was pre-eminent. And second, political representation, civil service composition, and the allocation of public funds were to be made on a proportional basis. Why did the Sunningdale settlement fail? Its Irish dimension, the Council of Ireland, created a furore among those Unionists opposed to power-sharing (35.5 per cent of the total electorate of 1973), and left Faulkner without the backing of his party as the experiment began. Then the British general election of February 1974 intervened at a critical stage. The plurality electoral rule meant that anti-Sunningdale Unionists were able to rout Faulkner Unionists, and obtain 51 per cent of the popular vote and eleven of the twelve Northern Ireland seats at Westminister. While poll evidence showed that strong Protestant support for the experiment had dropped after the general election to 28 per cent of their bloc,[21] the SDLP's understandable discontent at internment and repression meant that they were neither willing nor able to save Faulkner by making concessions over the Council of Ireland. Finally, the new Labour government proved especially spineless during the Ulster Workers' Council (UWC) strike which led to the collapse of the Executive. More generally, the Sunningdale settlement's fate showed that the conditions for voluntary power-sharing were not present. There was no multiple balance of power among the blocs, and there was asymmetry between the majority of the unionist bloc's attitudes towards power-sharing and that of the majority of the nationalist bloc. Moreover, the blocs were fragmenting just when their cohesion was essential to facilitate power-sharing. The political elites of the nationalist and especially the unionist bloc were not sufficiently autonomous to bargain and make concessions, even if they wanted to do so, because they had good reason to fear being outflanked by counter-elites favouring their bloc's version of 'no surrender'.[22] These features of Northern Ireland precluded voluntary power-sharing. They were brought into even bolder relief during the failed Constitutional Convention of 1975, and have remained constants of

---

[20] A. Lijphart, Typologies of Democratic Systems, *Comparative Political Studies* 1 (1968), pp. 3–44. Sue Halpern's essay, 'The Disorderly Universe of Consociational Democracy', *West European Politics*, Vol. 9, No. 2 (1986), surveys well the major criticisms of Lijphart's model, but instead of trying to reconstruct it chooses to condemn it to the dustbin of unscientific concepts.

[21] NOP Market Research Ltd, *Political Opinion in Northern Ireland* (London, 1974), p. 16.

[22] E. Nordlinger, *Conflict Regulation in Divided Societies*, Occasional Papers in International Affairs, No. 29 (Harvard University, 1972) plausibly argues that both elite motivation and autonomy are essential for successful conflict-regulation in open regimes.

the political system right up until the signing of the Anglo-Irish Agreement.

It is possible to understand the Anglo-Irish Agreement as an attempt to create the conditions for power-sharing to work, as a master-plan to coerce key factions of the unionist bloc to accept some version of the 1973–4 settlement as the least of several evils. On the one hand the Anglo-Irish Agreement confronts the unionists with an Irish dimension, the IGC, which is of far greater political salience than the Council of Ireland proposed in 1973. But, on the other hand, the Agreement offers unionists devolution as a mechanism for removing the agenda-setting scope of the IGC provided they are prepared to bite the bullet of agreed devolution—which would have to mean power-sharing because the SDLP cannot settle for anything less. The Anglo-Irish Agreement alters the structure of the incentives facing the elites of both blocs. The Irish dimension leaves the SDLP leadership free to negotiate the type of power-sharing which might be acceptable to unionists precisely because the Agreement has strengthened them against SF. And the unpalatable choices that the Agreement puts before the unionist bloc (discussed below) look designed to divide them, and to create a faction sufficiently significant and autonomous to do business with the SDLP and the APNI after ultra-loyalism has been tried and defeated. Unlike 1973–4, the unionist ultras are being given the initiative to do what they will first, in the hope that their defeat will create a new and more stable Faulkner-style grouping. Thatcher's remarks in her famous interview in Belfast certainly lend credence to such an interpretation: 'The people of Northern Ireland can get rid of the inter-governmental conference by agreeing to devolved government'.[23] This Machiavellian interpretation of the Anglo-Irish Agreement makes certain sense. The political education of the British and Irish elites since 1973 must have persuaded them that a voluntary internal settlement was impossible as long as salient groupings of unionists outside the APNI have no selective incentives to induce them to accept power-sharing, and as long as the SDLP have felt threatened on their green flank.

The Machiavellian story is, unfortunately, implausible if it is understood as a deliberately conceived rational game-plan in which all costs and benefits were calculated and all permutations of possible consequences known in advance. To take one counter-example, the scale and depth of unionist opposition to the Anglo-Irish Agreement was not anticipated by the Northern Ireland Office or the relevant cabinet

---

[23] *Belfast Telegraph*, 17 Dec. 1985.

ministers in the UK.[24] Likewise, Garret FitzGerald was startled by the intensity of the reaction of moderate unionists to the Anglo-Irish Agreement. These surprised reactions on the part of both states' officials are not what one might anticipate if they were playing the subtle power-game, and, unless one builds in further assumptions about current dissimulation in both Dublin and London, are incompatible with the Machiavellian story. While the consequences of the Agreement may eventually conform to the pattern expected if the British and Irish policy elites did plan coercive power-sharing, the reasons for signing the Agreement do not wholly conform to the rational actor story.

State self-presentations: Reconciliation and security?

The British and Irish states have highlighted peace, reconciliation, and security as their principal objectives in presenting the Anglo-Irish Agreement to their respective societies. The British government has constantly highlighted the security dimensions of the Agreement to both dissident Conservatives and the Ulster Unionists. Increased cross-border security liaison, the Republic's accession to the Suppression of Terrorism convention, and the American extradition bill have all figured prominently in British rhetoric. Embarrassing incidents such as the Glenholmes affair[25] and the emergence of the Stalker affair,[26] have not stopped both governments claiming early successes from the increased harmonization of the intelligence and resources of the RUC and the Garda Siochána. However, as a glance at Fig. 2.1 (Political murders in Northern Ireland 1969–85) and Fig. 2.2 (Breakdown of political murders 1969–84) should make apparent, there was no overwhelming case for a security offensive on the part of the British and Irish states before the signing of the Anglo-Irish Agreement. The most intense phase of political violence was in the early 1970s, during the collapse of Stormont and the failure of the Sunningdale settlement. Since the mid-1970s the IRA has altered its organization and military strategy. Economic targets have been abandoned to concentrate on attacking local security forces. The reasons for this change were the

---

[24] Interview with NIO official.

[25] Evelyn Glenholmes, a suspected IRA activist, walked free from a Dublin court in March 1986 largely because the British failed to prepare their extradition papers properly.

[26] The Stalker affair, which was still unfolding at the time of writing, centred on whether the RUC, MI5, the Home Office, or others conspired to obtain the suspension from duty, on unclear charges, of the Deputy Chief Constable of Manchester Police, John Stalker. He had been assigned the task of investigating whether or not the RUC had operated an illegal 'shoot-to-kill' policy against suspected terrorists during 1982 in Armagh. If Stalker's findings were affirmative their publication in the summer of 1986 would have been extremely embarrassing for the RUC and the government in the midst of the loyalist marching season.

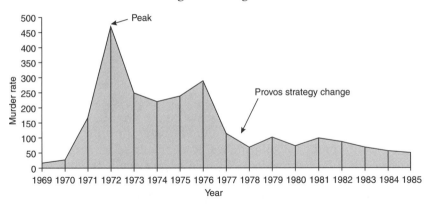

Fig. 2.1 Political murders in Northern Ireland 1969–85.

Source: *New Ireland Forum*, updated to 1985.

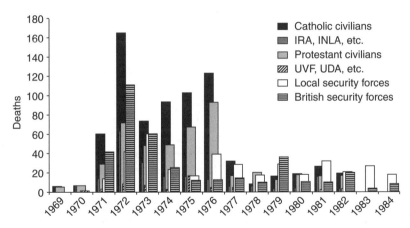

Fig. 2.2 Breakdown of political murders 1969–84.

Source: *New Ireland Forum*, updated by the author, from whom detailed figures are available.

comparative success of British repression in the mid-1970s, and the Provisionals' need for a strategy less likely to alienate their own social base. A cell structure and attacks on local security forces served both goals. The consequence has been a dramatic fall-off in civilian deaths. The policy of 'Ulsterisation' (the replacement of the British Army by the Royal Ulster Constabulary, RUC) had also led to a considerable reduction in the numbers of army personnel killed since the mid-1970s. True, the brunt of the IRA's strategy is now carried by local security forces (the RUC, the

Ulster Defence Regiment, UDR, and prison officers), but their fate does not have the same salience to British policy-making elites as those of civilians or army personnel. In other words, it is perfectly sensible to suggest that British strategists had achieved their goal of 'acceptable levels of violence' within Northern Ireland before the signing of the Anglo-Irish Agreement. But the high-risk initiative embarked upon at Hillsborough puts Catholic civilians at risk, has caused ferocious conflicts of loyalty within the RUC and the UDR, and compels the British to increase the army presence. As Figs 2.1 and 2.2 graphically illustrate, Catholic civilians are never at greater risk than when Protestants feel that their supremacy is being eroded, as during 1972–6. And the Anglo-Irish Agreement has put the greatest moral and intimidatory pressure on the local security forces who suffered most at the hands of the IRA in the late 1970s and early 1980s. Consequently, it is difficult to believe that the conventional security forces were whole-heartedly behind the Hillsborough agreement.

On the Irish side, the Anglo-Irish Agreement left the FG–ILP coalition government exposed to FF charges of violating the Republic's sover-eignty, giving retrospective recognition to RUC cross-border pursuits, and abandoning a well-established constitutional freedom for the pro-tection of political exiles. When one recalls that Haughey's deft playing of the 'green card' over RUC cross-border incursions in the last Irish general election of 1982 caused severe damage to FG, there are also reasons for suggesting that the security dimensions of the Agreement were not in the short-run rational interests of the Irish government. Furthermore, as John Taylor of the Official Unionist Party pointed out with sublime subtlety, the prospects of bombs and carnage on the streets of Dublin have risen greatly since the Agreement was signed.[27] And finally, the Irish government's presence at the IGC to some extent binds them against making wholesale criticisms of the RUC and the UDR. Their desire for the RUC to stand firm in the summer of 1986 seems to have restrained them from making political capital over the Stalker affair. King's abuse of the IGC, to mislead Barry over whether Stalker's report on RUC conduct in Armagh in 1982 was 'final' or 'interim', resulted in an ultimatum from the Irish requesting 'clarification'[28]—but the progress of the affair so far shows that the Irish government is tied to the British style of security/repression management, and has lost its past freedom of action. The loyalist marches through Catholic areas of Portadown in July 1986 put severe stress on the Irish government, but even this very

[27] *Irish Times*, 18 June 1986.   [28] *Guardian*, 23 June 1986.

traditional form of loyalist provocation led to very sensitive criticism of the British government. Such constraints must have been foreseen.

The Anglo-Irish Agreement did not bring peace and reconciliation instantly with the prime ministerial signatures. No one was naive enough to believe otherwise. However, the prelude to the Anglo-Irish Agreement did not help matters. The exclusion of the unionists from participation in the negotiation of the agreement, while entirely practical, has made their opposition all the stronger. In the short run the Anglo-Irish Agreement has undoubtedly exacerbated rather than ameliorated the existing levels of polarization, raised sectarian attacks on Catholics, induced Protestant assaults on the RUC, and encouraged the IRA to reap the whirlwind. There is also evidence that both the British and Irish governments have been—genuinely—surprised by the levels of animosity towards the Anglo-Irish Agreement among the Unionists, and by the apparent intransigence of John Hume to those 'feelers' which some unionists have made towards the SDLP.[29] If both governments believed their own rhetoric, they have miscalculated the scale of short-run conflict which the Agreement would produce. And at least on the conventional security front it is difficult to believe that their administrators' advice suggested anything other than that it would worsen matters, at least for the time being.

The organizational process approach

The second standard mode of analysing foreign policy decisions suggests that states or governments should not be assumed to be unitary actors who pursue specified goals and objectives. Rather, any decision will bear the hallmarks of the state agencies involved, their standard operating procedures, their established repertoires for defining problems, and their favoured solutions. Unlike the rational actor approach, the organizational process model will not leave us with perfectly lucid explanations of how rational actors reached optimal decisions.

On the British side, the relevant state agencies involved in the prelude to the Anglo-Irish Agreement were the Foreign Office, the Northern Ireland Office (NIO), the Cabinet Office, and, judging from the professional role of the civil servants involved in the negotiations, the pertinent intelligence services. While the Northern Irish NIO officials were not

---

[29] Harry West, the former leader of the OUP (1974–9), Austin Ardill, and David McNarry are the first group within the OUP to have offered power-sharing to the SDLP. Hume dismissed their informal talks with SDLP leaders because the Unionists still wanted the suspension of the IGC, and because the West group are no longer influential within the OUP (*Irish Times*, 6 March 1986).

influential, the NIO's British officials certainly were. Interviews have established a most interesting NIO jargon for defining their standard repertoires for dealing with Northern Ireland. Since the early 1970s they have developed what they call *internal* and *external* tracks. The former tells them to pursue the broadest possible agreement within Northern Ireland for an internal settlement. The latter tells them to pursue the maximum feasible good relations with the Irish Republic and the United States of America on the Ulster crisis, and to ensure minimum feasible international embarrassment.[30] These two tracks have often been in conflict or difficult to reconcile, especially given their third track, the maintenance of 'an acceptable level of violence'. However, the jargon of 'internal and external tracks' captures the basic thrust of British policy-making, or more strictly the administrative advice of the NIO, since 1972. And the Anglo-Irish Agreement has both standard NIO repertoires clearly built into it (agreed devolution and good relations with the Irish Republic). Consequently, apart from timing and formality, it is feasible to argue that the Anglo-Irish Agreement is consistent with the 'broad thrust' of the developed routines of British policy-making. It made sense to the British because it fitted their existing definitions of the 'problem' and their pre-established routines for managing it. Such an interpretation makes better sense of the facts than the Machiavellian coercive power-sharing story because it does not assume a comprehensive master-plan on the part of the British policy elite.

On the Irish side, it is apparent that since the partial success of the modernization programmes embarked upon in the late 1950s and early 1960s, the standard modes of defining the Northern Ireland question have altered, among both administrators and the policy elite. The legitimation of the Irish state is altering from the assertion of national sovereignty through cultural autonomy and separateness from the United Kingdom to achieving support through the material prosperity of advanced industrial capitalism. Irish state officials outside the ranks of FF have come to define Northern Ireland as a problem for the stability of their state, as a threat to their programmes of modernization, as an anachronism rather than a question of burning injustice or uncompleted national revolution. These changes in attitude are also reflected in the Republic's citizenry. For Irish state officials the Northern Ireland conflict

---

[30] Paul Arthur, 'Anglo-Irish relations and the Northern Ireland Problem', *Irish Studies in International Affairs*, 2,1, 1985, has cogently argued that British policy-making has been characterized by two features: quarantining the Irish issue from mainstream politics and maintaining international respectability. These features exemplify the NIO's internal and external tracks respectively.

has generally come to be managed through two strategic routines: playing the role of guardian of the Northern Ireland minority rather than prospective ruler of Ulster Unionists (advocating reform and power-sharing within Northern Ireland and using the international stage to proclaim this guardian role) and increasing cooperation with the British state, through the EEC and other forums, to contain the conflict ('unique relationships among these islands', and 'interdependence is not dependence' provide the bureaucratic codes here). The Anglo-Irish Agreement again fits neatly with these well-established routines, and also makes better sense of the facts than the rational actor models. Fianna Fáil, the party which has not yet made the full transition from the party of cultural nationalism to the party of economic nationalism, is the only major organization yet to accept in its rhetoric these decisive alterations in the foreign policy routines of the Irish state. In practice, in government, FF has both initiated such changes and furthered them, but in opposition has retained the scope to play the Green card for electoral opportunism.

The organizational process story is very plausible. Ensconsed in the vacillations of personalities and crisis-episodes, behind the zig-zags in British policy-postures highlighted by Bew and Patterson,[31] buried under the rapid turnover in Irish governments during 1980–2, and indeed behind the aberration of Thatcher's reaction to the New Ireland Forum proposals ('Out! Out! Out!'), compatible strategies for managing the Northern Ireland conflict have developed within the agencies of both states. With the Thatcher and FitzGerald administrations both in mid-term and both determined to make a symbolic initiative, 1985 was an opportune year for the cementing of the two states' approaches. It was also opportune because memories of the hunger strikes and the Irish Republic's studied neutrality during the Falklands/Malvinas war were fading.

The political approach

Politics is never solely a tale of rational state actions or bureaucratic routines. It is also a tale of personalities, symbolism, party manoeuvres, and *post hoc* rationalization in an uncertain environment. That the symbolic dimensions of a major initiative and agreement appealed to both prime ministers is on the record. FitzGerald claims to have entered politics to solve the Northern Ireland problem and to hasten the

---

[31] Op. cit., pp. 39–131.

secularization and pluralization of the Irish Republic. The rationality of Thatcher's political project is always greatly exaggerated on the left, but she has displayed a penchant for tackling head on what are perceived to be the major unresolved crises of the British state as well as a preparedness to break through existing conventional wisdom and inertia.[32] Her narrow escape from death at Brighton also concentrated Thatcher's mind on the Northern Irish question in a way that the IRA did not anticipate. NIO officials describe her commitment to the Anglo-Irish Agreement as total, and Peter Jay has remarked that when it was suggested that she was prepared to backtrack 'the divine anger was wonderful to behold'. Both leaders not only enjoyed the symbolism of a major initiative but shared a similar resolution to embark upon a 'leap into the dark', a propensity which few of their predecessors have displayed, and their personal beliefs and styles must be taken into account in any complete explanation of the signing of the Agreement.

The Anglo-Irish Agreement was good domestic politics in both states. Playing skilled statecraft to their respective electorates during mid-term opinion-poll blues brought rewards. The Irish coalition enjoyed a brief renewal of support and enjoyed overwhelming approval for the Agreement in opinion polls. Such a response could well have been anticipated. A split in FF, its opposition to the Agreement in the Dail, and the formation of the Progressive Democrats amounted to an unexpected, and briefly enjoyed, bonus. The Conservative government counted on, and received, all-party support in the Commons and thrived playing the role of acting in the national interest. However, successive governments have shown Northern Ireland does not matter electorally (unless one MP or TD can affect the stability of the executive), and as the Anglo-Irish Agreement comes under pressure while producing few immediate tangible results, much more radical initiatives might be acceptable to both the British and Irish electorates. As a result, some contend that both leaders have set in train a policy fiasco which will defeat their respective objectives. This story also makes sense, and might be rooted in the

---

[32] Talk of Thatcher as the British equivalent of de Gaulle is wildly exaggerated. There are few appropriate parallels between the Irish government and the Algerian national liberation movement, still less in terms of legitimacy between the Provisionals and the FMLN (unless one makes Islam and Catholicism the basis of comparison). The impact of Northern Ireland in the 1970s and 1980s, with the exception of attempted assassinations of key political figures, has not been anything as dramatic as that of Algeria on French politics in the 1950s. There is also no evidence that Thatcher or the British state are preparing to withdraw—such speculation misreads the effective administrative integration of Northern Ireland into the United Kingdom since 1972 and underestimates the *Realpolitik* of successive Irish governments.

activist compulsion of liberal democratic elites to do something rather than nothing, and to blunder in consequence.

There are two sophisticated versions of current left analyses of the character of direct rule since 1972 relevant to explanations of the Anglo-Irish Agreement. The first, a rational actor approach, argues that British policy-making has *reproduced* rather than *reformed* sectarian relations in Northern Ireland, and implicitly regards the British state as functionally structured to do so.[33] This school of thought essentially has a functionalist account of the state, and an auxiliary rational–actor imperialist model which it deploys to 'explain' policy outputs. The second, a political approach, contends that the *unintended* consequences of British policy-making have been to exacerbate sectarian conflict between Catholics and Protestants.[34] The second school is more theoretically and empirically sophisticated, unspoiled by the functionalist fallacies of much Marxist thought,[35] and is a good version of political approaches to policy-making. The logical extrapolation of the second school is to suggest that the Agreement may end up reinforcing sectarian relations, but that it must itself be explained by the decisions of politicians and administrators who genuinely thought themselves to be engaged in a process designed to weaken sectarianism. By contrast, this analysis will contend, in conclusion, that the unintended consequences of the Anglo-Irish Agreement could be the playing out of the Machiavellian power-game and the creation of conditions for the eventual dissolution of sectarianism.

Whatever the truth of these contentions, the decisive actor in the politics of the signing of the Anglo-Irish Agreement has been the SDLP and its leader John Hume. Content that the British and Irish premiers obtained whatever short-run glory it would bring, the SDLP leader has been reticent about his role. But as the instigator of Anglo-Irish discussions and the New Ireland Forum, as the leader who advocated abstaining from Prior's Assembly on the grounds that a boycott would produce something more, as an actively consulted adviser to the Irish government during the negotiations, Hume has contributed more than any other political leader towards the Agreement. Ulster Unionists are far more aware of this fact than the Republic's or British commentators who have vied to give credit to Cabinet Secretaries, Foreign Affairs or Cabinet

---

[33] Liam O'Dowd, Bill Rolston, and Mike Tomlinson, *Northern Ireland, Between Civil Rights and Civil War* (London: CSE Books, 1980).   [34] Bew and Patterson, op. cit.

[35] J. Elster, 'Marxism, functionalism and game theory', *Theory and Society*, 11 (1982), pp. 453–82.

Office staff, ambassadors, Thatcher, or FitzGerald. To Ulster Unionists, Hume is the evil genius behind the Agreement. Hume has always said that agreed devolution is acceptable to the SDLP, provided that it is part of a broader Anglo-Irish process. The SDLP's welcome for the Agreement, its willingness to give both the RUC and the British government some trust, and the distance opening up between the SDLP and FF all confirm both their prior interest in the Agreement and their willingness to exploit it to maximum advantage within the nationalist bloc. The SDLP is the party with most to gain and lose from the Agreement, and its relations with both governments were critical in its making, and will be crucial to its evolution. These facts explain why Hume has been condemned by the Official Unionist Party, the DUP, SF, and even the Workers' Party as the villain behind the agreement, glorying in his opportunity. There is some plausibility in the SF charge that the Anglo-Irish Agreement was made to save the SDLP, but there is also truth in the Unionist charge that it was the SDLP's minimum price for abandoning abstentionist politics.

In conclusion, on current evidence, it seems best to conclude that the Anglo-Irish Agreement was signed because of the confluence of well-established bureaucratic strategies, incremental and exploratory manoeuvres by politicians and administrators interested in symbolic initiatives, and jockeying for position on the part of the SDLP. Hume's description of the Agreement as a 'framework' rather than a solution or Machiavellian master-plan is correct, but he also knows that it is a framework potentially weighted in favour of SDLP solutions.

INTERIM RESULTS

After seven months of existence, the policy-outputs resulting from the deliberations of the IGC could be written on the back of a new pound coin. The most significant result of the Anglo-Irish Agreement so far has been its own survival, the regular inter-ministerial meetings, the institutionalization of an administrative Secretariat at Maryfield, and striking evidence of attempts to harmonize their statements by both governments. As yet it is quite impossible to assess objectively the consequences of formal increases in police cooperation, which like American 'aid' is difficult to measure, may come in unexpected forms, and indeed may never materialize. The major move on the Irish side has been to sign the Convention on the Suppression of Terrorism, but that was specifically promised in the communiqué accompanying the Anglo-Irish Agreement.

The British have so far reciprocated with two very minor changes: ensuring that Irish citizens will have the same rights in Northern Ireland that they enjoy in the United Kingdom, and facilitating the use of the Irish language in street-naming.

The most conflictual items on the policy-agenda of the IGC are acknowledged to be the following:

(1) whether there should be a new code of conduct for the Royal Ulster Constabulary, the 90 per cent Protestant police force;

(2) the existence and character of the locally recruited and almost entirely Protestant regiment of the British Army, the UDR, whose members have often been involved in sectarian murders and overlapping membership with paramilitary loyalist organizations;

(3) whether there should be a Bill of Rights to protect all traditions from each other and the state;

(4) whether the Flag and Emblems Act of 1954, which makes the flying of the tricolour of the Irish Republic an offence within Northern Ireland, should be repealed;

(5) whether the special, emergency legislation introduced by successive British governments, especially the Diplock (no-jury, one judge) courts which have been a major source of the alienation of the nationalist minority, should be reformed or scrapped; and

(6) whether 'supergrass' (paid-informers' evidence forming the sole basis for conviction) trials should cease.

In all these items on the agenda, movement so far has been largely confined to chairs, helicopters, and press-briefings. The Irish government has promised that major changes in the administration of justice would be forthcoming at the end of 1986—signalling to the nationalist minority that they should wait until Unionist civil disobedience ends before they can obtain their just deserts. The British government, while willing to move on the RUC's code of conduct, has remained adamant on the retention of the UDR, has shown little willingness to make a minor concession on the reform of the Diplock courts (the Irish government has asked for three judges instead of one), and is procrastinating on all dimensions of emergency legislation in the face of Unionist opposition to the Anglo-Irish Agreement. However, 'supergrass' trials, repugnant to both nationalists and loyalists, do seem likely to come to an end.

The bind that the British government faces now can be simply expressed: to display to the Unionists that the IGC does not amount to joint authority the Secretary of State for Northern Ireland must show himself capable of ignoring Irish representations at its deliberations. But in order to show the Irish government that the IGC is worthwhile he must make concessions to nationalist feelings. However, he must present any concessions that he does make as measures he would have taken without Irish intervention. The Secretary of State is thus obliged to take a zig-zag course. To date, King has chosen to show that the IGC is operational, and will not be suspended or postponed, but has refused to make rapid reforms in order to ease his most visible task, that is, managing Unionist discontent. Apart from his statement on the Union's perpetual existence and 'misleading' the Irish Foreign Minister over the Stalker inquiry, the Irish government has shown comprehension, even empathy, for the complex logic of King's position—but with an election imminent is likely to become impatient for more tangible results by the end of 1986.

PROSPECTS: WILL THE ANGLO-IRISH AGREEMENT SURVIVE?

The Northern Ireland conflict has both exogenous (outside Northern Ireland) and endogenous (within Northern Ireland) dimensions.[36] The survival of the Anglo-Irish Agreement will depend on how these exogenous and endogenous variables interact.

Endogenous actors

Unionists
Since December 1985 British media attention has understandably focused upon the most visible threat to its success, the Ulster Unionists. How has the Unionist opposition fared so far? When the Anglo-Irish Agreement was signed the Official Unionist Party (OUP) and DUP embarked upon a united opposition strategy. The Unionist campaign began constitutionally (if one discounts an attempted mugging of Tom King by DUP councillors). They resigned their Westminster seats, emphasized legitimate opinion-mobilization, and attempted to challenge the Anglo-Irish Agreement's legality in the courts. This first phase culminated in the January 1986 by-elections. The by-elections backfired, both because the Unionists lost one seat when Seamus Mallon, the deputy leader of the SDLP, and its impressive spokesman on law and order, successfully

[36] D. B. O'Leary, 'Explaining Northern Ireland', *Politics*, 5,1 (1985). See also J. Whyte, 'Interpretations of the Northern Ireland Problem', paper presented at a conference of the British Association for Irish Studies at the University of Keele, 2–4 April 1986.

contested the Newry and Armagh seat, and because the Westland affair overshadowed whatever media attention the by-elections might otherwise have generated in Great Britain. Moreover, the evidence of increased electoral support for the SDLP at the expense of Sinn Fein allowed both the Irish and British governments to suggest that the by-elections proved that the Anglo-Irish Agreement was actually working: moderate nationalism was re-establishing itself.[37] The unionists then moved their campaign up a gear, and eventually called for a general strike on 3 March. Molyneaux and Paisley, the leaders of the OUP and DUP, for a brief moment, looked as if they were prepared to accept some fudge which Thatcher and King were prepared to offer, but were quickly brought back into line by the led when they returned to Belfast. Despite evidence of widespread support among Protestants for the strike, media reports successfully highlighted coercive action and managed to brand the strike as wholly intimidatory in much the same manner as British trade-union disputes are usually treated. With the APNI openly bidding for the middle-class Protestant vote, the media presentation of the strike quickly opened up divisions within the Unionist bloc, especially among the OUP. Molyneaux felt compelled to dissociate the OUP from the strike organizers. Although an *Irish Times*/MRBI opinion poll showed 81 per cent of Protestants disapproving of the Anglo-Irish Agreement in February 1986, Unionist leaders, especially those in the OUP hierarchy, obviously felt constrained over what means they could use to attack the British government without opening up divisions within their supporters. Just as the OUP and DUP were trying to restructure their campaign, ultra-loyalist paramilitaries, with the apparent approval of senior figures in the DUP, began coordinated attacks on RUC officers. They were deliberately capitalizing on evidence of hostility to the Anglo-Irish Agreement among the rank-and-file of the RUC—openly articulated by the RUC Federation chairman—and inflammatory rhetoric about 'our police' which elected Unionist politicians had engaged in both before and after the strike. These attacks, which reached a peak between March and May 1986, were accompanied by a renewed spate of sectarian murders against Catholics. As predicted by Andy Tyrie, the leader of the Ulster Defence Association (UDA), the largest loyalist paramilitary organization, the

---

[37] S. Elliott, 'A Post-Mortem on an Unprecedented Poll', *Fortnight*, 10 Feb. 1986, shows that since its high-tide in 1983 there has been a swing from SF to the SDLP in those four constituencies where both SF and SDLP candidates stood. It should be noted that the growth of the SF vote after the hunger-strikes led them to participate in electoral politics was mostly based on a non-voting, militant republican vote rather than upon inroads into the SDLP's electoral base.

official Unionist politicians quickly played Pontius Pilate on their paramilitary brethren, and the first wave of assaults on the RUC has come to
an end. The summer marching season, when Protestants traditionally
march through Catholic areas to commemorate their past victories, was
not as confrontational as some had feared during July, but at the time of
writing the Apprentice Boys march in August was yet to come. The
history of this century (1911–14, 1920–5, and 1972–6) shows that
loyalists are at their most militaristic and bloodthirsty when they feel
under siege.

The local government strategy of the Unionists, like their dual strategy
of constitutionalism and civil disobedience, is also misfiring. They had
threatened to make local councils ungovernable and not to set rates (the
local property tax). But talk of 'Gideon's army' [38] soon waned as key
Unionist politicians folded under the threat of action by auditors in
Belfast and elsewhere. Currently (summer 1986), Unionist politicians
have embarked upon a campaign in Britain designed to win support for
their position. The fate of Boyd Black who stood in the Fulham by-
election in April 1986 with the backing of Unionists (he received fewer
votes than Screaming Lord Sutch of the Monster Raving Loony Party),
and the 100 people who attended the first 'mass-meeting' in Liverpool,
have given Unionists a sense of their complete isolation from all but the
lunatic fringe of the English public. The unionists' best hope of significant British mobilization is in the threats that the Scottish Orange
Order will pose to a handful of Conservative MPs in Scotland. The
Friends of the Union Group, established in late May 1986 to coordinate
the 'mainland' campaign, has so far shown no signs of having an impact
upon elite or public opinion. Unionists' opposition has won them nothing more than the postponement for a couple of days of scheduled
meetings of the IGC, while the assaults on the RUC have lost them the
potential sympathy of numerous right-wing Conservatives. But their
opposition has severely curtailed the pace and prospects of reforms
wanted by Northern nationalists, as both governments have agreed to
ride out the storm of protests.

What is the likelihood that Unionists can be sufficiently effective to
bring down the Anglo-Irish Agreement? There are good reasons for
supposing that their bloc cannot stay united. First, about 20 per cent of
Protestants, judging from poll evidence, are not against the Anglo-Irish
Agreement. If the Anglo-Irish Agreement pays dividends on the security

[38] The allusion is biblical: Gideon reduced the size of his army to its most valiant core and
was more successful in war as a result.

front against the IRA, that figure might grow. Second, unlike 1974, unionists are not mobilizing against an internal power-sharing executive in which some unionists are participating. They are mobilizing against the British government, against Margaret Thatcher and Tom King not Harold Wilson and Merlyn Rees, which as the British left can testify is a much more daunting prospect. And when one recalls that the second UWC strike in 1977 failed because it had unclear objectives and no internal target to overthrow, unionists' difficulties become even more apparent. Third, the organizational and strategic requirements for a repeat of 1974 do not seem to be present. The Conservative administration, the army, and the bulk of the RUC's leadership seem to have the motivated leadership to defeat any extended strike. Fourth, among those sections of the Protestant bloc aware that their material prosperity is desperately dependent upon the retention of the British connection, there is much furrowing of the brow over attacking a British government. The enthusiasm for strike action on 3 March 1986 was undoubtedly damped by high levels of unemployment, and the fact that only a one-day strike was called was significant.

Finally, the stakes for unionists are strikingly different from those in 1974. Their effective range of options is no longer circumscribed to either internal power-sharing along Sunningdale lines or the continuation of direct rule. Assuming for the moment that the Thatcher administration stands firm and that the coalition government in the Republic does not collapse, Unionist choices seem to be as follows:

1. Go down to defeat and accept the possible evolution of full British–Irish joint authority.
2. After defeat accept power-sharing with an unimportant Irish dimension and thereby reduce the role of the IGC.
3. Go for independence.
4. Stay in a state of permanent rebellion against the British government until the Anglo-Irish Agreement is repudiated.

The first choice is the most ignominious and galling for them. The second choice has the built-in carrot of allowing power-sharing to reduce the salience of the IGC, but requires sufficient Unionist politicians from the OUP to accept power-sharing, and be confident that they will not be instantly outflanked on their ultra-loyalist flank and meet the fate which befell Brian Faulkner. The third choice would split the unionists. They are, after all, unionists. They do not seek sovereignty over themselves. They are not nationalists but rather anti-nationalists. Unionists will only contemplate independence if and only if they are coerced into a united

Ireland. Most OUP and APNI voters might even baulk at considering independence if joint authority were being imposed. The DUP, thus, stand at the crossroads. Rhetorical demands for a nuclear strike on the Irish Republic notwithstanding,[39] the DUP are not currently sufficiently cohesive to raise independence as a threat. They know that to raise the option of UDI would split the unionist bloc. Paisley has cried 'wolf' so often that when the genuine article arrived in the person of Margaret Thatcher he has seemed strangely paralysed. His most radical statements to date have been to repeat the traditional loyalist cry in times of English perfidy: allegiance to Parliament must be withdrawn without ending loyalty to the Crown.[40] This call may well be treason, but so far it is not a declaration of independence: it is a bargaining posture, 'We want our Union on our terms'. During the occupation of the dissolved Assembly chamber at Stormont he increased the scope of his 'call to arms', but whether he will actively lead an armed struggle for independence still remains very dubious.[41]

If the DUP do not raise UDI as a serious alternative, Thatcher and King can call their bluff, see off their counter-mobilization, and subsequently look out for a power-sharing deal with a reconstituted OUP leadership. If the DUP raises the UDI option prematurely it will not only split the unionist bloc but also face the threat of a war on two fronts, against the British state and the IRA. The DUP has to build a 'coalition for unreasonableness', prevent the prospect of an OUP sell-out, and yet remain credible to large sections of Protestant opinion. The only way that unionists opposed to the Anglo-Irish Agreement can avoid defeat is to follow their fourth option, permanent rebellion on a negative programme of 'Ulster says No!', and to hope that something will turn up. This option, upon which they have been embarked for eight months, is very difficult to sustain. The OUP may cut and run when blood flows this summer, and when the British government has remained unmoved. The strategy also threatens to create a decisive impetus for British withdrawal, precisely the outcome all unionists want least. The success of the fourth option depends, as we shall see, upon critical external variables. The success of unionist opposition mostly depends upon the future evolution of the British and Irish governments.

---

[39] *Irish Times*, 21 April 1986. Rev. Ivan Foster, Assembly Member for Fermanagh, made his case at the DUP Conference with strained logic: if Gaddafy's haven for terrorism merited Reagan's raid, then surely a nuclear strike on the Irish Republic by Britain was in order. The Reverend seemed to be unaware that a nuclear strike on IRA bases would have considerable fallout on his Fermanagh electorate...

[40] *Irish Times*, 20 June 1986.   [41] *Evening Standard*, 24 June 1986.

Nationalists

How the SDLP can play its cards is somewhat less dependent upon the British and Irish governments, but can critically affect the stability of the Anglo-Irish Agreement. Indeed, Northern Catholics have more say in its stability than they had in maintaining the power-sharing executive in 1974. Adams, the clever leader of SF, was well aware that the Anglo-Irish Agreement had dealt the SDLP an ace. Initially most SF spokesmen filled the air with accusations that the SDLP was selling out the 'Irish [i.e. Northern Catholic] people'. Adams was more subtle when it became plain that the Unionists were going to force by-elections. He offered the SDLP an electoral pact. His strategy was obvious. He wanted either to prevent the SDLP from benefiting electorally from the Anglo-Irish Agreement through successful negotiation of a pact, or to gain the chance of accusing the SDLP of splitting the nationalist bloc should the offer of a pact be refused. Adams 'bearing gifts' did not deceive the SDLP's leadership. The by-elections gave them the opportunity to distance themselves from their acts of cowardice during the hunger strikes of 1980–1,[42] and the Anglo-Irish Agreement has given them the opportunity to lead the nationalist bloc away from the militaristic, sectarian, and romantic vices of Irish nationalism, and to re-earn the label 'social democratic and labour'. So far, the SDLP has reaped electoral rewards, revived at the expense of SF, and has used its freedom of manoeuvre to state its willingness to go into talks for devolved government provided the Anglo-Irish Agreement and its Irish dimension remains intact. The SDLP, nonetheless, faces two strong sources of pressure. First, the Northern Ireland Office and the Conservative government have not been slow in demanding SDLP support for the forces of law and order, especially the RUC, as a quid pro quo for the Anglo-Irish Agreement. The SDLP showed itself willing in the first few months of the agreement. But the RUC's handling of the 3 March 1986 strike and loyalist Marches in Portadown in July, the failure of the IGC to reform Diplock courts, the general maladministration of justice in Northern Ireland and the status of the UDR, and finally the controversy over the Stalker inquiry into the RUC's 'shoot-to-kill' policy in Armagh during 1982 have all compelled the SDLP into its understandable traditional posture on 'law' and 'order' in Northern Ireland. It is unprepared wholeheartedly to endorse the RUC and the legal system until they are seen to be impartial. Until the British government engages in serious reforms of Northern Ireland to add to the symbolic promises in the Anglo-Irish

---

[42] In 1981 the SDLP did not run a candidate against the IRA prisoner Bobby Sands, and thereby ensured his election as MP for Fermanagh and South Tyrone.

Agreement, the SDLP will not feel free to support the RUC without major reservations. If the SDLP is to maintain its newly acquired advantages over SF then the Agreement must be seen to make a difference to the minority population: 'all talk and no action' could quickly bring the IGC into disrepute among the nationalists who have been prepared to give the Anglo-Irish Agreement the benefit of the doubt. Second, the SDLP still has tensions between its green and reformist wings, and will remain united only if the Agreement makes a material as well as a symbolic difference to the position of the minority. SDLP support for it over the long run is contingent upon a British willingness to coerce the Unionists into accepting both the Agreement and the reform of Northern Ireland. The Anglo-Irish Agreement cannot work, of course, if the SDLP develops a hard line on eventual reunification, and regards it as a stepping stone to negotiated unification in the immediate future. It might become tempted to rely on a future British Labour government to execute such a strategy, especially in the face of permanent Unionist intransigence, but its primary objective remains power-sharing and reform within the framework of the Agreement.

The success of the Anglo-Irish Agreement is not in any way dependent upon the IRA or SF for support, but can they damage its chances of success? And can the Agreement, as intended, damage both SF and the IRA? Several factors are relevant to such questions. First, there is no doubt that SF is more vulnerable than the IRA. Entry into electoral politics has constrained the IRA's military options that SF can freely endorse. Ensnared in the search for electoral legitimacy, it must attempt to defeat the Agreement by pointing up the failure of the IGC to deliver promised reforms, and by suggesting that the SDLP have become trapped into supporting British imperialism. However, Sinn Féin cannot endorse the sorts of actions which might cause hardships to its natural constituencies in West Belfast and Derry. Moreover, if the Anglo-Irish Agreement makes a material difference to the civil liberties and economic welfare of the Catholic working class the social base of SF will be vulnerable. Second, after the Brighton bombings and trial, it will be some time before the IRA will be able to launch a sustained mainland bombing campaign, so that military efforts to cause a dramatic change in British policy are unlikely. Third, since the Anglo-Irish Agreement, like the IRA's own strategy, is a long-term framework rather than a solution, it has the potential to be a far more resilient British initiative than previous quick-fire recipes, and might undermine the credibility of the SF/IRA using a 'wear them down' strategy. Fourth, while it is true that the IRA can survive with minuscule active support among the Catholic minority, loss of support for SF will undoubtedly undermine its morale, and astute use of partial amnesty offers could throw the 'armalite and ballot box' camp into confusion.

Exogenous actors

One reason why both British and Irish officials like the Anglo-Irish Agreement is that its survival seems much less dependent upon the actors within Northern Ireland than previous attempted solutions. However, the other side of the coin is that the maintenance of the Agreement is much more dependent upon the stability of the postures of future British and Irish governments. External stability is critical if it is to act as a framework for an internal settlement. The most obvious threat to the Agreement is that within its first three years there have to be general elections in both the United Kingdom and the Republic. When we recall the consequences of the 1974 general election upon the Sunningdale settlement, the significance of these forthcoming elections cannot be doubted.

Logically, there are four relevant feasible outcomes which will affect the future of the Anglo-Irish Agreement. First, the election of British and Irish governments in favour of maintaining it. Second, the election of a British government in favour of the Agreement, but the election of an Irish government wanting to reject it. Third, the election of a British government in favour of repudiating the Agreement, but an Irish government which wants to retain it. Fourth, the election of British and Irish governments in favour of ending it. We can discount the third and fourth of these possibilities. These logical outcomes neglect a more subtle variation: the desire on the part of one or both elected governments to renegotiate the terms of the Agreement.

The election of two governments in favour of retaining the accord
This outcome remains likely. On the British side, a general election must take place by June 1988. All three major party groupings—Labour, Conservative, and the Liberal–SDP Alliance—expressed bipartisan support for the Anglo-Irish Agreement in its passage through Parliament. The return of a majority Thatcher administration for a third term of office will ensure the survival of the Anglo-Irish Agreement provided a possible Fianna Fáil government has not repudiated it. The longer Thatcher delays the calling of a general election the more likely it is that the unionists will be beaten down by the plenitude of state resources which the Conservatives can wield against them. Whatever their enthusiasm for Thatcher's departure from British political life, no one doubts that she and the Conservatives are far more able to coerce the unionists into

accepting the Anglo-Irish Agreement (and power-sharing) than any other British party, coalition, or minority government. The unionists hope that a new Conservative government might repudiate the Agreement, or not renew it. But the election of a FF government in the South, elected on a manifesto committed to ending it, is the only circumstance in which that Unionist hope might be realized.

In July 1986 it seemed that the three most likely outcomes of a British general election are a Labour majority government, a Labour minority government sustained by one or a combination of minor parties, or else a coalition government of a character impossible to predict with any confidence. In the first case, the current Labour front-bench team who would take over the Northern Ireland Office are supporters of the Anglo-Irish Agreement. Only the election of an overwhelming Labour majority (and, therefore, a very large swathe of left-wing MPs who look at Irish politics through ultra-left eyes) might produce a thrust in Labour policy-making towards a negotiated withdrawal from Ireland. However, even such an unlikely scenario will not lead to the end of the Anglo-Irish Agreement. Labour's manifesto is unlikely to differ from the position agreed by the NEC in 1981, namely, unification by consent, and will therefore put a considerable constraint on even thinking about the withdrawal option. It is also unlikely that any Irish government will want Labour to take such a high-risk strategy. On the other hand, a Labour minority government which repeated the unholy alliance constructed by James Callaghan with Ulster Unionists between 1976 and 1978 seems improbable, although nobody has ever lost money betting on the fecklessness of Labour governments. A minority Kinnock government would be far more likely to be forged through a pact with some permutation of the Scottish or Welsh Nationalists or some dissident Liberals (or indeed the SDLP who could have three seats in the next Parliament—including Adams' seat in West Belfast). Any such Kinnock minority government would maintain the Anglo-Irish Agreement, provided the Irish government were willing.

On the Irish, side, the re-election of the FG–Labour coalition government, or the formation of a FG–Progressive Democrats coalition government, or the election of a FF minority government, would bring back an Irish government in favour of the Anglo-Irish Agreement, or unable to repudiate it even if it wanted to do so. However, on current poll evidence[43] the most probable outcome of the next Irish general election is

---

[43] An *Irish Times*/MRBI poll gave FF 51 per cent of first preference votes of those who expressed a definite preference (*Irish Times*, 27 June 1986).

a FF majority government, which leads us to consider the second scenario.

British government in favour, Irish government against

Fianna Fáil currently opposes the Anglo-Irish Agreement, and is widely considered likely to form the next Irish government by mid-1987. However, the party's record and the capacity of its leaders to execute policy-cycles is notorious, so their current posture is no guide to their position in office. FF's toughness on the Anglo-Irish Agreement seems to have varied in correlation with the party's place in the opinion polls. Moreover, Haughey would be likely to be forced into stating his position on the Anglo-Irish Agreement before the general election. With the SDLP so strongly in favour, and the Irish electorate approving the Agreement by over 60 per cent, Haughey would have a difficult time explaining the concurrence of his position with that of Sinn Fein. Refraining from maximalist 'oral republicanism' might prove the better part of electoral valour, and Haughey could be expected to raise the option of politicians in difficulties—renegotiation. Haughey is aware that repudiating the Anglo-Irish Agreement with a Thatcher administration would produce a strongly pro-Unionist response on the part of the British government, or evern the forced repartition which Thatcher has been rumoured to have considered.[44] He would also face the prospect of rupturing the fragile unity of his party. Facing a Labour government, even one committed to unification by consent, would leave Haughey with a painful dilemma: either to go for negotiated independence and face the prospect of a civil war or, while proclaiming unification as a goal, to settle for something less. Like de Valera in 1940,[45] Haughey would choose the security and stability of his own state over reunification: the proclaimed uncompleted task of his party. Even if he wanted to take risks there would be strong voices around him propheysing disaster and urging caution. Haughey's most rational option, then, would be to call for the renegotiation of the Anglo-Irish Agreement, including, ironically, full joint authority, the option least liked by FF during the New Ireland Forum.

The defeat of the FG–ILP-sponsored referendum to permit civil divorce in the Irish Republic's constitution, held on 26 June 1986, showed dramatically that the levels of tolerance and pluralism in the South are accurately captured by the loyalist designation 'Rome rule'. The collapse

[44] *Sunday Press*, 4 Nov. 1984.

[45] Robert Fisk, *In Time of War: Ireland, Ulster and the Price of Neutrality, 1939–45* (London: Granada, 1985), tells how de Valera preferred the maintenance of partition to the abandonment of neutrality, despite Churchill's offer of unification in return for the use of Irish naval bases.

of a component of Fitzgerald's constitutional crusade has been the greatest symbolic blow to the Anglo-Irish Agreement to date, weakening the capacity of any Irish government to argue for minority interests in the North without hypocrisy. The referendum result has been a blow to all forms of republicanism, suggests that Catholicism is the dominant ideological component of Irish nationalism, and has cemented partition much more than the Anglo-Irish Agreement itself. While an abundance of condoms, abortions, and divorces will not alter unionists' attitudes towards unification, the referendum victory for the forces of Catholic reaction shows that the cultural conditions for pluralism are not present. Fianna Fáil's studied neutrality (against divorce) during the referendum, while bringing it closer to government, has left the party incapable of a serious programme for reunification by consent, and leaves its promises to Protestants in a future New Ireland utterly unconvincing both to unionists and to all British governments.

This analysis suggests that the accord can survive its first three years, albeit with intermittent tension between the two states. The Agreement will face civil disobedience on a large scale from unionists, further strikes, divisions within the RUC, especially if the Stalker inquiry were to indict senior officers, sectarian attacks against Catholics, as well as efforts by the IRA to disrupt the settlement. Managing the contradictions of reform and repression will continue to present problems to British governments, but, along with Irish governments, they will be obliged to play the Machiavellian power-game, even if they did not plan to do so. Agreed devolution will be regularly offered to those Unionists prepared to bargain with the SDLP. Naturally, the longer there is no internal settlement, the greater the prospect that loyalist mobilization against the Agreement will turn into a half-cocked bid for independence. But, rather than destroy the Anglo-Irish Agreement, a unilateral declaration of independence would produce a panicked rush for a deal with the SDLP and the APNI on the part of the leadership of the OUP. This benign scenario predicts short-run protest and reaction followed by a successful internal settlement incorporating power-sharing and an Irish dimension. The benign scenario is most critically dependent upon the role that a FF government would decide to play. The malign scenario, by contrast, predicts that loyalist rebellion will eventually unite the whole Unionist bloc in an unstoppable drive towards a declaration of independence, and the long-heralded bloodbath of civil war and repartition. However, the malign scenario is improbable, both because it assumes unionist cohesion, and because it forgets that both the British and Irish governments can put an end to a unionist uprising either by force or by repudiating the

Agreement. Consequently, the risks of allowing the benign scenario the opportunity to play itself out are worthwhile.

SHOULD THE AGREEMENT BE SUPPORTED?

That the Anglo-Irish Agreement should work, that is, for it to result in an internal power-sharing settlement within Northern Ireland, with an Irish dimension, is plainly the wish of the present author. That objective is shared by both the British Conservative and the Irish coalition governments. But why should democrats of the left and centre-left support such a policy? After all the standard orthodoxies of the British left are either to support Irish unification and adopt an ultra-nationalist stance which follows Sinn Féin,[46] or to take a class-based line such as the Workers' Party or Militant and adopt a de facto unionist position on the border while arguing for democratic reforms (Workers' Party line) or else take a common economic class-based revolutionary strategy (Militant line). These positions exemplify the two standard faults in socialist analyses of national questions. The first, the romantic nationalist line, is to swallow national self-determination rhetoric, identify the underdog, and support the people so chosen in their national liberation struggle. The second, the class-utopian line, is to ignore nationalist consciousness, to attempt to bypass it or transcend it through promoting a class-based strategy. It is instructive to refer here to the Austrian social democrats who were exceptional in falling into neither the nationalist nor the class-sectarian traps, and in not accepting the doctrines of sovereignty associated with the rise of the capitalist nation-state, and indeed of the contemporary state-socialist regimes. They argued cogently that socialists must consider questions of national identity without necessarily accepting wholesale 'self-determination' ideologies. National identity cannot simply be dissolved by class-unity or wither away in a prospective socialist paradise. This Austrian tradition is worth reinventing.

A power-sharing settlement in Northern Ireland, with an Irish dimension, or cooperative devolution on, the Kilbrandon lines, tackles head-on the central symbolic grievances of a considerable majority of northern Nationalists while maintaining the British citizenship of Northern Protestants. It ends Protestant supremacy, not their identity—and those who believe that all unionists' identity consists solely of triumphal

---

[46] G. Bell, *The British in Ireland (Arguments for Socialism). A suitable case for withdrawal* (London: Pluto Press, 1984), articulates the emotions of most Labour constituency activists.

supremacism are deluded. A power-sharing settlement recognizes that the central cleavage is between nationalists and unionists, but its evolution need not preclude other cleavages, based on socialist and liberal ideology, or class, from making themselves felt. The evidence of other states, such as Belgium or Holland, which have experienced power-sharing coalitions across religious, cultural, or ethnic divides, shows not only that they are feasible, but also that they are frequently transitional—their very success eventually leads to the weakening of the non-class based cleavages and permits the evolution of politics around a liberalism/socialism cleavage. Accordingly, if the bulk of the British left can stifle its usual impatience and romanticism, and reflect upon its strange and 'unholy' partisanship for Catholic nationalism against Protestant Unionism, there is every reason why they should come to support the opportunities opened by power-sharing arrangements.

These abstract arguments may seem absurdly optimistic in the face of contemporary realities, but they have been outlined to suggest that there is no reason why socialists and liberals, in common with FG and British Conservatives, should not consider power-sharing and an Irish dimension as sensible ways of ensuring democratic progress in Northern Ireland. Liberal democrats and democratic socialists should stop analysing Northern Ireland as a set of traffic lights where the choices are green, red, or orange. Normative advocacy of power-sharing need not imply *naïveté*, but rather should be accompanied by determined support for the political defeat of both ultra-loyalists and ultra-nationalists, the institutional recognition of both national identities without supremacism, and the end of illiberal and unnecessary repressive legislation and administrative practices. A programme of economic and social policies to end Catholic material disadvantage[47] while improving the aggregate welfare of both the Catholic and the Protestant working class is also desirable and feasible. Contrary to left mythology, Northern Ireland is reformable,[48] and contrary to Richard Rose's liberal pessimism[49] the problem is certainly not that there is no solution. There are multiple solutions, many of them close to final solutions: whether the Anglo-Irish Agreement provides the framework for one which democrats can support remains to be seen.

---

[47] Giving teeth to the FEA and the EOA is not beyond the competence of a reform-minded Labour government.

[48] M. Farrell, *Northern Ireland: The Orange State* (London: Pluto, 1976), expounds the unreformability thesis.

[49] R. Rose, *Northern Ireland. A Time of Choice* (London: Macmillan, 1975), p. 139.

3

The Limits to Coercive Consociationalism in Northern Ireland

Brendan O'Leary

Irish history is something Irishmen should never remember, and Englishmen should never forget.

(Oscar Wilde)

The merits of consociation as a means of solving the Northern Ireland conflict are presented through contrasting it with other ways of stabilizing highly divided political systems. Why voluntary consociation has been unsuccessful in Northern Ireland and unfortunately is likely to remain so is explained. The signing of the Anglo-Irish Agreement (AIA) must be understood against the background of the failure of previous consociational experiments. The AIA partly represented a shift in British strategy from voluntary to coercive consociationalism. The prospects for this coercive consociational strategy and variants on it are evaluated.

STABILIZING SEGMENTED SOCIETIES: THE CASE FOR CONSOCIATION

Northern Ireland is a 'segmented society'. Segmented 'societies' are not real societies. They are, in extreme cases, divided into parallel societies with endogamous marriage, which school themselves, organize separate

This chapter is a radically revised version of a paper presented in April 1988 at the IALS Conference on Anglo-Irish Legal Relations. I thank the following for helpful criticism: P. Arthur, B. Barry, A. Beattie, P. Dunleavy, S. Greer, G. W. Jones, D. King, T. Lyne, C. McCrudden, J. McGarry, P. Mitchell, J. Peterson, G. Smith, C. Symmons, the anonymous referees, and the editor of *Political Studies*. I also acknowledge the benefits of a Nuffield Foundation travel grant.

exclusive voluntary associations, read separate media, have different cultures and languages, and exclusively work with and service their own kind. The cleavages dividing the segments may be racial, ethnic, religious, linguistic, or ideological, or some cumulative permutation, but all dispose people towards war. Segmented as opposed to homogeneous societies are more likely to experience civil war because their divisions are not conducive to consensus. They are unsuited to the Westminster model of simple majoritarian or minimum-winning coalitions, single-party governments, and a disproportional voting system which creates a governmental executive able to impose its will within a unitary state.[1] The home rule government of Northern Ireland (1920–72) was a pathological specimen of majoritarian 'democracy', a tyranny of the majority, in which the Ulster Unionist Party (UUP)[2] won every parliamentary election held in the region.

Consociation by contrast is primarily distinguished by cooperation amongst political elites,[3] but has four key institutional traits. First, the state in a consociational system is governed by a power-sharing coalition of parties which enjoys the support of more than a simple majority of those who vote.[4] Second, consociation endorses segmental autonomy, permitting the blocs which divide the regime freedom to make autonomous decisions on matters of profound concern to them. Third, proportionality applies throughout the public sector: there is proportional representation in elections, in assembly committees, in public employment; and proportional allocation of public expenditure. Finally, mutual veto or concurring majority principles operate, permitting the minority segment(s) the ability to protect its (their) most important interests.[5] Consociational democracy is, therefore, the antonym of majoritarian democracy.

Consociational theory explores how segmented societies may be stabilized and operated with liberal democratic institutions. It suggests, by

[1] A. Lijphart, *Democracies: Patterns of Majoritarian and Consensus Democracy in Twenty-One Countries* (New Haven, Yale University Press, 1984).

[2] I use UUP to refer also to the Official Unionists (or the OUP), as they became known in the 1970s.

[3] A. Lijphart, *Democracy in Plural Societies: A Comparative Exploration* (New Haven and London, Yale University Press, 1977), p. 1.

[4] This requirement is less than a 'grand coalition' of all parties. Consociational requirements arguably are also met if all segments are proportionately represented within parties which compete for (rather than share) state power: see E. Aunger, *In Search of Political Stability: A Comparative Study of New Brunswick and Northern Ireland* (Montreal, McGill-Queen's University Press, 1981).

[5] The elements of consociation are elaborated in Lijphart's many publications: A. Lijphart, *The Politics of Accommodation: Pluralism and Democracy in the Netherlands* (Berkeley and Los Angeles, University of California Press, 1968); 'Typologies of democratic systems',

implication, six ideal-typical strategies for stabilizing segmented societies: hegemonic control, integration, partition, internationalization, arbitration, and consociation.[6] According to consociational theorists, regions like Northern Ireland must have consociation or no effective democracy at all, a claim this chapter seeks to reinforce. To see why, consider the alternatives to consociation in Northern Ireland.

Hegemonic control

This has been the most common mode through which segmented societies have been stabilized in world history.[7] Imperial or authoritarian regimes control multicultural territories through elite cooption and coercive domination. The control capacities of such regimes suppress latent divisions between segmental groups which might otherwise be manifested in conditions of modernization. The control is hegemonic if it makes an overt violent segmental contest for state power 'unthinkable' or 'unworkable' on the part of the subordinated.

In liberal democracies hegemonic control is less feasible for obvious reasons. Such regimes permit, indeed facilitate, segmental organization and mobilization; and in democratic conditions segmental contests for

Comparative Political Studies, 1: 1 (1968), 3–44; 'Consociational democracy', *World Politics*, XXI (1969), 207–25; 'Consociation: the model and its application in divided societies', in D. Rea (ed.), *Political Cooperation in Divided Societies: A Series of Papers Relevant to the Conflict in Northern Ireland* (Dublin, Gill and Macmillan, 1982), pp. 166–86; *Power-Sharing in South Africa* (Berkeley, Institute of International Studies, 1985).

[6] Lijphart mentions three strategies—integration, partition, and consociation—in a review article, 'The Northern Ireland problem: cases, theories and solutions', *British Journal of Political Science*, 5 (1975), p. 105, while G. Lehmbruch, 'Consociational democracy in the international system', *European Journal of Political Research*, 3 (1975), p. 378, mentions two—arbitration and consociation. Internationalization is my own term. I developed my classification of six stabilization strategies before reading Lijphart's latest book where he argues: 'There are five logical solutions to the problems of violence and democratic weakness in plural societies: assimilation, consociation, partition, mass emigration and genocide. I mention the last possibility merely in order to make the list exhaustive': *Power-Sharing in South Africa*, p. 31. Assimilation is what I call integration. Like Lijphart I do not regard mass emigration or genocide as solutions worth considering; however, unlike him, I believe that hegemonic control, arbitration, and internationalization are 'logical' solutions to the problems of segmented societies which are worth consideration.

[7] The distinction between consociationalism and control as means of stabilizing divided societies was pioneered by Ian Lustick, 'Stability in deeply divided societies: consociationalism versus control', *World Politics*, XXXI (1979), 325–44. Christopher McCrudden does not use this language, but shows how the British constitutional tradition permitted hegemonic control in Northern Ireland, 'Northern Ireland and the British constitution', in J. Jowell and D. Oliver (eds.), *The Changing Constitution* (Oxford, Clarendon Press, 2nd ed., 1989).

state power become 'thinkable' and 'workable'. However, we may speak of hegemonic control in nominal liberal democracies where one segment can dominate another segment (or segments) through its political, economic, and ideological resources; and where this superordinate segment can extract what it requires from the subordinated, or prevent redistributive demands being made by the subordinated. Nationalist, ethnic, and religious minorities in liberal democracies invariably claim in their rhetorics of protest that hegemonic control has been exercised over them. Not all such claims are true. However, few observers deny that Northern Ireland between 1920 and 1968 was an example of a society in which hegemonic control was exercised by Ulster Protestants. Historians, government-appointed commissions, political scientists, and Marxists all agree that political, economic, and cultural domination, discrimination, and monopoly were widespread in the province.[8] The current conflict resulted from the breakdown of Unionist control in the late 1960s, culminating in the abolition of the Stormont Parliament by the British government in 1972. Ever since, the recreation of such control, through the restoration of 'majority rule', has remained a central objective of Unionists, especially the Democratic Unionist Party (DUP). However, no one, except perhaps the majority of Ulster Protestants, considers the recreation of hegemonic control a desirable, democratic, or indeed feasible 'solution' to the conflict.

Integration

Integration of segmented societies can be achieved through voluntary cooperation or through coercion. Northern Ireland Catholics could be integrated into the United Kingdom or Northern Ireland Protestants into the Republic of Ireland.[9] Voluntary integration in an ethnic conflict requires at least one segment to surrender its identity (or at least that part of its identity which is the cause of the conflict) or it requires the creation of a transcendent identity. Peace must be the starting point if it is to be successful because some predisposition towards consensus rather than conflict is essential. By contrast, coercive integration is likely to succeed

---

[8] See *inter alia* P. Buckland, *The Factory of Grievances: Devolved Government in Northern Ireland* (Dublin, Gill and Macmillan, 1979); the Cameron Report, *Disturbances in Northern Ireland: Report of the Cameron Commission* (London, HMSO Cmd 532, 1969); J. Darby, *Conflict in Northern Ireland: The Development of a Polarized Community* (Dublin, Gill and Macmillan, 1976) and M. Farrell, *The Orange State* (London, Pluto Press, 1976).

[9] Catholics and Protestants could be integrated into an independent Northern Ireland but this prospect is even more fantastic.

only at the cost of producing some of the violence which it is designed to avoid.

The opportunities for integration strategies (whether voluntary or coercive) in Northern Ireland have passed. There is currently a low-level civil war, restrained by the presence of British troops, hardly ideal circumstances for voluntary integration. Government is carried on without consensus.[10] The conflict stems from the historical refusal of Unionists to be integrated with the rest of a self-governing Ireland, and the current refusal of nationalists to be integrated into Britain.[11] There is no viable transcendent identity on the cultural agenda.

Opportunities for voluntary integration, of Catholics into the United Kingdom or Protestants into Ireland, existed in the past. They might even exist at some future date. They do not exist now. If voluntary integration is a pious aspiration it might be thought that coercive integration is feasible. However, integrating Protestants into the Republic of Ireland, whether peacefully or forcefully, is advocated only by practitioners of wishful thinking.[12] The Republic has neither the appropriate motivations nor the capacity to integrate Northern Protestants. Its citizens' desire for Irish unity is a 'low-intensity aspiration'.[13] Referendum outcomes confirm that appeals to the electorate to make the Irish constitution more pluralist cut insufficient ice.[14] Moreover, the Republic's military capacity to conquer and hold Northern Ireland in the wake of a British withdrawal must be doubted. Following a British unilateral withdrawal the most probable scenario is one in which the Republic's forces stand 'idly by', awaiting the liquidation of the IRA, before intervening to repartition the island.[15] The alternative prospect of a joint British and Irish coerced

[10] R. Rose, *Governing Without Consensus: An Irish Perspective* (London, Faber and Faber, 1971), and *Northern Ireland: A Time of Choice* (London, Macmillan, 1976).

[11] To compound matters, the population has become more segmented since 1969: M. A. Poole, 'Religious residential segregation in urban Northern Ireland', in F. W. Boal and J. N. H. Douglas (eds.), *Integration and Division: Geographical Perspectives on the Northern Ireland Problem* (London, Academic Press, 1982), pp. 281–308 and F. W. Boal, 'Segregating and mixing: space and residence in Belfast', in Boal and Douglas, *Integration and Division*, pp. 249–80.

[12] See B. Rowthorn and N. Wayne, *Northern Ireland: The Political Economy of Conflict* (Oxford, Polity Press, 1988).

[13] 'Just as in the Republic the aspiration to acquire Northern Ireland is a low-intensity aspiration, so in Great Britain the aspiration to get rid of Northern Ireland is a low-intensity aspiration'. C. C. O'Brien, *Neighbours* (London, Faber & Faber, 1980), p. 39.

[14] B. Grivin, 'Social change and moral politics', *Political Studies*, 34 (1986), 61–81, and 'The divorce referendum in the republic, June 1986', *Irish Political Studies*, 2 (1987), 93–6.

[15] Sinn Féin (SF) recognizes these facts, but does not think about them. Its manifesto for the June 1987 Westminster elections called on the British government to 'declare that its military forces and political administration and system (sic!) will remain only for as long as

integration of Protestants into a united Ireland, floated in a recent blueprint,[16] rests on three wishful thoughts: the belief that Protestants will not fight (or not fight convincingly) if they are coercively integrated into the Republic; the belief that Irish policy-makers might wish to embark upon such a strategy; and the belief that a withdrawing British government will be prepared to invest the blood of its soldiers and its citizens' taxes to support the project.

The converse strategy, the coercive integration of Catholics into Britain, is more feasible, given the organizational resources of the British state, the fact that the Catholic minority are already in the United Kingdom, and that a significant proportion of Catholics do not wish to become part of the Republic.[17] However, successful integration requires the crushing and transformation of the nationalist identity of the minority. It would probably generate considerably more violence than currently exists. Even if coercive integration were to be carried out through British party competition in Northern Ireland, with both main parties offering programmes of reform to make formal equal citizenship a substantive reality,[18] the goodwill generated would be more than offset by the repression required to crush the IRA, and its social base, built and articulated by Sinn Féin (SF). It would also require the abandonment of the Anglo-Irish Agreement (AIA), lead to a breakdown in Anglo-Irish relations with serious repercussions for cross-border security, compel the Social Democratic and Labour Party (SDLP) to become more nationalist, and produce worldwide embarrassment for the British state, especially in European and American capitals. Such coercive integration is not on the agenda. British governments show no desire to crush the minority's Catholic identity and have increasingly recognized the legitimacy of its nationalist identity. British policy-makers consistently emphasize that

it takes to disarm and disband the RUC and UDR, transfer power to sovereign authorities, and withdraw': Sinn Féin, *For Freedom, Justice, Peace* (Derry, Sinn Féin Director of Elections, 1987). This demand calls on the British state to crush Unionists/Protestants' armed power, so that the 'true' self-determination of the 'Irish people' can be achieved. The idea that before a prospective withdrawal a British government would wish to conduct another, fiercer, and more bloody war with Unionists illustrates SF's capacity for self-deception.

[16] Rowthorn and Wayne, *Northern Ireland.*

[17] The best normative case for such a strategy is made by H. Roberts, *Northern Ireland and the Algerian Analogy: A Suitable Case for Gaullism?* (Belfast, Athol Books, 1986), and 'Sound stupidity: the British party system and the Northern Ireland question', *Government and Opposition*, 22: 3 (1987), 315–35. However, Roberts seems blind to the coercive implications of his arguments.

[18] However, it is a matter of fact that *most* enthusiasts for integration for Northern Ireland into Britain are not enthusiasts for authentic equal citizenship (i.e., programmes of affirmative action to rectify existing segmental inequalities).

Northern Ireland is a *conditional* unit of the United Kingdom: it is part of the United Kingdom so long as a majority of its inhabitants so wish. Such statements demonstrate that departure from Northern Ireland is 'thinkable' for British policy-makers. This long-standing mentality, which is not likely to be eroded, is not favourable to the integrationist strategies favoured by Robert McCartney and the Campaign for Equal Citizenship. Integration, however it is understood, is not a feasible starting point for stabilizing Northern Ireland.[19]

Partition

A logical solution for the problems of segmented societies is partition. The territory in which rival segments live can be partitioned (with internationally binding agreements, boundary commissions, local referendums, and funded population transfers) to remove all prospect of interactions which precipitate violence. This option of last resort has been carried out, usually very badly, in many ex-British colonies (notably in Cyprus, Palestine, and the Indian subcontinent).[20] Northern Ireland itself was created in 1920 through the partition of the island of Ireland, and the province of Ulster.

Partition requires careful management if it is not to induce more conflict than it is designed to prevent. It has often imposed horrendous costs: the partition of India cost half a million lives.[21] Partition also has long-run costs if it is carried out 'imperfectly': it creates Northern Irelands.[22] The 1920 partition of Ireland was not perfect. Indeed nationalists argue that the contemporary violence stems from a partition which produced a politics based upon 'a sectarian headcount'. The territory of Northern Ireland was carved out by Unionists in 'those districts which they could control'.[23] However, nationalists (constitutional or otherwise) do not argue for a better partition; rather, they oppose repartition and argue instead for the complete reversal of partition. Unionists, while also

[19] This argument implies no hostility to the promotion of 'cross-community relations' policies such as *voluntary* integrated education. It is merely sceptical about their political pay-offs.

[20] For a good discussion of British-managed partitions, see T. G. Fraser, *Partition in Ireland, India and Palestine: Theory and Practice* (London, Macmillan, 1984).

[21] G. D. Khoshla, *Stern Reckoning: A Survey of the Events Leading up to and Following the Partition of India* (New Delhi, Bhawnani, 1950).

[22] 'Without a minority in Northern Ireland the 1920 settlement would have been perfect': John Hume cited in P. O'Malley, *The Uncivil Wars: Ireland Today* (Belfast, Blackstaff, 1983), p. 100.

[23] D. Miller, *Queen's Rebels: Ulster Loyalism in Historical Perspective* (Dublin, Gill and Macmillan, 1978), pp. 122 ff.

opposed to repartition, are vehemently hostile to the reversal of partition. By contrast, less partisan observers argue that the imperfect partition of 1920 might be rectified by an improved repartition.[24]

What is common to the nationalist and unionist traditions is that neither want repartition, both for principled and strategic reasons. The practical difficulties of repartition, spelled out by various demographers, geographers, lawyers, and political scientists,[25] are known to both the British and Irish governments, and help explain why there has been no serious move to explore its merits. However, while it is an 'unthinkable' strategy for Irish governments (bound by the constitution of 1937 and the shibboleths of Irish nationalism), on the British side Mrs Thatcher is said to have commissioned papers on repartition[26] and it is obviously an option which will increase in attractiveness to British governments if the AIA does not induce an attractive settlement. However, the costs of a second and drastic partition of Ulster currently inhibit policy-makers from considering it.

Cooperative internationalization

Another means by which conflict in segmented societies can be regulated is through cooperative internationalization. States external to a conflict, even if they have interests at stake, can agree jointly to manage it; or international organizations, such as the United Nations, can provide peacekeeping forces and organize diplomatic negotiations between the contending segments. This option is one which the British and Irish governments have increasingly explored, culminating in the Intergovernmental Conference, with its administrative secretariat at Maryfield, established by the AIA. However, as yet, cooperation has not extended as far as the creation of a joint security force or joint emergency judicial administration, let alone the joint authority envisaged by the *New Ireland Forum Report*.[27]

Comparison with other segmented societies in which there is an internal replication of international conflicts suggests that cooperation between the British and Irish governments has lessened the scale of the

---

[24] P. Compton, 'The demographic background', in D. Watt (ed.), *The Constitution of Northern Ireland: Problems and Prospects* (London, Heinemann, 1981), pp. 74–92.

[25] See *inter alia* Compton, 'The demographic background'; Boal, 'Segregating and mixing'; K. Boyle and T. Hadden, *Ireland: A Positive Proposal* (Harmondsworth, Penguin, 1985), pp. 34–7; B. Walsh, 'Comment', in D. Watt, *The Constitution of Northern Ireland* (London, Heinemann, 1981), pp. 93–9; and Rose, *Northern Ireland*, pp. 160–3.

[26] *Sunday Press* (4 Nov. 1984).

[27] *New Ireland Forum Report* (Dublin, Stationery Office, 2 May 1984), ch. 8.

conflict. Sceptics should consider what the levels of violence might have been in the absence of British–Irish cooperation. The Republic's initial encouragement of traditional nationalism, in the aftermath of loyalist pogroms against Catholic ghettos in 1969, rapidly gave way to the recognition that consociation in the North was a precondition of unification. The Irish signature to the Sunningdale communiqué of December 1973 confirmed this acknowledgement. The position of successive Irish governments remained the same, although Fianna Fail, under Haughey's leadership, vacillated in the 1980s. The *New Ireland Forum Report* showed the degree to which traditional nationalist tenets had been revised. Moreover, no serious analysts deny that the overriding interest of the Irish Republic has been to prevent the conflict destabilizing its regime.[28] Since 1972, on the British side, international embarrassment, security considerations, and the need to assuage the Northern minority compelled governments to recognize Dublin's central role and interest in the containment of the conflict. Increasing British and Irish collaboration, after multiple hiccoughs, imbroglios, and scandals, precluded demands for cooperative internationalization through agencies like the United Nations or the EEC, which might otherwise have received greater attention.

However, cooperative internationalization is normally a short-run strategy of crisis management, a stop-gap solution in the aftermath of wars or geopolitial conficts. It primarily provides a breathing space to facilitate the evolution of one of the other strategies for stabilizing segmented societies: especially integration, partition, arbitration, and consociation. Maintaining cooperative internationalization over the medium to long run requires a combination of exceptional harmonization of the policies of the states concerned, with a willingness jointly to shoulder the burdens of accountability, resource commitments, and lives lost through security operations. For these reasons internationalization strategies cannot be expected to provide long-run solutions, but can at best be stimulants to other solutions. The AIA does represent a very definite and distinct mode of cooperative internationalization. However, it cannot be expected to solve the conflict; rather, it can at best contain it, while providing a framework within which a more lasting settlement can be built.

---

[28] O'Brien exaggerates when he argues that the official policy of the Irish Republic towards Britain has amounted to the following: *'please say you're going, but for God's sake stay'*: *Neighbours*, p. 45, italics in original. However, it is an insightful characterization. On the basis of my interviews, it accurately captures how the official Irish position is seen in Britain.

Arbitration

A fifth strategy for stabilizing segmented societies is arbitration, where conflict is refereed 'by a supposedly neutral authority above the rival sub-cultures'.[29] The authority's disinterestedness enhances its capacity to act autonomously, unswayed by the partisan preferences of the rival sub-cultures. Thereby the arbiter dampens the violence which would occur in its absence and permits governmental effectiveness to be maintained.

Arbitration has been the dominant British strategy since the onset of the current 'troubles'. Direct rule of Northern Ireland from Westminster has been in existence since 1972, complicated only by the brief power-sharing experiment in the first five months of 1974 and the modifications resulting from the AIA. Government is currently carried out largely through the office of the Secretary of State for Northern Ireland, a 'pre-fectoral' plenipotentiary of Westminster. He is not beholden to any local interests, and has the capacity to make laws and policy through Orders in Council and executive action without the consent of any locally elected representatives. All Secretaries of State claim to be 'neutral arbiters' of the conflict, and until 1985 pursued four basic policies consistent with their self-image as neutral arbiters.

First, as 'honest brokers' they encouraged the rival segments to work towards a political accommodation. 'Neutrality' rested upon the refusal to countenance majority rule (the anti-Unionist premise) in anything resembling its pre-1972 manifestation or to contemplate coercing Unionists into a united Ireland (the anti-nationalist premise). In the absence of a willingness on the part of the rival segments to accom-modate one another, the British government, unwillingly, would con-tinue direct rule as a second-best option, thereby ensuring no tradition could dominate the other. Second, they proclaimed the reform of Northern Ireland. Reform entailed modernizing along the lines of the post-war British consensus. Social problems were to be solved through public expenditure, economic growth, and professionalized administra-tion. Public expenditure and economic growth would allow Catholics' relative deprivation to be rectified while simultaneously improving the absolute levels of Protestants' welfare. Professionalized administration of the welfare state, especially in housing policy and the security forces, especially in the RUC, was to replace the parochial, clientelist, and supremacist sectarianism which had marred the conduct of government in Northern Ireland before 1972. Equal citizenship in the modern welfare

---

[29] Lehmbruch, 'Consociational democracy in the international system', p. 378.

state would enable the citizens of Northern Ireland to transcend the traditional ascriptive social relations which had been removed through the same policies elsewhere in the United Kingdom, notably in central Scotland. Third, criminalizing political violence was central to the strategy. Impartial hostility towards violence was proclaimed. After some initial hesitations on the part of policy-makers, political violence was treated as 'criminal'. However, according to their own statements, the exigencies of the situation prevented the British from using standard legal instruments to repress those prepared to engage in violence. The use of internment without trial was abandoned in 1975, discredited both by its past association with Unionist hegemonic control and its evident counter-productive ineffectiveness.[30] Nonetheless, an awesome array of security forces and legal instruments had made Northern Ireland exceptionally repressive amongst liberal democracies by the late 1970s.[31] Finally, quarantining Northern Ireland[32] from mainstream British political considerations whilst maintaining international respectability held the arbitration strategy together. British governments wanted to ensure that conflict did not spill over into Great Britain, and to avoid international embarrassment. The former concern was demonstrated by their refusal to organize British political parties in the province, and legally expressed in the Prevention of Terrorism Acts (1974, 1976, 1984, and 1989). The latter concern was shown in regular public relations missions to the United States. Northern Ireland's 'exceptionality' was emphasized to justify political and legal practices otherwise 'foreign' to British political culture. Bipartisan consensus was encouraged to prevent party controversy over British management of Northern Ireland. Broadcasting organizations and the press were subjected to unprecedented pressure, in 'peacetime', to portray government policy-making in the image of the 'honest broker'.

Arbitration seemed to work in the late 1970s. A 'concurrent majority' saw direct rule as preferable to either power-sharing (Protestants) or majority rule (Catholics).[33] There were hopes that the welfare and

[30] B. O'Leary, review article in *British Journal of Criminology*, 28: 1 (1988), 97–107.

[31] K. Boyle, T. Hadden, and P. Hillyard, *Law and State: The Case of Northern Ireland* (Oxford, Martin Robertson, 1975) and *Ten Years On in Northern Ireland* (Nottingham, Cobden Trust, 1980); C. Scorer and P. Hewitt, *The Prevention of Terrorism Act: The Case for Repeal* (Nottingham, Cobden Trust, 1981); and D. Walsh, *The Use and Abuse of Emergency Legislation in Northern Ireland* (Nottingham, Cobden Trust, 1983).

[32] P. Arthur, 'Anglo-Irish relations and the Northern Ireland problem', *Irish Studies in International Affairs*, 2: 1 (1985), 37–50.

[33] R. Rose, I. McAllister, and P. Mair, *Is There A Concurring Majority About Northern Ireland?* (Glasgow, Studies in Public Policy No. 22, Centre for the Study of Public Policy, University of Strathclyde, 1978).

security apparatuses had become more professional and that the Fair Employment Agency would implement effective anti-discrimination measures. The levels of violence, measured on all indicators (deaths, explosives, shootings), receded after the abandonment of internment. Finally, although Northern Ireland did cause international embarrassment it did not arouse major anxieties in Whitehall and Westminster. The conflict had apparently been quarantined with the defeat of IRA operations in Britain.

However, arbitration came unstuck in the 1980s. Direct rule, intendedly or otherwise, was biased. It was a Unionist status quo, even though most Unionists were not enamoured by it. Direct rule meant *British* rule of Northern Ireland.[34] Catholics saw it as, at best, a temporary expedient: a pause before power-sharing and the constitutional transition to a united Ireland (the SDLP perspective), or a pause before British withdrawal (the IRA perspective). The longer direct rule persisted the more British government became the primary target of minority discontent and blamed for all discreditable features of Northern Irish society.[35] The British were perceived to rely upon sectarian instruments of government: the Protestant-dominated RUC and Ulster Defence Regiment and the 'extraordinary' legal system. Roy Mason's years as Secretary of State (1976–9) were not seen as arbitration by the Catholic working class: 'Ulsterization', 'criminalization', and 'normalization' suggested the British were on the side of the Unionists. The minority Labour government's expedient concession of extra Westminster seats to Northern Ireland confirmed Catholics' belief that direct rule was another bastion of Protestant privilege.[36] In the absence of power-sharing, direct rule prompted greater nationalist sentiment amongst the minority and undermined local and international perceptions of British 'neutrality'. It also allowed unionists to veto significant accommodation. They preferred direct rule to conceding power-sharing and/or an 'Irish dimension'.

The insufficiency of reform pushed many in the SDLP away from accommodation towards more full-blooded, albeit constitutional, nationalism; especially because reform often appeared no more than

---

[34] A similar problem existed with the Army, fondly portrayed as an umpire: D. Hamill, *Pig in the Middle: The British Army in Northern Ireland* (London, Methuen, 1985). There is a telling Catholic saying: 'There are two things wrong with the British Army. First, it is British. Second, it is an Army'.

[35] Nationalist academics supported this argument: L. O'Dowd, B. Ralston, and M. Tomlinson, *Northern Ireland: Between Civil Rights and Civil War* (London, CSE Books, 1980).

[36] The extra seats were awarded under plurality rule, guaranteeing Unionist over-representation if they maintained a modicum of unity.

symbolic. The achievement of the goals of the civil rights movement ('one person one vote' and the end to gerrymandering in local government) did not legitimate direct rule because the reformed institutions had ceased to be centres of power. Catholic unemployment remained dramatically higher than Protestant unemployment: the male Catholic rate being 2.5 times the male Protestant rate.[37] Catholics blamed all the differential upon discrimination.[38]

Criminalization backfired most spectacularly. The IRA were on their knees in 1976–7, in danger of losing their social base and future recruits.[39] However, both Labour and Conservative governments failed to realize that their handling of emergency legislation, interrogation procedures, judicial processes, and prison management would rebuild support for the Provisionals. It was embarrassing to argue that those convicted by Diplock courts were 'ordinary' criminals. The Maze protests, followed by the hunger strikes of 1980–1, allowed SF to emerge as a serious political force, mobilizing the abstentionist Catholic electorate but also eating into the SDLP's vote. The martyrdom of the hunger strikers fuelled the growth of SF and legitimated the IRA, in the eyes of some of the world's media, as an authentic national liberation movement.[40] The electoral rise of SF, which did not peak until they had obtained 43 per cent of the nationalist vote, was firm evidence of the failure of criminalization.

Direct rule embarrassed Britain. It appeared remarkably like colonial administration. Efforts to promote power-sharing failed. The lack of progress in reforming Northern Ireland became increasingly visible. Finally, the delegitimation of criminalization won the IRA publicity. The world's press, Amnesty International, Irish-American Congressmen, and European Community parliamentarians regularly visited Northern Ireland and reported in ways which cast British policy-makers in an unflattering light. The quarantining of Northern Ireland came unstuck. The Conservatives and then Labour broke from bipartisan consensus. The current Conservative government was elected to office in May 1979 on an integrationist manifesto pledge but the policy did not survive Airey

[37] Standing Advisory Commission on Human Rights, *Religious and Political Discrimination and Equality of Opportunity in Northern Ireland: Report on Fair Employment* (London, HMSO, 1987), and D. Smith, *Equality and Inequality in Northern Ireland* (London, Policy Studies Institute, 1987).

[38] Objective analysis demonstrates that indirect discrimination through informal recruitment remains the major factor in explaining differential unemployment (see previous note).

[39] V. Browne and V. O'Toole, 'The ballot and the bullet', *Magill*, 10: 3 (1986), 8–15.

[40] D. Beresford, *Ten Men Dead: The Story of the 1981 Irish Hunger Strike* (London, Grafton Books, 1987).

Neave's murder by the INLA. The Conservatives contemplated majority-rule devolution for Northern Ireland (1979–80) before deciding to improve relations with the Republic in the Thatcher–Haughey summits of 1980. Labour embraced the 'unity of Ireland by consent' in 1981. Conservative policy-makers impatiently began to explore with the Irish government alternative longer-run strategies. Finally, after detours and false starts, such as 'rolling devolution' in 1982, the Conservatives embarked upon negotiating the AIA, their minds concentrated by the *New Ireland Forum Report* and the attempted assassination of the cabinet in 1984. Arbitration had run its course.

Consociation

The final strategy for stabilizing segmented societies which I shall consider is consociation or power-sharing. It has the following general advantages. First, it is based upon agreement rather than coercion (unlike hegemonic control, coercive integration, or enforced partition). Second, conflict-regulation is by the actors themselves rather than by external powers (unlike internationalization or arbitration). Third, it enjoys democratic legitimacy.[41] Fourth, it has a partially successful track record in stabilizing segmented societies. Finally, if it succeeds, it becomes dispensable. Consociational democracy facilitates a transition to 'normal' democratic competition, as has occurred in the Netherlands and Austria.[42]

Power-sharing in a devolved government, that is, local consociation, has been widely prescribed as the most desirable solution for Northern Ireland. It has been consistently advocated by the Alliance Party (APNI, the small, middle-class, cross-sectarian party) and by the SDLP (the moderate nationalist party). On occasions it has been advocated by members of the UUP, and even by members of the Ulster Defence Association (UDA). Successive British governments, both Labour and Conservative, have supported it. I share the conviction that Northern Ireland's constitutional choice is between consociational democracy and

---

[41] Critics like Barry and Lustick question its democratic credentials because it does not permit participation; but 'participation' in segmented societies does not produce a functioning democracy.

[42] Few political scientists reject the idea that consociation is an excellent normative solution to the problems of segmented societies. A Marxist, Ronald Kieve, argues that consociational democracy inhibited class struggle in the Netherlands, and was therefore a bad thing: R. Kieve, 'Pillars of sand: a Marxist critique of consociational democracy in the Netherlands', *Comparative Politics* (1981), 313–37.

no democracy, but the key question is whether consociation is feasible in Northern Ireland.

WHY VOLUNTARY CONSOCIATIONALISM HAS FAILED

All the vexed questions about consociation cannot be discussed here,[43] but three matter. First, is consociational democracy *necessary* to stabilize segmented societies? The answer is 'no'; there are other solutions. Second, is consociational democracy *sufficient* to stabilize segmented societies? The answer is again 'no'; consociation may not be enough, and consociational systems may well disintegrate, as has occurred in both Lebanon and Cyprus. The Sunningdale power-sharing experiment of 1973–4 in Northern Ireland did not end the terrorist actions of the Provisional IRA or loyalist sectarian assassinations. Consociation is, therefore, neither necessary nor sufficient to stabilize segmented societies. The consociational argument is more modest: in certain cases consociation can help stabilize segmented societies.

The third question is more important: are there certain necessary and sufficient conditions for the emergence of consociation? There are conflicting answers from Lijphart and his critics. Lijphart identifies background conditions 'conducive to the establishment and maintenance of consociational democracy'.[44] First, a multiple balance of power must exist among the segments, no segment having a majority and/or the segments being of approximately equal size. Second, a multiparty system with segmental parties is beneficial. Third, a relatively small population facilitates cooperation. Fourth, cooperation is easier when external

---

[43] Debate over consociational theory is extensive: B. Barry, 'Political accommodation and consociational democracy', *British Journal of Political Science*, 5 (1975), 477–505 and 'The consociational model and its dangers', *European Journal of Political Research*, 3 (1975), 393–412; H. Daalder, 'The consociational democracy theme', *World Politics*, XXVI (1974), 604–21; S. Halpern, 'The disorderly universe of consociational democracy', *West European Politics*, 9: 2 (1986), 181–97; Lustick, 'Stability in deeply divided societies'; K. McRea (ed.), *Consociational Democracy: Political Accommodation in Segmented Societies* (Toronto, McLellan and Stewart, 1974); E. Nordlinger, *Conflict Regulation in Divided Societies* (Cambridge, MA, Harvard University, Occasional Papers in International Affairs, 1972); A. Pappalardo, 'The conditions for consociational democracy: a logical and empirical critique', *European Journal of Political Research*, 9 (1981), 365–90; and M. van Schendelen, 'The views of Arend Lijphart and Collected Criticism', *Acta Politica*, 19: 1 (1984), 19–55. Debate centres on whether consociational concepts (grand coalition, segmental autonomy, proportionality, minority veto, stability) are well defined and whether the theory provides necessary and sufficient conditions for consociational systems.

[44] Lijphart, *Democracy and Plural Societies*, ch. III, and 'Consociation', p. 183.

threats are perceived as a common danger by the different segments. Fifth, society-wide loyalties, especially a sense of common national identity, support power-sharing. Sixth, the absence of extreme socio-economic segmental inequalities is important. Seventh, the relative isolation of the segments from each other is conducive. Finally, the existence of prior historical traditions of political accommodation facilitates consociation.[45]

Most of these favourable conditions are absent in Northern Ireland.[46] First, until 1972 there was no stable multiple balance of power. The UUP enjoyed hegemonic control commanding the loyalites of just less than two-thirds of the voters. Second, the creation of a multiparty system since 1972 has not been conducive to power-sharing. The fragmentation of the Unionist segment (into the UUP, the DUP, and the APNI) and the nationalist segment (into the SDLP and SF) created a five-party system. However, it is not based on strictly segmental lines (given the cross-denominational support for the APNI). More importantly, a multiple balance of power does not exist because the bulk of the unionist bloc (the UUP and DUP) has generally been united in its hostility to compromises with nationalists and commands a majority of the electorate. Third, the rival segments do not share a common external threat. For Unionists the external threat is posed by the Irish Republic (abetted by the Vatican, Moscow, the American State Department, and the British Foreign Office), whereas for nationalists the external threat is manifested in the British presence in Ireland. Fourth, the few society-wide loyalties do not lessen differences between the segments. Their shared adherence to Christianity also divides them.[47] Their traditionalist anti-cosmopolitan and anti-metropolitan values do not significantly cross-cut what divides them. The most important society-wide loyalty, common national identity, is absent. Fifth, socio-economic differences between the rival segments reveal sufficient inequality, discrimination, and belief in discrimination to sow immense distrust.[48] Very considerable socio-economic inequalities have been recently documented.[49] These inequalities are historically rooted in

[45] Here Lijphart follows Daalder, 'The consociational democracy theme'.

[46] Lijphart, 'The Northern Ireland problem'; and *Democracy in Plural Societies*, pp. 134–41.

[47] Lijphart calculates that the angle and index of cross-cutting between the religious and party cleavage systems in 1968 were both very low: 2° and 0.21 respectively: *Democracy in Plural Societies*, p. 125.

[48] Lijphart calculates that the angle of cross-cutting between religion and social class is 68° and that the index of cross-cutting equals 0.50: *Democracy in Plural Societies*, p. 138. These measures, based on 1960s data, indicate considerable but not extreme inequalities between the segments.   [49] See n. 37.

the relations of domination established during the plantation of Ulster and the wars of conquest in the seventeenth century and explain why Northern Ireland had no strong traditions of political accommodation before the advent of mass democracy or the creation of the regime.[50] The foundation of Northern Ireland took place against a background of armed communal mobilization and civil war. The only conducive background conditions, which Northern Ireland apparently possesses—small size and the relative isolation of the segments—are unfortunately the ones which, Lijphart's critics have argued, are based on implausible premises.[51]

The implications are bleak. Lijphart's checklist of conducive conditions suggests that voluntary consociational experiments in Northern Ireland are bound to fail. So far, all such experiments *have* failed. Successive attempts to establish a devolved settlement commanding widespread cross-community agreement have been unsuccessful: the Sunningdale settlement of 1973–4; the Constitutional Convention of 1975; the all-party talks of 1979–80; and Prior's rolling devolution scheme which under-pinned the Northern Ireland Assembly (1982–6).[52] Policy-makers per-suaded by Lijphart's theory seem to face two options: either promote partition (which he suggests might be the best option) or engineer the conducive conditions.

Consociational engineering entails creating at least the following favourable conditions: a multiple balance of power, a commonly per-ceived external threat, socio-economic equality between the segments, and overarching society-wide loyalties. There are two ways in which a multiple balance of power might be realized. The first is through pro-voking a deep split between the UUP and the DUP, deep enough to make the UUP favour power-sharing with the APNI and SDLP. However, this outcome, if feasible, would at best create a cross-sectarian majority, rather than a grand coalition (since the DUP and SF would be excluded from power-sharing). The second way is through a significant growth in the SDLP and SF electorate, fostered by higher Catholic population growth. This much predicted outcome has yet to materialize. Even if it did, it is not obvious that it would promote consociation. Rather, it might

---

[50] See *inter alia* I. Lustick, *State-Building Failure in British Ireland and French Algeria* (Ber-keley, Institute of International Studies, 1985) and R. F. Foster, *Modern Ireland 1600–1972* (London, Allen Lane, 1988).

[51] Pappalardo, 'The conditions for consociational democracy', p. 379.

[52] See *inter alia* R. Fisk, *The Point of No Return: The Strike Which Broke the British in Ulster* (London, André Deustsch, 1975); Rose, *Northern Ireland*; P. Bew and H. Patterson, *The British State and the Ulster Crisis* (London, Verso, 1985); and C. O'Leary, S. Elliot, and R. A. Wilford, *The Northern Ireland Assembly, 1982–1986: A Constitutional Experiment* (London, Hurst, 1988).

intensify nationalism amongst Catholics. The only easily imaginable way to create a common external enemy is to threaten a second partition of Ulster, in the hope that this threat to Protestants in western and southern Northern Ireland, and to Catholics in west Belfast, might generate consociational motivations.[53] Working on removing socio-economic inequalities, as experience has demonstrated, is equally difficult. It produces animosity amongst the majority, who deny that discrimination exists, and it increases their hostility to power-sharing. Moreover, even if reforms were to be successful they do not guarantee more accommodating attitudes on the part of the minority. Finally, 'overarching society-wide loyalties' are values which consociational engineers seem unlikely to induce. Manufacturing a shared national or Christian identity is beyond the grasp of policy-makers.

Promoting consociation on Lijphart's model seems unlikely to succeed, so power-sharing has been widely dismissed as an unworkable solution.[54] However, Lijphart himself advocates consociation when the background conditions are not at all favourable, even in South Africa![55] Should policy-makers follow his normative advice, despite the pessimism which his analysis induces? We seem to be faced with a contradiction. Political science determinism tells us that the conditions for consociation are absent, therefore it is not viable. Yet, Lijphart suggests that idealist goodwill on the part of well-motivated elites can create consociation, even in unfavourable conditions.

I want to develop an argument, based on synthesizing Lijphart's critics, which postpones this analytical choice. The validity of Lijphart's set of 'conducive background conditions' is widely disputed.[56] The critique of Lijphart suggests that three hypotheses, reconstructed from his speculations, remain plausible. First, consociation can be achieved only by elites sufficiently motivated to engage in conflict regulation: 'the independent actions of political élites, often taken in opposition to their followers' demands, rather than societal variables, ... best account for

---

[53] I may be the sole eccentric publicly to have recommended such a strategy: B. O'Leary, 'Exploring the roads to consensus', *Irish Times* (3 Dec. 1988).

[54] Consociation is not extensively discussed in a deservedly influential book, K. Boyle and T. Hadden, *Ireland: A Positive Proposal* (Harmondsworth, Penguin, 1985). They dismiss power-sharing as requiring 'a highly unrealistic degree of consensus'; requiring politicians 'to agree on everything all of the time'; and as incapable of providing 'any mechanism for resolving the differences of opinion that are bound to arise within a cabinet or executive' (pp. 49, 73, 84). These are 'Anglo'-centric legalistic judgements. If they were true, much of Western Europe would be ungovernable. Power-sharing may not be capable of working in Northern Ireland, but the causes of its fragile prospects are more deeply rooted.

[55] Lijphart, *Power-Sharing in South Africa*.   [56] See n. 43.

conflict regulation successes and failures in democratic regimes'.[57] Second, consociation is favoured where political elites enjoy pre-dominance over a deferential and organizationally encapsulated fol-lowing.[58] Finally, consociation is promoted not so much by a multiple balance of power, but rather by the stability of the subcultures in the segmented society.[59] The logic behind these hypotheses is straight-forward. The first is the simplest: conflict regulation can take place when elites are motivated to engage in it. However, the firmest proponent of this argument does not believe that goodwill is enough. Elites must be confident they can carry their followers with them. The conditions in the second hypothesis must be met. Finally, if well-motivated elites, enjoying some autonomy from their followers, are to engage in successful conflict regulation, they must be sure both of their social bases and of the intentions of their rivals. These hypotheses explain more convincingly the failure of attempts to promote consociation in Northern Ireland.

The absence of the required elite motivations

There are four reasons why elites might consider consociation. They may desire to fend off a common external threat, maintain the economic welfare of their segment, avoid violence, or obtain office. These moti-vations have evidently not been present in a 'critical mass' amongst Northern Ireland's politicians. There is no agreed external threat. The radical economic decline of the region has not concentrated enough minds on the merits of accommodation.[60] The desire to avoid war has not been sufficiently intense. Despite (or because of?) the historical experi-ence of segmental antagonisms, the strategies of unionist and nationalist leaders between 1969 and 1972 could not have been better designed to create violence.

The desire to obtain office has also been insufficiently strong. The APNI's leaders alone have remained consistently interested in sharing governmental office. SF leaders want a united Ireland or nothing. The SDLP's leaders, by contrast, desired local office, especially between 1972

---

[57] E. Nordlinger, *The Autonomy of the Democratic State* (London, Harvard University Press, 1981), p. 225.

[58] This is the central theme of Nordlinger's *Conflict Regulation in Divided Societies*. See also Pappalardo, 'The conditions for consociational democracy', p. 387, and Barry, 'The con-sociational model and its dangers', p. 396.

[59] Pappalardo, 'The conditions for consociational democracy', p. 387.

[60] For descriptions of the Northern Ireland economy, see the essays by Rowthorn and by Canning, Moore, and Rhodes in P. Teague (ed.), *Beyond the Rhetoric: Politics, the Economy and Social Policy in Northern Ireland* (London, Lawrence and Wishart, 1987).

and 1975, not only as proof of Unionst willingness to share power, but also to demonstrate to their segment that the reform of Northern Ireland was possible. However, since the rise of SF in the early 1980s the SDLP's leaders have played abstentionist politics. They boycotted the Assembly of 1982–6, and sought a guaranteed 'Irish dimension' ahead of local power-sharing. Amongst Unionists the DUP have generally been seen to be the most consistent local office-seekers, eager to build patronage and to win hegemony over the UUP, but they are not prepared to pay the price of sharing power with nationalists. Some of the leaders of the UUP have strong integrationist sympathies (many of them want Northern Ireland to be governed exactly like Britain), which dampen their enthusiasm for local office (attitudes strengthened by their over-representation at Westminster). Direct rule gave Unionists no reason to accommodate the minority, and they continue to 'believe that total victory [could] be achieved at an acceptable cost',[61] hardly the sort of motivation required for political compromise. Although the SDLP and the DUP have wanted devolution and local office for instrumental and ideological reasons, they have not been able to overcome their enormous differences. The SDLP wanted consociation with an Irish dimension; whereas the DUP have wanted majority rule devolution, 'precisely as a veto on Britain's untrustworthy intentions',[62] to prevent an Irish dimension.

British arbitration also negatively affected elite motivations. There was an excruciating dilemma. The absence of the British was essential if the appropriate motivations for consociation (fear of bloody war) were to emerge. However, far from promoting consociation, it would promote a bloodier civil war.[63]

The absence of sufficient elite predominance

A story from the French Second Republic applies to Northern Ireland. Ledru-Rollin was asked what he was going to do about a crowd protesting the violation of the constitution. He replied: 'As I am their leader, I shall follow them'. Northern Ireland's political elites have frequently resembled Ledru-Rollin in their willingness to put themselves in front of their crowd as opposed to leading them. There are good reasons for this behaviour. The key political leaders of Northern Ireland do not enjoy

---

[61] Barry, 'The consociational model and its dangers', p. 411.
[62] E. Moloney and A. Polack, *Paisley* (Dublin, Poolbeg Press, 1986), p. 338.
[63] The best-known statement is C. C. O'Brien, *States of Ireland* (London, Panther, 1974).

'structured elite predominance', that is, the ability to lead their followers in directions which they initially would oppose.[64]

Structured elite predominance can exist in four circumstances, at least one of which must be present to ensure it. The masses have to be apolitical, deferential, integrated into pyramidical patron–client relations, or integrated into modern mass political parties.[65] In any of these circumstances political elites enjoy some autonomy from their followers, sufficient to allow them to make compromises. The first two sets of circumstances are not present in Northern Ireland. The third, the existence of patron–client networks, is latent in Northern Ireland's political culture, but the Unionist network of patronage was weakened in 1972 and, in the absence of a share in political power, nationalist political elites have found it very difficult to build powerful clientelist relations.

What of the fourth condition? One of the obstacles to consociation in Northern Ireland is that the parties are highly democratic, in the sense of being representative of and responsive to their members. Rather than the conventional iron law of oligarchy, there exists a high degree of democracy from below. This leaves political leaders constantly looking over their shoulders, both to their electorate and to potential rival elites in their party.[66] The major political parties in Northern Ireland *either* do not display structured elite predominance *or*, if they do, either the party is too small to matter, or, worse still, the autonomy of its elites is counterproductive for consociation.

The UUP does not display structured elite predominance. The once hegemonic party which governed Northern Ireland without serious challenge for fifty years has forced out four of its five leaders since 1969 (O'Neill, Chichester-Clark, Faulkner, and West), and its current leader (Molyneaux) cannot be described as authoritative, let alone charismatic. The UUP is divided over whether to pursue devolution (McCusker,

---

[64] For this reason consociation has been called 'government by elite cartel': segmental leaders make the key decisions 'from above' so as to avoid democracy 'down below' producing civil war.   [65] Nordlinger, *Conflict Regulation in Divided Societies*, pp. 79–82.

[66] There is perhaps one exception: the DUP seems to enjoy 'structured elite predominance achieved through an hierarchical and disciplined party organization, as well as a considerable degree of deference towards party elites largely fostered by its ancillary organizations': P. Mitchell, *Conflict Regulation in Divided Societies: Northern Ireland, A Consideration* (Unpublished MSc thesis, London School of Economics 1986), p. 13. However, far from being a modern mass party whose bureaucratic structures generate autonomy for its leadership, the DUP seems more like a charismatic organization built around an individual and his church. It displays some structured elite predominance, but does so because of its charismatic rather than bureaucratic traits; and Paisley is wary of going to extremes ahead of his supporters.

Taylor, and the recently departed Millar) or integration (the line backed by Molyneaux, Powell, and the recently departed McCartney). It has endured several breakaway factions (Faulkner's UPNI and Craig's Vanguard Party in the 1970s, and McCartney's integrationists in the wake of the AIA). It seems to be in a permanent leadership crisis. The UUP's lack of positive ideological direction undermines whatever prospects might exist for structured elite predominance.

The SDLP displays greater structured elite predominance than the UUP, but the autonomy of its leaders is still limited. The first study of the party gave the impression of a modern party with extensive discretion vested in its leadership.[67] However, the party leadership, partly because of its constitution, has not always been able to impose its wishes upon its local branches. Moreover, the SDLP has not been without its leadership crises. John Hume and Seamus Mallon, the current leader and deputy-leader respectively, are more closely tuned to the party's grass roots than were social democrats like Gerry Fitt and Paddy Devlin, but this makes them less disposed towards concessions to the unionists. The tension over the relative importance of power-sharing and the Irish dimension, evident in the SDLP's 1979 leadership turmoil, remains latent. Hume's decision to engage in talks with SF during 1988 brought out this tension.[68] Since the signing of the AIA the SDLP's leaders do not seem clear about what concessions they are prepared to make to the unionists to produce a tangible internal settlement. The failure of secret discussions at Duisburg suggests that Hume is not prepared to trade even a temporary suspension of the AIA in return for a consociational deal.[69]

Structured elite predominance in the other three major parties—APNI, DUP, and SF—is less analytically important in considering the prospects for consociation. The autonomy of the APNI's leadership

---

[67] I. McAllister, *The Social Democratic and Labour Party of Northern Ireland* (London, Macmillan, 1977).

[68] The extensive formal discussions, involving the exchange of papers and face-to-face dialogue between SDLP and SF representatives in 1988, were significant. The talks were initiated by Hume, apparently to persuade SF that their strategy made Irish unification ever more unlikely. SF participated to show they were prepared to argue their case. The talks lasted until Hume felt confident that ending them would reflect upon SF rather than the SDLP. He argued forcefully that SF/IRA are the greatest obstacles both to an accommodation with unionists *and* to a united Ireland. However, some unionists contended that Hume's organization of the talks was designed to sabotage discussions about devolution between the Secretary of State and the unionist parties.

[69] These doubts about structured elite predominance in the SDLP do not suggest that Hume, the most impressive of Northern Ireland's politicians, is a weak leader. 'Structured elite predominance' is not a synonym for strong leadership; it refers to organizational and social conditions which allow strong leaders to make autonomous decisions.

is less relevant because it supports power-sharing. The DUP may well enjoy the structured elite predominance of Ian Paisley, but nobody believes his eminence is beneficial for the prospects of power-sharing. Finally, SF (which has also had major leadership and doctrinal crises) is led by people who do not desire to shift towards a wholly political strategy (which would mean abandoning terrorism), and are incapable of delivering such a strategy even if they were persuaded of its merits.

The absence of intra-segmental stability

Even with the existence of the appropriate motivations and structurally predominant elites, consociation would not automatically follow. Political elites must be secure in their segmented bases before hazarding compromise. Northern Ireland's political elites have obviously not felt secure. The twenty-year crisis and the change in the electoral system have encouraged the fragmentation of the rival segments. When the Protestant/Unionist monolith collapsed it broke into five fractions (the UUP, DUP, APNI, Vanguard, and UPNI) and then into three (the UUP, DUP, and APNI) competition for hegemony within this segment has weakened any impetus for power-sharing and accommodation. The DUP (and Vanguard before it) forced the UUP to be as bellicosely anti-consociational and loyalist as themselves. The Catholic/nationalist bloc consolidated behind the SDLP (as the civil rights activists and traditional nationalists made their peace) in the early 1970s but then fragmented under the lack of political progress. Competitive pressure, first from the Irish Independence Party and then SF, left the SDLP looking over its shoulder. The pattern of fragmentation within the majority and minority has also not been beneficial for consociation. The fraction of the Catholic/nationalist bloc prepared to consider power-sharing has been consistently higher than the fraction so disposed amongst the Protestant/Unionist bloc.

Northern Ireland has not only lacked Lijphart's conditions conducive for power-sharing but also the conditions specified in the reconstructed theory of consociationalism which I built through synthesizing the arguments of Lijphart's critics. This conclusion must inspire further pessimism. However, there is no need to aband on all hope. The question is whether elite motivations, elite autonomy, and segmental structures can be reshaped by British and Irish policy-makers in ways which are conducive to consociation. Can the AIA promote consociation?

FROM VOLUNTARY TO COERCIVE CONSOCIATIONALISM

The AIA has been interpreted in radically different ways.[70] However, no one disputes that it formalized British and Irish cooperation, internationalized the conflict, and gave the Irish government a role in the government of Northern Ireland (which was less than executive but more than consultative in its scope).[71] The AIA was also a notice that whilst the unionist guarantee remained (Northern Ireland is and will be part of the United Kingdom as long as a majority so wish), unionists no longer had the de facto right to veto British policy in Northern Ireland.[72]

However, the AIA also marked the abandonment of attempts to achieve consociation through voluntary means. It was, in part, a new experiment in coercive consociationalism. Many of its framers, on both the British and Irish sides, saw it as an attempt to create the conditions for power-sharing to work, as a master plan to coerce key fractions of the Unionist bloc into accepting some version of the Sunningdale 1973–4 settlement, as the lesser of several evils. On the one hand, the AIA confronted the unionists with an Irish dimension, the Inter-Governmental

---

[70] For the diverse academic reactions see P. Arthur, 'The Anglo-Irish agreement: conflict resolution or conflict regulation?', *Bulletin of Peace Proposals*, 18: 4 (1987); A. Coughlan, *Fooled Again? The Anglo-Irish Agreement and After* (Dublin, Mercier Press, 1986); W. H. Cox, 'The Anglo Irish agreement', *Parliamentary Affairs*, 40: 1 (1986); T. Hadden and K. Boyle, 'Hopes and fears for Hillsborough', *Studies*, 75: 300 (1986); B. Hadfield, 'The Anglo-Irish agreement 1985—blue print or green print?', *Northern Ireland Legal Quarterly*, 37: 1 (1986); A. Kenny, *The Road to Hillsborough* (London, Pergamon Press, 1986); B. O'Leary, 'The Anglo-Irish Agreement: statecraft or folly?', *West European Politics*, 10: 1 (1987); W. V. Shannon, 'The Anglo-Irish agreement', *Foreign Affairs*, 64: 4 (1986); and the essays in P. Teague (ed.), *Beyond the Rhetoric* (London, Lawrence and Wishart, 1987) and C. Townshend (ed.), *Consensus in Ireland: Approaches and Recessions* (Oxford, Clarendon Press, 1988).

[71] This formulation is Dr Garret FitzGerald's.

[72] The AIA was signed because of a range of rational considerations (stemming the growth of SF and securing Irish cooperation in security on the British side; stemming the growth of SF and securing British reform of Northern Ireland on the Irish side); the confluence of well-established bureaucratic repertoires; incremental and exploratory manoeuvres by politicians and administrators interested in symbolic initiatives; and jockeying for position by the SDLP. Elsewhere, I have examined three modes of explaining the Agreement: rational actor explanations; organizational process explanations; and political explanations; see O'Leary, *The Anglo-Irish Agreement*. Rational actor explanations are offered by the British and Irish governments who argue that the Agreement is designed to advance conciliation and improve security (see the Hillsborough Communiqué, November 1985); by nationalists, and republicans who argue that the Agreement is a counter-insurgency plan designed to break Sinn Féin and the IRA—see Coughlan, *Fooled Again?*; and by Unionists who believe it is the first stage of British withdrawal from Ireland—see P. Smith, *Why Unionists Say No* (Belfast, Joint Unionist Working Party, 1986) and E. Haslett, *The Anglo-Irish Agreement: Northern Ireland Perspectives* (Belfast, Joint Unionist Working Party, 1987).

Conference (IGC), of far greater political salience than the Council of Ireland of 1973–4. This measure, agreed over the heads of the Unionist population, was (and was perceived to be) coercive. It was imposed against the wishes of Unionists. On the other hand, the AIA offered Unionists a mechanism for removing the agenda-setting scope of the IGC, provided they were prepared to bite the bullet of *agreed devolution*, as specified in Article 4 (b) and (c) of the AIA. A devolutionary settlement would mean consociation because the British and Irish governments, and the SDLP, would not settle for less; and because the AIA's terms would not permit anything else.[73] The hope was that the SDLP, having secured an Irish dimension (the IGC), would be happier to reach a consociational accommodation. Strengthened in their segmental rivalry with SF, the SDLP would be freer to negotiate. The unpalatable choices which the AIA put before the unionist bloc, by contrast, were designed to force their leaders to rethink their political attitudes and to sow divisions amongst them. The AIA was designed to change the structure of the incentives facing the elites of both blocs, to encourage elite autonomy within Northern Ireland's political parties, and, by shifting the political terrain, to allow the 'unthinkable' to be thought. It was also hoped that the AIA would affect intra-segmental relations in ways conducive to power-sharing. The hope was widespread that the culs-de-sac offered by loyalist overreaction to the AIA would produce more accommodating political responses from unionists. The AIA aimed at both sides of the intransigent divide, albeit differentially: attempting to coerce unionists into consociation, while inducing the SDLP into welcoming it.

The AIA was not as coherent as the above reasoning suggests. British policy-makers were divided in their interpretation of its functions. There were those who saw the AIA as a counter-insurgency operation with good international public relations benefits; those who saw it as a stepping stone to withdrawal; and those who saw it as an attempt to engineer consociation.[74] Irish policy-makers were similarly differentiated,

---

[73] Articles 4(b) and 4(c) of the Agreement are as follows: '(b) It is the declared policy of the United Kingdom Government that responsibility in respect of certain matters within the powers of the Secretary of State for Northern Ireland should be devolved within Northern Ireland on a basis which would secure *widespread acceptance* throughout the community. The Irish government support that policy. (c) Both Governments recognize that devolution can be achieved *only with the co-operation* of constitutional representatives within Northern Ireland *of both traditions there*. The Conference shall be a framework within which the Irish government may put forward views and proposals on the modalities of bringing about devolution in Northern Ireland, in so far as they relate to the interests of the minority community' (Italics added).

[74] Non-attributable interviews with British officials in 1986 and 1989.

although few policy-influentials saw the AIA as a stepping stone to British withdrawal. These differences in motivation and interpretation subsequently led to a great deal of uncertainty and conflict. However, the experiment of coercive consociationalism is certainly being tried, even if not all framers of the AIA intended to try it.[75]

IS COERCIVE CONSOCIATIONALISM WORKING?

The preconditions of successful coercive consociationalism flow from the previous analysis. First, on the external front, both the British and Irish governments must commit themselves to supporting consociation, as envisaged in Article 4 of the AIA. Secondly, on the internal front, the British and Irish governments must create appropriate elite motivations, elite autonomy, and segmental balances.

The external front

The serious contestants for political power in Britain (the Conservatives, Labour, and the Democrats) and Ireland (Fianna Fáil, Fine Gael, Labour, and the Progressive Democrats) are committed to the AIA. However, if both governments disagree substantially over its nature and the priorities of the work of the IGC, little except 'crisis management' is likely to be achieved. British priorities at the IGC have followed this order: improved security (which has mostly meant promoting measures to weaken SF and the IRA); persuading Unionists that the AIA has entrenched rather than weakened the union; the promotion of consociation; and the reform of Northern Ireland by measures to increase equality of opportunity.[76] The objectives of Irish governments have differed. The Fine Gael–Labour coalition had four goals, ranked equal in importance: to reform Northern Ireland by advancing minority interests and aspirations, especially in the administration of justice and equality of opportunity; to promote consociation with an Irish dimension; to improve security (prevent the growth of SF in both parts of Ireland) but not at the expense of the first two objectives; and, finally, to develop and extend good Anglo-Irish relations in the context of the European Community. The Fianna Fáil government elected in February 1987, although not explicitly opposed to devolution in Northern Ireland (since such opposition would violate the AIA), has been more sceptical of its prospects of success and more

---

[75] Non-attributable interviews with Irish and British officials in 1986 and 1989.

[76] This reasoning is based upon communiqués, press-releases, and non-attributable interviews.

insistent that any such initiative must be accompanied by a North–South settlement incorporating all-Irish relations.[77]

These conflicting priorities contributed to public difficulties in Anglo-Irish relations, especially in 1988, but what is important to note here is that they are not helpful to consociation. To facilitate the latter Irish governments must commit themselves to 'agreed devolution', as envisaged under Article 4 of the AIA, and put more pressure on the SDLP to pursue it. This commitment would not be incompatible with the long-run aspirations of constitutional nationalists. If Catholics and Protestants cannot share power in Northern Ireland they are not going to share power in a united Ireland.[78] Consociation in Northern Ireland is a pre-condition of a stable and democratic united Ireland, even if that is envisaged as occurring at some date in the future-perfect.

The internal front

What has been the internal impact of the AIA on elite motivations, elite autonomy, and segmental stability? First, let us consider the nationalists. The SDLP responded favourably to the AIA. To sustain the SDLP's belief in its merits and its interest in consociation, it is imperative that the British government follow three consistent policies: reform the administration of justice, reform Northern Ireland's employment practices, and facilitate functional cross-border cooperation to make meaningful the Irish dimension of the AIA. These measures are necessary to make the SDLP willing to compromise on a consociational settlement, to enable its leaders to avoid the loss of electoral support, and to rebuild the SDLP as the dominant segmental party of Catholics/nationalists.

There have been perceptible but small-scale changes in the direction of reforming Northern Ireland. However, this programme has not yet built Catholic confidence in British government of Northern Ireland and it has often been set back by British 'counter-insurgency' initiatives. In an interview with a Northern Ireland Office official I posed the following question: 'Will future historians say that the British government missed a key opportunity to promote power-sharing in the immediate aftermath of the Agreement? During this period, when Unionists were unwilling to

---

[77] In his first major interview on his role in the IGC, Brian Lenihan, the Irish Foreign Minister, claimed to have three equal priorities: the promotion of the welfare of the minority, easing the fears of the majority, and reforming Northern Ireland: *Irish times* (11 May 1987).

[78] A point made clearly in a widely misinterpreted British Labour Party policy statement, K. McNamara, J. Marshall, and M. Mowlam, *Towards a United Ireland: Reform and Harmonisation: A Dual Strategy for Unification* (Front Bench Statement of the British Labour Party) (London, House of Commons, 1988).

talk, surely the reform of Northern Ireland could have been accelerated? If that had happened, and had been seen to be happening, then the SDLP's gains at the expense of SF might have been greater, and the SDLP would have found compromising on a devolutionary settlement much easier when Unionists eventually began to have "talks about talks" in 1987–8?' The official replied that the question was unfair. Some reforms, especially those on fair employment, needed lengthy consultation and deliberation and could not be achieved overnight. However, he conceded that accepting three-judge, as opposed to single-judge, Diplock courts would have consolidated support for the AIA amongst nationalists. Moreover, he made the following point: 'I have been ever more conscious of the contradiction of talking of the "achievements of the Agreement" against a background of current government policy of not attributing developments specifically to the Agreement, and implying that most of them would have happened in any case'.[79] This contradiction, which exists because of the British government's desire to suggest that the AIA has not weakened British sovereignty and its concern to minimize Unionist hostility, is obviously not good for supporters of the Agreement. As a result, Catholic support for the AIA has remained predicated more upon Unionist hostility to it than upon the concrete changes it has delivered.

The maladministration of justice, emergency legislation, and the policing system remain fundamental obstacles to Catholic confidence in British intentions to reform Northern Ireland. The same is true of British efforts to reform employment opportunities in Northern Ireland. Sixteen years after the van Straubenzee Report[80] and thirteen years after the establishment of the Fair Employment Agency, Catholics remain over-represented in semi- and unskilled occupations, and in those industries most susceptible to recession and high unemployment.[81] Moreover, the Conservative government has failed to stiffen employment legislation in ways which might satisfy its critics.[82] The Government White Paper, *Fair*

[79] Non-attributable interview with a NIO official in January 1989.

[80] W. van Straubenzee, *Northern Ireland Department of Health and Social Services, Report and Recommendations of the Working Party on Discrimination in the Private Sector of Employment* (Belfast, HMSO, 1973).

[81] The percentage level of unemployment amongst Northern Ireland Protestants hovers around the UK average (12.5%). They enjoy equal citizenship. The percentage level of unemployment amongst Catholics (35%) at times has been nearly three times as high as in the 1980s, and Catholic males have standardly been two-and-a-half times as likely to be unemployed as their Protestant counterparts.

[82] Fears of the consequences for racial and sexual discrimination laws in Great Britain, as well as ideological hostility to regulation, may be constraining the government's willingness to countenance radical steps: C. McCrudden, 'Equal employment opportunity in Northern Ireland', *Equal Opportunities Review*, 10 (1986), 17–21.

Employment in Northern Ireland (May 1988), and a 1989 bill designed to strengthen fair employment law and administration, have fallen short if they are designed to win Catholic support. As predicted by critics of the White Paper, the bill makes reverse discrimination illegal, makes certain types of affirmative action illegal, and omits prescribing the use of statistics for setting goals and timetables to create representative employment patterns.[83] Based on the minority report of the Standing Advisory Commission on Human Rights, which was clearly influenced by standard Unionist assumptions, the bill seems better designed for public relations than changing employment patterns. Such short-sighted policymaking may well give SF a future advantage in the competition for 'hearts and minds' within the Catholic community, making the argument that 'Northern Ireland is unreformable' sound more convincing.

The IRA and SF are violently opposed to consocation. Their actions are also one of the most significant factors in Unionist hostility to consociation. The British and Irish governments, and the SDLP, are not likely to be able to change the minds of these self-styled 'national liberators'. However, SF are more vulnerable than the IRA. Entry into electoral politics has constrained the IRA's military options that SF can freely endorse. Moreover, SF will find it difficult if Britain reforms Northern Ireland. They cannot easily reject actions which improve the lives of their constituents in West Belfast and Derry. Improving the civil liberties and economic welfare of the Catholic working class will threaten SF but these objectives are not at the forefront of the strategy of the British government. The AIA has produced better elite motivation amongst SDLP nationalists, which might favour eventual consocation. At the moment, however, the SDLP's leadership considers the Irish dimension of the AIA more valuable than agreed devolution. Therefore, it will be some time before we can conclude that consociational motivations and intra-segmental stability of the right sort exist within the nationalist minority. The growth of SF support has been stopped but there is no reason to suppose that it cannot rise again. After all, British policy-makers have shown an unerring knack of helping them when they are in difficulties.

What of elite motivations, elite autonomy, and segmental stability on the unionist side? The APNI, after painful divisions which split them on sectarian lines, decided to back the AIA. They remain the only Unionists to have accepted the AIA and consocation. However, the SDLP and the APNI could not form a majority in Northern Ireland, let alone a grand

---

[83] C. McCrudden, 'The Northern Ireland Fair Employment White Paper: a critical assessment', *Industrial Law Journal* 17: 3 (1988), 162–81.

coalition. Together, at best, they could obtain the support of 30–35 per cent of the Northern Ireland electorate. The key actors, the UUP and the DUP, remain opposed to the AIA. 'Ulster', meaning Protestant Ulster, 'says No'. Unionist opposition to the AIA has embraced legal actions (forced by-elections, mass demonstrations, and mass petitions), civil disobedience (political strikes, refusals to set rates or to pay taxes), and violence (by paramilitaries). The legal actions have proved fruitless. Unionists have lost two Westminster seats to the SDLP, while their mass demonstrations and mass petitions have confirmed British and international public opinion in their estimations of unionist unreasonableness. The Thatcher administration has faced down both legal protest and civil disobedience. Unionist politicians have surrendered when faced with the prospect of extensive fines for not setting local government rates. Finally, the degree of violence by loyalist paramilitaries has been remarkably low by the standards of unionist reaction to previous British 'sell-outs' in this century (1911–14, 1920–5, and 1972–6).

Amongst the UUP and DUP there was tacit acquiescence by 1987 in the existence of the AIA, recognition that it did not entail joint authority, but no signs whatever of acceptance of its legitimacy. Yet with the failure of the campaign against the AIA Unionist politicians faced increasing hostility from below, from people who enquired where they were being led. In January 1987 the UDA, through the Ulster Political Research Group, produced *Common Sense*, which accepted the idea that power-sharing was the way to remove the impact of the AIA, thus putting pressure upon Paisley and Molyneaux. Unionist leaders were sufficiently impressed to set up a Task Force, comprised of Harold McCusker and Frank Millar of the UUP and Peter Robinson of the DUP, and required it to consult their community as to what they should do. In July 1987 the Task Force reported with *An End to Drift*, which was hailed by some as proof that the AIA had induced unionists to accept power-sharing. Careful attention to the text suggested that it was little more than a restatement of the dilemmas and divisions facing unionists, as opposed to a constructive statement confirming that coercive consociationalism had worked. There was little dissent when Paisley and Molyneaux chose to interpret the Task Force report in a very limited way, although Millar and Robinson were later to resign from their party posts, the former permanently. The Unionists opened 'talks about talks' with the British government in the autumn of 1987, which petered out in 1988. Both the UUP and DUP remain insistent that the AIA must be suspended before they will engage in discussing a constitutional settlement with the minority and Paisley remains insistent that power-sharing is unacceptable.

The AIA has shown that it can survive Unionist opposition. However, coercive consociationalism has not worked so far, even if there are occasional episodes like the Duisburg discussions which show that the key elites are less far apart than is often supposed. Unionist motivations have certainly been worked upon. Their choices have been circumscribed. They can stay in their current state of disaffection and general withdrawal of consent against the British government in the hope that the AIA is repudiated, if only through a breakdown in Anglo-Irish relations. The danger with this option is that their own fears may become self-fulfilling. The British reaction might well be to accept full joint authority, consider repartition, or prepare to withdraw entirely. Second, unionists can advocate integration. However, this option divides them and has no significant takers in Britain. Over the long run, it might produce exactly the same reaction in Britain as the first option. Third, they can advocate independence. This option is the least popular. They are after all unionists; they do not seek sovereignty over themselves. They are anti-nationalists. Unionists will contemplate independence only if they are being coerced into a united Ireland. The final choice is the most ignominious and galling for them. It is what coercive consociationalism is designed to achieve. The AIA has a built-in carrot: a devolved consociational government would reduce the importance of the IGC and the direct influence of the Irish government on British policy-making in Northern Ireland.

There are no signs, yet, that elite autonomy and intra-segmental stability of the sort required are emerging on the Unionist side. Elite motivations are better than they were but leaders still lack the necessary autonomy. The DUP remains too big, too influential, and too intransigent for optimism. The UUP remains too uncertain and divided, and far from having split with the DUP it seems to be closer to it than for a long time. Their uncertainty is mirrored by the SDLP's confidence. Its leaders are relatively content with the AIA, and therefore less ready to make the concessions which might promote consociation. Having called for the removal of the unionist veto on policy within Northern Ireland, the SDLP are now exercising a veto on consociation.

WHAT IF COERCIVE CONSOCIATIONALISM DOES NOT WORK?

Coercive consociationalism has not yet worked. It nonetheless deserves more time and better Anglo-Irish cooperation to see if it can succeed.

There are also several variants on coercive consociationalism which have yet to be fully explored before we deny its prospects of ultimate success.

The first, radical direct rule, implies reforming Northern Ireland to make consociation easier to achieve in the future. It would work through persuading Catholics that Northern Ireland can be reformed through programmes of affirmative action and justly administered through the restoration of civil liberties, the creation of a bill of rights, and the reform of the courts; and through persuading them that sacrificing the objective of Irish unity in return for power-sharing is worthwhile. On the other hand, it would work through forcing what some regard as disagreeable change in Northern Ireland, persuading Unionists that power-sharing might be a better way of protecting their interests.[84] This strategy was latent in the terms of the AIA and deserves to be tried more vigorously.

Such a strategy should also be accompanied by a systematic change in the election systems in Northern Ireland. All elections, to the European Parliament, Westminster, a new Northern Ireland Assembly, and local councils, should take place under the same system: a party-list system of proportional representation. This change would have several advantages. The first is uniformity. Currently Westminster elections are first past the post, whereas other elections take place under the STV system. Second, the change would alter elite motivations amongst the UUP. Competition rather than cooperation with the DUP, at least during Westminster elections, would become more likely. Third, the list system, by contrast with STV, enhances the authority of party leaders as opposed to voters,[85] and might make compromise easier. Fourth, the list system is genuinely proportional, unlike STV which is a system which counts preference rankings and the intensity of preferences. Fifth, the list system is used in successful consociational systems. Finally, the list system is the European norm.

Radical direct rulers intent on producing consociation should also take advantage of British and Irish membership of the European Community to promote maximum feasible functional cross-border cooperation (in attracting investment and European Social and Regional Funds, in agricultural policy, energy production and distribution, and public transport) and maximum feasible legal harmonization (in bills of civil and social rights). The direction of more political attention to Brussels,

---

[84] The aim of the Labour Party's front-bench spokespersons on Northern Ireland (*Towards a United Ireland*) is to achieve consociation through radical, reforming direct rule. The party's policy is for Irish unity by consent (a less realistic aspiration), but it is evident that this unity is not expected within the lifespan of a Labour government.

[85] Lijphart, *Democracy in Plural Societies*, p. 137.

away from London and Dublin, will be doubly beneficial. European arbitrators of interests in Northern Ireland are less likely to be regarded as enemies of either segment and greater European integration will make the differences between membership of the British and Irish states less salient over time. Such developments will not provide a panacea for Northern Ireland but will make consociation more rather than less feasible; in any case, they are desirable on other grounds.

By contrast, the other variants on coercive consociationalism should not be tried. Joint authority is one way of increasing the coercive content of coercive consociationalism. The introduction of the Irish government into full sharing of authority in Northern Ireland might force upon Unionists the merits of power-sharing.[86] However, this strategy would not work for two reasons. Under joint authority, nationalists would have reduced incentive to share power with Unionists. Joint authority would also be destabilizing, as it would be interpreted, correctly, as the end of sole British sovereignty of Northern Ireland. It would not, therefore, produce a consociational response amongst Unionists; rather, it would create support for a unilateral declaration of independence.

The other variant of coercive consociationalism, forced independence designed to produce power-sharing, might also be considered a viable strategy on the grounds that nationalists and unionists would have to agree to accommodate one another without British arbitration. However, I believe that this variant would also be destabilizing and productive of greater civil war. Nobody wants independence, even as their second-best option. There would be insufficient incentives for Protestants to share power in an independent Northern Ireland where they would be hegemonic. Nationalists would still seek, by gun and/or ballot box, to unite the entire island. The new regime would also not be recognized by the Irish Republic or by the European Community unless it had the full support of the SDLP, which it would not get.

Non-consociational options

If consociation cannot be engineered in any of the modes outlined, then there are three feasible political and constitutional strategies available for the consideration of British policy-makers.[87] The first entails the *status quo ante*, maintaining a modified form of direct rule, downplaying the

---

[86] M. Dent, 'The feasibility of shared sovereignty (and shared authority)', in C. Townshend (ed.), *Consensus in Ireland* (Oxford, Clarendon Press, 1988), pp. 128–56.

[87] I lack the space to explain why I consider these options the most plausible alternatives to consociation.

importance of the AIA and reverting to the 'crisis management' much criticized by the Irish government before November 1985. Over the longer run this policy is unsustainable. Policy-makers in liberal democracies are under constant pressures to 'do something'. The famous fallacy 'something must be done; this is something; let's do this' operates regularly in politics. Irish policy-makers want to solve a conflict which threatens the stability of their state. British policy-makers want to end a conflict in which they have no major economic, geopolitical, or political stakes. I assume, perhaps erroneously, that British policy-makers believe themselves to have exhausted this option's possibilities.

The second option involves a unilateral abandonment of the AIA by the British government, in order to integrate Northern Ireland into the British political system. This strategy is very unlikely to be embarked upon by British policy-makers who have always been anxious to quarantine Irish affairs from mainstream British politics.[88] British political parties do not regard Northern Ireland as anything other than a conditional unit of the United Kingdom and there are no obvious material or ideological reasons why this outlook is likely to change. British political parties are not going to be prepared to pay the price of integration: drastic deterioration in relations with the Irish Republic, international condemnation, increasing the likelihood that Northern Ireland MPs hold the balance of power at Westminster, and permanent coercion of the recalcitrant Irish nationalist minority.

The final feasible initiative, repartition, entails abandoning both voluntary and coercive consociationalism and facing a different set of dilemmas. Although it is not on the immediate agenda, it is clear that should efforts to engineer consociation fail in the next decade then repartition will become increasingly attractive to British policy-makers. Repartition is the drastic but logical solution to consociational failures. It is also a solution which British policy-makers have been associated with before: in Palestine, India, and Ireland. If partition is executed properly, that is, creates relatively homogeneous states, it solves ethnic conflicts. Indeed it is such a drastic solution that threatening a major repartition of Ulster might actually produce the change in elite motivations, elite autonomy, and segmental relations required to generate a consociational settlement. It would concentrate nationalist minds in west Belfast and unionist minds west of the Bann and south of Armagh. The threat would have to be made credible by the appointment of a boundary commission,

---

[88] See R. D. Boyce, *The Irish Question and British Politics 1868–1986* (London, Macmillan, 1988).

by a public declaration of the willingness on the part of both states to carry out some small adjustments *pour encourager les autres*. Immediate clarification of the choice between partition and power-sharing through the *threat* of partition just *might* produce a consociational settlement.

Advocates of consociation in Northern Ireland have simple duties. They must persuade others that fewer people will die and fewer lives will be blighted by consociation and to persuade the parties in both islands that there are only two ways to stabilize the region: through consociation or through another partition. The knowledge that there is no feasible democratic alternative to consociation within the existing boundaries and structures of sovereignty of Northern Ireland might concentrate minds, after which hearts might follow.

4

Comparing Northern Ireland

John McGarry

> We tried to answer, spoke of Arab, Jew,
> of Turk and Greek in Cyprus, Pakistan
> and India, but no sense flickered through
> that offered reason to a modern man
> why Europeans, Christians, working-class
> should thresh and struggle in that old morass
>
> (John Hewitt, Ulster Poet)[1]

> Northern Ireland is truly a place apart.
>
> (editorial staff, *Belfast Telegraph*, 5 April 2000)

> For 30 years the politicians...of Northern Ireland have insisted their conflict cannot be compared to others.
>
> (Kevin Cullen, journalist, *Irish Times*, 13 May 2000)

> 'Ulster', the world's best laager!
>
> (sign in Ulster Unionist Party leader
> David Trimble's Westminster office)

> Say it once, Say it loud, I'm Black an' I'm proud...The Irish are the niggers of Europe, lads.
>
> (Roddy Doyle, author, *The Commitments*)[2]

For many people, like the editorialists of the *Belfast Telegraph* or the audience of John Hewitt's poem, Northern Ireland is a place apart, its conflict the result of some unique pathology. This view was particularly dominant from the outbreak of the troubles until the early 1990s, and it is still maintained. Northern Ireland has been seen, variously, as a

---

[1] J. Hewitt, *Out of my Time* (Belfast, 1974), cited in T. Nairn, *The Break-up of Britain* (London: Verso, 1981), 224.

[2] R. Doyle, *The Commitments* (New York: Vintage Books, 1989), 9, cited in B. Dooley, *The Fight for Civil Rights in Northern Ireland and Black America* (London: Pluto Press, 1998), 6.

'sui generis, untypical and even anachronistic phenomenon',[3] a 'peculiarly local conflict',[4] an 'outlandish exception to all the rules',[5] or as possessing a 'peculiar intractability'.[6]

However, many people, not just John Hewitt and Roddy Doyle, reject the idea that Northern Ireland is incomparable. Political partisans, contrary to Kevin Cullen's claim, have been drawing parallels with other divided societies since before the conflict began in the 1960s, and increasingly in recent decades. In addition, some of the best academic work on the Northern Ireland conflict, written by leading scholars from both outside and inside Northern Ireland, is comparative in focus.[7] Northern Ireland has been used as a test case for leading comparative theories, and compared with many other divided societies.

This chapter provides an overview of the use of comparative analysis in Northern Ireland. The point is not to critique any particular analogy or analysis, but to dispel the idea that the Northern Irish are parochial and their conflict unique or anachronistic. The first section shows how nationalist and unionist partisans have drawn links between Northern Ireland and other divided societies. These analogies are tied to particular international norms, and their use by Northern Ireland's communities reflect the importance of such norms. Both communities have used analogies, and their implicit normative arguments, to cement group solidarity and to influence international opinion, but their own actions and positions have been influenced by the analogies/norms they select. As Northern Ireland's rival groups have come to identify with those in other struggles, the latter's behaviour has impacted on them. Similarly, to the extent that analogies, and therefore the moral principles in the different parties' positions, have been accepted by outsiders, including the

---

[3] R. Pearson, cited in R. Kearney, *Postnationalist Ireland* (London: Routledge, 1997), 76. Pearson thought that the tendency to see Northern Ireland as peculiar would change as a result of the end of the cold war and the outbreak of several conflicts in Eastern Europe.

[4] J. Darby, cited in J. Whyte, *Interpreting Northern Ireland* (Oxford: Oxford University Press, 1990), 196.

[5] T. Nairn, *The Break-up of Britain* (London: Verso, 1981), 222. Nairn noted, to his credit, that Northern Ireland was becoming less peculiar.

[6] The Report of the Alliance Commission on Northern Ireland, cited in Whyte, *Interpreting Northern Ireland*, 199.

[7] A. Guelke, *Northern Ireland: The International Perspective* (Dublin: Gill and Macmillan, 1988); A. Lijphart, 'Review Article: The Northern Ireland Problem: Cases, Theories, and Solutions', *British Journal of Political Science*, 5 (1975), 83–106; I. Lustick, *State-Building Failure in British Ireland and French Algeria* (Berkeley: Institute of International Studies, 1985); R. Rose, *Governing Without Consensus: An Irish Perspective* (London: Faber and Faber, 1971); F. Wright, *Northern Ireland: A Comparative Analysis* (Dublin: Gill and Macmillan, 1987).

British and American governments, they have influenced public policy outputs. When outsiders accept the validity of a parallel, it has pushed them to adopt similar approaches towards both cases. These exogenous dimensions to the Northern Ireland conflict are missed not just by the authors cited at the beginning of this chapter, but by all who subscribe to what John Whyte once characterized as the dominant 'internal' or endogenous interpretation of the conflict.[8]

The second section discusses and categorizes the most prominent academic approaches over this same period. It serves to underline that the Northern Ireland conflict is not sui generis but that there are many dimensions along which it can be compared to other societies and other conflicts.

PARTISANS AND PARALLELS

The use of parallels by ethnic partisans is widespread.[9] Particular parallels are selected because they are considered appropriate: the partisans

---

[8] J. Whyte, *Interpreting Northern Ireland* (Oxford: Oxford University Press, 1990), 194–205.

[9] Israelis, particularly the Israeli right, have recently associated their struggle with Palestinians with that of America against Al-Qaeda. Some Palestinians, and Palestinian sympathizers, have compared the tactics of Israel towards Palestinians to that of colonizers, and even to Nazis. Canadian federalists compare Quebec separatists with the 'ethnic nationalists' of Eastern Europe, warning that the secession of Quebec may be followed by violence and partition or the mistreatment of minorities, as occurred in Yugoslavia and elsewhere. See M. Ignatieff, *Blood and Belonging: Journeys into the New Nationalism* (London: Viking, 1993). Quebec sovereigntists respond that they are civic nationalists and that their future would be like those parts of western Europe, like Iceland or Norway (or an independent Scotland) where sovereignty was attained peacefully and which are liberal, democratic, and prosperous. See K. Neilsen, 'Liberal nationalism and secession', in M. Moore (ed.), *National Self-Determination and Secession* (Oxford: Oxford University Press, 1998), 103–33. Also see 'Landry ridicules Dion as "despised politician"', *Globe and Mail*, 24 January 2001. In the early 1970s, Quebec nationalists described themselves as 'the White Niggers of America'. See P. Vallieres, *White Niggers of America* (Toronto: McClelland and Stewart, 1971). The comparison identified them with progressive movements for civil rights in the United States and decolonization in Africa and Asia, and it identified Canada's English majority as akin to Deep South racists and imperialists. In case the point was missed, Quebec's Anglos were labeled as 'Westmount Rhodesians', after a part of Montreal dominated by wealthy English-speakers. More recently, Canada's leading native chief, Matthew Coon Come, has compared the federal government to 'racists in the deep South'. While the US federal government had intervened to enforce a US Supreme Court decision to promote the rights of blacks, Coon Come argued that the Canadian federal government was opposing a Canadian Supreme Court decision to extend native fishing rights. 'Anger flares over native fishing', *Toronto Star*, 30 January 2001.

see the cases as essentially similar. Parallels are employed as heuristic devices, to illustrate to strangers how the conflict should be understood. They are also used for their instrumental value: as the parallel depicts the group positively and its rivals negatively, it is thought to strengthen group solidarity and win the support of outsiders.

Nationalist analogies

During the 1960s Northern Ireland's nationalists, particularly moderates, identified their plight with that of American blacks struggling for civil rights.[10] This had the advantage of associating Northern Ireland's Unionist regime with the white racist regimes of Alabama, Mississippi, and other parts of the Deep South. The parallel embarrassed Britain on the world stage and encouraged pressure from the United States for the reform of Northern Ireland. Like the US campaign, the appeal for civil rights in Northern Ireland was aimed at metropolitan citizens. The Northern Ireland Civil Rights Association (NICRA), which began to challenge the Unionist regime in 1964, was based on its American counterpart, although it was also inspired by the UK-based National Council for Civil Liberties. Catholics used the same slogans, 'One man, one vote' and 'The world is watching', and the same song, 'We shall overcome', as the Americans. More importantly, they employed the same tactics: civil disobedience and peaceful protest marches. It was thought that these tactics would have the same effect in Northern Ireland as in the United States, that is, that they would appeal to moderates in the dominant group and expose the intransigence of local chauvinists to liberal metropolitans. This was what happened.

Nationalists have been less inclined to portray their situation as similar to that of American blacks in recent years. This is because the American case, which featured a minority peacefully demanding civil rights, became less appropriate as the struggle of Northern Ireland's Catholics developed into a violent campaign for national rights. It is also because the American civil rights campaign lost its salience, partly because its core demands were conceded. However, nationalists continue to compare themselves to American blacks when it suits them. Nationalists who want to stop Orange parades through their neighbourhoods frequently refer to the Orange Order as akin to the Ku Klux Klan (KKK) and to the idea of it marching through a nationalist neighbourhood as the

---

[10] For a readable account of the ways in which Northern Ireland's Catholics and America's blacks have compared their plights, see B. Dooley, *The Fight for Civil Rights*.

equivalent to the Klan parading through a black neighbourhood in the United States.[11] Observers are reminded that Paisley, a leading defender of the Orange Order, received his doctorate from 'redneck segregationists in the Deep South of the U.S.'.[12] During congressional hearings into police reform in Northern Ireland in April 1999, at which I was a witness, a nationalist woman giving evidence claimed that Northern Ireland reminded her of Alabama in the 1950s.[13] The parallel resonated with several of the black congressmen in attendance, and they accordingly condemned the RUC. If a report in the *Guardian* is to be believed, President Clinton also accepts that the two cases are similar. He apparently rebuffed a request from Tony Blair to put pressure on Irish republicans to make concessions on police reform because he believed that bowing to Unionist demands on the RUC 'would be like leaving Alabama and Georgia under all-white cops'.[14] When loyalist thugs blocked the passage of young school children to the Holy Cross school in north Belfast in September 2001, an action that did not enhance their international reputation, Sinn Féin seized the opportunity. The incident was, in its view, a rerun of Little Rock, Arkansas, where white reactionaries had prevented the access of black children to integrated schools.[15]

By the 1980s, the favourite parallel of nationalists and republicans was between their struggle and that of the anti-apartheid movement in

[11] See 'SF says Order is like Ku Klux Klan', *Irish News*, 25 October 2000. One article in *An Phoblacht/Republican News* drew a direct parallel between the lynching of James Byrd, a black man in Jasper, Texas, and the killing of Robert Hamill, a Catholic in Portadown. The article suggested that it would be as ridiculous in the wake of this to allow an Orange Order March through Portadown as it would be to permit a KKK rally in Jasper. See 'Absurd Analogies'. *An Phoblacht/Republican News*, 9 July 1998. For more comments linking the Orange Order and the KKK, see Tim Pat Coogan, 'Unionist veto still the big rock on the road to peace', *Irish Times*, 18 January 2001. American blacks appear to accept that the Orange Order and KKK are related organizations. US Congressman Donald Payne, one of the most influential black politicians in Congress, told the *Sunday Times* recently that 'there are many parallels between the situation of Catholics in Northern Ireland and the situation the black community faced in the United States'. He confirmed that he would be present at Drumcree in July 2000 to observe the Orange Order's attempt to march through the Catholic Garvaghy road area. The *Sunday Times* suggested that Martin Luther King's daughter, Bernice, would also be there. 'King daughter may observe Drumcree', *Sunday Times*, 18 June 2000.

[12] 'Absurd Analogies'.

[13] *The Need for New and Acceptable Policing in Northern Ireland*, Hearing before the Committee on International Relations, House of Representatives, One Hundred Sixth Congress, First Session, 22 April 1999, Serial No. 106-16 (Washington, 1999), 11 and 13.

[14] 'Clinton refuses to back Blair's deal for RUC', *Guardian*, 25 May 2000. The words in quotation marks were spoken by a senior Administration official closely involved with the Northern Ireland peace talks. They reflect this official's view of the President's position.

[15] See 'When you face fascists, weasel words won't do', *Sunday Business Post*, 9 September 2001, and 'Holy Cross wasn't Little Rock', *Observer*, 9 September 2001.

South Africa.[16] Ironically, at the beginning of the century Irish republicans identified with Boers, who, like them, were engaged in a militant
campaign against British imperialism.[17] This comparison lost its appro-
priateness after the apartheid regime came to power in 1948, and after the
salient conflict in South Africa became that between whites and blacks
rather than that between Afrikaners and Britain. The comparison with
the anti-apartheid movement was pressed into service as early as the
1970s. Michael Farrell, a leader of the civil rights movement, pointed out
in an important book published in 1976 that the South African prime
minister had offered, when introducing a new Coercion Bill in the South
African parliament in 1963, to 'exchange all the legislation of that sort
for one clause of the Northern Ireland Special Powers Act'.[18] However, it
was not until the 1980s that this parallel became widespread. The
emerging violent anti-state protests in South Africa; the even more
violent response from Pretoria; the armed, even if relatively low-key,
campaign of the ANC's Umkhonto we Sizwe; and the greater profile of
the conflict against apartheid, all helped to make South Africa a more
compelling analogy for nationalists than the American civil rights
movement.

Republicans constantly refer to the similarity between their struggle
and that of the ANC, as can be seen from Belfast wall murals celebrating
ANC/IRA solidarity, and from their speeches and books.[19] When the
rival Northern Ireland parties were invited to South Africa in 1997,
Sinn Féin's newspaper delightedly reminded readers that Unionists
insisted on being kept separate from Sinn Féin at all times, 'an ironic
demand in the land that invented apartheid'.[20] It has also pointed to
Unionist sympathy for the apartheid regime and to the fact that loyalist
paramilitaries turned to it for arms.[21] The analogy has been given the
blessing, to the consternation of the British government, of Nelson Mandela

---

[16] Much of what I have to say about the analogy between South Africa and Northern
Ireland is derived from reading Adrian Guelke's excellent work on the subject. See
A. Guelke, 'The Political Impasse in South Africa and Northern Ireland: A Comparative
Perspective', *Comparative Politics*, (January 1991), 143–62; 'The Peace Process in South Africa,
Israel and Northern Ireland: a Farewell to Arms?', *Irish Studies in International Affairs*, 5
(1994), 93–106; 'The Influence of the South African Transition on the Northern Ireland Peace
Process', *South African Journal of International Affairs*, 3/2 (1996), 132–48; 'Comparatively
Peaceful: the Role of Analogy in Northern Ireland's Peace Process', unpublished manuscript, 1998.   [17] A. Guelke, 'Comparatively Peaceful', 3.
[18] M. Farrell, *Northern Ireland: The Orange State* (London: Pluto Press, 1976), 93–4.
[19] A. Guelke, 'The Political Impasse', 147.
[20] 'Sinn Féin impressed by South African experience', *An Phoblacht/Republican News*,
6 June 1997.   [21] 'Absurd Analogies'.

and other ANC leaders.[22] It is also accepted by constitutional nationalists. In a book published two years before the Good Friday Agreement was reached, the Social Democratic and Labour Party leader, John Hume, claimed that what Northern Ireland needed was a unionist version of F. W. de Klerk, the leader of the South African whites who negotiated an end to apartheid with Nelson Mandela.[23] Two years after the Agreement was signed, Hume continued to see Unionists as possessing an 'Afrikaner mindset'.[24]

Equating unionists with the defenders of apartheid is intended to suggest that it is for unionists, as defenders of the status quo, to make concessions. However, it is also meant to convey a *nationalist* interpretation of the conflict, and of the prescription that was necessary to end it. It infers that unionists, like whites, not only defend the status quo, but are also a *minority*, who should seek agreement with the nationalist *majority* in the island of Ireland. Just as South Africa's majority was denied its right to self-determination by the apartheid regime, Ireland's majority has been similarly deprived by the British state. The attempt to carve Northern Ireland out of Ireland is seen as analogous to attempts by whites to carve out a white dominated South Africa through the creation of black 'Homelands'.[25] Just as the context for the solution to South Africa's conflict was the reintegration of these territories into South Africa, so the context for a solution to the conflict in Northern Ireland is an end to the partition of Ireland (the hardline nationalist version) or a process which leads to this (the moderate and currently dominant version).

Towards the end of the 1960s and early 1970s, some radical republican groups drew parallels between Northern Ireland and Vietnam, and this had echoes on the British left. It was never a dominant comparison, however, perhaps because there was concern that its use would alienate

---

[22] 'Mandela's IRA remarks criticised', *Irish Times*, 21 October 1992. 'South African peace an inspiration to Irish movement, says President', *Irish Times*, 6 January 1998.

[23] John Hume, *A New Ireland: Politics, Peace and Reconciliation* (Boulder, CO: Roberts Rinehart, 1996), 117.

[24] 'Hume likens unionists to Afrikaners', *Irish Times*, 19 June 2000. According to Ruth Dudley-Edwards, a pro-unionist journalist, writing in the *Sunday Independent* on 25 June 2000, Hume was misquoted.

[25] In the same paragraph in Hume's book where he refers to the need for a Unionist de Klerk, he puts forward the conventional nationalist position that partition is the root of Northern Ireland's problems: 'There are parallels between the South African situation and our own. If the solution to the problem in South Africa had been to draw a line on the map, create a small white state, with two whites to every black person, and to make the rest of South Africa independent would there ever have been the possibility of peace? Would not the whites have been forced to discriminate totally against the black minority in order to ensure that it never became a majority? This is precisely what happened in Ireland, and we are still living with the consequences'. *A New Ireland*, 117.

Irish-American support. Republicans have also compared Ireland and Israel/Palestine. In the first half of the century, republicans were sympathetic to Zionists, who, like them, were being blocked from self-determination by British authorities. However, after Israel conquered the West Bank and Gaza Strip in 1967, and particularly after the outbreak in 1987 of the *intifada*, the Palestinian uprising against Israeli control, nationalists began to draw parallels between themselves and Palestinians.[26] This comparison, however, has not been as popular as that with black South Africans.[27] There are two obvious reasons: the PLO's greater proclivity for using indiscriminate terror made them a less attractive parallel; and Israeli Jews have been considered less of a pariah people than South African whites, at least in a West that continues to harbour guilt about the Holocaust. Israeli Jews may indeed be a pariah people in certain Arab societies, but Irish republicans are not primarily interested in influencing them.

More generally, Northern Ireland has been seen by its nationalist population, and in particular by republicans, as a colony, like those in pre-1960s Africa and Asia. This has helped to underline the republican position that Ireland, unlike Scotland and Wales, had never been a candidate for integration into the British nation. It has further suggested that the conflict is unfinished business left over from the imperial era, and that the appropriate prescription is a British withdrawal. Labeling Ireland as a colony entitled to national self-determination has the additional advantage of calling international law in aid. Colonies are entitled in international law to the right of self-determination, but integral parts of states are not. Designating Northern Ireland as a British colony is also consistent with the traditional nationalist argument that the conflict is externally imposed, and masks over internal divisions between unionists and nationalists.

A twist on the colonial argument is that Unionists are colonizers with their own independent interests, rather than the dupes of metropolitan imperialists. In this view, it is Unionists and not the British who are the main obstacle to a resolution of the conflict. The reason why Britain remains in Ireland has less to do with metropolitan interests than with the difficulty of cutting adrift its 'colons'. This position appears close to that of the moderate nationalist leader, John Hume. He has not only

---

[26] See 'The Death of a Peace Process', *An Phoblacht/Republican News*, 21 August 1997. The article gives a pro-Palestinian account of the the breakdown of the Middle East Process that followed the election of Benyamin Netanyahu as Israeli prime minister.

[27] A. Guelke, 'The Influence of the South African Transition', 140.

compared unionists with Afrikaners, but told republicans that they must negotiate with unionists and not simply the British government. The perspective is, arguably, making inroads among republicans.

Regarding the unionists as colons also informs the view, however, that they are incapable of accepting equality for nationalists (natives).[28] One nationalist journalist, pointing to the recent withdrawal of unionists from Northern Ireland's executive in spite of the many concessions they had won in the Agreement, compared them to the French in Algeria and the British in southern Africa.[29] This view of unionists as utterly intransigent presumably explains why some of those who regard them as colons think they should be 'repatriated'.

The international community largely accepts the colonial analogy, which helps explain why nationalists and republicans have received more support from outsiders than have unionists.[30] Many Americans, Europeans, and people from developing countries regard Northern Ireland as a colony of Britain. Even more damaging for the unionist cause, there is considerable evidence that people in Britain accept the colonial analogy. The public in Britain do not consider Northern Ireland an integral part of the United Kingdom. London has exclusion clauses in the Prevention of Terrorism Act that allow people from Northern Ireland to be denied entry to Britain. The main British political parties have not contested elections in Northern Ireland. Regular comments by British political elites suggest that many of them think of Northern Ireland in a colonial context. Reginald Maudling, when commenting on the failure of Stormont, said that it showed the Westminster constitution was not

---

[28] M. MacDonald, *Children of Wrath: Political Violence in Northern Ireland* (Oxford: Polity Press, 1986).

[29] Tom McGurk has this to say about rejectionist Unionists within the Ulster Unionist Party: 'Exactly like the French in Algeria and indeed the British in southern Africa, yet again we see a colonial minority bypassed by a new economic and political age incapable of seeing its plight in anything other than traditionally imperial and iconoclastic terms. To them "Ulster" is not the most devastated economic region of a second division European economy...but some imagined biblical lotus land where the Fenians are in their box and the children's swings are locked up in the park'. 'Time to bypass unionism', *Sunday Business Post*, 26 March 2000. Even Mary Holland, a leading journalist who is more sympathetic to Unionists than McGurk, has compared them to whites in Ian Smith's Rhodesia. See 'Zimbabwe has lessons for parties in the North', *Irish Times*, 27 April 2000. The *Independent's* editorialists, while mainly pointing to the differences between Northern Ireland and South Africa, nonetheless noted that 'Ulster's plantation Protestants and the Boer settlers of southern Africa do have some things in common, and not just a desire on both their parts to live in Orange Free States'. See 'Leader—ANC's lesson for Sinn Féin', *Independent*, 30 April 1998.

[30] A. Guelke, *Northern Ireland*.

'easily exportable'. In 1969, Jim Callaghan, the British home secretary who introduced troops into Northern Ireland, compared it with Cyprus, suggesting that it was much easier to get involved in these conflicts than to get out of them. In the mid-1990s, Home Secretary Douglas Hurd sounded a similar note to European Union foreign ministers: they should avoid military intervention in Bosnia lest they end up with a protracted commitment like the British government's in Northern Ireland.[31] More generally, British politicians have acted as if Northern Ireland was a type of trusteeship in which they were holding the ring between rival bands of squabbling natives. London's decision, in the Joint Declaration for Peace in 1993, and in the Good Friday Agreement of 1998, to grant the right of self-determination to the people of Ireland (North and South) and to allow a united Ireland as soon as a majority in Northern Ireland assents, is further evidence that the British government sees Northern Ireland as a colony. States have granted such rights to colonies, but seldom, if ever, to integral parts of their territory.[32] In turn, Britain's preparedness to make these concessions has focused nationalist minds on the autonomy of Unionists, on the view that they are colons.

Sinn Féin supporters argue that they are 'republicans', that is, that they are 'civic' nationalists committed to an inclusive vision of the nation in which Protestants and Catholics are treated equally.[33] This argument treats Irish nationalism, at least implicitly, as similar to French or American nationalism, both of which are predominantly civic in character. Unionists, by contrast, are identified as ethnic chauvinists, or as locals would put it, 'sectarian' bigots.[34] The message is that they are more

---

[31] The comments from Maudling, Callaghan, and Hurd are cited in J. McGarry and B. O'Leary, *Explaining Northern Ireland: Broken Images* (Oxford: Blackwell, 1985), 312–13.

[32] The constitutions of various communist states, including that of the USSR, included the right to secede. However, these were 'sham' rights and were not meant to be taken seriously by national minorities. The Canadian constitution now includes provision for a province of Canada to secede. The Canadian federal government is required to negotiate with the government of Quebec, or any province, that wins a 'clear majority' in a referendum that has a 'clear question' on secession. If the two parties negotiate in good faith, and the negotiations fail, the province is entitled to seek international recognition as an independent state. An important aspect of Canada's provision for secession is that it is judge-made, that is, it was inserted into the constitution by the courts, not politicians. This is an ironic example of Canadian judges invoking American-style judicial activism to reach a very un-American decision.

[33] 'Republican' is preferred to 'nationalist', as the latter is an ambiguous term that is applied to supporters of both ethnic and civic nationalism. The use of violence by the Irish *Republican* Army, however, has tainted the term.

[34] Nationalists often refer to bigoted Protestants as '*black*' and the Protestant-dominated RUC as '*black* bastards' a term that is probably derived from the 'Royal Black Preceptory', the elite of the Loyal Orders. Describing a neighbourhood as 'Black', therefore, is akin to

like militant Serbs than Americans. This civic/ethnic distinction pervades the other analogies favoured by nationalists. It may be another reason why republicans prefer identification with the ANC, a civic nationalist movement, over the PLO, which is more clearly ethnic nationalist. It is consistent with the colonial analogy, as colonial movements were generally multi-ethnic and inclusive national liberation movements. It is implicit in the common description of Unionists as analogous to South African Boers/whites, the KKK, or European fascist organizations. In each of these cases, the consistent nationalist message is that they are on the right side of enlightenment values while unionists cling to old prejudices.

Unionist analogies

A key theme running through nationalist comparisons is the depiction of Northern Ireland as a colony and of British rule as illegitimate. Unionists reject such arguments. Before political correctness became fashionable, Brian Faulkner famously explained that Northern Ireland was not a 'coconut colony'.[35] Unionists have consistently rejected the idea that Ireland was a colony before 1921. It was, rather, an integral part of the United Kingdom governed by the same legislative procedures as the rest of the state. What happened in 1921 was not decolonization but secession from the United Kingdom by ethnocentric nationalists. One academic who is sympathetic to unionism, Hugh Roberts, has devoted a short book to rejecting the argument that Northern Ireland is similar to the French colony of Algeria and that the appropriate prescription is an end to metropolitan rule.[36]

However, since 1972, and especially after 1985, many Unionists have come to see Northern Ireland as an 'internal colony' whose inhabitants have been treated as second-class citizens.[37] They are referring here to the British government's use of special 'Order in Council' procedures to limit debate on legislation pertaining to Northern Ireland and to its decision in 1985 to allow a 'foreign' government, the Irish Republic, a say over the affairs of Northern Ireland. Unionists have also criticized the major British parties, those with the only chance of winning office, for

describing it as very 'loyalist', or, to confuse matters even more, as very 'orange'. One imagines that nationalist politicians must have considerable difficulty explaining this to their allies in the US civil rights movement and South African anti-apartheid campaign.

[35] B. Faulkner, *Memoirs of a Statesman* (London: Weidenfeld and Nicolson, 1978), 157.

[36] H. Roberts, *Northern Ireland and the Algerian Analogy: A Suitable Case for Gaullism?* (Belfast: Athol Books, 1986).   [37] Ibid.

refusing to organize in Northern Ireland.[38] The use of the term 'internal colony' is deliberate, because the solution for this condition is integration, whereas 'decolonization' is the remedy for a colony.

While nationalists identify with the internationally recognized right of colonies to self-determination, unionists rest their case on an even older international principle: the right of states to sovereignty and territorial integrity. The conflict, from this perspective, is a result of irredentism and external aggression from the Irish Republic, and parallels are chosen to make this point. During the Gulf Crisis in the early 1990s former Ulster Unionist Party (UUP) leader James Molyneaux compared Northern Ireland with Kuwait, casting the former Irish prime minister Charles Haughey in the role of Saddam Hussein. His colleague Chris McGimpsey likened Northern Ireland with the Sudetenland, with Irish nationalists as Nazi aggressors and the Unionists as doughty liberal Czechs. McGimpsey claimed that 'the South's demand for the destruction of Northern Ireland—Eire's claim to *Lebensraum*—is equivalent to Hitler's claim over Czechoslovakia'.[39]

Antony Alcock, a member of the UUP, provides another version of this argument.[40] He explains that unionists traditionally refused to accommodate nationalists only because the latter rejected the territorial integrity of the United Kingdom and because the Irish Republic, in Articles 2 and 3 of its Constitution, expressed an irredentist claim to Northern Ireland. He draws on a number of cases from continental Europe to show that Unionist behaviour is not deviant. Alcock claims that the accommodation of the Swedish minority in the Aland islands and the Austrian minority in South Tyrol was greatly facilitated when Sweden and Austria dropped their claims to these respective areas. In Cyprus, Slovakia, and other parts of eastern Europe, on the other hand, continuing uncertainty over territorial integrity has prevented majority–minority settlements.

---

[38] See H. Roberts, 'Sound Stupidity: The British Party System and the Northern Ireland Question', in J. McGarry and B. O'Leary (eds.), *The Future of Northern Ireland* (Oxford: Clarendon Press, 1990), 100–36. See also Gary Kent, 'Left, Right, Centre', *Fortnight*, June 2000.

[39] McGarry and O'Leary, *Explaining Northern Ireland*, 98. McGimpsey was referring to Articles 2 and 3 of the Irish constitution. *Irish Times*, 29–30 October, 1990. An Irish nationalist could respond that both cases—the Sudetenland and Northern Ireland—are similar in that both flout the norm of self-determination. Large numbers of Irish and Germans were left on the wrong side of new borders because they were the weaker parties in peace agreements.

[40] A. Alcock, 'From Conflict to Agreement in Northern Ireland: Lessons from Europe', in J. McGarry (ed.), *Northern Ireland and the Divided World: Post-Agreement Northern Ireland in Comparative Perspective* (Oxford: Oxford University Press, 2001), 159–80.

Alcock's account helps to explain, from a pro-Agreement unionist perspective, why unionists signed the Good Friday Agreement. It was because the Republic agreed to remove its constitutional claim to sovereignty over a united Ireland; and because nationalists accepted that Northern Ireland required the consent of a majority within Northern Ireland. Alcock also offers an explanation of why many unionists are ambivalent about the Agreement or opposed to it. This is because Irish irredentism remains a potent political force. It is also because the Irish government, while it no longer has the right to be consulted in areas of jurisdiction that have been devolved to the Northern Ireland Assembly, continues, under the Agreement, to be able to 'put forward views and proposals' on 'non-devolved Northern Ireland matters'.[41]

Their concern with the territorial integrity of states has led Unionists to be skeptical of 'internationalising' conflicts. Their opposition to international intervention led some of them to denounce the North Atlantic Treaty Organization (NATO) intervention in Kosovo (or, as they would have it, Yugoslavia) in 1999. During the parliamentary debate on NATO's bombing campaign, the UUP's deputy leader, John Taylor, stated that he condemned it 'without hesitation'. In a defence of Yugoslavia's territorial integrity, he argued that it was as wrong to recognize Kosovo as it had been to recognize Croatia, Bosnia, and the other states of the former Yugoslavia.[42] A member of the Democratic Unionist Party, Ian Paisley Jr., complained that the Kosovo Liberation Army, like the IRA, had got its way 'by internationalising the crisis in the Balkans, and just like their Irish counterpart in the IRA, they are looking for a way of seizing power in this region of the Balkans' in the name of a 'mystical-romantic nationalism'.[43] While the younger Paisley relied on secular arguments, other Protestants did not. According to a 'Professor' Arthur Noble, writing on the elder Paisley's website, internationalization must be resisted because it is orchestrated by the

---

[41] Unionists also remain concerned, as is well-known, about issues relating to policing reform, prisoner release, and the decommissioning of paramilitary weapons.

[42] 'If the recognition of Croatia, Bosnia and the other states of the former Yugoslavia was wrong—if we were bounced into it—why is that now the basis on which we foresee a settlement being made? Recognition was wrong then and it is still wrong today'. Cited in D. Conversi, 'Moral Relativisim and Equidistance—British Attitudes to the War in the Former Yugoslavia', in T. Cushman and S. Metrović (eds.), *This Time We Knew: Western Responses to Genocide in Bosnia* (New York: New York University Press, 1999), 257. I am grateful to Daniele Conversi for drawing this to my attention.

[43] I. Paisley Jr., 'Kosovo and Ulster—The alarming parallel', *Belfast Telegraph*, 28 April 1999.

Vatican. What links the bombing of Serbia and the Good Friday Agreement in Northern Ireland, in this view, was that both were directed by Rome. The Vatican, apparently, is planning a papal 'super-state' in Europe, and has ordered its vassals in Washington and London to subdue the Serbs and Ulster's Protestants, the two groups who 'refused to bow the knee' to Rome.[44]

Given the support among unionists for an integrated United Kingdom, it is hardly surprising that their favourite parallel is with Scotland and Wales. Integrationist Unionists have long argued that Northern Ireland should be treated in the same way as these other parts of the United Kingdom. They have criticized the British government's practice of passing legislation for Northern Ireland in ways that are different from those used for Scottish and Welsh legislation, and the tendency of the major British parties to organize in Scotland and Wales, but not in Northern Ireland. Northern Ireland's distinctiveness, including the fact that it has a large Irish nationalist population, can be managed, it is claimed, within the United Kingdom, which also has sizeable Scottish and Welsh nationalist populations. As Britain would not allow a foreign government a say in Scottish or Welsh policy, unionists argue that it should not allow a 'foreign' government a say over Northern Ireland policy. Prior to the Labour government's decision in 1997 to devolve power to a Scottish parliament and a Welsh assembly, Unionist integrationists used the fact that Scotland and Wales had no such institutions to argue against devolution for Northern Ireland. Since devolution, anti-Agreement Unionists have expressed a preference for the Welsh over the Scottish model, as the powers Wales received were relatively insubstantial and, therefore, more compatible with integrationism.

Some unionists go beyond the Scotland and Wales analogy to compare Northern Ireland with parts of England. Margaret Thatcher once famously asserted that Northern Ireland is 'as British as Finchley', her suburban London constituency, although her autobiography suggests, her views on Northern Ireland were more traditionally British than this statement suggests. A Marxist integrationist clique, the British and Irish Communist Organization, once supported its case for integration by arguing that 'parts of Ulster' were physically similar to parts of England and could 'be placed in Worcestershire without arousing comment'.[45]

[44] A. Noble, 'Popery, NATO and the Yugoslav War: Our analysis vindicated!', located at http://www.ianpaisley.org/article.asp?ArtKey=nato

[45] British and Irish Communist Organization, *Against Ulster Nationalism* (Belfast: Athol Books, 1977).

Just as nationalists occasionally deviate from the rule of comparing their conflict with national liberation struggles, as when they identify with American blacks, Unionists also stray from a consistent defense of the territorial integrity of states. Rather than defending the territorial integrity of Cyprus and opposing outside interference in Cypriot affairs, two leading unionist politicians, John Taylor and Ken Maginnis, support the partition of Cyprus by Turkish forces and are sympathetic to the claims of Turkish Cypriots in the northern part of the island. Steven King, an adviser to the UUP leader, David Trimble, has argued the merits of partition not only in Ireland and Cyprus, but also in India and the former Yugoslavia. King claims that partition can maintain peace between warring enemies and that 'people who cannot hang together are better hanging apart'. His solution to the recent Kosovo conflict is the creation of a Greater Serbia and a Greater Albania, and an end to the illusion that one can have multi-ethnic states in this region.[46] This support for partition represents a divergence from the traditional unionist position that it was Irish nationalists who were partitionists, not unionists. The support for homogeneous states is also inconsistent with civic unionist support for the United Kingdom as a multicultural and multinational state.

Unionists have been less adroit, or less concerned, than republicans about selecting politically correct analogies. In the 1960s, in particular, they expressed sympathy with the white regime in Rhodesia, which they viewed as analogously under siege from a larger group and without friends. Ulster loyalists made contact with the South African apartheid regime during the 1980s, and currently have links with fascists in Great Britain.[47] As we have just seen, some unionists are happy to associate themselves with Milošević's Serbia. However, mainstream Unionists have become increasingly disenchanted with such comparisons, possibly because of the propaganda pitfalls associated with them. Since the Anglo-Irish Agreement of 1985 unionist politicians and intellectuals have increasingly presented their position in modern inclusive language.[48] They claim that unionists want a modern and tolerant multi-ethnic state capable of accommodating all its citizens, including Irish Catholics and nationalists. It is Irish nationalists who are said to seek a

---

[46] Steven King, 'Partition back in vogue', *Belfast Telegraph*, 13 May 1999.

[47] A. Guelke, 'The Influence of the South African Transition', 143–4; 'English fascists to join loyalists at Drumcree', *Observer*, 2 July 2000.

[48] See John McGarry 'Northern Ireland, Civic Nationalism, and the Good Friday Agreement', in J. McGarry (ed.) *Northern Ireland and the Divided World: Post-Agreement Northern Ireland in Comparative Perspective* (Oxford: Oxford University Press, 2001), 109–36.

homogeneous nation-state on the eastern European model.[49] To the nationalist accusation that they are like the KKK, the Loyal Orders have responded by framing their demand to march through nationalist areas in the liberal language of rights of assembly. One of these Orders, the Apprentice Boys, claims it wants the 'right' to march while nationalists want to impose 'apartheid' on Northern Ireland by keeping Orangemen and nationalists separate.[50] Another approach has been to argue that the Orange Order is a cultural organization, engaged in 'cultural preservation'.[51] Those who oppose the Orange Order's marches through nationalist neighbourhoods are thus, in Ruth Dudley-Edwards' view, guilty of 'cultural genocide'.[52] Launching his bid for the UUP leadership in March 2000, Unionist right-winger Martin Smyth suggested that it was Sinn Féin which was fascist, and claimed that the European Union was being hypocritical in opposing the inclusion of Joerg Haider's Freedom Party in the Austrian government while permitting Sinn Féin's participation in Northern Ireland's government.[53] One journalist, who is sympathetic to Unionism, pointed to Irish nationalist support for the Palestinians cause to argue that nationalists have been traditionally anti-Semitic.[54] When told by a reporter that John Hume had called for a Unionist de Klerk, David Trimble responded that the analogy was incorrect: it was a *nationalist* de Klerk that was necessary. Trimble was making the point that if one took Northern Ireland, or the United Kingdom, as one's point of reference, it was the nationalists who were in a minority, but his response also had the advantage of associating nationalists with an erstwhile pariah people.

---

[49] See Eoghan Harris, 'The tragedy of John Hume: a tribal leader, not a statesman', *Sunday Times*, 2 January 2000.

[50] 'Marching Orders: Ulster "apartheid" criticised', *Guardian*, 25 April 2000. See also Gary McMichael, 'Drumcree is all about rights', *Ireland on Sunday*, 9 July 2000.

[51] George Patton, executive officer of the Grand Lodge of Ireland, has lamented that 'in every other part of the world people who try to preserve their culture are lauded for it. But what happens when the culture is Orange? It is derided, the institution is demonised', *Irish Times*, 5 June 2000.

[52] 'Prejudice, ignorance barrier for NI Protestants', *Irish Times*, 29 June 1999.

[53] 'Smyth urges support ensure electoral gains', *Irish Times*, 25 March 2000. It is a common position among Unionists and their sympathizers that republicans are 'fascists'. Take this recent statement from Ruth Dudley-Edwards: 'I've hated the fascist strain in Irish republicanism since my Dublin childhood. My paternal grandmother lived and breathed hatred of Britain and worship of its enemies: until her death in 1956 she had a photograph of Hitler at the end of her bed. She even wrote 'Sinn Féin' on the ballot-paper if it had no candidate standing', 'Trimble on the Wire', *Belfast Telegraph*, 19 May 2000.

[54] Henry McDonald, 'The Beast is Back: The Bombing of Children in Israel sees the Return of Latent Anti-Semitism', *Observer*, 15 December 2002.

Unionists have sought in the past to depict republicans as 'terrorists'. They have also claimed that the IRA is part of an 'international terror network', drawing on evidence that it received funding from rogue regimes like Libya, and on the express sympathies of republicans for the PLO and the ANC. Parallels between the IRA and international terrorist organizations increased in 2001 with the news that three republicans had been charged with collaborating with anti-US FARC rebels in Colombia, and after the subsequent attacks by Al-Qaeda on New York on 11 September.

Analogies with international terrorists are now the dominant type of analogy used by Unionist politicians. After 11 September, David Trimble called for the British government to end its 'spurious distinction between domestic and international terrorism'.[55] The prominent pro-Unionist commentator, Conor Cruise O'Brien, uses his weekly column in the *Irish Independent* to focus on the association between the IRA and anti-American terrorists. Ruth Dudley Edwards, after condemning republicans for drawing parallels between themselves and oppressed peoples for political advantage, pointed in the same article to the following similarities between the IRA and Al-Qaeda: both targeted armed forces; both killed civilians; both attacked the centres of democratic states; both attacked important commercial targets; both were involved in global terrorism; and both supported suicide as a political weapon.[56] Robert McCartney used the opportunity to remind readers that Sinn Féin held seats in the Stormont executive, something he saw as analogous to 'Osama Bin Laden occupying a cabinet seat in Downing Street'.[57]

Such parallels are aimed at international opinion and the British government. However, they are directed in particular at the American people and government. They reflect Unionist awareness of the importance of the United States in influencing British policy towards Northern Ireland, especially since the early 1990s, and their concern that Americans have been traditionally pro-nationalist. They are meant to reinforce the position of both anti- and pro-Agreement Unionists that

[55] 'Trimble call over terrorism', *BBC News*, 4 October 2001. Also see R. McCartney and J. Skelly, 'What now for Ulster, Mr. Blair?', *Belfast Telegraph*, 20 September 2001. According to a report in the *Guardian* newspaper in February 2003, Trimble was going to tell Blair at an upcoming meeting that it was ironic he was going to wage war on Iraq when 'the Taliban in the shape of the IRA are in his own backyard', *Guardian*, 13 February 2003.

[56] 'The only difference, Gerry, is one of scale', *Sunday Independent*, 30 September 2001. Also see 'McGimpsey on US terror view', *UTV News*, 15 December 2002, http://www.u.tv/newsroom/indepth.asp?1d=26775&pt=n

[57] McCartney and J. Skelly, 'What now for Ulster, Mr. Blair?'

republicans cannot be trusted and should not be accommodated until there is convincing evidence that the IRA has decommissioned its weapons or disbanded. These Unionist arguments, which are heavily endorsed by Britain's right-wing press, resemble similar parallels drawn by the governments of Israel, India, and the Phillipines with respect to Palestinian, Kashmiri, and Mindanao insurgency movements, respectively: all are said to be part of an international terrorist network with links to Al-Qaeda.

The Bush administration shares some of these Unionist views, although it appears to have drawn the parallel independently. It has been a good deal more chilly towards republicans than its predecessor. Bush's special adviser on Northern Ireland, Richard Haass, claimed that the 11 September attacks had brought about a 'sea change' in how America viewed the IRA.[58] In an interview in the *Chicago Tribune* in December 2002, Secretary of State Colin Powell associated the IRA with Al-Qaeda and FARC, and suggested that 'these kinds of organisations are committed to destroying democracy in our hemisphere'.[59] This is a radical divergence from the traditional American view that the IRA was a parochial and anti-colonial group committed to forcing the British out of Ireland.

Do parallels matter?

One should be very careful about exaggerating the effect of parallels. Developments in divided societies, whether of a violent or peaceful kind, are usually influenced by a myriad of exogenous and endogenous factors. However, there is evidence that a comparison, once accepted, can have an independent effect on subsequent developments. In the 1960s, the norm spread by the US civil rights movement that second-class citizenship was unacceptable helped to motivate Catholics, after decades of passivity, to challenge the Stormont regime. The event that is thought by many to have started the Troubles, the Belfast to Derry march of January 1969, was modelled consciously on the Selma–Montgomery march undertaken by the American civil rights movement in 1965. The use of tactics of civil disobedience had roughly the same effect in Northern Ireland as in the American South: it exposed the illiberalism of the local governors, split the dominant group, and provoked metropolitan intervention. If the *Guardian* report referred to above is accurate, the

---

[58] *BBC News*, http://news.bbc.co.uk/1/hi/northern_ireland/1625061.stm
[59] *Irish News*, 18 December 2002.

analogy between Northern Ireland Catholics and American blacks continues to influence US policy on Northern Ireland.

The Northern Ireland–South Africa parallel was used explicitly by Irish Americans to shape US policy towards Northern Ireland. The MacBride principles, adopted to promote regulation of US investment in Northern Ireland, were modelled on the Sullivan principles established to govern trade between the United States and apartheid South Africa. This American pressure helped to secure anti-discrimination reforms in Northern Ireland, including the Fair Employment Act of 1989. By the 1990s, the ANC's decision to suspend its armed struggle, and to a lesser extent the PLO's decision to embrace the Oslo process, made it easier for the IRA to explore peace. According to Guelke, the ANC's decision to abandon its armed struggle was one of the factors that persuaded the IRA to declare a ceasefire in 1994.[60] Others, including Padraig O'Malley, have argued that the ability of South Africans to settle their conflict exercised a positive influence on Northern Ireland nationalists (and unionists) as they negotiated the Good Friday Agreement.[61] A number of journalists attributed the IRA's commitment in May 2000 to put its arms 'beyond use' to pressure from the ANC, particularly from one of Mandela's leading lieutenants, Mac Maharaj. It was noted by anti-Agreement unionists and others that an important aspect of the IRA's statement was that one of the two international inspectors appointed to examine some of its arms dumps be the former ANC Secretary-General, Cyril Ramaphosa.[62] A reporter from the *Boston Globe* claimed, albeit without naming any sources, that 'there is little doubt that [the IRA statement] would not have been issued if not for the influence of Maharaj and Ramaphosa, and if Ramaphosa had not been chosen by the British and Irish governments as one of their arms inspectors'.[63]

Several commentators have tied the IRA's decision to begin actual decommissioning in October 2001 to the events of 11 September.[64]

---

[60] A. Guelke, 'The Influence of the South African Transition', 145. Gerry Adams has publicly acknowledged that the ANC decision to choose dialogue over war helped to inspire Sinn Féin. See 'US attacks "exploited" to disarm IRA', *Irish Examiner*, 3 October 2001.

[61] P. O'Malley, 'Northern Ireland and South Africa: Hope and History at a Crossroads', in J. McGarry (ed.), *Northern Ireland and the Divided World*, 276–308.

[62] 'You are fools to believe IRA, Robinson tells MPs', *Belfast Telegraph*, 17 May 2000.

[63] Kevin Cullen, 'Boston, South Africa figure in Irish road to peace', *Boston Globe*, 17 May 2000. See also 'ANC brokered IRA peace offer', *Observer*, 14 May 2000.

[64] See 'US terror attacks, "led to decommissioning"', *BBC News*, 28 October 2001, http:// news.bbc.co.uk/1/hi/northern_ireland/1625061.stm; 'IRA disarmament springs from Sept. 11', *Boston Herald*, 28 October 2001; 'How America held the IRA over a barrel', *Observer*, 28 October 2001.

Apparently, the IRA, already damaged by its association with FARC rebels, and now associated explicitly and implicitly with Al-Qaeda, moved to assuage American opinion by starting to destroy its weapons. Certainly, there was tremendous pressure from the American government and from prominent Irish Americans, including several who were sympathetic to Sinn Féin. The Sinn Féin leadership was put on the defensive, arguing that it, unlike Al-Qaeda, was not a 'terrorist' organization, that the attacks on America were a 'crime against humanity', and that terrorism was 'ethically indefensible'.[65] Gerry Adams even claimed that the IRA, unlike Al-Qaeda, had not targeted innocent civilians. Given the obvious importance of the United States, as a source of republican fund-raising and as an influence on the British government, it seems plausible to attribute the *timing* of the IRA's move to 11 September.[66] The IRA's prior commitment to put its arms 'beyond use' suggests, however, that there were additional reasons for decommissioning.

Unionists also appear to have been affected by their choice of self-parallels. After years in which they argued that Northern Ireland should be treated the same as Scotland and Wales, their case for integration was dealt a serious blow when the Blair government devolved power to Edinburgh and Cardiff in 1997.[67] This created space for UUP moderates to support proposals for devolution in the Good Friday Agreement. The fact that the arrangements for Scotland and Wales were asymmetrical, reflecting the particular circumstances of each case, made it easier to accept, or at least more difficult to argue against, peculiar institutions for Northern Ireland, including a power-sharing executive and a North–South Ministerial Council and all-island 'implementation bodies'.[68]

[65] See 'Adams: Terrorism ethically indefensible', *BBC News*, 29 September 2001, and 'Adams: IRA are not terrorists like US hijackers', *The Herald*, 6 November 2001.

[66] Some thought that the IRA were prepared to decommission, but wanted to delay this until just before the Irish Republic's general election, which had to be called before the summer of 2002. See 'How September 11 forced the pace', *Guardian*, 23 October 2001, and 'World's drive against terrorism focused minds', *Irish Independent*, 23 October 2001. If this view is correct, the 11 September attacks brought forward decommissioning by a number of months.

[67] One effect of this was that integrationist opponents of the Agreement, such as Robert McCartney MP, shifted their arguments against the Agreement to the fact that it allowed Sinn Féin into government before the IRA had decommissioned its weapons rather than to the fact that it provided for power-sharing devolution.

[68] Traditionally, support for decentralization has been much higher in Scotland than in Wales. As a consequence, while Scotland received a Parliament with law-making powers and the (limited) ability to raise taxes, Wales received an Assembly with power to pass only secondary legislation (administrative regulations) and no money-raising powers.

Supporters of reform sought to take advantage of these parallels, pointing out that a new oath to be sworn by police constables from 1998, and proposed changes to the prosecution system, were based on Scottish precedents.

It is not only in Northern Ireland that partisan parallels have influenced events. In the Middle East, the success of the Israeli right in depicting Palestinians as a local branch of the Al-Qaeda network has coloured American opinion, and the policies of the Bush administration. This has allowed the Israeli government and military a relatively free hand in the West Bank and Gaza. It also helps to explain why Americans are more hostile to the Palestinian cause than Europeans. The Palestinian leadership has tried to resist the parallel by publicly disassociating itself from Al-Qaeda,[69] but it has not been able, or willing, to prevent the suicide bombings that give the parallel resonance.

There is also some evidence that the Basque nationalists of ETA have been influenced by their association with the IRA. Michael Keating has argued that Basque nationalists followed the Northern Ireland peace process closely, and it was not a coincidence that ETA called a ceasefire shortly after the signing of the Good Friday Agreement.[70] However, parallels between the IRA and ETA did not prevent a subsequent breakdown of ETA's ceasefire, unless one accepts the *Telegraph*'s line that ETA had learned from the IRA that breaking a ceasefire could bring a stream of concessions from a spineless government.[71] The difficulty here is that while ETA supporters liken their conflict to that in Northern Ireland, the Spanish authorities reject this analogy. Madrid, which sees part of its territory (Gibraltar) as colonized by Britain, is happy to accept the Irish republican argument that Northern Ireland is Britain's colony. Its view of the Basque Country, however, is analogous to the Unionist view of Northern Ireland: it is not a colony, but an integral part of the state.

[69] *Toronto Star*, 16 December.

[70] M. Keating, 'Northern Ireland and the Basque Country', in J. McGarry (ed.), *Northern Ireland and the Divided World*, 181–208. This position is also taken by the *Daily Telegraph*, which has consistently pointed to links between the IRA, ETA, and other members of an international terrorist network. See 'ETA's "indefinite" ceasefire meets a wary response', *Daily Telegraph*, 18 September 1998.

[71] 'Just as the announcement of the ETA ceasefire was heavily influenced by the IRA, so the ending of its truce in December and yesterday's return to killing mirrors events in Northern Ireland. When the IRA ended its ceasefire with the Docklands bomb in February 1996, the British government rushed to make concessions in order to restore the peace', 'A "war of liberation" inspired by IRA's bloody tactics', *Daily Telegraph*, 22 January 2000.

ACADEMICS AND COMPARATIVE ANALYSIS

Comparisons are not a preserve of partisans, of course. Northern Ireland has also been a focus of study for several intellectuals who have used comparative analysis. The most prominent of these approaches are based on classical pluralist theory, consociational theory, integrationist theory, linkage theory, and settler colonial theory. My intention here is to offer a brief summary of these approaches rather than a lengthy analysis and critique.[72]

Classical pluralist theory

Classical pluralist theory dominated political science during the 1950s and 1960s.[73] Sometimes referred to as 'cross-pressures' theory, it explained instability as resulting from the absence of a balanced distribution of conflicting interests. Conflict flowed, in this view, when social divisions, whether linguistic, racial, religious, or otherwise, reinforced rather than cross-cut each other, when, for instance, memberships in different voluntary associations were cumulative rather than overlapping.[74] Given its dominance in the 1960s, it is not surprising that it shaped some of the early prominent attempts to explain the conflict in Northern Ireland. In one of the first major works on Northern Ireland, Richard Rose argued that its reinforcing pressures accounted for its surplus of republican 'rebels' and loyalist 'ultras'. It had, according to Rose, insufficient cross-pressures to generate enough allegiant or passive citizens, and it consequently lacked the consensus required for legitimate democratic government.[75]

Edmund Aunger, a French-Canadian political scientist, also employed cross-pressures theory in a comparative study of Northern Ireland and the Canadian province of New Brunswick. According to Aunger, New Brunswick was stable, despite its English–French ethnic cleavage, because the language division was cross-cut by others based on religion

---

[72] Those interested in the latter should see the discussion by McGarry and O'Leary in *Explaining Northern Ireland*, particularly chapter 8.

[73] S. M. Lipset, *Political Man* (London: Hutchinson, 1960).

[74] According to Eric Nordlinger, the cross-pressures account of political stability was 'probably the explanatory hypothesis most widely accepted among American political scientists', *Conflict Regulation in Divided Societies* (Cambridge, MA: Harvard University Press, 1972), 93.

[75] R. Rose, *Governing Without Consensus* (London: Faber and Faber, 1971).

and class. Northern Ireland was unstable, by contrast, because its various social divisions were reinforcing.[76] In a comparative study of Belfast and Glasgow which used survey evidence, Ian Budge and Cornelius O'Leary emphasized that there was much lower cross-cutting between party and religion in Belfast than between party and any social characteristic in Glasgow.[77] In their view, the fact that political parties in Belfast were subject to fewer cross-pressures than their Glasgow counterparts helped explain why Belfast politics were unstable while Glasgow's were not.

Consociational theory

Consociational theory was developed by Arend Lijphart in reaction to what was seen as a sociological bias in pluralist theory.[78] According to Lijphart, social divisions by themselves did not necessarily condemn regimes to instability. Otherwise, he argued, how could one account for stability in states like Belgium, Switzerland, Austria, or the Netherlands—none of which, in his view, possessed cross-cutting social cleavages? While Lijphart accepted that certain social and political conditions were more conducive to consociational democracy than others, he claimed that the only essential conditions were the presence of strong political elites who were willing to accommodate each other and who were capable of winning their followers support for the resulting bargain. While the design of consociational institutions could vary, they included four basic features: (i) a grand coalition, an executive inclusive of all the state's main subcultures; (ii) proportional representation for the state's subcultures in public institutions, including the legislature and bureaucracy; (iii) group autonomy, allowing subcultures to be self-governing where possible; (iv) minority vetoes, at least where vital interests were concerned.

Consociational theory was first applied to Northern Ireland by Lijphart himself in 1975, although consociational thinking was implicit in the Sunningdale Agreement of 1973. Lijphart was pessimistic about the prospects for consociational democracy, claiming it was 'unworkable'.[79]

---

[76] E. Aunger, *In Search of Political Stability: A Comparative Study of New Brunswick and Northern Ireland* (Montreal: McGill-Queen's University Press).

[77] I. Budge and C. O'Leary, *Belfast: Approach to Crisis* (London: Macmillan, 1973).

[78] A. Lijphart, 'Consociational Democracy', *World Politics*, 21 (1969), 207–25.

[79] A. Lijphart, 'Review Article: the Northern Ireland Problem', 105.

The key problem in his view was the absence of support for it among the Protestant leadership and rank and file.[80] However, he added that Northern Ireland also lacked a number of conducive conditions: rather than being divided into groups none of whom could govern by itself, Northern Ireland had a (Protestant) majority that was 'capable of exercising hegemonic power'; Protestants were normatively attracted to the Westminster majoritarian tradition and rejected continental power-sharing norms; there was no overarching national consensus.[81]

By the mid-1990s, Lijphart was more confident about the prospects for consociationalism and claimed that it was the only 'viable option' for Northern Ireland.[82] Rather than being 'unworkable', he now argued that it was wrong to conclude that power-sharing 'cannot be successful'. His new optimism was due to his observation that the British government now appeared committed to power-sharing and that none of Northern Ireland's political parties were seriously proposing 'a return to majoritarianism'.[83]

Consociational theory has also been applied to Northern Ireland by Brendan O'Leary and me.[84] While broadly supportive of Lijphart's claim that a Northern Ireland government should be constructed on consociational principles, we have been critical of some of his arguments. One problem with traditional consociational research is its tendency to treat political systems as closed entities. This has led to a focus on endogenous factors when explaining conflict, and a stress on internal institutions, modelled on the traditional 'Westphalian' state, when proposing prescriptions. This focus limits the explanatory and prescriptive power of consociational theory when applied to conflicts like Northern Ireland's, which have been influenced by exogenous as well as endogenous factors, and where satisfactory prescriptions require institutions that transcend state frontiers.

---

[80] A. Lijphart, 'Review Article: the Northern Ireland Problem', 99.   [81] Ibid.
[82] A. Lijphart, 'The Framework Document on Northern Ireland and the Theory of Power-Sharing', *Government and Opposition*, 31/3 (1996), 268.   [83] Ibid., 274.
[84] Chapters 2 and 3 above, and see J. McGarry, 'A Consociational Settlement for Northern Ireland?', *Plural Societies*, 20 (1990), 1–21; B. O'Leary, 'The 1998 British–Irish Agreement: Consociation Plus', *Scottish Affairs*, 26 (1999), 1–22; B. O'Leary, 'The Limits to Coercive Consociationalism in Northern Ireland', in R. Rhodes (ed.), *The International Library of Politics and Comparative Government: United Kingdom* (Aldershot: Ashgate, 2000), 475–502; B. O'Leary and J. McGarry, *The Politics of Antagonism: Understanding Northern Ireland*, (London: Athlone, 1996); B. O'Leary, 'Afterword: What is framed in the Framework Documents?', *Ethnic and Racial Studies*, 18 (1995), 862–72.

In our view, an important reason why unionists refused to share power with nationalists was not because they were committed normatively to the Westminster model of government but because, as British nationalists, they preferred the default of direct rule from Westminster to the risk of power-sharing with Irish nationalists. Direct rule also helped to block what Lijphart calls a 'self-denying prophecy', a decision by elites to share power because the alternative is chaos and deepening violence. London paid the costs of the conflict and the British army helped to prevent it from reaching Bosnian levels of violence. Even if unionists had embraced consociationalism, this would not have sufficed for nationalists, who also demand institutions linking Northern Ireland with the Irish Republic. Agreement was reached in 1998 on a consociational government and North–South institutions in part because London made it clear to unionists that the default to a settlement was no longer unalloyed direct rule from Westminster but, instead, deepening Anglo-Irish cooperation in the governance of Northern Ireland. Unionist flexibility was facilitated by the growth of the nationalist population, by an IRA decision to declare a ceasefire, by the Irish government's preparedness to drop formal irredentist claims in return for a settlement, and by pressure from the United States to compromise.[85]

Integrationist theory

The classical pluralist accounts described above are explanatory in nature. However, there is a branch of pluralist theory that has an important normative and prescriptive dimension. This branch can be described as integrationist, as it seeks to transform divided societies into integrated ones. Integrationists, like pluralists, attribute conflict to the salience of divisive identities, such as those based on ethnicity or race, and the absence of cross-cutting identities, such as those based on class. However, integrationists believe that cross-cutting identities can be constructed, if the correct policies are followed. Such policies include combatting the divisive appeals of self-interested ethnic elites through the mobilization of organizations in civil society that promote transcendent identities; integration in schools, workplaces, and residential neighbourhoods; an end to discrimination; and the removal of economic inequality through economic growth and/or distribution.

---

[85] For more details on this, see Chapter 8.

Integrationism was advocated in one of the earliest books on Northern Ireland politics, written in 1961,[86] and it has been a theme of a number of works since then.[87] One complication, however, is that integrationists in Northern Ireland are themselves divided: there are some who support an integrated Ireland and some who support an integrated United Kingdom.[88] Others are post-nationalists who back the process of European integration in the belief that it will contribute to cross-cutting divisions by creating new functional allegiances across state boundaries and a new European identity that both communities in Northern Ireland can embrace.[89]

Integrationists are sceptical of consociational theory and regularly criticize it.[90] Consociationalists are accused of exaggerating the depth and resilience of social divisions, and of downplaying the capacity of humans to develop new identities. From the integrationist perspective, consociational institutions often worsen matters by strengthening the position of sectional elites who are responsible for division in the first place. Because consociational institutions are thought to entrench and deepen divisions, they are seen not simply as undesirable, but also as unstable and ultimately unworkable.

This integrationist critique of consociationalism is popular among academics specializing in the Northern Ireland conflict. Several of them oppose the British government's long-standing commitment to

---

[86] D. Barritt and C. Carter, *The Northern Ireland Problem: A Study in Group Relations* (Oxford: Oxford University Press, 1961).

[87] D. Smith and G. Chambers, *Inequality in Northern Ireland* (Oxford: Oxford University Press, 1991); C. Irwin, *Education and the Development of Social Integration in Divided Societies* (Belfast: Queen's University, 1991).

[88] For an Irish nationalist account, see G. FitzGerald, *Towards a New Ireland* (London: Charles Knight, 1972). For an academic perspective that resembles that of Irish republican dissidents, see R. Taylor, 'Northern Ireland: Consociation or Social Transformation?', in J. McGarry (ed.), *Northern Ireland and the Divided World*, 36–52. For a Unionist account, see A. Aughey, *Under Siege: Ulster Unionism and the Anglo-Irish Agreement* (Belfast: Blackstaff, 1989). For an analysis that discusses the shortcomings of these rival forms of integrationism, see J. McGarry, 'Northern Ireland, Civic Nationalism, and the Good Friday Agreement', in J. McGarry (ed.), *Northern Ireland and the Divided World*, 109–36.

[89] For a post-nationalist account, see R. Kearney, *Postnationalist Ireland*. Elizabeth Meehan argued in her inaugural lecture at Queen's University in Belfast in 1992 that European integration was having the desired effect: 'a new kind of citizenship is emerging [in Europe] that is neither national or cosmopolitan but which is multiple in enabling the various identities that we all possess to be expressed, and our rights and duties exercised, through an increasingly complex configuration of common institutions, states, national and transnational interest groups and voluntary associations, local or provincial authorities, regions and alliances of regions'. Cited, approvingly, in R. Kearney, *Postnationalist Ireland*, 84.

[90] For a discussion of this critique, see A. Lijphart, *Power-Sharing in South Africa* (Berkeley: University of California, Institute of International Studies, 1985), 106–8.

consociational institutions, and criticize the central part these play in the Good Friday Agreement. Anderson and Goodman claim that the consociational model at the heart of the Agreement has 'very serious defects', overemphasizes 'the primacy and the permanency of ethnic divisions', and 'actively excludes other perhaps more fruitful social categories, other bases of political mobilisation such as gender and class which cross-cut ethnic divisions'.[91] Wilford condemns consociational theory as conveying a 'rather bleak view of humanity' and as threatening to cast divisions in 'marble'.[92] He endorses an alternative strategy of promoting 'pluralistic rather than monolithic thinking' through ending discrimination in the workplace and educational integration.[93] Dixon criticizes consociationalism as 'elitist' and 'segregationist' and recommends mass participation and social integration as a more appropriate way forward.[94] In an article that rejects consociational prescriptions for Northern Ireland and South Africa, Rupert Taylor condemns Lijphart's 'uncritical acceptance of the primacy and permanency of ethnicity', argues that divisions in the two cases were constructed by self-interested elites, and calls for 'economic growth and the removal of discrimination' as an alternative strategy for conflict-resolution in both countries.[95]

A distinct variety of integrationism has been proposed for Northern Ireland by Donald Horowitz, an international authority on ethnic conflict. He believes that integration is best achieved by elites appealing across ethnic lines, and he recommends electoral systems that make such appeals necessary for electoral success. Horowitz regards consociational

[91] J. Anderson and J. Goodman, 'Nationalisms and Transnationalism: Failures and Emancipation', in J. Anderson and J. Goodman (eds.), *Dis/Agreeing Ireland: Contexts, Obstacles, Hopes* (London: Pluto Press, 1998), 21–2.

[92] R. Wilford, 'Inverting consociationalism? Policy, pluralism and the post-modern', in B. Hadfield (ed.), *Northern Ireland: Politics and the Constitution* (Buckingham: Open University Press, 1992), 31.   [93] Ibid., 41.

[94] P. Dixon, 'The politics of antagonism: explaining McGarry and O'Leary', *Irish Political Studies*, 11 (1996), 137–8. Also see his 'Consociationalism and the Northern Ireland Peace Process: The Glass Half Full or Half Empty?', *Nationalism and Ethnic Politics*, 3/3 (Autumn 1997), 20–36.

[95] R. Taylor, 'A consociational path to peace in Northern Ireland and South Africa', in A. Guelke (ed.), *News Perspectives on the Northern Ireland Conflict* (Aldershot: Avebury, 1994), 161–74. Both Taylor and Paul Dixon like the South African constitution that was adopted after 1999, that is, after it had been stripped of a number of consociational features that were part of a transitional constitution in operation between 1994 and 1999. See P. Dixon, 'Consociationalism and the Northern Ireland Peace Process', 32–3. The problem with the current constitution, however, is that it seems to have entrenched, for the foreseeable future, a one-party system. It is difficult to see how this, which bears some comparison with the Stormont regime, would suit Northern Ireland.

arrangements as inconsistent with integration, as they reward politicians who appeal only to their own ethnic communities. He is particularly troubled by the consociational concept of grand coalition, which is present in Northern Ireland's Agreement. This provides for the inclusion of radical parties from rival blocs in government, a result which, in Horowitz's view, is inimical with integration or even stable government.[96]

To these academic critiques of consociationalism can be added partisan attacks from both nationalists and Unionists: Irish republican Kevin Rooney claims that the Agreement's consociational institutions have 'put an end to the prospects for overcoming [Ireland's] divisions and institutionalise[d] the differences between Catholics and Protestants'; the leading Unionist Robert McCartney criticizes the same institutions as 'dysfunctional', 'undemocratic', and 'impermanent'. [97] Their alternatives, of course, are diametrically opposed.

Linkage theory

One problem with much political science work on ethnic conflict is that it puts an exaggerated stress on endogenous factors. As John Whyte has pointed out, this stress is an important feature of the general academic literature on Northern Ireland.[98] There is an important body of work, however, that has been undertaken at the interface between comparative politics and international relations and that emphasizes the role of exogenous factors in the Northern Ireland conflict. This can usefully be described as 'linkage' theory because it focuses on the linkages between exogenous pressures and internal political developments in Northern Ireland.

Linkage theories are a rather mixed bag. They range from some of the worst 'scholarship' on the Northern Ireland conflict to some of the best. In the former category are works that attribute much of the conflict to funding for paramilitary groups from rogue-states and diasporas,[99] as well as partisan accounts that attribute the conflict exclusively to

---

[96] D. Horowitz, 'The Northern Ireland Agreement: Clear, Consociational and Risky', in J. McGarry (ed.), *Northern Ireland and the Divided World*, 89–108.

[97] Rooney, 'Institutionalising Division', *Fortnight*, (June 1998), 21–2; R. McCartney, 'Devolution is a sham', *Observer*, 20 February 2000. For a similar Unionist perspective, see D. Kennedy, 'Evidence is growing that agreement did not work', *Irish Times*, 16 February 2000. [98] See Whyte, *Interpreting Northern Ireland*, 194–205.

[99] See C. Sterling, *The Terror Network: The Secret War of International Terrorism* (New York: Holt, Rinehart, and Winston, 1981).

'perfidious Albion' or to the Irish Republic's irredentism.[100] In the latter category are a number of books that, while acknowledging the importance of internal factors, take the position that the conflict cannot be explained without reference to the actions of both the British and Irish states. An influential short book by the lawyers Tom Hadden and Kevin Boyle, published in 1985, falls into this category.[101] So does a more substantive volume by Joseph Ruane and Jennifer Todd, published in 1996.[102] In our various works on Northern Ireland, Brendan O'Leary and I have also emphasized that the conflict cannot be explained adequately without recourse to British and Irish nation- and state-building failures.

Adrian Guelke looks beyond the role of Britain and Ireland. In a book published in 1988, he argued that the violence and constitutional stalemate in Northern Ireland was crucially shaped by the international norm of self-determination.[103] In his view, the international perspective that Northern Ireland is illegitimate, a legacy of colonialism, is an important factor underlying unionist insecurity and republican aggressiveness. Guelke has also done important work on linkages between South Africa's conflict and Northern Ireland's, and has claimed that events in the former influenced developments in the latter.

The most ambitious example of linkage theory is Frank Wright's *Northern Ireland: A Comparative Analysis*.[104] For Wright, Northern Ireland is best understood as an 'ethnic frontier', a site of contested sovereignty between the British and Irish national communities. In an ethnic frontier, conflict is crucially affected by the actions of external powers beyond the frontier. If one external power intervenes to side with an internal protagonist then the other will also seek external help, compelling a dramatic escalation in conflict. Wright holds an unstable regional environment responsible for the ferocity of past and present conflicts in the Balkans, Cyprus, and Lebanon.[105] The relative stability of Belgium and Switzerland, by contrast, flows from a tradition of non-interference and restraint by larger neighbours who have avoided intervention on behalf of their co-ethnics. When ethnic communities in a frontier zone are locked in conflict, the best that can be hoped for, according to Wright, is that

---

[100] See J. McGarry and B. O'Leary, *Explaining Northern Ireland*, Part I, chapters 1–4.

[101] K. Boyle and T. Hadden, *Ireland: a Positive Proposal* (London: Harmondsworth, 1985).

[102] J. Ruane and J. Todd, *The Dynamics of Conflict in Northern Ireland: Power, Conflict and Emancipation* (Cambridge: Cambridge University Press, 1996).

[103] A. Guelke, *Northern Ireland*.

[104] F. Wright, *Northern Ireland: A Comparative Analysis*.

[105] Ibid., 276–7, 282–3, and 285.

interested external powers will cooperate with each other to contain the conflict rather than siding only with their co-nationals. Northern Ireland's most benign feature, in Wright's view, is that the British and Irish governments, particularly since 1985, enjoy amicable and cooperative relations. His prescription is that this cooperation should be consolidated into full-blown British and Irish joint authority over the region.

The British and Irish states remain unquestionably the most influential exogenous actors in the Northern Ireland conflict. In recent years, however, academics have also pointed to the impact of Europe and the United States. In a number of accounts, which overlap with the integrationist accounts discussed above, European integration is seen as promoting multiple or post-national identities in place of the old nationalist–unionist polarities.[106] Intellectuals who are sympathetic to Irish nationalism put forward a variant of this: European integration will erode the identity of unionists in a way that will promote a united Ireland.[107] One unionist writer has argued that European integration is

---

[106] See note 89. Kevin Boyle has expressed a belief that the 'Europeanization of both islands...will force a reassessment of all relationships on these islands and in particular of the two principal influences on the present tragedy of Northern Ireland, "Britishness" as an historical integrating force and the reactive tradition of Irish separatism'. K. Boyle, 'Northern Ireland: Allegiances and Identities', in B. Crick (ed.), *National Identities: The Constitution of the United Kingdom* (Oxford: Basil Blackwell, 1991), 69, 78. Boyle and his colleague, Tom Hadden, have since tempered their Euro-enthusiasm. See K. Boyle and T. Hadden, *Northern Ireland: The Choice* (Harmondsworth: Penguin, 1994); Richard Kearney and Robin Wilson argue that European integration will allow Northern Ireland's citizens to evolve beyond nationalism and unionism and irreconcilable loyalties to different nation-states. They envisage Europe evolving into a federation of regions, including Northern Ireland, which will foster allegiances 'both more universal and more particular than the traditional nation-states', in 'Northern Ireland's future as a European Region', reprinted in R. Kearney, *Postnationalist Ireland*, 79. Cathal McCall claims that European integration has the potential to erode unionism and nationalism in Northern Ireland, particularly in the absence of sectarian violence, in 'Postmodern Europe and the resources of communal identities in Northern Ireland', *European Journal of Political Research*, 33 (1998), 406. Rupert Taylor writes that 'increasing European integration has led to the erosion of absolutist conceptions of national sovereignty [and there] has been an erosion of ethno-nationalism on both sides, a fading of Orange and Green, in favour of a commonality around the need for genuine structures of democracy and justice', in 'Northern Ireland: Consociation or Social Transformation?', 45. Also see J. Goodman, *Nationalism and Transnationalism: The National Conflict in Ireland and European Union Integration* (Aldershot: Avebury, 1997).

[107] G. FitzGerald, *Towards a New Ireland*, 111–12. A Cambridge economist, Bob Rowthorn, argues that closer economic cooperation between Northern Ireland and the Irish Republic in the context of the European Union will lead Unionists to shift their loyalties from London to Dublin. B. Rowthorn, 'Foreword', in R. Munck, *The Irish Economy* (London: Pluto Press, 1993). Sammy Smooha claims that the option of a united Ireland 'will be less and less resisted' by Unionists 'as Ireland, a member of the prospering European Union, [comes to]

having a negative impact: it is facilitating Anglo-Irish cooperation over Northern Ireland and, by eroding traditional notions of state sovereignty, weakening the union.[108] Other, more impartial observers agree that European integration is diluting state sovereignty, but see this as a useful development that creates the space for imaginative institutional arrangements suited to the needs of nationally divided societies like Northern Ireland.[109]

A number of scholars have focused on the influence of the United States, which is generally thought to have escalated after the Clinton administration assumed power in 1992.[110] Even before this, the US government was credited with persuading London to embrace a policy of power-sharing devolution in 1979 and to sign the Anglo-Irish Agreement in 1985.[111] Irish-American pressure groups are said to have played an important role in persuading London to implement far-reaching employment legislation in 1989.[112] Clinton's administration, it has been argued, played a crucial

enjoy economic growth, expand its welfare services and secularizes'. See S. Smooha, 'The Tenability of Partition as a Mode of Conflict Regulation: Comparing Ireland with Palestine-Land of Israel', in J. McGarry (ed.), *Northern Ireland and the Divided World*, 309–36.

[108] Denis Kennedy, a unionist who is hostile to Dublin's growing role in Northern Ireland, argues that Anglo-Irish cooperation would have been impossible outside of the EU: 'the experience of working together in the institutions of the Community, particularly at Council of Ministers and senior diplomat and official level, was slowly transforming the relationship…The patron-client pattern was dissolved; in the new circumstances British ministers and diplomats could see their Irish counterparts as clever partners in Europe. Without this transformation it is almost impossible to see how Dublin-London relations could have been transformed as they were between the mid-seventies and the mid-eighties'. D. Kennedy, 'The European Union and the Northern Ireland Question', in B. Barton and P. Roche (eds.), *The Northern Ireland Question: Perspectives and Policies* (Aldershot: Avebury, 1994), 177.

[109] 'Anglo-Irish Relations. Entente Cordiale', *Economist*, 28 November 1998; see J. McGarry, 'Globalization, European Integration and the Northern Ireland Conflict', in M. Keating and J. McGarry (eds.), *Minority Nationalism and the Changing International Order* (Oxford: Oxford University Press, 2001, 295–324).

[110] A. Wilson, *Irish America and the Ulster Conflict 1968–1995* (Washington: The Catholic University of America Press, 1995); 'From the Beltway to Belfast: The Clinton Administration, Sinn Féin, and the Northern Ireland Peace Process', *New Hibernia Review*, 1/3 1997: 23–39; 'The Billy Boys meet Slick Willy: The Ulster Unionist Party and the American Dimension to the Northern Ireland Peace Process, 1993–1998', *Policy Studies Journal*, 11 Spring 1999: 121–36; A. Guelke, 'The United States, Irish Americans and the Northern Ireland Peace Process', *International Affairs*, 72/3 (1996); 'Northern Ireland: international and north/south issues', in W. Crotty and D. Schmitt (eds.), *Ireland and the Politics of Change* (London: Longman, 1998); R. MacGinty, 'American Influences on the Northern Ireland Peace Process', *Journal of Conflict Studies*, 1997: 31–50; J. O'Grady, 'An Irish Policy Born in the USA', *Foreign Affairs*, May/June 1996.

[111] A. Wilson, 'From the Beltway', 23; R. MacGinty, 'American influences', 33; A. Guelke, 'The United States', 531–2. Also see A. Guelke, *Northern Ireland*, 147.

[112] A. Guelke, 'The United States', 528.

part in the IRA's decision to declare a ceasefire in 1994,[113] and Clinton's delegate, George Mitchell, is widely seen as having contributed to the successful outcome of the interparty negotiations that produced the Good Friday Agreement. While the United States is usually seen by unionists as biased against them, one commentator notes that Clinton had a good relationship with UUP leader David Trimble and that the president's last-minute assurances helped convince Trimble to sign the Good Friday Agreement.[114]

Settler colonial theory

A final prominent comparative approach to the Northern Ireland conflict is based on settler colonial theory. As O'Leary and I have argued, settler societies are normally extreme examples of plural societies and the fact that Ireland and later Northern Ireland was a site of settler colonialism helps to explain the intensity of divisions there.[115] The legacy of the settlement of Ireland contributed to the prevalence of segregation, endogamy, and segmented labour markets. The initial act of dispossession bequeathed a legacy of inequality that continues to poison intergroup relations. The parallels between the establishment of a hegemonic control system by the dominant settler group in Ireland, and later Northern Ireland, with dominant settler control systems in South Africa, Algeria, and Rhodesia helps explain the focus of several works by comparativists.[116]

Three of these works are especially noteworthy. Ian Lustick has compared French state-building failures in Algeria with British state-building failures in Ireland. In both cases, he claims, the large-scale introduction of settlers into the two regions fundamentally disrupted a

---

[113] A. Guelke, 'The United States', 534; R. MacGinty, 'American Influences', 34; J. O'Grady, 'An Irish Policy', 5; A. Wilson, 'From the Beltway', 32.

[114] A. Wilson, 'The Billy Boys'.

[115] J. McGarry and B. O'Leary, *Explaining Northern Ireland*, 333.

[116] D. Akenson, *God's Peoples: Covenant and Land in South Africa, Israel and Ulster* (Ithaca: Cornell University Press, 1992); P. Clayton, 'Religion, Ethnicity and Colonialism as Explanations of the Northern Ireland Conflict', in D. Miller (ed.), *Rethinking Northern Ireland: Culture, Ideology and Colonialism* (New York: Longman, 1998), 40–54; I. Lustick, *State-Building Failure in British Ireland*; M. MacDonald, *Children of wrath: Political Violence in Northern Ireland* (Oxford: Polity Press, 1986); D. Miller, 'Colonialism and Academic Representation of the Troubles', in D. Miller (ed.), *Rethinking Northern Ireland*, 3–39; B. Schutz and D. Scott, *Natives and Settlers: A Comparative analysis of the Politics of Opposition and Mobilisation in Northern Ireland and Rhodesia* (Denver: University of Denver, 1974); R. Weitzer, *Transforming Settler States: Communal Conflict and Internal Security in Northern Ireland and Zimbabwe* (Berkeley: University of California Press, 1990).

prerequisite for successful state-building: the elicitation of loyalties from the newly acquired area. At several crucial junctures, such as the Treaty of Limerick in 1691 and the Act of Union in 1801, Protestant settlers intervened to obstruct conciliatory gestures by the state towards natives.[117] This helps to explain why, when Catholic mass mobilization occurred in the late nineteenth century, it took off in a separatist direction.

Don Akenson's historical research emphasizes the important fact that Ulster's settlers were religiously inspired, like the Afrikaners who settled southern Africa and the Jews who settled Palestine. All three groups, Akenson argues, saw themselves as 'chosen peoples' who had a biblical covenant with God. This helped to explain Ulster Protestants' sense of superiority to Catholics, their willingness to discriminate, their endorsement of endogamy, their cohesiveness, their intransigence, their rejection of ecumenism, and their attachment to their soil, which they saw as a promised land. Akenson is careful to note that, while religion was crucial for Protestants, it is now a much less important influence.

Ronald Weitzer, who compares Northern Ireland with Zimbabwe, is concerned with the coercive dimensions of state power in divided societies with histories of settler rule. He shows that dominant settler groups can maintain control over sometimes much larger native populations through the construction of a highly sectarian security apparatus. With obvious relevance to contemporary Northern Ireland and contemporary Zimbabwe, Weitzer claims that substantive democratization—after a transition—requires a radical overhaul of inherited security structures.[118]

Weitzer argues that Zimbabwe at independence lacked a democratic political culture and a strong civil society. It had a regime that wanted to retain the repressive character of the security apparatus inherited from Rhodesia for use against its new (Ndebele) enemies. The result was that the transition from white minority rule to majority rule, while it increased democracy, did not create a liberal democracy. The new (British) regime that took over Northern Ireland in 1972 was much more willing than its Harare counterpart to transform the police into a professional and impartial agency. However, it was impeded on the

---

[117] William of Orange's original Treaty of Limerick, which was conciliatory towards Irish Catholics, was converted, at the insistence of settlers, into the Penal system. Pitt's proposal to link the Union of 1801 with Catholic Emancipation was also blocked by Protestant settlers, with help from King George.

[118] R. Weitzer, *Transforming Settler States*, 1.

one hand by opposition from a strong Protestant civil society, and on the other by a Catholic minority that was strong enough to resist strengthened security measures. The result was that the British engaged in limited reforms that did not go far enough.

These accounts are different from the partisan nationalist portrayal of Ireland as a colony. In the traditional nationalist account, Ireland is seen as exploited by outsiders—British imperialists. The existence of profound internal divisions in the colony are downplayed. Settlers, to the extent that they are acknowledged, are portrayed as the dupes of metropolitan forces without their own interests or identity. There is an inference, although often delivered *sotto voce*, that those who are descended from settlers have less legitimacy than natives. The above accounts, by contrast, emphasize that Northern Ireland has important *endogenous* divisions based on the historic distinction between settlers and natives. Britain is not the only obstacle to a resolution of the conflict: the different identities and interests of settlers and natives are also factors. Following from this, none of these accounts think the conflict can be resolved simply by Britain's withdrawal and none advocates a one-sided solution that favours nationalists.[119] These differences are sometimes overlooked by unionist sympathisers who (incorrectly) regard any portrayal of Protestants as settlers as a nationalist argument and as implying a demand that they be discriminated against or repatriated.[120]

CONCLUSION

This overview shows that Northern Ireland has not been regarded by everyone as a place apart. Rather, many of those involved in the conflict, as well as many of those who have studied it, have insisted on comparing Northern Ireland with other divided societies.

Partisans have drawn parallels between Northern Ireland and a wide range of other cases. The popularity of the practice reflects an absence of parochialism, and should put to rest the charge that the people of Northern Ireland are self-absorbed and out of touch. The widespread use of comparative analysis by academics, including numerous comparisons between Northern Ireland and other divided societies, also indicates that

---

[119] Thus, while arguing for the usefulness of comparing Algeria and Ireland against Unionist accounts which deny any similarities, Ian Lustick does not accept the arguments of 'troop out' advocates that the Algerian analogy means the British should withdraw.

[120] P. Dixon, 'The politics of antagonism', 133.

the political actors within Northern Ireland are right to see Northern Ireland as comparable, and analogous, to other societies and other conflicts. It should dispel the notion that its conflict is 'untypical' or 'anachronistic'. Rather, it is clear that there are many societies with similar difficulties, although there is no consensus on the appropriate comparison, and on the kind of division that characterizes Northern Ireland.

The widespread use of analogies and comparisons between Northern Ireland and other societies, particularly by politicians, also reflects the increasingly important role that international norms play in contemporary politics. This is further support for 'linkage' theory, the argument that the Northern Ireland conflict cannot be properly viewed through an endogenous lens alone. The use of analogical reasoning to stress the legitimacy of one's cause has been purposely employed by Northern Ireland's politicians to strengthen group solidarity and influence outside actors. There is also evidence that analogies, and the norms implicit in them, have influenced the behaviour of the Northern Irish parties themselves, as well as the behaviour of outsiders.

Northern Ireland is, as we have seen, a site of *competing* analogies and norms. Neither of its communities, unlike South Africa's blacks, the blacks of the Deep South, or Algeria's Arabs, have been able to achieve hegemonic legitimacy. This is one reason why the conflict continues, and why the best that is likely is an agreement rather than a settlement.

5

Five Fallacies: Northern Ireland and the Liabilities of Liberalism

John McGarry and Brendan O'Leary[1]

Five fallacies in the misinterpretation of conflict in Northern Ireland, which are characteristic of liberal readings of ethno-national conflicts, are identified and criticized in this article: (i) blaming the conflict on extremist political and religious elites; (ii) assuming that the conflict has fundamental economic and material foundations; (iii) assuming that the conflict flows from archaic religious or non-religious political cultures; (iv) assuming that segregation is the key social and structural cause of conflict; and (v) assuming that individual discrimination is the primary motor of antagonisms. The authors insist on the ethno-national nature of the conflict and the need for appropriate political means to address it.

Liberal explanations of ethnic and ethno-national conflicts and liberal prescriptions for their resolution enjoy wide currency in the academic world. In the classical liberal perspective properly ordered states are composed of individuals who are self-interestedly rational; for instance, they establish states to provide for their security, and they join groups or political parties to advance their own interests. Society itself is perceived as an arrangement to satisfy pre-existing individual interests, a 'co-operative venture for mutual advantage' (Rawls 1971: 4). In liberal ideology it is only in benighted and backward societies that individuals put an unchosen group identity—such as membership of an ethnic group or nation—ahead of their interests as individuals. Such societies are irrational, pre-modern, 'tribal', or 'primordial', outside the pale of the civilized liberal world (Ignatieff 1993). Ethnic and ethno-national

---

[1] This article abbreviates some of the principal arguments in McGarry and O'Leary (1995), to which interested readers are referred for defence in depth.

identifications lead to 'mindless' conflict—characteristic of Bosnia, Rwanda, the Middle East, and, of course, Northern Ireland. Communities sunk in illusory primordial identifications are seen as over isolated from the Enlightenment; their hostilities explained by isolation and ignorance which cause negative stereotyping and the spread of disapproving myths about those outside the ethnic *laager*. Ghettoization, segregation, sectarianism, and pillarization obscure the fundamental interests which humans have in common, especially those economic interests which cross-cut ethnic cleavages.

There are variations in the liberal world view. Ethnic attachments and conflict are not always explained by underdevelopment, ignorance, isolation, and unreasoning communalism. They may, on occasion, be attributed to opportunistically rational individuals pursuing their political or economic self-interest. Thus, instrumental machinations of self-interested elites, eager to exacerbate (or even to create) ethno-national divisions for their own narrow ends, are often 'exposed' by liberal authors. For example, the conflict in the former Yugoslavia is held to stem from the ambitions of Tudjman and Milošević, among other 'warlords', who saw in the collapse of Communism the opportunity to gain power by stirring up national antagonisms (Ignatieff, 1993: 6). Similarly, conflict in South Africa in the run-up to the transitional constitutional deal was attributed to the scheming of Buthelezi, who, it was said, had chosen to promote Zulu nationalism as a means to power rather than accept the more progressive liberal agenda of Mandela and de Klerk. Exposing rational and amoral opportunism is not limited to individuals when liberal muckrakers are in full flow. Entire ethnic collectivities may be seen as aggregates of individuals who have organized to ensure a greater share of scarce material resources. In this respect they are treated as no different from other 'rent-seeking' associations, like trade unions or interest groups. The closely related argument often follows that ethno-national conflict is caused by disputes over material resources; or it is said to be determined by inequality, deprivation, or the desire to profit. Conflict, in a more broad-minded liberal view, may be rooted in injustice, the result of opportunistic ethnic elites capturing state power and using it in a discriminatory fashion. Injustice often causes material inequality, and thereby causes resentment, but can extend beyond material concerns, touching on more abstract notions of fair play. Thus, discrimination along ethnic, religious, or racial lines promotes what is otherwise an artificial solidarity: winners defend the status quo; losers organize to dismantle it.

Liberal prescriptions for ethno-national conflict flow from these premises. If conflict is caused by backwardness, salvation lies in the bracing free air of modernity. If the problem is segregation, liberals seek to break down the barriers, including trade barriers, which exist between groups, and to expose them to each other. They espouse measures which 'reduce differences' between groups, and believe in what Steve Bruce has termed a 'mix and fix' philosophy (1994: 135). If the problem is scheming elites, the solution is opening the polity to alternative liberal voices. Thus, liberals advocate the formation of liberal political parties to counter ethnic entrepreneurialism. They launch liberal newspapers to combat ethnic propaganda. A recent article in the *Economist*, entitled 'Try words, they come cheaper', put matters thus: the 'warlike tribal myth[s]' of ethnically partisan media must be countered with stories of 'inter-tribal respect, co-operation and solidarity'. This prescription is intended to help ethnic divisions in places like Rwanda and the former Yugoslavia (*Economist*, 3 September 1994). Liberals also advocate electoral systems which facilitate 'vote-pooling' to make it more difficult for ethnic entrepreneurs to win with exclusivist appeals, and to help make 'moderation pay' (e.g. Horowitz 1989, 1991).

Alternatively, populist liberals advocate the bypassing of opportunistic political elites by appealing to the fundamentally individualist (and more moderate) sentiments of the people, and therefore support referendums or other instruments of direct democracy. If ethnic conflict is caused by material deprivations or inequalities, liberals seek to remove these causes and to create material incentives for peace. They call for economic aid for conflict zones, or, alternatively, for economic sanctions to bring warring factions to their senses. If conflict is caused by ethnic elites' discriminatory use of state power, the liberal solution is civic integration: the creation of a neutral state in which discrimination is banned. With equal citizenship guaranteed, irrespective of people's ethno-national origins, it becomes irrational for political elites to make ethnic appeals, and so ethnic bonds wither away. The key instrument in the construction of such a liberal state is an individualist Bill of Rights which bans discrimination. Some liberals go beyond neutrality and require the liberal state to redress the consequences of historic discrimination through affirmative action policies. Such 'temporary' policies will create 'a level playing field' in which the difference-blind rules of egalitarian liberalism can apply. Whatever the method employed, the goal of liberals is straightforward: the erosion of ethnic solidarities, at least in the public realm, and the promotion of a more rational state and society based on equal individual rights.

LIBERAL PERSPECTIVES ON NORTHERN IRELAND

Liberal views have shaped analysis of and prescription for Northern Ireland in a rich variety of ways. Here, we summarize five liberal theses about Northern Ireland. We label each of them fallacious, for reasons which we shall subsequently defend.

Fallacy one: The conflict is the responsibility of extremist elites

There is a popular journalistic view that the conflict can be traced to the machinations of political or religious elites rather than to differences among the people. Such thinking is prevalent in Northern Ireland's 'independent' magazine, *Fortnight*,[2] which regularly launches editorials on the need to unleash 'people power' to circumvent the politicians—as if the conflict is analogous to that which led to the downfall of the Marcos regime in the Philippines, or the Communist regimes of Eastern Europe. Supporters of this view cite opinion polls which consistently appear to show overwhelming popular support for compromise and peace. The view that the political class is to be blamed for the conflict informed the establishment of the Opsahl Commission in 1992 whose self-appointed task was to bypass the stonewalling of local elites by appealing to the people directly, and by allowing them to express their views before the Commission. The report of this self-appointed liberal elitist Commission was called, with no hint of irony, 'A Citizens' Inquiry' (Pollak 1993). It argued that politicians in Northern Ireland had much more latitude for compromise than they imagined (or pretended), and that they would benefit from educational courses on democratic conduct, available from the American, Scandinavian, and German governments.

Calls for a referendum to create political progress have also been informed by the belief that beyond the voices of divisive politicians can be found a more rational and moderate electorate. We predict that in 1995–6 the British and Irish prime ministers will hear multiple liberal voices, in the media and elsewhere, encouraging them to go for double referendums, North and South, to break any logjam in interparty nego- tiations. In doing so they will endorse the fallacy that the leaders are distinctly unrepresentative of their followers—even though in local government, assembly, and European parliamentary elections Northern

---

[2] The independence of the magazine has become questionable, since it now receives a subsidy from the British government.

Ireland has an electoral system, the single transferable vote (STV), which punishes unrepresentative leaders.

Linked to the belief that progress lies in shunting aside local extremist political elites is the electoral integrationist argument that *the* source of conflict is the unwillingness of the two major British parties to organize (or organize seriously) in the region. This, it is alleged, has left the field open to local 'sectarian' parties. Given a genuine choice between these parties and their British liberal counterparts, it is suggested that Northern Ireland's rational electorate would opt for the modernizing British parties. One academic has argued that the British party boycott was 'the fundamental reason' for continuing conflict in the region (Roberts 1990: 132). Their presence, on the other hand, would allegedly lead to a 'normal', modern, public policy oriented politics, in which divisions would be based largely on rational and deliberative political principles (Aughey 1989; Wilson 1989; Roberts 1990).

When local elites are not being blamed directly for the conflict, they are held responsible for the social segregation which allegedly causes it. The segregated school system is sometimes seen as the direct by-product of church elites with interests in sustaining religious and ethnic differences. Characteristically, opinion polls are invoked to show substantial parental support for integrated education (Irwin 1991). High rates of endogamy are also sometimes attributed to the Roman Catholic Church because of its traditional position that the children of 'mixed' marriages should be brought up as Catholics. One study concludes that the Church's role in fostering segregated education and endogamy 'is the most significant aspect of the role of religion in the divisions and conflicts in Ireland and goes to the heart of the matter' (Fulton 1991: 131; see also Jenkins 1986: 6–7).

Fallacy two: The conflict has fundamental economic and material foundations

Liberal economists and other liberals share with Marxists the temptation to suggest that ethno-national conflicts are fundamentally rooted in economic and material interests. Some claim that it is the existence of economic deprivation in Northern Ireland, particularly in working-class ghettos, which has caused conflict. The evidence seems strong: in numerous socio-economic indicators Northern Ireland is by far the most deprived region of the United Kingdom (Smith and Chambers 1991: 51–2); a considerable amount of violence originates from people who live in deprived Catholic and Protestant 'ghettos'; and the most militant political parties—Sinn Féin (SF) and the Democratic Unionist Part (DUP)—draw disproportionate support from the less well-off. The reasoning is also straightforward. Those with little stake in society have little interest in stability and are more likely to be lured into militant ethnic organizations.

These views are popular within the British labour movement and within Conservative Party circles. Northern Ireland Office minister Richard Needham claimed in 1989: 'If work can be found for 10,000 unemployed boys in West Belfast,... that in itself will do more to impact on the political and security areas than anything else' (*Fortnight*, no. 276, 1989). The supposedly liberal prime minister of Northern Ireland put the logic a little more memorably in 1969: 'If you give Roman Catholics a good job and a good house, they will live like Protestants, because they will see neighbours with cars and television sets' (*Belfast Telegraph*, 5 May 1969). Sometimes it has been argued that the conflict is not only caused by deprivation, but that the goal of those engaged in conflict is to end deprivation. In hearings held by the Opsahl Commission in the Shankill area in early 1993, some speakers attributed republican violence to the calculation that it would lead the government to transfer (financial) resources to Catholic areas. They attributed the more recent escalation in loyalist violence to the fact that Protestants had learned this lesson (*Fortnight*, no. 316, 1993, 29–30). If the cause of the conflict is deprivation, then, so it seems, its resolution requires prosperity or economic growth—executed through greater governmental intervention on the left-wing view, or by the development of an 'enterprise culture' on the right-wing view.

The more cynical liberal economic perspective detects economic opportunism at the root of the conflict. Political elites, it is said, refuse to compromise because they derive material perks from continuing antagonism. There is a popular view that the paramilitaries, or an important section thereof, are interested only in personal profit, and secure it through criminal rackets. Governmental officials from Britain and the Republic of Ireland have freely used terms like 'Mafia', 'gangster', 'racketeer', 'God-father', and 'mob rule' to describe the paramilitaries, implying that the profit motive is more transparent than nationalist or loyalist ideology. The view of the governments is supported by allegedly more dispassionate sources, including a significant number of journalists and academics (e.g. Clare 1990; Ryder 1990: 126; Dillon 1991: 419; Anderson 1994). One journalist expresses the thesis thus:

Assigning [Northern Ireland's] violence to religious hatreds or skewed nationalism or mere senselessness is too easy. In fact, the hardmen have a very good reason for wanting to sabotage any prospect of peace, one that has less to do with flags or gods and more to do with money.

(Anderson 1994: 46)

The prescription, implicit or explicit, is for tougher anti-racketeering measures and a clamp-down by the security forces.

Fallacy three: The conflict flows from archaic cultures

The region's cultural backwardness and lack of exposure to the forces of modernization are dominant liberal orthodoxies. Many liberals confidently assert, for example, that the conflict is pristinely religious—a rerun of struggles which more modern regions fought and resolved in previous centuries. This claim is buttressed by evidence of high levels of religiosity in the region, by the fact that the rival political parties and paramilitary organizations draw their support almost entirely from different religious groups (Catholics and Protestants), and by the high profile of certain clergymen in politics, such as the Reverend Ian Paisley.

The view that the conflict has a fundamental religious dimension is endorsed by humanist organizations, ecumenical groups, journalists, historians, psychologists, political scientists, and sociologists. Four distinct variants exist. First, liberal humanists blame the peculiar, anachronistic, and uncompromising devoutness of both Catholics and Protestants. This view, endorsed by some local atheists, is especially popular with outsiders. Here is a leading moralizing English journalist: 'The passions which are shared by Mass-going Gael and Calvinist planter, which sustain them indeed in the fashion of two drunks tilted out of the horizontal into a triumphal arch, are nothing to us' (Pearce 1991). Second, ecumenists, inside and outside the region, blame the conflict on the churches because they stress their differences and act as sectarian apologists for the political communities in their midst (Mawhinney and Wells 1975; Gallagher and Worrall 1982). Third, there is the thesis of sociologists of religion (and of liberal Irish nationalists) that it is the exclusivist and peculiar nature of Protestantism in Northern Ireland which underlies the conflict. In this perspective unionism is Protestantism, pre-national and religiously contractarian, whereas Irish nationalism is a secular ideology in which Irish Catholics can separate their faith and politics (Rose 1971: 216–17; FitzGerald 1972; O'Brien 1974; Heskin 1980: 47; Buckland 1981: 100; O'Malley 1983: 178; Bruce 1986). Finally, evangelical Protestants and liberal Unionists blame the conflict on the authoritarian Roman Catholic Church which they claim underpins an exclusivist and culturally coercive Irish nationalism (Aughey 1989: ch. 7; Wilson 1989: 213–14).

Prescriptions follow. Humanists see secularization as the best chance for peace. Ecumenists seek the promotion of common Christian values.

Those who regard Unionism and Protestantism as identical divide in their proposals. If they are sympathetic, they defend the status quo; if they are unsympathetic, they argue either that unionists need not be taken seriously in a modern secular world, or that unionists would have no national objections to a united Ireland provided that their religion was protected (e.g. FitzGerald 1972). Those who blame the conflict on the Roman Catholic Church (and who fear its influence within a united Ireland) seek the reconstruction of the 1688 Protestant theocracy if they are evangelicals, and a secular integrated United Kingdom if they are liberal Unionists.

However, the conflict is also attributed to a general cultural back-wardness, rather than to religion per se. There is a long-established view in Great Britain that the Irish are 'culturally' primitive and disposed towards violence. In international folklore, from the bar-rooms of Chicago to the bar-rooms of Melbourne, the Irish male can be found displaying the alleged traits of his people: aggressive and unreasoning violence, facilitated by excessive alcohol consumption. What could be more natural, therefore, that in the homeland of the 'fighting Irish' there should be endless violence and intransigence. In this view, the Northern Ireland conflict is a protracted 'donnybrook'.

Related to this 'argument' is the view that the local politicians, rather than being scheming Machiavellians, are archaic political dupes, incap-able of making deals without help from more sophisticated outsiders. In the 1970s the British government sent some local politicians to the Netherlands' legislature to learn how Catholics and Protestants could get along together. In 1993 the Opsahl commissioners suggested that local politicians are simply ignorant, poorly socialized in democratic skills, and would benefit from appropriate training programmes in Germany, Sweden, and the United States of America (Pollak 1993: ch. 10, para. 1.4). The alleged inability of the Irish to engage in the modern politics of 'give and take' is often put down to atavism, or an irrational preoccupation with the past. The Northern Irish, like the peoples of the Balkans, are said to indulge in 'ancient hatreds', as if they are incapable of putting their past behind them. The two communities are portrayed as encased in historic myths: Protestants in the myth of a besieged people, obsessively remembering 1690 as the date of their partial deliverance; Catholics in the myth of an oppressed people, obsessively recalling their conquest and subordination by British Protestants, recycling their grievances rather than looking forward.

The claim that the Northern Irish are unhealthily preoccupied with the past is, understandably, closely associated with professional historians.

Oliver MacDonagh turns Oscar Wilde's witty dictum that 'Irish history is something which Irishmen should never remember, and Englishmen should never forget' into a sober cultural observation: the Irish never forget and the English never remember (MacDonagh 1983). Other historians, much less sympathetic to Irish nationalism, add that Irish republicans interpret their past through the distorting lens of Gaelic romanticism and Catholic mysticism (Dudley-Edwards 1977; Foster 1988; Elliott 1989). The thinly veiled implication is that the Provisional IRA is the current bearer of an irrational, romantic, religiously enthused communal hatred, which takes its 'cultural' polish from the Gaelic and Catholic revivals of the nineteenth century. Religious and romantic spiritualism are identified as key traits of Irish political culture, and implied to be culpable for its lack of modernization. Nationalist violence stems from this romanticism. Young people join paramilitary organizations after being schooled in histories of oppression and sacrifice or after imbibing republican songs on similar themes. In one account, even the hunger strikes of 1980–1, in which ten men died, are attributed to Gaelic and Brehon cultures, the sacrificial themes in Christian thought, and the tradition of republican protests and hunger striking stretching back to the Fenian movement founded in the 1850s (O'Malley 1990). The homily for Irish nationalists is clear: abandon the culture which caused these suicides and which still fuels mayhem and antagonism.

A leading historian of Ulster unionism places special emphasis on the historically rooted siege mentality of the Protestant settlers and their descendants, and maintains that 'it is precisely because the most cruel and treacherous warfare has broken out over and over again, and usually after a period of relative security, as in 1641 or 1798 or 1920 or 1969, that the besieged suffer such chronic insecurity'. They fear insurrection by the natives/Catholics; betrayal from within their own ranks—the archetypal figure here being Governor Robert Lundy, the traitorous governor at the siege of Derry in 1690 and betrayal by Britain. 'The factor which distinguishes the siege of Derry from all other historic sieges in the British Isles is that it is still going on' (Stewart 1986: 56–7).

Fallacy four: The conflict is caused by segregation

Another liberal interpretation of Northern Ireland, often influenced by the history of black–white and Christian–Jewish relations in North America and Europe, is that conflict is caused (or at least exacerbated) by the isolation of the two communities from each other, an isolation more important than their alleged isolation from modernity. Numerous commentators highlight the denominational education system, in which 98 per cent of pupils are segregated by their religion of origin. These voluntarily (and state-subsidized) segregated schools are seen as indoctrination camps for the rival ethno-national communities. Teaching different histories causes hostile feelings towards the other community; segregation facilitates negative stereotypes and myths of the Other, and prevents the establishment of cross-communal friendships; learning culturally specific sports inhibits mixing even after graduation; and segregated education reinforces residential segregation. The high rates of endogamy are also reinforced— research suggests that mixed marriages formed 6 per cent of the total in Northern Ireland during the four decades 1943–82 (Fulton 1991: 199).

The liberal cure for segregation is to expose the rival groups to each other. Steve Bruce describes this 'mix and fix' mentality:

> Liberals get on well with each other. In such middle-class suburbs as the Malone Road area of Belfast, in such organizations as the [moderate] Alliance Party, and in such associations as Protestant and Catholic Encounter, Protestant and Catholic liberals mix and find they have much in common. They are thus readily drawn to the idea that the conflict is caused by misunderstanding and ignorance. If working-class people also mixed, they would learn that their stereotypes are mistaken—"they" do not have horns—and that they are just like us. End of conflict.
>
> (Bruce 1994: 134)

The 'mix and fix' prescription is naturally espoused by the integrated education lobby. A psychologist endorses their case: integrated education would be 'the single potentially most helpful step' at a social level (Heskin 1980: 155; see also Irwin 1991). In recent years, the British government has given some (though not total) support to this view, funding integrated schools and establishing a compulsory cross-curricular programme entitled 'Education for Mutual Understanding'. In 1993 the University of Ulster proposed a new campus at Springvale in West Belfast—the sales-pitch being that the site straddles the 'peace-line' and would draw students and staff from each community. In the view of its backers, including the Secretary of State, it would help to break down barriers (*Economist*, 29 October 1994, p. 68). Liberals also urge the Catholic Church to remove religious obstacles to inter-marriage to facilitate exogamy and the erosion of exclusivist group attachments.

Besides campaigns to loosen church control over education and marriage, liberal charities organize holidays where children from Protestant and Catholic ghettos can meet and erode their respective stereotypes. The Churches themselves are encouraging increasing contact through the ecumenical movement (Gallagher and Worrall 1982; Radford 1993). 'Contact' groups have been established, such as the well-known Corrymeela community or Protestant and Catholic Encounter (PACE), and a number of commentators and agencies have urged the government to make sure that integrated public housing is made available to those who want it, or have supported the creation of 'pilot' cross-community housing projects (SACHR 1990: paras. 4, 53–4, and 6.19; Pollak 1993: ch. 10).

Fallacy five: Individual discrimination is the primary motor of antagonism

Perhaps the most important liberal explanation of the conflict is that it is caused by discrimination—it is the one with which we have most intuitive sympathy. In the 1960s the Northern Ireland Civil Rights Association (NICRA) sought equal citizenship for Catholics to end their second-class status and their exclusion from the institutions of the devolved government at Stormont. A government inquiry into the violence which flowed from the civil rights demonstrations attributed it to the absence of civil rights for Catholics (Cameron 1969). According to one distinguished political scientist, had there been a Bill of Rights and judicial enforcement of its provisions against discrimination, as in the United States of America, there might have been no sustained political violence (Rose 1976). American civil rights leaders were able to pursue a successful strategy of non-violence because they could secure redress of black grievances through the courts. The Northern Ireland civil rights movement, denied similar opportunities, had no alternative strategy to offer militants, and the region became embroiled in violent conflict.

The British government has periodically expressed sympathy for this perspective and has introduced a range of measures to prevent discrimination against the Catholic minority. After a Fair Employment (Northern Ireland) Act (1976) failed miserably to achieve its objectives the British government, under pressure, eventually introduced a tougher law in 1989. It not only bans discrimination in hiring but also requires employers to monitor the religious composition of their workforce and to take affirmative action if necessary. Liberal critics argue for a vigorous pursuit of this logic: they call both for explicit employment targets and a timetable for these to be achieved.

The most comprehensively researched statement that discrimination is at the centre of the conflict has been made by researchers from the Policy Studies Institute working for the Standing Commission on Human Rights (Smith and Chambers 1991). The work of Smith and Chambers is not, like that of many commentators, ahistorical. They observe that the seventeenth-century plantation of Ulster gave the best land to Protestants and relegated the Catholics to less fertile hilly land or to the status of landless labourers. Colonial disparities were reinforced by penal legislation which prevented Catholics from owning land and thereby acquiring wealth in the period preceding industrialization (pp. 1–3, 368). Discrimination in employment and the allocation of public housing after 1921, the result of informal social practices and overt exhortations by successive Unionist leaders, reinforced the legacies of colonialism. The result has been persistent and significant divergences between Catholics and Protestants in unemployment rates, quality of employment, and overall living standards. For instance, Catholic men have standardly been about two and a half times more likely to be unemployed than Protestant men (pp. 161–2, 212).

In this liberal reading the current troubles erupted because of economic inequality and economic discrimination rather than nationalism or religion (p. 12). The NICRA campaign began over a dispute about public housing in 1964, and the Cameron Commission concluded that the minority's protests had little to do with the national question. This socioeconomic basis to the conflict was obscured by the emergence of the Provisional IRA, which has defined the key question as the existence of the state, and reinforced by the attitude of the British government which accepted the conflict as constitutional in nature, and by the flawed reasoning of those analysts who contend that the dispute about inequality springs from national or religious identities (pp. 56–7). The bulk of Smith and Chambers' work is devoted to successful demonstrations of economic inequalities between the two communities. Their survey, conducted in the middle of Unionist protests against the Anglo-Irish Agreement, when one would have expected considerable interest in constitutional questions, seemed to reveal that socio-economic inequalities remained central to many people. Asked to choose the biggest problem in Northern Ireland, the most popular answer from Catholics was unemployment (p. 75). Asked what change would be most likely to end 'the troubles', the most popular answer chosen by Catholics was 'equal opportunities for Protestants and Catholics' (p. 77). Having identified inequality as a central cause of conflict, Smith and Chambers rejected the unionist contention that this is a result of unequal abilities, or that it is a hangover from a bygone age which will gradually dissipate without corrective measures. Instead, they argued that it can be accounted for significantly by continuing direct and indirect discrimination in the private and public sectors. Their prescription is for more effective policies for equal opportunity.

THE LIABILITIES IN LIBERAL READINGS
OF ETHNO-NATIONAL CONFLICTS

All the foregoing liberal explanations have flaws. They either ignore or gloss over one or more of three essential facts: first, that the conflict is fundamentally rooted in ethno-national antagonism; second, that there is nothing pre-modern about conflicts which flow from such antagonism; and, third, that these antagonisms are intense because of their political and institutional setting. Liberals often make the mistake of reducing ethno-national conflicts to religious, cultural, or material differences between the ethno-national groups (Connor 1994). Such conflicts are better understood as socio-psychological, rooted in historically established collective identities and motivated by the desire to be governed by one's co-nationals, both for security and for collective freedom. These motivations have not been absent from liberal bastions like the United States, Great Britain, or France. What distinguishes these territories from those presently embroiled in conflict are that their national questions have (largely) been settled. There is also nothing pre-modern about ethno-national conflicts. Western Europe has been embroiled in them for the best part of this century, and Canada's unity is currently threatened by nationalist separatism. Northern Ireland's ethno-national antagonisms have been intense, more like Bosnia's than Belgium's or Canada's, and that must largely be explained by its political setting rather than its cultural environment. These considerations, simply asserted here, render the preceding liberal explanations and prescriptions problematic (see O'Leary and McGarry 1993; McGarry and O'Leary 1995).

Are political or religious elites to blame?

Elites play an important role in mobilizing nationalist movements. However, these movements usually have some pre-existing collective bases—the Achilles heel in most instrumentalist readings of ethno-nationalist conflicts. What is more important is that once mobilized, and especially after protracted violence, ethno-national divisions become rooted and are not easily dismantled without mutual collective security. In a deeply divided territory, with a long history of conflict, elites are more likely to reflect the divisions than to be responsible for them. Moreover, they respond to the incentives which they face. Leaders who underestimate the extent of those divisions and assume moderate positions often find themselves jobless or worse. Moderates in Northern Ireland have found no significant electoral niche. If moderate to begin with, they cannot compete with more chauvinistic leaders—as is evident in the electoral performances of the moderate Northern Ireland Labour Party (NILP) in the late 1960s and the Alliance Party (APNI) since the 1970s. If politicians experience Pauline conversions to moderation, as with Unionists like Brian Faulkner in 1974 and William Craig in 1975, or nationalists like Gerry Fitt in 1980, they may be abandoned by their grass roots. Contrary to the Opsahl commissioners, little in the recent history of Northern Ireland suggests that political elites can easily compromise on the national question while retaining support (see Mitchell 1995). If in conditions of peace it becomes evident that public opinion has changed, then political elites will be capable of greater flexibility—but this change will not suggest that conflict was sustained by unrepresentative elites.

The popular moderation that is often displayed in opinion polls must also be treated with scepticism. Polls are imperfect, especially so in deeply divided territories where respondents may be unwilling to tell the pollster what they really think. They may judge their views to be outside conventional norms, or that their real views, given to a stranger, may put them at considerable risk. The evidence from Northern Ireland is that opinion polls tend to overemphasize moderation and downplay extremism. Consider the following facts:

1. opinion-poll support for the moderate Alliance party is roughly twice what it receives in elections (Whyte 1986: 232).
2. cross-community power-sharing has received high cross-community support in opinion polls while Unionist politicians advocating it have so far floundered at elections.
3. support for SF and the DUP in elections has always exceeded their support in opinion polls.
4. huge numbers of Unionists vote for Ian Paisley while hesitating to admit it in public.

It, therefore, cannot be confidently asserted that a referendum on a constitutional settlement will produce the same moderation we sometimes see in surveys.[3] To put matters another way, selling any negotiated settlement successfully a referendum will have to

---

[3] When Canadians have been consulted in referendums they have always shown themselves to be more divided than their elites. Two referendums on prohibition and conscription split the country along linguistic lines. In a third referendum the political elites (the prime minister, ten provincial premiers, two territorial leaders, and four native leaders) submitted a package which they had unanimously negotiated. The package was rejected outside Quebec because it gave too much to that province, and within Quebec because it did not give enough.

offer security to both ethno-national communities and not just to their moderates.

The argument that Northern Ireland's rational electorate would seize the opportunity to vote for British political parties does not withstand scrutiny. First, Northern Ireland had a reasonable facsimile of the British Labour Party—the NILP—for a significant part of its history. It never made significant inroads into the nationalist or Unionist vote and disintegrated in the wake of the polarization of the late 1960s (McGarry and O'Leary 1995: ch. 4). Second, the region has had an explicitly liberal party, the Alliance Party, linked to the British Liberal Democrats, contesting elections since the early 1970s. Its support base has been restricted to 10 per cent of the electorate, and in the last decade to less than 10 per cent. Third, the Conservative Party, which has organized in Northern Ireland since 1989, has performed very poorly except in one unrepresentative local government district, North Down. Finally, the electoral integrationist case rests on the assumption that voters who would vote for British parties would do so for 'non-national' reasons. Polling evidence suggests, however, that the Conservatives appeal most to those in favour of the Union, that is, Protestants; whereas the Labour Party appeals most to those in favour of Irish unification, that is, Catholics, because Labour favours achieving Irish unity by consent (O'Leary and McGarry 1993: 297–9).

The view that segregated education and endogamy can be blamed in any significant fashion on self-interested communal elites must also be treated with caution. Despite the existence of polls showing support for integrated education, there has been no significant public response to various government initiatives to facilitate integrated education. The high rate of endogamy, at least in urban areas, is probably caused as much by residential segregation and the lack of social interaction as it is by church policy (Whyte 1986, 1990: 33–9). If Catholics do not meet Protestants, they are unlikely to want to marry them. Where there is an emphasis on ethnic solidarity and maintaining demographic numbers, and a distrust of the 'other side', endogamous practices prevail even among those who do not practise their religion. One sociologist of religion, while attaching primary blame to the Catholic Church policy for endogamy, acknowledges that Catholics may have non-religious reasons for not marrying Protestants: they may consider them 'bigots, or oppressors or ethnic aliens' (Fulton 1991: 226). Endogamy, after all, helps to ensure that the offspring will not only be of the same religion, but also of the same national and political persuasion. Marriage across religious lines carries more than dangers of religious censure: it can mean ostracism, accusations of treachery, and, in the more extreme cases, assassination (Whyte 1990: 41).

Has conflict been economically rooted?

Few commentators have reduced the conflict to deprivation. This is just as well, because there are many areas of the world much more deprived than Northern Ireland but are free of intense national conflict. Deprivation without the mobilizing glue provided by insecure ethno-national identity is mostly associated with apathy and criminal violence rather than with the organized and goal-oriented political violence character-istic of Northern Ireland (see O'Duffy 1995). Moreover, Unionists and nationalists draw support from right across the social spectrum, and not just from the deprived. Last, if deprivation was an important cause of conflict, we would expect the conflict to be worse in bad economic times than in good. Conflict should have been at its most intense during the Great Famine, rather than in 1798 or 1916–21 or after 1969. The current conflict broke out during a period of rising prosperity, suggesting a political trigger rather than an economic one. Similarly, its fluctuations in intensity have been more closely related to political events, such as internment without trial or the deliberations of the Constitutional Con-vention, for example, than to changes in the economic cycle (see McGarry and O'Leary 1995: ch. 7). These arguments suggest that giving a repub-lican a house and a TV set is unlikely to turn that republican into a Unionist, certainly not in the short to medium term (see also Rose and McAllister 1983).

Opportunistic explanations are also suspect. The view that Catholics engage in conflict because it 'pays' overlooks the destruction which violence has wrought in Catholic areas and the economic plight of the Catholic community. The claim that the pursuit of personal profit is an important motive for paramilitaries downplays their ethno-national motivations: the paramilitary groups are ethnically exclusive, and direct practically all of their violence against other ethnic groups or state officials. Unlike mobsters, they have political goals and react to political stimuli. They also receive more support from their respective communities than those significantly engaged in criminal activities, and they have been resistant to prison management methods that criminals normally accept without rancour. By suggesting that the paramilitaries are opportunistic criminals, analysts overlook the contributions of repression and the behaviour of the security forces to the popularity of paramilitarism. They also encourage the delusion that the conflict can be contained by anti-racketeering gestures. Even the British government, between 1972 and 1976, recognized explicitly the inadequacy of depicting the para-militaries as mere criminals. It abandoned this policy only for reasons of expediency, but now has for all practical purposes returned to it. In the wake of the recent ceasefire, the RUC are predicting an increase in 'ordinary crime'—which is an implicit admission that the paramilitaries were engaged in some non-criminal activities before the ceasefire (*Economist*, 22 October 1994, p. 70), and sounds explicitly like an attempt to protect police budgets.

Protection rackets are, of course, organized by both sets of paramilitaries, as are construction rackets, but the proceeds have been mostly directed towards political goals and are even regarded as 'legit-imate taxation' by some within their respective communities. Personal racketeering is relatively rare among paramilitaries, especially on the republican side. Life as an IRA volunteer is hardly designed to appeal to those interested in maximizing profits (Bishop and Mallie 1987: ch. 1). Apart from the privations involved, those engaged in the 'pursuit of happiness' are likely to incur the wrath of their colleagues in addition to that of the security forces. While the loyalist side has had its notorious gangsters, they are less prevalent now than in the past. In the late 1980s the Ulster Defence Association was taken over by young Turks eager to restore the organization's political integrity. Their takeover corresponded with a significant increase in loyalist violence, which suggests that political motivations are more lethal than criminal ones.

Finally, within the United Kingdom, Northern Ireland has the lowest levels of criminal violence per capita but the highest levels of political or ethnic violence. The conflict over the last twenty-five years has also not produced the 'societal disintegration' associated with the triumph of anarchic and anomic criminality in some of the world's cities, which further underlines the national and political nature of the conflict (O'Leary and McGarry 1993: ch. 1).

Are backward cultures the problem?

Religion in Northern Ireland (or in Bosnia) is best seen as an ethno-national marker rather than as an important independent motivator of violent conflict. Religious labels distinguish the ethno-national groups, the descendants of settlers and natives, from each other. While the ethno-national groups are composed largely of 'Catholics' and 'Protestants', in many cases individuals do not practise their religion or do not allow their religion to determine their politics. It is this which occasions the well-known oxymoron of the 'Catholic (or Protestant) atheist'. Religious beliefs clearly play some role in shaping people's politics, and they may even be predominant for some, but there is significant evidence that they are less important than national identity in motivating behaviour and political dynamics.

First, the conflict started, escalated, and has continued during the start of significant secularization[4] which has done little to undermine ethno-national conflict, and so it is questionable whether more secularization will make a significant difference. Second, there is no noticeable correlation between those areas most affected by violent conflict and areas of intense religious devoutness. In West Belfast, an epicentre of conflict, there have been significant declines in church-attendance in both communities (Wilson 1989: 204; Whyte 1990: 27). The spatial and per capita distribution of violence is highly concentrated in urban sites, which are, as elsewhere in the world, less religious than rural zones. Third, relations between the Churches were improving when conflict erupted in the late 1960s. The second Vatican Council had formally abandoned the Roman Catholic claim that 'outside the Church there is no salvation', and there has been considerable ecumenical activity and inter-church cooperation during the current conflict, very different from what occurred in earlier crises. Fourth, political activists avoid religious labels and make non-religious claims. The organizations of the minority embrace secular political values in their titles: 'nationalism' or 'republicanism', 'social democracy' and 'socialism' provide their vocabularies. No minority party or paramilitary group describes itself religiously. Politically, they describe themselves as 'the northern nationalist community', and have shown willingness on many occasions to support individuals who enjoyed a closer relationship with Trotsky than with the Pope. Contemporary nationalist politicians call for constitutional change, for economic reforms or changes to the policing and judicial systems, and leave religious issues, such as full-funding for segregated education to the Catholic Church. The formal targets of republican paramilitaries have been those who defended the Union, not those who defended Protestantism. The other community's political organizations define themselves as 'loyalist' or 'unionist'. There is only one example since 1969 of a major unionist party describing itself religiously, Paisley's Protestant Unionist

---

[4] Weekly church attendance among Catholics and Protestants has fallen since the 1960s. The divorce rate, while absolutely lower, has been increasing at about the same rate as in Great Britain. The rate of births outside marriage has also increased.

Party, and it changed its name to the Democratic Unionist Party in 1971 because of the limited attractiveness of its title. Loyalist paramilitaries also generally shun religious appellations, with the exception of the Protestant Action Force.

The absence of denominational titles in political and paramilitary organizations is more remarkable given their existence in other countries which are not racked by conflict, religious or otherwise. The high profile of Protestant clerics notwithstanding, the overwhelming majority of unionist politicians are lay people. They address secular issues, calling for a strengthening of the Union and for stronger security policies. The clerics who are politicians are best known for being hardliners on the union and security policy. Of course, national preferences might be dictated partly by religious motivations—a united Ireland, after all, would be 80 per cent Catholic, while the UK is over 80 per cent Protestant or secular—but if most nationalist and Unionist politicians are primarily interested in these religious agendas, they have done a good job of concealing it, from their followers as well as from others. Loyalist paramilitaries generally shun overtly religious targets. Catholic churches have remained relatively inviolate and priests have not been targets. It must be perplexing for those who believe that the paramilitaries are involved in a jihad that 'Protestant' gunmen assiduously have avoided clearly marked, accessible, and unarmed priests and nuns when searching for targets. Individuals engaged in authentic religious wars— during the Inquisition, the Reformation, and the Counter-Reformation— had no difficulty in dispatching heretics to hell.

The view that the Irish are culturally more disposed to be violent than other peoples is a colonial stereotype. The English, in the classic imperialist tradition, maintained that the Irish were murderous savages while murdering and savaging many of the natives. Such arguments justified conquest and expropriation in Ireland as they did in the Americas and elsewhere (Williams 1990). As for their alleged prowess with the beer glass, paramilitaries are more likely to be recruited for their disciplined, ascetic, and puritanical characters. English stereotypists are best directed to the mirror of world history, in which they will find that they (and their American cousins) have a much more widespread reputation for being an aggressive, warlike, piratical, and imperial people. They are also well advised to ask themselves which nation's soccer fans are most welcome outside the islands of the North Atlantic?

The argument that the Irish are preoccupied with history overlooks the tendency of most societies to engage in celebrations and commemorations of pivotal moments in their past. The view that they are too fixated on old battles to be able to reach accommodation gets the direction of causality wrong: it is because nationalists and unionists are locked in an unsolved conflict that their past antagonistic encounters are seen as being of continuing relevance. Unionists continuously recall past sell-outs and victories to strengthen group solidarity and to remind themselves that there is an *ongoing* threat. Nationalists recall past oppressions and griev-ances because their aspirations have still not been addressed. That the conflict has not been settled satisfactorily explains the present-centred preoccupation with history. If a settlement is reached now it would be odd if past quarrels continued to have the same resonance. If the political context was agreed and peaceable there is no reason why the Irish in Ireland should be any less adept at the wheeling-dealing politics of compromise than their cousins in America—the United States Congress contains many Irish-Americans who are consummate log-rollers. The counter-argument, that these Irish-Americans have embraced a new culture, is less persuasive than the argument that they operate in a radically different structural and institutional context.

Liberals who see the Northern Irish as unusually preoccupied with the battles of their ancestors usually live in states which are reasonably homogeneous or which have reached institutional accommodations between previously antagonisitic groups. Liberal Irish elites from the fabled 'Dublin 4', who now find their northern cousins embarrassing, come from an area which settled its national quarrel over seventy years ago. Rather than insulting the Northern Irish, they and others like them would be better advised to reflect on their good fortune.

Is segregation the problem and mixing the answer?

The idea of social mixing as a useful prescription faces major problems. To begin with it is impractical on a very significant scale. Residential segregation, particularly in working-class areas, is both extensive and voluntary. The desire to live among 'one's own' has been reinforced by twenty-five years of violence. Those who suffered most at the outbreak of the conflict in the late 1960s were those housed outside their respective ghettos. They experienced the Irish version of 'ethnic cleansing'. Without significant residential integration, however, there is unlikely to be sup-port for integrated education. This would require bussing into threaten-ing territory or at least out of the ghetto, and few parents will buy this idea. The same holds for workplace integration. There is also unlikely to be significant exogamy, because people from both communities are unlikely to meet and interact in the required fashion.

Even if social integration could be increased, it is questionable whether the consequences would necessarily be beneficial. In deeply divided territories, increased exposure to the 'other' may make group members more aware of what their group has in common and what separates them from the others. Exposure may cement group solidarity rather than diffuse it. There may, sadly, be something in the North American folk wisdom that white liberals are those whites who do not live near blacks. Analogously, Richard Rose warns that in Northern Ireland:

A Catholic in a mixed school many learn that when Protestants say 'Not an Inch' they mean it, just as a Protestant may learn that his Catholic schoolmates refuse to regard the Union Jack as the flag to which they give allegiance.

(Rose 1971: 337)

As Connor writes, 'the idea of being friends presupposes knowledge of each other, [but] so does the idea of being rivals' (1994: 48).

The research on whether mixing encourages tolerance is mixed. In the 1960s those who experienced integrated education were not significantly more tolerant than those who did not, a conclusion consistent with studies in other countries (Rose 1971: 336–7). This view has been supported by subsequent studies in Northern Ireland (Darby *et al.* 1977; Gallagher and Worral 1982). An anthropologist claimed that Protestants who had attended a Catholic school in one particular community got on well with their Catholic neighbours, but she also pointed out that

it would be idle to pretend that the ensuing contacts between Protestant and Catholic children spread only sweetness and light—boys everywhere gang up and what more natural than that at this school the gangs should be recruited on a sectarian basis.

(Harris 1972: 137).[5]

One recent study, however, claims that children do develop more moderate attitudes as they progress through integrated schools (Irwin 1991). Yet integration may also simply provide a new interface for protracted conflict.

The alternative to regarding 'mixing and fixing' as a panacea is to encourage it where it is feasible and wanted, but also to recognize durable divisions and ensure that both groups are treated in an equal manner and that both can be sure of their collective and cultural security. Just as many blacks in the USA now realize, ironically, that an authentic

---

[5] One psychologist observed that the interaction of blacks and whites in the United States increased prejudice there, but does not believe this would happen in Northern Ireland where differences are not ascriptive (Heskin 1980: 145).

version of the separate but equal doctrine in *Plessey v. Ferguson* may be more attractive than the separate means unequal doctrine of *Brown v. Bd. of Education*, so many northern nationalists insist that they want equality and autonomy rather than equality and integration. Full funding for denominational and state schools, and a fair allocation of resources for job creation and public housing, are more important for them than integration. Lest we are misinterpreted, we should spell out that we believe that sufficient provision must be made for all those who wish to be schooled, live, or work with members of the other community.

Is individual discrimination the problem?

The existence of significant economic inequality between Catholics and Protestants is undeniable. It has been convincingly argued that this gap exists because of discrimination, direct or indirect, that discrimination needs to be ended to reduce minority alienation, and that British efforts have not been far-reaching enough (e.g. Smith and Chambers 1991).

However, we take issue with the implicit liberal individualist supposition that the conflict centres on individual inequality and discrimination, and the implication that treatment of these matters will lead to a settlement. The liberal assumption is that people exist primarily as individuals with a fundamental (and moral) desire to be treated equally by others, and that states act justly and enjoy stability to the extent that they satisfy this yearning. This prescription is appropriate in societies where there is a consensus on national identity—in ethnically homogeneous states or in multi-ethnic immigrant societies with a shared civic identity, that is, where citizens see their relationship with the state through individualist lenses. However, in bi-national or multinational states, where there is no agreement on a common national political identity, matters are rather different. When the national nature of the state is at stake, many see themselves not just as bearers of individual rights but also as members of distinct communities.

Unable to recognize the importance of national identity or argue for the equal validity of rival versions of it, conventional liberalism not only fails to grasp what is at stake, but ends up accepting the nationalism of the dominant community by default (Kymlicka 1991, 1995; Taylor 1992, 1993). In Northern Ireland, liberals characteristically prescribe that members of the nationalist minority should enjoy equality as individual citizens within the United Kingdom. However, by failing to recognize what most Catholics consider integral to their conception of the good life, that is, the appreciation, recognition, and institutional equality of their

Irish national identity, this prescription falls short of authentic collective equality, including equality of individual self-esteem. Authentic collective equality requires that both groups' (national) identities be accepted as equally valid and legitimate—an argument refused by individualist liberalism.

Yet, it has been the denial of the national identity of the minority community, the denial of institutional recognition and equality for that national identity, and the denial of their right of national self-determination as a result of a poorly conceived partition of the island in the 1920s which has regularly occasioned conflict. There is endless evidence for this proposition. Consider just this: minority alienation from the political process remained intact under British direct rule despite the existence of laws and agencies designed to combat discrimination, and despite the provision of greater equality in the allocation of public housing and access to education.

As for surveys and opinion polls which show that individual grievances are highly salient, we must first observe that it is not unusual for national protests to be cloaked in the language of 'personal' grievances over issues like discrimination. Moreover, in the crucial act of voting, as opposed to responding to surveys, the vast majority of Catholics vote overwhelmingly for parties whose *raison d'être* is Irish nationalism, and not mere individual equality within the United Kingdom. Parties which espouse the latter goal receive derisory support from the minority. Non-party integrationist organizations, such as the Campaign for Equal Citizenship, are overwhelmingly Protestant, and what Catholic membership they have is not representative. As for republican paramilitaries, their campaign of violence has patently been waged over the issue of the border and the right of the Irish people 'as a whole' to national self-determination, rather than over fair employment. Sinn Féin links economic inequalities to the existence of the border and the denial of Irish national self-determination, but the latter are its most important concerns. It is very unlikely that nationalist political parties will lose significant support or that republican paramilitaries will be satisfied if the British government merely passes and implements more effective fair employment legislation.

While there are no survey data on the importance which paramilitaries attribute to unemployment compared with constitutional matters, their statements rarely refer to the need for jobs as a key goal. Smith and Chambers' survey does, however, measure the attitudes of the supporters of SF, the party which has supported the IRA until recently. It shows that 23 per cent of SF voters felt unemployment to be the biggest problem in Northern Ireland, but also reveals that 68 per cent of them chose straightforwardly nationalist responses: 'British rule' (44 per cent), 'the presence of British troops' (13 per cent), or 'the existence of the border' (11 per cent).[6] It is not clear why 'equality of opportunity' within the United Kingdom will satisfy this group. It makes sense, therefore, to conclude that a comprehensive settlement of the Northern Ireland conflict, which incorporates SF's supporters, needs to address the rights and aspirations of both national communities as well as the rights and aspirations of individuals.

Just as 'Unionist' civic integrationism downplays the national identity of the minority community, Irish nationalist civic integrationism, such as that represented by Dr Garret FitzGerald in the 1970s, downplays the British national identity of Unionists. Unionists do not want to be treated as equal citizens within a united Ireland any more than Irish nationalists want to be treated equally within the United Kingdom. They want the preservation of their nation through the preservation of the United Kingdom.

CONCLUSION

There have been two conflicts going on in and over Northern Ireland: the conflict between the parties and paramilitaries of the ethno-nationalist communities and their respective patron-states, and the conflict about what the conflict has been about. It is this latter conflict, the meta-conflict, waged primarily by intellectuals, with which this article has been concerned. The two conflicts are intimately connected because misinterpreting the conflict has consequences for public policy. The premise of this article is that five liberal fallacies have persistently blocked a surer understanding of Northern Ireland. The conflict is primarily ethno-national and it is this dimension which must be addressed, and addressed fairly if the conflict is to be ended, and durably satisfy the nationalism of the current minority while protecting the nationalism of the current majority. The construction of such a settlement will be difficult, of course, though not impossible (see McGarry and O'Leary 1995: ch. 9). The present opportunity to achieve a settlement seems better than any others since the 1960s and it seems likely that in their joint framework documents both governments will seek to exploit this opportunity.

[6] In the table that reports responses from party supporters on which change is needed to end the troubles, the option of a united Ireland has been accidentally omitted. Elsewhere, Smith and Chambers tell readers that nearly one half of Sinn Féin supporters thought creating a united Ireland was the change most needed.

Liberalism should not be tossed away with its bath water. There is clearly independent merit in the arguments that deprivation should be targeted by public and employment policy, that discrimination should be firmly tackled and affirmative action vigorously pursued, and that obstacles to voluntary interaction between the two communities should be dismantled. There is, however, no merit in the smug 'cosmopolitan' view that the conflict has been caused by unrepresentative and extremist elites, or by religiously or culturally retarded peoples incapable of the reasonable compromises allegedly characteristic of moderns. Analysts should always analyse themselves as a check on their interpretations of ethno-national conflicts.

REFERENCES

Anderson, Scott (1994). 'Making a killing: the high cost of peace in Northern Ireland'. *Harpers Magazine* 288: 1725, February, 45–54.

Aughey, Arthur (1989). *Under Siege: Ulster Unionism and the Anglo-Irish Agreement*. London: Hurst.

Bishop, Patrick and Eamon Mallie (1987). *The Provisional IRA*. London: Hutchinson.

Bruce, Steve (1986). *God Save Ulster! The Religion and Politics of Paisleyism*. Oxford: Oxford University Press.

—— (1994). *The Edge of the Union: The Ulster Loyalist Political Vision*. Oxford: Oxford University Press.

Buckland, Patrick (1981). *A History of Northern Ireland*. Dublin: Gill and Macmillan.

Cameron, Lord (1969). *Disturbances in Northern Ireland*. Report of the Commission appointed by the Governor of Northern Ireland. Belfast: HMSO.

Clare, Paul (1990) 'Subcultural obstacles to the control of racketeering in Northern Ireland'. *Conflict Quarterly*, 10(4): 25–50.

Connor, Walker (1994). *Ethnonationalism: The Quest for Understanding*. Princeton: Princeton University Press.

Darby, John, D. Murray, D. Batts, S. Dunn, S. Farren, and J. Harris, (1977). *Education and Community in Northern Ireland: Schools Apart?* Coleraine: New University of Ulster.

Dillon, Martin (1991). *The Dirty War*. London: Hutchinson.

Dudley-Edwards, Ruth (1977). *Patrick Pearse: The Triumph of Failure*. London: Gollancz.

Elliott, Marianne (1989). *Wolfe Tone: Prophet of Irish Independence*. New Haven: Yale University Press.

FitzGerald, Garret (1972). *Towards a New Ireland*. London: Charles Knight.

Foster, Roy (1988). *Modern Ireland: 1600–1972*. London: Allen Lane.

Fulton, John (1991). *The Tragedy of Belief: Division, Politics, and Religion in Ireland*. Oxford: Oxford University Press.

Gallagher, Eric and S. Worrall (1982). *Christians in Ulster, 1968–1980*. Oxford: Oxford University Press.

Heskin, Ken (1980). *Northern Ireland: A Psychological Analysis*. Dublin: Gill and Macmillan.

Horowitz, Donald (1989). 'Making moderation pay: the comparative politics of ethnic conflict management'. In J. P. Montville (ed.), *Conflict and Peacemaking in Multi-ethnic Societies*. Lexington, MA: Heath.

——(1991). *A Democratic South Africa? Constitutional Engineering in a Divided Society*. Berkeley: University of California Press.

Ignatieff, Michael (1993). *Blood and Belonging: Journeys into the New Nationalism*. Toronto: Viking.

Irwin, C. (1991). *Education and the Development of Social Integration in Divided Societies*. Belfast: Queen's University of Belfast.

Jenkins, Richard (1986). 'Northern Ireland: In what sense "religions" in conflict?' In R. Jenkins, H. Donnan, and G. McFarlane (eds.), *The Sectarian Divide in Northern Ireland Today*. London: Royal Anthropological Institute of Great Britain and Ireland.

Kymlicka, Will (1991). *Liberalism, Community, and Culture*, Oxford: Oxford University Press.

——(1995). *Multicultural Citizenship: A Liberal Theory of Minority Rights*. Oxford: Oxford University Press.

Macdonagh, Oliver (1983). *States of Mind: Two Centuries of Anglo-Irish Conflict, 1780–1980*. London: Pimlico.

Mawhinney, B. and R. Wells, (1975). *Conflict and Christianity in Northern Ireland*. Grand Rapids: Erdman.

McGarry, John and Brendan O'Leary (1995). *Explaining Northern Ireland: Broken Images*. Oxford and Cambridge, MA: Basil Blackwell.

Mitchell, Paul (1995). 'Party Competition in an Ethnic Dual Party System'. In Brendan O'Leary and John McGarry (eds.) *A State of Truce: Northern Ireland after Twenty-Five Years of War*. Special Issue of *Ethnic and Racial Studies*, vol. 18, 4: 773–96.

O'Brien, Conor Cruise (1974). *States of Ireland*. London: Panther Press.

O'Duffy, Brendan (1995). 'Violence in Northern Ireland 1964–94: Sectarian or Ethonational?' In Brendan O'Leary and John McGarry (eds.) *A State of Truce: Northern Ireland after Twenty-Five Years of War*. Special Issue of *Ethnic and Racial Studies*, vol. 18, 4: 740–72.

O'Leary, Brendan and John McGarry (1993). *The Politics of Antagonism: Understanding Northern Ireland*. London and Atlantic Heights, NJ: Athlone.

O'Malley, Padraig (1983). *The Uncivil Wars*. Belfast: Blackstaff.

——(1990). *Biting at the Grave: The Irish Hunger Strikes and the Politics of Despair*, Belfast: Blackstaff.

Pearce, Edward (1991). 'One Long piece of perplexity'. *Fortnight*, no. 296, p. 15.

Pollak, Andy (ed.) (1993). *A Citizen's Inquiry: the Opsahl Report on Northern Ireland*. Dublin: Lilliput.

Radford, Ian (1993). *Breaking Down Divisions: The Possibilities of a Local Church Contribution to Improving Community Relations*. Northern Ireland Community Relations Council.

Rawls, John (1971). *A Theory of Justice*. Oxford: Oxford University Press.

Roberts, Hugh (1990). 'Sound stupidity'. In J. McGarry and B. O'Leary (eds.), *The Future of Northern Ireland*. Oxford: Oxford University Press.

Rose, Richard (1971). *Governing Without Consensus: An Irish Perspective*. London: Faber and Faber.

—— (1976). 'On the priorities of citizenship in the Deep South and Northern Ireland'. *Journal of Politics*, 38(2): 247–91.

—— and Ian McAllister, (1983). 'Can political conflict be resolved by social change?' *Journal of Conflict Resolution*, 27(3): 533–57.

Ryder, Chris (1990). *RUC: Force Under Fire*, London: Methuen.

SACHR (1990). Second Report on Religious and Political Discrimination and Equality of Opportunity in Northern Ireland. Standing Advisory Commission on Human Rights.

Smith, David and Gerald Chambers (1991). *Inequality in Northern Ireland*. Oxford: Oxford University Press.

Stewart, A. T. Q. (1986). *The Narrow Ground: Patterns of Ulster History*. Belfast: Pretani.

Taylor, Charles (1992). 'The politics of recognition'. In C. Taylor and A. Gutman (eds.), *Multiculturalism and 'The Politics of Recognition'*. Princeton: Princeton University Press.

—— (1993). *Reconciling the Solitudes: Essays in Canadian Federalism and Nationalism*. Montreal: McGill—Queen's University Press.

Whyte, John (1986). 'How is the boundary maintained between the two communities in Northern Ireland?' *Ethnic and Racial Studies*, 9(2): 219–34.

—— (1990). *Interpreting Northern Ireland*. Oxford: Clarendon Press.

Williams, R. (1990). *The American Indian in Western Legal Thought: The Discourses of Conquest*. New York: Oxford University Press.

Wilson, Tom (1989). *Ulster; Conflict and Consent*. Oxford: Basil Blackwell.

6

The Labour Government and Northern Ireland, 1974–9

Brendan O'Leary

The Callaghan government was defeated on a motion of 'no confidence' in the House of Commons in May 1979, precipitating the general election that brought the Conservatives to power for eighteen years. This parliamentary humiliation was caused by two pivotal abstentions, that of Frank Maguire, an independent Irish nationalist MP, and that of Gerry Fitt, the then leader of the Social Democratic and Labour Party of Northern Ireland. The latter explained and justified his abstention as direct retaliation for Roy Mason's conduct as Secretary of State for Northern Ireland. Within a year Fitt had resigned his leadership position, and John Hume, a more intelligent, dynamic, and nationalist figure, renewed the SDLP. After Maguire's death in 1981 his Fermanagh and West Tyrone seat was won by Bobby Sands, an IRA prisoner convicted of scheduled offences—then leading a hunger strike that would end his own life. Sands's triumph at the ballot box and his subsequent martyrdom were the decisive moments in the electoral breakthrough of contemporary Sinn Féin. These stories affirm a forgotten truth: the radicalization of Irish nationalism in the 1980s was a by-product of the outgoing Labour government, and not the exclusive responsibility of the Thatcher cabinet. Many Irish in Great Britain and their sympathizers were also radicalized by the Irish policies of Callaghan's government. By 1981 the National Executive Committee of the Labour Party had embraced a policy of seeking Irish unification (by consent), the same policy as the SDLP—a platform commitment that would not be dropped until Tony Blair became leader of the party.

*****

The first Wilson government (1964–70) had intervened in Northern Ireland, politically and militarily, to redress the worst of the institutional discrimination and policy legacy of fifty years of government by the Ulster Unionist Party.[1] In so doing, Harold Wilson had partly acted from conviction, and partly reflected the dispositions of his Liverpool constituents. He had also been animated by the fact that during 1964–6 (when he had a parliamentary majority of three) the Ulster Unionist MPs at Westminster had acted as a loyal platoon of the Conservatives. When Wilson's government intervened in response to the civil rights movement, and the Unionist backlash against it, Richard Crossman, its most subsequently distinguished diarist, made the following entry: 'We have now got into something which we can hardly mismanage'.[2] This statement now sounds as ironic as imaginable, but in 1969–70 there was a widespread hope that London would preside over substantive reform in the region. Wilson handed responsibility to James Callaghan as Home Secretary, and thereby revived his fading career—as he enjoyed his only unambiguous moment as a reformer. Callaghan would hold all four of the great offices of state, the Premiership, the Chancellorship, and Foreign and Home Secretary, and have an unenviable record in all of them, but his brief flurry of constructive activities in Northern Ireland in 1969–70, especially in housing and policing policy, were the exceptions amongst his disappointing ministerial performances—even prompting a mildly self-congratulatory book on the subject.[3] Subsequent events collectively put paid to the optimism that had surrounded Callaghan's actions: the surprise return of the Conservatives to office in June 1970; Reginald Maudling's conduct as Home Secretary; the British Army's hardline conduct, especially in Belfast; the rise and aggression of the Provisional IRA; the independent aggression of loyalist paramilitaries; and the fateful and foolish decision to permit internment without trial in 1971.

The Army's murder of unarmed civilians, protesting against internment on January 30th 1972, Bloody Sunday, paved the way for the suspension of the Stormont parliament later that spring. Heath's Tories were forced to think, and rethink. Eventually, in late 1973, prompted by the goodwill of Willie Whitelaw and one of Heath's rare acts of skilled

---

[1] For an account of the UUP's regime of control see Brendan O'Leary and John McGarry, *The Politics of Antagonism: Understanding Northern Ireland* (1996, 2nd edition), pp. 107–80.

[2] Richard Crossman, *The Diaries of a Cabinet Minister*, Volume III (1977), p. 620.

[3] James Callaghan, *A House Divided* (1973). Callaghan creditably initiated the construction of a new, non-discriminatory Housing Executive that materialized in 1971. He records Crossman as having told him that he would be dismissed in an autumn reshuffle in 1969, but was reprieved because of his management of Northern Ireland; James Callaghan, *Time and Chance* (1987), p. 272.

statecraft, a power-sharing settlement was negotiated at the civil service college in Sunningdale.[4] Three major Northern Irish parties, the official UUP, the Alliance, and the SDLP, under the watchful auspices of both the UK and Irish governments, endorsed power-sharing in Belfast and a Council of Ireland to link the Dublin and Belfast parliaments. Brian Faulkner of the UUP and Fitt of the SDLP led the Executive, established by the Sunningdale agreement. It had been in office since 1 January 1974 when Heath called a general election for Westminster the following month, only to lose almost as surprisingly as Wilson had in 1970. In both 1970 and February 1974 the change of incumbent government at Westminster had adverse consequences for Northern Ireland. Whereas in 1970–2 the Conservatives fanned the flames of conflict through partisanship towards the Unionists, especially by introducing internment and soft-pedalling on loyalist violence, in 1974 Labour would undermine the Sunningdale settlement through abject spinelessness before the strike of the Ulster Workers Council (UWC); and after October 1974 it would start to renew the repressive errors of the Tories, albeit with more finesse and hand-wringing regret.

The Wilson (1974–6) and the Callaghan (1976–9) premierships differed in style and underlying preferences, but much less in substantive decisions and non-decisions. As regards Northern Ireland both prime ministers acted as if they were in office but not in power, devoting little but frustrated attention to the region. Statements they made before and after their premierships showed they had formulated preferences substantively different from the status quo, but in office did nothing that significantly advanced these goals. Wilson would have preferred a united Ireland, and in November 1971 had put forward a fifteen-point programme to that effect when Labour was in opposition.[5] Point two included a creditable proposal to generate tripartite talks between Great Britain, Northern Ireland, and Ireland, the formula that would eventually be adopted in the making of the Sunningdale agreement in 1973, and more comprehensively and inclusively in the making of the Good Friday Agreement during 1995–8. In Opposition Wilson rejected internment without trial, and would, to his credit, make good on that pledge when he returned to office. He went so far as to meet with IRA personnel in 1972—though he managed to exclude this episode from the relevant

[4] For a treatment of Sunningdale's differences with the Good Friday Agreement, see Stefan Wolff, 'Context and Content: Sunningdale and Belfast Compared', in *Aspects of the Belfast Agreement* (2001), edited by Rick Wilford, pp. 11–27.

[5] Harold Wilson, *Final Term: The Labour Government, 1974–1976* (1979), pp. 68–70; see especially the chapter 'John Bull's Other Island', pp. 66–80.

section of his memoirs.[6] The head of his policy unit, Bernard Donoughue, described Wilson as having had 'radical instincts' on the Irish question,[7] and he was permitted, along with Wilson's press secretary, Joe Haines, to develop dramatic policy options, including (a) an 'Algerian solution'— i.e. withdrawal; and (b) imposed dominion status, i.e. independence with connections to the Crown. In May 1974 Wilson drafted his own 'Doomsday Scenario'—though Donoughue describes his premier as being frightened by his own thinking, which sounds typical of the man.[8] Tony Benn's diary entry of 10 April 1974 records the following after a Cabinet meeting: 'It was agreed, again under the highest secrecy, that we would begin considering the implications of a total withdrawal. Of course, if that got out, it would precipitate bloodshed but we felt we simply had to do it. Roy [Jenkins] took that view. Jim [Callaghan] looked very doubtful but thought it needed to be done. Fred Peart, Peter Shore and Willie Ross are 100 per cent pro-Protestant. So the cabinet would divide on Catholic– Protestant lines in the event of this happening'.[9] The sole significant public evidence that the Wilson government was contemplating such radical options came, ironically in light of later developments, from Roy Mason, then Secretary of State for Defence. He made a speech on 24 April 1974 warning that pressure in Great Britain was mounting for a pullout of troops and to set a date for withdrawal. His Ministry promptly issued a statement denying that there had been any change of policy. One wonders whether Mason simply made an error, flew a kite for Wilson, or whether he sabotaged the withdrawal option in the light of opinion within his ministry.[10] Benn's diary records the following for the Cabinet meeting of 25 April: 'The first item was a speech by Roy Mason yesterday in which he had hinted that British troops might be withdrawn... Harold [Wilson] said that Ministers must consult with the FO, and in particular with the Northern Ireland Secretary before saying anything. Merlyn [Rees] told me he was desperately worried... it encouraged the idea that the British Labour Government was a soft sell. Harold said the speech was a breach of the Procedure for Ministers'.[11] This admonishment would appear to exclude the idea that Mason flew a

[6] See note 3.

[7] Bernard Donoughue, *Prime Minister: The Conduct of Policy under Harold Wilson and James Callaghan* (1987), p. 128. Donoughue opens his narration on 'the problem' of 'Ireland' by saying that as a 'former professional historian' he knew it to be 'insoluble'. Why professional historians, former or otherwise, might have such knowledge is not explained.

[8] Ibid., p. 129.   [9] Tony Benn, *Against the Tide, Diaries 1973–76* (1989), pp. 137–8.

[10] Rees describes himself as 'left wondering why the speech had been made', *Northern Ireland: A Personal Perspective*, p. 61.   [11] Benn, op. cit., p. 142.

kite for Wilson. These months aside, in which he made a rhetorical attack on the UWC's strikers as 'spongers', Wilson was to show no determination to pursue any radical, or indeed simply ambitious, agenda on Northern Ireland during the rest of his premiership—a Cabinet sub-committee did consider the withdrawal option but rejected it. From May 1974 'Wilson and his successor tried not to get too deeply involved in the Irish problem. Our policy became one of consolidation, trying to contain terrorism and just get through from year to year. The Irish situation regularly appeared on the agenda of the Cabinet Committee... but it was mainly a question of reporting information... and rarely was anything taken higher to Cabinet... [T]he Cabinet Committee... never after 1974 actually discussed Northern Ireland *policy*: it only discussed law and order'.[12] Callaghan, by contrast with Wilson, entertained no radical options on Northern Ireland as premier. His memoir *Time and Chance* conveys his world-weary resignation: 'At no time did I feel we were doing more than breasting the tide'.[13] He blamed the locals, albeit in polite language: 'It was frustrating to watch every initiative destroyed from within, and I can but repeat the opinion I expressed to my Cabinet colleagues eighteen years ago at the outset of the present troubles in January 1969: "The cardinal aim of our policy must be to influence Northern Ireland to solve its own problems"'.[14] Out of office he had a change of heart, making a speech in July 1981 that proposed a timetabled period for a negotiated agreement before an ordered British withdrawal and the formation of an independent Northern Ireland.

The stylistic differences between the premiers were reflected in the personnel they chose to manage the region. The two Secretaries of State, Merlyn Rees (1974–6) and Roy Mason (1976–79), were remarkably different in personality and profile,[15] though both were on the right of the party and associated with Callaghan's patronage. An LSE alumnus, Rees had the shambolic gait of a badly dressed and over-promoted head-master—he had been a teacher. His indecisiveness made it difficult to believe he had been an RAF officer during the Second World War. His Welsh name and roots belied a largely English persona—he had been the MP for Leeds South since 1963. His heavily lined face was 'lived in',

---

[12] Donoughue, *Prime Minister*, p. 132, emphasis in the original.

[13] Callaghan, op. cit., p. 500   [14] Ibid. p. 500.

[15] The former kindly agreed to be interviewed by the author (18 Dec. 1990), and generously reviewed one of his co-edited books for the *LSE Magazine*. The latter refused all requests for interviews, the sole ex-Secretary of State to refuse the author such a request in the 1980s and 1990s.

worried, and anxious—with his glasses constantly threatening to fall off his nose. He was a sincere man, thoughtful, capable of listening, but held by his civil servants to be incapable of decision-making; and when he did decide, caution usually triumphed over his intellect. His memoirs are a copy-edited version of the man—garrulous, intermittently coherent, a collection of anecdotes and episodes, but with little eye for the main story. Nevertheless, they display occasional flashes of genuine insight, showing the intelligence and moral commitment that had brought him to political office.[16] He held, for example, the interesting view that Britain stopped just outside of the Belfast region; and he observed of his abusive and threatening correspondence that 'There was little to choose between the two sides except that more religious sectarianism was shown by the majority population and more anti-unionism by the minority'.[17] Ideologically, he was right-wing Labour, but with a touch of romanticism. He referred to trade unionist and nonconformist people as 'my kind of people'.[18] He was at home with trade unionists, and briefly entertained naive beliefs that working class loyalist Protestants could be won to non-sectarian socialism. He developed a detailed knowledge of the region, still evident many years after his exit from office, but remained burdened by the memory of his role—in my interviews he was very defensive about Labour's crisis decision-making of 1974. One would have to be very tough, cynical, and world-weary not to have liked Merlyn Rees, even if one disagreed with his politics. He could provoke irritation and exasperation, but active animosity towards him was difficult. 'Dithering' was the term of criticism most often applied in interviews with British and Irish officials that I conducted in the late 1980s and early 1990s. A contemporaneous newspaper description quoted one of his officials declaring: 'I don't mind Merlyn wrestling with his conscience for ages over every issue. What I mind is that the result always seems to be a draw.'[19]

Such evaluations did not apply to Roy Mason, whom friend or foe regarded as decisive. He too was right-wing Labour, a Yorkshireman, also with a military past. The former Secretary of State for Defence was the true political thug of the Callaghan administration—a description normally and wrongly applied to the brilliant, loquacious, and effortlessly intelligent Denis Healey. Mason was educated, but did his

---

[16] Merlyn Rees, *Northern Ireland: A Personal Perspective* (1985).

[17] Rees, op. cit., p. 317.   [18] Rees, op. cit., p. 71

[19] Cited in David McKittrick and David McVea, *Making Sense of The Troubles* (2001), p. 106.

best to hide it—in a manner once common in the class-conscious north of England. Whereas Rees agonized, Mason appeared barely to reflect, during or after his tenure in office. He spoke in clipped, blunt language, with none of Rees's verbosity or warmth. The MP for Barnsley was an embarrassing example of working-class royalism and authoritarianism. Hosting the Queen in Northern Ireland on the occasion of her Jubilee in 1977 was plainly the highlight of his life. That his evident pleasure in toe-curling deference to the Crown might be politically offensive to Irish nationalists, 'Greens' as he called them, either did not deter him or occur to him. 'He's probably the Protestants favourite Secretary of State', said Roland Moyle, a Labour junior minister in the Northern Ireland Office (NIO).[20] Not until Peter Mandelson's appointment would so many Unionists be so happy with a Secretary of State. Whereas Rees was mildly and tacitly unionist—he would later not support the passage of the Anglo-Irish Agreement of 1985[21]—he was, however, genuinely interested in conflict-resolution. While ultimately willing to follow the advice of counter-insurgents and those suggesting that civil liberties should be traded for order, he took no self-indulgent pleasure in his difficult brief for the Union. Rees, like Callaghan, was willing to con-template 'radical' steps *after* he had left office: expressing his willingness to cede South Armagh to Ireland.[22] Mason, by contrast, revelled in the prefectoral nature of the Secretary of State's role, beholden to no local parliament. He was a unionist and a trade unionist, with the repertoire of imagination associated with both of these traditions. His civil servants thought of him as a viceroy, Irish nationalists as vice-Roy.

*****

Between 1972 and 1985 successive UK governments presented them-selves as neutral arbiters of conflict in and over Northern Ireland.[23] It was not an unfamiliar self-designation. In retreat from empire, mandates, and protectorates, UK governments had claimed to be neutral arbiters of the rival claims of Hindus and Muslims in the Indian sub-continent, Arabs

---

[20] Interview, 3 January 1991. Donoughue described him as seeming more 'Protestant' than the 'Prods', op. cit., p. 131.

[21] In his memoir he declared that 'Grandiose Anglo/Irish solutions will not work', op. cit., p. 352. This too was defensive. The Anglo-Irish Agreement, which paved the way for the Good Friday Agreement, stemmed from the two sovereign governments taking action, precisely the path Rees and Mason closed off after the 1974 strike.

[22] Rees, op. cit., p. 351.

[23] What follows draws upon joint work with John McGarry, especially *The Politics of Antagonism*, chapter 5, 'Deadlock, 1972–85: the limits to British arbitration'.

and Jews in Palestine, and Greek and Turkish Cypriots. This self-designation was usually accompanied by a functionally appropriate amnesia over the contribution of imperial governance to national, ethnic, and communal conflicts. Northern Ireland was problematic, however, because it was not a colony that could be differentiated by the twin tests of salt-water *and* skin-colour differentiation from Great Britain. It was plainly the oldest colonial legacy, but it was not immediately clear to Westminster and Whitehall whether to treat it as an internal or external matter, British or colonial, or both. They decided in general on an internal treatment, especially in the NIO, which soon become unionist with a small 'u', and would seek to exclude the Foreign Office from its brief as much as possible. The border would not, it was said, be an issue. The elephant in the room would not be discussed with the British public. It was comforting for London to treat the conflict as fundamentally religious rather than as ethno-national or colonial. Such typification made the conflict the sole responsibility of the locals. Self-presentation as neutral arbiters had other attractions. It was in keeping with traditional British rhetoric on Irish matters. It offered a mode of crisis-management less drastic than that entailed by imposing Irish unification, Northern Ireland's independence, a new partition, or joint sovereignty. Arbitration avoided the problematic option of treating Northern Ireland as unambiguously British. As all now know better, the notion of British, or British homogeneity, is itself ambiguous. If Northern Ireland was to be British did that mean it should be governed as England, Scotland, or Wales—or as Northern Ireland? Was it not the case that the British, historically, were Protestants, unified by their opposition to the Catholic powers of Europe and the Catholics of these islands? Arbitration as neutrality between the Reformation and the Counter-Reformation offered UK governments the chance to present themselves as tolerant, reasonable, and post-religious, if not wholly secular. Arbitration also had international presentational advantages. It was acceptable—if not always ideal—to Irish governments, and to the US State department. It had the benefits of ambiguity—London could opt to see any Northern Ireland item as internal or as external, as judged most convenient. Labour had intervened with troops in 1969 because the Royal Ulster Constabulary (RUC) had been partisan—and was exhausted with riot-control (or riot-creation, depending upon one's perspective). But, it had also intervened because the Irish government appeared likely to mobilise on the border, and because a further Protestant backlash was feared. The story of this intervention was rewritten, in part accurately, as being motivated to keep the warring factions apart.

Three fundamental premises comprised the arbitration orientation under the Wilson and Callaghan cabinets:

(i) encouraging Protestants and Catholics to work together towards an agreed largely internal political accommodation, while retaining the stance of the honest broker;

(ii) reforming or modernizing Northern Ireland along the lines of the post-war British consensus; and

(iii) impartial security policies that eventually rested on the criminalization of political violence.

Rees tried the first element with some determination, even though he and Wilson had wholly failed to stabilise the Sunningdale settlement, a failure treated separately below. After the destruction of the Sunningdale enterprise Rees paved the way for elections to a constitutional convention in 1975. They were designed to exclude the involvement of the Irish government, and put the UK in the role of mediator rather than as the active director of a political initiative. Neutrality on the part of the Secretary of State consisted of refusing to enforce a reunification of Ireland (the anti-nationalist axiom), and refusing any restoration of a devolved government on the strongly majoritarian lines of the Stormont regime (the anti-unionist axiom). When the convention's Unionist majority in its final report insisted on a majoritarian executive, and described the SDLP as fundamentally republican and incapable of being loyal members of a Belfast government, Rees dissolved the body in March 1976— leading to twenty three years of direct rule from Westminster.

Mason, by contrast, pursued no significant power-sharing initiatives, directly or otherwise. He believed they heightened expectations and created instability. Benevolent direct rule on the second premise of arbitration policies constituted his understanding of his mission. He declared he was more worried by the region's economy than its political or security problems. Rees and Mason, like some of their Conservative predecessors and successors, saw one of their key tasks to be the institutionalization of professionalized public services, cleansing the partisan, clientelist, and supremacist conduct of local governments and state organizations prevalent under the Stormont parliament. The police were detached from their role as the armed wing of the Ulster Unionist Party. The appointments of magistrates and judges, public prosecutions, and the franchise for local government and regional elections were put under Westminster's control. Fairer administration of education and health-boards flowed from direct rule, it was thought. Human rights watchdogs, ombudsmen, and anti-discrimination legislation, under both the Tories and Labour, showed formal evidence of good intentions. Public expenditure and employment would no longer be overtly dictated by the political patronage imperatives of the UUP.

If professionalizing public bureaucracies was regarded as evidence of Labour's determination to provide good instead of agreed government, its security policies were eventually intended to show ministers as firm governors. The Labour government had been seen to respond to coercion. Nationalists judged, correctly, that Wilson and Rees had capitulated before the coercion of the Ulster Workers Council strike. A determined loyalist minority, which eventually mobilised a majority of the majority community, was able to dictate outcomes to a cross-community majority within Northern Ireland—irrespective of the local Assembly's election returns, mandate, or current preferences. Unionists also judged that the government was negotiable before the assaults of republicans. Ceasefires and experiments in negotiations with the IRA were tried in 1975—and fed loyalist fears of a sell-out. But while the constitutional convention was in progress Rees and his officials reconsidered security policy—reflecting the tendency for British policy-makers to partition party-political and security matters without deep appraisals of their mutual connections. These reconsiderations would be implemented under Mason.

They involved three themes: criminalization, Ulsterization, and normalization. In part, they stemmed from the Gardiner Report, which had been commissioned to rid London of the embarrassment of internment without trial. Initiated in August 1971, internment had been overtly incompetent and partisan. The first loyalist was not interned until February 1973. While the policy operated between 1971 and 1975, 2060 republicans were detained, by comparison with 109 loyalists.[24] Readers can appraise for themselves the bias in this policy from one piece of comparative data: whereas republicans were twenty times as likely as loyalists to be interned, they were responsible for just over twice as many deaths in this period.[25] Gardiner recommended the restoration of judicial processes, insisting that suspects should be dealt with through the courts, and, fatefully, that the 'special status' category for the targeted prisoners should be phased out. The Gardiner Report softened the Diplock Report

---

[24] G. Hogan and C. Walker, *Political Violence and the Law in Ireland*, 1989, pp. 93–4.

[25] Between 1971 and 1975 all republican paramilitaries were responsible for 806 deaths in and over Northern Ireland, whereas loyalists were responsible for 385. In 1974 and 1975 the death tolls caused by each set of paramilitaries were very close in number. The data and the simple calculation in the text are based on the definitive work of David McKittrick, Seamus Kelters, Brian Feeney, and Chris Thornton, *Lost Lives: The Stories of the Men, Women and Children who died as a result of the Northern Ireland troubles* (2001) 3rd edition, p. 1496.

of 1972, which had recommended the suspension of the right to a jury-trial for certain indictable offences, new relaxed rules on the admissibility of evidence and on the onus of proof, and enhanced powers for the security forces—the police and the army. These commendations had been duly incorporated in the Emergency Provisions Act (EPA) of 1973, which had retained the power of internment. While the EPA had been portrayed as a reform, because it was accompanied by the repeal of the hated Special Powers Act of the Stormont parliament, it was widely and rightly diagnosed as containing many of the same threats to the fair adminiration of justice: up to one half of the new Act was directly inspired by the older legislation.[26] Criminalization, of course, depended for its success on two contentious predictions, that the UK would be able to present itself as relying on normal legal processes, and that the efforts to delegitimise political violence as criminal violence would work within the constituent populations of republicans and loyalists. The first prospect was destroyed because the government continued to depend on juryless single-judge Diplock courts, and to derogate from the European Convention on Human Rights on the grounds that there was an emergency—which contradicted the suppositions of 'normalization'. In addition, the abandonment of internment led to an increased reliance on confessions, extracted by coercive and dubious questioning techniques.[27] This prompted the embarrassment of vigorous criticism by Amnesty International in 1978.[28] Mason was forced to permit an inquiry and the Bennett Committee proposed new controls on police conduct, which did lead to a decline in complaints after Mason had left office. The second prospect, winning legitimacy for the criminalization of paramilitaries, had some limited effect within the loyalist working class; resistance within the republican constituency would wholly defeat it.

'Ulsterization' involved the use of locally recruited police and military in the management of security—and sought a downsizing in the role and numbers of the British Army in the region. The policy had obvious public relations advantages for Whitehall. Between 1969 and 1975, 270 British soldiers were killed in the conflict, compared with 148 of the local security forces; between 1976 and 1984 the figures were 150 and 235 respectively.[29] The use of locals in security duties helped press briefings intended to fend off interpretations of the conflict as colonial. It was thought that the British Army's vanguard role made it easier for the IRA to argue that it was fighting a national war of liberation. Presentation of

---

[26] Hogan and Walker, op. cit., p. 197.   [27] Peter Taylor, *Beating the Terrorists?* (1980).
[28] *Report of an Amnesty International Mission to Northern Ireland 1977* (1978).
[29] Calculated from McKittrick, *et al.*, Table 1.

Ulsterization was bolstered by the adoption of 'police primacy' as part of 'normalization' in 1976. The police had doubled in size between 1969 and 1972. Mason oversaw another dramatic expansion: by 1982 the RUC comprised 7,700 regulars and 4,800 reservists. The ratio of police officers to residents in Northern Ireland's small population was soon over four times that in the South-east of England. This comparison rightly suggests that 'normalization' was not with respect to some English norm. The police did develop greater responsibility for security, but this was accomplished by militarizing the police. The flak-jacketed, heavily armed, armoured Land-Rover-borne RUC did not resemble English bobbies. Plastic-bullet firing police were less lethal, and usually more circumspect, than soldiers using live ammunition, but they were still engaged in political repression. The RUC made little use of normal police methods of gathering intelligence, especially in Catholic dominated areas, and used military snatch-operations rather than low-key modes of arrest. The Army was fully present in a back-up role, but almost exclusively deployed in republican dominated districts—thereby undermining both police primacy and efforts to portray impartiality in the administration of policing.

'Ulsterization' and 'normalization' were not confined to the RUC. In 1969 Callaghan as Home Secretary had overseen reports and measures intended both to disarm the RUC and to disband the B-Specials, the exclusively Protestant paramilitary auxiliary back-up to the RUC. The latter objective was formally achieved; the former was rapidly reversed, in part in response to IRA actions. By 1979 Mason, Callaghan's appointee as Secretary of State, had professionalized but militarized the RUC, and had overseen the expansion and extensive deployment of the Ulster Defence Regiment, the UDR, a locally recruited and deployed section of the British Army. The UDR had a highly partisan name, as offensive in nationalist ears as that of the RUC's; and they were seen as the new B-Specials. Within a decade of Labour's first intervention Mason was presiding over nearly 20,000 jobs in the RUC and UDR establishments, mostly staffed by working-class Protestants. Once again Catholics and nationalists were being policed, para-policed, and soldiered by the local majority of Protestants and Unionists. 'Ulsterization' had predictably become Unionist-ulsterization; and it had other foreseeable consequences. The IRA (and the INLA) switched their focus of attack towards the most visible security personnel, i.e. the RUC and the UDR. The result was that the conflict was waged more directly between locals, imparting an apparently greater sectarian colouration to a mutually dirty war, making it even more difficult for Unionist politicians to contemplate power-sharing with their nationalist neighbours. The credibility of normalization was further undermined by the government's public deployment of the Army's most feared specialist intelligence unit, the SAS, in Armagh; and the decision either to permit a dirty war opened by MI5, MI6, the SAS, and specialist units of the RUC, or not to look closely into the actions and inactions of the said agencies.[30]

'Criminalization' posed a serious threat to the IRA. The first response of its prisoners arrested and convicted under the new rationalized legal procedures was to go 'on the blanket', refusing to bear prison uniforms. This was followed by the 'dirty protests', smearing their prison walls with their own excrement—again in a determined rejection of the criminal designation. The 'H blocks', the recently designed high-security prison units, became locally and then internationally notorious: and plainly the site of incarceration of the politically motivated. 'Criminalization', however, would not be decisively defeated by the IRA until after Labour had left office. In the struggle between the UK authorities and republican prisoners, culminating in ten dead hunger strikers in 1981, the prisoners would win de facto recognition of their special status while the government would formally avoid the concession of political status.[31] But no one was fooled. The prisoners won at the ballot box. The outcome was Sands's and subsequently Sinn Féin's electoral breakthrough—Sinn Féin was able to widen the battlefields, and the IRA was able to shake off the criminal label within its own constituency and beyond. The long-run repercussions of Rees's and Mason's criminalization policies were to build Sinn Féin a strong political constituency, one that threatened the SDLP's nationalist flanks, and would eventually resend London's negotiators back towards an accommodation with the

---

[30] For diverse materials on the dirty war, especially works dealing with British intelligence, informers, and loyalist paramilitaries, see Anthony Bradley, *Requiem for a Spy: the Killing of Robert Nairac* (1993); Steve Bruce *The Red Hand: Protestant Paramilitaries in Northern Ireland* (1992) and "Terrorists and Politics: The Case of Northern Ireland's Loyalist Paramilitaries." *Terrorism and Political Violence* 13, no. 2 (2001): 27–48; Martin Dillon, *The Dirty War* (1990); Paul Foot, *Who Framed Colin Wallace?* (1989); Fred Holroyd with Nick Burbridge, *War Without Honour* (1989); Raymond Murray, *The SAS in Ireland* (1990); Peter Taylor, *Stalker: The Search for the Truth* (1987); Marc Urban, *Big Boys Rules: the Secret Struggle Against the IRA* (1992); and Peter Wright and Paul Greengrass, *Spycatcher* (1987).

[31] On the IRA and the hunger strikes, see especially David Beresford, *Ten Men Dead: The Story of the 1981, Irish Hunger Strike* (1987); and on republicans see, *inter alia*, Patrick Bishop, and Eamon Mallie, *The Provisional IRA* (1987), Brendan O'Brien, *The Long War: The IRA & Sinn Fein from Armed Struggle to Peace Talks* (1995); Tim Pat Coogan, *The IRA* (1970, 1980, 1987); Padraig O'Malley, *Biting at the Grave: The Irish Hunger Strikes and the Politics of Despair* (1990); critically reviewed by the author in *Irish Political Studies* (1991); and Peter Taylor, *Provos: The IRA and Sinn Féin* (1997). On Sinn Féin see Brian Feeney's fine study, *Sinn Féin: A Hundred Turbulent Years* (2002).

government of Ireland. Ulsterization, like criminalization, bought short-run gains at the expense of long-run contradictions. Direct rule became overtly *British* rule through local Ulster Unionist instruments. The image of the impartial arbitrator would be shredded as the UDR replaced the B-Specials; as the RUC became a rationalized, expanded, and overwhelmingly Protestant force—its reform primarily confined to its detachment from the UUP; and as a steady stream of episodes and scandals persuaded nationalists of extensive collusion between the security forces, intelligence agencies, and loyalist paramilitaries. Above all, a social democratic government might have been expected to have strongly endeavoured to achieve significant reform in employment—in eradicating direct and indirect discrimination; in encouraging the development of genuinely bi-national or non-sectarian trades unions; and in encouraging the confrontation of public prejudices and stereotypes. A Fair Employment Act was passed in 1976; the legal framework would prove naive and ineffective, while the agency it established would lack sufficient powers to make a difference. Catholic male unemployment would remain over twice that of Protestants for the next two decades. Labour did nothing of importance with its trade union allies to build common ground within the working class. Its initial dalliance with the Northern Ireland Labour Party, which disappeared amidst the polarization of the 1970s, had given its leaders concrete evidence that British Labour could not perform the types of cross-community mobilization it had managed in Scotland. Thinly funded and anaemic efforts to promote good community relations, and to encourage integrated education on the part of Lord Melchett, a junior minister under Mason, symbolised good intentions. But they were comprehensively undermined by the failure to stabilize Sunningdale, or to deliver a positive outcome from the constitutional Convention of 1975–6, and, of course, by the repercussions of Ulsterization and criminalization.

What of order, if not law and the rule of law? How might one evaluate Labour's governance of security? Within Northern Ireland the years 1972–6 were marked by the highest levels of political violence in the current phase of the conflict, as tracked by the key indicators of killings, injuries, explosions, shootings, and armed robberies. Levels of violence on all these indicators in general fell sharply from 1977 onwards, thereafter reaching a generally steady state until the IRA and loyalist ceasefires of 1994–7. Should these data be deployed in defence of the Labour government? It at least dampened levels of violence—including in Great Britain, where the horrors of the Guildford and Birmingham pub-bombings were to trigger the passage of the Prevention of Terrorism

Act. But several caveats need to be entered into any such appraisal. The high death-toll in the early years is best explained by three factors. The first is the decision of the Provisional IRA to engage in urban and rural guerrilla warfare and urban terrorism—producing large numbers of casualties amongst inexperienced police and army personnel—whereas its commercial bombings led to a large number of civilian deaths. The second was the loyalist backlash, first against civil rights demonstrations in the late 1960s, and then in the form of very high levels of sectarian assassinations against Catholics between 1971 and 1975. The third factor was the introduction of internment without trial in August 1971: initially targeted exclusively (but inaccurately) at the nationalist community, the policy acted as a recruitment agency for the IRA.

The reductions in all major indicators of conflict from 1977 are related to these three factors. The IRA changed its strategy. Weakened by the ceasefire of 1975, on which more below, it reorganized in small cells, or active service units. It settled down for a 'long war', abandoning its hopes of rapid victory. It switched its foci towards military and political targets—reducing its scale of commercial bombing, with its indiscriminate consequences for civilians and where the impacts had often adversely affected their own base of support. Second, loyalist paramilitaries reduced their assassinations of Catholics, in part because their fears of a British withdrawal had diminished. Moreover, over time they were more likely to be arrested than before, and their organizations became more factionalized, corrupt, and directionless. Third, greater numbers and effectiveness on the part of the security forces dampened down levels of violence. Police primacy reduced the Army's propensity to be more trigger-happy. The price was high: huge investments in security devices, surveillance systems, cordoned-off town-centres, checkpoints, forts, observation posts, and computerized civilian screening on a massive scale. Urban landscapes and housing were redesigned to be less friendly to the urban paramilitant. Emergency legislation that became permanent removed certain standard civil liberties and judicial safeguards (notoriously those accused and convicted of the Guildford and Birmingham pub-bombings were entirely innocent of the charges against them).

This brief appraisal suggests why purely on order criteria some are tempted to assess the Mason years positively—they turned the corner on the worst of the violence. This is a verdict especially held by many unionists. The Labour cabinets certainly deserve credit for abandoning internment without trial. Conflict-reduction is not, however, conflict-resolution, and nor is it proof of sensible conflict-management. The reduction in violence was partly caused by perversities and actions for which governments were not responsible; and government actions created new perversities. Residential segregation increased extensively as people chose to live safely with 'their own': the early 1970s reduced radically the numbers of genuinely 'mixed areas'. The absence of a politically negotiated settlement encouraged a long war of attrition, a 'non-result', a continuous and bleeding stalemate—bringing up whole new cohorts of mutually distrustful citizens and politicians. The sealing off of the Protestant middle class and better-off working class, both from the visible signs and the economic costs of the conflict, reduced their incentives to engage in power-sharing, let alone accept an Irish dimension. The institutionalized interests of large sections of the Protestant working class in security and security-related occupations made them more indifferent towards peace. A distinguished Cambridge economist, Professor Bob Rowthorn, would come to describe Northern Ireland as having a 'workhouse economy', in which the participants in an unproductive economy either engage in surveillance of one another or exchange non-marketed services. The growth of Sinn Féin and the radicalization of the SDLP were by-products of the policies of Rees and Mason. The government's manipulation of the IRA's ceasefire in 1975, while seen as tactically acute by counter-insurgents, had negative long-run costs. Merlyn Rees in his memoirs maintains that the government's quasi-negotiations during the IRA's ceasefire were coherent, 'to create the conditions in which the Provisional IRA's military organization might be weakened. The longer the ceasefire lasted, the more difficult it would be for them to start a campaign from scratch and in this period of peace I hoped political action would be given a chance'.[32] The rationale of his officials was certainly to distract and demobilize the IRA by discussing withdrawal but not negotiating it. And the IRA was weakened by the ceasefire, but that only ensured that after its reorganization it would become wholly overtly hostile to ceasefires or truces without a British commitment to withdrawal, and would treat NIO officials as deceitful counter-insurgents. The summer that Labour lost office saw the INLA and the IRA succeed in their most spectacular killings to date: the INLA blew up Airey Neave in the House of Commons car-park, while the IRA blew up Lord Louis Mountbatten, and killed eighteen British soldiers, at Warrenpoint. The ceasefire experience of 1975 partly explains why the IRA broke its 1994 ceasefire; it suspected the Major government of stringing it along in the way that Rees's officials had done two decades

---

[32] Rees, *Northern Ireland*, op. cit., p. 224.

before. This culture of suspicion still drives the current IRA's leadership's reluctance to complete the decommissioning of its weapons until the British government has comprehensively and unambiguously delivered on all its public and legal obligations under the Good Friday Agreement. Lack of trust in New Labour amongst Irish republicans is not just the result of Peter Mandelson's dreadful performance as Secretary of State; it is rooted in entrenched memories of the IRA's manipulation at the hands of Rees's officials. The entrenchment of distrust was not confined to nationalist quarters. Unionists had seen the Labour government as negotiable, and as willing to bend to coercion. Once Labour had lost its parliamentary majority at Westminster the UUP extracted concessions of an integrationist kind, notably an expansion in Northern Ireland's representation at Westminster, and could rely on its veto power on the floor of the Commons to inhibit any prospect of power-sharing or an Irish dimension. The Labour government, under both its premiers, therefore reduced the capacity of UK ministers to provide credible commitments to the locals, let alone the Irish government. Being distrusted and disliked by both communities was seen by some as a badge of honour; a more sensible appraisal is that earning contempt and distrust all around earns no politicians worthy reputations, either at the time or later.

*****

The collapse of the Sunningdale experiment was the decisive event of the Labour Government of 1974; it haunted the rest of Labour's term of management; and it is the event by which Labour's ministers should be judged. That is why it is addressed at the end rather than the beginning of this chapter. Evaluation requires a rapid analytical narrative. The Sunningdale Agreement was both an agreement and an agreement about further possible agreements. It included immediate consent to the formation of a cross-community coalition government in Northern Ireland, comprising Faulkner's Official Unionists, Fitt's SDLP, and the Alliance party, a unionist party in lower case 'u', which drew support from cultural Protestants and Catholics. An eleven-member Executive was formed with six UUP, four SDLP and one Alliance ministers. In this respect the Agreement was a voluntary consociation. The three parties had between them won nearly 61 per cent of the first preference votes cast in the Northern Ireland Assembly elections held in the summer of 1973, and the UUP (though divided) and the SDLP were the largest parties in the Unionist and nationalist blocs, respectively. The Agreement also envisaged a Council of Ireland, at the SDLP's insistence, but with the support of the UK and Irish governments. The Council harked back to unfulfilled elements of the Government of Ireland Act of 1920.[33] It was to consist of a Council of Ministers, seven from each of the two jurisdictions on the island, a secretariat, and a sixty-member consultative assembly (with thirty members from Dáil Éireann and thirty from the Northern Ireland Assembly). Decisions of the Council of Ministers were to be unanimous, thus providing veto powers to both sides—and indeed sub-sections of both delegations. The Council was to be experimental, vested with minor consultative and research functions, but it was to have a 'harmonizing' role, and the door was left open for it to become the embryonic institution of a reunified Ireland—though plainly only through mutual cooperation. Sunningdale also had an agenda too often forgotten today—including consideration of major reforms of the RUC and a review of the policy of internment without trial. A commission was promised to examine the contentious issue of cross-border extradition of those suspected of terrorist offences. Faulkner and his colleagues hoped to win acceptance for power-sharing and the Council of Ireland amongst Unionists by emphasizing the potential security benefits from coopera-tion with the Irish government, the largely symbolic nature of the Council, the Unionist veto over the Council's evolution, and the de facto recognition of Northern Ireland's current status contained in Article 5: 'The Irish Government fully accepted and solemnly declared that there could be no change in the status of Northern Ireland until a majority of the people of Northern Ireland desired a change in that status'.

The Agreement got off to an inauspicious start, even though many of its ministers were to prove effective holders of their portfolios. It was evident that it would be opposed by both sets of paramilitaries. On 4 January 1974, four days after the Executive took office, the Ulster Unionist Council of the UUP voted to reject the Agreement. Three days later Faulkner resigned from the UUP, forming the Unionist Party of Northern Ireland (UPNI). He managed to bring over only seventeen of his initial supporters in the Assembly to his new party, leaving the three parties in the executive with the unambiguous support of forty-five of the seventy-eight Assembly members,[34] a majority, but now with only a majority of nationalists on its side. Within the Assembly many of the anti-Agreement Unionists would behave boorishly and thuggishly, especially

---

[33] Mansergh, Nicholas. "The Government of Ireland Act, 1920", in *Historical Studies*, edited by J.G. Barry. Belfast: Blackstaff, 1974.

[34] The NILP's one Assembly member meant that the power-sharing parties had forty-five of the Assembly on their side, compared with thirty-three opposed Unionists.

towards Faulkner's Unionists. At the end of January a constitutional challenge to Ireland's signature to the Agreement was placed before Dublin's Supreme Court (*Boland v. An Taoiseach*). The Court would uphold the constitutionality of the Agreement; it was not in breach of Articles 2 and 3 of Ireland's Constitution; but the Irish government was obliged in the case to defend its position as de facto rather than de jure recognition of Northern Ireland's status as part of the United Kingdom. The Taoiseach, Liam Cosgrave, insisted in the Dáil on 13 March that 'Northern Ireland . . . is within the United Kingdom and my Government accepts this as a fact'. Ireland's Attorney General declared more emphatically that 'any person living in this island and knowing our history could not possibly construe the Sunningdale declaration as meaning that we did not lay claim over the six counties'.[35] These statements, while true, could not help Faulkner's unionists.

The Westminster general election of February 1974 displaced the Conservatives who had negotiated the Sunningdale settlement. In his first Cabinet post, Rees was therefore in charge of a settlement that Labour had not made. Worse, Westminster's backward electoral system, plurality rule in single-member districts, served to weaken the position of the power-sharing parties. They had benefited from proportional representation in multi-member districts in the Assembly elections, but they could not agree common pro-Agreement candidates in winner-takes-all contests. By contrast, all the anti-Agreement Unionists mobilized behind the United Ulster Unionist Council (the UUUC) with an agreed candidate in each constituency. Their platform declared that 'Dublin is only a Sunningdale away'. They won eleven out of twelve of Northern Ireland's seats at Westminster. It bears emphasis, however, that this 92 per cent share of the available seats was won with just 51 per cent of the votes cast, in an election that had no mandated authority over either the Sunningdale agreement or the jurisdiction of the Assembly. Obviously from then on Faulkner's UPNI would be in serious trouble. By the end of April the UUUC had held a conference that agreed the following platform: the abolition of the power-sharing Executive and the Sunningdale Agreement; immediate new Assembly elections; and the return of security policy management to a new Assembly. This agenda was directly hostile to the agreement just negotiated by the two sovereign governments, and to the majority of the Assembly elected in 1973.

---

[35] *Irish Times*, 22 April 1974, cited in O'Leary and McGarry, *The Politics of Antagonism*, op. cit., p. 200.

Within three weeks, on 14 May, the Ulster Workers Council (the UWC) called a general strike in support of the objectives of the UUUC. A shadowy confluence of trade unionists and loyalist paramilitaries, it was not then—or later—a major body. It called the strike, even though many of the politicians within the UUC had cold-shouldered them, doubtful of their success and reluctant to embrace such overt militancy. On the first day of the strike it seemed those politicians had judged correctly: the overwhelming majority of workers went to their enterprises, offices, and shops. The major loyalist paramilitary organization, the UDA, then deployed its militants, marshalled by their leader Andy Tyrie. The UDA's orchestrated intimidation, witnessed by the author as a young man of sixteen, made the strike bite, extensively in eastern Northern Ireland, and then wherever Protestants were demographically dominant. Roads were blocked. Masked men, hooded men, men with sunglasses and parka jackets 'visited' factories and blocked the exits to housing estates. Toughs and aspiring toughs in the tartan fashions of the time manned makeshift barricades. The UWC had critical support within the electricity power-stations. What began as a largely unsupported strike soon became very effective. As it spread, Protestants supported it more. For many, especially for Catholics, it became a lockout, not a strike. The Army did nothing about the intimidation. The police matched their indifference. General Sir Frank King later admitted: 'When the strike started I remember having a conference and deciding not to get mixed up in it...we never had any aggro at all with the strikers. Dealing with intimidation was a police job. The fact that the RUC didn't do too much about it was no concern of ours. We were angry at the time but it wasn't our job. If Rees had ordered us to move against the barricades we would have said: "With great respect, this is a job for the police. We will assist them if you wish, but it's not terrorism".[36] The head of the Army did not regard organised thuggery by the UDA as terrorism, or not the type of terrorism to which he was mandated to respond. The Ministry of Defence and the Army claimed that they could not run the power stations properly or comprehensively. Pessimistic scenarios flooded into Rees and Wilson—warning them of sewage in the streets, epidemics,

---

[36] Cited in McKittrick and McVea, *Making Sense of the Troubles*, op. cit., pp. 103–4. Another general later rationalized matters differently: the 'Executive was doomed before the strike began...I think it was a mercy Merlyn Rees was there...He didn't make any decisions of any kind. If you'd had a decisive man who had arrested the strikers on the first day it would have created chaos', *Irish Times*, 15 May 1984, cited in Paul Bew and Henry Patterson, *The British State and the Ulster Crisis: From Wilson to Thatcher*, p. 67, n. 118. One wonders whether the general ever considered that chaos was created by his colleagues' inactions.

food-shortages, and power-free hospitals. In Dublin and Monaghan loyalists planted bombs, the most devastating in the conflict to that date—killing twenty-five people in the Irish capital and seven in the border town. Many would subsequently believe the loyalists had had the assistance of British intelligence operatives—operating to 'encourage' the Irish government to move on extradition, or pursuing some other agenda of their own.[37] Within the Executive nationalists made compromises: the Council of Ireland would be postponed until after the next Assembly election. It did not stop the strike. The UK government at last moved to control oil and petrol supplies and distribution; Wilson condemned the strikers as 'spongers', which upset the relevant targets; but two weeks into the strike Faulkner resigned after Rees refused to open negotiations with the strikers. Rees then dissolved the Executive and the Assembly.

How should we assess this event over a quarter of a century later? The most incisive journalist account of the time, by a brilliant reporter, Robert Fisk, is surprisingly irresolute in its conclusions, and wrong that the strike had broken the will of the British to stay. What the strike broke was the will of London governments to have a significant Irish dimension in addressing the conflict, a will that would not be recovered until Margaret Thatcher and Garret FitzGerald negotiated the Anglo-Irish Agreement in 1985. *The Point of No Return: The Strike Which Broke the British in Ulster* is, correctly, highly critical of the Northern Ireland Office, the police, and the Army—the latter, of course, as we have seen is condemned from its commanding officer's own words. Not all responsibility can be attributed to these agencies or their leading personnel, but they were responsible for allowing a strike to bite through intimidation. It was not their duty to have an opinion on the Executive's future prospects; that was the job of their masters. Political communications from the NIO and Number 10 were very poor, but if there is no decisive message communications cannot help. Whether or to what extent the NIO's officials, the police's senior ranks, or the Army's top brass colluded with loyalists, or whether such collusion occurred at lower ranks, is something we may know more about later, but whatever we may learn in these respects, in the absence of vigorous political direction from the top the conduct of the security forces was less appropriately focused than it might have been. It was

---

[37] The victims' accounts and campaigns for an inquiry are narrated in Don Mullan, *The Dublin and Monaghan Bombings: The Truth, The Question and the Victims' Stories* (2000). An inquiry on the subject in Ireland, under the direction of Justice Barron, is scheduled to report in September 2003; see also J. Bowyer Bell, *In Dubious Battle: The Dublin and Monaghan Bombings 1972–1974* (1996).

after all loyalist violence that escalated during early 1974; republican violence remained at much the same pitch. It is, of course, evident that popular unionist support for the Agreement had fallen dramatically before the Executive collapsed, and that there would have been continuing difficulties between the UPNI and the SDLP within the Executive over internment, police reform, extradition, and the implementation of the Council of Ireland. But the fact remains that before the strike developed there was still a majority in the Assembly available to support the Executive. Sunningdale need not have died in May 1974, even if it may have had an inevitable later rendezvous with a coroner.

It has to be said: Rees, as the local Secretary of State, Wilson, as Prime Minister, and to a lesser extent Mason as the Secretary of State for Defence were the key officials with political responsibility for what happened. Rees did not believe in Sunningdale. He thought it lost from very early on, well before the strike. Later, he would damn Sunningdale before his cabinet colleagues as a piece of 'British suburban illusion, a sort of *Guardian* solution which was no solution.'[38] When a Labour politician casually attacks the *Guardian*, cheap and desperate arguments are being mustered. Sunningdale was no illusion; it was the fruits of both the cities and the suburbs of Great Britain and both parts of Ireland. Rees was not only incapable of credible commitment; he simply lacked conviction— and he would not have been the best in any crisis, to put it mildly. Later, he would claim in a television interview 'I didn't let them win. They were going to win anyway. It could not be done, that's the short answer. The police were on the brink of not carrying out their duties and the middle class were on the strikers' side'.[39] This is just unconvincing. The police initially were not given direction. The Protestant middle class were won to the strike; they did not start in its ranks. Rees, with his trade union sympathies, was politically incapable of thinking about how to break the strike, a reactionary strike against three elected governments—he did not think of an early crack-down, instructing his senior military and police commanders to behave accordingly; nor did he think later of martial law, or of taking powers to order workers and managers to man the electricity-stations; or, indeed, of letting the strikers live with what would have been the devastating and delegitimizing consequences of full-scale power-cuts. In 1977 Roy Mason would prove far more resolute in response to a second loyalist strike orchestrated with Paisley's support; in 1986–7 Margaret Thatcher would resist even more widespread initial

---

[38] Tony Benn, *Against the Tide, Diaries 1973–76* (1989), p. 526.
[39] Cited in McKittrick and McVea, op. cit., p. 106.

Unionist antipathy to a British and Irish constitutional initiative. Decisive action by Rees and his colleagues might have made the lives of his successors easier. The loyalist strike leaders certainly expected a crackdown; they went into hiding in anticipation; theirs was an unexpected victory. Wilson too lacked the courage of his convictions—choosing not to withhold funds for Northern Ireland's loyalist-dominated shipyards in response to the strike (even though he contemplated the idea in private). The head of his policy unit would find the craven response of his government and the sudden collapse of the Executive perplexing, inexplicable, and suspicious.[40] In 1974, as the minister responsible for Defence and the Army, Mason arguably did not prompt the senior military to prepare properly for manning power stations or get them to link strike-breaking to breaking paramilitarism. None of the three men, or their biographers, have any compelling riposte to John Hume's comment in his memoirs: 'The establishment of power-sharing was a tribute to the political courage of the then Conservative government...Unfortunately the Labour administration which succeeded it...showed no similar courage, and in May of that year, in what was one of the most squalid examples of government irresponsibility, it surrendered its policy in the face of a political strike organised by a paramilitary minority on the Unionist side.'[41] Thus far the Blair government has proven much more robust in defence of the Good Friday Agreement than its predecessors were in defence of Sunningdale. Blair's government helped make the Good Friday Agreement, and whatever its subsequent deficiencies, occasional acts of cowardice, and misjudgements, especially under Mandelson, it is most unlikely to earn the disrespect attached to the conduct of Northern Ireland policy and administration under Wilson, Callaghan, Rees, and Mason.

[40] Interviews and conversations with Bernard Donoughue, including at Bishopsgate Investments and LSE, spring 1991; and see 'Ireland', in his *Prime Minister*, op. cit., *passim*.

[41] John Hume, *Personal Views—Politics, Peace and Reconciliation in Ireland* (1996).

7

The Conservative Stewardship of Northern Ireland 1979–97: Sound-bottomed Contradictions or Slow Learning?

Brendan O'Leary[1]

Oscar Wilde thought it took a heart of stone not to laugh at the demise of the heroine of one of Dickens' sentimental novels. The same idea arises when asked to reflect upon eighteen years of Conservative government on the politics of Northern Ireland.[2] Solemnity is called for, but the oddities of these years mean that horselaughs are tempting.[3] Remarkable inconsistencies or contradictions, as Marxists say, have characterized the Northern Irish policy-making and implementation of the four

[1] The author thanks Amanda Francis for help and absolves her of responsibility.

[2] Spatial constraints prevent concessions to those unfamiliar with Northern Ireland. The necessary materials are in the following books and surveys: Kevin Boyle and Tom Hadden, *Northern Ireland: a Positive Proposal* (Harmondsworth, Penguin, 1984); Kevin Boyle and Tom Hadden, *Northern Ireland: the Choice* (Harmondsworth, Penguin, 1995); John McGarry and Brendan O'Leary, *Explaining Northern Ireland: Broken Images* Oxford and Cambridge, MA, Basil Blackwell, 1995); John McGarry and Brendan O'Leary (eds.), *The Future of Northern Ireland* (Oxford, Clarendon, 1990); Brendan O'Leary and John McGarry (eds.), 'A state of truce: Northern Ireland after twenty five years of war', *Ethnic and Racial Studies* 18 (1995), 4; Brendan O'Leary and John McGarry, *The Politics of Antagonism: Understanding Northern Ireland* (London and Atlantic Heights, NJ, Athlone, 2nd ed., 1996); Joseph Ruane and Jennifer Todd, *The Dynamics of Conflict in Northern Ireland: Power, Conflict and Emancipation* (Cambridge, Cambridge University Press, 1996); and John Whyte, *Interpreting Northern Ireland* (Oxford, Clarendon, 1990).

[3] For detailed treatments of these years, see Paul Bew and Henry Patterson, *The British State and the Ulster Crisis* (London, Verso, 1985); Peter Catterall and Sean McDougall (eds.), *The Northern Ireland Question in British Politics* (Basingstoke, Macmillan, 1996); Michael Cunningham, *British Government Policy in Northern Ireland 1969–89* (Manchester, Manchester University Press, 1991); Brendan O'Duffy, *Violent Politics: A Theoretical and Empirical Examination of Two Centuries of Political Violence in Ireland* (PhD dissertation, London School of Economics, 1996); and McGarry and O'Leary, *The Politics of Antagonism*.

Conservative governments since 1979, and provide the food for the occasionally ribald analysis which follows. But, it will be maintained, these inconsistencies and contradictions mask a deeper reality, the slow development of a more consistent and sensitive approach to the management of Northern Ireland—and for these reasons mockery must be suitably restrained.

THE INCONSISTENCIES OR CONTRADICTIONS

Consider in succession five related and partially overlapping contradictions in the Conservative stewardship: (i) the integrationist–devolutionist contradiction; (ii) the sovereignist–intergovernmentalist contradiction; (iii) the cherished but indifferent Union contradiction; (iv) the talking and not talking to terrorists contradiction; and (v) the defence of capitalism and social justice contradiction.

The integrationist–devolutionist contradiction

Margaret Thatcher and her Shadow Secretary of State for Northern Ireland, Airey Neave, shifted the Conservatives from bipartisanship between 1975 and 1979—though they found it difficult to outflank the then Secretary of State, Roy Mason, on law, order, authoritarianism, and thoughtless contributions to local community relations. Thatcher and Neave advocated the full administrative integration of Northern Ireland into the United Kingdom. To be more precise, they advocated regional and local government on the Scottish model, and left others to imagine the remaining details. They were much influenced by two men.

The first was Enoch Powell, the British nationalist ideologue, former Conservative, and then Ulster Unionist Party (UUP) MP for South Down. An exponent of the 'logic' of integration, of making Northern Ireland less different from the rest of the United Kingdom, this former professor of Greek espoused a simple dialectic. Integration implied a British 'nationalizing' policy for Northern Ireland, unitary centralized Unionism, what would later be called Thatcherite statecraft in Great Britain. It meant dealing with Northern Ireland's minority as if it was not serious about its Irish nationalism, but merely unconsciously hankering after the benefits of good government—Westminster-style. The smack of firm government was necessary to criminalize and marginalize Irish nationalist militants. This thinking contributed significantly to Thatcher's mishandling of the republican hunger strikes in 1980–1. The second man was Edward

Heath, though, unlike Powell, Thatcher was counter-suggestive to his influence. Heath had suspended the Stormont parliament in 1972 in order to reconstruct it as a power-sharing devolved assembly, a task he had succeeded in doing by the end of 1973. His success, however, was short-lived, not least because he called and lost a Westminster general election in February 1974 that enabled hardline Unionist opponents of the new system, with 51 per cent of the regional vote, to win eleven out of the then twelve Northern Irish seats.[4] The malleable spine of Merlyn Rees, appointed Secretary of State by Harold Wilson in February 1974, made it easier for the anti-Sunningdale United Ulster Unionist Council to destroy the power-sharing executive in May 1974—with a little help from loyalist, and indeed republican, paramilitaries. As Thatcher was allergic to all things Heathite, and disposed towards Powellite logic, it appeared that Northern Irish policy would depart radically from that of her predecessor; it would be integrationist rather than devolutionist.

Yet the moment Thatcher became Prime Minister the Conservatives changed their constitutional though not their security policy. The manifesto commitment to administrative integration was abandoned—and not just because Airey Neave was murdered by the Irish National Liberation Army in the House of Commons car park during the 1979 general election campaign. Each of Thatcher's Secretaries of State for Northern Ireland—Humphrey Atkins (1979–81), James Prior (1981–4), Douglas Hurd (1984–5), Tom King (1985–9), and Peter Brooke (1989–92)—attempted to promote a devolved assembly, though without using the dreaded name 'power-sharing'. The Conservatives in government, if not within their party or their rhetoric, recognized that neither integrationist 'logic', nor a miniature Westminster parliament on the lines of the old Stormont regime, were appropriate to Northern Irish conditions. Peter Brooke and Sir Patrick Mayhew (1992–7), the Secretaries of State appointed by John Major, felt freer to acknowledge these realities, at least in inter-election periods. Sir Nicholas Scott, one of Thatcher's most robust and effective security ministers at the Northern Ireland Office (NIO), put the governing logic actually pursued by the Conservatives lucidly: 'Northern Ireland is different, so it must be governed differently'.[5]

---

[4] After 1921 the number of Westminster seats for Northern Ireland was kept lower than its population might otherwise have warranted. In horse-trading with the UUP, to prolong the Labour government, James Callaghan and Michael Foot agreed to increase Northern Irish representation at Westminster to seventeen seats. The measure took effect in the 1983 general election, and increased the potential leverage of the UUP. From 1997 the region will have eighteen seats.   [5] Interview with the author, 3 January 1991.

Prior managed to set up an elected Assembly in 1982, despite ill-tempered opposition from his Prime Minister.[6] The 'rolling' scheme enabled the delegation of a set of powers (excluding security) which an extraordinary majority of the prospective Assembly might choose to exercise—promoting power-sharing devolution by other means. The election for the Assembly facilitated Sinn Féin's entry into competitive politics more than the creation of a power-sharing government. In 1982 to some people's surprise, especially Thatcher's, 10 per cent of those who voted in Northern Ireland, over 30 per cent of nationalists, backed the party which supported the IRA's right to engage in 'armed struggle'— and did so in the immediate aftermath of the death of ten republicans who had starved themselves to death to win recognition as political prisoners. The Assembly did not last its full term. One of Prior's successors, Tom King, felt obliged to suspend it. Boycotted by all nationalists from its inception, it ended its days as a site of Unionist protest against the Anglo-Irish Agreement of 1985.[7] Yet King declared, without irony, that it was his intention to establish talks about talks between political parties (excluding those which condoned violence)—in which a devolved government would be a central objective. His successors have continued in the same vein. Mayhew managed to set up an elected Peace Forum some ten years later, in May 1996. It was not an assembly, though it was hoped that it would lead to one; but it was an elected body. It was boycotted by all elected nationalists, like the previous Assembly, and became a site of protest for Unionist opposition to Conservative policy on the peace process. The Forum has not been wound up, and might one day perform a useful role, but it has not yet been a success—and the election which set it up enabled Sinn Féin to win its best ever share of the regional vote, 15.5 per cent.[8]

So when not creating elected bodies boycotted by nationalists, who feared that they would become Stormont Mark IIs, and when not helping Sinn Féin's vote by setting up such bodies at inauspicious moments, Thatcher and Major sought to promote a devolved government— anathema elsewhere in the Kingdom. The world, that is, the government

---

[6] For accounts which diverge on facts and opinions, see James Prior, *A Balance of Power* (London, Hamish Hamilton, 1986) and Margaret Thatcher, *The Downing Street Years* (London, HarperCollins, 1995), esp. p. 394.

[7] Cornelius O'Leary, Sidney Elliott, and Rick Wilford, *The Northern Ireland Assembly, 1982–86: A Constitutional Experiment* (London, Hurst, 1988).

[8] See Geoffrey Evans and Brendan O'Leary, 'Intransigence and flexibility on the way to two forums: the Northern Ireland elections of May 30 1996 and public opinion', *Representation*, 34 (1997), 208–18.

and media of the United States of America, was told that the prospective devolved government would enjoy cross-community support, be formed from an assembly elected by proportional representation, and take the form of a multiparty coalition—in short, it would be consociational. The successive Secretaries of State who pursued this elusive goal were not, however, entirely inconsistent in practice, even if they were inconsistent in formal intent.[9] Some of their deeds corresponded much better with the image of a unitary, British national integrationism. They centralized and 'de-democratized' local Northern Irish public life in multiple ways, further diminishing the 'powers' of local governments; expanded quangocracy on a scale comparable to, and indeed in excess of, that in Great Britain;[10] placed increasing administrative and legislative discretion in the hands of the Secretary of State; and, last but not least, gradually integrated Northern Ireland into multiple aspects of British administrative, policy-formulation, and parliamentary routines— measures inconsistent with the aim of creating a meaningful devolved assembly! The last significant steps of Major's government in 1996–7 included regularizing the scrutinizing of legislation, hitherto passed mostly through Orders in Council, and establishing a Grand Committee for Northern Ireland. These measures, critics observed, were at odds with the government's promotion of agreed devolution in what were then hoped to be 'all-party' negotiations—in which nothing, apparently, had been decided in advance. They were, however, consistent with the government's desperate need to shore up its parliamentary position, and make concessions to the UUP in return for its support in the lobbies.

The most piquant dimension of the integration–devolution contradiction was electoral. The fall-out with Heath, who terminated Unionist one-party rule in Northern Ireland, led the UUP's MPs to stop taking the Conservative whip at Westminster. By 1986, the last organizational linkage between the two parties, joint youth membership, was broken after the Anglo-Irish Agreement. In its aftermath, the Conservative party hierarchy strongly resisted independent electoral organization in Northern Ireland. But faced by an activists' protest-movement— identified as 'a peasant's revolt' by one aristocrat who could be relied

[9] Locals devised nicknames for all the Tory Secretaries of State—the printable ones include Willie Whitewash, Humphrey Who?, Gentleman Jim, Tom Cat King, Babbling Brooke, and Paddy Mayhem.

[10] These 'de-democratizing' measures were often welcomed by Catholics and nationalists in the SDLP—who preferred progressive and professionalized public administration under direct rule to clientelist and discriminatory local government by the UUP.

upon to recognize the species[11]—the occasionally impressive and always urbane Brooke was required, on behalf of a pro-devolution government, to witness the local creation of pro-integration branches of his party. The new members organized with enthusiasm. They wrapped themselves in the Union Jack more tightly than on 'the mainland'—the Unionist term for Great Britain. They described themselves as integrationist Thatcherites; and as opponents of devolution and of the Anglo-Irish Agreement—in short, of the local policies of the Conservative government. They argued that giving the Northern Irish the chance to vote Conservative would enable them to break from local ethno-religious tribalism, and spent much time arguing that the British Labour party should do the same— though organizing in Northern Ireland remains one of the few Conservative policies that Labour's modernizers have not imitated. The new local Conservatives maintained that the 'community charge' should be transferred forthwith to the denizens of Northern Ireland, as proof of its status as an integral part of the United Kingdom, but the NIO's Conservative ministers avoided adding the poll tax to their woes.

The results of electoral integration were unimpressive: peaking with 5.7 per cent of the regional vote for the Conservatives in the 1992 Westminster election. Their electoral 'successes' were confined to North Down—often described by journalists as 'like Surrey', a sure sign that they have travelled extensively in neither county. In the May 1996 Forum elections the Conservatives, fortunately for their masters at Westminster and Smith Square, failed to figure in the top ten parties. Their share of the total vote registered half of one per cent, and the local branches of the party face losing their deposits in the 1997 Westminster election. Contradictory preferences between a governing party's leadership and its activists are not uncommon in parliamentary democracies, but it is rare for a governing party to permit new branches of its organization to be established that it knows will oppose its own policies in the relevant locality. It is not, however, rare for activists to discover that their preferences have less popular resonance than they imagine. It might all even have been amusing, had matters of war and peace not been at stake.

The sovereignist–intergovernmentalist contradiction

The Conservative and Union Party is nothing if it is not the party of Westminster sovereignty and of British nationalism. In 1979 its

---

[11] Author's unattributable interview with a senior Conservative MP in 1990.

designated Prime Minister opposed external interference in the internal affairs of the United Kingdom, and was unenthusiastic about 'Irish dimensions'. Yet by the end of Thatcher's premiership, and throughout Major's, it had become unthinkable to consider managing Northern Ireland except through the cooperation of the 'the two Governments', the standard parlance. The major achievement, for good or ill, of the Conservatives in eighteen years of office was the negotiation of an international treaty with the Republic of Ireland in 1985,[12] now known as the Anglo-Irish Agreement. It granted the Irish government, in Article 2, rights of consultation, through a regular and fully serviced Intergovernmental Conference, on all aspects of Westminster's Northern Irish policy; and promised in the same article to make 'determined efforts' to agree with this foreign government.[13] The Agreement fell short of cosovereignty or joint authority, and in its first years was often implemented in a manner that disappointed Irish nationalist hopes and expectations, but it was the first occasion that a foreign state had been granted such privileges over London policy-makers within their own jurisdiction since the Danegeld was paid by earlier lords of the realm.

The explanation for this remarkable volte-face, from insisting on unilateral sovereign prerogatives to embracing intergovernmentalism, is complex, and cannot be related in detail here.[14] To increase security within Northern Ireland and Great Britain, and to contain fears about militant and electoral republicanism expanding in both parts of Ireland—aggravated by the mismanagement of the Maze hunger strikes—Thatcher was persuaded to change tack by successive Irish premiers (Charles Haughey and Garret FitzGerald), by fellow Conservatives (Sir, now Lord, Geoffrey Howe and Douglas Hurd), and by her civil servants in the Foreign Office and the Cabinet Office (especially, but not only, Robert, now Lord, Armstrong). She agreed the development of an institutionalized Irish dimension—which she had prevented Prior including within his rolling devolution plans in 1982, not least because of Ireland's stance during the Falklands/Malvinas war.

---

[12] For different discussions of the meanings, making, and impact of the Anglo-Irish Agreement, see Arthur Aughey, *Under Siege: Ulster Unionism and the Anglo-Irish Agreement* (London, Hurst, 1989); Tom Hadden and Kevin Boyle (eds.), *The Anglo-Irish Agrement* (London, Sweet and Maxwell, 1989); Anthony Kenny, *The Road to Hillsborough* (Oxford, Pergamon, 1986); and O'Leary and McGarry, *The Politics of Antagonism*, chs. 6–7.

[13] Lord Tebbitt described the Irish government as 'a county council' to the author, who pointed out that Conservative governments are not in the habit of signing treaties with county councils—*BSkyB*, 13 February 1996.

[14] See O'Leary and McGarry, *The Politics of Antagonism*, chs. 6–7.

Thatcher was also persuaded to sign the Agreement because it would later enable an agreed devolved government in Northern Ireland.[15] As told in her memoirs she still seems slightly surprised that she ever signed it, rather like her memory of the Single European Act, but unsurprised that 'the wider gains for which I had hoped from greater support by the nationalist minority in Northern Ireland or the Irish government and people for the fight against terrorism were not going to be forthcoming'.[16] For once the Iron Lady despaired too soon. It was the Agreement that created the conditions for the paramilitary ceasefires of 1994–6, and the more hopeful prospects for a political settlement and interethnic peace that remain features of the late 1990s, evidence to the contrary notwithstanding.

The one long-run benefit of the Agreement, from Thatcher's perspective, was that 'the international dimension [of Northern Ireland] became noticeably easier to deal with'.[17] True, but the Agreement had price-tags in return for the reductions in Britain's international embarrassment, especially in the United States of America. The Irish government acquired greater potential leverage than before, which it was to use to the maximum under Taoiseach Albert Reynolds (1992–4), who took significant risks for peace, and successfully persuaded John Major to take them with him, and thereby helped orchestrate the republican ceasefire of August 1994, which lasted until February 1996. Northern nationalists appreciated the symbolic, and some of the material, benefits from the active consultation with their patron-state from 1986 onwards. They became more willing to believe in the possibility that Northern Ireland could be reformed, as demonstrated by the second Fair Employment Act (1989). Many saw less merits in the IRA using the Armalite while Sinn Féin used (and abused) the ballot box. Ultimately, the Agreement led republicans to reconsider their strategy and goals. They ceased to believe that they, or the IRA, could win a united Ireland through war, or indeed through war and electoral competition.

---

[15] This strategy, backed by some senior civil servants, was called 'coercive consociation' by this author, not by the policy-makers (as some Unionists imagine the author to have claimed)—see O'Leary, 'The limits to coercive consociationalism in Northern Ireland', *Political Studies* 37 (1989), 452–68. The strategy aimed to push Unionists into a devolved power-sharing government by confronting them with the threat that British–Irish intergovernmental cooperation might lead to something worse. Critics of this interpretation are commended to reread the text of the Agreement: Article 4 states that agreed devolved government is the preferred policy of the United Kingdom, and that the Irish government supports the policy; Articles 2 and 4 limit the scope of the Inter-Governmental Conference if there is a devolved government.   [16] Thatcher, *The Downing Street Years*, pp. 406–7.
[17] Thatcher, *The Downing Street Years*, p. 407.

They moved instead, albeit slowly, to create a pan-nationalist coalition for 'change' in favour of northern nationalists, rather than an immediate united Ireland.[18] Not the least of the achievements of the Agreement was that Sinn Féin's activists sought to internationalize their struggle, in America and Europe, through appeals to the discourses of international law, self-determination, and democracy—later to prove helpful in assisting the verbal transformations of the Agreement into the Joint Declaration for Peace of December 1993,[19] an important feature of what we can optimistically call the first peace process.

It was precisely because the Conservatives were *the* British sovereignist party, the party of 'no surrender' to foreigners, and the hegemonic owners of British patriotism, that it was a Conservative government that successfully presided—albeit painfully, and with many a reluctant twist—over the 'inter-governmentalization' and 'inter-nationalization' of the management of Northern Ireland.[20] The process began with the Thatcher and Haughey summit of 1980, and culminated in 1994–5 in still ongoing three-stranded, two-state, and multiparty negotiations. These talks, like the talks of 1991–2, have been facilitated by international third parties. Today a former US Senate majority leader, George Mitchell, a Canadian general, John de Chastelain, and a former Finnish Prime Minister, Harri Holkeri, handle constitutional minutiae and the intricacies of the possible decommissioning of parliamentary weapons, while in 1992 the Australian Sir Ninian Stephen made available his good offices. Even Dr Paisley's Democratic Unionist Party now participates, albeit without fulsome enthusiasm, in trips to the White House, and in formal negotiations which include the Irish government as the co-chair—assisted by semi-official representatives and promises of small-scale funds from the United States of America and the European Union. Moreover, when their minds are focused, the British and Irish governments now have the organizational capacity and intelligence to interact with one another with greater sensitivity and skill than they did in the

---

[18] Kevin Bean, 'The New Departure: Recent Developments in Irish Republican Ideology and Strategy', *Occasional Papers in Irish Studies*, No. 6 (University of Liverpool, Institute of Irish Studies, 1994); Eamonn Mallie and David McKittrick, *The Fight for Peace: the Secret Story Behind the Irish Peace Process* (London, Heinemann, 1996); Fionnula O'Connor, *In Search of a State: the Catholics of Northern Ireland* (Belfast, Blackstaff, 1993), and the author's interviews suggest that the Agreement compelled a rethink amongst republicans, first visible in Sinn Féin's *Scenario for Peace* (1987), and consolidated with the publication of *Towards a Lasting Peace in Ireland* (1992).

[19] See McGarry and O'Leary, *Explaining Northern Ireland*, appendices A and B.

[20] See W. Harvey Cox, 'Managing Northern Ireland intergovernmentally', *Parliamentary Affairs*, 40 (1987), 80–97.

early stages of the present conflict—when, apparently, an Irish government contemplated military intervention in defence of its co-nationals, and when, apparently, British intelligence operatives could conspire with loyalist paramilitaries to bomb the Republic.

The sovereignist–intergovernmentalist contradiction has, therefore, been resolved in practice, if not yet fully in Conservative doctrine. The United Kingdom's sovereignty over Northern Ireland remains formally intact, but intergovernmentalism, or rather bi-governmentalism, is the management method. Treaty arrangements and formal inter-prime ministerial statements are in place, enabling agreed transition to British and Irish co-sovereignty or eventual Irish sovereignty, if and when demography and democratic head counts of northern nationalists create a different majority. The process, of course, is not a one-sided surrender. Arrangements are in place for a possible renunciation of Ireland's formal claim to sovereignty over Northern Ireland—expressed in Articles 2 and 3 of *Bunreacht na hÉireann* (1937). But, it is agreed, that must await confirmation in a referendum endorsing a comprehensive political settlement—transitional or permanent—that will establish greater functional cooperation between the two parts of Ireland, through both British–Irish intergovernmentalism and North–South interparliamentarism. The prospective, complex, and heterogeneous institutional networks, sketched in the joint Framework Documents of February 1995, may materialize as outlined, or may one day be credited as the textual origins of a federal Ireland, functioning within a more confederal British Isles, themselves within a confederal European Union.[21]

The cherished but indifferent Union contradiction

If the sovereignist–intergovernmentalist contradiction has been resolved in practice in favour of bi-governmentalism, the 'cherished but indifferent Union' contradiction looks more stably unresolved. This contradiction is easy to state; and can be found in the public language of staunchly British Unionist Conservatives like Thatcher and Andrew Hunter, the most recent Chair of the Conservative backbench Northern Ireland Committee, in the more lofty Europeanist tones of the former Foreign Secretaries Lord Howe and Douglas Hurd, and in the 'dripping green' speeches of Sir Nicholas Scott and Peter Temple-Morris. The Conservative and Unionist Party warmly espouses the Union of Great

---

[21] For the possibilities, see Brendan O'Leary, 'Afterword: what is framed in the framework documents?', *Ethnic and Racial Studies*, 18 (1995), 862–72; and McGarry and O'Leary, *Explaining Northern Ireland*, ch. 10.

Britain and Northern Ireland, and yet is indifferent about it. It is warmly and passionately uxorious about the Union, yet it would permit a quick divorce tomorrow.

We can take as our text the Conservative Party manifesto of 1997. Under the heading of 'a confident, united and sovereign nation', in which Northern Ireland is impliedly part of the British nation, the reader is told that 'While we cherish the Union and Northern Ireland's place within it, we recognize that there exist within the Province special circumstances which require further action to be taken'.[22] These special circumstances include 'local accountable democracy'—which implies an elected assembly, an idea which the previous page of the manifesto warns 'could well pull apart the Union' if implemented in Scotland and Wales. Pulling apart that other Union, the one that binds Great Britain, is obviously of greater emotional concern. 'We cherish... but' statements loom large in Unionist indictments of the last eighteen years of Conservative government. They have also been noted, naturally in more ironic tones, by Irish nationalists.

In cherishing mode the Conservatives insist that Northern Ireland is British—which it is not, geographically, historically, or legally, though it does contain a majority of British people. In indifferent mode the Conservatives treat it as a region which is not British—which it is not; or one that requires 'special circumstances', that is, non-British institutions, which is true. Cherishing means that Northern Ireland deserves the best of British: in government and public services, which it gets, aside from its policing. Indifference means constitutional idiosyncrasy piled upon legal and political oddity. Northern Ireland's status as part of the United Kingdom has always been conditional: it has a legal right to secession, or more precisely to unification with the Republic of Ireland, a fact underlined in the last eighteen years and entrenched in the Anglo-Irish Agreement. England, Scotland, and Wales are not declared in law or in international treaties to be part of the United Kingdom as long as their local parliaments or local peoples desire. They are not subject to treaties which specify how they might become part of another state. In the Joint Declaration for Peace of 1993, known in this island as the Downing Street Declaration, 'the people of Ireland' are defined impliedly in a way which differentiates them from 'the people of Britain'. The people of Northern Ireland, irrespective of whether they support the Union, are explicitly not defined as British, but as Irish.[23] This, to put it mildly, suggests

---

[22] Conservative Central Office, *You Can Only Be Sure with the Conservatives: The Conservative Manifesto 1997* (Westminster, 1997), p. 51.

[23] McGarry and O'Leary, *Explaining Northern Ireland*, pp. 409, 420.

indifference to the self-professed identities of those the Conservatives claim to cherish. The Union has become a loveless marriage according to its Unionist critics—in which the partner with the greater status, money, and power sustains the polite fictions only because the weaker party insists upon it.

This analysis may, of course, allow too much for sentiment and prejudice. One Conservative told the author in 1994, off the record, that it was best to understand the Conservative position as 'the sort of hypocrisy demanded by *realpolitik'*. As the party in charge of the state, a state which needs the cooperation of the Republic of Ireland, it must declare that the United Kingdom is neutral in the conflict between Irish nationalists and (British) Unionists, and about the long-run constitutional future of 'the Province'. However, reason of state does not bind the parliamentary party, or the party-at-large, whose sentimental members oppose such neutrality. In short, the contradiction dissolves once one realizes that the state of the Conservatives is neutral on the Union, whereas the party of the Conservatives is not.

The talking and not talking to terrorists syndrome

The most publicly embarrassing contradiction of the last eighteen years has been the syndrome of 'talking and not talking to terrorists (and their supporters)'. Thatcher and Major regularly declared that they would not talk to terrorists, or their spokesmen; indeed Major told the House of Commons that the idea would turn his stomach. They publicly refused to talk to terrorists, and their more palatable alleged 'fronts', Sinn Féin, the Progressive Unionist Party, and the Ulster Democratic Party, even though Sinn Féin had a considerable electoral mandate. The two Conservative Prime Ministers encouraged other democracies to follow their example, and stand firm against the scourges of local and 'international' terrorism. And yet Thatcher must have authorized both Atkins' indirect contacts with republicans in 1980–1 and Brooke's with republican sources after 1989; and in 1993 Major and Mayhew were exposed as having lied to Parliament about their communications with republicans.

The Conservatives in office were not, of course, complete hypocrites on the subject of terrorism. They were tougher on terrorism than on its causes. Thatcher's memoirs reveal her obsession with security, almost to the exclusion of every other Northern Irish topic: the relevant chapter is entitled 'Shadows of Gunmen'. She faced down the hunger-strikers until she had created so many martyrs that the republicans switched into politics. Her governments deployed the SAS in Northern Ireland and in

Gibraltar, and authorized a range of covert actions in what became called the dirty war. Her governments introduced a broadcasting ban on Sinn Féin, required all councillors to take an oath repudiating the use of violence, and made the Prevention of Terrorism Act permanent—despite its being in conflict with the judgements of the European Court of Human Rights.

It was, perhaps, because of its natural dispositions on terrorism that the Major government failed constructively to exploit the opportunity created by the republican and loyalist ceasefires in 1994. It was not wholly prepared for them, because its intelligence-information and its judgement were not as good as the Irish government's. For the same reasons, it was unprepared for the breakdown of the IRA's ceasefire in February 1996. By political tradition and instinct the Conservatives were understandably biased in ways which affected their judgements. They hated the prospect of publicly negotiating with the spokespersons of Irish republicans. Major had to assuage the right wing of his party throughout the Irish peace process; and felt he had to bend over backwards to reassure constitutional unionists that they were not being sold out—unionists who were divided over whether to treat the IRA's cessation of violence as a surrender, a trap, or a ripe moment for negotiations.

The Major government walked a fateful path. In the aftermath of the IRA's ceasefire, and the reciprocal loyalist ceasefire six weeks later, it engaged in important confidence-building measures, but, more significantly, began to erect an ever-changing obstacle course to inclusive multiparty negotiations. It broke its promises to the Irish-American Morrison delegation, to the Irish government, and to republicans about the prospective timing of such negotiations. Flying in the face of sensible advice from key figures in the Army and the RUC, it became fixated on seeking symbolic surrenders of *materiel* from the undefeated paramilitaries; and, most disastrously and incompetently, in January 1996 it played manipulative politics with the report of the international body chaired by Senator Mitchell that it had jointly set up with the Irish government to resolve the impasse it had itself created over the 'decommissioning' of paramilitary weapons.

These successive errors of judgement—over-negotiating, and pre-conditioning prospective negotiations—were aggravated by Major's progressively diminishing parliamentary majority. By the summer of 1995 he was wholly exposed to pressures from his Europhobic and ultra-Unionist right wing, and increasingly disposed to keeping the UUP sweet in case its MPs were needed in the lobbies. From 1995 the new leader of the UUP, David Trimble, sought to postpone negotiations as long as possible and followed crowds of angry, fearful, and law-breaking Orangemen and women in his capacity as their leader. He demanded, and got, an election in May 1996 to precede negotiations. He rejected outright the Framework Documents, carefully devised by the two governments as flexible but strongly recommended proposals, without receiving any British governmental admonishment. He supported the Orange Order's rights of territorial machismo, and sought the further normalization of Northern Irish business at the House of Commons, the politics of 'creeping integration'.

The first peace process ended in a bloody but messy renewal of republican violence, punctured with occasional loyalist actions of a similar nature. It had produced two so far fruitless political outcomes: an elected Forum boycotted by all nationalists; and a hamstrung multiparty and intergovernmental talking shop that without Sinn Féin has so far been going nowhere, slowly. And yet... within weeks of the breakdown of the IRA ceasefire the Major government was, with the Irish government, concerned to re-establish, or to be seen to re-establish, the peace process, bi-governmentally, on similar promises, and it prepared legislation to facilitate amnesties for the decommissioners of paramilitary weapons. Indeed until the 1997 general election was called Conservative ministers avoided precluding the possibility of ever negotiating with Sinn Féin. For their part, a range of republicans and loyalists sought to revive the peace process, mindful that the Conservative government's difficulties were not entirely of its volition, and that the killings executed by their ultras were at least as culpable as the government

The capitalist party unfrees the labour market

The least widely noticed contradiction of the Conservative hegemony was that the party of unfettered free markets and deregulation, especially of free markets in labour, introduced the most vigorous, if not perfect, affirmative action programmes in the European Union. The 1989 Fair Employment Act was demanded of the Conservative government, in response to Irish Americans who had mobilized a threatened investment-strike under the 'MacBride principles'. It was demanded by the Irish government, which was consulted at length, and before the House of Commons, on the details of the relevant legislation; and it was advocated and sketched by a range of non-Conservative anti-discrimination experts. Last, but not least, the Conservatives made unusual concessions to the Labour Party's front-bench spokesmen during the passage of the Bill that rectified Labour's much more feeble 1976 Act.[24] This outcome was not one that any one would have predicted from a New Right, free-market, British nationalist party. Like the other contradictions it demands explanation.

EXPLAINING OR EXPLAINING AWAY
THE CONTRADICTIONS

How should one react to these apparent contradictions and incon-sistencies? Three partially overlapping accounts present themselves: (*a*) historical garbage can or foul-up explanation; (*b*) reactive crisis management within a pluralist liberal democratic state; and (*c*) ethno-national policy learning.

Historical garbage can or foul-up explanation

One historical garbage can explanation would be that matters could not have been otherwise—an insoluble policy problem will have useless and incoherent technologies (policies) thrown at it. Alternatively, it might be suggested that to look for consistency in Conservative politicians engaged in 'high politics' is to be a victim of rationalist fallacies. The Conservative record on Ireland in this century is, after all, multiply inconsistent. They began as stout opponents of home rule, and sought to kill the idea 'with kindness'—the killing administered by 'bloody Balfour'.[25] Against devolu-tion (home rule), the party's leaders encouraged illegal paramilitarism and insurrection against the will of the House of Commons.[26] The consequent Irish republican insurrection found the Conservatives as the coalition partners of the Liberals whom they had once accused of treason over Ireland. They supported harsh repression from 1916 to 1921, before conceding the need to negotiate with the Sinn Féin of their day, whose growth they had fertilized. During and after the Irish war of independence

---

[24] See Christopher McCrudden, 'The Evolution of Fair Employment (Northern Ireland) Act 1989 in Parliament', in R. J. Cormac and R. D. Osborne (eds.), *Discrimination and Public Policy in Northern Ireland* (Oxford, Clarendon, 1990), pp. 244–64.

[25] Eunan O'Halpin, *The Decline of the Union: British Government in Ireland, 1892–1920* (Dublin, Gill and Macmillan, 1987).

[26] Ian Lustick, *Unsettled States, Disputed Lands: Britain and Ireland, France and Algeria and the West-Bank-Gaza* (Ithaca, NY, Cornell University Press, 1993); O'Leary and McGarry, *The Politics of Antagonism*, ch. 2.

key Conservatives constrained Lloyd George's settlement with Sinn Féin,[27] and gifted devolution (home rule), of all things, to the novel and widely unwanted entity of Northern Ireland, ensuring lasting bitterness in Irish–British relations.[28] From 1922 until 1964 the Conservatives were in the UK cabinet for all but eight years, and were happy to leave Northern Ireland devolved and governed by a provincial quasi-branch of their party whose representatives took the Tory whip at Westminster.

Yet, garbage can reasoning, in the light of these historical inconsistencies, is not enough. The Conservatives as a party have, after all, generally been consistent in their Unionism. They have differed mostly over the means to support the Union—though, when the chips were down, they were willing to transfer Northern Ireland to the Irish Free State as a side-payment for the latter's entry into the Second World War. But the point still stands. They have been consistent, throughout most of the century, in opposing the break-up of the United Kingdom—though any part of Ireland has been much less integral to their vision of the British nation than Scotland, Wales, or England.

Reactive crisis management in a pluralist state

It is, perhaps, more tempting, and illuminating, to see many of the foregoing contradictions as the by-products of the policy-making dynamics of a pluralist state. The Conservatives, in government, have responded like a weathervane to the relevant political pressures—from the Irish and US governments, from Northern Irish parties in Westminster and without, from paramilitaries aiming bullets or planting bombs, from the Irish diaspora in America and Britain, and from the British media. The resultants of these pressures have varied and twisted their political intentions and indeed their preferences. The autonomy of Conservative policy-makers was constrained and rendered inconsistent, especially in reactive crisis management compounded by the low salience of Northern Ireland in cabinet decision making. As former Taoiseach Dr FitzGerald memorably complained: 'The failure of the Irish to understand how stupidly the British can act is one of the major sources of misunderstanding between our countries ... Their system is uncoordinated. Because there's a Northern Ireland Secretary people think there's a Northern Ireland policy—but there isn't'.[29] Such suggestions

---

[27] Michael Laffan, *The Partition of Ireland, 1911–25* (Dundalk, Dundalgan, 1983).

[28] McGarry and O'Leary, *Explaining Northern Ireland*, ch. 1.

[29] David McKittrick, 'FitzGerald attacks inept Britain', *Independent*, 7 June 1989.

regularly feature in Irish diplomatic and undiplomatic complaints—and were formally expressed in the *Report* of the New Ireland Forum in May 1984.[30]

This reasoning, while illuminating, especially on the daily management of crises, is nevertheless ultimately unsatisfactory. Beneath the contradictions there have been consistencies. The Conservatives, in government, have accepted that Northern Ireland is different and that integration, while preferable for the party faithful, is ultimately infeasible. As governors the Conservatives have recognized that Northern Ireland must be treated as 'a place apart' in the light of its distinctive conflict. They have reformed, and sought to reform, some of the most overtly majoritarian and discriminatory aspects of public institutions and public life in the region—many of which were embarrassing reminders of the dispositions of ancestral Tories. Conservative office-holders think, at least tacitly, that Northern Ireland should be consociationalized. The Conservatives have been generally consistent, if not always intelligent, in security policy between 1979 and 1994—though it was not always coherently coordinated with the promotion of power-sharing democracy or the winning of political consent. The Conservatives were also generally consistent between 1979 and 1997 in regional economic policy— though the generous subvention of the region probably reduced the incentives facing local political elites to settle the conflict.

There have, of course, been inconsistencies: Secretaries of State varied in their initiatives and local micro-management; Thatcher presided over the shift from the focus on an internal resolution to externalizing the management of the conflict with the Irish government; Major did, and did not, accept the normalization of interactions with Sinn Féin; and the bulk of this article has examined five apparent contradictions in some depth. But it would be unsatisfactory to conclude merely that the Conservatives have been consistent in some, and inconsistent in other policies—even though there is truth in this suggestion.

Ethno-national policy learning

It is an odd feature of much explanation in political science that so little credence is given to cognition or learning as independent variables. One way of explaining the inconsistencies in the Conservative stewardship is to maintain that policy learning, albeit painfully slow learning, has been taking place—learning that has been maintained and developed in the

---

[30] New Ireland Forum, *Report* (Dublin, Stationery Office, 1984).

memory banks of the senior ranks of the civil service, the military, and the police; and transmitted with increasing success to successive elected office-holders.

Many of the contradictions and inconsistencies discussed above can be explained against the background of ethno-national policy learning. Amongst British policy-makers the definition and understanding of the conflict has been transformed in the last eighteen years. It has been recognized as ethno-national and bi-governmental, as well as bi-national, in nature. It has been recognized that the fundamental conflict is between rival nationalisms; and does not derive primarily from religious conflicts between Protestants and Catholics, or from economic deprivation, or from economic discrimination, or from the absence of good British government, or just from terrorism—even though all these variables have been and are at play, and even though things have been done to address these other dimensions of the conflict.

Better prescriptions, and policy dispositions, have followed better analysis—albeit slowly, and in some cases only after lessons have been relearned by new office-holders. It is known, though not always stated in this language, that the internal promotion of consociational arrangements can only be successful if matched by bi-governmentalism and cross-border institutions that ensure that both Irish nationalists and British Unionists have approximate equality in national recognition, and have parity of esteem. It is recognized that a political settlement requires that unionists and nationalists, and their governments, must be coerced, in their own best interests, to drink at the well of institutional concessions. It has become known, albeit reluctantly acknowledged and against ingrained beliefs, that political violence has political causes, and should not merely be treated as ordinary criminality. It is understood that British arbitration cannot ever be seen as neutral, even when it is benign, by non-British people—the promise of 'rigorous impartiality' has had to be matched by real and promised Irish dimensions.

This is not, perhaps it is necessary to say, a pious commendation of Conservative policy-makers. They could have learned these matters much earlier and much better. Many of them took two decades to learn what Edward Heath mostly understood in 1973. Moreover, their learning was not, unfortunately, significantly promoted by the dissemination of independent academic research. The Conservatives were, of course, not alone in being slow learners—the same could be said of many in the British opposition parties, and of Northern Irish nationalists, republicans, Unionists, loyalists, and the parties in the Republic of Ireland. The acquisition of useable knowledge, relevant to the possible resolution of the region's ethno-national conflict, has come from the experience of protracted war and conflict; from the understanding that no one can 'win' outright, and that the opponents are political, with identities as well as interests and passions.

It will be intriguing to see when they go into Opposition whether the Conservatives' policy learning will be maintained, either by them or by their successors in office. If they go into Opposition it seems most likely that their learning will be at least temporarily sacrificed to the party's opposition to the wider constitutional restructuring of the United Kingdom envisaged by Labour and the Liberal Democrats. Conservative leaders will certainly be freer to express their party faithful's inclinations on Northern Ireland, which are less burdened by learning.

8

Political Settlements in Northern Ireland and South Africa

John McGarry

This chapter examines comparisons between Northern Ireland's recent peace process and agreement and similar developments in South Africa. On the one hand, the analogy has been used to explain Northern Ireland's conflict and the type of prescription it requires. On the other, it has been employed to suggest ways in which agreement might be achieved in Northern Ireland, or, more recently, why agreement has been reached. These uses of the analogy ignore or downplay crucial contextual differences between the two cases. The most important of these is that, while South Africa's conflict took place largely within a single state, Northern Ireland's occurs within a wider British–Irish space. This contextual difference is crucial for understanding the Northern Ireland conflict, the type of institutions required there, and why agreement was reached.

Many academics and political activists have compared the conflicts in Northern Ireland and South Africa.[1] Until the 1990s, a dominant theme of

Thanks are due to the referees from *Political Studies*, and to Margaret Moore and Brendan O'Leary, for their helpful comments. I would also like to thank the Social Science and Humanities Research Council of Canada (SSHRCC) and the United States Institute of Peace (USIP) for financial help with my research.

[1] H. Adam and K. Moodley, *The Opening of the Apartheid Mind: Options for the New South Africa* (Berkeley, University of California Press, 1993); H. Adam, 'The politics of ethnic identity: comparing South Africa', *Ethnic and Racial Studies*, 18 (1995), 457–75; H. Dickie-Clark, 'The study of conflict in South Africa and Northern Ireland', *Social Dynamics*, 2 (1976), 53–9; H. Giliomee and J. Gagiano, *The Elusive Search for Peace. South Africa, Israel, Northern Ireland* (Cape Town, Oxford University Press, 1990); A. Guelke, 'The peace process in South Africa, Israel and Northern Ireland: a farewell to arms?', *Irish Studies in International Affairs*, 5 (1994), 93–106; A. Guelke, 'Promoting peace in deeply divided societies: Frank Wright Commemorative Lecture' (Dept. of Political Science, Queen's University Belfast, 1994); A. Guelke, 'Comparatively peaceful: the role of analogy in Northern Ireland's peace process', unpublished manuscript (1997); M. Macdonald, *Children of Wrath: Political Violence in Northern Ireland* (Cambridge, Polity, 1986); and R. Taylor, 'A Consociational Path to Peace in Northern Ireland and South Africa?' in A. Guelke (ed.), *New Perspectives on the Northern Ireland Conflict* (Aldershot, Avebury, 1994), pp. 161–74.

these studies was that both conflicts, along with one going on in Israel/ Palestine, were intractable.[2] After this, however, South Africa reached a settlement, and comparisons between the two cases shifted to stressing how the South African experience could be used to help achieve a settlement in Northern Ireland. Some commentators have used the South African analogy to bolster their explanation of the Northern Ireland conflict, and their prescription for it. At least three distinct perspectives have been put forward: one nationalist, one unionist, and a third approach that is associated with liberalism, Marxism, and postmodernism and that rejects both nationalism and unionism.

Others, eager to see peace, have suggested that Northern Ireland's politicians should take a lesson from the example of South Africans, who, after years of intransigence, agreed to negotiate a settlement. The Forum for Peace and Reconciliation, meeting in Dublin in November 1995, invited South Africa's Deputy President F. W. de Klerk to address them on the South African example.[3] During a state visit to South Africa in 1996, the Irish President, Mary Robinson, pointed out that the warring parties in Ireland had much to learn from South Africa's lesson in reconciliation.[4] In 1997, leading South African politicians from both the ANC and Nationalist Party invited Northern Ireland's politicians to their country so that they could benefit from their experience in reaching accommodation.[5] And when Northern Ireland's politicians reached agreement on 10 April 1998, two leading British newspapers claimed that the South African trip had evidently done some good.[6] Implicit in such views is a popular but lazy theory of conflict resolution: warring groups reach agreement when they see reason or when they learn it from others.

---

[2] The alleged intractability of the conflict in South Africa and Northern Ireland (and Israel/Palestine) explains the title of Giliomee and Gagiano's book, *The Elusive Search for Peace*.

[3] The invitation to de Klerk is cited in Guelke, 'Comparatively peaceful', p. 7. South Africa is not the only society that is supposed to have held lessons for Northern Ireland. In the early 1970s, the British government believed that Northern Ireland's politicians would benefit from travelling to the Netherlands to see how its Protestants and Catholics worked out their differences.

[4] 'South African peace an inspiration to Irish movement, says President', *Irish Times*, 27 March 1996.   [5] *Irish Times*, 16 June 1997.

[6] 'Leader—ANC's lesson for Sinn Fein', *Independent*, 29 April 1998. An *Observer* journalist opened an article which purported to explain Trimble's embrace of the Good Friday Agreement with the claim that 'It was on the distant veld of a South African game park that David Trimble began the journey in earnest from leader of one tribe to the architect of a new inclusiveness in Ulster', 'Trimble's long march to a new Unionism', *Observer*, 4 July 1998.

This chapter examines these uses of the South Africa analogy in light of the recent agreement in Northern Ireland. The argument is that the comparisons insufficiently acknowledge the many differences between the two cases. While South Africa's primary conflict was among groups whose aspirations are confined to the territory of South Africa, Northern Ireland's primary conflict involves groups who wish to belong to different states, the United Kingdom and the Republic of Ireland. The governments of these two states, particularly the former, have exercised an influence over Northern Ireland far beyond that which any outside agents have over South Africa. The problem with the three explanations referred to is that they underestimate the strength (and undervalue the legitimacy) of one or both of Northern Ireland's unionist and nationalist traditions, and they argue, incorrectly, that Northern Ireland's problems can be resolved within one state. Agreement was reached in April only because both nationalists and unionists were accommodated, and because the bi-statal dimension was explicitly recognized and institutionalized.[7]

The problem with the other accounts is that they downplay the role of contextual factors in reaching agreement. Accords were reached in South Africa and Northern Ireland not because their dominant (white and Unionist) groups came to their senses, but because it became sensible for them, because of the changing environments they faced, to reach agreement. Yet their respective environments were different. As the governing group in an independent state, South African whites were brought to negotiate because of a range of domestic crises and diffuse international pressures. While unionists also faced endogenous pressures and incentives, as a dependent group within a region of the United Kingdom they were particularly susceptible to British government policy, reached in cooperation with the Irish government. It was largely British–Irish policy which produced unionist flexibility, although unionists' acceptance of the new status quo is not as total as that of South Africa's whites.

WHAT SORT OF PROBLEM? WHAT SORT OF SETTLEMENT?

The analogy with South Africa has been used by nationalists, Unionists, and a group of commentators who are (allegedly) opposed to both

[7] See the series of articles by C. McCrudden, J. McGarry, and B. O'Leary in the *Sunday Business Post*: 'Answering some big questions', 19 April 1998; 'Dance of the ministries', 26 April 1998; 'All-Ireland bodies at work', 3 May 1998; 'Equality and Social Justice', 10 May 1998; 'The heart of the agreement: a bi-national future with double protection', 17 May 1998.

nationalism and Unionism to reinforce their explanations of and prescriptions for the Northern Ireland conflict.[8]

Nationalists in Northern Ireland attach considerable importance to the South African analogy.[9] Ironically, while Irish nationalists in the early part of the century identified themselves with Boers, who, like them, were engaged in a struggle against British imperialism, since the 1960s nationalists have identified almost totally with the anti-apartheid movement. Republicans constantly refer to the similarity of their struggle with that of the ANC, as can be seen from Belfast wall murals celebrating ANC/IRA solidarity and from their speeches and books. The analogy has been given the blessing, to the consternation of the British and Irish governments, of Nelson Mandela and other ANC leaders.[10] According to Guelke, the strength of republicans' identification with the ANC was so intense that the latter's decision to enter negotiations and 'suspend' its armed struggle was one of the factors which influenced the IRA to declare its ceasefire.[11]

The analogy is also accepted by constitutional nationalists. In the late 1960s, civil rights leaders compared the unionist government to the apartheid government of John Vorster. In the same vein, John Hume, the leader of the SDLP, has claimed that what Northern Ireland needs is a unionist version of F. W. de Klerk, the South African whites' leader who freed Mandela, entered negotiations with the opposition, and ultimately reached a settlement with it.[12]

---

[8] These three uses of the South African analogy are not the only ones, but I think they are the most important. Each of them is associated with a comprehensive explanation of, and prescription for, the Northern Ireland conflict. Other uses of the analogy seek to draw detailed, rather than broad, lessons, such as whether Northern Ireland would benefit from a Truth Commission or whether South Africa's experience with the decommissioning of weapons or police reform is relevant for Northern Ireland. See, for example, 'What the Irish can learn from South Africa', *Boston Globe*, 16 April 1998; 'Time not right for truth commission', *Irish Times*, 14 May 1998; 'ANC's lesson for Sinn Féin', *Independent*, 30 April 1998.

[9] For a summary of the ways in which Irish nationalists have compared themselves with the anti-apartheid movement in South Africa, see Guelke, 'Comparatively peaceful', pp. 1–2 and 4. I have relied on Guelke's account in writing parts of the next two paragraphs.

[10] 'Mandela's IRA remarks criticised', *Irish Times*, 21 October 1992. Kader Asmal, a leading ANC minister who lived in Ireland, has likened the penal system with apartheid and Cromwell's policy of deporting Catholics to Connacht with the apartheid regime's homelands policy, *Irish Times*, 27 March 1996.

[11] Guelke, 'Comparatively peaceful', p. 8.

[12] J. Hume, *A New Ireland: Politics, Peace and Reconciliation* (Boulder, CO, Roberts Rinehart, 1996), p. 117. A case can be made for separating nationalist uses of the analogy into distinct republican and constitutionalist categories. Both prefer that the context for a settlement be Ireland, but the latter is more prepared than the former to accept a continuing UK context also.

Equating unionists with South Africa's pre-1994 white community is not just meant to suggest that it is for Unionists, as defenders of the status quo, to make concessions. This is a suggestion many non-partisans could safely endorse. It also conveys a *nationalist* version of the conflict and the prescription that is necessary to end it. Thus, it infers that unionists, like whites, not only defend the status quo, but are also a *minority*, who should seek agreement with the nationalist *majority* in the island of Ireland. Just as South Africa's majority was denied its right to self-determination by the apartheid regime, Ireland's majority has been similarly deprived by unionists. The attempt to carve Northern Ireland out of Ireland is seen as analogous to attempts by whites to carve out a white-dominated South Africa through the creation of Black 'Home-lands'.[13] Just as the context for the solution to South Africa's conflict was the reintegration of these territories into South Africa, so the context for a solution to the conflict in Northern Ireland, it is suggested, is an end to the partition of Ireland (the hardline version), or a process which leads to this (the moderate version).

Not surprisingly, this use of the analogy is rejected by Unionists. While Unionists may sympathize with the white population of South Africa (and of Rhodesia) as a similarly besieged group, and loyalist para-militaries have collaborated with the apartheid regime's security forces, they have never conceded that their position is similar to that of South Africa's whites in the way conveyed by nationalists. The crucial difference for unionists is that they consider themselves a *majority*, and not a minority like South Africa's whites.[14] This is because they use Northern Ireland, and not Ireland, as the basis for any comparison. In the Unionist view, the partition of Ireland, which allowed Northern Ireland to remain part of the United Kingdom, was a legitimate exercise of self-determination. Predictably, therefore, when in mid-1997 UUP leader David Trimble was informed by a reporter about Hume's desire for

---

[13] In the same paragraph where Hume refers to the need for a unionist de Klerk, he puts forward the conventional nationalist position that partition is at the root of Northern Ireland's problems: 'There are parallels between the South African situation and our own. If the solution to the problem in South Africa had been to draw a line on the map, create a small white state, with two whites to every black person, and to make the rest of South Africa independent, would there ever have been a possibility of peace? Would not the whites have been forced to discriminate totally against the black minority in order to ensure that it never became a majority? This is precisely what happened in Ireland, and we are still living with the consequences'.

[14] One of the consequences of this difference in perception is that while a number of South African whites came to regard the apartheid regime as illegitimate, unionists remain solidly united on the legitimacy of the Union. This may be one reason why unionists have been more reluctant to negotiate a compromise with the opposition than South African whites.

a unionist de Klerk, he responded that the analogy was flawed as nationalists were the minority in Northern Ireland. What was needed, in Trimble's view, was not a unionist de Klerk, but a republican version.[15] From this perspective, conflict-resolution in Northern Ireland requires the nationalist minority to accept the constitutional preferences of the unionist majority, that is, Northern Ireland as an integral part of the United Kingdom and without political links to the Republic of Ireland.

A third version of the South African analogy is radically different from the other two. It allegedly rejects partisanship. Whereas nationalists and unionists suggest that what is needed is action by leaders (unionist or nationalist 'de Klerks'), the 'third wayers' reject such a 'top-down' view of conflict resolution. The third view is instead associated with what might be described as a 'social transformation' school in Northern Ireland, a significant group of commentators who argue that if there is to be a settlement, Northern Ireland society needs to be—and can be—transformed from the 'bottom-up'.[16] 'Transformers' start from the understanding that the cause of Northern Ireland's difficulties is the presence of the two identities outlined above, and they normally regard the political demands associated with these rival identities as irreconcilable. The identities are seen, not as deep-rooted, but as constructed by political and intellectual elites. They are amenable, therefore, to deconstruction. What is needed to achieve this is a concerted campaign by associations in 'civil society' to transcend nationalism and unionism and to create a common society divided only along lines of individual (or class) interest. Social transformation theory is popular among traditional liberals and Marxists, who have been hostile to ethnicity and nationalism, and among postmodernists, who have rejected the notion of fixed group boundaries.

The use of the South African analogy to support 'social transformation' theory in Northern Ireland is associated with the work of Rupert Taylor.[17] Taylor argues that the reason why the South African conflict,

---

[15] *Irish Times*, 29 April 1997; cited, Guelke, 'Comparatively peaceful', p. 1.

[16] The social transformation movement enjoys considerable support among Northern Ireland's chattering classes. It includes those who champion integrated education, 'normal' class politics over 'sectarian' politics (the Worker's Party, union groups, the Alliance Party), and gender politics (Women's movement). Its latest intellectual champions include the following: (the appropriately named) M. Love, *Peace-building through Reconciliation in Northern Ireland* (Aldershot, Avebury, 1995); J. Ruane and J. Todd, *The Dynamics of Conflict in Northern Ireland: Power, Conflict and Emancipation* (Cambridge, Cambridge University Press, 1996); S. Ryan, 'Peace building strategies and intercommunal conflict: approaches to the transformation of divided societies', *Nationalism and Ethnic Politics*, 2 (1996), 216–31.

[17] Taylor, 'A consociational path to peace'.

like Northern Ireland's, was considered intractable was because of the reification of racial/ethnic difference. In the 1960s, South Africa was regarded, particularly by its dominant white community, as being fundamentally divided along racial lines, and the contest for power was perceived in zero-sum terms. From the perspective of whites, a democratic settlement was a nightmare in which the black majority would turn the tables on them. A negotiated settlement only became possible, according to Taylor, because South African society was transformed between the 1960s and early 1990s from a society that thought in racial ways to one that was significantly non-racial. The credit was due to numerous groups in civil society who rejected the apartheid state's reification of race and ethnicity, and who worked to promote the idea of a common society in which racial and ethnic differences were irrelevant.[18] This made possible agreement on a constitutional settlement in which all South Africans were protected as equal individuals and group rights were largely ignored.

According to Taylor and other 'transformers', there can be no solution to Northern Ireland's 'zero-sum' conflict unless a similar social metamorphosis takes place there. The prescription from this perspective is for civil society groups (NGOs, churches, unions, and other voluntary associations) to work to erode existing (nationalist and unionist) partisan identities. At the micro-level, transformers support public policies, which, in their view, dissolve support for ethnic identities, such as anti-discrimination legislation, integrated education and housing. At the macro (constitutional) level, they advocate constitutional change similar to that achieved in South Africa: a Bill of Rights which proclaims the centrality of the individual over the group and political arrangements which encourage the emergence of non-ethnic parties. They are resolutely opposed to consociational (power-sharing) arrangements which, in their view, privilege ethnicity and the representatives of particular ethnic groups.

These three uses of the South African analogy cannot all be right. In fact, they all have important flaws. Let me explain their defects in order.

Ironically, the use of the South African analogy by Northern Ireland's leading nationalist and unionist politicians illustrates the nature of the conflict and the shortcomings in these partisan accounts: it is a struggle

---

[18] R. Taylor, J. Cock, and A. Habib, 'Projecting peace in apartheid South Africa', Paper presented at the meeting of the International Political Science Association, Seoul, South Korea, 1997; R. Taylor and M. Orkin, 'The Racialisation of Social Scientific Research on South Africa', in P. Ratcliffe (ed.), *The Politics of Social Research* (London: Palgrave Macmillan, 2001); R. Taylor and M. Shaw, 'The Dying Days of Apartheid', in A. Norval and D. Howarth (eds.), *South Africa in Transition* (London, Macmillan, 1998).

between two political communities who identify with different states, Ireland in the case of nationalists and the United Kingdom in the case of unionists. This crucial bi-statal dimension is absent from South Africa's conflict. The latter's communities do not seek to belong to different states. All of its main factions, including the Zulus of the Inkatha Freedom Party, consider themselves to be South African, although some of them have additional sub-South African identities. As a consequence, what South Africa required was a settlement *in* South Africa. The main negotiations there centred on how power should be organized at the centre and how much power should be decentralized.

While Northern Ireland's nationalist and unionist parties held rigidly to their rival versions of the South African analogy, agreement between them was impossible. The nationalist/republican version—a united Ireland or something clearly transitional to this—was unacceptable to Unionists, and the Unionist version—an integrated United Kingdom without links to the Irish Republic—was unpalatable for nationalists. This was clearly understood by important politicians and officials in the British and Irish governments, and since the early 1980s both governments have been agreed on an institutional framework for Northern Ireland that connects it to both Britain and the Irish Republic.[19] Agreement became possible in April 1998 because key nationalist and unionist agents moved away from their traditional view that the other's aspirations, like those of South Africa's whites, were illegitimate. All the major Irish nationalist parties, including both the SDLP and Sinn Féin, accepted an agreement which softened the Republic's irredentism,[20] accepted that Northern Ireland should remain part of the United Kingdom for as long as a majority of its population wanted, and established British–Irish institutions that would, presumably, continue in place even if a united Ireland came into existence. Those Unionists who endorsed the Agreement accepted not only the principle of power-sharing within Northern Ireland, but the establishment of all-Ireland political institutions which would cooperate in several functional activities, and a continuing role for the Irish government in any matter which had not been devolved to the new Northern Ireland Assembly. There is, now, a difficult transition period to be weathered before these institutions take root. However, it is extremely difficult to envisage a workable alternative.

[19] B. O'Leary and J. McGarry, *The Politics of Antagonism: Understanding Northern Ireland* (London, Athlone, 1996), chapters 7–9.

[20] The Republic did not abandon irredentism. It abandoned its claim to have the right to exercise legal jurisdiction over Northern Ireland without the consent of a majority there, while retaining an 'irredentist' aspiration to unity.

The popularity of transformation theory in Northern Ireland can be explained by the difficulty of achieving an agreement that has—and can keep—the support of Northern Ireland's two ethno-national communities. But is the transformers' version of the South African analogy any more feasible than the traditional nationalist and Unionist varieties? Taylor's account of the South African 'transformation', in which preoccupation with race and ethnicity have been replaced with universalism, is hardly part of a factual consensus. In fact, it is rejected by leading international experts on ethnicity, operating from different political positions,[21] as well as by several South African academics.[22] An important part of Taylor's case for the transformation of South Africa rests on depicting South Africans' electoral behaviour, as measured in the country's first (and only) democratic election, as non-racial. Yet this is a highly contestable reading, given that the overwhelmingly white Nationalist Party secured only 3–4 per cent of the (black) African vote, the overwhelmingly black ANC won 2–3 per cent of the white vote, and a largely ethnic party, the Inkatha Freedom Party, won around half of the Zulu vote.[23] And even if Taylor is right that ethnicity and race are weak

---

[21] Two of the leading experts on ethnic conflict, Donald Horowitz and Arend Lijphart, who disagree on almost everything else, share the view that ethnic and racial divisions will be of importance in the future South Africa. Horowitz, who believes the notion of a non-racial society in South Africa is 'utopian' and the plural society's analogue to the search for a classless society, writes that 'South Africa's politics will not be non-racial and non-ethnic but multiracial and multiethnic', D. Horowitz, *A Democratic South Africa? Constitutional Engineering in a Divided Society* (Berkeley, University of California Press, 1991), pp. 29, 85. According to Lijphart, writing in 1985, a future South Africa will be an 'ethnically plural society on a par with most of the black states in Africa. [Intra-black ethnic cleavages] currently muted by the feelings of black solidarity in opposition to minority rule... are bound to reassert themselves in a situation of universal suffrage', A. Lijphart, *Power-sharing in South Africa* (Berkeley, Institute of International Studies, University of California Press, 1985), pp. 19–20.

[22] Guelke dismisses the idea of a non-racial South Africa as a 'myth', A. Guelke, 'Dissecting the South African miracle: African parallels', *Nationalism and Ethnic Politics*, 2 (1996), pp. 142–5. In his view, South Africa's major current division is between Africans and non-Africans (Afrikaners, English, Asians, Coloureds). Giliomee criticizes the idea that 'racial and ethnic cleavages will quickly dissipate', arguing, variously, that Afrikaners form 'a clearly defined group', the white community 'displays a powerful group consciousness', and that there are '[p]otentially serious ethnic divisions... among Africans', H. Giliomee, 'Democratization in South Africa', *Political Science Quarterly*, 110 (1995), pp. 100–1.

[23] Figures from Guelke, 'Dissecting the South African miracle', p. 145. Taylor's response is that what appears to be a racial vote is really a class vote, given the huge socio-economic disparities between white and black. However, he provides no evidence that it is class rather than race, or rather than class and race, which motivates voters. Intuitively, it seems more plausible to suggest that both class and race played a part in voting decisions. This would make South Africa what Horowitz describes as a 'ranked' society, one in which class and race or ethnicity are reinforcing, D. Horowitz, *Ethnic Groups in Conflict* (Berkeley, University of California Press, 1985), p. 22.

in South Africa currently, it seems somewhat premature to declare a South African 'transformation' after one free election, less than a decade of freedom of association, and the pronounced tendency in the rest of Africa for sub-state ethnic divisions to cause havoc once the glow of national liberation has faded.[24]

Let us assume for the sake of argument that Taylor is correct about South Africa. And let us also accept that ethnic attachments are neither obviously primordial nor biological, but socially and politically constructed, and that identities can evolve depending on context.[25] Even with this, however, there are significant reasons for doubting whether such a transformation is possible in Northern Ireland in the foreseeable future. Northern Ireland's ethno-national divisions are long-standing, the result of British and Irish nation-building failures in the eighteenth and nineteenth centuries.[26] Unlike South Africa's divisions, Northern Ireland's have become consolidated in a democratic system in which purveyors of other forms of identity, such as class, have failed utterly to compete with nationalists and unionists. In every election in the north of

Similar arguments—that what appears to be an ethnic division is really a class division— have been made about voting patterns in Northern Ireland. For criticism of such arguments, see J. McGarry and B. O'Leary, *Explaining Northern Ireland: Broken Images* (Oxford, Blackwell, 1995), chap. 4.

[24] The divisions in South Africa, in Horowitz's view, 'are very much on the order of the cleavages that in some countries translated into serious post-independence conflict and violence...To ignore them in planning for a future South Africa would be to repeat the same fallacy of assuming in the 1950s and 1960s that an inclusive "nationalism" would be the universal solvent of differences in post-colonial Africa, a fallacy for which many people paid dearly', Horowitz, *A Democratic South Africa?*, p. 85.

[25] Transformers sometimes seek to undermine consociationalism by identifying it with radical views based on primordialism or socio-biology. Thus, Taylor claims that Lijphart's writings are 'tied to plural society theory, in which, reflecting the prevailing academic consensus of the late colonial period, the key underlying source of conflict in societies marked by social and cultural pluralism is taken to lie in deep primordial forces of ethnic identity', 'A consociational path to peace', p. 162. Also see Paul Dixon's critique of work by Brendan O'Leary and John McGarry, 'The politics of antagonism: explaining McGarry and O'Leary', *Irish Political Studies*, 11 (1996), 130–41. Such a criticism if accurate would be serious, given the evidence that ethnic and national identities are politically and socially constructed, albeit over a considerable time period. Reasonable consociationalists, however, do not claim that ethnic ties are primordial or biological, but that in deeply divided societies they are durable, cannot be imagined out of existence, and must be accommodated in political institutions. The consociationalist argument is that particularly in certain contexts—deeply divided societies, where divisions are long-standing and when there is intra-group violence—it is more realistic to accept that different groups will continue to exist than to seek the 'deconstruction' of group ties.

[26] B. O'Leary and P. Arthur, 'Introduction. Northern Ireland as a Site of State- and Nation-Building Failures', in J. McGarry and B. O'Leary (eds.), *The Future of Northern Ireland* (Oxford, Clarendon, 1990), pp. 1–47.

Ireland from 1886, the population has divided into ethno-national camps with only a small middle ground. Its 'civil society' is similarly divided, which is why it is an error to put too much faith in 'bottom-up' solutions (or in referendums 'over the politicians' heads'). Given the failure of non-nationalist parties or civil society groups to compete seriously in Northern Ireland for over a century, the belief that a 'transformation' is possible within the foreseeable future seems wishful.[27]

Moreover, Northern Ireland has just experienced almost thirty years of polarizing inter-ethnic violence in which large numbers of unionists have been killed by nationalists, and vice versa. One of the remarkable aspects of South Africa's recent past is that it has had relatively little inter-racial violence, at least not by blacks against whites.[28] Inter-group violence in Northern Ireland is a further barrier to the emergence of a transcendent identity there. There is also a question as to whether Northern Ireland's *national* identities should be equated with South Africa's *racial* identities in the way Taylor does. As a principle for group membership, racism is almost universally abhorred, which is one of the reasons the apartheid regime crumbled. As a principle of group membership, nationalism is almost universally subscribed to, which helps explain why unionists and nationalists do not face the same pressures as South African racists to abandon their identities.[29]

Even if it was practical to eliminate Northern Ireland's two antagonistic identities in the foreseeable future, this would still leave the problem of how it should be governed in the interim, and what sort of institutions it should have. To incorporate South Africa's individualist and majoritarian constitution into Northern Ireland under present circumstances would have disastrous consequences, as its practical effect would be a unionist majority governing a nationalist minority. This minority, over 40 per cent of the population, would be more strongly placed and more likely than South Africa's white minority (13 per cent of

---

[27] The Stormont government did seek to reinforce the nationalist–Unionist divide, but it can hardly be credited with inventing it. There is no counterpart in Northern Ireland, or anywhere else for that matter, for the apartheid's state's massive attempt to engineer and reinforce identities through policies based on the Population Registration Act, including pass laws, Bantustans, and the proscription of inter-racial marriage and sexual relations.

[28] See Taylor and Shaw, 'The Dying Days of Apartheid'.

[29] There is a related normative question of whether we should seek to overcome national identities in the same way we should seek to eliminate racism. Racism is exclusionary and almost always hierarchical. Nationalism, however, is often consistent with inclusive appeals and respect for other nations. Nationalisms can produce conflict, but it is possible to prevent this through institutional arrangements which accommodate rather than transcend national identities.

the population) to oppose such a settlement.[30] The likelihood of such opposition explains why the British government has insisted since 1973 that any Northern Ireland government be consociational in character. The necessity of consociationalism has long been acknowledged by Northern Ireland's loyalist parties, and in the Agreement of April 1988 it was accepted by the bulk of the UUP.

Transformers' prescriptions for Northern Ireland are suspect on another front also. Because they abstract from the question of boundaries/states, they accept the Union by default. While it is compatible with neutrality to advocate equal citizenship within a single state in a racially divided society like South Africa, it is hardly impartial to advocate this in a nationally divided society like Northern Ireland. The fact that transformers are associated with majoritarian prescriptions on both political institutions and boundaries explains why they are often regarded by nationalists in Northern Ireland as politically correct Unionists. The political prescriptions of transformers, in fact, are very similar to those of one of the most prominent Unionist opponents of the recent agreement, Robert McCartney.[31]

Transformers, such as Taylor, claim that consociationalism is not only undesirable but 'dangerous' because, through rewarding ethnic parties with seats in legislatures and government, it entrenches ethnic divisions.[32] Such an argument would have some relevance if political settlements were designed to reward *only* ethnic parties with the privileges of power. In fact, many power-sharing formats, including the transitional power-sharing arrangements in South Africa (1994–9) and that included in Northern Ireland's Agreement, are designed to allow *any* political party that wins significant support to have a share of seats in the legislature and cabinet.[33] Such provisions may be criticized for ruling out substantial oppositions, but hardly for advantaging ethnic parties over their non-ethnic counterparts.

[30] Arguably, South Africa's whites, controlling the security apparatus, were also well-placed to reject majoritarianism. They could take solace, however, in their power in the private sector and in the bureaucracy, a luxury which Northern Ireland's nationalists do not possess.

[31] McCartney, leader of the UK Unionist Party and an MP, advocates the need for individual rights within a single (British) state. Like transformers, he criticizes consociationalism (power-sharing) as rewarding sectarianism. His 'anti-sectarianism' does not stop him from maintaining a close political alliance with the Rev. Ian Paisley!

[32] Taylor, 'A consociational path to peace', p. 166.

[33] In both South Africa, 1994–9, and Northern Ireland, from 1998, executive seats are distributed proportionally among parties represented in the legislature.

Northern Ireland's Agreement more clearly privileges nationalist and unionist parties through provisions that key measures need not only majority support in the Assembly, but the support of a proportion of both nationalists and unionists.[34] Such provisions should be seen, however, as transitional steps necessary to build the level of trust required to over-come historic divisions. If this can be achieved, the ground will have been prepared for a genuine transformation and there will be no further need for such special measures.[35]

A final criticism that transformers make about consociational arrangements of the sort contained in the Agreement is that they are unstable and depend for their survival on unrealistically high levels of cooperation. However, the elections of May 1998 returned enough pro-Agreement politicians to give it reasonable prospects for survival over the short to medium term, and the British and Irish governments will work, in most conceivable scenarios, to ensure there is no backtracking. In any case, should the consociational institutions established by the Agreement collapse, the alternative is not the South African model preferred by transformers, but either cantonization within Northern Ireland, with each community governing its own localities, or direct rule from Westminster with continuing or increased input from the Irish government.

FROM INTRANSIGENCE TO AGREEMENT: EXPLAINING THE BEHAVIOUR OF WHITES AND UNIONISTS

The agreements reached in South Africa and Northern Ireland involved significant shifts from the status quo towards the position of blacks and nationalists, respectively. One way to explain the agreements, therefore,

---

[34] The Agreement provides for two decision-making rules in the Assembly: (i) either 'parallel consent', that is, a majority of those voting, including a majority of the Unionist and nationalist designations voting; (ii) or a 'weighted majority', that is, 60% of members voting, including at least 40% of each of the Unionist and nationalist designations voting. At the first meeting of the Assembly, members were required to designate themselves as nationalist, Unionist, or 'other'.

[35] Successful consociational arrangements are 'biodegradable'. If they succeed in establishing trust in a divided society, and there is agreement, normal majoritarian institutions can be established. This is what happened in the Netherlands—see A. Lijphart, *The Politics of Accommodation: Pluralism and Democracy in the Netherlands* (Berkeley, University of California Press, 1968). As the *Economist* put it just after the May referendum, 'the long-term task [is] clear: to help Northern Irish politics evolve into a condition in which this fragile constitutional structure can be ditched', 30 May 1998, p. 17.

is to explain why the status quo's defenders, whites and Unionists, came to accept such shifts.[36]

An ethnic group's acceptance of compromise over intransigence does not flow from a belated discovery of reason or from exposure to others' accommodative behaviour, but from rational calculations about group interests, first articulated by intellectuals and politicians, and then more broadly accepted. Nor does it flow exclusively from elite voluntarism, as calls for a nationalist or unionist 'de Klerk' suggest: while the willingness of leaders to consider compromise can be important, this is unlikely to exist, or to be sufficient to carry along followers, unless other conditions are favourable.[37] Both whites and unionists were exposed to a range of pressures (and incentives) to seek accommodation with blacks and nationalists respectively. There were important differences, however, in the source and nature of these pressures. As a governing minority in an independent state, South Africa's whites were subjected to a range of endogenous and diffuse international pressures which eventually forced them to negotiate. Unionists, however, are a small minority within the United Kingdom whose main political goal is to remain part of that state. As a result they have been relatively immune from some of the pressures that whites faced, but particularly susceptible to direct British government policy. Since 1985, British policy has been influenced by, and largely implemented in cooperation with, the Irish government. Appreciating the British–Irish context in which Northern Ireland exists is as vital, therefore, to understanding why the Agreement came about as it is to understanding the conflict and the prescription required.

South Africa's whites: To 'adapt or die'[38]

South Africa's whites reached a settlement in 1994 not so much because they had become transformed into liberals by civil-society activists (as de Klerk's consistent refusal to apologize for apartheid indicates), but because of changes in their circumstances that made the decision to reach

---

[36] This is not to say that only the dominant group need show flexibility. Unless one side has been defeated, conflict resolution normally requires flexibility on all sides. The flexibility of one group, moreover, is often related to the flexibility of its enemies, that is, accords flow out of a dynamic and interactive environment. In the following account, I explain that the moderation of whites and unionists was influenced by the moderation of their adversaries, although this was not the only, or the most important, influence on their actions.

[37] Think of what would have happened if F. W. de Klerk had led whites in the 1960s. Would he have advocated an end to apartheid? Would he have remained leader if he had suggested this?

[38] P. W. Botha warned his fellow Afrikaners in a celebrated speech in 1979 that they must 'adapt or die'. Cited in D. O'Meara, *Forty Lost Years* (Randburg, Ravan, 1996), p. 255.

a settlement more palatable than the status quo, and better than any of the alternatives. De Klerk's decision to settle was crucially influenced by a number of interrelated pressures. The white share of the population, which had held steady at 20 per cent between 1910 and 1960, dropped to 15 per cent by 1985 and was projected to fall to 11 per cent by 2010, endangering their ability to occupy strategic positions in the state apparatus and economy. The demographic crisis allowed de Klerk to peddle successfully a negotiated settlement as 'indispensable for the survival of whites as a shrinking minority'.[39]

Economic growth in the 1960s and 1970s gave way to stagnation in the 1980s and 1990s.[40] The decline could be linked to apartheid, as it flowed from internal instability—which made international and even domestic investors reluctant to invest—and from external economic sanctions. The crisis threatened whites' material privileges, narrowed the government's options for dealing with the political crisis—such as buying off the black middle class—and even, given the rising cost of defence expenditures, threw into question the state's ability to defend itself. International economic sanctions were reinforced by cultural, academic, and sporting boycotts. Together, these international measures effectively cut whites off from the western community with which they identified.

From the mid-1980s also, it was clear that white control, which had been hegemonic since Sharpeville in 1960, was breaking down. Continuing white rule became incompatible with order. The opposition increasingly challenged the regime, through civil disobedience, strikes, and riots. The growing internal resistance empowered opposition groups, while the increased reliance on emergency measures helped to delegitimize apartheid as a form of control, opening up important divisions among whites. As an ideology, apartheid had been embraced by Afrikaners as a way to ensure peace and stability between the races. These justifications evaporated after the 1984–6 insurrection made it clear that apartheid, rather than providing order, gave rise to serious opposition and unrest.[41]

---

[39] H. Giliomee, 'South Africa's democratic surprise', paper delivered to a conference on 'Good Surprises: Peace Processes in South Africa, Northern Ireland and Israel/Palestine', Duke University, November 1995, p. 12. Also see Giliomee, 'Democratization in South Africa', pp. 86–8, and Guelke, 'The peace process', p. 100.

[40] There is a consensus among experts on South Africa that economic collapse and the collapse of apartheid were inextricably linked. See R. Price, *The Apartheid State in Crisis: Political Transformation in South Africa 1975–1990* (New York, Oxford University Press, 1991), p. 232; Giliomee, 'South Africa's democratic surprise', p. 7; Adam and Moodley, *The Opening of the Apartheid Mind*, p. 56; O'Meara, *Forty Lost Years*, p. 463.

[41] For the importance of stability as a foundation of apartheid ideology, see H. Giliomee and L. Schlemmer, *From Apartheid to Nation-Building* (Cape Town, Oxford University Press, 1990), chapter 2.

Also important was the stance of the opposition. We can put it counterfactually. Had the Pan-Africanist Congress, with its call for 'one settler—one bullet', been the dominant opposition group, there would have been no settlement. But Mandela's ANC was dominant, and went out of its way to assuage the fears of whites and to reassure them that South Africa belonged to all its citizens. His moderation reinforced the development of a 'stitch in time' mentality among whites, as he was ageing and there were fears his successors would be less accommodating. Although Mandela suspended the ANC's 'armed struggle' only after the start of negotiations, this struggle had been tame to begin with, and had hardly ever been directed against the white population. While the ANC insisted on, and ultimately achieved, majority rule, it reassured Afrikaners that their culture would be accommodated. In short, a settlement with the ANC posed no obvious existential threat to whites, whether physically or culturally. In addition, the ANC's movement away from socialist economics in the late 1980s helped to reassure whites that they could retain private power while releasing their grip on the public variety.

Unionists and British–Irish cooperation

As a non-governing group in a region of the United Kingdom, Unionists escaped many of the pressures faced by Afrikaners and whites. Because the United Kingdom is committed to an equitable distribution of services throughout its territory, unionists (and nationalists) have been sheltered from the economic consequences of conflict and political intransigence.[42] The United Kingdom has also been on hand to prevent a spiral into a Bosnia-scale catastrophe, thus blocking what Lijphart describes as a 'self-negating prophecy' by leaders—a decision to draw back from the

There is also a consensus among academic commentators that the end of the cold war reinforced whites' willingness to negotiate, although there is debate about whether this strengthened the government and made it more confident about negotiations or bolstered the opposition and made negotiations with it more necessary. In the view of most commentators, the main effect of the collapse of Eastern European communism was to increase white confidence about negotiations, as it rolled back the communist threat in Africa, deprived the ANC/SACP of external support, and, by casting considerable doubt on socialist economic planning, made the ANC retreat from left-wing positions. Guelke argues, however, that it was the ANC which benefited from the end of the cold war. A. Guelke, 'The impact of the end of the Cold War on the South African transition', *Journal of Contemporary African Studies*, 14 (1996), 87–100.

[42] B. O'Leary, T. Lyne, J. Marshall, and B. Rowthorn, *Northern Ireland: Sharing Authority* (London, Institute for Public Policy Research, 1993), pp. 81–2.

abyss by compromising with the enemy.[43] Northern Ireland's position as a region of a relatively important state, coupled with no strong local political institutions, has meant that there has been less international pressure on unionists to compromise than was applied to South African whites. There is no counterpart in Northern Ireland to the international economic, cultural, and sporting boycotts which brought whites to negotiate. Most importantly, Northern Ireland's position within the United Kingdom meant for unionists that their inflexibility did not mean a 'future too ghastly to contemplate', the warning South African whites were familiar with. Rather, for most of the period after 1972, the default to compromise was the essentially Unionist option of direct rule from Westminster. Unionists may have disagreed about whether direct rule was better than pre-1972 arrangements, when they governed Northern Ireland without interference from Westminster, but they agreed it was preferable to a deal with nationalists. For most of the period before Good Friday 1998, it was this latter scenario which invoked Unionist nightmares.

Unionists are facing emerging demographic problems, although these are not as severe as South African whites'. While those who gave their religion as Protestant, an accurate marker of unionist sympathies, declined from 63.2 per cent in 1961 to 50.6 per cent in 1991, those who gave their religion as Catholic increased from 34.9 per cent to 38.4 per cent. The remainder (11 per cent) refused to give a religious designation.[44] These figures correspond remarkably closely with recent election results. In three Northern Ireland-wide elections held in 1996–7, unionist parties (the UUP, DUP, UKUP, PUP, UDP, and Conservative Party) averaged 50.3 per cent of the vote, whereas nationalist parties averaged 38.2 per cent.[45] The rest of the vote, which presumably includes a high proportion of those who refuse to give a religious designation, was split among a middle and moderate bloc made up of the Alliance Party, Women's Coalition, and others. The unionists' share of the vote has been declining steadily. In the seven province-wide elections which took place between 1982 and 1989, in contrast to those in 1996–7, the average

[43] Of course, violence does not always produce such self-negating actions. There are plenty of examples where it results in profound polarization and greater violence, as in Rwanda, Burundi, Bosnia, or Sri Lanka.

[44] Figures from P. Doherty, 'The Numbers Game: The Demographic Context of Politics', in A. Aughey and D. Morrow (eds.), *Northern Ireland Politics* (London, Longman, 1996), p. 202.

[45] Figures from B. O'Leary and G. Evans, 'Northern Ireland: la fin de siècle, the twilight of the second Protestant ascendancy and Sinn Féin's second coming', *Parliamentary Affairs*, 50 (1997), p. 673. In the last election before the Agreement, the Westminster elections of 1997, nationalists won 40.2% of the province's vote.

unionist vote was 55.4 per cent and the average nationalist vote, 32.5 per cent.[46]

While a subject of dispute among academics, there is a popular perception that there will be a Catholic majority early in the next century. Whether that happens, Unionists are in such imminent danger of losing their electoral majority, and so divided, that it now makes sense to see Northern Ireland as having several political minorities rather than a majority and a minority. These demographic and electoral facts helped to undercut the traditional Unionist argument for majoritarian institutions and to make the consociational arrangements at the heart of the Agreement palatable. They also made it increasingly rational for unionists to seek to win Catholic support for the Union by agreeing to political concessions. And finally, the weakening unionist position made it likely that the next offer from the British and Irish governments would not be as generous as the present one. Unlike de Klerk, unionist leaders have not publicly admitted that demographic arguments influence their behaviour, although some do privately.[47] In any case, it seems unlikely that thinking unionist politicians would have ignored these changing demographic realities.

While Northern Ireland's position within the United Kingdom shielded unionists from the need to compromise in the period after 1972, their desire to preserve the Union meant, paradoxically, that they were vulnerable to British pressure to seek accommodation with nationalists. In this way their position was not as strong as that of separatists, or groups like the Rhodesian whites who were prepared to defy the UK government and unilaterally declare independence rather than bow to London's pressure. While South Africa's whites were amenable to western pressure because they identified with the west and sought membership of it, Unionists were amenable to British pressure for the same reason. Britain, as the sovereign power in Northern Ireland, was also in a stronger position to apply its power than outside states in South Africa. It was the successful exercise of British policy, influenced by the Irish government and implemented in cooperation with it, that induced the bulk of the UUP to accept the Good Friday Agreement.

[46] Figures based on Brendan O'Leary, 'Party Support in Northern Ireland, 1969–1989', in J. McGarry and B. O'Leary (eds.), *The Future of Northern Ireland* (Oxford, Clarendon, 1990), Table A4.1, p. 343.

[47] According to one confidential source, loyalist paramilitaries gave weakening Protestant numbers as a reason for seeking compromise during private conversations (personal communication, 5 December 1997).

The British–Irish cooperation, which contributed significantly to the recent agreement, began in 1985 with the signing of the Anglo-Irish Agreement (AIA). This was a reaction to the failure of Unionists and nationalists to reach an internal power-sharing accommodation, and it was designed, at least in part, to create the conditions for this. The Agreement committed the British and Irish governments to cooperate over Northern Ireland, gave the Irish government input into the governance of Northern Ireland through an Intergovernmental Conference, and established an intergovernmental secretariat in Northern Ireland. A key aim of the Agreement was to induce unionist compromise by altering the structure of the incentives they faced: They were to be offered the carrot of a reduction in the Irish government's role in the North if they agreed to an internal settlement with nationalists.[48] The AIA was bitterly opposed by Unionists, but it proved invulnerable to their protests, and created divisions among them on how to counter it. Rather than being destroyed or dissipating, cooperation between the two states deepened and became entrenched.

The recent political negotiations which resulted in the Agreement grew out of interactions between the two nationalist political leaders, Hume and Adams, and the Irish government. An Irish government initiative led to the Joint Declaration for Peace, released by Dublin and London in December 1993, which paved the way for the IRA and, subsequently, the loyalist ceasefires. The institutional outline of the Good Friday Agreement was laid out by the two governments, in advance of serious negotiations among the internal parties, in the 'Framework' proposals of February 1995. Changes were made as a result of input from the local parties in January 1998 and again in the text laid before the parties during the final week of negotiations, but the governments' institutional design remained largely intact in the final agreement.

The negotiations did not begin, and this is a point often overlooked by journalists who compare Northern Ireland and South Africa, as a result of Unionists deciding to negotiate with nationalists.[49] Because the governments' approach envisaged changes to a unionist status quo, and was

[48] As Brendan O'Leary and I have written, 'The choice offered by the AIA to unionists was: negotiate a power-sharing devolved government which will make irrelevant the proceedings of the intergovernmental conference or allow the intergovernmental conference to become the bridgehead of a very significant Irish dimension', *The Politics of Antagonism: Understanding Northern Ireland* (London: Athlone, 1993 and 1996), p. 235.

[49] None of the constitutional initiatives undertaken since the conflict began in 1969 have originated from Unionists. Initiatives in 1973–4, 1975, 1979, and 1982 all failed, as a result of Unionist unwillingness to change the constitutional status quo and nationalist unwillingness to accept it.

linked to the Hume/Adams dialogue, it was broadly supported by nationalists, particularly by the largest nationalist party, the Social Democratic and Labour Party. However, the negotiations, like the AIA, produced a split within Unionism as to how best to counter the British–Irish approach. One of the major unionist parties, the DUP, refused to participate, with its leader arguing, with some plausibility, that the governments had already fixed the result. UUP leaders calculated, correctly in my view, that staying out of the negotiations was riskier than being included. A boycott would jeopardize unionist standing with the British public, leave the intergovernmental conference fully intact, and possibly give rise to the deepening of Anglo-Irish cooperation. This was also the position of two small but important loyalist parties, the PUP and UDP, which emerged in the wake of the loyalist ceasefires.

The UUP's participation in the negotiations, however, could hardly be misunderstood as enthusiastic. Rather than negotiating, the UUP, as well as Unionists outside the negotiations, focused on challenging the sincerity of one of the nationalist parties' (Sinn Féin) commitment to constitutionalism. Their tactics bore resemblance to those of the Israeli right who, rather than engage in substantive negotiations, sought to stall, and ultimately destroy, the Oslo process by challenging the PLO's commitment to fighting terrorism.[50] As late as January 1998, the *Economist* stated that 'unionist politicians... have never been happy with the peace process'.[51]

A key reason why there was no discernible movement towards agreement between the IRA ceasefire in August 1994 and the summer of 1997 was the pivotal position of unionists in the Westminster parliament, which weakened the Conservative government's ability to bring pressure to bear and made it thinkable that the British–Irish initiative could be successfully resisted. This changed, however, with the election of the Labour government with a large majority in June of 1997. By most accounts, Blair looked set to hold onto power for a decade, a time in which unionist numbers would continue to decline. His party was committed to the Framework proposals, and his Secretary of State, Mo Mowlam, had indicated in Opposition considerable flexibility towards Sinn Féin and a commitment to reforming Northern Ireland, including its predominantly Protestant police force. Unionists were

---

[50] See I. Lustick, 'Ending protracted conflicts: The Oslo peace process between political partnership and legality', *Cornell International Law Journal*, 30 (1997), 741–57.

[51] The *Economist*, 10 January 1997, p. 47. To be precise, Unionists liked the peace very much, it was the process they were unhappy with.

delivered a clear message, although it was already implicit in the Anglo-Irish Agreement: they had no veto over the deepening of North–South cooperation or over internal reforms. It was this message, and Blair's room for manoeuvre, not his charm or charisma, which induced Unionist flexibility. Unlike Major, Blair indicated he would not allow the issue of decommissioning to prevent progress. He set a deadline of May 1998 for an agreement to be arrived at by the negotiating parties and ratified by a referendum, and this is what occurred.[52]

Pressure from the two governments to negotiate a settlement, and the danger that Unionists would be worse off if they did not, played an important role in driving Trimble to negotiate. However, his task, like de Klerk's, was made easier by the flexibility of his (nationalist) opponents. The IRA's ceasefire in August of 1994 created an atmosphere which was more conducive to Unionist compromise. It also ushered in a loyalist ceasefire and the participation of refreshingly flexible loyalist parties in the political negotiations. Their presence acted as a crucial cushion for Trimble against DUP accusations that his involvement in talks jeopardized the Union. Sinn Féin contributed to the momentum which produced agreement by its public acceptance that it need not include a united Ireland. By agreeing to revise the Republic's irredentist claim over Northern Ireland and accepting the establishment of a British–Irish Council, two important UUP demands, nationalists allowed Trimble to market the Agreement to his followers as a balanced compromise.

The pressures on Unionists to accept the agreement, however, were more subtle than those which forced whites to accept a settlement in South Africa. To a significant extent, they rested on speculation about the future behaviour of the British and Irish governments rather than on obvious facts like demographic collapse, international boycotts, and economic decline. As a result, while South African whites have overwhelmingly accepted the end of white rule, significant numbers of unionists have continued to reject Northern Ireland's accord.[53] An alternative strategy of resisting agreement, hoping for (or engineering)

[52] In the final days of the negotiations, the *Economist* described the British pressure on Trimble as 'intense'. The UUP's deputy leader, John Taylor, explained that rejecting the deal 'would have left the party almost completely isolated within British politics', 18 April 1998, p. 19.

[53] South Africa may not have experienced a shift from racialism to non-racialism, Taylor's analysis notwithstanding, but it has experienced a remarkably peaceful transition from white rule to majority rule. Serious opposition to the transition among whites never emerged. The white Freedom Front, which sought a better deal for whites than that won by de Klerk, achieved only 2.1% of the vote in the 1994 elections, compared to the Nationalist Party's 20% (Guelke, 'Dissecting the South African Miracle', p. 144). White extremist

a breakdown in British–Irish cooperation and a return to direct rule from Britain, remains rational for them, even if risky. This differential endorsement by the two groups exists notwithstanding the fact that whites, having given up a monopoly of power and agreed to majority rule, have conceded much more than unionists. It is the sizeable proportion of rejectionists among the unionist community that represents the most serious obstacle to the success of the Agreement.

Rejectionism, however, faces significant obstacles. The British and Irish governments know how the Agreement was reached, and understand the basis of the opposition to it. They will realize that they have to maintain a solid partnership if the institutions established by the Agreement are to survive attempts by unionist rejectionists to undermine them, and if the unionists who have accepted the agreement are to be kept onside. They will seek to emphasize cooperation and keep disagreements private in order to weaken rejectionism and to encourage more unionists to work with the new institutions.

The two governments have tacitly made it clear that the alternative to the survival of the institutions established by the Agreement is not the *status quo ante*, but a deepening and consolidation of British–Irish cooperation over Northern Ireland. This has included the message that all aspects of the Agreement which do not necessarily require local political institutions, such as the commitments to release prisoners, reform the police, and pursue economic, legal, and political equality between the two groups, will be undertaken regardless of whether local institutions exist. Thinking unionists will also be aware that North–South institutions cooperating in the areas envisaged by the Agreement could be established and run by civil servants if they refuse to participate. The risk for rejectionists is that by destroying (or boycotting) the Agreement's institutions, they lose input into the coming reforms, while seeing them being implemented anyway.

The prospects for the survival of the Agreement will be enhanced if other groups play a constructive role. As rejectionists will be encouraged if they can establish political alliances, it will be important for the international community and the British parliamentary opposition to maintain support for British–Irish cooperation in general and the

opposition, after an abortive show of force just before the 1994 elections, effectively evaporated. In Northern Ireland, on the other hand, the agreement has divided Unionism in half. Exit polls from the Referendum on 22 May indicated that only a slight majority of unionists voted 'yes'. In the elections of June 1998, unionists supporting the Agreement won thirty seats and 23.9% of the vote, while unionist rejectionists won twenty-eight seats and 24.9% of the vote.

Agreement in particular. The actions of the Conservative party in June 1998, when it broke with the tradition of 'bipartisanship' on Northern Ireland over a bill dealing with the Agreement's provisions on prisoner release, was serious because it sent a clear message to rejectionists that they have allies at Westminster. Fortunately, William Hague does not seem to share the ideological convictions of Bonar Law.

Finally, the Agreement's prospects will be strengthened if Irish nationalists appreciate the difficulties of Unionist moderates and refrain from maximalist goals. The issue of police reform, on which the two communities are polarized, will be particularly important here. While the police need to be radically reformed, and this has been accepted in the Agreement, Sinn Féin calls for the RUC to be 'disbanded' will only strengthen opposition to the Agreement among Unionists and weaken its prospects.

In summary, the supporters of the Agreement should be able to consolidate unionist support for it by continuing and strengthening the logic that produced the Agreement in the first place, that is, by strong and purposeful British–Irish cooperation combined with nationalist sensitivity to the unionist position.

CONCLUSION

Several commentators on Northern Ireland's conflict have made analogies with South Africa, usually to offer a particular explanation of the conflict, or a prescription for it, or to suggest how Northern Ireland's politicians might learn from the South African example. I have argued that the conclusions drawn from these analogies are often misleading, superficial, or inappropriate. The Northern Ireland conflict is a conflict between two national groups who identify with different states, whereas the South African conflict is a dispute among different ethnic and racial groups within a single state. Following from this, an agreement in Northern Ireland required institutions which went beyond the boundaries of a single state to include the United Kingdom and the Republic of Ireland. These are the type of institutions proposed by the British and Irish governments and accepted by those parties participating in Northern Ireland's negotiations in April 1998. As Northern Ireland is a deeply divided society, it also requires power-sharing institutions that are quite unlike the majoritarian institutions in place in South Africa. Whether majoritarian institutions are appropriate even for South Africa will become clear only over time.

Just as an understanding of Northern Ireland's position within a British–Irish context is important for understanding its conflict and the type of prescription it requires, it is also important for understanding why agreement came about. While whites were driven to negotiate in South Africa by a range of domestic and international pressures, it was largely British–Irish policy that induced Unionist flexibility, although demographic pressures and nationalist flexibility also played a role. Whereas negotiations in South Africa were initiated by the governing whites, negotiations began in Northern Ireland as an initiative of the British and Irish governments, with input from the leaders of the nationalist minority. Unionists were reluctant to take part in those negotiations and were induced into reaching agreement largely because their incentive structures were altered by British and Irish policy. If the Agreement is to be consolidated, and the institutions established by it are to thrive in the face of opposition from Unionist rejectionists, continuing British–Irish cooperation will be essential.

9

The Nature of the Agreement

Brendan O'Leary

INTRODUCTION

It is an academic, personal, and political honour to give the Ninth John Whyte Memorial Lecture. It is an academic honour because John Whyte was the most dispassionate of the interpreters of our conflict. In these respects and many others he is a hard act to follow. His major survey, *Interpreting Northern Ireland*,[1] posthumously published in 1990, conveys his marvellous gifts of clarity and concision in exposition. Commemorating John Whyte comes with a warning: be clear. It is a personal honour to give this lecture because John Whyte was one of my mentors as a young academic. He was very helpful, very generous, and robust in argument, as is his son, Nicholas.

This lecture is a belated act of homage to the Whyte family, not least because Jean Whyte is here to hear it. She, like Nicholas, is under no obligation to agree with my arguments, but I do want to make one unfalsifiable claim. I think that John Whyte would have agreed with the analysis that follows. Last, this is a political honour. John Whyte worried

Note: This chapter is in U.S. spelling, and is edited in accordance with the conventions of U.S. legal journals.

Text Accompanying the Ninth John Whyte Memorial Lecture, Nov. 26, 1998, Queen's University of Belfast. This essay draws on, but significantly modifies, a series of articles written with Dr Christopher McCrudden and Prof. John McGarry for the *Sunday Business Post* (Dublin), 19 and 26 April and 3, 10, and 17 May, 1998. It also draws on two other articles by the author, *The 1998-British Irish Agreement: Power Sharing Plus*, published by the Constitution Unit (School of Public Policy: UCL, London, 1998), and *The 1998 British-Irish Agreement: Consociation Plus*, Scottish Affairs, 26, 1–22 (1999). A United States Institute of Peace grant facilitated research. Thanks are especially owed to John McGarry and Chris McCrudden, and to Katharine Adeney, Pia Chaudhuri, Prof. John Coakley, Prof. Walker Connor, Prof. Conor Gearty, Prof. Robert Hazell, Prof. Donald Horowitz, Prof. David McCrone, Dr Tom Nairn, Dr Mads Qvortrup, members of the Constitutional Unit at UCL, and multiple Irish and British public officials, politicians, and journalists who are too numerous to be named here. The usual disclaimer applies.

[1] John Whyte, *Interpreting Northern Ireland* (1990).

whether social scientific research on Northern Ireland was worthwhile, but contributed extensively and successfully to public deliberation in defiance of his occasional despair on this matter. He would have been quietly pleased at the extent to which at least some social science, including political science, helped in the making of the Agreement.

The name of the Agreement

The Agreement Reached in the Multi-Party Negotiations[2] is a major achievement, both for its negotiators and for the peoples of Ireland and Britain. To make it, many politicians, officials, paramilitaries, and ordinary citizens had been through trials by ordeal. It emerged from a political desert whose only landmarks were failed initiatives. Yet, the Agreement that emerged from that desert has no agreed name. It carries no person's name, British or Irish, or American, and the names of no roles, be they Prime Ministers, *Taoisigh*, Secretaries of State, Foreign Ministers, or Party Leaders. Some know it by the place that it was made, as the Belfast Agreement, or, more controversially, as the Stormont Agreement. Yet, it was not signed by all of its supporters in the final negotiating chambers, and it was actually made in many places, including Dublin, London, and Washington; in smaller cities, towns, and villages; and in airports, airplanes, airwaves, by mobile-phone, and unofficial communications. Some just know it by its date: the 10 April, 1998 Agreement, or the Good Friday Agreement. The former seems too limited, while the latter gives too much credit to Christianity—both as a source of resolution and as a cause of conflict.

It is also known as the British–Irish Agreement, after the peoples who confirmed it in referendums in both parts of Ireland—though strictly speaking only the British in Ireland as well as the Irish in Ireland were asked to ratify it. I prefer to call it the British–Irish Agreement. This name reflects the importance of the fact that the Agreement is the fulfillment of a previous Agreement, known as the Anglo-Irish Agreement.[3] We Irish and British know that much resides in names, and so to avoid giving any further offense to anyone's sensibilities, I will refer to it simply as the Agreement.

---

[2] Agreement Reached in the Multi-Party Negotiations, Apr. 10, 1998 [hereinafter Agreement].
[3] Agreement Between the Government of the United Kingdom of Great Britain and Northern Ireland and the Government of the Republic of Ireland, Nov. 15, 1985, U.K.-Ir., Cmnd. 9657, *reprinted in* Tom Hadden and Kevin Boyle, The Anglo-Irish Agreement 15–48 (1989) [hereinafter Anglo-Irish Agreement].

The institutional nature of the Agreement

What kind of Agreement is it? What is its nature? It is not an example of 'the third way', as Charles Leadbetter recently argued at the feet of Tony Blair. It is much more interesting than a courtier's claims. The correct answer for a student of political science, as John Whyte would have recognized, is that it is a consociational agreement. In other words, it is a political arrangement that meets all four of the criteria laid down by that doyen of political science, the Dutchman Arend Lijphart: cross-community executive power-sharing, proportionality rules applied throughout the relevant governmental and public sectors, community self-government or autonomy and equality in cultural life, and veto rights for minorities.[4]

A consociation is an association of communities. In this case, the communities are British unionist, Irish nationalist, and others. A consociation can be created without any explicit consociational theory to guide it, and indeed that has often happened.[5] More often consociations are the outcomes of bargains or pacts between the political leaders of ethnic or religious groups. The Agreement is the product of tacit and explicit consociational thought,[6] and of bargaining, or of what is sometimes called pacting.

The Agreement, however, is not just consociational. It also departs from Lijphart's prescriptions in important respects that have practical implications for Northern Ireland and for regulating ethnic and national

[4] See, e.g., Arend Lijphart, Democracy in Plural Societies (1977).

[5] Lijphart claims that consociational rules were created by Dutch politicians in 1917, Lebanese politicians in 1943, Austrian politicians in 1945, Malaysian politicians in 1955, Colombian politicians in 1958, Indian politicians in the 1960s and 1970s, South African politicians in 1993–4, and by British politicians addressing Northern Ireland in 1972. One does not have to agree with the citation of any or all of these cases to accept Lijphart's point that politicians are more than capable of doing theory without the aid of theorists. See, e.g., Arend Lijphart, *Foreword: One Basic Problem, Many Theoretical Options—And a Practical Solution?, in* The Future of Northern Ireland at viii (John McGarry & Brendan O'Leary eds., 1990); James Currey, *Prospects for Power-Sharing in the New South Africa, in* Election '94 South Africa: The Campaigns, Results and Future Prospects 221–33 (Andrew Reynolds ed., 1994); Arend Lijphart, *The Puzzle of Indian Democracy: A Consociational Interpretation*, 2 Am. J. Pol. Sci. 258 (1996).

[6] One of the makers of the Agreement, Dr Mowlam, the United Kingdom Secretary of State for Northern Ireland since 1997, has an academic consociational heritage. She wrote about Swiss federal and consociational practices in her educational career, and at least one of her advisers has had an abiding interest in the subject. Consociational thinking not only formed part of the background thinking of the United Kingdom Labour Party. It had an impact on the drafting of the Framework Documents of 1995. The novel executive formation in the Agreement, based on the d'Hondt rule, reflects consociational coalition principles used elsewhere in Europe and in the European Parliament.

conflict elsewhere. It is a consociational agreement with important external dimensions. It is one made with national and not just ethnic or religious communities, and it is one endorsed by both leaders and the led.

To be formulaic, the Agreement establishes an internal consociation built within overarching confederal and federal institutions. It has imaginative elements of co-sovereignty, and it promises a novel model of double protection. It rests on a bargain derived from mutually conflicting hopes about its likely long-run outcome, but that may not destabilize it. One supplement must be added to this already lengthy formula, the fact that the Agreement is vulnerable both to post-Agreement bargaining and to legalism.

THE FOUR CONSOCIATIONAL ELEMENTS

Executive power sharing

At the heart of any consociational arrangement is executive power-sharing. The Agreement establishes two semi-presidential figures in a devolved Northern Assembly—a First Minister and a Deputy First Minister. Once elected, they have presidential characteristics because it is almost impossible to depose them until the next general election. Presidentialism means an executive that cannot be destroyed by an assembly except through impeachment.

Let me make this clear through a currently relevant illustration. Even if David Trimble's party colleagues were to vote unanimously to depose him from the leadership of the Ulster Unionist Party (UUP), he could not be forced to resign his position as First Minister. That could happen only if enough nationalists collude with enough Unionists to enforce it. To do that, however, nationalists in the Assembly would have to bring down their own Deputy First Minister. This is a fact because the First Minister and the Deputy First Minister are elected together by the parallel consent cross-community consent procedure (see Appendix 9A.1). This procedure requires them to have the support of 50 per cent of registered nationalists and unionists as well as a majority of the Assembly. Critically, this rule gives very strong incentives to unionists and nationalists to nominate a candidate for one of these positions that is acceptable to at least a majority of the other bloc's members in the Assembly. So even if in the future Gerry Adams leads Sinn Féin into surpassing the SDLP in seats won in the Assembly, unionists will be able to block his nomination as Deputy First Minister. Likewise, nationalists can veto an unacceptable hardline unionist.

In the first elections for these posts, pro-Agreement unionists in the UUP and the Progressive Unionist Party voted solidly for the combination of David Trimble of the UUP and Seamus Mallon of the SDLP. Naturally, so did the SDLP. Sinn Féin deliberately abstained to avoid the First and Deputy First Ministers being chosen by more nationalists than by unionists—an outcome that might have endangered Trimble's status with the unionist public, and a sign of Sinn Féin's maturing avoidance of provocation.

The rules practically ensure that a Unionist and a nationalist share the top two posts. The Agreement makes it clear that both posts have identical symbolic and external representation functions. Indeed, both posts have identical powers, and their only real difference is in their titles. Both, for example, will preside over the Executive Committee of Ministers and have a role in coordinating its work. The Agreement does not make it clear whether the two will have any of the existing departmental responsibilities in Northern Ireland, though it might make sense for them to run jointly and be served by the existing Finance and Personnel Ministry.[7]

With one notable exception that I will discuss in a moment, David Trimble and Seamus Mallon have successfully and carefully coordinated their statements and actions since their joint election, especially in the management of the Drumcree crisis in the first two weeks of July 1998. They are showing how this new diarchy will critically depend upon the personal cooperation of the two holders of these posts. The Northern Ireland Act of 1998, which has just gone through Westminster's last procedures, has reinforced their interdependence by requiring that 'if either the First Minister or the Deputy First Minister ceases to hold office, whether by resignation or otherwise, the other shall also cease to hold office'.[8] The one major exception to the pattern of dyarchic cooperation has arisen over the implementation of the rules for executive formation. Indeed, as I speak, we have a crisis of executive formation.

Unlike some Presidents and most Prime Ministers, neither the First Minister nor the Deputy First Minister formally appoint the other Ministers to the Executive Committee. Instead, under the plain meaning of the Agreement, these posts should be allocated to parties in proportion to their strength in the Assembly, according to a mechanical rule called the d'Hondt rule (see Appendix 9A.2). The rules are simple in their

---

[7] The Northern Ireland Act makes it plain that the top two Ministers can hold functional portfolios. Northern Ireland Act, 1998, ch. 47, § 16 (Eng.).   [8] Id. § 16(7).

consequences. Any party that wins any significant share of seats and is willing to abide by the Agreement has a reasonable chance of access to the executive. This appears a subtle form of what Lijphart calls grand coalition government, though it is a coalition government without a coalition agreement and no-one is obliged to join it.

This is how it should work in law. The d'Hondt rule means that parties get the right to nominate Ministers according to their respective strength in seats, and there is no vote of confidence required by the Assembly. It also means that parties get to choose, in order of their strength, their preferred ministries. An individual minister can be deposed from office by cross-community rules (see Appendix 9A.1), but the party that held the relevant ministry will be able to appoint his or her successor from amongst its ranks. Parties, of course, have the right to refuse a ministry to which they are entitled and may voluntarily exclude themselves from their automatic right to a share in executive power.

The current crisis of executive formation has arisen for political and constitutional reasons. Politically, it has arisen because David Trimble has insisted that Sinn Féin must deliver some IRA decommissioning before its members can take seats in the Executive Committee. Under the Agreement, he has no constitutional warrant to exercise this veto. The Agreement does not require prior decommissioning on the part of any paramilitaries or of any parties connected to them, though it does require the completion of decommissioning by 22 May 2000. Trimble has been given the opportunity to exercise this unconstitutional veto, which has led to a breach in the formal requirements of the Agreement, because the SDLP did not make immediate executive formation a condition of its support for the Mallon–Trimble ticket for Deputy First Minister and First Minister. The SDLP failed to do so because it wished to shore up Trimble's political position. The price has so far been rather high, and it has yet to be repaid.

One flexible provision in the Agreement has given Trimble room for this manoeuvre. The Agreement states that there must be at least six other Ministers, but that there can be up to ten. The number of ministries are to be decided by cross-community consent, presumably after the First and Deputy First Ministers agree on a proposal. That has given Trimble the opportunity to delay on executive formation. The more Ministries there are in the Executive Committee then the more proportional the representation of parties on the Executive. The UUP has been holding out for a seven seat Executive, under which Unionists would have an overall majority. The SDLP is holding out for a larger Executive (see Appendix 9A.2).

Imagine for the moment that the crisis of executive formation is eventually resolved. How will the Executive Committee work? Individual ministers will enjoy executive powers under existing UK legislation and can operate without collective responsibility, except where the Executive Committee and the Assembly have agreed on a broad programme and where they are obliged to engage in cross-departmental activities. No method of reaching agreement within the Executive Committee is specified, though the program must enjoy cross-community support in the Assembly. In practice, agreements within the Executive minimally will require majority support, including the agreement of the First and Deputy First Ministers.

In short, the consociational criterion of cross-community executive power sharing is clearly met in the Agreement. There are, though, special features of the new arrangements that differ from previous consociational experiments in Northern Ireland and elsewhere. Ministers will take a Pledge of Office, not an Oath of Allegiance. This bi-nationalism is at the heart of the Agreement. Nationalist ministers do not have to swear an Oath of Allegiance to the Crown or the Union. The Pledge requires Ministers to discharge their duties in good faith, to follow exclusively peaceful and democratic politics, to participate in preparing a programme of government, and to support and to follow the decisions of the Executive Committee and the Assembly.

The duties of office include a requirement to serve all the people equally, to promote equality, and to prevent discrimination. This means, according to the doctrine of ministerial responsibility, that civil servants will be bound to run their departments consistently, with these obligations. The duties of office also include a requirement that the relevant Ministers serve in the North-South Ministerial Council. This duty, in conjunction with other clauses, will prevent parties opposed to this aspect of the Agreement from taking Ministerial office in good faith.

How should we appraise the executive design that is at the heart of the Agreement? The special skill of the designers is that they have created strong incentives for executive power sharing and power division but without requiring parties to have a formal coalition agreement. In these respects, the Agreement differs from the Sunningdale experiment of 1973. What some makers of the Agreement did not foresee, though, was that failure to timetable the formation of the rest of the executive immediately after the election of the First and Deputy First Ministers could precipitate a protracted crisis of executive formation.

Amendments to the Northern Ireland Act of 1998 could be adopted by the UK parliament or the Northern Ireland Assembly. Such an adoption would be consistent with the Agreement as it would prevent any recurrence of this type of crisis. In the future, candidates for First Minister and Deputy First Minister could be obliged to state the number of executive portfolios that will be available in the Executive Committee, and the formation of that Committee should be required within a week. Otherwise, the election of the First Minister and Deputy First Minister should be rendered null and void. That would plug this particular constitutional hole. It may, however, be unnecessary. It is not likely that any future candidates for First Minister or Deputy First Minister will agree to be nominated without a firm agreement from their opposite number on the number of portfolios and the date of cabinet formation.

Proportionality

Consociational arrangements are built on principles of proportionality. The Agreement meets this test in three clear ways, on the executive in the manner that I have discussed (see also Appendix 9A.1), in the elections to the Assembly, and in public sector positions. All future elections to the 108-member Assembly will use a proportional representation system, the single transferable vote (STV) in six-member constituencies. The Assembly, though, may choose by cross-community consent procedures to advocate change from this system later. The Droop quota in each constituency is, therefore, 14.3 per cent of the vote, which squeezes the very small parties or alternatively encourages them to form electoral alliances.[9]

Thus, the smaller of the two loyalist parties, the Ulster Democratic Party (UDP) led by Gary McMichael, won no seats in the first Assembly election. Conceivably, the rival loyalist parties, the PUP and the UDP, may see the need to coalesce in the future to achieve better representation. Very small parties that can gather lower order preferences from across the unionist and nationalist blocs, such as the Women's Coalition, have shown that the system need not preclude representation for small parties among the 'Others'.

This system of voting is not what Lijphart recommends for consociational systems. Lijphart is instead an advocate of party list PR systems because he believes that they help make party leaders more powerful and better able to sustain inter-ethnic consociational deals. Those who would like to see David Trimble in greater control of his party might covet this form of proportional representation. If, however, a region-wide list

---

[9] The Droop quota used in single transferable vote ('STV') is (Total Vote/$N+1$)+1, where N = number of Assembly members to be elected.

Table 9.1 The shares of blocs in the 1998 Assembly

Bloc	Seats won	First preference vote (%)	Seats won (%)
Nationalists	42	39.8	38.8
'Yes' Unionists	30	25.0	27.7
'No' Unionists	28	21.3	25.9
Others	8	9.4	7.4
Total(s)	108	100[a]	100[a]

[a] Percentages do not add up to 100 because of rounding.

system had been in operation in June of 1998, then the UUP would have ended up with fewer seats, as well as less seats than the SDLP. The STV system, moreover, has the merit of encouraging 'vote-pooling'.[10] In principle, voters can use their transfers to reward pro-Agreement candidates at the expense of anti-Agreement candidates.[11] Some of the SDLP's and Sinn Féin's voters, have found it advantageous to reward David Trimble's Ulster Unionist Party for making the Agreement by giving its candidates their lower-order preferences. In this way, they helped some of the Ulster Unionist Party's candidates pip the candidates of the DUP and UKUP.[12]

Tables 9.1 and 9.2 illustrate the outcome of the June 1998 elections to the first Assembly under the Agreement. The proportionality of the results is evident, both with respect to blocs and with respect to parties. The deviations in seats won compared to the first preference vote benefited primarily the pro-Agreement parties. Candidates of such parties gathered support through the transfers of lower order preferences.

The UUP was the principal beneficiary of the transfer of lower order preferences, taking its seat share (25.9 per cent) significantly above its first-preference vote share (21.3 per cent). These lower order preferences, however, came from voters who voted both for and against the Agreement. The Northern Ireland Women's Coalition was the most

[10] Donald Horowitz, *Ethnic Groups in Conflict*, 628 (1985).

[11] This option is also open to anti-Agreement voters, but DUP and UKUP voters are unlikely to give their lower order preferences to Republican Sinn Féin should that party ever choose to stand for elections.

[12] The STV system has arguably helped encourage Sinn Féin on its current path. In the past, it won over few supporters from other parties. Since the early 1990s, that is no longer true because SDLP voters have been rewarding Sinn Féin for its increased moderation. STV also has the great merit of having been used in Northern Ireland for local government elections since 1973, and European Parliamentary elections since 1979, so voters do not need to learn a new system.

Table 9.2 Party performances in the 1998 Assembly election

Party	Seats won	First preference vote (%)	Seats won (%)
SDLP	24	22.0	22.2
Sinn Féin	18	17.7	16.6
Other nationalists	—	0.1	—
UUP	28	21.0	25.9
PUP	2	2.5	1.8
UDP	—	1.2	—
Other 'Yes' Unionists	—	0.3	—
DUP	20	18.0	18.5
UKUP	5	4.5	4.6
Other 'No' Unionists	3	3.0	2.8
Alliance	6	6.4	5.5
Women's coalition	2	1.7	1.8
Others	—	1.3	—

Percentages do not add up to 100 because of rounding.

widespread beneficiary of lower-order preferences, winning two seats despite a very low first-preference vote share. The transfers by voters to the pro-Agreement candidates, though not as significant as had been hoped, performed one very important task. They converted a bare anti-Agreement majority of the first preference vote (25.5 per cent) within the unionist bloc of voters into a bare pro-Agreement majority (27.7 per cent) amongst seats won by unionists, a result that was essential for the stabilization of the Agreement.

Proportionality rules, combined with accommodative incentives, do not stop with the executive, the committee system in the Assembly, or the electoral system. The Agreement is consistent with past and future measures to promote fair employment and affirmative action in the public sector that will, one hopes, eventually ensure a proportional and non-discriminatory civil service and judiciary.

The Agreement also envisages a representative police force. It is the task of the Independent Commission on policing, headed by former Hong Kong Governor Christopher Patten, to ensure the creation of a police service that is representative of Northern Ireland. The RUC's mononational culture, and indeed its monopoly on policing services, must end if the Agreement is to be fully consistent with a consociational model.

Democratic consociation cannot exist where those of military age in one community are almost the sole recruitment pool to police all of those in another community. A fully representative and preferably two-tier model of federal and democratic policing is the best way to ensure that proportional policing supplements the other political institutions of the Agreement.[13]

Communal autonomy and equality

Consociational settlements avoid the compulsory integration of peoples. Instead, they seek to manage differences equally and justly. To be liberal, such settlements must also protect those who wish to have their identities counted differently as well as those who do not want to be identified by collective identities.

The Agreement leaves in place the new arrangements for schooling in Northern Ireland in which Catholic, Protestant, and integrated schools are to be equally funded. In this respect, Northern Ireland is fully consociational and liberal. Only the very small minorities of non-Christian religious believers (less than one per cent of the population) lack full and equal funding, and it would be generous and just to make such provisions for them where numbers permit. The Agreement also makes new provisions for the educational use, protection, and public use of the Irish language, along the lines used for Welsh in the United Kingdom. It, therefore, adds linguistic protections to educational protections of Irish nationalist culture.

Most importantly, the Agreement completes the equalization of both major communities as national communities. Specifically, the Agreement refers to British and Irish communities and not just, as is so misleadingly said, to Protestants and Catholics. The European Convention for the Protection of Human Rights and Fundamental Freedoms (European Convention on Human Rights), which is weak on the protection of collective rights and equality rights, will be supplemented by measures that will give Northern Ireland its own tailor-made Bill of Rights, to protect both national groupings as well as individuals. The worst illusion of parties to the conflict and some of its successive managers, based in London, Belfast, or Dublin, was the belief that Northern Ireland could be stable and democratic while being either British or Irish. The Agreement makes Northern Ireland bi-national and opens up the prospect of a fascinating jurisprudence, not least in the regulation of parades and marches.

---

[13] See John McGarry and Brendan O'Leary, Policing Northern Ireland: Proposals for a New Start (1999).

The Agreement does not neglect the non-national dimensions of local politics, nor does it exclude the 'Others' from what I have heard described in Alliance party circles as a squalid communal deal. All aspects of unjustified social equalities, as well as inequalities between the national communities, are recognized in the text of the Agreement, and given some means of institutional redress and monitoring. The Agreement addresses national equality, the allegiances to the Irish and British nations, and social equality. In other words, it addresses other dimensions that differentiate groups and individuals in Northern Ireland, such as religion, race, ethnic affiliation, sex, and sexuality.

Equality issues, be they national or social, are not left exclusively to the local parties to manage and to negotiate, which might be a recipe for stalemate. Instead, the UK government has signalled its intention to create a new statutory obligation on public authorities. They will be required to carry out all their functions with due regard to the need to promote equality of opportunity in relation to people's religious background and political opinions. They will be required also to promote equality with respect to people's gender, race, disabilities, age, marital status, and sexual orientation. This commitment entails what Dr Christopher McCrudden labels mainstreaming equality. The UK government is also likely to establish a Human Rights Commission tasked with an extended and enhanced role, including monitoring, promoting litigation, and drafting a tailor-made Bill of Rights for Northern Ireland.

Minority veto rights

The final dimension of a consociational settlement is the protection of minorities through giving them veto rights. The Agreement fulfills this criterion in the Assembly, in the courts, and through enabling political appeals to both the UK and Irish governments.

The Assembly has cross-community procedures, including parallel consent, weighted majority, and petition procedures (see Appendix 9A.1) that protect nationalists from Unionist dominance. Indeed, they do so in such a comprehensive manner that before the election of the First and Deputy First Ministers, there were fears that the rules designed to protect the nationalist minority might be used by hardline Unionist opponents of the Agreement to disable its initiation and to destroy its development.

This possibility remains alive, but is somewhat diminished because the weighted majority rule requires a lower level of Unionist consent than was required for the election of the First and Deputy First Ministers. The 'Others' are less protected in the Assembly. They can, for instance, be outvoted by a simple majority and any nationalist–Unionist super-majority. In addition, their numbers leave them well short of being able to trigger a petition on their own. The 'Others', however, have not been at the heart of the conflict. It is therefore not surprising if they are not at the heart of the resulting pacts, though it is not accurate to claim that they are excluded from the Agreement.

In the courts, the 'Others', disaffected nationalists, and Unionists will have means to redress breaches of their human and collective rights. The content of the European Convention on Human Rights is well-known. What is less clear is what package of collective rights the new independent Northern Ireland Rights Commission will recommend. What has also not been addressed directly and immediately is the composition of the local judiciary. The Agreement provides for a review of the criminal justice system that will include 'arrangements for making appointments to the judiciary'.[14] It will, however, be of great importance that the judiciary reflects the different communities in the North and is committed to the human and minority rights provisions that it will increasingly interpret.

Other non-national minorities have not been forgotten. In the Civil Society Forum to be created in the North with a Southern counterpart, and through the Intergovernmental Conference of the British and Irish governments, mechanisms have been established to ensure that the 'Others' will be able to express their voices and to ensure that the new rights culture does not exclude them. It would be helpful if progress in establishing these forums were expedited.

CONFEDERAL AND FEDERAL ELEMENTS OF THE AGREEMENT

The Agreement is not only internally consociational, but it is also confederalizing and federalizing. This meshing of internal and external institutions highlights it as novel in comparative politics. Let me make it plain why I regard the Agreement as both confederalizing and federalizing, though my emphasis is on the former.

Confederations exist when sovereign jurisdictions voluntarily delegate powers and functions to bodies that can exercise power across all jurisdictions. I believe that the Agreement creates two new confederal relationships. I also believe that the Agreement has subtle federalist dimensions if we agree that a 'federacy' exists when there are at least two separate tiers of government over the same territory and when neither tier can unilaterally alter the constitutional capacities of the other.

---

[14] Agreement, *supra* note 2, Policing and Justice, Annex B: Review of the Criminal Justice System, Terms of Reference.

The all-Ireland confederal relationship

The Agreement creates a new confederal relationship that is all-Ireland in nature—the North-South Ministerial Council. When established, it will bring together those with executive responsibilities in Northern Ireland and in the Republic. It will be established after the Assembly has come into being and completed a programme of work to establish the Council. The specific deadline for that body of work to be agreed on passed on 31 October 1998. That date passed without an agreement because no executive has been formed in Northern Ireland to engage with its counterpart in the Republic.

Consequently, the signatories to the Agreement are now in breach of their treaty obligations. This breach opens the entire Agreement to constitutional challenge in the Republic, enabling, *in extremis*, any aggrieved citizen to argue for the retention of the old Articles 2 and 3 of the Irish Constitution on the grounds that the United Kingdom is in breach of its treaty obligations.

What is intended by the Agreement is clear. Nationalists were concerned that if the Assembly could outlast the North-South Council, it would provide incentives for Unionists to undermine the latter. Unionists, by contrast, worried that if the Council could survive the destruction of the Assembly, nationalists would seek to bring this about. The Agreement is a tightly written contract with penalty clauses. Internal consociation and external confederalism go together; the Assembly and the Council are mutually interdependent, meaning that one cannot function without the other. Unionists cannot destroy the Council while retaining the Assembly, and nationalists cannot destroy the Assembly while keeping the Council.[15] If the Assembly does not create the Council, then it will effectively destroy itself, enabling, *in extremis*, any aggrieved citizen in Northern Ireland to argue for the suspension of the Northern Assembly until the North-South Ministerial Council is established.

The North-South Ministerial Council is the means by which nationalists hope to persuade Unionists of the attractions of Irish unification.

---

[15] The Agreement does not mention what happens if both institutions, and thus the Agreement itself, collapse. This author's opinion is that Northern Ireland would be governed, as at present, by the British government with input from Dublin through the British–Irish Intergovernmental Conference. The two governments would likely pursue the promotion of equality of esteem, reductions in the employment gap between Catholics and Protestants, and the reform of policing. Eventually, there would be a shift towards direct co-sovereignty over the region. If the Agreement's core institutions are not established, then any legal challenge to the implementation of changes to Articles 2 and 3 of the Republic's Constitution is likely to be successful. Unionists opposed to the Agreement would do well to bear these considerations in mind.

In addition, it will satisfactorily link northern nationalists to their pre-ferred nation state. Consistent with the Agreement, the Irish government has agreed to change its Constitution to ensure that the North/South Ministerial Council will be able to exercise island-wide jurisdiction in those functional activities where Unionists are willing to cooperate.

The North-South Ministerial Council will function much like the Council of Ministers in the European Union, with ministers having considerable discretion to reach decisions but remaining ultimately accountable to their respective legislatures. The Council will meet in plenary format twice a year, and in smaller groups to discuss specific sectors (say, agriculture or education) on a regular and frequent basis.

Provision is also made for the Council to meet to discuss matters that cut across sectors and to resolve disagreements. In addition, the Agree-ment provides for cross-border or all-island implementation bodies, meaning the same as executive. These bodies are to be responsible for implementing decisions taken in at least six as yet unspecified areas. These areas were to be agreed on during a transitional period between the Assembly elections and October 31 1998, but are currently under discussion. The Agreement provides an Annex that lists twelve possible areas for implementation.

The North-South Ministerial Council differs from the Council of Ireland of 1974, and not just in name. There is no provision for a North-South joint parliamentary forum, as there was in the Sunningdale Agreement of 1973. The Northern Assembly and the Irish *Oireachtas*,[16] however, are asked to consider developing such a forum. Nationalists wanted the North/South Ministerial Council to be established by legis-lation from Westminster and the *Oireachtas* in order to emphasize its autonomy from the Northern Assembly. Unionists preferred that the Council be established by the Northern Ireland Assembly and its counterpart in Dublin. The document produced on April 10 1998 split the differences between the two positions.

The North-South Council and the implementation bodies are to be brought into existence by British–Irish legislation. During the transitional period now extended beyond October 31 1998, it is for the Northern Ireland executive and the Republic's government to agree how cooperation should take place and in what areas the North/South institutions should coop-erate. Once this body of work is agreed on, the Northern Ireland Assembly will be unable to change it unless both communities there consent.

[16] This is the collective name in Gaelic for the two chambers of the Irish parliament, *Dáil Éireann* and *Seanad Éireann*.

The question of what scope and powers these North-South institutions will have remains to be decided. Some of this was supposed to have been already decided by October 31 1998. The Agreement does, however, require a meaningful Council. It states that the Council will, rather than may, identify at least six matters where existing bodies will be the appropriate mechanisms for cooperation within each separate jurisdiction. The Agreement also identifies at least six matters where cooperation will take place through cross-border or all-island implementation bodies. The Agreement also links Ireland, North and South, to another confederation, the European Union. It requires the Council to consider the implementation of EU policies and programmes as well as proposals under way at the European Union and makes provisions for the Council's views to be taken into account at relevant EU meetings.

The signatories to the Agreement have promised to work in good faith to create the North-South Ministerial Council. There has not been sufficient good faith to prevent the first material break in the timetable scheduled in the Agreement. The signatories are required to use best endeavours to reach agreement and to make determined efforts to overcome disagreements in functions where there is a mutual cross-border and all-island benefit.

The crisis over executive formation may have prolonged consequences. The Agreement explicitly envisaged a timetable that would have enabled an interim Northern executive to establish itself and enabled it to make binding agreements with the Republic's ministers. Once North-South cooperation was agreed, any future unionist majority in the Assembly would not be able formally to block it, since any scaling back of the Council's powers would require the consent of both nationalists and Unionists.[17] Nationalists are beginning to fear that the crisis of executive formation will throw the entire content of North-South cooperation open to the veto of both 'No' unionists and soft-'Yes' unionists in the Assembly, which is due to have a full life in February.

But again, let us imagine that this crisis is eventually overcome. If that happens, then several current facts will support the new constitutional

[17] The possibility of a Unionist Minister refusing to serve on the Council will appear to some as very grave, given that Unionist parties that oppose the Agreement, especially the DUP, are in principle eligible for ministerial portfolios. This, however, is ruled out in practice. Participation in the North-South Ministerial Council has been made an essential responsibility attaching to relevant posts in the two administrations. Relevant posts are, presumably, any portfolio a part of which is subject to North-South cooperation. This leaves open the possibility that a politician opposed to the North-South Ministerial Council might take a seat on it with a view to wrecking it. Ministers, though, are required to establish the North-South institutions in good faith and to use best endeavours to reach agreement.

confederalism. As the Republic's Celtic Tiger continues to expand, Northern Ireland's Ministers and citizens should see increasing benefits from North-South cooperation. In addition, as the European Union continues to integrate, there will be pressure for both parts of Ireland to cooperate. This pressure comes from their shared peripheral geographical position, similar interests in functional activities such as agriculture and tourism, and in having regions defined in ways that attract funds.[18]

The British–Irish confederal relationship

There is a second, weaker confederal relationship established by the Agreement that affects all the islands of Britain and Ireland. Under the new British–Irish Council the two sovereign governments, all the devolved governments of the United Kingdom, and all the neighbouring insular dependent territories of the United Kingdom can meet and agree to delegate functions. They may also agree on common policies. This proposal meets Unionists' concerns for reciprocity in linkages and provides a mechanism through which they may in the future be linked to the United Kingdom even though Northern Ireland has become part of the Republic of Ireland.

Unionists originally wanted any North-South Ministerial Council to be subordinate to a British–Irish, or East–West, Council. This has not happened. There is no hierarchical relationship between the two Councils. Indeed, there are two textual warrants for the thesis that the North/South Ministerial Council is more important and far-reaching than its British–Irish counterpart. The Agreement requires the establishment of North-South implementation bodies, while leaving the formation of East–West bodies a voluntary matter. While the Agreement states explicitly that the Assembly and the North-South Ministerial Council cannot survive without each other, it makes no equivalent statement concerning the British–Irish Council.

The development of this confederal relationship may be stunted by an Irish Governmental reluctance to engage in a forum where it may be

Because these requirements are presumably subject to judicial review, it is unlikely that potential wreckers, like Ian Paisley or Peter Robinson, would be able to take part in the North-South Ministerial Council in a destructive manner, even if they wanted to. One of the requirements for membership of the Executive is that ministers must 'support ... all decisions of the Executive Committee,' and they can be removed if they do not show such support. Removal, though, presupposes decisions being made by the Executive Committee. Whether these provisions will be justiciable remains to be seen.

[18] Northern Ireland could, in principle, even go into Economic and Monetary Union ('EMU') with the Republic if Britain itself remained outside, providing there was agreement in the Assembly and the Secretary of State and the Westminster parliament assented.

outnumbered by at least seven other governments, including the governments of Westminster, Scotland, Wales, Northern Ireland, Jersey, Guernsey, and the Isle of Man. The development of these relationships may be stunted though rules may develop to ensure the joint dominance of the sovereign governments. The British–Irish Council, however, may flourish as a policy formulation forum if the devolved governments of the United Kingdom choose to exploit it as an opportunity for intergovernmental bargaining within the United Kingdom, or to build alliances with the Irish government on European public policy, in which case it will give added impetus to other federalist processes.

A United Kingdom–Northern Irish federalizing process

The Agreement is the penultimate blow to unitary Unionism in the United Kingdom, a political persuasion already dented by the 1997–8 referendums and legislative acts establishing a Scottish Parliament and Welsh Assembly.[19] Does the Agreement simply fall within the rubric of devolution within a decentralized unitary state? Arguably not. Two Unions make up the United Kingdom—the Union of Great Britain and the Union of Great Britain and Northern Ireland. The constitutional basis of the latter Union is now distinctly different than the former.

The Agreement is a treaty between two states and it is based on Irish national self-determination as well as British constitutional convention. The United Kingdom officially acknowledges in the Agreement that Northern Ireland has the right to secede into the Republic on the basis of a local referendum. The United Kingdom also recognizes in a treaty the authority of Irish national self-determination throughout the island of Ireland.

Moreover, the Agreement's institutions are being created by the will of the people of Ireland, North and South, and not just by the people of Northern Ireland, considering the interdependence of the North/ South Ministerial Council and the Assembly. Consequently, the United Kingdom's relationship to Northern Ireland regarding international law is explicitly federal because the Westminster parliament and executive, except through breaking its treaty obligations and denying Irish national self-determination, cannot exercise power in any manner in Northern Ireland that is inconsistent with the Agreement.

This federalizing process will be enhanced if the United Kingdom and Northern Irish courts treat Northern Ireland's relationship to

---

[19] The formation of an English Parliament would be the last blow.

Westminster as akin to those of the former Dominions, which had a federal character, as they did in the period of the Stormont Parliament (1921–72). Moreover, the nature of devolution in Northern Ireland is not closed by the United Kingdom's Northern Ireland Act of 1998. The Act has created an open-ended mechanism for Northern Ireland to expand its autonomy from the rest of the United Kingdom, albeit with the consent of the Secretary of State and the approval of Westminster. No such open-ended provision has been granted to the Scottish Parliament or the Welsh Assembly. In short, Northern Ireland can gain maximum autonomy while remaining within the Union provided that there is agreement within the Northern Assembly. Legalist Diceyians may insist that Westminster's sovereignty in Northern Ireland remains ultimately intact. If, however, the Agreement beds down the political development of a federal relationship between the United Kingdom and Northern Ireland, then it is assured for the near future whatever might be said in the dry recesses of the Constitution's ancient regime.

Irish federalizing processes

The Agreement opens federalist avenues in the Republic of Ireland, hitherto one of the most centralized states in Europe. The North-South Ministerial Council is seen by nationalists, North and South, as the embryonic institution of a federal Ireland. Nationalists consider that a confederation must be built first, and then, after trust has been established, a federation should be created. This stepping stone theory is articulated most emphatically by 'No' Unionists. These 'No' Unionists are not wrong in their calculation that many nationalists see the North/South Ministerial Council as transitional. Sinn Féin says so, and so does Fianna Fáil.

The Irish government and its people did not abandon Irish unification when they endorsed the Agreement. Indeed, it has become, in the words of the new provisional Article 3 of the Irish Constitution:

the firm will of the Irish nation, in harmony and friendship, to unite all the people who share the territory of the island of Ireland, in all the diversity of their identities and traditions, recognising that a united Ireland shall be brought about only by peaceful means with the consent of a majority of the people expressed, in both jurisdictions in the island.[20]

The amended Irish Constitution, therefore, officially recognizes two jurisdictions that jointly enjoy the right to participate in the Irish nation's exercise of self-determination. Unification is no longer linked to unitarism and is entirely compatible with either full confederation or federation.

[20] Ir. Const. art. 3 (1937), as proposed for amendment.

Irish unification cannot be precluded because of present demographic and electoral trends, which have led to a steady rise in the nationalist share of the vote across different electoral systems.[21] The nature of any eventual unification envisaged in the redrafted Irish Constitution is now very different. It no longer provides for anything resembling a programme of assimilation. Respect for the diversity of identities and traditions connects with both consociational and con/federal logic. The Republic is bound by the Agreement to structure its laws and its protection of rights in order to prepare for the possibility of a con/federal as well as a unitary Ireland.

The Agreement recognizes Northern Ireland as a legal entity within the Irish Constitution.[22] Its ultimate demise in status as a political unit is no longer a programmatic feature of *Bunreacht na Eireann*. The Agreement also envisages the subjection of both jurisdictions in Ireland to the same regime for the protection of individual and group rights, a situation entirely compatible with a subsequent formal confederation or federation.

It is, perhaps, worth speculating on what might happen if a majority emerged for Irish unification within Northern Ireland. If nationalists acquired local majority support within Northern Ireland, it would not necessarily be in their considered interests to promote the region's immediate administrative and legal assimilation into the Republic. Nationalists would then have an interest in preserving Northern Ireland as a political entity within a federated Ireland. They would after all be a local majority, as would the governing coalition in the Republic whose calculations might be disturbed by the entry of Northern participants. Conversely, some Unionists faced with this prospect might prefer a unitary Ireland as the lesser evil, calculating that their chances of being key players in government formation in a bigger arena might protect them better than being a minority in Northern Ireland.

Meanwhile we all know that the con/federal dimensions of the Agreement are not merely pan-Irish or pan-British. They will evolve within a European Union which has its own strong confederal relationships, as well as many ambitious federalists. There will be no obvious organizational contradictions that will arise from this extra layer of con/federalizing, and they might help to transfer some of the heat from binary considerations of whether a given issue is controlled by London or Dublin.

---

[21] See John McGarry and Brendan O'Leary, Explaining Northern Ireland: Broken Images ch. 10 (1995); *see also* Brendan O'Leary and Geoffrey Evans, *Northern Ireland: La Fin de Siècle, the Twilight of the Second Protestant Ascendancy and Sinn Féin's Second Coming, in* Parliamentary Affairs 672–80 (1997).   [22] Ir. Const.

DOUBLE PROTECTION AND CO-SOVEREIGNTY

The subtlest part of the Agreement, its tacit double protection model, goes well beyond standard consociational thinking and is laced with elements of co-sovereignty. The Agreement is designed to withstand major demographic and electoral change. It promises to entrench the identical protection of rights, collective and individual, on both sides of the present border. In effect, it promises protection to Northern nationalists now on the same terms that will be given to Ulster Unionists should they ever become a minority in a unified Ireland. Communities are to be protected whether they are majorities or minorities, and whether sovereignty lies with the United Kingdom or the Republic, hence the expression double protection.

The two states not only promise reciprocity for the local protection of present and future minorities, but also have created two intergovernmental devices to protect those communities. One such a device is the successor to the Anglo-Irish Agreement, the intergovernmental conference that guarantees the Republic's government access to policy formulation on all matters not yet devolved to the Northern Assembly or the North/South Ministerial Council. The other device is the British–Irish Council. If Irish unification ever occurs, then the Republic's government would find it politically impossible not to offer the British government reciprocal access in the same forums.

It is important to note what has not happened between the two sovereign governments. Formal co-sovereignty has not been established. Unionists claim that they have removed the 1985 Anglo-Irish Agreement in return for conceding a North/South Ministerial Council. This claim is, at best, exaggerated. Under the new Agreement, the Irish government will retain a say in those Northern Irish matters that have not been devolved to the Northern Assembly, as was the case under Article 4 of the Anglo-Irish Agreement.[23] As with that agreement, there will continue to be an intergovernmental conference, chaired by the Minister for Foreign Affairs and the Northern Ireland Secretary of State, to deal with non-devolved matters. This conference will continue to be serviced by a standing secretariat.

The new Agreement, moreover, promises to intensify cooperation between the two governments on all-island or cross-border aspects of rights, justice, prison, and policing, unless and until these matters are

---

[23] Anglo-Irish Agreement, *supra* note 3, art 4.

devolved to the Northern executive. There are provisions for representatives of the Northern Assembly to be involved in the intergovernmental conference, which would signify a welcome proclivity for democratization. The Anglo-Irish Agreement fully anticipated these arrangements.[24] Therefore, it is more accurate to claim that the Anglo-Irish Agreement has been fulfilled than it is to say that it has been removed.

THE MILITARY AND POLITICAL NATURE OF THE AGREEMENT

The institutional nature of the Agreement is complex, but it accurately matches the conceptual categories that I have deployed. There is no need to use new terms for what has already been agreed on, except, perhaps, for what I have called the double protection model. The Agreement is wide-ranging, multilateral, and has something in it for everyone who signed it. Its institutions address the totality of relationships between nationalists and unionists in Northern Ireland, between Northern Ireland and the Republic, and between Ireland and Britain. It is neither a victory for nationalists nor for unionists. Both can maintain their central aspirations, their core identities, and protect or express better their interests. While describing constitutional architecture is one thing, informal political reality is often very different.

The Agreement may be an immensely subtle institutional construction, but everyone asks, 'Is it a pack of cards, vulnerable to the slightest pressures?' 'Is it vulnerable to the play of either Orange or Green cards by hardline loyalists or republicans, or to miscalculations by softer-line politicians?' 'Will its successful implementation prove more difficult than its formulation?'

These are hardly foolish concerns, as revealed by the fracas at Drumcree on 4 July, the massacre at Omagh in August, and the continuing crisis over executive formation and decommissioning. There are, however, reasons to be cheerful about the robustness of these institutions if we analyse the military and political nature of the settlement. There are also reasons to be cautious.

The Agreement on ending the armed conflict

The Agreement is a political settlement that promises a path to unwind armed conflict and to create a peace settlement. Formally speaking, however,

---

[24] See Brendan O'Leary and John McGarry, The Politics of Antagonism: Understanding Northern Ireland, chs. 6–7 (2nd ed. 1996).

no military or paramilitary organizations negotiated the Agreement. The Agreement encompasses decommissioning, demilitarization, police reform, and prisoner release. It addresses these issues in this textual order, and it is plain that though all these issues are interlinked, they are not explicitly tied to the construction or timing of the new political institutions.

Decommissioning

The Agreement is clear on decommissioning. No paramilitaries that abide by the Agreement have to engage in formal surrender to those they opposed in war. The Independent International Commission on Decommissioning, chaired by Canadian General John de Chastelain, is to assist the participants in achieving the total disarmament of all paramilitary organizations. The parties that informally represented paramilitary organizations in the negotiations are required to 'use any influence they may have, to achieve the decommissioning of all paramilitary arms *within 2 years* following endorsement in referendums North and South of the agreement and *in the context of the implementation of the overall settlement'*.[25]

The emphasized passages clarify the termination point for decommissioning, not the moment of commencement. The passages also make it clear that decommissioning is linked to the implementation of the overall settlement, including the establishment of the North, North/South, and East–West governance structures, and to police reform. That is why David Trimble's demand that Sinn Féin achieve a start to decommissioning by the IRA before executive formation in the North is regarded as a breach of any reasonable interpretation of the text of the Agreement. Without executive formation in the North, none of the formal institutions of the Agreement that require the cooperation of the local parties can get under way.

Sinn Féin has nominated a representative to the International Commission. It has issued a statement effectively stating that the war is over. For the first time it has issued an outright condemnation of other republicans, namely the Real IRA, whose members carried out the Omagh bombing. It is even assisting ETA in its organization of a ceasefire and political negotiations in Spain. Evidently, David Trimble and some of his senior colleagues are unprepared to regard this activity as sufficient evidence of good intentions. Each move on Sinn Féin's part has merely led the UUP to request more. On the basis of current postures, only one obvious resolution of this crisis presents itself, namely that

---

[25] Agreement, *supra* note 2, Decommissioning ¶ 3 (emphasis added).

executive formation should be announced in the morning, and material progress on decommissioning should be announced in the afternoon.

Demilitarization, police reform, and prisoner release

The Agreement promises, and the United Kingdom government has begun, a series of phased developments to demilitarize Northern Ireland. Normalization is explicitly promised. The Agreement promises reductions in army deployments and quantity, as well as the removal of security installations and emergency powers. The Agreement also addresses personal firearms regulation and control, as an extraordinary proportion of Northern Ireland's citizens, mostly Protestants and unionists, have legally held lethal weapons.[26]

Police reform is addressed in the Agreement through an Independent Commission,[27] which must provide a report by the summer of 1999. The terms of reference of the Independent Commission require that the commission propose how to establish a police service that is representative, routinely unarmed, professional, effective and efficient, fair and impartial, free from partisan political control, accountable, and conforms with human rights norms.[28] This commission is to report a year before decommissioning is finished. It is difficult to believe that the choice of timing on the part of the makers of the Agreement was an accident. Plainly, the public outline of police reform was to be available as a confidence-building measure for nationalists before the major part of republican decommissioning could be expected. Bringing forward this outline fast might be one way to resolve the crisis of executive formation, though the necessary radicalism will be difficult for David Trimble and his colleagues to swallow.

The early release of paramilitary prisoners sentenced under scheduled offences, and of a small number of army personnel imprisoned for murders of civilians, has proceeded with less disruption than might have been anticipated. Measures to assist the victims of violence have helped ease the pain occasioned in some quarters by these early releases. The early release scheme has also worked in creating incentives for such ultra-paramilitary organizations as the Loyalist Volunteer Force to agree to a ceasefire in order to benefit their prisoners.

The political nature of the Agreement

There is, then, agreement on how to unwind the military and paramilitary conflict. Movement is taking place on some dimensions but not

[26] Id., Security ¶¶ 1–4.   [27] *See* McGarry and O'Leary, *supra* note 13.
[28] Agreement, *supra* note 2, Policing and Justice, ¶¶ 1–2.

on others. Before we address the obstacles to a final resolution, let us briefly examine the political nature of the Agreement. The Agreement is based on multiple forms of recognition, including recognition of the balance of power. It is an act of statecraft, but it is also based on hard-headed calculations rather than pious sentiments.

Recognition

The Agreement is an act of recognition between states and national communities. The Republic of Ireland has recognized Northern Ireland's status as part of the United Kingdom, subject to the implementation of the Agreement. The United Kingdom has recognized the right of the people of Ireland to exercise their national self-determination, albeit conjointly and severally. It has confirmed that Northern Ireland has the right to secede, by majority consent, to unify with the Republic of Ireland. The Republic of Ireland has recognized Unionists' British political identity. The United Kingdom has recognized Northern nationalists as a national minority, not simply as a cultural or religious minority, and as part of a possible future Irish national majority. The two states have recognized the paramilitaries that have organized ceasefires as political agencies. The Agreement has not required them to surrender to their respective authorities and has accepted the release of their prisoners on the assurance that their organizations will participate in ceasefires. The paramilitaries have, with some minor exceptions, recognized one another when it comes to ceasefires.

Unionists have recognized nationalists as nationalists, not simply as Catholics or as the minority. Nationalists have recognized Unionists as Unionists, and not just as Protestants. Nationalists and unionists have recognized others who are neither nationalists nor unionists. This bounty of recognition in contemporary Northern Ireland would warm the cockles of Hegel's and Charles Taylor's hearts.[29] The identity dimension of the conflict that John Whyte emphasized is undoubtedly being addressed.

Balance of power

The Agreement also rests on recognition of a balance of power. The Anglo-Irish Agreement of 1985 led to a new but ultimately productive stalemate. Republicans were left with no immediate prospect of significant electoral growth and their military capacity to sicken the British proved limited.

[29] For sophisticated discussions of recognition, see, for example, Erik Ringmar, Identity, Interest and Action: A Cultural Explanation of Sweden's Intervention in the Thirty Years War (1996), and Charles Taylor, Multiculturalism and the Politics of Recognition (1992).

Loyalists reorganized in the late 1980s, and by the early 1990s were able to raise the costs of sustaining violence within the republican constituency. Unionists discovered the limits of just saying no as British or bi-governmental initiatives were created over their heads. There was a military stalemate and a political stalemate, but there were also under-ground structural changes beneath the 'frozen surface' that were noted by John Whyte in his last essay.[30] These changes included greater equality of opportunity and self-confidence among nationalists, as well as a shift in the demographic and a resulting shift in the electoral balance of power within the communities. Together, these changes underlined the fact that any political settlement could not return nationalists to a subordinate status. The initiative of John Hume and Gerry Adams con-structively responded to this new stalemate. Much work had to be done before their initiative bore fruit.

The bargain
There is a bargain at the heart of the Agreement. Nationalists have endorsed it because it promises them political, legal, and economic equality now, plus institutions in which they have a strong stake, with the possibility of Irish unification later. The Agreement provides that nationalists co-govern Northern Ireland, rather than their being gov-erned by either unionists or the British government. Moreover, they get promises of further reforms to redress past legacies of direct and indirect discrimination. Republicans in Sinn Féin and the IRA can trade a long war that they could not win or lose for a long march through institutions in which they can reasonably claim that only their means have changed, not their end, the termination of partition.

Nationalist support for the Agreement is not difficult to comprehend. For nationalists, it is a satisfactory bet either way. Why, then, did the UUP and the loyalist parties make this consociational pact with the nationalist devil? The charms and latent threats of Tony Blair and Bill Clinton, the diplomacy of George Mitchell, and the process of multiparty inclusive negotiations are not enough to account for David Trimble's decision to lead his party where it was most reluctant to go, nor do these factors allow for his intelligence.

In this author's judgment, the unionists who supported the Agreement were concerned not so much with ending the IRA's long war. Rather, they were concerned with protecting and safeguarding the Union. Their

---

[30] John Whyte, *Dynamics of Political and Social Change in Northern Ireland, in* Northern Ireland and the Politics of Reconciliation 103–16 (Dermot Keogh and Michael Haltzel eds., 1993).

calculations suggest that only by being generous now could they reconcile nationalists to the Union and protect themselves against possible seismic shifts in the balance of demographic power. Unionists would get a share in self-government now, avoid the prospect of a British government making further deals over their heads with the Irish State, and have some prospect of persuading northern nationalists that a newly reconstructed Union offers a secure home for them. They made an Agreement to stave off something worse.

Ideas

Recognizing identities and interests are necessary, but not sufficient conditions of a constitutional settlement. Ideas, however loosely understood or flexibly deployed, were also important in the making of the Agreement. Their development, dissemination, and impact is harder to trace, but that does not mean the task cannot be accomplished. Fresh language and policy learning were evident in the making of the Agreement. Policy obstinacy and recalcitrance within the highest echelons of the dying Major government and of the spread-eagled rainbow coalition in Dublin between 1995 and 1997 were also evident.

The crafters of the ideas were many and varied, including politicians, public officials, and many unofficial advisers. Defining the sources of the conflict in national terms, rather than as issuing from religious extremism or terrorism, was vital. Without this shift, the Anglo-Irish Agreement, the Framework Documents, and the Agreement itself would not have been possible. The end of the cold war and political change in South Africa and the Middle East registered in and effected the region. The traditional explanations of the causes of the conflict had increasingly ceased to move the local participants. Many were open to compromises and political institutions that would mark a shift from the limitations of either London's or Dublin's conceptions of good governance.

The beauty of the Agreement as a bargain is that both nationalists and Unionists have sound reasons for their respective assessments of its merits, namely for believing that they are right about the long term. They cannot be certain that they are right, and so they are willing to make this elaborate settlement now. Does Yeats' phrase, 'a terrible beauty', apply here? Will the Agreement wither and die once it has become apparent who is right about the long term? That possibility cannot be excluded, but that is why the Agreement's architecture repays careful inspection. It is not a consociation like the model in Lebanon, that is vulnerable to the slightest demographic transformation in the make-up of its constituent communities.

There are incentives for each bloc to accommodate the other precisely in order to make its vision of the future more likely. For example, both have reasons to act creatively on the basis of self-fulfilling prophecies. The benefit of the double protection model is that it eases the pain for whoever gets it wrong about the future. The confederalizing and federalizing possibilities in the Agreement ensure that both national communities will remain linked, come what may, to their preferred nation-states. Moreover, the Agreement does not preclude the parties agreeing at some future juncture to a fully fledged model of British and Irish co-sovereignty in and over Northern Ireland.

There will, of course, be difficulties ahead, but Northern Ireland has a new, if slightly precarious and slightly unbalanced, bi-national super-majority. The Assembly and its Executive Committee are workable, and they can become mechanisms for accommodating the diverse peoples of the North. There will be difficulties in agreeing on a budget and a broad programme of government, and die-hards or kill-hards will be hoping to capitalize on them. Managing the twilight of the second Protestant ascendancy in Irish history and the re-interment of militant republicanism are not easy tasks, but the Agreement may deliver many impossibilities before its first birthday.

THE SHORT-TERM POLITICS OF THE TRANSITION: A COUNSEL ON THE GAMES OF UNLIKELY PARTNERS AND THE TEMPTATIONS OF LEGALISM

Before the optimistic picture can materialize, much work remains to be done. The Agreement's political entrenchment requires that some short-term advantage-maximizing and game-playing temptations be avoided. At the heart of this Agreement lie four internal political forces—the SDLP, the UUP, Sinn Féin, and the PUP/UDP.[31] The SDLP and the UUP comprise the historically moderate nationalists, while Sinn Féin and the PUP/UDP are the more moderate republicans and loyalists. Maintaining the Agreement requires that these political forces evolve as informal coalition partners while preserving their bases. Considerations of brevity oblige this author to focus on just two of these constellations.

---

[31] In the new dispensation there are now eight minorities. Five support the Agreement: nationalists, republicans, yes unionists, yes loyalists, and others. Three are against the Agreement: no unionists, no loyalists, and no republicans. The latter are in objective alliance.

The UUP is the most likely short-term maximizer and game-player. The party split most under the impact of the making of the Agreement. It lost votes to the 'No' Unionists, and it has lost some further dissenters that were elected on its platform. The temptation of its leaders is to renegotiate the Agreement in the course of its implementation. That way they can hope to refortify the party and draw off support from the soft-'No' camp amongst Unionists.

The UUP would have preferred an Agreement that was largely internal to Northern Ireland. It also would have preferred an Agreement that provided for their co-governing Northern Ireland with the SDLP. It would strongly prefer to govern Northern Ireland without the formal participation of Sinn Féin. Consequently, the UUP's most tempting game plan is to use the decommissioning issue to split what their supporters see as a pan-nationalist bloc. If they achieve decommissioning, then they assume that they will split the republican base of Sinn Féin, and they can live with that. If they do not achieve decommissioning, they may think that they can sabotage the more radical agenda of the Agreement if they can retain British support on the issue of decommissioning. The temptation of the UUP is towards post-Agreement negotiation, motivated by an opportunism aggravated by perceived political weakness. The signs of this game will be a phony legalism, an adversarial and petty-minded interpretation of the Agreement, postponement and prevarication, and brinkmanship. These signs may appear familiar.

The other constellation is republican. Republicans may be tempted to engage in game-playing of a different kind. They can and may insist on the full letter of the Agreement to sustain their constituency and their long-term political strategy, even if this insistence creates great difficulties for the UUP and the SDLP, their informal partners. They may think that they have an each-way bet. If the UUP delivers on the Agreement, well and good. If the UUP does not deliver, then Sinn Féin will position itself to ensure that Unionists are blamed for its non-implementation. For hardliners, non-implementation of the Agreement may provide a pretext for a return to war. In contrast, softer-liners will argue that any return to violence could only be sanctioned if governmental or loyalist forces were responsible. Many softer-liners would argue that Sinn Féin would have more to gain electorally both within Northern Ireland and the Republic through remaining a wholly constitutional opposition to a defunct Agreement. Sinn Féin may ironically be tempted by hard legalism, extracting the full letter of its contract with the UUP at the risk of damaging the informal political coalition that made the Agreement.

CONCLUSION

Three things must happen in order for this consociational and con/federal Agreement to survive. Immediate, daily, vigorous, and continuing British and Irish oversight is required to encourage the Agreement's fulsome implementation before the looming prospect of a constitutional time-bomb in a Dublin court. The governments must use all their available tools, from rhetorical appeals to politicians' salaries and expenses, in order to reach this end.

The Agreement also requires an immediate end to the Northern Ireland Office's new meta-administrative principle that any disagreement over the meaning of the Agreement and its accompanying legislation must be subject to cross-community consent procedures, an incredible invitation to legalism on the part of parties tempted to renegotiate the Agreement continually. The Agreement also requires greater recognition among the informal coalition partners, especially within the UUP and Sinn Féin, that they may benefit more in the long run from not seeking maximum short-term advantage from one another's difficulties and from not over-hyping their own. They should reflect on the fact that a Northern Assembly election is not required before 2002.

The benefits of these requirements will be demonstrated if two crises are resolved. One is the present crisis linking decommissioning and executive formation. The other is the widely anticipated future crisis over police reform. If they are not resolved, we will have a constitutional and policy mess that will require all the patience and national and religious ecumenism of another John Whyte to interpret. I hope that this will not be necessary, not least because there will never be another John Whyte.

APPENDIX 9A.1: HOW WILL THE ASSEMBLY AND ITS CROSS-COMMUNITY VOTING RULES WORK?

The Assembly and its Executive will have full legislative and executive competence for economic development, education, health and social services, agriculture, environment, and finance (including the Northern Ireland civil service). Through agreement the Assembly is able to expand these functions; and, again through agreement, and with the consent of the Secretary of State and the Westminster Parliament, the Assembly may legislate for any non-devolved function. So, if the Assembly works well, then maximum feasible devolved self-government is possible and a convention might arise in which the Secretary of State and Westminster 'rubber stamp' legislative measures coming from the Assembly. The road is open to one in which public policy in Ireland, North and South, is made without direct British ministerial involvement—though the British budgetary allocation will continue to be pivotal as long as Northern Ireland remains in the United Kingdom.

Assembly members have to designate themselves as nationalist, unionist, or 'Other'. This ruling poses difficult questions for the Alliance and other 'cross-community' parties, such as the Northern Ireland Women's Coalition. If they choose to register as unionist, then they increase the number of moderate unionists in the Assembly, but with the attendant risk that they may lose the support of some Catholic voters. If they choose to designate themselves as 'Other', then they may, by contrast, weaken their power in critical votes in the Assembly and run the risk of losing the support of some Protestant voters. In this Assembly they have determined that they are 'Other', though they are free to change their classifications in the future.

The Assembly through majority rule passes 'normal laws', though there is provision for a minority, of thirty of the 108 Assembly members, to trigger special procedures. But 'key decisions', that is, the passage of controversial legislation, including the budget, automatically have these special procedures that require 'cross-community' support. Two rules have been designed.

The first is 'parallel consent'. This requires, among those present and voting, both an overall majority of Assembly members and a majority of both unionist and nationalist members to endorse a proposal. Table 9.2, which records the numbers in each bloc returned in the June 1998 election, suggests that parallel consent with all members present will require the support of twenty-two nationalists and twenty-nine Unionists, as well as an overall majority in the Assembly.

The second rule is that of 'weighted majority'. This requires, among those present and voting, support from 60 per cent of members, that is, sixty-five members when all members vote, or sixty-four excluding the Speaker. It also requires the support of 40 per cent of nationalist members and 40 per cent of unionist members. The data in Table 9.2 suggest that at least seventeen nationalists must consent under this procedure, and at least twenty-four unionists. It also suggests that all nationalists (forty-two) and the minimum necessary number of unionists (twenty-four) have the necessary combined support in the Assembly as a whole for any measure passed in this way (sixty-five). The same figures strongly suggest that in the first new Assembly moderate pro-Agreement unionists are vulnerable to pressure from anti-Agreement unionists. They could even refuse to be part of a predominantly nationalist super-majority necessary to work the parallel consent rule. But there is fat built into the Assembly. The bottom line is that David Trimble can survive and deliver a workable portion of the new cross-community majority even with six dissidents in his own party—providing he can be certain of the support of the PUP (which is likely), and providing that he can live with support from Sinn Féin (which is evidently much more uncomfortable for him).

The cross-community rules are vital but not entirely predictable in their consequences. The legislation implies that the parallel consent procedure must be attempted first, and then the weighted majority procedure can be followed. That, however, may have to be clarified when the transitional Assembly decides its rules of procedure—by cross-community consent! The operation of the cross-community rules depends not just on how parties register, but also on how disciplined parties are within the Assembly—the widespread fears that have been expressed about the discipline and unity of the UUP reflect knowledge of this fact.

The Assembly will have committees scrutinizing each of the departments headed by Ministers. Committee Chairs and Deputy Chairs will also be allocated according to the d'Hondt rule (see Appendix 9A.2). Each committee will have to approve any proposed new law within its jurisdiction tabled by Ministers, and indeed the committee can initiate legislative proposals. In consequence, a committee dominated by other parties may block the legislative initiatives of a dynamic Minister, and it may initiate legislation not to that Minister's liking—though the success of such proposals are subject to the possibility of cross-community special procedures!

APPENDIX 9A.2: THE MYSTERIOUS WORK OF VIKTOR D'HONDT IN BELFAST

Viktor d'Hondt is the best answer to the Trivial Pursuit challenge to name a famous Belgian. He was a mathematician who devised a proportional method that is used for many purposes, including allocating political offices according to the shares of seats held by parties in the European Parliament. The method works by iteration, using a simple series of divisors, 1, 2, 3, etc. Rules like this are needed because assembly-persons do not come in convenient fractions. Table 9.3 shows how the allocation works, assuming parties have the seats previously displayed in Table 9.2 (see page 269 above) and assuming all parties are willing and entitled to take their seats. The party with the largest number of seats, the UUP, must get the first ministry, and then its seat share would then be divided by two. We then look for the next largest number of seats, held by the SDLP, and they get the second Ministry. Allocation proceeds until all ministries are filled. In Table 9.3, ten ministries are allocated. The numbers in square brackets in the *M* columns indicate the order in which parties win ministries of their choice, whereas *S* is the number of seats each party has during each stage of the allocation.

In this scenario, Unionists are entitled to five ministries (three UUP and two DUP), while nationalists are entitled to five (three SDLP and two SF). If, by contrast, the First Minister and Deputy First Minister decide that there should only be six Ministries, then unionists would have three (two UUP, one DUP) and nationalists would have three (two SDLP and one SF). If they opted for seven, the UUP's current negotiating preference, then there would be four unionist Ministries and three for the nationalists.

What happens if the DUP does not take its ministries because it will not accept the obligations of office? If there are to be ten ministries, then the UUP would win one more ministry and the Alliance would win a

Table 9.3 The distribution of Ministries (assuming all parties use their entitlements)

Divisors	UKUP		DUP		PUP		UUP		APNI		NIWC		SDLP		SF	
	S	M	S	M	S	M	S	M	S	M	S	M	S	M	S	M
1	5	—	20	[3]	2	—	28	[1]	6	—	2	—	24	[2]	18	[4]
2			10	[7]			14	[5]					12	[6]	9	[9]
3			6.6				9.3	[8]					8	[10]	6	
4			5				7						6		4.5	
All			20	2			28	3					24	3	18	2

Table 9.4 The allocation of ministries (with a DUP boycott or exclusion)

Divisors	UKUP		DUP		PUP		UUP		APNI		NIWC		SDLP		SF	
	S	M	S	M	S	M	S	M	S	M	S	M	S	M	S	M
1	5	—	20	n/a	2	—	28	[1]	6	[10]	2	—	24	[2]	18	[3]
2			10	n/a			14	[4]					12	[5]	9	[7]
3			6.6	n/a			9.3	[6]					8	[8]	6	
4			5				7	[9]					6		4.5	
All			20	n/a			28	4	6	1			24	3	18	2

ministry. Nationalists would keep the same number of ministries as before, but would improve their position in the pecking order. If, by contrast, there are to be six ministries, then unionists would have three ministries (all UUP), whereas nationalists would have three (two SDLP and one SF) but with an improved pecking order (Table 9.4).

There is only one important ambiguity in the Agreement about how the d'Hondt rule will operate. Two possibilities exist. Either the First and Deputy First Ministers count as part of the allocation of Ministers, or they do not. If they do count, then in the examples above the UUP would start the allocation with twenty-seven seats and the SDLP with twenty-three. In some possible scenarios this method would have the important consequence of helping other parties. But if they do not count, as I think is the most reasonable reading of the text, then allocations would proceed as in the above examples.

The d'Hondt rule is also to be used to allocate Committee Chairs and Deputy Chairs. It would be fair to do so with the figures resulting from the subtraction of Ministers from parties' seats in the Assembly, but the Agreement is not clear on this. It is also not clear if the d'Hondt rule will be used to allocate all committee places. I am assuming that that will happen—in which case some committees may not have Unionist majorities.

The UUP and the SDLP have provisionally agreed on the creation of junior ministers, presumably to be allocated places on the d'Hondt rule. If so, then every major pro-Agreement party will have most of its members having prizes of one sort or another—something that can only assist the cementing of the Agreement—and will provide incentives for a shift of posture on the part of ambitious anti-Agreement assembly members. It will also mean that the new Assembly is likely to have a rather small part of its membership free for standard adversarial parliamentary debating in the classical Westminster mould. Perhaps that is also to the good.

10

Globalization, European Integration, and the Northern Ireland Conflict

John McGarry

This chapter is concerned with the impact of globalization and European integration on the Northern Ireland conflict and its resolution. By 'globalization', I refer to a number of related phenomena: the development of global communications (satellite television and the internet); the increased mobility of labour, goods, and capital; the new move to integrated economies within regional economic associations—the European Union (EU), North American Free Trade Area, Association of South East Asian Nations (ASEAN), Mercosur; the development of supra-state political institutions—the EU, North Atlantic Treaty Organization (NATO); the spread of democratic and human rights norms; and an emerging global regime, in which international action in defence of these norms is countenanced against 'sovereign' states. 'European integration' covers aspects of these phenomena that are focused on Europe and that involve European institutions.

There are two broad approaches to answering the question of how these developments affect, or will affect, national conflicts like Northern Ireland's. Some claim that they have identity-transforming or difference-eliminating effects. Others view them as providing a context in which differences can be more effectively managed.[1]

I would like to thank Margaret Moore and Brendan O'Leary for insightful comments on this chapter, and Patti Lenard for her invaluable research assistance. The Social Sciences and Humanities Research Council of Canada funded the research.

[1] For a discussion of difference-eliminating and difference-managing methods of ethnic conflict regulation, see J. McGarry and B. O'Leary, 'Eliminating and Managing Differences', in A. Smith and J. Hutchinson (eds.), *Ethnicity* (Oxford: Oxford University Press, 1996) 333–41.

These two approaches are related to an important debate on the development of nationalism. On a modernist conception of the construction of nations and national forms of identity, associated with the work of Gellner, Anderson, and Hobsbawm, among others, nations developed in the modern period because they were functional to the economic imperatives of modernization and the large bureaucratic state.[2] In Gellner's formulation of this argument, the modern economy and the accompanying rise of the modern bureaucratic state presupposes mass literacy and increasingly standardized modes of communication and cultural practices. Whereas, in the pre-modern period, cultural and linguistic communities were politically irrelevant, national forms of identity become important in the modern period, because they are functional to the imperatives of industrialization and modernization. Anderson elaborates on this basic thesis: he claims that vernacular reading communities created through print capitalism came to shape the boundaries of national identities.

This description of the construction of national identities by broad economic and social forces suggests that global economies, and the institutional changes that accompany globalization, will transform nations and national identities. As states give up their powers to supra-state institutions and transnational corporations, we end up in a condition of postmodernity in which national identities become less relevant and dysfunctional and where they are superseded by other kinds of association and identity. This thesis is put forward most starkly by Hobsbawm, who argues that nationalism is largely a nineteenth-century phenomenon, associated with the construction of national economies and of declining relevance in the new economic order: 'The owl of Minerva which brings wisdom, said Hegel, flies out at dusk. It is a good sign that it is now circling around nations and nationalism.'[3]

Another variation of this argument emphasizes the role of globalization in increasing interactions among different peoples, and claims that it is this that leads to a reduction of cultural diversity, to overlapping and multiple identities, and even to the creation of a global cosmopolitan culture.[4] This view has its roots in an older argument, shared by thinkers

---

[2] B. Anderson, *Imagined Communities: Reflections on the Origin and Spread of Nationalism* (London: Verso, 1983); E. Gellner, *Nations and Nationalism* (Ithaca, NY: Cornell University Press, 1983); E. Hobsbawm, *Nations and Nationalism since 1870: Programme, Myth, Reality* (Cambridge: Cambridge University Press, 1990).

[3] Hobsbawm, *Nations and Nationalism*, 183.

[4] J. Waldron, 'Minority Cultures and the Cosmopolitan Alternative', in W. Kymlicka (ed.), *The Rights of Minority Cultures* (Oxford: Oxford University Press, 1995); M. Castells, *The Power of Identity* (Oxford: Blackwell, 1997).

on the left and right, that industrialization and urbanization would erode regional identities *within* states.[5]

The view that changes associated with globalization and European integration have a difference-eliminating potential is not restricted to intellectuals: it was uppermost in the minds of the statesmen who established the European Common Market. This was constructed not only, or even mainly, for its purported economic benefits, but because it was thought it would erode the rival nationalisms that had produced two World Wars.[6]

A second and quite different view is that globalization, and especially the institutional structures that accompany it, permits us to *manage* national divisions more effectively. Thus, it has been argued that the construction of the EU has provided national minorities in Scotland, the Basque Country, and Catalonia with the opportunity to enhance their autonomy by establishing direct links with the EU in Brussels. An increase in regional cooperation across state frontiers has allowed national groups divided by these boundaries to (re-)establish links. A new internationalized rights regime, associated in Europe with the European Court of Human Rights and the European Convention on Human Rights, has made it more difficult, though clearly far from impossible, for states to engage in the repression of minorities. Increasingly, states are becoming signatories to international treaties that commit them to respect a variety of human and minority rights. International non-governmental organizations, such as Amnesty International and Helsinki Watch, aided by technological advances in communications, are becoming more adept at exposing abuses. Multigovernmental organizations such as the Organization for Security and Cooperation in Europe, the EU, and NATO have taken steps to protect the position of particular minorities, the latter two by making respect for minority rights a prerequisite for membership. The United Nations and NATO seem increasingly prepared, in the aftermath of the cold war, to intervene directly in conflict zones, such as Bosnia, the Kurdish area of northern Iraq, and Kosovo, to enforce equitable settlements on warring national communities. Majority–minority relations, it appears, are less likely to be regarded as purely domestic matters.[7]

---

[5] K. Deutsch, *Nationalism and Social Communication: An Inquiry into the Foundations of Nationality* (Cambridge, MA: MIT Press, 1966); K. Marx and F. Engels, *Manifesto of the Communist Party* (Moscow: Progress, 1977).

[6] E. Haas, *The Uniting of Europe: The Role of Political, Social and Economic Forces* (Stanford: Stanford University Press, 1958).

[7] As the UN Secretary-General Kofi Annan put it recently, an international norm against ethnic repression is emerging 'that will and must take precedence over concerns of state

The view that globalization is primarily a difference-managing device does not presuppose a particular position on the debate about the history of nationalism. It is consistent with the view that nations have premodern origins, with roots in ancient *ethnie*.[8] It is also compatible with the modernist view that nationalism is economically functional, as long as it is accepted that its economic utility remains relevant in spite of globalization. Thus, Michael Keating, who argues that globalization has several difference-managing benefits, also claims that new or re-emergent nationalisms in places like Scotland, Catalonia, and Quebec are largely attempts to ensure these territories are favourably situated in the global economy.[9] Finally, the difference-managing hypothesis is consistent with the view that globalization has not yet proceeded far enough to have difference-eliminating effects.

This debate about the origins of nationalism, and its relation to modernity and postmodernity, has affected thinking on the Northern Ireland conflict. As elsewhere, there is an influential view that identities are being transformed by the forces of globalization, and by European integration in particular. My goal in this chapter is to show the shortcomings of such thinking and to demonstrate that, while globalization has had no noticeable difference-eliminating effects, it has helped to provide a context in which differences can be more effectively managed.

GLOBALIZATION AND DIFFERENCE EROSION IN NORTHERN IRELAND

The argument that globalization and European integration are transforming, or will transform, identities in Northern Ireland comes in both modernist and postmodernist variants.

Modernist (Irish and British) accounts

Since the 1950s Irish nationalists have portrayed economic integration as conducive to securing unionist support for a united Ireland. This

sovereignty' (*Globe and Mail*, 17 May 1999). For a balanced and realistic view of how human rights norms are increasing in importance, see the special feature in the *Economist*, 'The World is Watching', 5 Dec. 1998. The *Economist* argues that state sovereignty still has 'plenty of life left in it' and that 'for most purposes, states will continue to respect each other's sovereignty'. However, it also argues that the sovereignty doctrine is being revised, is no longer absolute, and is becoming increasingly conditional on how states treat their citizens.

[8] A. D. Smith, *The Ethnic Origins of Nations* (Oxford: Blackwell, 1986).

[9] M. Keating, 'Nations without States: The Accommodation of Nationalism in the New World Order', in M. Keating and John McGarry (eds.) *Minority Nationalism and the Changing International Order* (Oxford: Oxford University Press, 2001), 19–43.

thinking was outlined by future Taoiseach Liam Cosgrave in a speech to Dáil Éireann in 1954. It played an important part in convincing Taoiseach Seán Lemass to abandon attempts at autarky in the Irish Republic, to sign a free-trade treaty with the United Kingdom, and, in 1965, to meet with Terence O'Neill, Northern Ireland's prime minister, to improve economic cooperation.[10] In a referendum on the United Kingdom's membership of the European Economic Community (EEC) in 1975, many nationalists voted yes because they thought it would weaken the border and bring a united Ireland closer.

To help convert Unionists, nationalists routinely argue that European integration has made a united Ireland more attractive from an economic perspective. They claim that Ireland and the United Kingdom's joint membership of the EU means that Protestants can now accept a united Ireland without losing access to British markets, a benefit they could not be assured of when Ireland was partitioned in 1921. It is noted that the disproportionate representation of small states in EU institutions means that the North as a relatively large part of Ireland would fare better in its political capacities than it does as a small and insignificant part of the United Kingdom.[11] It is argued that all-Ireland political institutions would represent Northern Ireland's interests better in Brussels than Whitehall, given that both parts of Ireland have common and important interests in agriculture and regional policy that are not shared by Great Britain.[12] In an attempt to offset Protestant fears about losing the substantial British subvention, it is sometimes added that Europe would be prepared to finance Irish unity.[13]

---

[10] T. Lyne, 'Ireland, Northern Ireland and 1992: The Barriers to Technocratic Anti-Partitionism', *Public Administration*, 68/4 (1990), 417–33.

[11] G. FitzGerald, *Towards a New Ireland* (London: Charles Knight, 1972), 111–12.

[12] Ibid. 110–11. As John Hume told the SDLP annual conference in 1997, 'By the way, does anyone believe that our interests in Europe would be better protected by London than by Dublin? Could anyone imagine Dublin failing so spectacularly and for so long on a priority matter like BSE?' Hume argued before the conference that Northern Ireland would have been granted an exemption from the EU ban on British beef had the British government asked for one from the European Commission. The government didn't ask, he argued, because of fears about the reaction of farmers in England, Scotland, and Wales, and despite the fact that agriculture is a much more important part of Northern Ireland's economy than it is of any other part of Britain's (*Irish News*, 17 Nov. 1997).

[13] 'It can scarcely be doubted that, in the event of a political solution being found to the Northern Ireland problem, which is by far the biggest single source of unrest and violence within the frontiers of the present community, that institution would be willing to contribute financially to the transitional arrangements towards such a settlement' (Fine Gael, *Ireland: Our Future Together* (Dublin: Fine Gael, 1979)). The 'political solution' that Fine Gael was recommending was a united (federal) Ireland.

This thinking was given a boost by the Single European Act of 1986, by the Maastricht Treaty of 1992, and by the recent economic performance of the 'Celtic Tiger'. From the nationalist perspective, Ireland's position on the periphery of an increasingly integrated Europe is making it more worthwhile for both parts of the island to establish all island political institutions.[14] When, in the early 1990s, the Chair of the Northern Ireland Institute of Directors proposed an integrated 'island economy' in the context of the single market, a nationalist newspaper (the *Irish News*) lauded the plan as 'paving the way for unity'.[15] Nationalists also point to the way in which Northern Ireland's Euro MPs work together at Brussels as evidence they are latently co-nationals.[16]

While nationalists claim that European integration will erode the British identity of unionists, unionists are less optimistic that it will erode the Irish identity of nationalists. Because international public opinion tends to favour a united Ireland, unionists normally see any form of internationalization as aiding their enemies.[17] However, some Unionist intellectuals argue that European integration, with its benefits of labour mobility, common European citizenship, and limited cross-border co-operation between adjacent parts of different states, has the potential to reconcile Irish nationalists to a future within the United Kingdom.[18]

---

[14] J. Hume, 'A New Ireland in a New Europe', in D. Keogh and M. Haltzel (eds.), *Northern Ireland and the Politics of Reconciliation* (Cambridge: Cambridge University Press, 1993), 227. Hume told the SDLP's 1997 party conference that 'Europe through the Single Market has created an economic space where we can grow together...In almost every sector—farming, business, tourism, energy—the main groupings and interests on both sides of the border are calling for a more integrating, harmonised and united approach to marketing, to planning, to taxation, to regulation' (*Irish Times*, 17 Nov. 1997).

[15] J. Anderson and I. Shuttleworth, 'Currency of Co-operation', *Fortnight*, 3/12 (Dec. 1992), 18.

[16] These nationalist arguments have some academic support. A Cambridge economist, Bob Rowthorn, argues that closer economic cooperation between Northern Ireland and the Irish Republic in the context of the EU will lead Unionists to shift their loyalties from London to Dublin (B. Rowthorn, 'Foreword', in R. Munck, *The Irish Economy* (London: Pluto Press, 1993)). An Israeli political sociologist, Sammy Smooha, who has examined Northern Ireland from a comparative perspective, claims that the option of a united Ireland will be less and less resisted by Unionists as Ireland, a member of the prospering European Union, [comes to] enjoy economic growth, expands its welfare services and secularizes (S. Smooha, 'The Tenability of Partition as a Mode of Conflict-Regulation: Comparing Ireland with Palestine—Land of Israel', in J. McGarry (ed.), *Northern Ireland and the Divided World* (Oxford: Oxford University Press, 2001) 328–30).

[17] See A. Guelke, *Northern Ireland: The International Perspective* (Dublin: Gill and Macmillan, 1988).

[18] Cadogan Group, *Northern Limits* (Belfast: Cadogan Group, 1992). D. Kennedy, 'The European Union and the Northern Ireland Question', in B. Barton and P. Roche (eds.), *The Northern Ireland Question: Perspectives and Policies* (Aldershot: Avebury, 1994), 186.

While an Irish cultural identity would survive, it would be shorn of much of its political nationalist content.

Postmodernist (Europeanist) perspectives

The postmodernist argument that continental integration will erode both Irish and British nationalism is made by a number of intellectuals. Elizabeth Meehan argued in her inaugural lecture at Queen's University in Belfast in 1992 that 'a new kind of citizenship is emerging that is neither national or cosmopolitan but which is multiple in enabling the various identities that we all possess to be expressed, and our rights and duties exercised, through an increasingly complex configuration of common institutions, states, national and transnational interest groups and voluntary associations, local or provincial authorities, regions and alliances of regions'.[19] Rupert Taylor claimed recently that 'increasing European integration has led to the erosion of absolutist conceptions of national sovereignty' and that there 'has been an erosion of ethno-nationalism on both sides, a fading of Orange and Green, in favour of a commonality around the need for genuine structures of democracy and justice'.[20] Taylor points, approvingly, to the EU's involvement in the establishment of new 'inclusive' partnerships through its peace and reconciliation programme. This funds collaboration between the voluntary community sector, local councillors, and representatives from trade unions, from both sides of the political divide and from both sides of the border.[21]

Other intellectuals have been more safely future-oriented. Kevin Boyle has expressed a belief that the 'Europeanization of both islands... will force a reassessment of all relationships on these islands and in particular of the two principal influences on the present tragedy of Northern Ireland, "Britishness" as an historical integrating force and the reactive tradition of Irish separatism.'[22] Richard Kearney and Robin Wilson argue that European integration will allow Northern Ireland's citizens to

---

[19] Queen's University Belfast inaugural lecture, 'Citizenship and the European Community', 14 May 1992, cited approvingly in R. Kearney, *Postnationalist Ireland* (London: Routledge, 1997), 84. E. Meehan, 'Citizens are Plural', *Fortnight*, 311 (Nov. 1992), 13–14. Perhaps it is not surprising that Meehan, a holder of a Jean Monnet Chair in European Social Policy at Queen's, believes that Europe is having a benign effect.

[20] R. Taylor, 'Northern Ireland: Consociation or Social Transformation', in McGarry (ed.), *Northern Ireland and the Divided World*, 45.   [21] Ibid.

[22] K. Boyle, 'Northern Ireland: Allegiances and Identities', in B. Crick (ed.), *National Identities: The Constitution of the United Kingdom* (Oxford: Blackwell, 1991), 69, 78. Boyle and his colleague Tom Hadden have since tempered their Euro-enthusiasm. See K. Boyle and T. Hadden, *Northern Ireland: The Choice* (Harmondsworth: Penguin, 1994).

evolve beyond nationalism and Unionism and irreconcilable loyalties to different nation-states. They envisage Europe evolving into a federation of regions, including Northern Ireland, which will foster allegiances 'both more universal and more particular than the traditional nation-states'.[23] Cathal McCall claims that European integration has the potential to erode unionism and nationalism in Northern Ireland, particularly in the absence of sectarian violence.[24]

These arguments also have a strong normative and prescriptive component. They are based on a view of nationalism as a form of tribalism, responsible for conflict, and as a threat to democracy and the universalist values of the Enlightenment. The claim is not only that nationalism is being transcended, but that it should be. Postmodernists champion the process of European integration and globalization because of its nation-eroding powers, and they oppose policies that they see as hindering the removal of national divisions within Northern Ireland. Thus, Taylor strongly opposes the consociational institutions in Northern Ireland's Good Friday Agreement, in which both nationalists and Unionists are given legislative vetoes, on the basis that this 'reinforces the belief in the centrality of ethnonational politics.'[25]

Dissolving nationalisms?

Modernist and postmodernist accounts of the demise of nationalism run up against observed reality.[26] Rather than eroding minority nationalisms, globalization has contributed to their emergence (or re-emergence) in several places, such as Quebec, Scotland, Catalonia, and the Basque Country. In each of these cases, the construction of transnational regimes has provided new reasons why the nation should have its own institutions, whether to take advantage of new economic interests or to protect itself against new dangers of economic dislocation or cultural uniformity.

Globalization has also played a role in the re-emergence of nationalism in Northern Ireland. The civil rights campaign that preceded the 'Troubles' was linked to spreading international norms about human rights,

---

[23] R. Kearney and R. Wilson, 'Northern Ireland's Future as a European Region', in Kearney, *Postnationalist Ireland*, 79.

[24] C. McCall, 'Postmodern Europe and the Resources of Communal identities in Northern Ireland', *European Journal of Political Research*, 33 (1998), 406.

[25] Taylor, 'Northern Ireland', 2.

[26] See M. Keating and John McGarry, 'Introduction: Minority Nationalism in the Changing International Order', in M. Keating and John McGarry (eds.) *Minority Nationalism and the Changing International Order* (Oxford: Oxford University Press, 2001), 1–15.

and particularly to the example of the civil rights movement in the United States. The Northern Ireland Civil Rights Association used the same song, 'We shall Overcome'; the same slogan, 'One man, One vote'; the same tactics, marches and civil disobedience; and the same demand, equal rights for everyone, as its US counterpart.[27] The Unionist regime's control of the minority was fatally undermined as images of policemen clubbing marchers were carried globally by satellite television.[28] The new circumstances ended Britain's traditional policy of quarantining Northern Ireland. London's intervention, and the eventual implementation of direct rule, was prompted by what Brendan O'Leary and I have described as 'the politics of embarrassment'.[29] It was in this context that Northern Ireland polarized into two rival (Irish and British) camps, as Irish nationalists (and republicans) stepped into the breach left by civil rights campaigners, and the unionist community mobilized in defence. In the resulting violence, over 3,200 people have been killed and many thousands seriously injured.

Given this violent 'inter-national' conflict, it would have been surprising if the simultaneous, often abstract, process of European integration had been able to dilute either side's national identity. That it did not is clear from evidence provided by opinion surveys and election results. The first significant survey of national identities in 1967 showed Protestants splitting between a British identity (39 per cent), an Ulster identity (32 per cent), and an Irish identity (20 per cent). Another major survey in 1978 recorded a significant increase in Protestants' Britishness, with 67 per cent choosing a British identity, compared to an Ulster identity (20 per cent) or an Irish identity (8 per cent). A third survey

---

[27] B. Dooley, *Black and Green: The Fight for Civil Rights in Northern Ireland and Black America* (London: Pluto Press, 1998).

[28] Apparently the civil rights marchers were aware of the benefits of satellite television technology. One of their chants was 'the whole world is watching'. Cited in Guelke, *Northern Ireland*, 1.

[29] '…contingent developments opened Westminister's ears and eyes. As in the USA, national and global television made the exercise of hegemonic control over a local minority embarrassingly visible' (B. O'Leary and J. McGarry, *The Politics of Antagonism: Understanding Northern Ireland* (Athlone: London, 1993, 1996), 172); also see Kennedy, 'The European Union', 178). Not all regimes, as anyone familiar with Afghanistan and Iraq will appreciate, are vulnerable to the spread of human rights and democratic norms. Contrary to traditional Irish republican thinking, it was probably fortunate for the nationalist minority that Westminster and not Stormont had sovereignty over Northern Ireland. The Unionists, with vital interests at stake as well as being profoundly antagonistic towards nationalists, were not prepared to relax control voluntarily. Their position was similar to that of whites in the Deep South of the United States, who were unwilling to relax control of blacks until forced to by the US federal government.

in 1989 showed no significant change from 1978 (68 per cent British, 10 per cent Ulster, 16 per cent Northern Irish, and 3 per cent Irish).[30] In other words, British national identity strengthened among Protestants during this period, probably as a result of the threat posed by violent Irish republicanism. Among Catholics, these surveys show consistently high support for an Irish identity. Seventy-six per cent of Catholics claimed an Irish identity in 1967 and 69 per cent did so in 1978. The proportion dropped to 60 per cent in the 1989 survey, but this was largely because a new category of 'Northern Irish' was introduced, which 25 per cent of Catholics chose.[31] A series of further surveys conducted in the 1990s show broadly similar results for both Protestants and Catholics.[32]

Northern Ireland's politics have been dominated throughout this period by nationalist and unionist political parties, as the election results in Fig. 10.1 indicate. Contrary to what the postmodernist thesis would suggest, the share of the vote won by parties outside the two ethno-national blocs has declined. The most important of these parties, the Alliance Party of Northern Ireland, averaged 8.4 per cent of the vote in its first five (Northern Ireland-wide) election campaigns (1973–5), but only 6 per cent in its last five election campaigns (1997–9). During the last two regional elections in 1996 and 1998, the total vote of parties outside the ethno-national blocs (Alliance, the Northern Ireland Women's Coalition, and the Labour Party) amounted to only 8.4 per cent on both occasions. While nationalist and Unionist parties won an average of 82 per cent of the vote during the five elections that were held between 1973 and 1975, they have received an average of 90.6 per cent in Northern Ireland's last five elections.[33] Non-ethnic parties do poorly in all types of election

[30] The 1967 survey was conducted by Richard Rose, and those in 1978 and 1989 by Edward Moxon-Browne. The results of all three are given in E. Moxon-Browne, 'National Identity in Northern Ireland', in P. Stringer and G. Robinson (eds.), *Social Attitudes in Northern Ireland: The First Report* (Belfast: Blackstaff, 1991). [31] Ibid.
[32] K. Trew, 'National Identity', in R. Breen, P. Devine, and L. Dowds (eds.), *Social Attitudes in Northern Ireland* (Belfast: Appletree, 1996), table 1.
[33] I have relied for these figures on the data reported on Nicholas Whyte's webpage http://www.explorers.whyte.com. The elections covered were different in their nature: in the 1973–5 period they include one local government election, two to Northern Ireland regional bodies (the 1973 Assembly and the 1975 Convention), and two Westminster elections; in the 1996–9 period they include one local government election, one Westminster election, two elections to Northern Ireland regional bodies (the 1996 Forum and 1998 Assembly), and an election to the European Parliament. One could make an argument that the data, as presented, exaggerate the increase in support for nationalist and Unionist parties, as they include an election in the earlier period, the local government election of 1973, in which 'others' did unusually well (16%), and one in the later period, the European election of 1999, in which they did unusually poorly (2%). Even if one takes away these two election results, however, the share of the vote won by nationalist and Unionist parties still

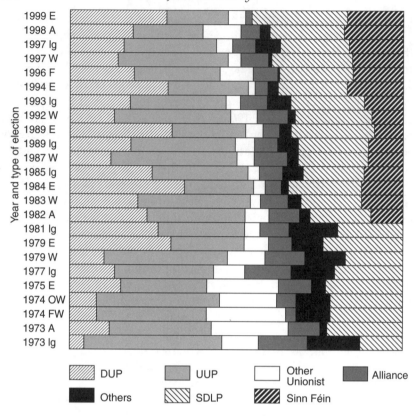

Fig. 10.1 Northern Ireland elections since 1973.

Key: E: European election; A: Assembly election; lg: local government election; W: Westminster election; F: February, O: October.

Source: Nicholas Whyte, http://www.explorers.whyte.com.

including those that are based on PR-STV, an electoral system that provides more openings for small and new parties than its main altern-ative, the single-member plurality (SMP) system.[34]

Nor is there any evidence from electoral data of softening identities *within* either of Northern Ireland's two ethno-national communities.

increased from an average of 85% in 1973–5 to 89.2% in 1996–9. One should remember that all I have to do to discredit the postmodernist argument is show that the share of the vote won by nationalist and unionist parties has increased over the last twenty-six years.

[34] Paradoxically, Alliance has done slightly better in recent Westminster elections, which employ SMP, than in Northern Ireland elections, which use PR. Another way to show the extent of national polarization in Northern Ireland is to examine transfers in those elections that are based on PR-STV. In the European election of 1999, of Ian Paisley's surplus of

Before 1982 the nationalist electoral bloc was dominated by the relatively moderate Social Democratic and Labour Party (SDLP), although largely because the more radical Sinn Féin boycotted elections. Since Sinn Féin began to contest elections after the 1981 hunger strikes, its share of the total nationalist vote has increased noticeably. In its first five election campaigns (1982–7) it won an average of 37.3 per cent of the nationalist vote, but in its last five campaigns (1996–9) it achieved an average of 41.8 per cent.[35] As the nationalist share of Northern Ireland's vote has expanded throughout this period, Sinn Féin's success means that it is also winning a greater share of the total vote: from an average of 11.8 per cent between 1982 and 1987 to an average of 16.6 per cent between 1996 and 1999.[36] It is possible that at least some of Sinn Féin's success within the nationalist bloc is a result of the party becoming more moderate rather than voters becoming more radical. However, as Sinn Féin remains clearly a radical nationalist party, its rise in popularity is difficult to reconcile with the view that identities are softening.

Within the unionist bloc, it is more difficult to measure electoral shifts between radical and moderate factions. This is because continuous fragmentation within unionism over the past thirty years has made it harder to compare party fortunes over time. It is also because there has been little to choose between the two leading unionist parties, the Democratic Unionist Party (DUP) and the Ulster Unionist Party (UUP), for much of this period, with both being equally intransigent. A gap between the two has only been apparent since the Good Friday Agreement of 1998, which was accepted by the UUP and rejected by the DUP. One consequence of the UUP's new 'moderation' is that its share of the

22,969, 22,162 were transferred to the Unionist candidate Jim Nicholson and thirty-two to the nationalist and republican candidate Mitchell McLaughlin. The latter figure can safely be attributed to mistakes or mental disorders.

[35] These figures have been calculated from the electoral data provided by Whyte, http://www.explorers.whyte.com

[36] In the 1973 election to the Northern Ireland Assembly, nationalists won 24.1% of the vote. In seven elections between 1982 and 1989, the nationalist share of the vote rose to 32.5%, and in five elections between 1996 and 1999, it increased to 39.8%. To the uninformed observer, this data might suggest support for the Irish nationalist argument that unionists are converting to nationalism. The shift, however, can be explained by Sinn Féin's participation in electoral politics since 1982, an increase in turnout among nationalist voters, and an increase in the nationalist share of the population. It is not because the scales have fallen from unionists' eyes, as nationalists might have hoped. See O'Leary and McGarry, *The Politics of Antagonism*, 192; B. O'Leary and G. Evans, 'Northern Ireland: La Fin de Siècle, The Twilight of the Second Protestant Ascendancy and Sinn Féin's Second Coming', *Parliamentary Affairs*, 50 (1997), 672–80.

UUP–DUP vote has gone down in the two elections that have been held since the Agreement was signed.[37]

If European integration is transforming Northern Ireland's politics, as Taylor has argued, one would reasonably expect this to register during election campaigns for the European Parliament. However, European elections in Northern Ireland are traditionally fought over the same constitutional issues as elections to Westminster, local government, and the Northern Ireland Assembly. The 1999 European election campaign, to take the latest case, was fought almost exclusively over the merits and demerits of the Good Friday Agreement and not European issues. As the *Irish News* put it crudely during the campaign, 'The European election [has] nothing to do with Europe . . . [it is] about how many Prods and how many Fenians there are in the north' (11 May 1999).[38]

As Fig. 10.2 indicates, the middle 'Europeanist' ground does not do any better in European elections than in other types of election in Northern Ireland. In fact, it does much worse. Whereas Alliance received 6.5 per cent of the vote in elections to the Northern Ireland Forum in 1996 and Northern Ireland Assembly in 1998, its share collapsed in the European election of 1999 to 2.1 per cent. This poor showing can be explained simply. Many of those who are prepared to vote for the middle ground in local government or Assembly elections, where they have some prospect of winning seats, choose to vote for nationalist or unionist parties, or to abstain, during European elections where, because of the size of the vote quota needed (169,703 in 1999), there is no prospect of electing a middle-ground candidate.

---

[37] There have been two elections since the Good Friday Agreement, to the Northern Ireland Assembly in June 1998 and the European Parliament in June 1999. In the Assembly election the UUP won 53.1% of the DUP–UUP vote compared to 56% in elections to the Northern Ireland Forum in 1996. In the European Parliament election it won 39.2% of the DUP–UUP vote compared to 45.3% in the preceding European election in 1994.

[38] The focus of European elections on constitutional issues is partly obscured by John Hume's 'post-nationalist Eurospeak'. Outsiders listening to Hume could come away with the impression that he wants European integration to dissolve both nationalism and unionism. However, insiders understand that it is the 'divisions' between nationalists and unionists that Hume wants to dissolve, and that he sees this dissolution as creating the basis for 'a new Ireland' within Europe. As one unionist insider writes, the basis of Hume's position 'is the territorial unit of the island of Ireland, and its objective is to secure some form of political unity for that territory, despite the fact that a clear majority in one of the two political units now existing on the island is resolutely opposed to any form of unity . . . it is a nationalist demand, not a post-nationalist one' (Kennedy, 'The European Union and the Northern Ireland Question', 185).

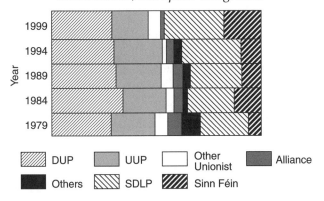

Fig. 10.2 Elections to the European Parliament.

Source: Nicholas Whyte, http://www.explorers.whyte.com (following Whyte, I have included Bernardette Devlin-McAliskey's vote in 1979 as a vote for Sinn Féin).

To the extent that Northern Ireland's people and politicians think about Europe at all, the tendency is for them to see it through a nationalist or unionist rather than post-nationalist lens. Nationalists, particularly supporters of the SDLP,[39] endorse European integration largely for instrumental reasons, just as nationalists do in Scotland, the Basque Country, and Catalonia. For them, European integration has the advantage of eroding British sovereignty over Northern Ireland and reducing the importance of the border with the Irish Republic. It is seen, as discussed earlier, as having the potential to weaken the identity of Unionists. European involvement is also welcomed because it internationalizes the conflict in a way that is generally helpful to the nationalist position. This explains why opinion surveys show nationalist voters as far more Europhile than their unionist counterparts,[40] and why nationalist

[39] Traditionally, the SDLP has been more Europhile than Sinn Féin. The latter has been relatively hostile to Europe because it sees European integration as weakening the sovereignty of the Irish state. In recent years Sinn Féin has moved closer to the SDLP position on Europe.

[40] A 1967 opinion poll in Northern Ireland found that Catholics were four to one in favour of joining the European Economic Community, while Protestants were marginally against. A 1992 Gallup poll found that Catholics were five to one of the opinion that membership of the European Union was advantageous, while Protestants believed so by two to one. Catholics were in favour of the Maastricht Treaty by almost two to one, while Protestants were narrowly against. Data from Kennedy, 'The European Union and the Northern Ireland Question', 166–7. A survey conducted by Evans and O'Leary in 1996 asked nationalists and Unionists if 'Governments from the European Union...should be involved in the forthcoming negotiations'. The survey recorded the surplus of 'yes' over 'no' respondents. The score for nationalists was −1. SDLP supporters were in favour, scoring 8, while Sinn Féin supporters scored −14. The Sinn Féin negative score reflects the view of

politicians in the early 1990s called for the EU to be given a direct role in the internal government of Northern Ireland.[41]

Unionists are significantly more reluctant to embrace Europe, because it threatens British sovereignty and because European politicians are more sympathetic to Irish nationalism than to unionism. This reluctance is recorded in survey data (see note 40) and in the actions of Unionist politicians. A strong majority of unionist MPs voted against the United Kingdom's accession to the EEC in the 1971 free vote at Westminster, and they have since allied themselves with the Euro-sceptic wing of the British Conservative Party.[42] While unionist MPs played, ironically, a crucial role in passing the Maastricht Treaty at Westminster in 1994, it was not because of latent pro-European sympathies, but rather because they knew a government defeat on this issue would mean an election, which was likely to result in a new and less sympathetic Labour government, and in the loss of their pivotal position in the British parliament elected in 1992. Both the DUP and UUP remain Euro-sceptic.[43] Despite this, pragmatic considerations have allowed unionist politicians to participate in some European initiatives, such as sitting on cross-community partnership bodies established as part of the EU's Peace and Reconciliation programme, and to cooperate with the nationalist MEP John Hume in Brussels.[44] The MEP Ian Paisley's position on constitutional issues is ample proof that this pragmatic cooperation is not, as some would have it, evidence of weakening unionism.

some republicans that the EU has weakened Ireland's political sovereignty, and that it involves Ireland in a body in which the United Kingdom plays a dominant role. By contrast, the Unionist response was −50. G. Evans and B. O'Leary, 'Frameworked Futures: Intransigence and Flexibility in the Northern Ireland Elections of May 30, 1996', *Irish Political Studies*, 12 (1997), 32.

[41] During 1991–2 John Hume tabled proposals for the creation of an executive to govern Northern Ireland modelled on the European Commission. The proposed executive would have included three elected representatives from Northern Ireland and three appointees, one each from the British government, the Irish government, and the European Commission.

[42] P. Hainsworth, 'Northern Ireland and the European Union', in A. Aughey and D. Morrow (eds.), *Northern Ireland Politics* (London: Longman, 1996), 131.

[43] For a UUP perspective, see 'United Ireland "will lose under emu"', *Irish News*, 20 Nov. 1997. In the European election of June 1999 David Ervine of the small Progressive Unionist Party became the first Unionist candidate to stand on a pro-Europe platform.

[44] Northern Ireland's representatives in the European Parliament may cooperate on economic matters, but they have also used the EU on several occasions as a platform for their opposing political aspirations. See E. Moxon-Browne, 'The Impact of the European Community', in B. Hadfield (ed.), *Northern Ireland: Politics and the Constitution* (Buckingham: Open University Press, 1992), 50–1.

The standard response of post-nationalists to the evidence presented by electoral data and party positions is that this detracts from evidence of post-national activity outside conventional politics. They claim that the preoccupation of political parties with constitutional issues has alienated significant numbers of people, who have instead channelled their energies into non-governmental organizations in what is called 'civil society'.[45] It is here, in organizations like the EU-sponsored partnership programmes, the Corrymeela Centre and All Children Together, that evidence for the transcendence of national identities is supposedly to be found.[46]

One problem with this argument is that it is not clear that Northern Ireland's people are 'alienated' from participation in conventional politics. If electoral turnout is used as a way of measuring alienation, Northern Ireland's electorate appears less alienated than Great Britain's. Turnout in local government and European elections in Northern Ireland is consistently much higher than in the rest of the United Kingdom, despite the fact that Northern Ireland's local governments have fewer powers than Great Britain's, and that Northern Ireland has more elections.[47] Turnout in elections to the Northern Ireland Forum in 1996 (64.7 per cent) and Assembly in 1998 (68.6 per cent) was higher than in the 1999 elections to the Scottish Parliament (59 per cent) and Welsh Assembly (45 per cent). Only in elections to the Westminster Parliament is turnout lower in Northern Ireland (67.4 per cent in 1997 and 69.8 per cent in 1992) than in Great Britain (71.4 and 77.9 per cent respectively).[48] Some of the variance here can be explained by the fact that elections to Westminster, unlike other elections in Northern Ireland, take place under the SMP electoral system. Given the absence of swing voters in Northern Ireland, SMP makes results fairly predictable, which can dampen

[45] A. Pollock (ed.), *A Citizen's Inquiry: The Opsahl Report on Northern Ireland* (Dublin: Lilliput, 1993), 90. The Opsahl Commission's views are cited approvingly by Taylor, 'Northern Ireland'. [46] Taylor, 'Northern Ireland'.

[47] In elections to the European Parliament in 1994 and 1999, the turnout in Northern Ireland was 49.4% and 57% respectively. In the United Kingdom the turnout was 36.4% and 24%. While turnout in local government elections in Northern Ireland in the 1990s ranged between 54.7% (1997) and 56.6% (1993), turnout in Britain ranged between 32.5% (Metropolitan Boroughs in 1992) and an unusually high 53.4% (Welsh districts in 1991). All Northern Ireland data are from http://www.explorers.whyte.com. Data for turnout in European elections in the UK are from http://www2.europarl.eu.int/election/results/uk taux.htm. Data for local government results in Britain are from C. Rallings and M. Thrasher (eds.), *Local Elections in Britain* (New York: Routledge, 1997), 53.

[48] Data for turnout in Great Britain for Westminster elections are from D. Butler and D. Kavanagh, *The British General Election of 1997* (New York: St Martin's Press, 1997), and D. Butler and D. Kavanagh, *The British General Election of 1992* (New York: St Martin's Press, 1992).

enthusiasm for voting. Nor is there clear evidence that Northern Ireland's electorate has become less participatory over time: while there has been some drop-off in local government turnout over the past quarter-century, participation in European, Westminster, and Assembly or Forum elections has remained reasonably constant.[49]

Even if we focus on civil society, as post-nationalists suggest, it is not clear that it is above the ethno-national fray. The two most popular mass organizations, the Orange Order and Gaelic Athletic Association, are partisan unionist and nationalist, respectively. Shane O'Neill observes that even Northern Ireland's politically active feminists, and activists from its gay and lesbian communities, seek to be recognized as one or other of the two national communities, with most of them 'freely [acknowledging] the political primacy of the national struggle'.[50] Many of the organizations in civil society that are committed to peace and conflict resolution understand that this will require the accommodation rather than the transcendence of nationalism and unionism. As Feargal Cochrane, the author of the most comprehensive study of these organizations, has pointed out, 'While some [peace and conflict resolution organizations] are working to erode the traditional political identities represented by unionism and nationalism, just as many (if not more) are committed to accommodating these alternative identities and establishing mechanisms that will allow them to coexist peacefully.'[51]

Those who believe that national identities are being eroded in Northern Ireland might well argue that the achievement of the Good Friday Agreement supports their claims. After all, both sides took major steps back in the Agreement from traditional positions on exclusive (British or Irish) state sovereignty, and the Agreement was endorsed in a referendum by an overwhelming majority of the electorate (71 per cent). Nationalists and republicans accepted there could not be a united Ireland without the consent of a majority in Northern Ireland. The unionists who endorsed the Agreement accepted a government in Northern Ireland in which nationalists are represented proportionately, a North–South

[49] See Whyte, http://www.explorers.whyte.com. The turnout data do not show any significant trend during the period under review (1973–99). The highest turnout for a local government election between 1973 and 1997 was in 1973 (68.1%). The highest turnout for a Northern Ireland regional election between 1973 and 1998 was in 1998 (68.6%).

[50] S. O'Neill, 'Mutual Recognition and the Accommodation of National Diversity: Constitutional Justice in Northern Ireland', MS, Queen's University, Belfast, 1999, 6.

[51] F. Cochrane, 'Unsung Heroes? The Role of Peace and Conflict Resolution Organizations in the Northern Ireland Conflict', in McGarry (ed.), *Northern Ireland and the Divided World*, 153.

Ministerial Council, and a number of all-Ireland 'implementation bodies' to administer various areas of public policy.[52]

It is more sensible, however, to see the Agreement as a *compromise* between rival national communities who grasped an opportunity for peace than as evidence of transformed or weakened identities. Nationalists embraced it overwhelmingly, even though it involved compromises on traditional demands, because it represented a significant advance from a unionist status quo. It also did not foreclose the achievement of a united Ireland, at least in the medium to long term. Indeed, in the weeks and months after the Agreement both the Irish Taoiseach, Bertie Ahern, and the leader of Sinn Féin, Gerry Adams, claimed there would be a united Ireland in their lifetime.[53]

Around half of the Unionist community rejected the Agreement outright, both in the referendum of May 1998 and in the elections to the new Northern Ireland Assembly, held in June 1998,[54] largely because they shared Ahern and Adams's analysis.[55] The Unionist politicians who accepted the Agreement did so in the face of considerable pressure from the British and Irish governments.[56] London and Dublin had laid out the framework for what a settlement should contain in early 1995 and made it clear to Unionists, particularly after Labour won office with a massive majority in May 1997, that the alternative to agreement was not the largely Unionist status quo of direct rule from London, but the deepening of Anglo-Irish cooperation over Northern Ireland and the implementation of a range of reforms, including a reformed police and a new equality agenda. Unionists were offered the choice of participating in these reforms, or alienating the British public and watching them being

[52] It was subsequently agreed that the six implementation bodies would deal with inland waterways, food safety, trade and business development, special EU programmes, the Irish and Ulster Scots languages, and aquaculture and marine matters.

[53] For Ahern's comments, see *Irish Times*, 27 Nov. 1998. For Adams's, see *Irish Times*, 20 Apr. 1998.

[54] Exit polls from the referendum on the agreement in May of 1998 showed that only a bare majority of Unionists voted 'yes'. In the Assembly elections of June 1998, Unionists supporting the accord won 23.9% of the vote and thirty seats while Unionist rejectionists won 24.9% of the vote and twenty-eight seats. One member of the 'yes' side has since voted with the 'no' camp on a number of important decisions, which means, effectively, that the two sides are level in the Assembly.

[55] The DUP claim that, under the Agreement, 'the Union would be fatally weakened... Unionists know that any deal so enthusiastically endorsed by the Dublin government and the SDLP is something which represents a dilution and diminution of the Union' (*Irish Times*, 16 Apr. 1998).

[56] For more details on this argument, see Chapter 8, 253–6.

implemented anyway. By itself, however, this pressure was insufficient, particularly to ensure grass-roots unionist support. There was also enough balance in the Agreement—including the removal of the Irish Republic's irredentist claim to Northern Ireland, a provision that Northern Ireland could only become part of a united Ireland if a majority of its people consented, and the creation of new British–Irish institutions—to allow pro-Agreement Unionist politicians to market it as securing and even strengthening the Union.[57]

Continuing national polarization in Northern Ireland helps to explain why the Agreement has not yet been consolidated.[58] It also makes clear, however, why the Agreement which treats both ethno-national communities in an even-handed manner, is an appropriate way forward. Rather than entrenching divisions, as some post-nationalists suggest, the Agreement's institutions offer the possibility of nationalists and unionists cooperating with each other and building the trust that will allow them to transcend their differences in the longer term. Presumably this is why, as Cochrane points out, many of the conflict resolution organizations that want to see nationalism and Unionism transcended support the Agreement.[59]

GLOBALIZATION AND DIFFERENCE MANAGEMENT

What, then, about the argument that globalization, while not reducing differences, facilitates their management? One version of this argument is that it has become more difficult for governments to repress minorities,

---

[57] The *Irish Times* recounted a Trimble speech to the Northern Ireland Forum in the week after the Agreement was signed: 'Mr. Trimble said the Agreement was a disaster for Sinn Féin and the IRA, and that it strengthened the North's position within the UK. Trimble claimed the alternative was the Anglo-Irish Agreement, and that he had achieved the ending of the Republic's territorial claim and a recognition of the territorial integrity of the UK' (18 Apr. 1998).

[58] Pro-Agreement Unionists won only a 'wafer-thin majority' in their bloc in both the referendum of May 1998 and the Assembly elections of June 1998 (see n. 53). Subsequently, even pro-Agreement Unionists refused to establish the Agreement's central institutions, the executive and North–South Ministerial Council, apparently because of the IRA's failure to decommission weapons. The institutions were not set up, and powers were not devolved to the Assembly, until December 1999, twenty months after the Agreement was signed. Even this success was temporary. The continuing failure to reach agreement on decommissioning resulted in the British government suspending the institutions on 11 February 2000, and they were not re-established until 30 May 2000.   [59] Cochrane, 'Unsung Heroes?', 30.

and less likely that they will want to do so. This is said to be a result of several related phenomena: the international spread of democratic and human rights norms in the context of the war against Hitler, the decolonization of Asia and Africa, and the American civil rights campaign; advances in communications technology and a proliferation of intergovernmental and non-governmental agencies that together facilitate the global exposure of human rights transgressions; and the demonstration effect, again carried globally, of minorities struggling for rights.

One should be very sceptical of the universal application of such arguments, as the evidence from Rwanda, Iraq, and the Kurdish region of Turkey suggests. However, a good case can be made that Northern Ireland's nationalist minority has benefited from these developments. While the spread of human rights norms helped to unleash a minority revolt in the late 1960s, it also produced a raft of reforms from the British government. London suspended the exclusionary Stormont regime in 1972 and argued that future governments in Northern Ireland would have to be power-sharing in nature. It also introduced a number of positive changes, including the disbanding of the B Specials, the creation of an independent police authority, and the establishment of an impartial agency charged with the allocation of public housing.[60]

Britain has since relied on often counter-productive emergency legislation, and its security forces have been involved in a number of excesses.[61] However, it is also clear that it has been restrained by its own commitments under an emerging international human rights regime, and by external pressures from non-governmental organizations, external governments, and multi-government organizations. Criticism in the late 1970s by Amnesty International, as well as by the government's own Bennett Committee, led to new controls on police interrogation procedures.[62] The adoption by a number of states in the U.S. states of the MacBride principles, which tied US investment in Northern Ireland to a range of anti-discrimination and affirmative-action measures, 'provided the main impetus', in the view of one commentator, for the robust measures contained in Britain's Fair Employment Act (1989).[63] Apart

---

[60] See O'Leary and McGarry, *The Politics of Antagonism*, 173–4.

[61] J. McGarry and B. O'Leary, *Policing Northern Ireland: Proposals for a New Start* (Belfast: Blackstaff, 1999), 35–9.

[62] Amnesty International, *Report of an Amnesty International Mission to Northern Ireland* (London: Amnesty International, 1977); Bennett Report, *Report of the Committee of Inquiry into Police Interrogation Procedures in Northern Ireland*, Cmnd. 7397 (1977).

[63] Guelke, *Northern Ireland*, 151. Also see O'Leary and McGarry, *The Politics of Antagonism*, 215.

from this, the UK government has been brought before the European Commission of Human Rights and the European Court of Human Rights on several occasions for its treatment of detainees and prisoners,[64] and has been criticized by a number of agencies, including the European Parliament, the United States Congress, the United Nations, Amnesty International, and British–Irish Human Rights Watch, for, among other matters, its handling of the 1981 hunger strikes, its use of plastic bullets, and the composition and practices of the Royal Ulster Constabulary.[65] As governments are normally reluctant to acknowledge the impact of external bodies on their decision-making, it is difficult to point to specific reforms resulting from these interventions. However, it is reasonable to argue that, at the very least, they contributed to 'non-decisions' and prevented matters from getting further out of hand.[66] As one knowledgeable commentator has pointed out, Britain's adherence to the European Convention on Human Rights helped to rule out 'the adoption of many of the security measures pressed for by unionists and the associated political strategy of trying to crush republican para-militaries by military means'.[67]

Another development in the domestic affairs of states that has bene-fited some minorities is the trend towards third-party intervention, not just to enforce human rights, but in the related field of ethnic conflict resolution. Such interventions have forced external agencies to look beyond the promotion of universal (individual) human rights to the design of macro-political arrangements and provisions for 'group' rights that will allow rival ethnic groups to coexist in peace and justice.[68] In Northern Ireland, external interventions have helped to establish more equitable political arrangements between nationalists and Unionists, and a more balanced relationship between the British and Irish governments. In 1978 the European Council agreed to give Northern Ireland three seats in the European Parliament, significant overrepresentation, to help

---

[64] For details, see Guelke, *Northern Ireland*, 165–8.

[65] See O'Leary and McGarry, *The Politics of Antagonism*, 214; Moxon-Browne, 'The Impact of the European Community', 51.

[66] A non-decision occurs when a government decides not to do something. In this case, the argument is that if Britain had not been scrutinized by these external agencies and/or did not care about its international reputation, it would have engaged in more radical repression of nationalists.　　　　　　　　　　　　[67] Guelke, *Northern Ireland*, 68.

[68] It is this trend, sometimes referred to in the international relations literature as 'peace-making', that explains the paradox whereby the United States, which champions individual rights over group rights at home, is forced to champion group rights and individual rights in places like northern Iraq, Bosnia, and Kosovo.

ensure there would be one nationalist MEP.[69] Pressure from the United States also played a crucial role in the Conservative government's decision in 1979 to drop its pro-unionist integrationist policy in favour of a more even-handed approach based on a power-sharing government in Northern Ireland.[70]

Since the late 1970s both the United States and the European Parliament have called consistently for the British government to cooperate with the Irish government towards a resolution of the Northern Ireland conflict. In 1977 President Carter took the unprecedented step of indicating that the internal politics of Northern Ireland was a legitimate concern of American foreign policy, and expressed support for a peaceful settlement involving the Irish government.[71] A report of the European Parliament on Northern Ireland published in 1984 emphasized the need for cross-border cooperation and for the British and Irish governments to work together in Northern Ireland in certain specified fields.[72] In the view of an opponent of these developments, the report and the growing consensus in European circles behind the need for Anglo-Irish cooperation helped persuade Margaret Thatcher to sign the Anglo-Irish Agreement in 1985.[73] She was also pushed in this direction by the Reagan Administration in the United States.[74] Each time Thatcher visited the United States before 1985, Northern Ireland was raised, often by President Reagan himself. Reagan continued a promise made by Carter to provide

[69] J. Ruane and J. Todd, *The Dynamics of Conflict in Northern Ireland: Power, Conflict and Emancipation* (Cambridge: Cambridge University Press, 1996), 281.

[70] See Guelke, *Northern Ireland*, 141–2. The volte-face was a response to concerns that Carter's campaign to secure the Democratic Party's presidential nomination would increase his administration's vulnerability to Irish-American pressure. News of the change in policy was first announced by the British ambassador to the United States, Sir Nicholas Henderson.

[71] O'Leary and McGarry, *The Politics of Antagonism*, 214. By the late 1990s, US intervention in the internal affairs of Northern Ireland had become 'humdrum', according to Niall O'Dowd. He was writing on the occasion of a visit to Belfast by the US First Lady, Hillary Clinton, when she called for the loyalist killers of Catholic lawyer Rosemary Nelson to be brought to justice. In O'Dowd's view, 'a few years back the notion of an American First Lady speaking out on any aspect of life in Northern Ireland would have been taboo' (*Ireland on Sunday*, 16 May 1999).

[72] N. J. Haagerup, *Report Drawn up on behalf of the Political Affairs Committee on the Situation in Northern Ireland*, European Parliament Working Documents, doc. 1-1526/83 (Strasbourg: European Parliament, 1984): Kennedy, 'The European Union and the Northern Ireland Question', 179.

[73] Kennedy, 'The European Union and the Northern Ireland Question', 179.

[74] See A. Wilson, 'From the Beltway to Belfast: The Clinton Administration, Sinn Féin, and the Northern Ireland Peace Process', *New Hibernia Review*, 1/3 (1997), 23. According to Guelke, the US role was a 'significant factor' in the making of the Anglo-Irish Agreement (*Northern Ireland*, 147).

aid in the event of a settlement, and praised the Report of the *New Ireland Forum Report*, a document on the way forward produced by Ireland's main constitutional nationalist parties. When the Anglo-Irish agreement was signed, it was quickly endorsed by the United States and the European Parliament, as well as by member states of the EEC, Canada, Australia, New Zealand, and Japan. This was a response that both vindicated the British approach and made it difficult for future governments to change course. There has been similar international approval for subsequent Anglo-Irish initiatives, including the Joint Declaration for Peace in December 1993 and the Good Friday Agreement of April 1998.

The American interest in conflict resolution in Northern Ireland increased dramatically in the 1990s, particularly after the election of President Clinton in 1992.[75] Clinton sent a special envoy to Northern Ireland during the early stages of the peace process; put some of his senior advisers, including National Security Adviser Anthony Lake, to work on Northern Ireland affairs;[76] regularly invited Northern Ireland politicians to the White House; persuaded the former Senate Majority Leader George Mitchell to chair a crucial committee on the decommissioning of paramilitary weapons and then to preside over the multiparty negotiations that produced the Good Friday Agreement; visited Northern Ireland three times in five years; and intervened directly during crucial periods of the negotiations. This close attention bolstered the position of the Irish government in negotiations with Britain. It also helped increase republicans' confidence about the utility of political

---

[75] Two sources attribute the increased American interest in conflict resolution in Northern Ireland to, among other things, international investment flows and European integration. From this perspective, America's intervention was due to its economic interest in stability in Ireland, which is the location of considerable and increasing American investment, and an important American foothold in the integrating EU. See R. MacGinty, 'American Influences on the Northern Ireland Peace Process', *Journal of Conflict Studies*, 43 (1997), and Wilson 'From the Beltway to Belfast', 36–7. Among the many additional, and complementary, reasons given for America's increasing role are: Clinton's perception of the importance of Irish-American votes in crucial primaries (J. O'Grady, 'An Irish Policy Born in the USA', *Foreign Affairs*, 75 (May–June 1996), 3, 6); a decline in the importance of the Anglo-American relationship in the context of the post-cold war era (ibid.); successful lobbying by Irish American groups (A. Guelke, 'The United States, Irish Americans and the Northern Ireland Peace Process', *International Affairs*, 72/3 (1996), 521); the idea that US success in brokering a settlement in Northern Ireland would enhance American credibility in other ethnic disputes (ibid. 536); Clinton's perception that the conflict was ripe for resolution and that he could play a useful role (Wilson, 'From the Beltway to Belfast', 25).

[76] It has been said that Lake devoted about one-quarter of his time to Northern Ireland (MacGinty, 'American Influences', 41).

negotiations.[77] In particular, Clinton's decision in early 1994 to issue a visa to Sinn Féin leader Gerry Adams helped give Adams the standing he needed to bring hardline republicans behind his peace strategy. Adams has claimed the visit to the United States brought forward the IRA ceasefire, which occurred in August 1994, by one year.[78]

Writing in the late 1980s, Adrian Guelke, Northern Ireland's foremost expert on the conflict's international dimensions, wrote that the impact of outside forces and international norms had been largely negative.[79] Guelke noted the prevailing international view that colonies should be independent, and that the conflict in Northern Ireland was a hangover from the colonial era. As a result, most outsiders favoured a united Ireland. This, according to Guelke, helped to explain the constitutional stalemate because it increased Unionist insecurities whilst reducing nationalists' incentive to compromise. It also helped to explain the violence. It promoted a siege mentality among unionists that provided a justification for the actions of loyalist paramilitaries. By bolstering the IRA claim that it was engaged in a legitimate anti-colonial struggle against British imperialism, and by facilitating fundraising activities among Irish Americans, it encouraged the IRA to fight on.

We can see now, with the benefit of hindsight, that this analysis was too pessimistic. Not only did external actors play a less direct role in the 1980s, when Guelke wrote, than they have done since, but their role over the last decade has been generally constructive. The United States not only bolstered Dublin's diplomatic position and helped to bring republicans into constitutional politics, it managed to do so in a way that kept, or even made, key unionist politicians interested in compromise. Senator Mitchell, who presided over the negotiations that produced the Good Friday Agreement, won praise as an honest broker from both sides.

---

[77] According to Wilson, 'the belief that Clinton might use his power to push Britain into a political formula for Northern Ireland favourable to republicans' was an important factor in republican thinking (Wilson, 'From the Beltway to Belfast', 32). A 1994 republican document on the peace strategy, TUAS, was explicit about the importance of the American role, noting that 'there is potentially a very powerful Irish-American lobby not in hock to any particular party in Britain or Ireland' and that 'Clinton is perhaps the first US President in decades to be influenced by such a lobby' (cited in MacGinty, 'American Influences', 34; also see Guelke, 'The United States, Irish Americans and the Northern Ireland Peace Process', 534).

[78] The announcement of the ceasefire closely followed a visit to Belfast by an American delegation led by Congressman Bruce Morrison, a close friend of Clinton's. According to O'Grady, the minutes of the meeting in which the IRA voted for the ceasefire indicated that the decision was taken 'mainly because of the power of the Irish-American lobby' (O'Grady, 'An Irish Policy Born in the USA', 5). This conclusion, however, appears to be O'Grady's interpretation and not a quote from the minutes themselves. O'Grady, not suprisingly, does not give a source for the minutes.   [79] Guelke, *Northern Ireland*.

Clinton's visit to Northern Ireland in November 1995, in which he visited both Protestant and Catholic areas and was careful not to give offence to either side in his speeches, was widely seen as a well-executed exercise in impartiality.[80] Unionist and loyalist politicians, not just nationalists, were given unprecedented access to the White House, and took it up.[81] While Clinton's success in coaxing republicans is often noted, he simultaneously managed to bring unionists along, with David Trimble acknowledging that a reassuring phone call from Clinton on the day the Agreement was reached helped convince him to sign it.[82]

The Anglo-Irish cooperation that has prevented the Northern Ireland conflict from escalating into something far worse,[83] and that produced the Anglo-Irish Agreement and eventually the Good Friday Agreement, was not just, or even mainly, a result of direct pressure from the European Parliament and Washington. It was also linked to the European integration process in indirect ways. By developing precedents of sovereignty-pooling, this helped to make thinkable the sort of trans-state institutions that are needed to govern Northern Ireland, and that are included in the Good Friday Agreement. In addition, the many meetings of European leaders that took place after Britain and Ireland's joint entry into the EEC in 1973 gave the Irish and British prime ministers opportunities to meet in the background to discuss Northern Ireland. This allowed friendships to develop and, more importantly, prevented megaphone diplomacy—the tendency of the two governments to communicate with each other through the media, usually with negative effects on their relations. The fact that Ireland is a member of the EU, with representation on a number of important bodies and veto power on the Council of Ministers, has led Britain to take it more seriously than in the past. The result has been a productive balance in the relationship that

---

[80] According to Unionist Roy Bradford, Clinton's visit 'significantly changed the feeling among unionists that the American agenda is exclusively nationalist'. A *Belfast Telegraph* poll showed that 73% of people in Northern Ireland thought the visit had been helpful. Both cited in MacGinty, 'American Influences', 39.

[81] See A. Wilson, 'The Billy Boys Meet Slick Willy: The Ulster Unionists and the American Dimension to the Northern Ireland Peace Process, 1993–98', *Policy Studies Journal* (Spring 1999).   [82] Ibid. 22.

[83] Northern Ireland is, in Frank Wright's term, an 'ethnic frontier', a site of contested sovereignty between two broader national communities, one Irish and one British. In such frontier zones the level of conflict is crucially affected by the actions of external powers close to the frontier region. As Wright explained, an unstable external environment contributed to ferocious and bloody conflicts in the Balkans, Cyprus, and Lebanon. He believed, in my view correctly, that Anglo-Irish cooperation was crucial to containing the Northern Ireland conflict. F. Wright, *Northern Ireland: A Comparative Analysis* (Dublin: Gill and Macmillan, 1987), 276–7, 282–3, 285.

has led Britain to take the concerns of nationalists more seriously. As the *Economist* put it recently, the 'shared membership of the European Union gives Britain and Ireland sufficiently comparable status to dissolve the mutual chippiness of the past'.[84] The British–Irish rapprochement led, in the months after the Agreement, to an address by Tony Blair to the Irish Parliament, making him the first British prime minister to have been awarded such an honour, and possibly the first who would have taken it up. Interestingly, Blair used the opportunity to call for a joint British–Irish body to defend their archipelago's interests in the EU. It should be noted, however, that this increased cooperation cannot be explained in crude economic terms, as a result of increased Anglo-Irish economic transactions within the EU. Rather the effect of EU membership for Ireland has been a radical reduction in its dependence on the United Kingdom.[85]

Finally, European integration has created a context in which the aspirations of nationalists for meaningful recognition of their national identity through all-island political institutions can be reconciled with Unionists' preparedness to accept such institutions providing they are functionally useful and do not threaten Northern Ireland's constitutional position as a part of the United Kingdom. At least some Unionists were persuaded during the negotiations that led to the Good Friday Agreement that all-island *economic* cooperation made sense in the context of Ireland's position on the periphery of the EU, and given the British government's handling of the BSE fiasco.[86] Unionist intellectuals, including one of Trimble's leading advisers, helpfully pointed out that

---

[84] 'Anglo-Irish Relations: Entente Cordiale', *Economist*, 28 Nov. 1998. A commentator who is relatively hostile to the Anglo-Irish entente, Denis Kennedy, a former head of the EU Commission Office in Belfast, argues that the enhanced Anglo-Irish cooperation would have been almost impossible outside the EU: 'the experience of working together in the institutions of the Community, particularly at Council of Minister and senior diplomat and official level, was slowly transforming the relationship... The patron–client pattern was dissolved; in the new circumstances British ministers and diplomats could see their Irish counterparts as clever partners in Europe. Without this transformation it is almost impossible to see how Dublin–London relations could have been transformed as they were between the mid-seventies and the mid-eighties' (Kennedy, 'The European Union and the Northern Ireland Question', 177).

[85] Whereas the United Kingdom took about 75% of Ireland's exports in 1960, by 1997 this share had dropped to approximately 21.4%. Imports dropped from 50% to 30.9%. While Ireland's recent economic miracle is closely tied to foreign direct investment, this is mostly from the United States rather than from the United Kingdom.

[86] See n. 12. The same thinking explains the cooperation between Unionists and nationalists in cross-border 'partnership' bodies set up as part of the EU's Peace and Reconciliation Programme. Rather than suggesting a weakening of identities, as Taylor seems to believe, this implies only a willingness to cooperate. As James Anderson writes about cross-border

cross-border cooperation occurred throughout the EU without threatening state sovereignty, and was a small price to pay, a 'fig leaf' as it was called, to win nationalist approval for the principle of majority consent.[87] Another unionist intellectual, who was a member of the UUP negotiating team and one of Northern Ireland's leading experts on the EU, argued that the cross-border arrangements accepted under the agreement fell in general 'into the pattern of existing European models'. He presented a paper to this effect to his colleagues during the negotiations.[88] European integration was one of the factors that made 1998 different from 1920 and 1974, when similar North–South institutions had been proposed but had been rejected by Unionists.[89] One way to appreciate the importance of European integration on this aspect of the Agreement is to look at it counterfactually: what if the UUP had been asked to accept cross-border institutions in a state system whose members practised autarky? In this scenario it would have been a great deal more difficult to sell the institutions to the Unionist community as economically pragmatic rather than as the straightforward political concession to nationalists depicted by the Agreement's Unionist opponents.

cooperation, 'The nationally "neutral" EU context was felt by some to be a crucial factor in getting together groups which would otherwise have been hostile to cross-border cooperation' (J. Anderson, 'Integrating Europe, Integrating Ireland: The Socio-Economic Dynamics', in J. Anderson and J. Goodman (eds.), *Disagreeing Ireland: Contexts, Obstacles, Hopes* (London: Pluto, 1998), 81–2).

[87] The adviser is Paul Bew. He and two of his colleagues, Henry Patterson and Paul Teague, argued in 1997 that 'the history of the EU suggests that despite all the integration that has taken place, member states remain stubbornly intact as political, economic and social units. The lesson for unionists is that economic cooperation does not necessarily mean that Northern Ireland's position within the UK or the Protestant identity will be compromised to any great extent' (*Northern Ireland: Between War and Peace* (London: Lawrence and Wishart, 1997), 196). Richard Kearney also noted that 'the process of European integration has the potential to make the "nationalist aspiration" less unpalatable to unionists. For it becomes possible, in this context, to present closer relations between north and south as pragmatically desirable in a single-market Europe without frontiers, where people, goods and capital move freely across former barriers' (*Postnationalist Ireland*, 86–7).

[88] This intellectual was Anthony Alcock, professor of modern languages at the University of Ulster. The importance of European precedents for Unionists can be gleaned through reading their literature. In a critique of the 1995 'Framework' documents, the Cadogan Group, a Unionist intellectual think-tank, accepted proposed cross-border arrangements but rejected all-island institutions, in part because, while there were precedents for cross-border cooperation between regions in the EU, there were no precedents for part of one state cooperating with another state (*Northern Limits*, 27–8). Alcock pointed out, on the other hand, that there are EU precedents for such arrangements (A. Alcock, 'From Conflict to Agreement in Northern Ireland: Lessons from Europe', in McGarry (ed.), *Northern Ireland and the Divided World*, 177).

[89] See also J. Anderson and J. Goodman, 'Nationalisms and Transnationalisms: Failures and Emancipation', in Anderson and Goodman (eds.), *Disagreeing Ireland*, 12.

CONCLUSION

There is little evidence that globalization or European integration has contributed to supranational identities anywhere, except in some intellectual circles. There is some evidence that European integration has weakened 'conglomerate' identities, such as those in Britain and Switzerland, in favour of Scottish identities or nested Scottish–British and French Swiss–Swiss identities. In Northern Ireland, however, European integration has not strengthened loyalties to Europe, or contributed to multiple, overlapping, or nested identities. Instead, Northern Ireland remains divided between British and Irish nationalists, as it has been since before the Treaty of Rome. Indeed, these divisions have become more polarized during three decades of European integration, which is hardly surprising given a simultaneous violent conflict in which over 3,200 people have been killed and many thousands seriously injured.

The resilience of Northern Ireland's divisions explains the need for the power-sharing and border-transcending institutions contained in the Good Friday Agreement. The Agreement is a compromise between nationalism and unionism, and an important part of its appeal is that it allows nationalists and unionists to believe, respectively, that it is a necessary step towards reconciliation in Ireland and securing the Union. It is not unthinkable that Northern Ireland's communities may develop overlapping identities in the future.[90] This is only likely, however, if the local context is changed from one of hostility to one of cooperation, and this will depend more on the success of the institutions in the Good Friday Agreement than on international economic integration.

While globalization has not diluted identities in Northern Ireland, it has contributed to conflict management. An emerging international rights regime has constrained those parts of the British state that favour coercion over kindness, although the constraints have not always been apparent. Changing norms on state sovereignty have unleashed a range of benign effects, including the positive use of the United States'

---

[90] Some identities will be easier for Unionists and nationalists to don than others. Just as David Laitin shows that Slavs in post-Soviet Kazakhstan found it easier to swap their 'Soviet' identity for one as 'Russian speakers' rather than as 'Kazakhs', one could envisage unionists and nationalists coalescing around a 'Northern Irish' identity rather than an Irish or British one. See D. Laitin, *Identity in Formation: The Russian-Speaking Populations in the Near Abroad* (Ithaca, NY: Cornell University Press, 1998).

diplomacy in Northern Ireland as well as increased cooperation between the British and Irish states.

It is impossible, however, to be precise about the effects of globalization, and these should not be exaggerated. It must be kept in mind that there were other pressures pushing in the same direction. A thirty-year nationalist insurgency indicated the counterproductive folly of infringing human rights or supporting a political status quo that was unacceptable to a (growing) nationalist minority. The Anglo-Irish cooperation that produced the Anglo-Irish Agreement and ultimately the Good Friday Agreement may have been made easier as a result of sovereignty-pooling and intergovernmental cooperation within the EU, but it was also due to a long learning curve on the part of London that Northern Ireland was a site of conflicting sovereignty claims that could not be managed within the traditional state system.[91] Globalization complemented these factors.

---

[91]   B. O'Leary, 'The Conservative Stewardship of Northern Ireland, 1979–97: Sound-Bottomed Contradictions or Slow Learning?', *Political Studies*, 45 (1997), 663–76. The sovereignty-pooling which lies at the heart of Anglo-Irish cooperation, while partly linked to European integration, also had older roots: similar North–South institutions were part of the Government of Ireland Act, 1920.

11

'Democracy' in Northern Ireland: Experiments in Self-rule from the Protestant Ascendancy to the Good Friday Agreement

John McGarry

Pierre van den Berghe has argued that democracy in divided societies can take five different forms: Herrenvolk democracy, ethnic democracy, liberal democracy, multicultural democracy, and consociational democracy. My chapter argues that each of van den Berghe's five versions of democracy, or relatives of them, has been experimented with in pre-partition Ireland and Northern Ireland. While all have clear limits, the one that is most suited to Northern Ireland's conditions is consociational democracy. This chapter discusses some limits of the consociational approach in Northern Ireland but also defends it against common criticisms.

According to van den Berghe, the state can be dominated by one group, as in a *Herrenvolk* or ethnic democracy; protective of individual equality, as in a liberal democracy; accommodative of minority group rights, as in a multicultural democracy; or co-governed by its different groups, as in a consociational democracy.[1] Northern Ireland (and pre-partition Ireland) provides a useful test case for weighing the relative merits and feasibility of these options, as it has experienced all of them, or relatives of them.

Ireland's eighteenth-century Anglican control system, the 'Protestant Ascendancy', has several features in common with van den Berghe's

As usual I am indebted to Margaret Moore and Brendan O'Leary for their many helpful insights. Thanks also to Sammy Smooha, who asked me to write this chapter and who offered several useful criticisms, and to the anonymous referees at *Nations and Nationalism*. Finally, I would like to acknowledge the help of the Social Sciences and Humanities Research Council of Canada (SSHRCC), the United States Institute of Peace, and the Carnegie Corporation of New York, all of which have funded my research.

[1] van den Berghe (2002)

concept of *Herrenvolk* democracy, although in Ireland only a small proportion of the *Herrenvolk* had the franchise. Northern Ireland approxi-
mated an ethnic democracy under the Stormont regime that existed
between 1921 and 1972. During the period of 'direct rule' between 1972
and 1999, Northern Ireland was governed from Westminster according to
liberal democratic and increasingly multicultural democratic principles.
Since December 1999, it has had brief experience of consociational
government.

Neither *Herrenvolk* nor ethnic 'democracy' are properly democratic or
capable of delivering justice and long-term stability. Both offend fundamental democratic principles of equal citizenship and self-determination.
In addition, the spread of civic equality norms mean that both are
increasingly likely to be challenged by excluded groups and by Western
states and international organizations. Liberal democracy has clear
advantages for minority groups as its institutions should shield their
members from discrimination and permit them certain freedoms. Its main
shortcoming, from the perspective of religious and cultural communities,
is that it offers relatively little positive protection for their collective cultural rights. This shortcoming helps to explain why many Western states,
under pressure from these communities, have been moving in recent
decades from liberal towards multicultural democracy (Kymlicka 1995).[2]

While multicultural democracy can accommodate religious and cultural minorities, it is unlikely to satisfy *national* minorities. National
minorities tend to resent the suggestion that they are mere cultural
communities.[3] Unlike the latter, whose needs can be satisfied by policies
of cultural protection, national minorities insist on institutions that
recognize and permit collective self-government. As a quid pro quo for
remaining part of the state, they seek to have it redesignated as a multinational state, not merely as a multicultural state.

Multicultural democracy is also unlikely to address the concerns of
minorities in *deeply* divided territories, particularly violently divided
ones, such as Sri Lanka, Lebanon, Bosnia, and Cyprus. Minorities in these
societies want and, if their bargaining position is strong, insist upon far-
reaching institutional measures that guarantee their group's security,
such as guaranteed autonomy, a share in executive power at the level of

---

[2] Some maintain by contrast that there is a continuing quiet tide of assimilation. See
Brubaker (2001).

[3] Take the Quebecois, for example, who find wholly unsatisfactory the notion that their
claims are on a par with mere cultural communities, such as Sikhs, Muslims, and German-
Canadians. They insist that they are a national, not a mere cultural, community, and they
distrust Canada's multiculturalism policy because it obscures this distinction.

the central government, a representative public sector (particularly a representative police and army), and vetoes over significant political change. These are the protections associated with consociational democracy.

Consociationalism also has limits, although the limits stressed in this article are not those that are highlighted by anti-consociationalists. Typically, critics oppose consociationalism because they believe it privileges certain divisive identities (such as ethnicity) over other integrating or cross-cutting identities (such as class), and that it institutionalizes and entrenches divisions based on these identities. They also argue that consociational coalitions, which require rivals to cooperate, are inherently unstable. However, it is possible to design consociational institutions so that they reward any identity group that has democratic support, and so that they provide a mechanism for narrowing rather than entrenching division. Consociational institutions may be unstable, but the alternatives associated with anti-consociationalism cannot resolve the problem of instability, and often compound it. Moreover, it may be possible to address problems of instability in consociational institutions.

The consociational approach is limited because it exaggerates the extent to which conflicts are self-contained. This has led consociationalists to downplay or ignore the importance of exogenous factors when explaining how consociational settlements emerge, or when seeking to bring them into existence.[4] It has also led them, when designing conflict-regulating institutions, to focus on intra-state institutions, at the expense of those that link states or parts of states. Yet, the latter may also be necessary in the many cases, including that of Northern Ireland, where national communities intersect with state frontiers (McGarry and O'Leary 1995).

Consociationalists have also focused too narrowly on the design of, and need for agreement on, political (legislative and executive) institutions. The achievement of political settlements normally requires agreement on transitional issues that go beyond such institutions, and the stability of political institutions may be affected by how these other issues are managed.

---

[4] Lijphart lists nine factors that make the establishment of a consociational democracy more or less likely: no majority segment; segments of equal size; small number of segments; small population size; external threats; overarching loyalties; socio-economic equality; geographical concentration of segments; and tradition of accommodation Lijphart (1985: 120). Eight of the nine are endogenous.

EIGHTEENTH-CENTURY IRELAND'S *HERRENVOLK* SYSTEM AND TWENTIETH-CENTURY NORTHERN IRELAND'S SYSTEM OF MAJORITARIAN (ETHNIC) DEMOCRACY

Van den Berghe defines a *Herrenvolk* democracy as one that limits the right to vote and to be represented in law-making bodies to a privileged racial or ethnic group. Apartheid South Africa, where whites enjoyed universal suffrage but blacks were denied any democratic rights, is the classic case. An ethnic democracy is defined as one that allows limited democratic rights to subordinate groups but clearly privileges one ethnic group over others. Israel, which allows Arab citizens of Israel the vote and representation in the Knesset, but officially discriminates against them and unofficially excludes them from participation in government, is an example. Several states in Eastern Europe, including Latvia, Croatia, and Estonia, also clearly privilege one community over another. While van den Berghe and others (Smooha 1999) stress the differences between ethnic and *Herrenvolk* democracy, the two are similar in profound ways. Both are at odds with fundamental priniples of civic equality and democratic accountability, and both are at best incomplete or partial democracies. In practice, a minority may be excluded just as effectively in an ethnic democracy as in the *Herrenvolk* variety.

There is also some evidence that dominant groups interested in monopolizing power choose between these alternatives for pragmatic rather than principled reasons: they are prepared to be ethnic democrats when in a majority, but *Herrenvolk* democrats when in a minority. Before 1994, the white minority in South Africa used a *Herrenvolk* democracy to control the state's black majority but an ethnic democracy to control its small Asian and Coloured populations. Blacks had no voting or representation rights at the level of the central government, but, after 1984, Asians and Coloureds were allowed to vote for their own racially based legislative chambers. In the same vein, Israel allows voting and representation rights to the Palestinian minority within its pre-1967 border, but did not extend these after 1967 to the much larger Palestinian population of the West Bank and Gaza.

Ireland's eighteenth-century Anglican control system bears some likeness to South Africa's *Herrenvolk* system under apartheid. As a result of the penal system that was introduced in Ireland after the Williamite settlement of 1691, Catholics were excluded from the (very limited) franchise and from any representation in parliament or government.

They were also excluded from the ownership of property and from membership of the professions and the social and religious establishments. Inter-marriage between Catholics and Protestants was banned (O'Leary and McGarry 1996: 69). During the eighteenth century, the island was owned and administered by a Protestant (Anglican) oligarchy with its own parliament in Dublin, although effective power remained vested in an executive officialdom appointed by the Crown.[5]

From 1782 to 1801, the Protestant-only Irish parliament enjoyed formal legislative independence from Westminster (although it remained curtailed by the power of Crown patronage and control over the executive). It was not until 1793 that Catholics were extended the right—on a restricted property franchise—to vote for MPs, but they continued to be prohibited from sitting in the Irish parliament.[6]

Faced with growing pressure to dismantle this colonial and sectarian system, and fearful of intervention from revolutionary France, Ireland's 'Protestant Ascendancy' acquiesced in the dissolution of its parliament, uniting Ireland with Great Britain in the Act of Union of 1801. To protect their political influence, leading Irish Protestants conspired with King George III against British Prime Minister Pitt's plan to allow Catholics to sit in the British parliament, and this concession was delayed until 1829. One of the consequences was that the Union became associated in Catholic minds with continuing exclusion, and by the time the franchise was extended to the (male) masses in the latter part of the nineteenth century, the Catholic population had become mobilized behind Irish nationalism.

In 1921, when Northern Ireland was established as a self-governing region within the United Kingdom, there was no question of Ireland's eighteenth-century *Herrenvolk* system being (re-)established there. The UK government, which, since 1918, had been elected on a universal franchise, and which retained overall responsibility for Northern Ireland, would not have permitted this. However, two factors meant that there was no need for formal exclusion of Catholics. First, Northern Ireland's borders were gerrymandered to ensure a comfortable Protestant/Unionist

---

[5] Presbyterians were intermittently persecuted by Anglicans in the seventeenth and eighteenth centuries, and were also excluded from the religious and political establishments.

[6] These similarities between penal Ireland and apartheid South Africa help to explain why leaders of the anti-apartheid struggle, including Nelson Mandela and Kader Asmal, have compared their plight to that of Ireland under British colonialism, to the chagrin of the British government and delight of Irish republicans: *Irish Times*, 27 March 1996.

majority of around 65 per cent. Second, the Northern Ireland parliament was established as a miniature version of the Westminster system. Under this system, the party (or parties) that enjoys a majority in the legislature has untrammelled executive and legislative power.[7] The executive is not constrained by a separate legislature, or a judicially enforced Bill of Rights, or constitutionally independent non-central governments, as happens in the United States.

Protestants/Unionists were capable, therefore, of excluding Catholics from power, de facto if not *de jure*, as long as they maintained ethnic solidarity. Such solidarity was forthcoming because the large Catholic/ nationalist minority refused to accept partition; because of irredentist activity from the Irish Free State (after 1937 Eire/Ireland and after 1949 the Irish Republic); and because the British government expressed considerable ambivalence about the Union, with some of its leaders regarding partition as temporary. In 1929, to reduce further the prospects of fissures among Protestants, the Ulster Unionist government abolished Northern Ireland's proportional representation electoral system and replaced it with one based on single-member plurality. This helped to ensure that smaller Unionist or class-based parties were unable to disrupt the Ulster Unionist Party's (UUP) legislative majority.

From 1921 to 1972, power was monopolised by the UUP. It established what Brendan O'Leary and I (1996: ch. 3) prefer to call a regime of 'hegemonic control'. It may also be seen as a version of what van den Berghe and Sammy Smooha define as an 'ethnic democracy' (Smooha 1977, 1990). The regime consistently acted in the Protestant/Unionist interest, and was permitted to do so by successive British governments, which seemed prepared to tolerate unionist control as long as it was effective. Catholics were discriminated against in public-sector employment and in public housing. Local government wards were gerrymandered to turn local Catholic majorities into minorities. A police force, the Royal Ulster Constabulary, was established that was almost exclusively Protestant. It was backed by emergency legislation, which was used to quell minority dissent. The Flags and Emblems Act of 1954 permitted police to take down displays of the Irish Tricolour but not the Union Jack. There was not a single Catholic cabinet minister appointed until 1968, a step taken when the regime was experiencing a terminal crisis. The only legislation passed as a result of an opposition (Catholic/ nationalist) motion was the Wild Birds Act of 1931.

---

[7] For details of Northern Ireland's political system between 1921 and 1972, see O'Leary and McGarry (1996: ch. 3).

Northern Ireland's control system collapsed in the late 1960s because of overlapping endogenous and exogenous developments. The minority reorganized and changed tactics. The British welfare state, and increasing access to post-secondary education in particular, contributed to a confident and growing Catholic middle class that was unwilling to accept second-class citizenship. Its resolve was strengthened by the norms of civic equality that flowed out of the campaign of the American civil rights movement. Catholics launched their own civil rights protests and challenged the unionist regime to reform (O'Leary and McGarry 1996: 167–8). They were supported by British civil liberties groups and, more importantly, by sections of the new Labour government elected in 1964. The Unionist regime split under these pressures and, when hardliners sought to repress the minority, an embarrassed British government was forced to intervene. Westminster prorogued the Stormont parliament in 1972 and implemented a system of 'direct rule' from London.

Despite reminiscences about the Stormont 'golden age' among hard-line Protestants, it is generally recognized that majoritarian (for which read 'control' or 'ethnic') democracy is no longer a feasible option for Northern Ireland. The British government has made it clear that a return to the Stormont system is out of the question. It would be resolutely opposed by the large and growing Catholic (nationalist) community— currently well over 40 per cent of Northern Ireland's population and electorate. Unionist politicians, especially in the UUP, appear to understand that the continuing growth of the Catholic population could make 'majority rule' a poisoned chalice. After the Good Friday Agreement, advisers to the UUP leadership pointed out that, because of a rising nationalist vote, it might soon be 'grateful' it had agreed to mandatory power-sharing.[8] These facts help to explain why no Unionist party, not even Ian Paisley's Democratic Unionist Party (DUP), calls for a return to majority rule.[9]

Virtually all Unionist politicians are now formally committed to some form of power-sharing. There is still disagreement, however, over whether this should be with the Social Democratic and Labour Party (SDLP) and Sinn Féin or just the former; if it should be based on a minimum winning

[8] 'Shock report has UUP reeling', *Irish Examiner*, 20 June 2000.
[9] Indeed in November 2001, the DUP was at pains to defend the cross-community consent procedures established by the Good Friday Agreement. See the *Northern Ireland Assembly Official Report (Hansard)* for 2 and 5 November 2001, at http://www.ni-assembly.gov.uk/hansard.htm

coalition or on the inclusion of all major parties; if the power-sharing government should have wide-ranging legislative powers or more narrow administrative powers; and if it should be based on an executive/cabinet or on a set of legislative committees, the latter system being similar to that which operates at local government level and in the new Welsh Assembly.

Northern Ireland's experience demonstrates the normative flaws of ethnic democracy. It also underlines the difficulty of sustaining such a regime, particularly when the minority that is being controlled is proportionally large and growing, and when the regime exists within a Western milieu where civic equality is an important value. Nonetheless, it is clear from developments in Eastern Europe in the 1990s that the practice of ethnic democracy has some life in it. The break-up of the communist multinational states of the Soviet Union, Yugoslavia, and Czechoslovakia has resulted in the emergence of a number of states that are dominated by one ethnic community. The cases include Estonia, Latvia, Slovakia, Croatia, and Serbia. All of these states have imposed second-class citizenship on (or, in some cases, denied citizenship to) at least some of their state's minorities.[10] They have established what Rogers Brubaker calls 'nationalising' states—states, the symbols, institutions, and policies of which reflect the interests of their dominant national communities (Brubaker 1996).

Even these new states have been susceptible, however, to spreading norms of equal citizenship and to Western pressure to relax discrimination against minorities. The European Union (EU) and NATO have insisted on improvements in minority rights as the price of entry into their clubs, or even as a cost of being put on waiting lists for entry. Both the EU and OSCE have applied pressure, including moral persuasion and sanctions, against states in Eastern Europe that treat their minorities unfairly, and there is some evidence that this is having benign effects.[11] In one case of extreme abuse, the repression of Kosovo's Albanians by Serbia's Milošević regime, the West intervened militarily, infringing previously sacrosanct principles of state sovereignty, to protect the minority in question. The intervention contributed to the downfall of Milošević's ethnic democracy and its replacement by what promises to be a democracy of the liberal or multicultural type.

---

[10] Denial of citizenship in the Baltic states has been based on the legal argument that some residents are illegal settlers under international law.

[11] For the effects of outside pressure in Estonia and Latvia, see Bernier (2001).

LIBERAL AND MULTICULTURAL DEMOCRACY IN NORTHERN IRELAND (1972–98)

Liberal democracy and multicultural democracy are both founded on the central liberal principles of freedom and equality of persons. In this respect they are radically different from, and superior to, *Herrenvolk* and ethnic democracy. The difference between them is that while liberal democracy is founded on the notion of individual equality, multicultural democracy is based on individual equality *and* protections for cultural communities. While a liberal democracy takes steps to protect individual rights, such as the right to vote, to assemble, or to be free from discrimination, a multicultural democracy takes additional steps to protect the culture of minority communities and to shield them from assimilation. Such steps might include the provision of public education in a minority's religion; affirmative action programmes to promote the number from minority groups in the public and private sectors; flexible dress codes to allow religious minorities (such as Sikhs) to serve in the police or armed forces; and government funding of minority cultural festivals and interest groups.[12] While Western states have been traditionally governed by liberal democratic principles, many of them, including Canada, Australia, and the United States, have moved toward multicultural democracy in recent years.[13]

Between 1972 and 1998, Northern Ireland was governed directly from Westminster, largely because the province's political parties could not agree on a formula for a return to devolved government. British rule began as liberal democratic, if one puts aside its excessive reliance on emergency legislation, but it gradually developed multicultural democratic tinges. Before implementing direct rule, London had already pressed the Stormont regime into making a number of standard liberal reforms to prevent discrimination: the allocation of public housing was transferred from the regional government to an impartial and autonomous agency; gerrymandering of ward boundaries at the local government level was ended; the police force, which had been an arm of the unionist state, was given a new arm's length relationship with politicians. Its impartiality improved as a consequence, although it continued to be rejected by nationalists, mainly because it continued to be associated with the defence of an illegitimate political order (McGarry and

---

[12] For a longer list of multicultural policies, see Kymlicka (1998: 42).
[13] For an argument that this trend is going into reverse, see Brubaker (2001).

O'Leary 1999: 25–42). There was also a law, in 1970, to prevent the incitement of hatred. Throughout the period of direct rule, the allocation of public expenditure and the location of publicly subsidized industry were conducted in a reasonably even-handed fashion, a welcome departure from the practice under the Stormont regime. A Standing Advisory Commission on Human Rights was appointed in 1973. In 1976, London passed fair employment legislation to overcome discrimination against Catholics in the workplace. These measures were strengthened considerably by new legislation in 1989, although neither Act contained provisions for affirmative action (reverse discrimination). The Public Order (NI) Order of 1987 strengthened the law on incitement to hatred and gave police the power to control marches likely to cause provocation.

On top of these standard liberal democratic reforms, and particularly from the 1980s, Britain offered a limited accommodation of Catholic and Irish culture. After 1972, it continued Stormont's policy of partly funding the Catholic separate education system. However, the position of the Catholic schools improved incrementally under direct rule, and in 1992 a decision was taken to fully fund the Catholic system, putting it on an equal footing with its public (in practice, Protestant) counterpart (McGrath 2000). The government also took steps from the 1980s to develop more balanced historical curricula in the schools, and more contact between the schools of both communities. The Flags and Emblems Act, which discriminated against the display of the Irish Tricolour, was repealed in 1986. A Community Relations Council was established in 1990, and it funded a number of initiatives aimed at the promotion of intercultural understanding. Steps were also taken to promote the use of the Irish language in Northern Ireland. Through the 1980s, the government offered funding to the independent and West-Belfast based Irish language organization, *Glór na nGael*. Funding was withdrawn in 1990 but restored in 1992. In 1989, it established a quasi-autonomous agency, the *Iontaobhas Ultach*/Ultach Trust, to promote the Irish language.

While London's view after 1985 was generally that direct rule should be replaced as soon as possible by consociational (power-sharing) devolution, unionist politicians and academics increasingly argued that Northern Ireland should be permanently integrated into the United Kingdom on a liberal or multicultural basis. Unionist 'integrationists' warned against any form of devolution, whether of the ethnic or consociational democratic variety. Even the latter, it was claimed, would repeat the main mistakes of the 1921–72 period: It would erect a distinction between Great Britain and Northern Ireland, thereby whetting the appetites of nationalists and marginalizing unionist liberals.

A consociational government, in this view, would become a forum for sectarian squabbling. It would be better for everyone concerned, inte-grationists argued, if the individual and cultural rights of all of Northern Ireland's citizens were equally protected within the United Kingdom (see Aughey 1989; and Wilson Foster 1995).

Towards this end, integrationists pressed for all remaining legislative, administrative and political distinctions between Northern Ireland and Great Britain to be removed. They pushed for legislation affecting Northern Ireland to be incorporated into British legislation rather than passed separately. There were also calls for Northern Ireland's representation at Westminster to be increased, and for Northern Ireland to be administered in the same way as regions in Britain. Any decentralization of powers to Northern Ireland, it was stressed, should be minimal in scope, and no different from the sort of powers enjoyed by regional or local governments in Britain. Some Unionists also lobbied for the main British political parties, the Conservatives and Labour, to organize in Northern Ireland.

The case of Northern Ireland, however, underlines the limits of liberal and multicultural democracy in nationally divided societies. While a British liberal democracy could accommodate Catholics as individuals, and a British multicultural democracy could accommodate Catholics or Irish-speakers as cultural communities, neither was compatible with the political aspirations of even moderate Irish *nationalists*. Throughout the 1972–98 period, the latter, represented by the Social Democratic and Labour Party, demanded not simply an end to discrimination against Catholics, full funding for Catholic schools, and steps to promote the Irish language, but also a consociational government in Northern Ireland, an assembly with law-making powers, and political links between Northern Ireland and the Irish Republic. The more radical Irish nationalists of Sinn Féin rejected any solution within the United Kingdom and instead offered alternative proposals for a multicultural united Ireland that was respectful of the individual rights and culture of Northern Ireland's Protestants. Sinn Féin's proposals, however, were at least as objectionable to Unionists as the latter's proposals for a British multicultural democracy were to nationalists.

British liberal or multicultural democracy was not only incapable of accommodating the political aspirations of nationalists in Northern Ireland, it also failed to satisfy (soft and hard) nationalists in Scotland and Wales. From the 1970s onwards, large numbers in both countries, particularly the former, made it clear that the minor provisions to protect their identity, culture, and interests at Westminster and Whitehall were insufficient. They instead demanded self-government, and in refer-endums held in 1997 voted for it. The British government's decision to concede a Welsh assembly and a Scottish parliament, and the various institutions established under Northern Ireland's Good Friday Agree-ment, indicate its awareness of the shortcomings of liberal or multi-cultural democracy as frameworks for governing its multi-*national* state.

NORTHERN IRELAND'S CONSOCIATIONAL AND BI-NATIONAL AGREEMENT (1998–)

The fact that Northern Ireland's Unionist and republican elites have been wedded to two irreconcilable versions of liberal or multicultural democracy for much of the past thirty years, goes a long way towards explaining the political stalemate during this period. Both sides decided to compromise because of a mix of endogenous and exogenous factors.

Some of the endogenous factors stressed by consociationalists as con-ducive to compromise did not apply in Northern Ireland. Its Agreement was not a result of leaders acting to avoid impending economic collapse, as happened in South Africa (McGarry 1998). The British Treasury lar-gely absorbed the economic damage caused by the conflict, and there was no particularly significant economic downturn in the years before 1998. It was not crucially a result of increasing violence, and a decision by leaders to pull back from the brink. Violence was generally lower in the 1990s than in previous decades, although some have argued that the unusually successful targeting of leading republicans by loyalist para-militaries helped to concentrate the minds of Sinn Féin.

An endogenous factor that did matter in Northern Ireland was demographic change.[14] Between 1961 and 1991, the number of those who gave their religion as Protestant declined from 63.2 to 50.6 per cent, while those who declared themselves Catholics increased from 34.9 to 38.4 per cent (Doherty 1996: 202). The remainder (11 per cent in 1991)

---

[14] The importance of this was pointed out as early as 1990 by Brendan O'Leary (1990). Also see McGarry and O'Leary (1995: 403–6). Demographic change has mattered elsewhere also. The decline of whites as a proportion of South Africa's population was an important factor in bringing F. W. De Klerk to the negotiating table. See McGarry (1998). The growth of the Palestinian population in the West Bank and Gaza helped to destroy the idea of *Eretz Israel*, an Israeli state stretching from the Mediterranean Sea to the border with Jordan. Virtually all Israeli Jews are now united around the argument that they need to be separated from (West Bank and Gaza) Palestinians, but they are still divided on where the borders should be.

gave no religion. At the same time, the nationalist share of the Northern Ireland vote increased steadily, from an average of 31 per cent in four elections between 1982 and 1985, to an average of 38 per cent in the four elections before the Agreement (1996–7). Both nationalist parties grew, the SDLP from 20 to 23.7 per cent and Sinn Féin from 11.5 to 14.2 per cent. The Unionist vote declined during the same period from 57.5 to 52 per cent, with the UUP's vote dropping from 28.5 to 26.5 per cent and the DUP's from 25.2 to 19.5 per cent.[15] These changes affected both republicans and Unionists. The growing Catholic share of the population and vote for Sinn Féin helped to convince republicans that there could be gains through constitutional politics and that political institutions within Northern Ireland need not mean Unionist dominance. For the UUP, the trend underlined that time was not on the Unionist side. The rising nationalist, and particularly the republican, vote showed that the Unionist option of an integrated British liberal (or multicultural) democracy was falling on deaf Catholic ears. It opened space for Unionist moderates to argue that compromise was necessary to win Catholics to the Union.[16] Demographic and electoral change also undercut arguments for majority rule and strengthened the case for power-sharing, as the UUP's advisers acknowledged after the Agreement was reached.[17]

However, exogenous factors were also crucial in producing agreement. The IRA's decision to declare a ceasefire, which paved the way for negotiations, was facilitated in a small way by the decision in the early 1990s of the ANC and, to a lesser extent, the PLO to abandon armed struggle (Guelke 1996: 145). These were organizations that republicans expressed solidarity with, and the precedents they created made it easier for republican leaders to sell constitutional politics to the grass roots. Much more importantly, republicans were induced to compromise by the intervention of the United States. Influenced by a large Irish-American

---

[15] I have started in 1982 because Sinn Féin did not contest elections before this. If I had contrasted the period before 1982 with the 1996–7 period, the growth in the nationalist vote would have been even more significant. I have also used similar types of elections in each period: in both cases I picked one European election, one Westminster election, one local government election, and one regional election. See Nicholas Whyte's elections webpage at http://explorers.whyte.com/ The gap between the share of the vote won by nationalists and Unionists continues to narrow. In the four elections that have taken place since the Agreement (again one of each type of election listed above), nationalists won an average of 42% and Unionists 50.2%.

[16] Addressing critics of the Agreement at the UUP's annual conference in 1999, David Trimble asked if their preferred alternatives had managed to stem Sinn Féin's growing vote, or if there was an alternative plan on how to achieve this: *Irish Times*, 14 October 1999.

[17] See n. 7.

lobby and by the end of the cold war, the US administration gave unprecedented attention to Northern Ireland after President Clinton took office in 1992. Clinton sent a special envoy to Northern Ireland during the early stages of the peace process; put several of his senior advisers to work on the Northern Ireland peace process, including the National Security Adviser, Anthony Lake; visited the province three times in five years; regularly invited the Northern Ireland political party leaders to Washington; persuaded former Senate majority leader George Mitchell to preside over the negotiations that led to the Agreement; and intervened personally in the political negotiations on several occasions. American pressure for an equitable settlement helped to boost the position of the Irish government in negotiations with the United Kingdom. It also increased the confidence of republicans about the utility of talks.[18] Clinton's decision in early 1994 to issue a visa to Sinn Féin leader Gerry Adams is credited with giving Adams the standing he needed to bring hardline republicans behind his peace strategy. Adams himself claimed that it brought forward the IRA ceasefire, which occurred in August 1994, by one year.[19]

While Clinton's role in coaxing republicans is often noted, he simultaneously managed to bring unionists along also. Like nationalists, they were given unprecedented access to the White House and the administration was careful to appear impartial throughout. UUP leader David Trimble acknowledged that reassurances from Clinton helped convince him to sign the Agreement.[20] However, the most important exogenous influence on unionists was the UK government. After a brief fling with integration in the late 1970s, London moved away from this option, though not consistently. After 1985, the government abandoned unalloyed direct rule from Westminster. Unionists had always considered this option, which was not radically different from their goal of an integrated United Kingdom, as preferable to the risks of a settlement with nationalists. In the Anglo-Irish Agreement of 1985, however, Britain gave the Republic of Ireland a limited role in policy-making in Northern

---

[18] A 1994 republican document on the peace strategy was explicit about the importance of the American role, noting that 'there is potentially a very powerful Irish-American lobby not in hock to any particular party in Britain or Ireland' and that 'Clinton is perhaps the first US President in decades to be influenced by such a lobby': cited in MacGinty (1997: 34).

[19] For a more extensive analysis of the exogenous factors that led to Northern Ireland's Good Friday Agreement, see O'Leary and McGarry (1995) and McGarry (2001).

[20] Personal communication from Professor Andrew Wilson, who interviewed Trimble on this matter.

Ireland, while offering to reduce this in the event of an agreement on devolution between nationalists and Unionists. The default to compromise, which had been direct rule from Westminster, shifted to London–Dublin cooperation in the governance of Northern Ireland, with the danger, from the Unionist perspective, that this would be consolidated and extended in the absence of agreement between the Northern Ireland parties. There was no immediate movement. At first, Unionists thought they could destroy the Agreement by protest, although it proved robust. There was also hope that the Agreement could be resisted or turned back while the Conservatives were in power in London, and particularly during the 1992–7 parliament when the Conservative government depended on Unionist support in the House of Commons.[21] The UUP began to negotiate seriously with nationalists only following Labour's landslide victory in 1997 and Tony Blair's signal that he was committed to achieving a settlement by May 1998.

The compromise arrived at on 10 April (Good Friday) 1998 involved republicans and Unionists converging on a package that had already been embraced (at least in its broad outline) by the British and Irish governments as well as the moderate nationalists of the SDLP. At the centre of the settlement was the devolution of substantial powers to Northern Ireland to be exercised by an executive and legislature constructed on consociational principles. The Agreement met all four of the criteria laid down by Arend Lijphart, the doyen of consociational theory (Lijphart 1977). First, there was to be *executive power-sharing*. The government was to be led by a dual premiership,[22] which was to be elected by a majority in the Assembly, including concurrent majorities of both nationalist and Unionist representatives—a formula that was designed to secure one post for each community. The executive was to be drawn proportionately from the parties in the Assembly, with executive seats allocated according to the d'Hondt procedure.[23] This resulted, albeit after a substantial delay, in the allocation of five ministerial positions to nationalists (three SDLP, two SF) and five to

---

[21] Indeed, the option of integration, which had been abandoned since 1979, was reconsidered during the Major years.

[22] Under the Agreement, the government is to be led by a first minister and a deputy first minister. Despite the inequality in status suggested by the titles, both ministers enjoy equal powers.

[23] The d'Hondt procedure, named after Belgian Viktor d'Hondt, is a proportional method for allocating offices to parties according to the number of seats they hold in the legislature. The method employs a simple series of divisors, 1, 2, 3, etc. The party with the largest number of seats gets its pick of the ministries available, and then its seat share is divided by

unionists (three UUP, two DUP). Second, *proportionality* norms prevailed throughout, in the electoral system, which was based on proportional representation–single transferable vote; in the rules for the formation of the executive and legislative committees; and in proposals for reform of the police service to make it 'representative' of the population. Third, *minority vetoes* were evident most clearly in rules for the passage of legislation. Important ('key') laws could only be passed by 'parallel consent', a majority of the Assembly plus a majority of both nationalist and unionist representatives, or by 'weighted majority', 60 per cent of the Assembly including at least 40 per cent of both nationalist and unionist representatives. Fourth, while *segmental autonomy* norms were least evident, given that Northern Ireland's two communities are interspersed, the Agreement left intact the existing separate but now equal Catholic, Protestant, and integrated schooling systems. It also provided increased governmental support for the Irish language (and for Ulster Scots).

The Agreement was ratified by 71 per cent of voters in a referendum in May of 1998, including a huge majority of nationalists and a narrow majority of unionists. The result appeared to vindicate Lijphart's claim that consociational democracy is the only kind of democracy that can gain widespread acceptance in the region.[24] However, there is a major caveat. Had the package put before the parties on 10 April 1998 contained *only* the consociational institutions outlined by Lijphart, there would have been no settlement.

two. The party with the next largest number of seats gets the next ministry, and so on. The table below shows how the d'Hondt procedure worked to allocate the ten ministries available in the Northern Ireland executive after the Assembly elections of June 1998. The table includes data on the four largest parties in the Assembly, the only parties large enough to qualify for ministries. As the table shows, the UUP and SDLP were entitled to three ministries each, while the DUP and Sinn Féin were entitled to two each. The UUP received the eighth ministry ahead of Sinn Féin because of a rule that in the event of a tie, the seat went to he party with the largest number of first-preference votes.

Divisors	UUP seats	Ministries	DUP seats	Ministries	SDLP seats	Ministries	SF seats	Ministries
1	27	1st	20	3rd	24	2nd	18	4th
2	13.5	5th	10	7th	12	6th	9	9th
3	9	8th	6.6		8	10th	6	

[24] Post-Agreement survey data reveal that 86% of Catholics and 62% of Protestants support power-sharing in principle: Evans and O'Leary (2000: table 14).

First, both moderate and radical Irish nationalists have always rejected any accord that does not address, in institutional form, their desire to be linked with their compatriots in the Republic of Ireland.[25] They signed the Agreement only because it also provided for a number of political institutions that joined both parts of Ireland. The most important of these was a North–South Ministerial Council (NSMC), a body to be comprised of the Republic's government and the Northern Ireland Executive. The NSMC was intended to function much like the Council of Ministers in the EU, with ministers having considerable discretion to reach decisions, but remaining ultimately accountable to their respective legislatures. It was to meet in plenary format twice a year, and in smaller groups to discuss specific sectors (say, agriculture or education) on a 'regular and frequent basis'. In addition, the Agreement provided for a number of cross-border or all-island 'implementation' bodies. There eventually turned out to be six in number, and they were given the task of cooperating over inland waterways, food safety, trade and business development, special EU programmes, the Irish and Ulster-Scots languages, and aquaculture and marine matters.[26]

Second, both communities had serious concerns that went beyond the sharing of power in Northern Ireland or all-island institutions, such as the questions of how to deal with paramilitary prisoners, paramilitary weapons, demilitarization, and policing reform. All of these issues were also covered in the Agreement, although in the case of the last three it was decided that the details of how they should be managed should be left to later.[27] The Agreement, then, delivered not only consociation but, as Brendan O'Leary has put it, 'consociation plus' (O'Leary 1999).[28]

---

[25] This need for extra-state institutions is a feature of the Northern Ireland conflict that Lijphart overlooks: in an otherwise incisive dissection of the Northern Ireland conflict in a 1975 article, in which he lists the obstacles to power-sharing, he ignores the fact that nationalists have always opposed any institutional arrangement restricted to Northern Ireland. See Lijphart (1975).

[26] The Agreement committed both parts of Ireland to a further six functional areas of cooperation—including some aspects of transport, agriculture, education, health, the environment, and tourism. It also provided for a British–Irish Intergovernmental Conference to promote bilateral cooperation between the Irish and British governments on all matters of mutual interest within their jurisdiction, and for a British–Irish Council, a forum to bring together not just the representatives of the British and Irish governments but also those within the various devolved institutions within the United Kingdom.

[27] For details on how the Agreement dealt with these issues, see O'Leary (1999).

[28] Brendan O'Leary has developed the term 'complex consociation' to describe Northern Ireland's Agreement. He correctly argues that Northern Ireland is not the only conflict zone that requires such complex attention. This is also the focus of a Carnegie-sponsored research programme at Cambridge University on 'complex power-sharing arrangements'. The programme is under the direction of Marc Weller.

DEFENDING NORTHERN IRELAND'S CONSOCIATIONAL INSTITUTIONS AGAINST THEIR (LIBERAL DEMOCRATIC) CRITICS

The Agreement's consociational institutions have been criticized by 'liberal democratic' intellectuals and politicians in the nationalist and unionist blocs. These positions, moreover, are representative of standard liberal democratic criticisms of consociationalism.[29]

Two broad and related objections are raised. The first is that, instead of resolving the conflict, consociational institutions promote sectarianism and entrench existing identities. Republican dissidents argue that they 'institutionalise' division (Rooney 1998: 21),[30] while Unionist rejectionists see them as 'divisive' (McCartney 2000). Small parties from outside the two ethno-national blocs criticize the Agreement as a 'pact' between the dominant sectarian political parties against the 'others' who are trying to transcend difference,[31] while a leftist intellectual claims that its consociational institutions 'solidify intra-communal networks' when the goal should be to promote 'inter-communal association' (Taylor 2001).

The second objection made is that the consociational 'grand coalition' executive at the heart of the Agreement is *inherently* unstable.[32] This is because it guarantees places not just to moderates from the opposing camps, but to all major parties. In Northern Ireland, this argument is associated with several Unionist commentators and politicians. Rather than a grand coalition, they recommend a voluntary coalition of moderates, by which they mean a coalition without Sinn Féin (Kennedy 2000; Roche 2000). Such an executive, it is claimed, would be more likely to

[29] See the speeches by Alliance Party representatives during the Northern Ireland Assembly debates of 2 and 5 November 2001, in the *Northern Ireland Assembly Official Report (Hansard)* at http://www.ni-assembly.gov.uk/hansard.htm

[30] Kevin Rooney (1998) worries that by establishing institutions that 'celebrate difference', the Agreement has 'put an end to the prospects for overcoming these divisions'.

[31] Spokespersons for Democratic Left and the Alliance Party have criticized the Agreement as, respectively, a pact 'between the two dominant sectarian and tribal blocs' and as emphasizing 'two communities' rather than all the people who share 'common values and principles'. See McLean (1998) and McGarry (1999).

[32] The Unionist intellectual and politician, Robert McCartney, ironically mimics anti-Agreement republicans in claiming that the power-sharing institutions are 'impermanent', 'dysfunctional', and 'unworkable', and that it is only a matter of time before this 'macabre parody of real democracy' is brought to a halt by its 'inherent defects and weaknesses' (McCartney 2000).

agree on a collective programme of government and more in keeping with British liberal democratic practices. A similar view has been argued by a prominent American political scientist, Donald Horowitz (Horowitz 2001).[33]

These criticisms are not convincing. The claim that the Agreement, or consociationalism in general, promotes sectarianism flows from a distorted view of sectarianism. There is a basic inability in the above accounts to distinguish between, on the one hand, policies that promote injustice and incite conflict between groups and, on the other hand, policies that are designed to promote equitable settlements and better inter-group relations.[34]

Northern Ireland's Agreement falls squarely into the latter category. It promotes mutual respect and peaceful coexistence between groups, principles that are the polar opposite of sectarianism and division. As liberal democratic critics on both sides acknowledge when questioning the Agreement's stability, it cannot work unless there is inter-community cooperation. Its central institutions have been deliberately crafted to rule out ethno-centric policies. This is clear in three crucial areas. First, the election of the first minister and deputy first minister requires 'parallel consent', support from a majority of the Assembly plus a majority of both nationalist and Unionist Assembly members. This is a formula that effectively creates a choice between no leadership and a bipartisan leadership.[35] Second, key legislation cannot be passed unless it is supported by a majority in the Assembly and by at least 40 per cent of both nationalists and unionists. Third, the favourite institutions of each community have been made interdependent. Nationalists cannot undermine the Northern Ireland Assembly in the hope that the NSMC will remain intact, and Unionists cannot destroy the NSMC and

---

[33] Opponents of the grand coalition model claim to have been vindicated by the problems that have beset the power-sharing institutions since 1998. For an example, see Wilford and Wilson (2001). Wilford and Wilson are good at describing the problems, but not at offering more viable alternatives.

[34] Some liberal democrats appear unable to appreciate the difference between ethnic cleansing and apartheid, on the one hand, and power-sharing between groups on the other. Thus, when Brendan O'Leary and I expressed our support for consociationalism in *Explaining Northern Ireland*, one critic wrote that these views could be seen as 'condoning . . . ethnic cleansing'. See Dixon (1996: 139). See also our reply (McGarry and O'Leary 1996). For a perspective that appears to equate the defence of the rights of multicultural minorities with the policies of the apartheid state in South Africa, see Piper (2000).

[35] The fact that 50% of either bloc can prevent the election of the first minister and deputy first minister, as happened on 2 November 2001, is a weakness in the Agreement's decision-making rules. I will address this below.

retain the Assembly. Both communities are required to work both institutions.[36]

The Agreement not only stresses equality ('parity of esteem') between nationalists and unionists, it also offers protection to individuals, including those who regard themselves as neither Unionist nor nationalist. Each minister is required under the Agreement to behave in a non-partisan way towards the citizens of Northern Ireland: 'to serve all the people of Northern Ireland equally, and to act in accordance with the general obligations on government to promote equality and prevent discrimination'. The Agreement provides for the entrenchment of the European Convention of Human Rights in Northern Ireland law, which will make it easier for citizens to bring cases against authorities; a new Northern Ireland Human Rights Commission; a Bill of Rights for Northern Ireland; and a new statutory Equality Commission. The British government is also committed to creating a statutory obligation on public authorities in Northern Ireland 'to promote equality of opportunity in relation to religion and political opinion; gender; race; disability; age; marital status; dependants; and sexual orientation'. Public bodies are to be required to draw up statutory schemes indicating how they will implement their obligations.

The criticism that the Agreement entrenches existing identities is directed at a requirement that members elected to the Assembly designate as 'unionists', 'nationalists', or 'others'.[37] Such designation was thought to be necessary to ensure that important measures had cross-community consent. The passage of important laws requires the support of a majority in the Assembly and the support of at least 40 per cent of both registered nationalist and Unionists. The election of the first and deputy first ministers requires, as mentioned above, concurrent nationalist and Unionist majorities. These rules, however, also privilege nationalists and Unionists over 'others'. Arguably, they create a minor incentive for voters to support nationalists or Unionists, or for elected members to register as nationalists or Unionists, as members from these groups will count more than 'others'. They also have the effect of pre-determining, in advance of election results, that nationalists and unionists are to be better protected than 'others'.

---

[36] For an analysis of the Agreement, see chapter 9 and the series of articles by McCrudden, McGarry, and O'Leary in the *Sunday Business Post* (1998).

[37] It is often argued that these provisions 'entrench sectarianism', but note that the Assembly's rules and procedures institutionalize political and not religious identities.

It should be noted, however, that privileging a particular group of members or predetermining beneficiaries in advance of elections is not recommended by consociationalists, even if, as in this case, the predetermined groups have constituted almost all of the electorate for the past century (Lijphart 1995). What consociationalists prefer is that minority vetoes be implemented in ways that do not specify which groups are to be protected. It would have been more in keeping with consociational principles if the Agreement had insisted on a simple weighted majority (say 60 per cent) for the passage of important legislation, large enough to protect the nationalist minority or a future Unionist minority.

In a number of other respects, the Agreement's institutions are more conducive to the emergence of new parties, including parties that are neither Unionist nor nationalist, than is the Westminster system. The Assembly uses an electoral system based on proportional representation–single transferable vote (PR–STV)—which allows parties to win seats with a much smaller threshold than is normally required under single-member plurality. As a result, voters in Assembly elections are less likely than are voters in Westminster elections to consider voting for a new party a waste of time. By allowing for the ranking of preferences, PR–STV also provides an opportunity for inter-communal or trans-communal voting on lower preferences. In this respect also, it is more conducive to extra-bloc voting than its Westminster counterpart. Under the Agreement, any party, not just the existing parties or nationalist or unionist parties, is entitled to seats in the executive if it meets the quota established by the d'Hondt system. Because the executive is constituted proportionately, a party is entitled to membership in government with a much smaller share of seats in the legislature than is normally required in the Westminster system. This means that new parties have a better chance to promote their visibility, influence public policy, and further demonstrate to their supporters that voting for them is a meaningful exercise.[38]

In addition, the Agreement establishes a Civic Forum alongside the elected Assembly. This institution is made up of representatives of organizations from outside conventional politics. It presents an opportunity for those who do not feel represented by conventional political

---

[38] There is an argument for making the executive even more inclusive by extending its size. A larger executive, constituted by the d'Hondt mechanism, would give a seat to the Alliance Party and might in future give seats to other small parties. Alternatively, the executive could be constituted by the Sainte-Lague mechanism, which is more advantageous for small parties than d'Hondt. For an explanation of the difference between d'Hondt and Sainte-Lague, see McGarry and O'Leary (1995: 373–5).

parties to have their voices heard, and has no counterpart elsewhere in the United Kingdom, including in the new devolved regimes in Scotland and Wales. If all these institutional features are considered together, it shows that while the Agreement recognizes nationalist and Unionist identities, it does not preclude the development of other identities.

More generally, while consociation is based on the accommodation of rival communities, an extended period of inter-group cooperation should reduce divisions rather than maintain or deepen them. If Northern Ireland's Agreement can be consolidated, there is a much greater likelihood of debate on socio-economic and related issues than existed in the political vacuum that preceded devolution. It is this understanding that explains why parties like Alliance and the Workers Party, while critical of some of the Agreement's allegedly sectarian features, nonetheless still strongly support it.

The second objection to a consociational package—that voluntary coalitions of moderates are more stable than consociational grand coalitions—appears intuitively plausible. However, the evidence is not strong, as Northern Ireland's experience illustrates. First, excluded radicals can also destabilize power-sharing institutions. In an ethnically divided society, excluded radicals are likely to accuse included moderates from their bloc of treachery, which may prevent the latter from making the compromises necessary for successful power-sharing. Excluded radicals can also engage in violence, creating a polarized atmosphere that squeezes moderates and makes compromise difficult. This, in fact, is what happened during Northern Ireland's only experiment with voluntary power-sharing between moderates: the Sunningdale experiment of 1973–4. The coalition was attacked by radicals on both sides. It found it difficult to reach substantive internal agreement amidst mounting violence, and collapsed after less than five months in office.[39] Other consociational coalitions have also failed because they have been undermined by radicals on the outside.

Second, inclusion in power-sharing coalitions can make radicals less extreme, because it provides them with opportunities to have their concerns addressed constitutionally, and gives them a stake in the system. Inclusion can strengthen the position of moderates within radical

---

[39] It does not follow from my argument that the inclusion of radicals in government in 1974 would have improved the stability of the power-sharing government. Indeed, in 1974 these radicals were virulently opposed to power-sharing and would have refused to take any positions offered to them. However, when radicals are prepared to participate in power-sharing institutions, and are not bent on their destruction, it makes sense to include them. I give reasons for this below.

factions, a possibility Horowitz and others appear to discount. The decision of the IRA to declare a ceasefire in 1994, and Sinn Féin's subsequent decision to participate in Northern Ireland's legislature and government, was closely related to the Adams/McGuinness argument that gains could be secured through politics. This position has been strengthened, and that of violent dissidents weakened, by Sinn Féin's rising electoral support and the rewards that this brings, including two positions in Northern Ireland's government.[40] Sinn Féin's moderates have also been strengthened by the prospect that, as long as Sinn Féin sticks to its constitutional tactics, it will supplant the SDLP as the largest nationalist party in the Northern Ireland Assembly and become a political force in the Irish Republic. The fruits of this became apparent in October 2001, when the IRA announced that it had begun decommissioning its weapons.[41] Sinn Féin's recent behaviour, ironically, and contrary to Horowitz's own views on the party, makes it a good example of Horowitz's best-known thesis: that parties will moderate if they have to in order to win office (Horowitz 1989).

The most serious threat to the stability of Northern Ireland's power-sharing agreement is not the inclusion of 'radical' parties in the executive. It is, rather, the voluntary exclusion (and semi-exclusion) of unionist rejectionists, whose aim is to replace the (bi-national) Agreement with something that is more Unionist. The way to respond to this problem is not to exclude Sinn Féin (or other parties with significant support) but to make it clear that rejectionism and boycott carries costs. Part of this will involve reapplying the logic that induced (some) unionists to accept the Agreement in the first place—that is, the government making it clear to unionist rejectionists that the collapse of the institutions will not result in something that is more palatable to them, such as integration or administrative devolution on the Welsh model, but in Anglo-Irish cooperation in the governance of Northern Ireland.

The Agreement's stability would also be reinforced if some of its rules were revised, under its provisions for review, so that participation is

---

[40] Anti-consociationalists tend to see Sinn Féin's rise as evidence of increasing extremism, and sometimes attribute it to the 'unworkable' nature of Northern Ireland's consociational institutions (see Wilford and Wilson 2001). However, it makes more sense, given Sinn Féin's clear movement from physical force republicanism to constitutional politics, to see its electoral growth as flowing from its increasing moderation. See Mitchell, O'Leary, and Evans (2001). Other factors are also responsible, such as the party's articulate and capable leadership, and the growing Catholic share of the population combined with the tendency of young Catholics to vote Sinn Féin.

[41] In the Irish Republic's general election of May 2002, which took place after this chapter was submitted, Sinn Féin increased its number of TDs from one to five.

made more rewarding than boycotts. One area of concern is the rule for electing the first and deputy first minister, concurrent majorities in the nationalist and unionist blocs. This rule was enacted to ensure that the top two positions commanded strong support among nationalists and unionists, but it also means that a small majority in either bloc can prevent the positions being filled and provoke major crises. The problems with the rule were laid bare on 2 November 2001 when the first and deputy first minister team of Trimble and Durkan failed to be elected, despite receiving support from over 70 per cent of the Assembly. The failure occurred because anti-Agreement rejectionists were able to command a narrow majority of one vote in the unionist bloc.

It would be better to retain the concurrent majority rule as a first resort as it is in the Agreement, but to implement a default rule, to be used if concurrent majorities are not available. The first and deputy first minister could be elected under the d'Hondt procedure, currently used for filling other ministerial portfolios, although there would have to be a provision to ensure that both positions could not be held by nationalists or unionists. The advantage of d'Hondt is that it would make it more difficult for any party to refuse to assume its position, as if it did the position would revert to another party. The use of d'Hondt for ministerial positions other than the first and deputy first minister helps to explain why the DUP, while rejecting the Agreement, has nonetheless felt compelled to take up its portfolios.[42]

Finally, the agreement will be further stabilized if there is continuing progress on the decommissioning of paramilitary weapons. Sinn Féin can

---

[42] At the time this article is being submitted (November 2001), a review of the Agreement's rules is about to begin. For an analysis of the rules, and our preferred changes, see McGarry and O'Leary (2001). There are alternatives to using d'Hondt as the default rule for electing the first and deputy first minister team. One is to use the Agreement's weighted majority rule: 60% of the Assembly plus at least 40% of both the nationalist and unionist blocs. Another is to rely on a *simple* weighted majority of 60%—a threshold that is high enough to ensure that support from both communities is required, but low enough to prevent vetoes by rejectionists. O'Leary and I prefer d'Hondt as a default rule because we believe these other defaults would result in moderate parties colluding to deprive Sinn Féin or the DUP of one of the top positions (should either come to command a majority in its bloc).

It would also be useful if the Northern Ireland Act was revised to remove the requirement that the resignation of one of the co-premiers automatically triggers the resignation of the other. This provision is not in the Agreement itself. The ability of one co-premier to bring the other down was used by both David Trimble and Seamus Mallon as a destabilizing bargaining chip during the 1999–2001 period. A resigning co-premier should be replaced in the first instance by someone from his or her party. If this is not an option, the vacant position should be filled by the d'Hondt procedure with the proviso that it could not be occupied by someone from the other co-premier's bloc.

make a constructive contribution here, and the British government can help by ensuring that there is progress on outstanding issues of concern to republicans, including demilitarization, police reform, and reform of the criminal justice system.

CONCLUSION

Northern Ireland's experience allows us to explore the feasibility and desirability of the various types of democracy described by van den Berghe. It is possible to see Northern Ireland's historical development as involving passage through all of his options or reasonably close relatives of them: from eighteenth-century Ireland's *Herrenvolk* system, to ethnic democracy in Northern Ireland between 1921 and 1972, to liberal and multicultural democracy between 1972 and 1999, to the current experiment in consociational democracy. As I have argued, this represents history as progress, although it is too early to say it means the end of history.

A study of Ireland shows that *Herrenvolk* and ethnic democracy can bring stability for lengthy periods, but they involve costs, not least in the protection of human rights and dignity, that proper democrats should be unwilling to pay. Moreover, the stability purchased often merely stores up grievances that eventually boil over into conflict. Northern Ireland's ethnic democracy became untenable as the Catholic minority grew in strength from the 1960s. It was also undermined by the spread of new international norms of civic equality, arising from the defeat of Nazi Germany, decolonization, and the American civil rights movement. The spread of these norms has not prevented the creation of new ethnic democracies in Central and Eastern Europe in the wake of the collapse of Communism, but these states are also coming under pressure to restrain themselves if they want to join prestigious Western institutions.

Northern Ireland's experience also indicates the limits of liberal or multicultural democracy as a method of conflict resolution in nationally divided or deeply divided societies. Neither offers the substantive institutional recognition and guarantees that minorities in such societies need. Another difficulty is that neither is determinate about the territory and state in which the liberal or multicultural democracy should exist. This is a problem in nationally divided societies, as minorities wonder why they should be included in someone else's liberal or multicultural democracy when they can have their own.

Consociational democracy, which offers minorities a variety of guarantees to protect their culture, identity, rights, and economic interests, is the only one of van den Berghe's variants that has been able to gain general acceptance in Northern Ireland. Moreover, it is possible to devise consociational institutions that do not favour predetermined groups but that reward whatever parties win democratic elections. Consociational institutions possess the potential to erode Northern Ireland's divisions, although this will take time. While consociational settlements may face problems of instability, there are usually ways to address these without abandoning consociationalism itself.

My chapter is not, however, uncritical of consociational theory. Had the document put before Northern Ireland's parties in April 1998 been limited to consociational institutions, there would have been no settlement. The Agreement is more complex than that described in the traditional consociational literature. It contains important inter-state institutions, while addressing a wide range of internal transitional matters, including policing reform, paramilitary prisoners, demilitarization, and the decommissioning of paramilitary weapons. The need for such complexity is not restricted to Northern Ireland. It is a fundamental requirement in other conflicts too, including those in Bosnia, Macedonia, Sri Lanka, the Basque Country, and elsewhere.

REFERENCES

Aughey, Arthur (1989). *Under Siege: Ulster Unionism and the Anglo-Irish Agreement*. Belfast: Blackstaff.

Bernier, Julie (2001). 'Nationalism in Transition: Nationalizing Impulses and International Counter-weights in Latvia and Estonia'. In M. Keating and J. McGarry (eds.), *Minority Nationalism and the Changing International Order*. Oxford: Oxford University Press, 342–62.

Brubaker, Rogers (1996). *Nationalism Reframed: Nationhood and the National Question in the New Europe*. Cambridge: Cambridge University Press.

—— (2001). 'The Return of Assimilation? Changing Perspectives on Immigration and its Sequels in France, Germany, and the United States'. *Ethnic and Racial Studies*, 24(4): 531–48.

Dixon, Paul (1996). 'The Politics of Antagonism: Explaining McGarry and O'Leary'. *Irish Political Studies*, 11: 130–41.

Doherty, P. (1996). 'The Numbers Game: The Demographic Context of Politics'. In Arthur Aughey and Duncan Morrow (eds.), *Northern Ireland Politics*. London: Longman, 199–209.

Evans, Geoffrey and Brendan O'Leary (2000). 'Northern Irish Voters and the British–Irish Agreement: Foundations of a Stable Consociational Settlement?' *Political Quarterly*, 71(1): 78–101.

Guelke, Adrian (1996). 'The Influence of the South African Transition on the Northern Ireland Peace Process'. *South African Journal of International Affairs*, 3(3): 132–48.

Horowitz, Donald (1989). 'Making Moderation Pay: The Comparative Politics of Ethnic Conflict Management'. In J. P. Montville (ed.), *Conflict and Peacemaking in Multiethnic Societies*. Lexington, MA: Heath, 451–75.

—— (2001). 'The Northern Ireland Agreement: Clear, Consociational and Risky'. In J. McGarry (ed.), *Northern Ireland and the Divided World*. Oxford: Oxford University Press, 89–108.

Irish News (2001). 'Burnside Pitches for Whole New Game'. 12 October.

Kennedy, Denis (2000). 'Evidence is Growing that Agreement did not Work'. *Irish Times*, 16 February.

Kymlicka, Will (1995). *Multicultural Citizenship*. Oxford: Oxford University Press.

—— (1998). *Finding Our Way: Rethinking Ethnocultural Relations in Canada*. Toronto: Oxford University Press.

Lijphart, Arend (1975). 'Review Article. The Northern Ireland Problem: Cases, Theories, and Solutions'. *British Journal of Political Science*, 5: 83–106.

—— (1977). *Democracy in Plural Societies*. New Haven: Yale University Press.

—— (1985). *Power-sharing in South Africa*. Berkeley: Institute of International Studies.

—— (1995). 'Self-determination Versus Pre-determination of Ethnic Minorities in power-sharing systems'. In W. Kymlicka (ed.), *The Rights of Minority Cultures*. Oxford: Oxford University Press, 275–87.

MacGinty, Roger (1997). 'American Influences on the Northern Ireland Peace Process'. *Journal of Conflict Studies*, 43: 31–50.

McCartney, Robert (2000). 'Devolution is a Sham'. *Observer*, 20 February.

McCrudden, Chris, John McGarry, and Brendan O'Leary (1998). 'Answering some Big Questions'. *Sunday Business Post*, 19 April.

——, ——, and —— (1998). 'Dance of the Ministries'. *Sunday Business Post*, 26 April.

——, ——, and —— (1998). 'All-Ireland Bodies at Work', *Sunday Business Post*, 3 May.

——, ——, and —— (1998). 'Equality and Social Justice', *Sunday Business Post*, 10 May.

——, ——, and —— (1998). 'The Heart of the Agreement: A Bi-national Future with Double Protection', *Sunday Business Post*, 17 May.

McGarry, John (1998). 'Political Settlements in Northern Ireland and South Africa'. *Political Studies*, 46(5): 853–970.

McGarry, John (2001). 'Globalization, European Integration and the Northern Ireland Conflict'. In M. Keating and J. McGarry (eds.), *Minority Nationalism and the Changing International Order*. Oxford: Oxford University Press, 295–324.

—— and Brendan O'Leary (1995). *Explaining Northern Ireland*. Oxford: Blackwell.

—— and —— (1996). 'Proving our Points on Northern Ireland'. *Irish Political Studies*, 11: 142–54.

—— and —— (1999). *Policing Northern Ireland: Proposals for a New Start*. Belfast: Blackstaff.

—— and —— (2001). 'Revising the Rules'. Unpublished paper.

McGarry, Philip (1999). 'Why the Agreement may Fail'. *Belfast Telegraph*, 16 September.

McGrath, Michael (2000). *The Catholic Church and Catholic Schools in Northern Ireland: The Price of Faith*. Dublin: Irish Academic Press.

McLean, Paddy-Joe (1998). 'Five Reasons why Socialists Should say Yes to the Deal'. *Irish News*, 9 May.

Mitchell, Paul, Brendan O'Leary, and Geoffrey Evans (2001). 'Northern Ireland: Flanking Extremists Bite the Moderates and Emerge in their Clothes'. *Parliamentary Affairs*, 54(4): 725–42.

O'Leary, Brendan (1990). 'Party Support in Northern Ireland, 1969–1989'. In John McGarry and Brendan O'Leary (eds.), *The Future of Northern Ireland*. Oxford: Oxford University Press, 342–57.

—— (1999). 'The Nature of the Agreement'. *Fordham Journal of International Law* 22(4): 1628–67.

—— *The British–Irish Agreement: The Second Peace by Ordeal* (provisional title). Oxford: Oxford University Press, (forthcoming).

—— and John McGarry (eds.) (1995). 'A State of Truce: Northern Ireland after Twenty-Five Years of War'. Special issue of *Ethnic and Racial Studies*, 18(4).

—— and —— (1996). *The Politics of Antagonism: Understanding Northern Ireland*. London: Athlone.

Piper, Laurence (2000). 'Whose Culture? Whose Rights? A Critique of Will Kymlicka's *Multicultural Citizenship*'. Paper presented at the IPSA XVIII World Congress, Quebec City, 1–5 August.

Roche, Patrick (2000). 'A Stormont without Policy'. *Belfast Telegraph*, 30 March.

Rooney, Kevin (1998). 'Institutionalising Division'. *Fortnight*, June: 21–22.

Smooha, Sammy (1977). 'The viability of ethnic democracy as a mode of conflict-management: comparing Israel and Northern Ireland'. In T. Endelman (ed.), *Comparing Jewish Societies*. Ann Arbor, MI: University of Michigan Press, 267–312.

—— (1990). 'Minority Status in an Ethnic Democracy: The Status of the Arab Minority in Israel'. *Ethnic and Racial Studies*, 13(3): 398–413.

—— (1999). 'The Model of Ethnic Democracy: Characterization, Cases and Comparisons'. Paper read in conference 'Multiculturalism and Democracy in Divided Societies', 17–18 March, Center of Multiculturalism and Educational Research, University of Haifa, Israel.

Taylor, Rupert (2001). 'Consociation or Social Transformation'. In J. McGarry (ed.), *Northern Ireland and the Divided World*. Oxford: Oxford University Press, 36–52.

van den Berghe, Pierre (2002). 'Multicultural democracy: can it work?' *Nations and Nationalism*, 8(4): 433–49.

Wilford, R. and R. Wilson (2001). 'A "bare Knuckle Ride": Northern Ireland'. In R. Hazell (ed.), *The State and the Nations: the First Year of Devolution in the United Kingdom*. Thorverton: Imprint Academic, 79–116.

Wilson Foster, John (ed.) (1995). *The Idea of the Union: Statements and Critiques in Support of the Union of Great Britain and Northern Ireland*. Vancouver: Belcouver.

12

The Protection of Human Rights under the Belfast Agreement

Brendan O'Leary

The full details of the Belfast Agreement are still being explored, interpreted, and reinterpreted.[1] With others, I believe that the Agreement, its legislative enactment in the (UK) Northern Ireland (1998) Act, and its protection in the British–Irish Agreement (1999) created consociational institutions within Northern Ireland and confederal institutions across these islands, and that it also sketched a model of 'double protection' of rights throughout Ireland compatible with a change in the sovereign stateholder in Northern Ireland.[2] It is not disputed by anyone that better human rights protection was a central promise of the Agreement. Here, I argue for some essential features of human rights protection under the Belfast Agreement. My focus is on the governmental, political, national, and ethnic dimensions of rights protection,

This chapter adapts and revises a lecture given to the SDLP's Conference on Human Rights in Belfast on 28 January 2001 and subsequently submitted to the Northern Ireland Human Rights Commission. It has benefited from criticism from Martin O'Brien of the Committee on the Administration of Justice, Law Professors Tom Hadden, Colin Harvey, Nicola Lacey, and Christopher McCrudden, and Professor John McGarry. Comments from my LSE colleague Dr Julia Black were very helpful. Shelley Deane and Simone Lewis were assiduous with research assistance. All named can be held responsible for improvements. Only Professor McGarry shares full responsibility for the views expressed.

[1] See e.g. 'Essays: Analysis of the Northern Ireland Peace Agreement', *Fordham International Law Journal*, April 1999; Joseph Ruane and Jennifer Todd, eds., *After the Good Friday Agreement: Analysing Political Change in Northern Ireland*, Dublin, University College Dublin Press, 1999; Brendan O'Leary, 'The Nature of the British–Irish Agreement', *New Left Review*, Jan.–Feb. 1999, pp. 66–96; Rick Wilford, ed., *Aspects of the Belfast Agreement*, Oxford, Oxford University Press, 2001; John McGarry, ed., *Northern Ireland in a Divided World*, Oxford, Oxford University Press, 2001.

[2] Brendan O'Leary, 'The Nature of the Agreement', *Fordham International Law Journal*, April 1999; 'The Nature of the British-Irish Agreement'; 'The Character of the 1998 Agreement: Results and Prospects', in Wilford, ed., *Aspects of the Belfast Agreement*, pp. 49–83; 'Comparative Political Science and the British–Irish Agreement', in McGarry, ed., *Northern Ireland in a Divided World*, pp. 53–88.

and my argument does not seek to juridify politics or absolutize rights in any naive fashion.[3]

Let me make it plain that what I suggest below claims to identify what minimally needs to be done and legally institutionalized to protect the *political* core of the Agreement. My argument should not, however, be interpreted as simply arguing for a minimal form of new rights protection—though it is logically compatible with such a view. With one caveat my argument is fully compatible with the ambitions of those who want Northern Ireland to have its own, novel, extensive, and comprehensive Bill of Rights,[4] one that elaborates many more forms of rights protection than are addressed here. It is, for instance, essential that the types of emergency regime that permitted abuses be rendered illegal under any new form of human rights protection. The fact that I do not focus, for example, on the rights of women, children, and the disabled, on criminal proceedings or on economic rights, to name but some topics, does not mean that I regard these rights as in any sense less important—though I am much less competent to discuss them. The caveat is this: I do not think that any new Bill of Rights, however progressive, should permit the judicial striking down of any feature of the Agreement; any changes should occur *within* the established institutions and terms of the Agreement.

CONSOCIATION

Internally the Belfast Agreement created a consociation. A consociation, especially a liberal consociation, is an association of communities based on recognition of the mutual equality of groups *and* individuals. Consociational, or complex cross-community power-sharing systems, when they work, help stabilize territories divided by national, ethnic, or religious antagonisms. They do so by recognizing differences, rather than by attempting to eliminate them through the imposition of one identity. 'Equality, proportionality, difference, and consensus' is their motto.

---

[3] For a salutary criticism of some naive views of rights protection, see Tom Hadden, 'The Pendulum Theory of Individual, Communal and Minority Rights', in S. Caney and P. Jones, eds., *Human Rights and Global Diversity*, London, Frank Cass, 2001, pp. 77–90.

[4] The Northern Ireland Human Rights Commission (NIHRC) has not yet taken either a minimalist or a maximalist position. Examples of distinctive and comprehensive suggestions include those of Amnesty International ('Northern Ireland: An Inclusive Bill of Rights for All', London, February 2001), the Committee on the Administration of Justice ('CAJ's Preliminary Submission to the Northern Ireland Human Rights Commission on a Bill of Rights for Northern Ireland', Belfast, March 2001) and Sinn Féin ('A Bill of Rights for the North of Ireland, Submission to the Human Rights Commission', Belfast, 27 February 2001).

The Belfast Agreement envisaged all four essential features of a regional consociation.[5] First, Northern Ireland has a *cross-community power-sharing executive*. This is built around two institutions: the dual premiership, elected by an absolute majority of members and a concurrent majority of registered nationalists and registered Unionists in the Assembly; and the inclusive Executive Committee, filled by the d'Hondt proportional allocation mechanism. Second, it is built on the application of *proportionality principles* throughout much of the political/public sector. This feature is manifestly evident in the Executive, built on the d'Hondt executive.[6] It is also true of the Assembly, elected by the single transferable vote (STV) electoral system, and with committee places partly allocated through the d'Hondt mechanism. Pending the full implementation of the Patten Report, to coin a phrase that echoes the old Irish Constitution, the police should, with political will from the UK government and others, eventually become representative of Northern Ireland society. Proportionality is also envisaged in both the public sector and the private sector; vigorous fair employment legislation and the strong emphasis on 'mainstreaming' equality contained in section 75 of the Northern Ireland Act (1998) suggest as much.[7] Third, the new system respects *community self-government and equality* in culture. Respect for religion, and parity of esteem and equality between different national identities, is part of the Agreement, and already partly built into public law. Existing provisions for full funding of different pre-tertiary education systems were (tacitly) respected by the Agreement, and new provisions create greater room for public use of, and education in, Irish and Ulster Scots as well as the English language. Finally, the new system respects a range of veto rights, or to put it more positively, a range of *consensual and participatory devices*. These exist explicitly in the cross-community consent procedures of the Assembly and the petition procedure.[8] They now exist for individuals in the form of the (UK) Human

[5] Arend Lijphart, *Democracy in Plural Societies: A Comparative Exploration*, New Haven, London, Yale University Press, 1977; see also O'Leary, 'The Nature of the British–Irish Agreement'.

[6] For a full discussion of the d'Hondt mechanism, see Brendan O'Leary, Bernard Grofman, and Jorgen Elklit, 'Divisor Methods to Facilitate and Sequence Portfolio-Allocation in a Multi-Party Cabinet Coalition: Evidence from Northern Ireland', paper presented at the European Public Choice Conference, Paris, 19 April 2001.

[7] See Christopher McCrudden, 'Equality and the Good Friday Agreement', in Ruane and Todd, eds., *After the Good Friday Agreement*, pp. 96–121; 'Mainstreaming Equality in the Governance of Northern Ireland', *Fordham International Law Journal*, April 1999; 'Equality', in C. Harvey, ed., *Human Rights, Equality and Democratic Renewal in Northern Ireland*, Oxford, Hart, 2001, pp. 75–112.

[8] For details, see O'Leary, 'The Nature of the British-Irish Agreement'.

Rights Act (1998); but they might also exist through the comprehensive or supplementary elements of a local Bill of Rights envisaged by the Agreement.

My claim, widely accepted, is that the Belfast Agreement was and is internally consociational, even if this terminology was not, and is not, explicitly used by its makers. It was a liberal consociational agreement because it did not mandate that individuals must have group identities— citizens are free to exit from, and to adopt other, recognized group identities, but are also free to insist that they belong to none (or 'others'). If that is accepted then the question that must arise is this: what system of human rights provision does this liberal consociation require?

The answer, most obviously, is a Bill of Rights and a legal system that is consistent with it. That, in turn, implies that each of the four elements of the consociational system must be appropriately protected where necessary. The Belfast Agreement envisaged that the new Northern Ireland Human Rights Commission (NIHRC) would consult and advise on the scope for defining, in Westminster legislation,

rights supplementary to those in the European Convention on Human Rights, drawing as appropriate on international instruments and experience . . . to reflect the principles of mutual respect for the identity and ethos of both communities and parity of esteem, and—taken together with the ECHR—to constitute a Bill of Rights for Northern Ireland.

On the preceding logic, the NIHRC needs to design supplements to the existing Bill of Rights that would protect, in an appropriate and mutually consistent manner, each of the four consociational elements, namely

- inclusive executive power-sharing
- proportionality principles
- community-self-government and equality
- mutual veto rights and consensual procedures.

INCLUSIVE POWER-SHARING AND PARTICIPATION IN GOVERNMENT

A legal determination by Justice Kerr in January 2001, currently being appealed, ruled that it was unlawful for the First Minister, David Trimble, to refuse to nominate two Sinn Féin ministers to carry out their official duties on the North–South Ministerial Council. The judge acted correctly in finding the First Minister's action unlawful, but in my view he did not ground his decision-making sufficiently in the text of the Agreement and its legislative enactment. Had he done so he would have paid much greater attention to the requirement that ministers engage in 'normal participation'. We shall have to wait to discover the reasoning that governs the decision at appeal. But, whatever the rights and wrongs of this case, the episode demonstrates that any Northern Ireland Bill of Rights should, so far as is possible, guarantee the power-sharing logic of the Agreement.

One way to realize this objective would be to have a general equal participation clause, for example,

The representatives of unionists, nationalists and others, are equal before and under the law, and have the right to equal protection and equal benefit of decision-making in the Northern Ireland Assembly and its Executive Committee, and related public bodies, and the right to expect partnership, equality and mutual respect as the basis of their relationships in government, and must use their best endeavours to ensure that these expectations are met. Nothing in this clause affects the validity of the decision-making rules agreed in the Belfast Agreement.[9]

This general equal participation clause, which draws upon some of the language of the Agreement, would need to be qualified by a commitment that the said representatives are committed to democratic politics. To be consistent with the Agreement, the clause may be worded:

No parties entitled to representation may be excluded from full participation in the workings of the Assembly and its Executive Committee and related public bodies save where their Ministers have been deemed by the Assembly, under the cross-community consent procedures, to be in breach of their obligations under that Agreement, including the obligations of the Pledge of Office.[10]

In this way cross-community power-sharing in the Executive and in the Assembly would be fairly and appropriately protected. Such logic would then extend to other public bodies such as the North–South

---

[9] This equal participation clause, especially 'equal benefit of decision-making', would need to be qualified by the positive or affirmative action equality clause (see below). This clause has been drafted without the benefit of legal advice, and may be improved through criticism. The last sentence is designed to prevent 'others' from challenging the con-stitutionality of the cross-community consent procedures. I propose it for consistency with the Agreement. It may indeed be necessary to have a general clause which would prohibit the (Northern Ireland) Bill of Rights, or any provision within it, from having the effect of 'striking down' any or all of the institutions of the Agreement, and their decision-making mechanisms.

[10] This clause has been drafted without the benefit of legal advice; I would be happy to have it improved through criticism.

Ministerial Council, the British–Irish Council, the Policing Board, and the District Policing Partnership Boards.

GENERAL EQUALITY AND PROPORTIONALITY

The second element of a consociational system is the presence of proportionality principles. In the circumstances of Northern Ireland this requires a general commitment to equality to be embedded in a local Bill of Rights—partly because the European Convention on Human Rights and Fundamental Freedoms is widely, and correctly, deemed deficient in its equality provisions. Any such general equality commitment would, of course, need to be complemented by a clause protecting positive or affirmative action undertaken to redress inequalities, and, possibly, by a clause requiring public authorities to achieve proportional representation of communities and individuals in public bodies.

A general equality clause might take the following form:

All persons are equal before and under the law and have the right to the equal protection and benefit of the law without direct or indirect discrimination, and, in particular, without direct or indirect discrimination based on religion, political opinion, race, national or ethnic origin, colour, sex, marital or family status, sexual orientation, age, or mental or physical ability.[11]

Any such general equality provision would require at least two further qualifying clauses to ensure its compatibility with consociational proportionality. One clause would be necessary to protect positive or affirmative action programmes that are designed to achieve proportionality—and which might therefore imply temporary inequalities in benefits under the law. It might be worded as follows:

The general equality right of all persons shall not preclude any law, public policy or activity, like the Fair Employment Act (1998), section 75 of the Northern Ireland Act (1998) or the Police (Northern Ireland) Act (2000), that has as its objective reducing inequalities or achieving the proportional representation in public or

---

[11] This clause has been drafted without the benefit of legal advice; I would be happy to have it improved through criticism. I draw on Brendan O'Leary, Tom Lyne, Jim Marshall, and Bob Rowthorn, *Northern Ireland: Sharing Authority*, London, Institute of Public Policy Research, 1993, pp. 39–41, influenced by the Canadian Charter of Rights and Freedoms (Ottawa, 1982), clause 15, and the thinking of Professor Christopher McCrudden at that time. Article 4.3 of the European Framework Convention on the Protection of National Minorities (1995) similarly states that measures intended to achieve full and effective equality do not constitute discrimination.

private bodies of disadvantaged groups or individuals, specifically those that have been disadvantaged or previously under-represented because of their religion, race, national or ethnic origin, political opinion, colour, sex, sexual orientation, age, mental or physical disability or past criminal conviction.[12]

An additional clause might place a positive onus on all public bodies to ensure as far as possible the proportional representation of specified groups. This, of course, would be much more controversial, but entirely consistent with the consociational logic of the Agreement. In particular, it would be sensible through supplementary rights provisions to extend the logic of section 75 of the Northern Ireland Act (1998) fully to bodies such as the police (scheduled for such attention pending the full implementation of the Patten Report) and the judicial system, including the Northern Irish judiciary. These considerations will be revisited.

Another clause is required on equality and proportionality. Citizens and parties have something to gain from reflecting on this proposal. This argument may be considered idiosyncratic, but needs to be put. Participation rights should include the right to a proportional representation electoral system for the Northern Ireland Assembly, local government elections, European Parliamentary elections, and elections to the Westminster Parliament, and for all other or future elected public bodies. The Sunningdale settlement was severely undermined in 1974 by the opposing logic of—and opposed mandates from—the use of the STV system in multi-member districts to elect the Assembly, and the 'winner-takes-all' system used in Westminster parliamentary elections. It is possible (indeed, on balance, likely) that the same scenario of competing electoral system logics and mandates may damage the Belfast Agreement, very shortly or subsequently.

Every voter and party in Northern Ireland—Unionist, loyalist, nationalist, republican, members of the women's coalition, and others (including Alliance)—would gain from having compatible, if not identical, proportional electoral systems for electing their representatives in different tiers of government. This idea would be consistent with the logic of the Agreement; and it would be inclusive. It would add a measure of stability to the current dispensation. Any such right would not, and should not, mandate communal representation or communal rolls.

---

[12] I would be happy to have this clause improved through criticism. I draw on O'Leary *et al.*, *Northern Ireland: Sharing Authority*, which was influenced by the Canadian Charter of Rights and Freedoms (Ottawa, 1982), clause 15, and the thinking of Christopher McCrudden at that time.

Citizens are and should be free to be 'others', and to elect 'others', that is, those who are neither registered nationalists nor registered Unionists in the current Assembly.

The Westminster Parliament might, of course, be unhappy with one part of the United Kingdom having a Bill of Rights mandating proportional representation electoral systems for all elections. The Prime Minister and the Secretary of State—who would introduce supplementary provisions for a Bill of Rights for Northern Ireland—will need to be persuaded of the merits of this idea. If Westminster and the Secretary of State were adamantly unhappy, then an exception for Westminster elections would have to be made to such a clause for it to have any prospect of success. But if the SDLP and the UUP jointly made such a case it would be difficult for any Westminster government to resist. Its predecessors did make exceptions for Northern Ireland when STV was introduced for European elections and for local elections; they might be persuaded to do so again.

An electoral participation-equality clause might be drawn up along the following lines:

Enfranchised citizens in Northern Ireland or those with enfranchised citizenship rights shall have the right to elect representatives to the Northern Ireland Assembly, the Westminster Parliament, the European Parliament, Local Government Districts and any other directly elected representative and public bodies as may be determined by law. In each case the electoral system shall be one of the systems of proportional representation, and in each case determined efforts made to ensure that as far as is feasible each person has a vote of equal value.[13]

The purpose of such a clause would be to assure current and possible future minorities that electoral system changes will not take place that would significantly disadvantage their prospects of representation. When newly independent Ireland considered how to protect the prospects of Irish Protestants, such thinking affected the constitutional design of the electoral provisions of the Irish Free State and of Bunreacht na hÉireann (Constitution of Ireland). It would be equally sensible to think like this for the new Northern Ireland—not least for ensuring 'double protection', a point that I will revisit. The sub-clause on making votes 'of equal value' is not just the historic demand of 'one person one vote' from the civil rights movement; it would act as a guide to legislators in designing electoral systems, including the design of constituency boundaries. A modern Bill of Rights should not specify any

---

[13] I would be happy to have this clause improved through criticism.

particular electoral system, but it is reasonable for it to specify a family of systems: there is an infinite supply of systems of proportional representation.

COMMUNITY SELF-GOVERNMENT AND EQUALITY

The third element of a consociation respects and institutionalizes groups' esteem, culture, and identity—granting each group self-government where appropriate, recognizing difference while protecting equality. How might this principle be embodied?

The NIHRC is doubly tasked with providing

- 'the formulation of a general obligation on government and public bodies fully to respect, on the basis of equality of treatment, the identity and ethos of both communities in Northern Ireland'; and
- 'a clear formulation of the rights not to be discriminated against and to equality of opportunity in both the public and private sectors'.

This paper has already partly addressed the NIHRC's second task. Professor McCrudden's counsel in his multiple publications is recommended on how to frame rights protections that outlaw unreasonable direct and indirect discrimination, and support equality of opportunity, in both the public and the private sectors.[14]

The first requirement raises different but related issues. The terms of reference of the Belfast Agreement specify two communities only. The text of that Agreement suggests that these communities should be construed as Irish nationalist and British Unionist. The way to give force to this part of the Agreement is to respect and legally recognize both of these political identifications equally, while recognizing that Northern Ireland is part of the United Kingdom as long as a majority so wish but may become part of Ireland if Irish people North and South so determine. That in turn suggests that the national insignia, symbols, emblems, anthems, and cultures of Great Britain and Ireland should be fully and equally respected in the government, administration, and public life of Northern Ireland. A preferable formula would be one which respected the use of both the British and the Irish communities' insignia, symbols, emblems, anthems, and cultures in public bodies, or of mutually agreed Northern Irish designated markers of identity, *or* none; but not just one. This will be, to put it mildly, a controversial suggestion in some quarters,

---

[14] For details see O'Leary, 'The Nature of the British-Irish Agreement'.

but it is consistent with the logic of the Agreement. It is, therefore, proposed that public authorities either fully and equally respect the national insignia, emblems, anthems, and symbols of the British and Irish states and nations, *or* that they deliberately choose insignia, emblems, anthems, and symbols that are disassociated from both states' or nations' traditions, *or* that they use such insignia, emblems, anthems, and symbols as are agreed by the Northern Ireland Assembly under cross-community consent procedures.

Professor Hadden (and other liberal unionists) believe there is an irreducible element of constitutional symbolism which attaches to state membership, and he believes therefore that the flying of two flags looks very much like a symbol of joint sovereignty, and that the argument for 'two flags or none' is partisan.[15] There is, I think, little merit in replying to this view by trying to distinguish state from national flags, as this would not be practical in Northern Ireland. The two flags in question reflect the respective national identifications, and are official state flags. Provided rights of symbolism in this domain are to be 'doubly protected'—so that they would be the same for Northern Ireland in a unified Ireland as they are in the United Kingdom—some may be satisfied. But that logic itself should persuade those unionists worried about the prospects of Irish unification of the merits of the 'two flags, neutrality, or none' approach. Professor Hadden and I have agreed on the need for an individual right to use which symbols may be preferred, subject to some sort of protection against stirring up communal divisions or hatred.

It would be constructive, and consistent with consociational logic and the Agreement, to have a general protection against coercive assimilation into another national identity built into Northern Ireland's Bill of Rights, for example,

Whether Northern Ireland remains in the UK or becomes part of a unified Ireland the sovereign government—including its actual and possible central, federal, federated, regional or devolved governments and public bodies—shall refrain from policies or practices aimed at the cultural assimilation of persons belonging to Irish or British national minorities against their will.[16]

Respecting national identity and ethos requires recognition and public support for the languages and schooling traditions of 'both communities', and of those who wish to belong to neither. In the judgement of

---

[15] Personal communication.

[16] I would be happy to see this clause improved through criticism. I draw upon the European Framework Convention on the Protection of National Minorities (1995), Article 5.

most, it also requires legal recognition and public support for the ethos and schooling of Catholics and Protestants, and of those who are neither.

It would be sensible to have national, religious, and linguistic identity and ethos appropriately and separately recognized, for example

- Every person shall have the right to choose freely to be described and treated as British or Irish or Northern Irish or other or not to be treated as such, and no disadvantage shall result from this choice, or from the exercise of the rights which are connected to that choice.[17]
- Every person shall have the right to choose freely to be described and treated as Catholic, Protestant, not religious, or other, including other types of Christian or of other religious conviction, or not to be treated as such, and no disadvantage shall result from this choice, or from the exercise of the rights which are connected to that choice.
- Every person shall have the right to choose freely to use the English, the Irish, and the Ulster-Scots languages in public and in private, and no disadvantage shall result from this choice, or from the exercise of the rights which are connected to that choice.[18]

Qualifications to these rights—to protect positive action for equality and to avoid unreasonable expenditures—would be necessary and appropriate, and can be suitably crafted.

Appropriate Northern-Ireland-wide public bodies, such as the universities, the police, local governments, public broadcasters, and public administrators, should under such clauses, or similar clauses, be required to give equal consideration and treatment to the Unionist, nationalist, and other identities; religious and non-religious convictions; and English, Irish, and Ulster-Scots language users. That might mean, for example, double or triple names for streets or public buildings. Many believe that these provisions must be there, but that they must not be over-done: for example, public authorities should be entitled to limit their commitments to demonstrated demand in the case of public services in Ulster Scots or Irish.

---

[17] This clause, and the one that follows, have been drafted without the benefit of legal advice: I would be happy to see them improved. I draw upon the European Framework Convention on the Protection of National Minorities (1995), Article 3. These clauses would need to be qualified by the positive or affirmative action clause above.

[18] This clause draws upon the European Framework Convention on the Protection of National Minorities (1995), Article 3. It would need to be qualified by the positive or affirmative action clause above, and may need to be qualified by considerations of demand and cost.

These suggestions draw to some extent from the European Framework Convention for the Protection of National Minorities (1995). It has several merits:

- It is designed to protect national minorities, not just ethnic, linguistic, or religious minorities—though it does not always follow through on this distinction, conceptually conflating national minorities with other kinds of minorities.
- The rights to be protected are to be exercised 'individually as well as in community with others' (Article 3.2).
- Its signatories agree to promote the conditions necessary for national minorities to 'maintain and develop their culture, and to preserve the essential elements of their identity, namely their religion, language, traditions and cultural heritage' (Article 5); and to take appropriate measures 'to protect persons who may be subject to threats or acts of discrimination, hostility or violence as a result of their ethnic, cultural, linguistic or religious identity' (Article 6.2).

Nevertheless, the Framework Convention has the following weaknesses:

- It supports rather weak public language rights for national minorities (Articles 9, 11, 14).
- It does not require its signatories to support the public funding of national minorities' 'own private educational and training establishments' (Article 13.2).
- It makes no mention of fair electoral/proportional electoral arrangements.
- Its linkages to 'strong equality' measures are not apparent (just like the document from which it stems, namely the European Convention on Human Rights and Fundamental Freedoms).

For these reasons, among others, Northern Ireland requires tailor-made provisions for the public funding of educational and training establishments; language rights; provisions on national cultures and markers; electoral participation rights; and stronger equality rights.

Any freedom of conscience clause in the Bill of Rights, or any reaffirmation that Northern Ireland endows no religion, needs to be qualified to permit the full public funding of teacher-training colleges for Catholic, Protestant, and integrated schools, and the full funding of all appropriate secondary and primary schools.

Suggested clauses are,

- Nothing in the Bill of Rights abrogates or derogates from any rights or privileges guaranteed under extant legislation in respect of denominational, separate, dissentient, or integrated schools.[19]
- Parents have the right to have full public funding, on a proportional basis, available to support schools for their children of a particular religion or ethos—Roman Catholic, Protestant (of whatever denomination), Jewish, integrated, Irish-medium, of another religious nature, and of a non-religious nature—provided that there is evidence of sufficient demand, and provided that such schools follow the minimal requirements of publicly examinable curricula in the United Kingdom, Ireland, or in member states of the European Union.

All schools, to protect their ethos and identity, will have to be entitled to determine their own teaching selection, which may require that they be exempt from certain equality of opportunity provisions. Schools may, as appropriate, be required to follow either the UK national curriculum or the Irish national curriculum, or indeed the European *baccalauréat*. But for any such clauses it will be reasonable to constrain rights provision and public policy, by considerations of demand, and equally reasonable to permit disproportionate expenditure on previously disadvantaged schools, to raise their standards of provision. (Whether primary or secondary education should be selective—and if so in what ways—is not something that should be elaborated in a Bill of Rights.)

Speaking from the experience of two types of schooling in Northern Ireland, I would suggest that the children of cultural Catholics, of cultural Protestants, and of parents who send them to integrated schools, should uniformly enjoy the right to refuse to attend religious services or religious education in their schools, provided they spend the relevant time in study. Professor Dickson and his colleagues on the Human Rights Commission, and the experts on the rights of children, should decide whether this stipulation warrants inclusion in the Bill of Rights.

Schools of all kinds, including Irish-medium schools, should be fully funded where there is appropriate demand, and where they follow the minimal expectations of at least one national curriculum. It would also be sensible to have a formal requirement that relevant public bodies be

---

[19] This clause is modelled on clause 29 of the Canadian Charter of Rights and Freedoms (Ottawa, 1982), which is designed to protect the full funding of religious schools and their rights to select their teachers.

competent to communicate with citizens in the Irish language, and Ulster Scots, with equivalent public funding for such persons as may be required where the numbers involved justify such expenditure.[20]

VETO RIGHTS OR CONSENSUAL PARTICIPATION RIGHTS

The last element of a consociational system is the existence of mutual veto rights, or consensual procedures. Most of the above proposals fit this description. The suggested rights protect difference as well as equality, and thereby give each major national and religious community—and the others—sufficient strength to maintain itself socially and politically. Other aspects of the Agreement, already in statutory form, have the same effects, notably the cross-community consent procedures in the Assembly. There are also opportunities for voice for the 'others' built into the Agreement—in the Civic Forum and through the British–Irish intergovernmental conference. You might reasonably ask: 'What more could possibly be sought of a consociational nature?'

To this, I would answer: 'At least two further provisions.' The first would need to be embedded in a British–Irish treaty, and in the Irish Constitution, as well as UK legislation:

Should the people of Northern Ireland in future determine, in accordance with section 1 of the Northern Ireland Act (1998), and in conjunction with the people of Ireland, to become part of a united Ireland then they will continue to enjoy all the rights and freedoms under this Bill of Rights—unless the representatives of the people of Northern Ireland determine otherwise through the parallel consent procedure in the Assembly.

Such a clause would have the virtue of reciprocity. The rights and freedoms agreed now, when the United Kingdom is the sovereign stateholder, would remain in being should a northern nationalist majority emerge and win sufficient support in a referendum for Irish unification.

The second provision that is needed is an obligation on all public office-holders in Northern Ireland—be they politicians, judges, police, or other officials—to pledge that they will conduct their work in a manner consistent with the Bill of Rights. That would not only suffuse public

---

[20] The predecessor of the NIHCR proposed provisions of this type. See the Standing Advisory Commission on Human Rights, *Religious and Political Discrimination and Equality of Opportunity in Northern Ireland: Second Report*, London, HMSO, 1990.

culture with rights consciousness, but also remedy one of the defective features of the Police (Northern Ireland) Act (2000), namely the failure to require all police, including serving officers, to commit to the codes of conduct required in the new order.

So far, this article has sketched how a model of human rights provisions might be constructed consistent with the consociational nature of the Agreement, and with what the negotiators for the most part agreed, explicitly or tacitly. The specific wordings and suggestions outlined may all be controversial, but they are consistent with the letter and spirit of the Agreement. Now, I must elaborate on how human rights provisions might be organized to be consistent with the Agreement's other core political features: its external confederal nature, and its model of double protection.

CONFEDERAL RIGHTS

The Agreement established two confederal relationships (across Ireland, and across Britain and Ireland) embedded in two institutions (the North–South Ministerial Council, and the British–Irish Council). Both are consistent with the European Framework Convention on the Protection of National Minorities, which endorses transfrontier cooperation (Article 18) and free and peaceful cross-border movement and political association (Article 17). But these Framework Convention clauses are of a negative, 'non-interfering' nature, rather than positive rights of participation; for example, 'The parties undertake not to interfere with the rights of persons belonging to national minorities to establish and maintain free and peaceful contacts across frontiers' (Article 17. 1). There would be no harm in incorporating these clauses, but they need supplementation.

A clause should be embedded in both UK and Irish legislation, and in Northern Ireland's Bill of Rights, which protects the rights of the current national minority and of a future possible national minority to meaningful cross-border institutional arrangements, for example,

- As long as Northern Ireland remains part of the United Kingdom the UK government will ensure the continuing functioning of the North–South Ministerial Council or of bodies with equivalent powers and functions to ensure transfrontier cooperation and free and peaceful functional cooperation between the nationalist minority and their co-nationals in Ireland.

- If the people of Northern Ireland in future determine, in accordance with section 1 of the Northern Ireland Act (1998), and in conjunction with the people of Ireland, to become part of a united Ireland then the Irish government will ensure the continuing functioning of the British–Irish Council, or of bodies with equivalent powers and functions (equivalent to those of the former North–South Ministerial Council), to ensure transfrontier cooperation and free and peaceful functional cooperation between the British Unionist minority and their co-nationals in the United Kingdom.[21]

DOUBLE PROTECTION

It should be clear that, to be consistent, I have been arguing that the SDLP and other northern nationalists should advocate that northern nationalists be entitled to the same rights now as British Unionists should enjoy in a united Ireland. This position is entirely consistent with the Agreement. It is 'double protection' because national communities would be protected as minorities and as majorities. Note that this argument does not require that Ireland should have exactly the same rights in place now, or shortly, as the United Kingdom should now, or shortly, protect in Northern Ireland. It merely requires that the provision and protection of such rights would be triggered by a change in sovereignty. A clause that would give this effect has already been proposed above. I stand by it.

A more immediately radical harmonizing strategy would also be consistent with this proposal and the Agreement. It would mandate the NIHRC and the Irish Human Rights Commission to develop an all-island Charter of Rights and Freedoms that would apply in the event of a change of sovereignty, but that could also be incorporated now in both jurisdictions. This too is consistent with the Agreement, but may face difficulties in winning sufficient support in both jurisdictions for immediate and wholesale incorporation. Alternatively, such a policy could be pursued incrementally, in stages. If so, it might be proposed that the provision and protection of rights and freedoms in the field of criminal justice and its regulation—and the severe delimitation of emergency regimes—should be the first priority for all-island harmonization. Other domains could be pursued serially. This would be consistent with the SDLP's and others' strategy of consensual cross-border cooperation.

---

[21] Dr Julia Black has pointed out that it would be useful to have a clause obliging both states to ensure cooperation in protecting confederal rights whether Northern Ireland is part of the United Kingdom or Ireland.

THE IMPLEMENTATION AND PROTECTION OF
A NEW BILL OF RIGHTS

The NIHRC was mandated by the Belfast Agreement to propose supplements to the European Convention. It is argued here that it should do
so, and design a Bill of Rights for Northern Ireland. Its exact statutory
form should be left to the experts; it might be attached to the Northern
Ireland Act (1998) which it would, of course, qualify; it might be
a separate Northern Ireland Human Rights Act, drawing on various
international instruments, including the European Convention, in Sche-
dules. (This would imply the repeal of the UK Human Rights Act for
Northern Ireland but would still meet the terms of reference of the
Agreement.) But rights provision and protection should be elaborated
that are consistent with the models of consociational, confederal, and
double protection institutions that make up the core of the political
institutional design of the Agreement. We may quibble over the details
and wording of clauses but not, I hope, about the broad vision.

But supposing that the NIHRC does produce such a draft Bill of
Rights which achieves these goals, and others, such as a novel, comprehensive Bill of Rights suited to the early twenty-first century, what
should happen then? The Commission should, I believe, argue that its
proposed Bill of Rights should be made part of an international treaty
between the UK and Irish governments, so that neither could unilaterally
repeal nor amend it without renouncing its treaty obligations. But, before
passage of the treaty through the UK Parliament and the Oireachtas, the
Northern Assembly should be free to propose amendments to the proposed Bill of Rights by the cross-community consent procedures—and
free to reject it outright by cross-community consent procedures. After
the treaty is signed the Assembly should also enjoy the right to propose
changes to the Bill of Rights, again by cross-community consent, and to
send such amendments to the UK Parliament and the Oireachtas for
incorporation in any modified treaty. Also, the UK and the Irish parliaments should declare that they would rule out any changes to the Bill of
Rights which had not previously been requested by the Northern
Assembly by cross-community consent—thereby adding domestic to
international entrenchment. In this way ownership of the Bill of Rights
would be Northern Irish but the two sovereign governments would
protect the Bill of Rights.

Therefore, it can be argued that a referendum on Northern Ireland's
Bill of Rights is not necessary—partly because the provision and

protection of rights are not entirely devolved functions, and partly because the Agreement, and the NIHRC and its mandate, have already received popular endorsement in the 1998 referendums. The promises in the Agreement of what would happen in the field of rights provision and protection were reasonably clear—certainly no more demanding than some of its other provisions. And, frankly, the danger of a referendum on the Bill of Rights becoming a second referendum on the Agreement itself is one that hopefully will be avoided: current or past opinion polls cannot assure us that this would not happen.

The Bill of Rights should also be incorporated within Northern Ireland differently from how the European Convention has been incorporated into the rest of the United Kingdom's political system. The UK government—or the Irish government in one possible future—should not be allowed to legislate 'notwithstanding these rights'. That, of course, would mean that the courts would obtain the right to strike down both UK legislation as regards Northern Ireland and the laws and executive actions of the Northern Assembly, its Executive, and the other institutions of the Agreement. Such a world would of course shine an intense spotlight on the judiciary—neglected in the negotiation of the Agreement, aside from the Criminal Justice Review.

The senior judiciary is not currently representative of Northern Ireland. To say so implies no criticism of the existing judiciary, either personally or in their decision-making. But if all other public bodies, including the police, are to be rendered consistent with the Agreement, why should the judiciary be exempted from reform, especially if they are inevitably to play a larger role in the determination of law and the qualification of public policy? Unless and until the composition of the judiciary is addressed, many will be reluctant to have the judiciary enjoy the power to strike down legislation or executive activity.

Here, too, it is hoped the NIHRC will be bold, and address the composition and appointment of the judiciary. On consociational and democratic logic, at least some of the following proposals should be considered:

1. The Lord Chancellor's Office—or its successor—should have section 75 of the Northern Ireland Act fully applied to it, as regards Northern Ireland's judiciary and judicial officials.
2. The composition of Northern Ireland's current supreme court (i.e. the High Court and the Court of Appeal) could be periodically proposed to the Northern Ireland Assembly by a joint resolution of the First and Deputy First Ministers. Their proposals would be

agreed or rejected by a judicial and human rights committee of the Northern Ireland Assembly—where the committee could reject a resolution only with cross-community consent procedures. If agreed, the court's composition would be sent to the UK cabinet and the Lord Chancellor for ratification. Each judge might be assured a ten-year term of office, rescinded only for an impeachable offence.

3. A new judicial appointments commission might operate to ensure a more representative and broad-ranging judiciary over time; its relations with the First and Deputy First Ministers, and the Assembly, would have to be the subject of further reflection.

4. Consideration might be given to a Constitutional Court charged with protecting the Belfast Agreement, the Bill of Rights, and the all-island Charter of Rights and Freedoms.

Of course, protection of the new Bill of Rights will require more than appropriate incorporation and appropriately designed, trained, and retrained judiciaries. It will require the NIHRC to have sufficient resources to educate the public in their rights, and sufficient resources to use its right to initiate legal cases, and act as a third party, and to have many of the powers of its new Irish counterparts. Indeed, a world in which both parts of Ireland compete in the expression and protection of human rights will provide excellent proof that our historic conflicts are being successfully managed—if not yet resolved.

13

The Politics of Policing Reform in Northern Ireland

John McGarry

Political scientists who specialize in ethnic conflict and its regulation normally do not focus on policing.[1] They are more interested in the design of formal political institutions, including legislatures, executives, and electoral systems, and on how power is distributed between tiers of governments. Policing is left to experts in law faculties and criminology institutes, who may abstract policing from its political context. Yet, satisfactory resolution of disputes over policing is often pivotal in the attainment of political settlements in divided territories. The Royal Ulster Constabulary (RUC) was at the core of the conflict in and over Northern Ireland and the negotiations that led to the Agreement of 1998. Policing proved less tractable in negotiation between the makers of the Agreement than even the management of paramilitary prisoners—who were released on licence.[2] Had policing details been included in the general negotiation formula that 'nothing is agreed until everything is agreed' then there would have been no settlement. The designs of key political institutions, including a power-sharing executive and assembly and two ministerial councils linking Northern Ireland with Ireland and Great Britain, were negotiated with relative ease. But policing was so divisive that the local parties and two governments could only agree to hand it

---

[1] The work of Ronald Weitzer is a significant exception. See Weitzer R. (1990). *Transforming Settler States: Communal Conflict and Internal Security in Northern Ireland and Zimbabwe*. Berkeley: University of California Press; and (1995) *Policing Under Fire: Ethnic Conflict and Police-Community Relations in Northern Ireland*. Albany: State University of New York Press. Also see J. Brewer, A. Guelke, I. Hume, E. Moxon-Browne, and R. Wilford (1988). *The Police, Public Order and the State: Policing in Great Britain, Northern Ireland, the Irish Republic, the USA, Israel, South Africa, and China*. New York: St. Martin's Press.

[2] A former Taoiseach, Dr FitzGerald, has described policing in Northern Ireland as having the status of Jerusalem in the Israeli–Palestinian peace process ('Watering Down of Patten Unnecessary'. *Irish Times*, 12 August 2000). We think it is closer to the controversies surrounding the right of return.

over to an independent commission on agreed terms of reference. The
Irish government and Irish nationalists insisted on an international commission, an idea unionists fiercely resisted, arguing for a UK-appointed
commission. An independent UK appointed commission was agreed, and
was eventually headed by Christopher Patten, a former Conservative
minister. The Irish government sought and received reassurances from
the UK government that the commission would be international in
composition, and that its recommendations for appointees would be
taken seriously, and that the terms of reference of the commission would
preclude negligible reform.[3]

   While the negotiators were able to agree the commission's terms of
reference, it turned out after the commission reported in September 1999
that this consensus was illusory. The UUP leader, David Trimble,
appears to have thought that the terms of reference would absolve the
existing RUC from requiring major changes. Five years after the Agreement, as this book goes to press (May 2003), consensus is still elusive,
though conceivable. Disputes over policing have contributed, directly
and indirectly, to the destabilization of the Agreement's formal political
institutions, which, as this book goes to press, have been suspended by
the British government for a fourth time. Here, we explain why reform
was necessary, critically analyse the reform process between 1998 and
2003, and make recommendations for settling policing.

WHY REFORM WAS SOUGHT: THE RUC AS AN INSTRUMENT OF CONTROL

The RUC was formed during the partition of Ireland and the formation
by Unionists of a regime of hegemonic control in the new Northern
Ireland (O'Leary and McGarry 1996: 107–52). It represented the coercive
arm of the Unionist regime, charged not simply with combating crime
but with policing and maintaining partition. From the outset, it was
armed and paramilitary in character, unlike police forces in Great Britain,
or even the new police in the Irish Free State, the Garda Síochána, which
had also been formed during a civil war. To assist it in its paramilitary
role, the RUC was equipped with some of the most draconian police
powers ever granted in a liberal democracy. These were contained in the
Civil Authorities (Special Powers) Act of 1922, renewed annually until
1928, then for five years until 1933, and then made permanent. The 'Special

---

[3] Information from Irish officials (April 1998).

Powers Act' was augmented by other legislation, notably the Public Order Act (1951) and the Flags and Emblems Act (1954). All three laws aimed at quelling nationalist dissent.

The RUC contravened the standard norm within the Anglo-Saxon constitutional tradition that the police exercise a semi-autonomous, or arm's length, relationship with political authorities. Its senior officers were subordinate in practice to the political direction of the Northern Ireland government. Between 1921 and 1972, this government was always comprised of the Ulster Unionist Party, and was always Protestant (with the exception of one cabinet minister appointed towards the end of what is now known as the Stormont era). It was heavily penetrated by members of the Orange Order. The RUC was closely supervised by the Ministry of Home Affairs, whose top officials, according to one source, were 'strident defenders of Protestant interests and whose policies with regard to law and order were sometimes purely political and biased against Catholics' (Weitzer 1995: 34). When Labour politicians first intervened in Northern Ireland in the late 1960s, they declared themselves 'stunned' by the lack of police independence from the ruling UUP (O'Leary and McGarry 1996: 127).

A committee established in 1922 to organize the new police recommended, somewhat surprisingly, that it be made representative of the population, but proportionality never materialized. Catholic representation in the ranks peaked at 21 per cent of the RUC in 1923, fell to 17 per cent by 1927, to 10 per cent by the outbreak of the present round of conflict in 1969, and to 8 per cent in 1999. Nationalists, as opposed to Catholics, did not apply to join the police. This was because of intimidation and fear of ostracism from their own community, but it was also because they opposed the regime the police defended. Institutional affiliations were developed between police units and Orange lodges. A significant proportion of the force (around one half in 1923, and one-third in 1951) were ex-members of the Ulster Special Constabulary, a Protestant and Unionist organization with roots in the Ulster Volunteer Force, the paramilitary organization established to prevent Home Rule. The Specials were back-up paramilitary auxiliaries.

The success of the control regime was measured by the fact that there was not much sustained and significant armed nationalist unrest between 1921 and 1972. Interactions between the RUC and Catholics were often civil in policing domains that were not directly ethnicized. But relations deteriorated seriously in the late 1960s, when the combination of partisan control, the use of emergency powers, and overwhelmingly Protestant personnel produced deep antagonisms. In October 1968, the

RUC ran amok in Derry/Londonderry in front of television cameras, attacking civil rights demonstrators who had refused to heed the Minister of Home Affairs' orders to remain within Catholic areas. In January 1969 marchers escorted by the police were ambushed at Burntollet Bridge by a loyalist mob, which included members of the police. In August of 1969, the RUC and Specials clashed with Catholic protestors, again in Derry/Londonderry, in an event that set the stage for Westminster's intervention in Northern Ireland.

PARTIAL REFORM 1969–98: THE LIMITS OF CIVIC INTEGRATION

British intervention produced a number of reforms aimed at introducing into Northern Ireland what was seen as the standard constitutional model of policing, that is, an impartial police primarily responsible for 'normal' crime prevention rather than paramilitary or political security duties. The reforms were aimed at demilitarizing, professionalizing, and depoliticizing the police. The RUC was disarmed—although it was soon rearmed, in early 1971, when the Provisional IRA became more organized. The Specials were disbanded. The Civil Authorities (Special Powers) Act was repealed. An independent Police Authority was created in 1970, to increase police accountability to the public, and to loosen the relationship between the RUC and the Unionist Ministry of Home Affairs. The removal of unionist partisan control was facilitated when the Stormont Parliament was prorogued in 1972 and the British government assumed direct responsibility for policing.

These liberal integrationist reforms were not without consequence. Some academic accounts noted a significant improvement in the quality of policing from the 1970s (Weitzer 1995; Brewer and Magee 1991). Party-political depoliticization was particularly successful: the UUP's control was ended, and the RUC's leadership increasingly prided itself on its belief that it was above politics. By the end of the 1980s, the Chief Constable, Jack Hermon, refused to meet with Unionist politicians lest it appear to compromise the police's neutrality. There were also advances in professionalism, the code-word for impartiality between the two communities. While the pre-1969 police had shown little enthusiasm for tackling loyalist protests, by the mid-1980s the RUC effectively handled loyalist protests against the Anglo-Irish Agreement. From the mid-1990s, it stood in the front line against loyalists demanding the right to march through Catholic areas in Portadown. One result was increasing animosity towards the police in working-class Protestant areas. Some members of the RUC were forced to leave their Protestant neighbourhoods, while the last police officer killed in the conflict died as a result of a blast-bomb thrown by loyalist protesters in Portadown during 1998.

These reforms and changed behavioural patterns, nevertheless, failed to win nationalist support for the police. There were two fundamental reasons for this: the association of the RUC in nationalist minds with unacceptable political arrangements, and the presence of violent conflict and its consequences. The reforms were based on the liberal premise that discriminatory policing was at the heart of the conflict and that impartial enforcement of law and order was the cure. This reasoning ignored the fact that nationalists were not simply seeking equal treatment before the law, like African Americans in the United States of America, but an entirely different political dispensation, preferably one with different borders. Even though reforms had broken the links between the RUC and the UUP, they did nothing to sever its association with the Union and the Crown, evident in its title. The reforms, moreover, occurred amidst a violent struggle between republican paramilitaries and the security forces. This had several damaging consequences for police–nationalist relations. Even if the law was applied impartially, nationalists were bound to take the brunt of police surveillance, but nationalists, by any criteria, were disproportionately searched, arrested, interned, and convicted. They were also disproportionately the victims of plastic bullets fired by both army and RUC, and of other forms of lethal force.

The violence of republican and loyalist paramilitaries prompted security-oriented responses that undermined many of the earlier reforms. While the B Specials were disbanded, the Ulster Defence Regiment (UDR), a locally recruited and deployed section of the British Army, was created. It was soon regarded as a straight substitution for the Specials. The RUC was massively expanded, and a full and part-time Reserve created. The Special Powers Act was repealed but replaced by the Emergency Provisions Act 1973 and the Prevention of Terrorism Act 1974. The RUC was rearmed and remilitarized within months of having been disarmed. From 1971 until 1976 it played a subordinate role to the Army, but then the British government introduced a policy of 'police primacy', handing the leading role in combating the IRA to the RUC. The UK government was anxious that its role should be regarded as impartial, and it may have been anxious to reduce losses of Army personnel. It would be more difficult for the IRA to depict the British as occupiers if it was confronted with a local police rather than a 'foreign' army. One obvious consequence of 'police primacy', or

'Ulsterization', was that the RUC's overt role as defender of the British state was highlighted.

Aggravating matters further, there were soon heard compelling allegations of a 'shoot to kill' policy practised by special units of the RUC against republican paramilitaries in the early 1980s. By the late 1980s files of IRA suspects were being given to loyalist paramilitaries. This confirmed suspicions of collusion between the police and loyalists (though Army intelligence units may have been more salient than the police in organized collusion). Nationalists were then antagonized anew by the RUC's role in forcing Orange parades through certain districts in the 1990s, particularly the Garvaghy road in Portadown in July 1996. In addition to these particular episodes, the RUC continued to rely on military-style snatch operations and a counter-insurgency style of policing.

The nationalist view that the RUC was a biased force, despite successive Chief Constables' protestations about professionalism and impartiality, was continually affirmed by its overwhelmingly Protestant composition, and by unsatisfactory accountability arrangements. The Catholic proportion of the RUC had declined to 8 per cent in the 1990s, despite a tripling of overall police numbers since the 1960s. Catholics that did join the RUC were not nationalists—if they were they kept their views muffled. The unelected and unrepresentative Police Authority, which had been given little authority, proved reluctant to use its limited powers. It was far more likely to defend the police, and even to praise it, than to be critical or indeed managerial. As a result, even moderate nationalists and trade union representatives refused to take their places.

Ulsterization, and police primacy, had other negative effects. The police became one of the two prime targets of the IRA, which did little for its attitude towards nationalists, or, indeed for relations between Unionists and nationalists. Violence made it difficult to introduce and entrench further reforms, because defenders of the status quo defined them as appeasement of republicans and argued that they would demoralize a force in the front line of maintaining law and order.

THE AGREEMENT AND THE ESTABLISHMENT OF THE INDEPENDENT COMMISSION

The peace process, the paramilitary ceasefires of 1994, and the Agreement of 1998 provided the possibility of a new beginning for policing. The Agreement envisaged a shared political order, a necessary condition for police that would have widespread legitimacy. But it was not a sufficient condition because many nationalists regarded the RUC as unacceptable. Nationalists confidently expected a settlement to include fundamental reforms to policing. Unionists, by contrast, had two views of the police, neither of which was conducive to agreement with nationalists. Partisan Unionists, strongly represented in the DUP and present in the UUP, saw the RUC as 'their' police. They opposed even the limited liberal reforms of the direct rule period, as they saw these as tying the police's hands. They had pushed for the police to be given carte blanche to fight the IRA. By contrast, liberal Unionists, present in the UUP and the Alliance Party, argued that the reforms of the previous quarter-century had been dramatically successful. They claimed that the RUC had become a fully impartial police service, 'the best police-force in Europe' according to one of their southern enthusiasts.[4] They believed they were fully professional, effective, and efficient; free from partisan political control; tough but fair; tough on terrorists, be they republican or loyalist; and tough on criminals. In short, most Unionists were more likely to find the RUC deserving of medals and hefty pay rises rather than requiring reforms. In four opinion polls conducted between 1995 and 1997, around 70 per cent of Unionists argued that the RUC should be able to carry on 'exactly as now' (McGarry and O'Leary 1999: table 1.4). Liberal Unionists often claimed that 'many Catholics' or (less often) 'many nationalists' found the RUC acceptable and that nationalist leaders exaggerated the degree of minority disgruntlement or were responsible for that disgruntlement (ibid.: 10–13). Liberal and partisan Unionists argued that the key reason for Catholic opposition to the RUC was terrorist intimidation: Catholics did not join the police because that would mean endangering their lives and those of their relations, and would leave them unable to return to their communities. Important secondary reasons included the failure of the Gaelic Athletic Association to allow RUC members to participate in their sports, and the opposition of Catholic clerical leaders and political parties to the RUC. These unionist arguments were shared by most of the police and by the unionist dominated Police Authority.[5] The latter used its resources to produce opinion surveys that demonstrated, to their satisfaction, that Catholics supported the RUC (for a critical analysis of this data see McGarry and O'Leary 1999: chapter 1).

---

[4] Ruth Dudley Edwards, *Sunday Independent*, 26 March 2000.

[5] In the RUC's *Fundamental Review of Policing*, released by it in summary form, 'intimidation' was the sole explanation offered for low numbers of Catholic police officers. RUC (1997). *A Fundamental Review of Policing: Summary and Key Findings*. Belfast: RUC, p. 9.

These arguments dominated Unionist discourse in the period preceding the 1998 Agreement (ibid.: 9–10), but they were not convincing. Catholics refused to join the RUC throughout its history, even when there was little or no republican violence, or any effective republican organizations that could have successfully intimidated them. The arguments are also contradicted by polling data, including the Police Authority's and other data collected by non-partisan academic sources. The latter indicated a widespread view among Catholics that the RUC was biased towards Protestants, and a conviction that the force should either be reformed or replaced/disbanded. One survey conducted for the Fortnight Educational Trust in December 1997 showed that 70 per cent of Catholics thought that 'complete reform' of the RUC was 'essential' to a lasting settlement, while a further 11 per cent thought it 'desirable'.[6] Another, conducted in May 1998, found that 60 per cent of Catholics were in favour of 'radical reform' of the RUC (*Belfast Telegraph*, 18 May 1998). The two parties that, between them, won all of the nationalist vote and most of the Catholic vote were strongly opposed to the RUC. For Sinn Féin, the RUC was a sectarian police force, an instrument of Unionist domination, a participant in the conflict rather than a neutral law enforcement agency. Republicans argued that the RUC's members had been linked to the repression, torture, and killing of nationalists, and highlighted the fact that RUC personnel had colluded with loyalist paramilitaries. In their view, the police could not be reformed, only disbanded. As one republican activist put it: 'A reformed RUC would amount to nothing more than painting a smile on the face of a corpse'.[7] The moderate nationalists of the SDLP were less forceful, and more inclined to acknowledge the enormous human price paid by police officers and their families during the conflict (over 300 police officers had died, and many had suffered long-term injuries or traumas). However, they too argued that the RUC was unacceptable. The SDLP did not demand that the RUC be disbanded, but insisted that policing could not be resolved by 'minor adjustments to the status quo'.[8]

It was hardly surprising, given these polarized positions, that the makers of the Agreement did not provide a detailed blueprint for policing reform. But rather than let deep disagreement prevent a settlement

---

[6] Catholics, in fact, were more likely to consider policing reform to be essential to a settlement than the disbanding of all paramilitary groups. Colin Irwin (1998). *The Search for a Settlement: The People's Choice*. Belfast: Fortnight Educational Trust, p. 3.

[7] Anthony McIntyre (1994). Cited in *Policing in a New Society*. Belfast: Centre for Research and Documentation, p. 40.

[8] SDLP (1995). *Policing in Northern Ireland*. Belfast: SDLP, p. 8.

of non-policing issues, the parties decided to hand the issue over to an independent commission, which was required to report no later than the summer of 1999. The negotiators were, however, able to agree on the Commission's terms of reference. The parties accepted the need for a 'new beginning to policing in Northern Ireland with a police service capable of attracting and sustaining support from the community as a whole'. The Commission was mandated to adhere to the following seven principles in making its recommendations. The police should be:

- representative
- impartial
- accountable
- decentralized
- infused with a human rights culture
- efficient and effective
- free from partisan political control.

By implication there was also an eighth principle, namely, that the new arrangements should be compatible with the Agreement. These proposals were part of the package ratified by referendum in May 1998. Agreement on general principles, however, did not reflect agreement on substantive details. While nationalists (and anti-Agreement Unionists) argued that the terms of reference presaged substantive changes, pro-Agreement Unionists appeared to believe that the RUC already satisfied these eight principles.

The Patten Report

The Commission was established in June 1998 under the chairmanship of Christopher Patten. He was considered suitable not only because of his obvious competence and experience as a former Northern Ireland minister, but also because he was a Catholic on the one hand, and a former senior member of the Conservative Party on the other.[9] His Commissioners included experts from Canada and the United States, as well as the United Kingdom. The Commission held a series of public meetings throughout Northern Ireland, invited written submissions, conducted a survey, researched through focus groups, met with police services and experts in other countries, and delivered its report in September 1999.[10]

---

[9] The notion that an English Catholic would be more acceptable to Irish nationalists than an English Protestant flows from the typical and mistaken view that the conflict is religious in basis.

[10] *A New Beginning: The Report of the Independent Commission on Policing for Northern Ireland*, Belfast and London, September 1999. The Commission held meetings in every district

Below we summarize how its recommendations reflected the terms of reference laid out in the Agreement.

Representative.   To build a representative police service, the Commission called on nationalist leaders to encourage Catholics to join a reformed police service, and on the GAA to rescind its Rule 21, which prohibited members of the police from joining the Association (it obliged). It recommended more imaginative marketing campaigns in nationalist areas, and lay involvement in recruitment panels. Most significantly, the commissioners proposed recruiting Catholics and non-Catholics in a 50 : 50 ratio from the pool of qualified candidates for the next ten years. This matched the population ratios in the younger age-cohorts. On their model—given early and scheduled retirements of serving officers—this policy would ensure that 30 per cent of the service would be of Catholic origin by year ten, and between 17 and 19 per cent within four years (above the critical mass of 15 per cent that they claimed was necessary to change the police's character). This was a significantly slower pace of change than we advocated. It meant that after ten years, Catholics, who represent well over 40 per cent of Northern Ireland's population, would still be underrepresented in the police. The commissioners justified their proposals by stressing that they wished to avoid a service that would have non-Catholic 'Chiefs' and Catholic 'Indians'. The commissioners argued that Catholic recruits should be broadly representative of the Catholic community, that is, that they should be nationalist or republican in political opinion. However, the recommended affirmative action measures applied to Catholics rather than nationalists, although the Commission did propose that the Part-Time Reserve be expanded from 1,300 to 2,500 officers, and that the additional recruits be drawn from areas where there were currently few recruits (i.e. nationalist areas). This territorial criterion, disappointingly, was not extended to the recruitment of the regular police.[11] The commissioners were aware that their

council area. It received 2,500 written submissions, 10,000 people attended their meetings, and 1,000 spoke at them.

[11] In arguing for a territorial criterion to be applied when recruiting to the Part-Time Reserve, the Commission pointed out that '[w]hole areas of Northern Ireland which are predominantly Catholic/Nationalists are underrepresented in the Part Time Reserve' (14.12). However, this argument applied equally to the regular police. The Commission appears to have recommended a territorial criterion for the Part-Time Reserve because these officers were likely to be asked to serve locally, and would, therefore, facilitate community policing. However, the use of a politically sensitive territorial criterion for recruitment of regular officers would have better ensured a representative police service. This is because Catholics who live in predominantly nationalist/republican areas are more likely to be nationalists/republicans than Catholics who live outside these areas.

proposed affirmative action measures applied only to entry-level recruitment, and that this would leave the senior ranks of the police dominated by Protestants for years to come. They, therefore, recommended a proactive strategy to recruit Northern Ireland Catholics serving in other police services, including the Garda Síochána (15.17). They also proposed to establish a programme of long-term personnel exchanges, between Northern Ireland's police and the Garda, in specialist fields, such as drugs and training (18.10). The principle of representativeness was extended to the civilian staff. The Commission called on the Northern Ireland Civil Service to facilitate representativeness by developing a policy of internal transfers of such staff, and proposed that people seeking civilian posts be recruited in the same way as officers.[12]

Impartial. The Commission understood that recruiting Catholics required more than simply making positions available or stopping republican intimidation. It stressed that the 'main' problem facing policing was the political divide between Unionists and nationalists and the fact that the latter associated the 'police with unionism and the British state'.[13] A widely accepted police, therefore, would have to be nationally impartial. It backed a principle of neutral impartiality, proposing that the name and symbols of the police be freed from 'any association with either the British or Irish states'—although conceivably it could have opted for a principle of bi-national impartiality in which the police used the symbols of both states. It was recommended that the name of the police, the Royal Ulster Constabulary, be changed to the neutral 'Northern Ireland Police Service'. The old name was triply inappropriate: Royal identified it with the Crown, the United Kingdom's legal equivalent of the idea of the state; Ulster signified a partisan understanding of Northern Ireland; and a Constabulary conveyed a nineteenth-century purveyor of order rather than a modern service. The proposed new name was neutral because nationalists in the 1998 referendum, North and South, had overwhelmingly accepted the current status of Northern Ireland as part of the United Kingdom, as long as a majority so determined. The badge and symbols of the police were also to be neutral,

---

[12] While the Commission recommended that civilian recruits to the police service 'should' be recruited in the same way and by the same process as police officers (14.16), it did not italicize this in the way it did its other recommendations. It also was not included in the Report's 'Summary of Recommendations'.

[13] Patten explicitly rejected the Unionist argument that because the police were funded and provided by the British state, its name and symbols should reflect that provenance (17.4 and 17.5). This did not stop Unionists from repeating this argument after the report was published.

and the Union flag was no longer to be flown from police buildings. Although it did not state so explicitly, its support for a 'neutral working environment', which was in any case required under existing fair employment legislation, also suggested an end to the practice of displaying the Queen's portrait inside police stations. Respect for both communities in Northern Ireland was, according to the report, to form an important part of police training, and new and existing officers were to be required to take an oath that accorded 'equal respect to all individuals and to their traditions and beliefs'. These recommendations, in addition to satisfying the Commission's terms of reference, also met the Agreement's explicit commitment to establishing 'parity of esteem' between the national traditions, and the United Kingdom's solemn commitment to 'rigorous impartiality' in its administration.

Accountable. The Commission responded to the view that the RUC was unaccountable for its actions by proposing a number of reforms. Democratic accountability was to be strengthened in two senses: the 'subordinate' (or obedient) sense and the 'explanatory and cooperative' sense. It recommended the establishment of a nineteen member 'Policing Board' to replace the discredited Police Authority, which was unelected and which, despite its name, had no authority. The Policing Board was to bring together ten elected politicians—allocated according to the d'Hondt rule among the parties that comprised the new Executive—with nine appointed members, representative of a range of sectors of civil society, 'business, trade unions, voluntary organisations, community groups and the legal profession'. The unelected members (under a devolved government) were to be appointed by the First and Deputy First Ministers. The Board was therefore envisaged as broadly representative, in both its elected and unelected members, and at one remove from direct executive power—so that it was less likely to become the mere instrument of ministers. It was to have 'robust' powers, including the power to set 'objectives and priorities' over the short to medium term (three to five years); to monitor police performance; to adopt an 'Annual Policing Plan'; and to negotiate the annual policing budget with the Northern Ireland Office. Importantly, it was to be able to require the Chief Constable to report on, and to hold an inquiry into, 'any' aspect of the police service or police conduct, including operational decisions. This was an attempt to pre-empt an attempt by the Chief Constable to block reports and inquiries on the traditional grounds that this infringed his 'operational independence'. Patten specified that the grounds on which a Chief Constable could appeal a request from the Policing Board for a report, or a decision by the Board to initiate and inquiry, should be 'strictly limited to issues such as those involving national security, sensitive personnel matters and cases before the courts' (6.22).

The Report, contrary to what scaremongers and the right-wing press suggested, was not intended to destroy the operational responsibility of the police, or indeed to party-politicize its management. It was intended to let police managers manage, but to hold them, post-factum, to account for their implementation of the Policing Board's general policing policy, and to enhance the audit and investigative capacities of the Board in holding the police to account for their implementation, financial and otherwise, of the Board's policy. In Patten's vision the police should become fully part of a self-governing democratic society, transparently accountable to its representatives, rather than a potentially self-serving, unaccountable group of budget maximizers, mission-committed to their own conceptions of good policing. The new service would have 'operational responsibility', but would have to justify its uses of its managerial discretion.

Local democratic accountability was to be provided by District Policing Partnership Boards (DPPBs), based on existing District Councils. Like the Policing Board, they were to have a majority of elected members reflecting the balance of local councils, with a minority of unelected members. Each DPPB was to be representative of the district's population. It was proposed that they hold monthly meetings at which local police commanders would present reports and answer questions. While they were not to be given the power to issue plans, insist on reports, and hold inquiries, it was recommended that their views be taken 'fully into account' by the police and the Policing Board. It was proposed that Belfast's DPPB have four sub-groups covering, respectively, North, South, West, and East Belfast.

To provide accountability in the 'explanatory and cooperative' sense, the Commission insisted on 'transparency' in police operations. It was recommended that the Policing Board and the DPPBs meet in public once a month, the former to receive a report from the Chief Constable and the latter to allow the public to address questions to the Board and the local police. This was to prevent a recurrence of the practice established by the Police Authority and its local counterparts (the Community–Police Liaison Committees), supposedly public representatives, of meeting in secret. The Commission recommended that policing documents, including codes of practice, be made publicly available, with the presumption that information should be withheld only when it is in the public interest—not the police interest.

Steps were also proposed to improve the *legal* accountability of the police. Much of the Commission's work in this respect involved endorsing the earlier recommendation of one of its members, Maurice Hayes. He had recommended that an adequately resourced Police Ombudsman be created with the power to react to complaints against the police and to initiate inquiries into police actions, even where no complaint had been received. Its need to re-endorse Hayes's proposals implied that the Police (Northern Ireland) Act 1998 (which the government had strangely passed while Patten's Commission was deliberating), which had established the office of Police Ombudsman, had not addressed the task adequately. In addition, Patten recommended a Commissioner to oversee covert law enforcement, who would ensure that this was practiced with due regard for the law and only when conventional policing techniques could not reasonably substitute.

Decentralized. The Patten Report expressed a desire to roll back the centralization of policing that had occurred both in the United Kingdom and Ireland during the last two centuries: 'An important theme of this report is that policing should be decentralised, and that there should be constant dialogue at local levels between the police and the community' (6.25). Patten's subject was 'policing Northern Ireland' not 'the police in Northern Ireland'. Policing, it was argued, should be organized by a plurality of agents and organizations, and not be exclusively the responsibility of a monolithic, centralized line-hierarchy, detached from the rest of society. Ultimate responsibility for the security of persons and property in society should remain with citizens and their representatives.[14] The report recommended that responsibility for policing be devolved to the Northern Ireland executive 'as soon as possible' (6.15). The desire to decentralize, to make the police accountable 'at all levels', also informed the proposal to establish DPPBs. The Report argued that a model of policing based on a partnership with local communities 'should be the core function of the police service and the core function of every police station'. Every neighbourhood, it was proposed, should have a dedicated policing team with the lead responsibility for policing this area. The members of the neighbourhood team should serve in that capacity for at least three years and their uniforms should bear their names and the name of their neighbourhood. It was also proposed that district

[14] 'We recommend that the Policing Board should coordinate its work closely with other agencies whose work touches on public safety, including education, environment, economic development, housing and health authorities, as well as social services, youth services and the probation service, and with appropriate non-governmental organizations' (6.10).

councils be allowed to contribute 'up to the equivalent of a rate of 3p in the pound' to meet the district's distinct policing needs. This was to be used to 'purchase additional services from the police or statutory agencies, or from the private sector'.

The decentralization of political accountability was to be matched by the internal decentralization of the police. It was proposed that its organizational structure be changed to match local district council areas.[15] Local commanders were to be given the autonomy to deliver sensitive policing according to local needs. The idea was to deliver policing geared toward crime prevention in conjunction with local agencies rather than reactive policing. The Commission shied away, however, from creating a federated police structure, involving *separate* local forces. This would have facilitated even stronger links between local communities and their police, and might have helped to attract nationalist recruits. It might have made the success of the new policing arrangements less dependent on the success of devolution. Federated, or 'two-tier', police services are the norm in Canada, the United States, and many parts of Europe. The objections to this idea—fears of 'balkanisation' and concerns that there would be a hierarchical relationship between the two tiers—were the least convincing part of the report.

Infused with a Human Rights Culture. The Commission recommended that the Policing Board and Ombudsman be given powers to monitor and investigate the police in relation to its respect for human rights. 'Bad apples', that is, officers who had committed human rights abuses in the past, should be 'dealt with' (5.18). Rafts of measures to prevent future abuses were included. New and serving officers should be required to take a new oath/declaration expressing commitments to upholding human rights. Officers should have to 'register their interests and associations', so that, presumably, it would be a bad career move to join sectarian organizations such as the Orange Order—the Commission stopped short of banning such membership outright. It recommended a 'programme of action' to focus policing on human-rights, and that respect for human rights be made an important part of officers' appraisals. Knowledge of human rights was to be built into training and retraining (which was to be provided by non-police personnel) and their codes of practice. The astonishing absence of legal personnel within the RUC with expertise in human rights was singled out for remedy. The incorporation of the European Convention into UK public law, and

---

[15] Belfast was to be subdivided into four districts, to coincide with the four sub-groups of the Belfast DPPB.

Northern Ireland's own forthcoming special provisions to strengthen the rights of national, religious, and cultural minorities, were welcomed as likely to ensure that policing and legal arrangements would perform at higher standards than in the past. But other international norms were also held out as benchmarks: 'compliance... with international human rights standards and norms are... an important safeguard both to the public and to police officers carrying out their duties' (5.17).

Patten proposed steps for normalizing and demilitarizing the police to address human rights objectives. It was recommended that the military appearance of police stations and patrol vehicles be transformed, that moves be made towards an unarmed police—although progress in these areas was to be linked to security considerations. A number of 'Holding Centres', used to detain and question people under emergency legislation, and associated by nationalists with the abuse of prisoners, were to be closed forthwith. The Commission recommended that Special Branch, which had been widely criticized as an independent 'force within a force', guilty of human rights infractions, and tainted by allegations of collusion, be reduced in size, with officers attached to it for relatively short periods. It was to be amalgamated with criminal investigations. The establishment of a commissioner for covert law enforcement was also consistent with the promotion of a human rights culture.

The report, however, was weak on emergency laws. Instead of repeal, it proposed that when the security situation had improved to a point where special measures were no longer necessary, Northern Ireland and the rest of the United Kingdom should be subject to a single uniform piece of emergency legislation. The Commission failed to recommend the banning of plastic bullets (plastic baton rounds) in spite of their lethal and counter-productive effects, instead proposing safeguards on their use and research into alternatives. While it recommended that officers who had committed past abuses should be dealt with, this was put in the narrative of the report rather than in the recommendations. No explicit proposals were put forward for weeding out 'bad apples', either in Special Branch or in the police as a whole. This loophole was later exploited by opponents of change.

Efficient and Effective. The commissioners deliberately avoided false economies, opting to retain an oversized police service of 7,500 police officers, much larger than existed in similarly sized regions in the rest of the United Kingdom. But such a service could fulfil the following tasks:

(1) begin a novel and far-reaching experiment in community policing;

(2) deter hardline paramilitaries opposed to the Agreement, and those tempted to return to active combat;

(3) manage large-scale public order functions (mostly occasioned by the Loyal Orders); and

(4) facilitate faster changes in the service's religious and gender composition than might otherwise be possible.

The provisions enabling local governments to experiment and outsource services were also designed to 'market-test' effectiveness, while proposals to produce greater 'civilianisation' were to free personnel for mainstream policing tasks and deliver long-run savings. There were also recommendations to improve the financial accountability of the police, to ensure better value for money. In addition, however, the Commission argued, correctly, that efficiency and effectiveness were not simply a matter of better manpower planning or financial management. All of its major recommendations were seen as necessary to promote a more efficient and effective police service.

Free from Partisan Political Control. The Commission's task was to ensure democratic accountability of policing at all levels while preventing any dominant political party or individual from being able to direct the police. This was why the Commission recommended a strong local Policing Board as a counterweight to the Secretary of State, as well as removing the Secretary of State's power to issue 'guidance' on the exercise of police functions. As the report stated, the Secretary of State's dominant position in the tripartite relationship with the Police Authority and the Chief Constable since 1972 had created an impression that the police was an instrument of British government policy rather than a service meeting local priorities.[16] Weakening the Secretary of State's position would, it was hoped, achieve a distinction between the police and the state, and thus complement the Commission's other recommendations for an impartial police.

To ensure that the Policing Board would not be partisan, Patten recommended that its political members be drawn proportionately from parties present in the Executive, according to the d'Hondt rule. The independent members were to be 'representative of the community as a whole'. The DPPBs were to be broadly representative of their district. They were to be composed of a majority of elected members, 'reflecting the balance' of the District Council. The Commission did not state how this

---

[16] See 5.9.

balance should be attained—although it would have been a simple step to have recommended the d'Hondt procedure used for the Policing Board.

Appraisal. Patten correctly saw these different recommendations as part of a coherent and holistic vision, interlinked and mutually reinforcing. There could be no representative police unless it was also impartial, and vice versa. An efficient and effective police service would be one that was accountable, impartial, representative, and imbued with a human rights culture. Wise to how governments could treat reports, the Commission warned that its recommendations should not be 'cherry-picked'. It recommended that the government appoint an 'Oversight Commissioner' to supervise the implementation of their proposals.

The report contained proposals with which we and many others disagreed. We would have liked faster affirmative action, an outright prohibition on membership of secret societies and sectarian organizations, a more radical experiment in federal or decentralized policing, the repeal of emergency legislation, and an immediate end to the use of plastic bullets (McGarry and O'Leary 1999: *passim*). The way the commissioners tied several of their recommendations—including those related to public order policing, civilianization, and even policing with the community—to improvements in the security situation may have appeared commonsensical, but it handed discretion on implementation to security officials in charge of assessing 'threat levels', people not noted for their openness to radical change and who may have been involved in past collusive and unlawful activities. The stress on security considerations failed to acknowledge fully the counter-productive effect of this approach during the course of the conflict. Recommendations that reports and inquiries could be vetoed on grounds of 'national security' handed a potentially strong blocking weapon to those against such openness. These supposed safeguards sat awkwardly with the Commission's mandate to deliver a policing service free from partisan political control, as they allowed the UK Secretary of State to decide when and if these changes should be implemented.

But the Report met its terms of reference. It was wholly consistent with the Agreement, and the recommendations were sensible for a territory primarily divided into two communities of almost equal size with rival national allegiances and significantly intermixed. They flowed straightforwardly from the Agreement's commitment to establishing 'parity of esteem' for the two national traditions. They represented an imaginative compromise between those Unionists who, remarkably, maintained that the existing RUC already met the terms of reference of the Agreement, and those nationalists, especially republicans, who maintained that the RUC's record mandated its immediate disbanding.[17] The Commission's recommendations opened up the possibility of a police service acceptable to nationalists and unionists. The SDLP accepted the Commission's report with enthusiasm, and its deputy leader, Seamus Mallon, indicated that in the context of the report's implementation, his party was prepared to participate fully in the new institutions and to recommend that young nationalists join the police service. Sinn Féin's initial response was more muted, because the report fell short of its traditional demands. However, helped by the rejection of the report by Unionists, it came round. By June of 2000, it was arguing, in a manner that appeared indistinguishable from the SDLP, that the government had to implement the entire report. Gerry Adams pointed out that if Patten was implemented in full, it was his hope that Sinn Féin could then urge republicans and nationalists to join the new police service.[18] This was a political advance that would have been unimaginable a short time earlier. Though critics suggested that Sinn Féin's endorsement of the report was part of a strategy to demoralize the police before a resumption of an IRA military offensive,[19] its position can be seen more plausibly as evidence of its increasing moderation and willingness to embrace constitutional politics.

Unionists, defending the status quo, rejected the report, with David Trimble describing it as a 'gratuitous insult' and as the 'most shoddy piece of work' he had seen in his 'entire life'. They were opposed in particular to the recommendations that dealt with the name and symbols of the police.[20] However, there was little immediate prospect that unionists would become anti-police, or anywhere near as anti-police as nationalists had been. This was not part of their tradition. The Patten Commission, then, could be said to have done its job well.

---

[17] We take pride in noting that the report followed closely the recommendations we put forward in our book *Policing Northern Ireland*. (Barry White of the *Belfast Telegraph* observed after reading the report: 'What really surprised me was the number of times Patten refers to a book by two academics, John McGarry and Brendan O'Leary, *Policing Northern Ireland*. Its summary makes 10 points, most of which find their way into the report in some form'. 'Patten . . . finding the gems in the detail', *Belfast Telegraph*, 18 September 1999.)

[18] 'Adams "dubious about RUC pledge"'. *BBC News Online*, 1 June 2000.

[19] See R. McCartney, 'Patten Report finishes what IRA started'. *The Times*, 28 October 1999.

[20] 'Trimble dismisses report as insult to the RUC'. *Irish Times*, 10 September 1999. The outburst prompted Patten to point out that his report had delivered on its terms of reference, which Trimble had accepted. Unionist rejectionists concurred with Patten. The most charitable interpretation of Trimble's reaction is that he had thought when he had signed up to the Agreement's terms of reference that he was endorsing the status quo: that is, the RUC was already impartial, free from partisan political control, imbued with a human rights culture, and so on.

NOT IMPLEMENTING AND IMPLEMENTING PATTEN

The British government's task at this juncture was clear. An independent commission, with terms of reference established under inter-party and bi-governmental agreement and ratified by referendum, had delivered its report. It presented an opportunity for a new start to policing. However, while publicly committed along with the Prime Minister to the full implementation of Patten, the Northern Ireland Secretary of State, Peter Mandelson, in introducing a Police Bill to the UK parliament in May of 2000, opted to leave out or amend several of Patten's key recommendations.

Mandelson's decision to dilute Patten resulted from two overlapping political considerations. The first was a calculation that weakening the report, particularly its recommendations on the name, emblems, and symbols of the police, was necessary to strengthen Trimble's position within Unionism and to secure his party's re-entry into the power-sharing executive. Mandelson had already suspended the Agreement's institutions, including the executive, in February 2000, because of a threat by Trimble to withdraw his party following the failure of the IRA to decommission its weapons. This unilateral suspension was a breach of international law and undermined the faith of nationalists in the integrity of the Agreement. The UK government, after negotiations with the parties, agreed that the institutions should be restarted in late May. However, it then faced the danger that Trimble would not be able to win his party's approval to re-enter the executive, in spite of an announcement by the IRA on 6 May 2000 that it was committed to putting its weapons 'completely and verifiably beyond use'.[21] This political uncertainty was used by pro-Agreement Unionists, particularly John Taylor, to negotiate with the government on policing reform.[22] The Police Bill was published on 16 May, a few days before an Ulster Unionist Council meeting over whether the UUP should re-enter the executive.[23] When it went through

[21] At a UUC meeting in March 2000, Trimble only narrowly retained his leadership against a last-minute, anti-Agreement, and unimpressive rival, Martin Smyth, by 57–43 per cent. The UUC passed a motion pledging that the UUP would not return to the executive unless the name of the RUC was retained.

[22] Taylor, Trimble, and other leading pro-Agreement Unionists argued that their ability to secure their party's agreement to re-enter the executive 'depended on the response to UUP concerns over the name and emblem of the reformed police'. 'Government prepared to make concessions on RUC'. *Irish Times*, 8 May 2000. Also see 'RUC row threatens deal: Trimble aims for concessions on police to secure key vote'. *Guardian*, 12 May 2000.

[23] The UUC met eventually on 29 May and voted by a narrow margin to re-enter the executive.

the Commons Mandelson accepted a UUP amendment to change the police's name to 'Police Service of Northern Ireland (incorporating the Royal Ulster Constabulary)'—one of the longest titles in the world.

Mandelson's second concern was that implementing Patten would compromise the security of the state. This concern was shared by Unionists, who had favoured giving the police a free hand to fight terrorism. The Secretary of State appears to have been influenced on these matters by his security officials and perhaps his civil servants. These were predictably supportive of the status quo: a 'counter-insurgency' model of policing where transparency and accountability are not cardinal values. They were, doubtless, concerned with preventing the unearthing of past and current scandals resulting from covert and collusive activities.[24] Influential in the early stages of the bill's drafting was the Patten Action Committee, a group whose title implied some connection to the Independent Commission, but were, in fact, Northern Ireland Office civil servants and the RUC's own Change Management Team.

The result was a bill that fell far short of what the Commission recommended in several fundamental areas, particularly impartiality; representativeness; accountability; the promotion of human rights; and decentralization. While Patten sought to ensure an impartial police, with a name and symbols free from 'any association with either the British or Irish states', and without the Union Jack on display over police stations, the bill left these matters to be decided by the Secretary of State (*Police (Northern Ireland) Bill*, S. 50 (2), S. 50 (1) and S. 69 (3)).[25] While Patten had recommended that the new police oath should include a commitment to show equal respect for all 'traditions and beliefs', this phrase was excluded from the bill's oath (ibid.: S. 36). These changes indirectly undermined the possibility of a representative police, but there were also direct attacks on this vista. The period in which the police were to be recruited on a 50:50 basis from Catholics and non-Catholics was reduced from ten to three years, with any extension requiring a decision by the Secretary of State. The bill was silent on aggregation, the policy proposed

---

[24] Moore and O'Rawe (2001) argued that the dilution of Patten was part of a broader British agenda—to hold the line against pressures to reform policing, not only in Northern Ireland, but also in the metropolitan London region. 'A New Beginning for Policing in Northern Ireland'. In C. Harvey (ed.), *Human Rights, Equality and Democratic Renewal in Northern Ireland*. Oxford: Hart, 185.

[25] On the same day the Police Bill was published, the Secretary of State took powers by Order in Council to regulate the flying of flags over government buildings. This was properly a decision that should have been made by Northern Ireland's parties in line with the Agreement's requirement that 'symbols and emblems are used in a manner which promotes mutual respect rather than division'.

by Patten for dealing with years in which there might be a shortfall in the recruitment of suitably qualified cultural Catholics, and it was also dangerously silent on targeting. Civilian posts in the police service were to be filled on a 50 : 50 basis, but only when ten positions were open at the same level. There was no statutory provision for disbanding the almost exclusively Protestant Full-Time Reserve, which Patten had recommended be 'phased out' (Patten: 13.11). There was no provision for enlarging the Part-Time Reserve in spite of Patten's arguments that these part-time positions 'could in principle be filled rapidly' in order to address the underrepresentation of Catholics/Nationalists (ibid.: 12.18).[26] These failures meant that the overall composition of the police would remain more Protestant and Unionist than the Commission had intended. As long as the Full-Time Reserve continued to exist, it reduced incentives to recruit to the regular police, which was to be recruited on a 50 : 50 basis.

The most serious tampering concerned Patten's mechanisms for democratic and legal accountability. Patten had envisaged a strong, independent, and transparent Policing Board to hold the police to account and to replace the discredited Police Authority (ibid.: 6.23). The Board was subordinated to the Secretary of State throughout the Bill, in spite of Patten's warning that the police should be seen as a service that met local priorities. Both the Secretary of State and the Board could set 'objectives' for the police and the latter's had to be consistent with the former's.[27] The Secretary of State could issue 'codes of practice' relating to the discharge by the Board of any of its functions. The Secretary of State, and not the Board, was given the power to set targets and performance indicators for the police. The Chief Constable, not the Board, was given the task of devising a Code of Ethics for the police. The bill gave the Chief Constable much wider latitude to appeal Board requests for reports to the Secretary of State than had been envisaged by Patten. While Patten had stated that the grounds for appeal 'should be strictly limited to issues such as those involving national security, sensitive personnel matters and cases before the courts', already nebulous categories, the Bill permitted appeals when a report would contain

---

[26] As Patten pointed out, the current Part-Time Reserve is the component of the police with the lowest proportion of Catholics—less than 5%, as opposed to 7% in the Full-Time Reserve and 8% in the regular police (14.12).

[27] Patten had recommended that the Board should have responsibility for short-term objectives (3–5 years) and stated that 'we see no justification for government to second-guess the Board in these matters' (6.16).

information relating 'to a matter that is being investigated by a statutory authority' or 'would be likely to prejudice the prevention or detection of crime, the apprehension or prosecution of offenders or the administration of justice' (S. 55 (3) (c) and (e)). The Bill even changed Patten's reference to 'personnel matters' to 'personal matters', a potentially broader category subject to privacy legislation. Board-initiated *inquiries* were subject to these same extensive restrictions. In addition, an inquiry could not be held if the Secretary of State considered it to be against 'the interests of the efficiency or effectiveness of the police force', a clause that effectively enabled him to prevent any inquiry. Inquiries into past misconduct were explicitly prohibited, in spite of Patten's conclusion that 'bad apples' should be 'dealt with'. The Secretary of State was given a veto over the appointment of anyone to head an inquiry, in spite of Patten's recommendation that the Board should have discretion on this matter.

As if these steps were not enough to prevent inquiries (or independent inquiries), the Bill stipulated that the Board should operate according to a weighted majority of twelve of its nineteen members when recommending an inquiry (Schedule 1, Part VI S. 17 (4) (b)). This recommendation was tantamount to giving Unionist and Unionist-nominated members of the Board a veto—not in Patten, and a clear infringement of the terms of the Agreement that the police should be free from 'partisan political control'. The provision meant that the Board could not necessarily initiate an inquiry even if its ten elected members unanimously endorsed it. While Patten had recommended that the Board meet publicly at least once a month, to facilitate transparency, no duty was imposed on it to do so.[28] The Board anticipated by the bill was so weak that its discredited predecessor, the Policing Authority, criticized it and claimed that the new Board 'could actually have less power' than it had.[29] This was a turn of events that no one could have anticipated when the Prime Minister and the Secretary of State indicated in public their intention to implement Patten. The Ombudsman, which Patten had recommended should have the power to 'initiate inquiries or investigations', did not have her powers enhanced by the Bill. Indeed, her powers were circumscribed further, with the Secretary of State being given

[28] The Chief Constable was not even required as a measure of transparency to declare his staff's individual participation in secret societies, ibid., S. 47 (6).

[29] The Authority found this to be 'ludicrous', which also summed up the feelings of nationalists about the Authority's intervention. *Press release issued by the Police Authority for Northern Ireland on the publication of the Police (NI) Bill, 19 May 2000.* The press release can be found at http://cain.ulst.ac.uk/issues/police/policeact/pani17500.htm

powers to limit the Ombudsman's ability to inquire into the past behaviour of the police.

Rather than a police service 'infused with a human rights culture', the Bill referred throughout to a police 'force'. The new policing oath, by which officers were to swear to uphold 'fundamental human rights', and which Patten had recommended be taken by all officers, was limited to new recruits on the spurious grounds that existing constables had already taken oaths and could not be required to take new ones. This appears to have been an attempt to allay Unionist concerns that the RUC was being disbanded de facto but it seriously undermined the perception among nationalists of a 'new beginning'.[30] In addition there was no requirement for even new officers to swear to show equal respect for 'all traditions and beliefs'. The weakness of the accountability institutions, particularly the inability to inquire into past abuses and weed out 'bad apples', inhibited the likelihood of a new human rights culture. The government failed to provide a statutory basis in the bill for the incorporation of human rights in police training, for a programme of action on human rights, or for the Northern Ireland Human Rights Commission to be allowed input on these questions. The bill was also silent on Patten's recommendations for Special Branch, which was a touchstone issue for nationalists and particularly republicans.

Instead of 'decentralising' the police, the Bill foresaw a centralized police, in keeping with the counter-insurgency, hierarchical model of policing favoured by the RUC. Patten's recommendation that District Police Commanders present 'reports and answer questions' at monthly meetings with the District Police Partnership Boards was not given a statutory basis.[31] The proposal to decentralize control over policing by giving district councils the power 'to contribute up to the equivalent of a rate of 3p in the pound' to allow the DPP to pay for extra policing services to meet their distinctive needs, was not included in the Bill, the victim of a hysterical claim that this would be used to hire paramilitaries on the rates. There was no follow-through on Patten's proposed experiment in community policing: that every neighbourhood should have a dedicated policing team, that its officers have their names and the names of their neighbourhood displayed on their uniforms, and that they should serve

---

[30] Republicans believed that Patten's recommendation that every officer take a new oath was a compromise between their call for the RUC to be disbanded and the Unionist call for it to continue without change. *Sinn Fein Response to the Revised Implementation Plan on Policing*, 25 August 2001.

[31] The Bill stripped the word 'Board' from their title, calling them instead District Policing Partnerships (DPPs), a title that suggested no authority.

three to five years in the same neighbourhood. The bill excluded ex-paramilitary prisoners from serving as independent members on the District Policing Partnerships, a step which had not been recommended by Patten and which erected an obstacle to republican (and loyalist) acceptance of the police.

British perfidy and back-pedalling

The result of the Blair government succumbing to pressures from Unionists and security officials was a bill that one of us described as a 'parody' of Patten.[32] It was incompatible with 'parity of esteem', 'rigorous impartiality' by the UK government, and the terms of reference established by the Agreement and ratified by referendum. We were not the only people who reached this conclusion. The Bill was denounced by members of the Patten Commission, one of whom, Professor Shearing, claimed the report had been 'gutted'.[33] It was criticized by other academics; the Women's Coalition; non-governmental and human rights organizations including the Committee on the Administration of Justice; the US House of Representatives; Irish Americans; the Irish government; and the Catholic Church.[34] Most importantly, it was rejected by the political representatives of Northern Ireland's nationalists. The SDLP announced that it would refuse to take its positions on the new institutions or to recommend that nationalists join the police. Sinn Féin did likewise. Its spokesperson claimed that Patten had been 'binned'.[35]

Secretary of State Mandelson had unilaterally rewritten the report to placate Unionists and his own security officials. The bill, moreover, appeared part of a pattern of measures aimed at conciliating Unionists, described by Seamus Mallon as 'government by concession'.[36] This included the decision to suspend the Agreement's institutions in February 2000 and a decision to allow the Secretary of State to rule on the flying of flags over public buildings in May 2000. Mandelson had not only

---

[32] Brendan O'Leary, 'What a Travesty: Police Bill is Just a Parody of Patten'. *Sunday Business Post*, 30 April 2000.

[33] The Bill was denounced by Gerard Lynch, Maurice Hayes, and Clifford Shearing. See 'Policing held up by political power play'. *Irish Independent*, 25 November 2000; 'Foundations of Patten Dismantled'. *Irish Times*, 15 November 2000.

[34] See P. Hillyard, 'Police Bill is not faithful reflection of Patten'. *Irish Times*, 2 August 2000; Moore and O'Rawe, 'A new beginning for Policing'; G. FitzGerald, 'Watering down of Patten was unnecessary and dangerous'. *Irish Times*, 12 August 2000; House Resolution 447, 106th Congress.   [35] G. Kelly, *Irish News*, 12 November 2000.

[36] S. Mallon, 'Filling unionist bowl at too high a price'. *Irish Times*, 18 May 2000.

prevented a 'new beginning' for policing, he had undermined nationalist faith in the Agreement and made it difficult to challenge the argument of dissident republicans that the British were partisans rather than impartial arbiters. He endangered the IRA's commitment to decommissioning because its offer of May 2000 had been proffered in the context of the full implementation of the Agreement. By promising to implement Patten in full but then delivering this parody of a bill, Mandelson undermined republicans' already tenuous belief in the government's *bona fides*—a problem that was later to dog the government when it promised to bring its position closer to Patten.

The UK government further destabilized the Agreement's political institutions by indicating to unionists that their decisions on participation in the executive could be used as a bargaining chip with which to extract concessions. It strengthened the unionist rejectionist argument that the Agreement, rather than a compromise, was a nationalist document that needed to be rewritten. This failure to implement the Patten Report in a timely and reasonable manner has been an important cause of the instability that has plagued the Agreement's political institutions since 2000. The failure to achieve rapid and significant progress on policing reform helps to explain the failure of the IRA to engage in substantive decommissioning. In turn, that made it difficult for David Trimble's Ulster Unionists to remain part of the power-sharing institutions, and to deflect outflanking criticisms from the DUP.

The UK government, however, eventually realized its political errors, and that Mandelson's actions had not helped anybody. Following the fall from office of Mandelson, Secretaries of State Reid and Murphy restored the integrity of the United Kingdom's claim to be implementing the Patten Report, albeit as a result of sustained pressure from the Irish government and Irish nationalists. The logic of argument eventually prevailed over partisan tactics as NIO officials were forced to acknowledge the plain meanings of the Patten report. The three years between May 2000 and May 2003 have produced a steady, albeit slow, repudiation of the government's initial position on policing reform. These changes were reflected in the *Police (Northern Ireland) Act 2000;*[37] the government's 'Updated Implementation plan' released in August 2001 after multiparty negotiations at Weston Park;[38] the *Police (Northern Ireland) Act*

---

[37] *Police (Northern Ireland) Act* 2000, at http://www.hmso.gov.uk/acts/acts2000/20000032.htm.

[38] *The Community and the Police Service: The Patten Report Updated Implementation Plan.* Northern Ireland Office, August 2001, p. 1.

$2003;^{39}$ and the 'Joint Declaration' by the British and Irish governments in April 2003.[40]

As a result of these changes, there has been progress in all areas. Impartiality has been improved. The Policing Board is now required, when carrying out its functions, to uphold the principle of an impartial police service. New officers must now attest that they will discharge their duties with 'impartiality, upholding fundamental human rights and according equal respect to all individuals and their traditions and beliefs'.[41] The RUC's name has been changed, for all 'operational purposes', to the 'Police Service of Northern Ireland'.[42] It has been given new symbols and emblems that are non-partisan.[43]

A number of steps have been taken to ensure a representative police. The *Police (Northern Ireland) Act* 2000 included Patten's recommendation on aggregation, allowing the Secretary of State to make up for a shortfall in Catholic recruits in a given year, by hiring more than 50 per cent (but not more than 75 per cent) in subsequent years. It took steps to improve the representativeness of the police service's civilian workforce.[44] The

---

[39] Police (Northern Ireland) Act 2003, at http://www.hmso.gov.uk/acts/acts2003/20030006.htm

[40] *Joint Declaration by the British and Irish Governments*, April 2003, at http://www.nio.gov.uk/pdf/joint2003.pdf

[41] *Police (Northern Ireland) Act* 2000, S. 38 (1). However, serving officers are still not required to make this declaration, contrary to Patten's explicit recommendation. The government's explanation, that 'existing officers have already been attested as constables and cannot be required to take the new oath', is hardly compelling. *The Community and the Police Service: The Patten Report Updated Implementation Plan*. Northern Ireland Office, August 2001, p. 1.

[42] The legal name of the police is now the 'Police Service of Northern Ireland (incorporating the Royal Ulster Constabulary)'. The government explained that the RUC had been retained in the official title because it wished to demonstrate, in line with Patten, that the RUC was not being disbanded, *The Community and the Police Service: The Patten Report Updated Implementation Plan*. Northern Ireland Office, August 2001, p. 59. Patten, however, had made clear that the link between the RUC and the new police service should be recognized through the colour of the uniform, not the name, *The Report*, 17.7. In August 2001, the government indicated its preparedness to revisit the issue of the title should the 'PSNI' come not to be used for all operational and working purposes. It is now generally agreed that the name of the police is the PSNI, except in republican circles where it is labelled the PSNI/RUC.

[43] The Secretary of State delegated his powers to issue emblems and flags for the police to the new Policing Board. Sinn Féin professes to be unhappy with the police's new badge, a Saint Patrick's Cross surrounded by six symbols—a harp, crown, shamrock, laurel leaf, torch, and scales of justice. It is doubtful that its objection, which is based on the retention of the crown, is a fundamental one.

[44] The Act provided for the 50:50 recruitment formula to be applied to the police's civilian workforce when six or more similar positions were being filled. In the Police Bill, the 50:50 provisions for civilian workers did not come into effect unless ten or more related positions were available.

British government is committed to phasing out the largely Protestant Full-Time Reserve and to building up the Part-Time Reserve in areas where there are currently few reservists (i.e. nationalist areas). The British and Irish governments are committed to legislation to allow lateral entry and secondments between the PSNI and Garda Síochána.

The accountability of the police to the public has been strengthened. The Policing Board is now responsible for setting short- and medium-term objectives for the police, while the Secretary of State is required to consult with the Board on setting his long-term objectives and on issuing codes of practice 'with a view to reaching agreement'. The Chief Constable is required to take account of the Board's policing plan in the discharge of his functions. The Board is responsible for developing measures to improve the 'economy, efficiency and effectiveness' of policing, a power that had—in the Policing Bill—rested with the Secretary of State. Eight of the Board's nineteen members can now initiate an inquiry, as long as they are a majority of those present and voting. This means that nationalists can initiate inquiries if some non-nationalists abstain.[45] The grounds on which the Chief Constable can appeal to the Secretary of State a Board request for a report or inquiry have been significantly reduced.[46] Local accountability has also been improved. Policing with the community is now to be a 'core function' of the police service, which means an enhanced role for DPPs. In a step designed to woo Sinn Féin, the Police (Northern Ireland) Act 2003 provides for ex-prisoners to serve as independent members on DPPs, and for the powers of Belfast DPP's sub-groups to be extended.[47] These changes, however, require an order in council. Such an order is to be made in the context of 'acts of completion', that is, convincing proof that paramilitary, particularly IRA, violence is over. Importantly, the British government

---

[45] Police (Northern Ireland) Act 2003, Section 12 (4).

[46] The Bill had proposed an appeal on the grounds that the request related to a matter that 'is being investigated by a statutory authority', but this was removed in the Police (Northern Ireland) Act 2000. The Bill had also proposed that the Secretary of State be able to veto or halt an inquiry if it would not be 'in the interests of the efficiency or the effectiveness of the police', but this was also removed. Under the Police (Northern Ireland) Act 2003, the sole grounds on which an appeal can be made are if it is in the interests of national security, relates to a sensitive personnel matter, or would be likely to prejudice proceedings which have commenced in a court of law. See Section 76A. A sensitive personnel matter is defined as a 'matter which relates to an individual's holding of, application for, or appointment to a relevant office or appointment', with a relevant office one which is under the direction and control of the Chief Constable. There remains some potential for this qualification to be abused. On the whole, however, the 2003 Act is a significant improvement on the 2000 Policing bill.   [47] Police (Northern Ireland) Act 2003, Section 16 and Schedule 1.

has also committed to devolving control over policing and justice during the term of the next Assembly, if this can be done on a 'basis that is robust and workable and broadly supported by the parties'.[48]

There is also to be a comprehensive 'programme of action' to focus policing on a human rights-based approach.[49] The Board has been given responsibility for devising a Code of Ethics, which will make police officers aware of their obligations under the European Convention of Human Rights. Before issuing or revising the Code, it is obliged to consult with the Northern Ireland Human Rights Commission and the Equality Commission. It has also been given responsibility for monitoring the Code's effectiveness. Finally, the government has strengthened the Ombudsman's powers, to allow her to 'investigate' current police practices and policies, and to make obstruction of such investigations a disciplinary offence.

Together, these changes have made possible, as the SDLP and Irish government have argued, the delivery of the 'substance and spirit of the Patten Report'.[50] There is now the potential for a fully legitimate police service, the first in Northern Ireland's history.

ONE LAST STEP

The delays and reversals in the British government's handling of policing reform have had costs attached. The SDLP agreed to join the Policing Board ahead of some of the changes being implemented, on the basis of promises made at the Weston Park negotiations in July 2001, but Sinn Féin has continued to refuse to endorse the police or take up its positions on the Policing Board. Currently (May 2003), Northern Ireland's political institutions are suspended by the British government. This action was taken in October 2002 to prevent the withdrawal of David Trimble's UUP from the executive, a step that would have resulted in elections within six weeks. The Policing Board continues to meet *sans* Sinn Féin.

One might ask if Sinn Féin's absence matters? It has been argued that the status quo, whereby the SDLP and Unionists cooperate on the Policing Board, is a sufficient advance on the past, and that Sinn Féin's participation would be mischievous and obstructive at best, or

---

[48] *Joint Declaration by the British and Irish Governments*, Annex 2, para. 1.

[49] http://www.nio.gov.uk/pdf/pnibill.pdf

[50] 'Governments' joint proposals can deliver the 'spirit and the substance of Patten report'. *Irish Times*, 1 August 2001.

destructive at worst.[51] But Sinn Féin is now Northern Ireland's largest nationalist party. Without its backing, the police will continue to lack legitimacy among republicans, a group whose alienation helped to give rise to violent conflict. A police service without Sinn Féin's backing cannot become a representative police service, as republicans and many other nationalists will not join it—even if there are generous provisions for affirmative action. Sinn Féin's refusal to endorse the police also has implications for the wider political process. Unless it backs the police, and persuades the IRA to fade away, Unionists are unlikely to see it as a party that should be in government.

Sinn Féin's refusal to endorse the police in return for the measures contained in the Joint Declaration of April 2003 may appear consistent with a position that has been articulated by Padraig O'Malley as well as many Unionists and serving police officers. This is that opposition to the police among republicans is so ingrained that it can never be overcome:

'the concepts of policing and being anti-Catholic are so intertwined in the Catholic mind that the state can do nothing to untangle the perceptions. Being anti-police is an integral part of the Catholic identity that no reform can address. Cosmetic or even genuinely structured reforms will never succeed, because they won't be able to change core attitudes. The issue is not about numbers but about identity. The Catholic sense of identity will always associate any police force, and in particular the RUC, as being Protestant and a de facto expression of Protestant power. Policeman and Catholic are antithetical in terms of identity. Catholics as police will always smack of being the worst of all things—pariah in your own community. And for what?'[52]

A version of this thesis is regularly expounded by Ireland's leading public intellectual, Conor Cruise O'Brien: republicans are anti-police and if they want onto the Policing Board or into the police service, it can only be to destroy it from within.[53]

However, republicans are not anarchists, and it is not true that they are incapable of supporting any police, regardless of how it is structured and the political context in which it works. To take this view is to embrace

---

[51] An opinion survey conducted in January/February 2003 reported that 38% of Protestants, including 72% of DUP supporters, did not want Sinn Féin on the Policing Board. 'The People's Verdict'. *Belfast Telegraph*, 21 February 2003.

[52] P. O'Malley, 'Northern Ireland's identity gulf can't be overcome by police reform'. *Boston Globe*, 19 June 1998.

[53] Two of O'Brien's favourite themes in his weekly column in the *Irish Independent* are: (i) how 11 September will turn the United states against Sinn Féin; and (ii) that the IRA pushes police reform in order to demoralize the police and/or take over the police in republican areas (see also C. C. O'Brien, 'Police Powers: How the IRA leverages the peace process', in *Atlantic Monthly*, December 2001—http://www.theatlantic.com/issues/2001/12/obrien.htm).

a type of primordialism—the belief that identities are etched in stone and cannot be changed. No serious academic subscribes to such views, and there is some survey evidence that concern among Catholics about policing is declining as the Patten Report is implemented.[54] Sinn Féin's leaders no longer complain that Patten is not being implemented. Nonetheless, they clearly face difficulties over claims that they'll be 'policing partition' and over supporting a police that will, for the foreseeable future, be comprised largely of ex-RUC officers.[55] These difficulties have been compounded by a number of recent events: the PSNI's failure to stop loyalist attacks on nationalist areas in North Belfast, Larne, and elsewhere; the Ombudsman's report on the Omagh bomb, which highlighted the independence and unacceptable behaviour of Special Branch; the raid by dozens of PSNI officers on Sinn Féin's offices in October 2002;[56] and plausible allegations, including by the Metropolitan Commissioner, Sir John Stephens, of police collusion with loyalists in the killings of Catholics, particularly the lawyer, Pat Finucane.

It is regrettable in this context that the British government has decided to postpone the assembly elections originally scheduled for May 2003. Electoral competition with the SDLP would augment the position of Sinn Féin's moderates. This is because the most obvious way for Sinn Féin to expand is by winning the support of moderate nationalists who have previously supported the SDLP. The government's decision to postpone the election also militates against compromise from republicans, because it contradicts the concept of Irish self-determination that is at the heart of the Good Friday Agreement. This is why London's acceptance in early May 2003 that it will repeal the Suspension Act 2000 is important, although we believe that its commitment to the Agreement should be entrenched by way of a treaty attached to whatever European constitution is agreed in the future. Moreover, the aftermath of elections, particularly if they confirm Sinn Féin as the larger of the two nationalist

[54] 'What now for the Agreement?' *Belfast Telegraph*, 21 February 2003. Pollster Colin Irwin reports here that police reform moved from being Catholics' number one priority in May 2000 to number eight in February of 2003.

[55] A poll conducted in January and February of 2003 found that 59% of Sinn Féin's supporters thought 'complete reform of the PSNI' was an 'essential' step towards a lasting peace and political stability. A further 27% thought it a 'desirable' step. See www.peacepolls.org.

[56] 'Sinn Féin will dig in after PSNI raid on HQ'. *Sunday Business Post*, 6 October 2002. The raid, captured by television cameras, was seen by Unionists as proof of Sinn Fein's perfidy. However, it was regarded throughout the nationalist community as politically motivated, an attempt to allow Unionists to collapse the political institutions while pinning the blame on Sinn Féin, and as evidence that the PSNI was merely the RUC under a new name.

parties, will create a context in which bargaining on policing and related issues would be likely. It may be that one of the reasons why republicans have been reluctant to endorse the PSNI or declare the IRA war over prior to an election is that crucial negotiations, including on the election of a First Minister/Deputy First Minister team, and on the devolution of policing, will not commence until *after* an election. So the sooner elections are held, the better.

There are two other steps that can be taken to facilitate a positive response from republicans, steps that are consistent with the Patten report and that would not be seen as rewarding Sinn Féin (at the expense of the SDLP) for staying off the Policing Board. First, the Chief Constable should endeavour to ensure that policing on the ground is as impartial as possible. The police will have to confront any loyalist attacks on, or attempts to force Orange marches through, nationalist neighbourhoods, as well as threats from republican dissidents. Second, given the currently low levels of threat against the police, there is a good argument for normalizing policing as soon as possible, that is, for expediting those changes that Patten linked to the security situation. These include the introduction of neighbourhood policing; the complete demilitarization of police vehicles and police stations; the establishment of a routinely unarmed police service; the introduction of a non-lethal alternative to the use of plastic baton rounds in public order policing; the merging of Special Branch and the Criminal Branch; and the phasing out of the Full-Time Reserve.

No one expects republicans to become uncritical supporters of the police, in the way that some unionists have been in the past, but this is not what is being requested of them. Rather, they are being asked to accept the legitimacy of a reconstructed police while holding its members strictly to account. This will require a transformation that is dramatic, but it can no longer be said to be unthinkable.

CONCLUSION

Policing and policing reform in Northern Ireland are revealing for a number of reasons. First, the police, along with the army, can be used as a crucial instrument of hegemonic control in an ethnically divided territory. Police repression may succeed in quelling minority dissent for a time, but it also stokes up grievances that, if left unchecked, can facilitate minority rebellions. Second, integrationist (liberal–democratic) reforms are seldom sufficient in ethnically divided territories. It is not enough to create a professional police. A representative police is necessary. In nationally divided societies, moreover, the symbols, name, and behaviour of the police should be nationally impartial. The police need not be wholly consociational—in which case each community would police only its own—but, ideally, they need oversight through executive power-sharing and they need to be proportionally representative.

Northern Ireland's experience shows how the issue of policing reform cannot be easily separated from other aspects of political settlements. Policing was one of the most intractable issues in the negotiations that produced the 1998 Agreement, and the Agreement was reached only because policing was left aside until later. The failure to resolve policing has since destabilized the assembly and executive established by the Agreement, which are now suspended. The IRA's reluctance to decommission its weapons or to disband has been connected to what republicans see as a reluctance to implement Patten's recommendations on policing. The unwillingness of unionists to share power with republicans is caused by the fact that the IRA will not decommission/disband, and to the related fact that the latter refuse to endorse the police. This connection between legitimate policing and political institutions has been overlooked in the literature on conflict regulation, and yet it is of paramount importance not just in Northern Ireland but in other divided territories, including Bosnia, Kosovo, and Afghanistan.

Bibliography of Writings by John McGarry and Brendan O'Leary on Irish Politics, 1985–2003

JOHN McGARRY AND BRENDAN O'LEARY

Books and edited collections

McGarry, John and Brendan O'Leary (1999). *Policing Northern Ireland: Proposals for a New Start*. Belfast: Blackstaff.

McGarry, John and Brendan O'Leary (1995). *Explaining Northern Ireland: Broken Images*. Oxford and Cambridge, MA.: Basil Blackwell.

McGarry, John and Brendan O'Leary (eds.) (1990). *The Future of Northern Ireland*. Oxford: Oxford University Press.

O'Leary, Brendan and John McGarry (eds.) (1995). *State of Truce: Northern Ireland after Twenty Five Years of War*. Ethnic and Racial Studies, Special Issue, 18, 4.

O'Leary, Brendan and John McGarry (1993; 1996—2nd revised and updated edition). *The Politics of Antagonism: Understanding Northern Ireland*. London and Atlantic Heights, NJ: Athlone.

Articles and chapters in books

McGarry, John and Brendan O'Leary (2003). 'Northern Ireland and the Liabilities of Liberalism'. In John Stone and Dennis Rutledge (eds.), *Race and Ethnicity in Global Society*. Oxford: Basil Blackwell, 171–186.

McGarry, John and Brendan O'Leary (1996). 'Proving our points on Northern Ireland (and giving reading lessons to Dr Dixon)'. *Irish Political Studies*, 11: 142–54.

McGarry, John and Brendan O'Leary (1995). 'Five Fallacies: Northern Ireland and the Liabilities of Liberalism'. *Ethnic and Racial Studies*, 18 (4): 837–61.

McGarry, John and Brendan O'Leary (1990). 'Northern Ireland's Future: What is to be done?'. *Conflict Quarterly*, 10 (2): 42–62.

McGarry, John and Brendan O'Leary (1990). 'Northern Ireland's Options: A Framework, Summary and Analysis'. In John McGarry and Brendan O'Leary (eds.), *The Future of Northern Ireland*. Oxford: Oxford University Press, 268–303.

Newspaper articles

McGarry, John and Brendan O'Leary (2003). 'Agreement Review Could Circumvent DUP Veto', *Irish Times*, 6 December.

McGarry, John and Brendan O'Leary (2002). 'One More Bold Step Required on Path to Policing Reform'. *Irish Times*, 5 December.

McGarry, John and Brendan O'Leary (1998). 'RUC Reform Must Not Repeat Boundary Commission Fiasco'. *Sunday Business Post*, 15 April.

McCrudden, Christopher, John McGarry, and Brendan O'Leary (1998). 'Answering Some Big Questions. Explaining the Agreement, Part 1'. *Sunday Business Post*, 19 April.

McCrudden, Christopher, John McGarry, and Brendan O'Leary (1998). 'The Dance of the Ministries. Explaining the Agreement, Part 2'. *Sunday Business Post*, 26 April.

McCrudden, Christopher, John McGarry, and Brendan O'Leary (1998). 'All-Ireland Bodies at Work. Explaining the Agreement, Part 3'. *Sunday Business Post*, 3 May.

McCrudden, Christopher, John McGarry, and Brendan O'Leary (1998). 'Equality and Social Justice. Explaining the Agreement, Part 4'. *Sunday Business Post*, 10 May.

McCrudden, Christopher, John McGarry, and Brendan O'Leary (1998). 'The Heart of the Agreement: A Bi-National Future. Explaining the Agreement, Part 5'. *Sunday Business Post*, 17 May.

JOHN McGARRY

Books and edited collections

McGarry, John, (ed.) (2001). *Northern Ireland and the Divided World: Post-Agreement Northern Ireland in Comparative Perspective*. Oxford: Oxford University Press.

Articles and chapters

McGarry, J. (2003). 'Consociational Theory and Northern Ireland's Good Friday Agreement'. In A. Morawa (ed.), *European Yearbook of Minority Issues*. Bozen/Bolzano: Kluwer Academic Press, 283–98.

McGarry, John (2002). 'Le nationalisme civique et le conflict en irlande du Nord'. In M. Seymour (ed.), *Etats-nations, multinations et organisations supranationales*. Montreal: Liber, 301–15.

McGarry, John (2002). '"Democracy" in Northern Ireland: experiments in Self-rule form the Protestant Ascendancy to the Good Friday Agreement'. *Nations and Nationalism*, 8 (4): 451–74.

McGarry, John (2001). 'Northern Ireland and the Shortcomings of Civic Nationalism'. In John McGarry (ed.), *Northern Ireland and the Divided World:*

Post-Agreement Northern Ireland in Comparative Perspective. Oxford: Oxford University Press: 109–36.

McGarry, John (2001). 'Globalization, European Integration and the Northern Ireland Conflict'. In Michael Keating and John McGarry (eds.) *Minority Nationalism and the Changing International Order.* Oxford: Oxford University Press, 295–324.

McGarry, John (2001). 'The Comparable Northern Ireland'. In John McGarry (ed.), *Northern Ireland and the Divided World: Post-Agreement Northern Ireland in Comparative Perspective.* Oxford: Oxford University Press, 1–33.

McGarry, John (2000). 'Police Reform in Northern Ireland'. *Irish Political Studies,* 15: 183–92.

McGarry, John (1998). 'Political Settlements in Northern Ireland and South Africa'. *Political Studies,* 46 (5): 853–70.

McGarry, John (1990). 'Northern Ireland and the Option of Consociationalism'. *Plural Societies,* Vol. XX, No. X, 1 June 1990.

McGarry, John (1988). 'The Anglo-Irish Agreement and Power-Sharing in Northern Ireland'. *Political Quarterly,* 59 (2): 236–50.

BRENDAN O'LEARY

Books

O'Leary, Brendan, Tom Lyne, Jim Marshall, and Bob Rowthorn (1993). *Northern Ireland: Sharing Authority.* London: Institute of Public Policy Research.

Articles and chapters

Evans, Geoffrey and Brendan O'Leary (2000). 'Northern Irish Voters and the British-Irish Agreement: Foundations of a Stable Consociational Settlement?' *Political Quarterly,* 71 (1): 78–101.

Evans, Geoffrey and Brendan O'Leary (1997). 'Intransigence and Flexibility on the Way to Two Forums: The Northern Ireland Elections of 30 May 1996 and Public Opinion'. *Representation,* 34 (3/4): 208–18.

Evans, Geoffrey and Brendan O'Leary (1997). 'Frameworked Futures: Intransigence and Flexibility in the Northern Ireland Elections of May 30 1996'. *Irish Political Studies,* 12: 23–47.

Hazell, Robert and Brendan O'Leary (1999). 'A Rolling Programme of Devolution: Slippery Slope or Safeguard of the Union?' In Robert Hazell (ed.), *Constitutional Futures: A History of the Next Ten Years.* Oxford: Oxford University Press, 21–46.

Mitchell, Paul, Brendan O'Leary, and Geoffrey Evans (2002). 'The 2001 Elections in Northern Ireland: Moderating "Extremists" and the squeezing of the Moderates', *Representation,* 39, 1: 23–36.

Mitchell, Paul, Brendan O'Leary, and Geoffrey Evans (2001). 'Northern Ireland: Flanking Extremists Bite the Moderates and Emerge in Their Clothes'. *Parliamentary Affairs*, 54, 4: 725–42.

O'Duffy, Brendan and Brendan O'Leary (1995). 'Tales from Elsewhere and an Hibernian Sermon'. In Helen Margetts and Gareth Smyth (eds.), *Turning Japanese? Britain with a Permanent Party of Government*. London: Lawrence and Wishart, 193–210.

O'Leary, Brendan (2002). 'The Belfast Agreement and the British-Irish Agreement: Consociation, Confederal Institutions, A Federacy, and a Peace Process'. In Andrew Reynolds, (ed.), *The Architecture of Democracy: Constitutional Design, Conflict Management, and Democracy*. Oxford: Oxford University Press, 293–356.

O'Leary, Brendan (2002). 'The Belfast Agreement: The Making, the Management and the Mismanagement of a Complex Association'. In Colin Hay (ed.), *British Politics Today*. Oxford: Polity, 259–305.

O'Leary, Brendan (2001). 'The Belfast Agreement and the Labour Government: How to Handle and Mishandle History's Hand'. In Anthony Seldon (ed.), *The Blair Effect: The Blair Government 1997–2001*. London: Little, Brown and Company, 448–88.

O'Leary, Brendan (2001). 'The Protection of Human Rights under the Belfast Agreement'. *Political Quarterly*, 72 (3): 353–65.

O'Leary, Brendan (2001). 'The Character of the 1998 Agreement: Results and Prospects'. In Rick Wilford (ed.), *Aspects of the Belfast Agreement*. Oxford: Oxford University Press: 49–83.

O'Leary, Brendan (2001). 'Comparative Political Science and the British-Irish Agreement'. In John McGarry (ed.), *Northern Ireland in a Divided World*. Oxford: Oxford University Press, 53–88.

O'Leary, Brendan (2000). 'L'accord britaniicoirlandes del 1998, I el plus del consensualisme'. In Montserrat Guibernau (ed.), *Nacionalisme: Debats I dilemes per a un mou mil-lenni*. Barcelona: Centre d'Estudis de Temes Contemporanis, 203–28.

O'Leary, B (2000). 'Quali armi contro i nazionalisme'. In Marco Moussasanet (ed.), *Dueemila: Verso una societa aperta, 2. Politica, migrazione, guerra epace, religione*. Milan: Il Sole 24 Ore, 221–4.

O'Leary, Brendan (2000). 'The Limits to Coercive Consociationalism in Northern Ireland'. In R. A. W Rhodes (ed.), *The International Library of Politics and Comparative Government: United Kingdom*. Aldershot: Ashgate, II, 475–502.

O'Leary, Brendan (1999). 'The 1998 British-Irish Agreement: Consociation Plus'. *Scottish Affairs*, 26 (Winter): 1–22.

O'Leary, Brendan (1999). 'The Implications for Political Accommodation in Northern Ireland of Reforming the Electoral System for the Westminster Parliament'. *Representation*, 35 (2/3): 106–13.

O'Leary, Brendan (1999). 'The Nature of the Agreement'. *Fordham Journal of International Law*, 22 (4): 1628–67.

O'Leary, Brendan (1999). 'The Nature of the British-Irish Agreement'. *New Left Review*, 233 (January–February): 66–96.

O'Leary, Brendan (1997). 'The Conservative Stewardship of Northern Ireland 1979–97: Sound Bottomed Contradictions or Slow Learning?' *Political Studies*, 45 (4): 663–76.

O'Leary, Brendan (1995). 'Afterword: What is Framed in the Framework Documents?' *Ethnic and Racial Studies*, 18 (4): 862–72.

O'Leary, Brendan (1995). 'Introduction: Reflections on a Cold Peace'. *Ethnic and Racial Studies*, 18 (4): 695–714.

O'Leary, Brendan (1993). 'Affairs, Partner Swapping and Spring Tides: The Irish General Election of 1992'. *West European Politics*, 16 (3): 401–12.

O'Leary, Brendan (1992). 'Public Opinion and Northern Irish Futures'. *Political Quarterly*, 63 (2): 143–70.

O'Leary, Brendan (1991). 'An Taoiseach: The Irish Prime Minister'. In George W. Jones (ed.), *West European Prime Ministers*. London: Frank Cass, 133–62; also as 'An Taoiseach: The Irish Prime Minister'. *West European Politics*, 14 (2): 131–62.

O'Leary, Brendan (1990). 'Appendix 4. Party Support in Northern Ireland, 1969–89'. In John McGarry and Brendan O'Leary (eds.), *The Future of Northern Ireland*. Oxford: Oxford University Press, 342–57.

O'Leary, Brendan (1990). 'Northern Ireland and the Anglo-Irish Agreement'. In Patrick Dunleavy, Andrew Gamble, and Gillian Peele (eds.), *Developments in British Politics 3*. Basingstoke: Macmillan, 269–91.

O'Leary, Brendan (1989). 'The Limits to Coercive Consociationalism in Northern Ireland'. *Political Studies*, 37 (4): 452–68.

O'Leary, Brendon (1987). 'The Anglo-Irish Agreement: Meanings, Explanations, Results and a Defence'. In P. Teague (ed.), *Beyond the Rhetoric: Politics, Economics and Social Policy in Northern Ireland*. London: Lawrence and Wishart, 11–40.

O'Leary, Brendan (1987). 'Towards Europeanisation and Modernisation? The Irish General Election of February 1987'. *West European Politics*, 10 (3): 455–65.

O'Leary, Brendan (1987). 'The Anglo-Irish Agreement: Statecraft or Folly?' *West European Politics*, 10 (1): 5–32.

O'Leary, Brendan (1985). 'Explaining Northern Ireland: A Brief Study Guide'. *Politics*, 5 (1): 35–41.

O'Leary, Brendan and Paul Arthur (1990). 'Introduction: Northern Ireland as the Site of State- and Nation-Building Failures'. In John McGarry and Brendan O'Leary (eds.), *The Future of Northern Ireland*. Oxford: Oxford University Press, 1–47.

O'Leary, Brendan and Geoffrey Evans (1997). 'Intransigence and Inflexibility on the Way to Two Forums. The Elections to the Northern Ireland Peace Forum May 1996 and Public Opinion'. *Representation*, 34 (3/4): 208–18.

O'Leary, Brendan and Geoffrey Evans (1997). 'Northern Ireland: La Fin de Siècle, The Twilight of the Second Protestant Ascendancy and Sinn Fein's Second Coming'. *Parliamentary Affairs*, 50 (4): 672–80.

O'Leary, Brendan and Geoffrey Evans (1997). 'Northern Ireland: La Fin de Siècle, The Twilight of the Second Protestant Ascendancy and Sinn Fein's Second Coming'. In Pippa Norris and Neil P. Gavin (eds.), *Britain Votes 1997*. Oxford: Oxford University Press, 164–72.

O'Leary, Brendan and Brendan O'Duffy (1990). 'Appendix 3. Political Violence in Northern Ireland'. In John McGarry and Brendan O'Leary (eds.), *The Future of Northern Ireland*. Oxford: Oxford University Press, 318–41.

O'Leary, Brendan and John Peterson (1990). 'Further Europeanisation and Realignment. The Irish General Election, June 1989'. *West European Politics*, 13 (1): 124–36.

O'Leary, Brendan, Bernard Grofman, and Jorgen Elklit (2004 in press). 'Divisor Methods to Facilitate and Sequence Portfolio-Allocation in a Multi-Party Cabinet Coalition: Evidence from Northern Ireland and Denmark', *American Journal of Political Science*.

Miscellaneous: Newspaper articles, reviews, ephemera

O'Leary, Brendan (2003). 'Lethal Mix of Armalite and the Ballot Box'. *Times Higher Education Supplement*. London, 3 October, 27–8.

O'Leary, Brendan (2002). 'British-Irish Council'. *The World Book Encyclopaedia*. Chicago: B, 632.

O'Leary, Brendan (2002). 'Give Northern Ireland's Voters a Choice'. *Financial Times*. London, 13 October.

O'Leary, Brendan (2002). 'Ireland'. *The World Book Encyclopaedia*. Chicago: I, 416–28.

O'Leary, Brendan (2002). 'North-South Ministerial Council'. *The World Book Encylcopaedia*. Chicago: N, 518.

O'Leary, Brendan (2002). 'Northern Ireland'. *The World Book Encyclopaedia*. Chicago: N, 521–25.

O'Leary, Brendan (2002). 'Shades of Green'. *Financial Times*. London, 16 May, 13.

O'Leary, Brendan (2002). 'United Kingdom'. *The World Book Encyclopaedia*. Chicago: U, 48–75.

O'Leary, Brendan (2001). 'Ireland after Hume'. *Financial Times*. London, 18 September.

O'Leary, Brendan (2001). 'Personal View: Ignore the Prophets of Doom'. *Financial Times*, London, 11 June.

O'Leary, Brendan (2001). ' Elections, not 'Suspensions'. *The Guardian*, London, 13, July.

O'Leary, Brendan (2001). 'How the Agreement Won through Despite Trimble'. *Punch*, 15, 7 November.

O'Leary, Brendan (2001). 'Reid Should Not Allow a New Unionist Boycott'. *Irish Times*, 4 October.

O'Leary, Brendan (2001). 'When Rights are Traded for Peace (Review of Peace Agreements and Human Rights, by Christine Bell)'. *Sunday Business Post*, Dublin, 11 February.

O'Leary, Brendan (2001). Agreement is Not Devolution in Unitary State'. *Irish Times*, Dublin, 11 October, 16.

O'Leary, Brendan (2001). 'A Big Step for N. Ireland'. *Philadelphia Inquirer*. Philadelphia, 25 October, 23.

O'Leary, Brendan (2000). 'Letter on Patten Report and Police Bill'. *Irish Times* Dublin, 9 August.

O'Leary, Brendan (2000). 'The Patten, the Whole Patten and Nothing but the Patten'. *Irish Times*, Dublin, 28 July.

O'Leary, Brendan (2000). 'Perfidious Britannia'. *The Guardian*, London, 15 June.

O'Leary, Brendan (2000). 'Suspension Would be a Potentially Fatal Blow'. *Irish Times*, 5 February.

O'Leary, Brendan (2000). 'What a Travesty: Police Bill is Just a Parody of Patten'. *Sunday Business Post*, Dublin, 30 April.

O'Leary, Brendan (2000). 'Trimble: Review of Henry McDonald's Trimble'. *Sunday Business Post*, Dublin, April 13.

O'Leary, Brendan (2000). '3,636 so far, and counting (Review of David McKittrick *et al. Lost Lives: The Stories of the Men, Women and Children who Died as a Result of the Northern Ireland Troubles)'. Times Higher Education Supplement*, London, 3 March.

O'Leary, Brendan (2000). 'Albion retains the right to be perfidious'. *Sunday Business Post*, Dublin, 30 April.

O'Leary, Brendan (2000). 'Better to hang on'. *The Guardian*, London, 2 February.

O'Leary, Brendan (2000). 'Death in a state of violence takes on Kafkaesque quality: Review of Fionnulla Ni Aolain'. *The Politics of Force: Conflict Management and State Violence in Northern Ireland. Sunday Business Post*, Dublin.

O'Leary, Brendan (2000). 'Foreword to Michael McGrath's'. *The Catholic Church and Catholic Schools' in Northern Ireland: The Price of Faith*. Dublin: Irish Academic Press.

O'Leary, Brendan (2000). 'History of North's Catholics Riddled With Inaccuracies (Review of The *Catholics of Ulster—A History* by Marianne Elliott)'. *Sunday Business Post*, Dublin, 22 October.

O'Leary, Brendan (1999). 'Answering to the People?' *The Irish News*. Belfast, 23 March.

O'Leary, Brendan (1999). 'A Bright Future and Less Orange (Review of 'A New Beginning' by the Independent Commission on Policing for Northern Ireland)'. *Times Higher Education Supplement*, London, 19 November.

O'Leary, Brendan (1999). 'Patten Report has Implications for All'. *Irish Independent*, Dublin, 15 October.

O'Leary, Brendan (1999). 'Remake, remodel'. *The Guardian*. London, 18 March.

O'Leary, Brendan (1999). 'Unionists' Move An Escape from Reality'. *Irish Independent*, Dublin, 15 October.

O'Leary, Brendan (1999). 'Review of Paul Mitchell and Rick Wilford eds. *Politics in Northern Ireland'. Irish Political Studies*, 14: 150–1.

O'Leary, Brendan (1999). 'Damit Gewalt nicht mehr notig ist'. *Tages-Anzeiger*, 3 December.

O'Leary, Brendan (1999). 'Four Options, One Way Forward'. *Financial Times*, London, 5 November.

O'Leary, Brendan (1999). 'How Can the Police Survive the Peace?' *The Irish News*, Belfast.

O'Leary, Brendan (1999). 'How to Share Power: The Friday Review'. *The Independent*, London.

O'Leary, Brendan (1999). 'Lost Nun and Closet Extremist, Review of Conor Cruise O' Brien, *Memoir*, of Olivia O'Leary and Helen Burke, *Mary Robinson*, and of *Ideas Matter: Essays in Honour of Conor Cruise O'Brien'*. *Times Higher Education Supplement*, London, 9 April, 24.

O'Leary, Brendan (1998). 'The 1998 British-Irish Agreement: Power-Sharing Plus'. London: Constitution Unit.

O'Leary, Brendan (1998). 'Bias in Memoirs Scores Political Own Goal'. *The Scotsman*, Edinburgh, 19 January.

O'Leary, Brendan (1998). 'British Opinion is Turning'. *Independent*, Dublin, 14 July.

O'Leary, Brendan (1998). 'Free the Gunmen'. *The Guardian*, London, 8 January.

O'Leary, Brendan (1998). 'Lessons for Academic Stalkers'. *Political Studies*, 796–8.

O'Leary, Brendan (1998). 'The Magic Number is 64'. *Times Higher Education Supplement*, 22 May.

O'Leary, Brendan (1998). 'A Muted Miracle'. *The Guardian*, London, 17 April.

O'Leary, Brendan (1998). 'No surrender (by us)'. *The Guardian*, July 11.

O'Leary, Brendan (1998). 'The Nobility of Hope . . . Not Despair'. *Irish Independent*, Dublin, 11 December.

O'Leary, Brendan (1998). 'The Northern Ireland Assembly'. *Monitor: The Constitution Unit Bulletin*, 3, May, 4.

O'Leary, Brendan (1998). 'Ulster, perche questa pace puo durare'. *Il Sole-24 Ore*, 24 April.

O'Leary, Brendan (1997). 'Has Gerry Adams Signalled What Sinn Fein Really Wants?' *The Scotsman*. Edinburgh, 24 July.

O'Leary, Brendan (1997). 'Unionists Will Lose Electoral Dominance'. *Irish Times*, 2 July.

O'Leary, Brendan (1997). 'After the Avalanche'. *Sunday Tribune*, Dublin, 4 May.

O'Leary, Brendan (1997). 'All is Not Yet Lost, It is Just Bloodier Than It Need Have Been'. *The Scotsman*, Edinburgh, 8 July.

O'Leary, Brendan (1996). 'War about talks and talks about war'. *LSE Magazine*, London, 4–6.

O'Leary, Brendan (1995). 'Brave New Worlds: The UK and Irish Governments' Proposals for Northern Ireland'. *The Parliamentary Policy Forum*, Spring (1): 29–31.

O'Leary, Brendan (1995). 'A Carefully Crafted Essay in Statecraft'. *Sunday Press*, Dublin, 5 March.

O'Leary, Brendan (1995). 'How Document Sees a New North'. *Sunday Press*, Dublin, 2 February.

O'Leary, Brendan (1994). 'The Best of Both Worlds'. *Parliamentary Brief*, October 31–2.

O'Leary, Brendan (1994). 'Fast Moves Now Needed to Find an Agreed Ireland'. *Sunday Press*, Dublin, 4 September.

O'Leary, Brendan (1994). 'An Irish Peace with Honour'. *Independent*, London, 23 September.

O'Leary, Brendan (1994). 'The North: One Way Forward'. *Sunday Press*, Dublin, 19 September.

O'Leary, Brendan (1994). 'Three Basic Obstacles Remain to a Durable Resolution in the North'. *Sunday Press*, Dublin, 2 February.

O'Leary, Brendan (1994). 'What Happens if the Provos Say Yes, Say No or Say Maybe'. *Sunday Press*, Dublin, 16 January.

O'Leary, Brendan (1994). 'When the Shooting Stops'. *Sunday Press*, Dublin, 28 August.

O'Leary, Brendan (1993). 'Parsing the Paragraphs'. *Sunday Press*, Dublin, 19 December.

O'Leary, Brendan (1993). 'Steps Towards a Constitutional Compromise'. *The Independent*, London, 28 January.

O'Leary, Brendan (1993). 'Review of David Smith and Gerald Chambers' "Inequality in Northern Ireland"'. *British Journal of Sociology*, 44 (1): 146–7.

O'Leary, Brendan (1992). 'Exploding the North's Employment Myths' (Review of R. Cormack and R. D. Osborne's *Discrimination and Public Policy in Northern Ireland*. *Irish Times*. Dublin, 28 March.

O'Leary, Brendan (1992). 'The Future of Northern Ireland'. *Current Issues in Focus*, 12: 25–6.

O'Leary, Brendan (1991). 'Contribution to Symposium on Brooke Talks'. *Fortnight*.

O'Leary, Brendan (1991). 'Reform Agenda Proves Popular'. *Fortnight*, 297: 16–17.

O'Leary, Brendan (1991). 'Review of Alan O'Day and Yonah Alexander's *Ireland's Terrorist Trauma*'. *Political Studies*, xxxix: 593–4.

O'Leary, Brendan (1991). 'Review of Bob Purdie's *Politics in the Streets*'. *Political Studies*, xxxix (2): 389–90.

O'Leary, Brendan (1991). 'Review of John Whyte's *Interpreting Northern Ireland*'. *Irish Times* Dublin, 5 January.

O'Leary, Brendan (1991). 'Review of Padraig O'Malley's *Biting at the Grave* and *Questions of Nuance*'. *Irish Political Studies*, 6: 118–22.

O'Leary, Brendan (1991). 'Review of Vincent McCormack and James O'Hara's *Enduring Inequality* and Arthur Aughey *et al Northern Ireland in the European Community*'. *Public Administration*, 69 (3): 410–12.

O'Leary, Brendan (1991). 'Temporary for Two Decades'. *Fortnight*, 299: 15.

O'Leary, Brendan (1991). 'Then Talk Some More'. *Fortnight*, 298: 18–19.

O'Leary, Brendan (1991). 'Unionists Must Give Much More than an Inch'. *Fortnight*, 297: 10–13.

O'Leary, Brendan (1990). 'A Hegelian Inspects the Laager: Review of Arthur Aughey's *Under Siege*'. *Irish Times*. Dublin, 6 January.

O'Leary, Brendan (1990). 'Ireland—Problem without a Solution?' *LSE Magazine*, 2, 4–12.

O'Leary, Brendan (1990). 'Lawyers' View of the Anglo-Irish Agreement'. *Irish Times*. Dublin, 16 April.

O'Leary, Brendan (1990). 'More Green, Fewer Orange'. *Fortnight*, 12–15 and 16–17.

O'Leary, Brendan (1990). 'Resolving Northern Ireland? The Options for British and Irish Policy-Makers in the 1990s'. *Wroxton Papers in Politics*.

O'Leary, Brendan (1990). 'Review of Conor Cruise O'Brien's *Godland: Reflections on Religion and Nationalism*'. *Ethnic and Racial Studies*, 12 (4): 586–8.

O'Leary, Brendan (1990). 'Review of Thomas Wilson's *Ulster: Conflict and Consensus*'. *Governance*, 3 (3).

O'Leary, Brendan (1990). 'Setting the Record Straight: A Comment on Cahill's Country Report on Ireland'. *Governance*, 3 (1): 98–104.

O'Leary, Brendan (1990). 'Solving Northern Ireland?' *Contemporary Record*, 4 (1 & 2): 19–22 and 8–11.

O'Leary, Brendan (1990). *Symposium on Brooke Talks. Belfast Fortnight*. September, Belfast.

O'Leary, Brendan (1990). 'United Ireland, United Europe?' *Tribune*. August

O'Leary, Brendan (1990). 'The Weight of the Dead Generations: Review of Henry Patterson's *The Politics of Illusion: Socialism and Republicanism in Modern Ireland*'. *Fortnight* (April).

O'Leary, Brendan (1989). 'Guiltless Passions of a Unionist Liberal: Review of Tom Wilson's *Ulster: Confluict and Consensus*'. *Irish Times*. Dublin, 7 October

O'Leary, Brendan (1989). 'Letter: Civilian Deaths in Ulster'. *The Observer*, London, 27 August, 30.

O'Leary, Brendan (1989). 'Northern Ireland through the Telescope: Review of Adrian Guelke's *Northern Ireland: The International Perspective*'. *Irish Times*. Dublin, 3 February.

O'Leary, Brendan (1989). 'Review Article: Twenty Years-a-Warring and Twenty Years-a-Writing'. *Government and Opposition*, 24, 1 (Winter 1989): 117–20.

O'Leary, Brendan (1989). 'Review of Cornelius O'Leary *et al*'s *The Northern Ireland Assembly, 1982–86*'. *Fortnight*, March.

O'Leary, Brendan (1989). 'Review of Frank Wright's *Northern Ireland: A Comparative Analysis*'. *West European Politics*, 12 (1): 169–171.

O'Leary, Brendan (1989). 'Review of John Hutchinson's *The Dynamics of Cultural Nationalism*'. *British Journal of Sociology*, 41 (1): 130–1.

O'Leary, Brendan (1989). 'Review of Tom Inglis's *Moral Monopoly: The Catholic Church in Modern Irish Society*'. *West European Politics*, 12 (2): 169–71.

O'Leary, Brendan (1988). 'Review of works on Political Violence and Terrorism'. *British Journal of Criminology*, 28 (1): 97–107.

O'Leary, Brendan (1988). 'Behind the Reforms: Review of John Ditch's *Social Policy in Northern Ireland, 1939–50*'. *Times Higher Education Supplement*. London, 25 November.

O'Leary, Brendan (1988). 'Exploring the Roads to Consensus: Review of Charles Townshend (ed.) *Consensus in Ireland: Approaches and Recessions'*. *Irish Times*. Dublin, 3 December.

O'Leary, Brendan (1988). 'Red, Green and Gold: Review of Austen Morgan's *James Connolly: A Political Biography'*. *Times Higher Education Supplement*.

O'Leary, Brendan (1988). 'Review Article on Terrorism'. *British Journal of Criminology*, 28 (1): 97–107.

O'Leary, Brendan (1984). 'Review of John McColgan's *British Policy and the Irish Administration, 1920–22'*. *Public Administration*, 62 (1): 126–7.

Ross, F. Stuart (2002). 'Brendan O'Leary on Policing Northern Ireland'. *Irish Edition*. Wyndmoor, PA: February.

Name Index

Note: A small 'n' refers to a footnote number.

Subject Index

Note: A small 'n' refers to a footnote number.